David C. Cook
Bible Lesson
Commentary

The Essential Study Companion *for* Every Disciple

David C. Cook
Bible Lesson
Commentary

NIV

David C Cook
transforming lives together

DAVID C. COOK NIV BIBLE LESSON COMMENTARY 2014–2015
Published by David C Cook
4050 Lee Vance View
Colorado Springs, CO 80918 U.S.A.

David C Cook Distribution Canada
55 Woodslee Avenue, Paris, Ontario, Canada N3L 3E5

David C Cook U.K., Kingsway Communications
Eastbourne, East Sussex BN23 6NT, England

David C Cook and the graphic circle C logo
are registered trademarks of Cook Communications Ministries.

All Scripture quotations are taken from the Holy Bible, New International Version®,
NIV®. Copyright © 1973, 1984 by Biblica, Inc™. Used by permission of Zondervan. All
rights reserved worldwide. www.zondervan.com.

Lessons based on *International Sunday School Lessons: The International Bible Lessons for
Christian Teaching*, © 2010 by the Committee on the Uniform Series.

ISBN 978-1-4347-0582-2

Written and edited by Dan Lioy, PhD
The Team: John Blase, Doug Schmidt, Amy Kiechlin, Tonya Osterhouse, and Karen Athen
Cover Design: Amy Kiechlin
Cover Photo: iStockphoto

Printed in the United States of America
First Edition 2014

1 2 3 4 5 6 7 8 9 10

022514

Contents

Remaining Steadfast in Hope

Unit I: A Brighter Day

Unit II: A Time of Difficulty

Unit III: A Vision of God's Grandeur

Offering Genuine Worship

Unit I: Revering the Lord

Unit II: Praying to the Lord

Unit III: Serving the Lord

Operating in the Spirit's Power

Upholding Justice

A Word to the Teacher

In 1521, Martin Luther appeared before the Diet of Worms. Holy Roman Emperor Charles V presided over the imperial assembly held at Worms, Germany. Luther's life was clearly in danger. While under oath, he acknowledged that he wrote the books the religious and civil authorities declared to be heretical. But he refused to renounce his teachings unless convinced that he had strayed from the Scriptures.

One tradition has held that Luther's concluding words in his heroic display of faith were as follows: "Here I stand. I cannot do otherwise." This solitary religious leader, filled with courage from his fresh reading of Scripture, dared to challenge the might of the church and state in his day. Through his writings and teachings, he (along with many others) helped to set in motion the Protestant Reformation.

Like the believers alive during the time of Luther, it is your privilege, as a Sunday school teacher, to present the whole counsel of God's Word. Sometimes you will discuss a positive subject, such as the promises the Lord made to His people. On other occasions, you will present a less pleasant topic, such as God's judgment. Both of these themes are emphasized in this year's *David C. Cook NIV Bible Lesson Commentary*.

Regardless of the subject matter the Spirit empowers you to present to your students, your job as a Sunday school teacher is eternally relevant. After all, you are not just giving the students important biblical information (even though the latter is true). The Spirit is also giving you the courage to be an agent of change in the students' lives. This is an awesome responsibility, and one I know you take seriously.

As you purpose to teach God's Word to your students, take a few moments to think about what the Spirit has done and is doing through you. Also, pray that your students will discover that the Scriptures are as relevant today as they were in the time of Luther and the other Protestant reformers. Then, watch in fascination as your students discover that the Lord is both just and merciful.

May God richly bless you as you share the riches of His truth and grace with your students!

Your fellow learner at the feet of the Master Teacher,
Dan Lioy

Using the *David C Cook NIV Bible Lesson Commentary* with Materials from Other Publishers

Sunday school materials from the following denominations and publishers follow International Sunday School Lesson outlines (sometimes known as Uniform Series). Because the *David C Cook NIV Bible Lesson Commentary* (formerly *Peloubet's*) follows the same outlines, you can use the *Commentary* as an excellent teacher resource to supplement the materials from these publishing houses.

NONDENOMINATIONAL:

Standard Publishing: *Adult*

Urban Ministries

Echoes Teacher's Commentary (Cook Communications Ministries): *Adult*

DENOMINATIONAL:

Advent Christian General Conference: *Adult*

American Baptist (Judson Press): *Adult*

Church of God in Christ (Church of God in Christ Publishing House): *Adult*

Church of Christ Holiness: *Adult*

Church of God (Warner Press): *Adult*

Church of God by Faith: *Adult*

National Baptist Convention of America (Boyd): *All ages*

National Primitive Baptist Convention: *Adult*

Progressive National Baptist Convention: *Adult*

Presbyterian Church (U.S.A.) (Bible Discovery Series—Presbyterian Publishing House or P.R.E.M.): *Adult*

Union Gospel Press: *All ages*

United Holy Church of America: *Adult*

United Methodist (Cokesbury): *All ages*

A Vision of the Future

DEVOTIONAL READING

Jeremiah 29:10-14

DAILY BIBLE READINGS

Monday September 1
*Jeremiah 22:1–9 Act with
Justice and Righteousness*

Tuesday September 2
*Jeremiah 11:1–10 Hear the
Words of This Covenant*

Wednesday September 3
*Isaiah 2:10–19 Only the
Lord Will Be Exalted*

Thursday September 4
*Jeremiah 18:1–10 Turn from
Your Evil Way*

Friday September 5
*Jeremiah 29:10–14 A Future
with Hope*

Saturday September 6
*Jeremiah 12:14–17 Hope for
Israel's Neighbors*

Sunday September 7
*Jeremiah 30:1–3, 18–22 The
Days Are Surely Coming*

Scripture

Background Scripture: *Jeremiah 30*
Scripture Lesson: *Jeremiah 30:1-3, 18-22*
Key Verse: *"'The days are coming,' declares the LORD, 'when I
will bring my people Israel and Judah back from captivity and
restore them to the land I gave their forefathers to possess,' says
the LORD."* Jeremiah 30:3.
Scripture Lesson for Children: *Jeremiah 30:1-3, 18-22*
Key Verse for Children: *"I will bring my people Israel and
Judah back from captivity and restore them to the land."*
Jeremiah 30:3.

Lesson Aim

To experience spiritual renewal in loving relationship
with God.

Lesson Setting

Time: 587 B.C.
Place: Judah and Jerusalem

Lesson Outline

A Vision of the Future
   I. God's Promise to Restore His People:
      Jeremiah 30:1-3
      A. The Command to Write: vss. 1-2
      B. The Declaration to Regather Israel and Judah: vs. 3
  II. God's Pledge to Fulfill His Promise: Jeremiah
      30:18-22
      A. Rebuilding of the Nation's Infrastructure: vs. 18
      B. Enabling God's People to Flourish: vss. 19-20
      C. Commissioning a New Leader: vs. 21
      *D. Living in a Covenant Relationship with God:
        vs. 22*

Introduction for Adults

Topic: *A Promise Assured*

In Jeremiah 30:22, the Lord promised the exiles living in Babylon, "So you will be my people, and I will be your God." Today, when we trust in the Lord Jesus, we become members of His body, the global church.

The preceding statement isn't just a truth we affirm. More importantly, by God's grace we are to live it out on a daily basis. Becoming God's people—both individually and collectively—takes a lot of work. We need to say *no* to our sinful desires and *yes* to God's will for us. We also devote as much time and attention to the interests of others as to what excites us.

Living in this way means God's priorities take precedence over ours. It also means we care so much about the community of faith that we do all we can to meet people where they are in the midst of their human brokenness.

Introduction for Youth

Topic: *A Connection Is Made*

Every four years the Olympic torch is passed hand-to-hand by runners from all over the world. People thrill when the last runner arrives at the stadium and ignites the Olympic torch to open the games.

Young people are on the receiving end of something far more precious than the Olympic torch. When they accept the Christian faith from their parents, they join themselves to the community of believers from every part of the globe and down through history. This is in keeping with Jeremiah 30:22, which declares, "So you will be my people, and I will be your God."

As members of the community of faith, it is the duty of saved young people to pick up the torch of the Lord Jesus and carry it, until they in turn pass it on to their children. For a parent, the most satisfying thing in life is to see one's children preparing to take up the torch of Christian faith!

Concepts for Children

Topic: *All Will Be Well*

1. God's people had sinned against Him.
2. God allowed His people to experience difficulty.
3. God's people felt sorry for their sins.
4. God promised to forgive His people and help them obey Him.
5. God is pleased when we thank Him for forgiving us when we sin.

Lesson Commentary

I. GOD'S PROMISE TO RESTORE HIS PEOPLE: JEREMIAH 30:1-3

A. The Command to Write: vss. 1-2

This is the word that came to Jeremiah from the LORD: "This is what the LORD, the God of Israel, says: 'Write in a book all the words I have spoken to you.'"

No biblical writer revealed more of his soul than Jeremiah. Through his often brash and pointed complaints to God, we see the exasperation of Jeremiah's heart. The Lord commanded Jeremiah never to marry and have children. He preached for years, only to be rebuked, insulted, and banished by leaders who hated him. Moreover, unlike other Old Testament prophets, Jeremiah did not have the benefit of miracles to validate his message. For Elijah, God brought down fire from heaven. Ezekiel, Isaiah, and Daniel had great visions. In contrast, God gave Jeremiah object lessons. The prophet used such ordinary items as a ruined belt, shattered pottery, and a wooden yoke to communicate an extraordinary message of impending judgment.

Jeremiah served the Lord in Jerusalem during the reigns of the last five kings of Judah. He was a confidant of Josiah (639–609 B.C.), Jehoiakim (609–597 B.C.), and Zedekiah (597–586 B.C.). These three relationships, however, were remarkably different. Josiah was a godly king who initiated broad spiritual reforms in Judah. Of course, Jeremiah supported the king with great enthusiasm. Josiah's son, Jehoiakim, toppled his father's reforms and led Judah headlong into idolatry. He despised Jeremiah and did everything he could to squelch the prophet's message. Zedekiah proved to be a weak king. While at times he seemed to favor Jeremiah, Zedekiah was afraid to oppose his court officials, who wanted to silence the prophet.

Jeremiah lived through the capture and destruction of Jerusalem by the Babylonian army under the command of Nebuchadnezzar (586 B.C.). The Babylonian conquest of Judah and of Jerusalem came in three waves. In 605 B.C., Nebuchadnezzar conquered King Jehoiakim and carried part of the temple treasures, along with Daniel, to Babylon. Then, in 597 B.C., Jehoiachin (son of Jehoiakim), the remainder of the temple's treasures, along with 10,000 of Judah's leaders, were taken to Babylon. Ezekiel was in this group.

Next, in 588 B.C., Nebuchadnezzar came a third and final time. For one and a half years, the Babylonian army whittled away at Jerusalem's defenses. Though confident at first, the Judahites began to lose courage when Egypt's rescue attempt was crushed and other fortified cities of Judah began to fall like dominoes. The end came in 586 B.C. when the Babylonians breached the walls of Jerusalem and burned the city. Nebuchadnezzer blinded King Zedekiah and carried him and more than 800 captives to Babylon in chains. Only a remnant of the poorest people was left to inhabit the rubble that Jerusalem had become.

One of the most obvious features of the Book of Jeremiah is that its messages are not arranged chronologically. With the exception of chapter 13, the first 20 chapters probably come from the period between the prophet's call by God (626 B.C.) and a critical battle between Egypt and Babylon (605 B.C.). Most of the material in chapters 21–39 appears to date from the reigns of kings Jehoiakim and Zedekiah. Within those broad boundaries, the prophetic messages cluster by topic or theme.

In chapter 29, after the second group of hostages had been taken away as captives to Babylon, Jeremiah turned his focus from warning the people of Judah to encouraging the exiles in Babylon. The prophet shifted his theme from judgment for sin to future restoration, sending his message in a letter with couriers from King Zedekiah. Jeremiah urged the exiles to settle down in Babylon and to disregard predictions of a rapid return to Judah. They would prosper and benefit as long as they worked for the peace and prosperity of Babylon. Besides, the Lord intended to take 70 years to reshape His people so that they would seek Him.

Jeremiah 30 through 32 have been called the Book of Consolation or Comfort because the message of future hope contrasts with the dominant note of judgment throughout the rest of the book. In chapter 30, the Lord summoned Jeremiah to record a divinely inspired message (vs. 1). These oracles of hope, which appear in chapters 30 and 31, came directly from the Lord and were to be placed in a scroll (that is, thin strips of leather or papyrus joined together in long rolls; 30:2). Jeremiah's prophecies would be a permanent record of God's pledge to redeem His chosen people from their lengthy time of deep distress in Babylon.

B. The Declaration to Regather Israel and Judah: vs. 3

"'The days are coming,' declares the LORD, 'when I will bring my people Israel and Judah back from captivity and restore them to the land I gave their forefathers to possess,' says the LORD."

The regathering and reunification of Israel and Judah foretold in Jeremiah 30:3 is in keeping with what Moses declared in Deuteronomy. For instance, in chapter 28, the lawgiver described how the Lord would bless the Israelites if they remained faithful to Him in the promised land or curse them if they were unfaithful. Repeatedly, Moses implored God's chosen people to obey His decrees. But the Israelite leader must have realized that at some future point, the nation might turn away from God and disregard His ordinances. And when it happened, God would allow foreign powers, such as the Egyptians, Assyrians, and Babylonians, to overrun Israel and Judah, remove many of the inhabitants, and disperse them around the known world.

Sometime after that period of deep distress had occurred, the Israelites would come to their senses and realize that their dispersion had taken place because of their disobedience. Moses revealed that, at that time, the people would recall

God's commands. The lawgiver also declared that if the Israelites returned to the Lord in obedience, He would bless them. Even though they would be scattered among the surrounding nations, God would regather them, forgive them, and again grant them prosperity in the promised land. Jeremiah 29:10-14 discloses that at the end of Babylon's 70 years of rule, the Lord would fulfill His pledge to restore His people. In particular, as they reflected on His promise of a future filled with hope, they would pray to God. Then, He would listen and respond by bringing "Israel and Judah back from captivity" (30:3) and reestablish them in the "land" He previously gave to their ancestors.

II. GOD'S PLEDGE TO FULFILL HIS PROMISE: JEREMIAH 30:18-22

A. Rebuilding of the Nation's Infrastructure: vs. 18

"This is what the LORD says: 'I will restore the fortunes of Jacob's tents and have compassion on his dwellings; the city will be rebuilt on her ruins, and the palace will stand in its proper place.'"

In Jeremiah 30:4-11, God promised to deliver His people from a period characterized by anguish and terror. The latter would be a time of panic, not peace, in which even those who were physically strong would grab their stomachs in pain like a pregnant woman giving birth. In that terrible circumstance, the all-powerful Lord pledged to free His people from their bonds of servitude to Babylon. This dramatic turn of events would enable them to serve Him under a restored Davidic ruler. The New Testament reveals this king to be the Lord Jesus, Israel's Messiah.

In light of these fantastic promises, God urged the exiles in Babylon not to be paralyzed with fear. After all, He was supremely powerful to deliver them from their captivity in faraway lands and establish them once again safely and securely in Judah. The Lord acknowledged that He would overturn such oppressors as Babylon to end the displacement of His chosen people. God also affirmed that He would chastise them in an equitable manner for their centuries of unfaithfulness. Yet He would not utterly wipe them out.

Jeremiah 30:12-17 recounts God's promise to heal the wounds He inflicted on His people for their insubordination. When the Lord allowed foreigners to overrun Israel and Judah and exile many of their inhabitants, the result seemed like an incurable injury. Their situation appeared to be utterly hopeless, especially in the absence of anyone to uphold their cause and bind up their wounds. In that terrifying circumstance, all the people's former political and religious allies (including Egypt, Edom, Moab, Ammon, Phoenicia, and Assyria) had forsaken them. God explained that His severe chastening of His people through the hands of their enemies was due to the extreme extent of the nation's iniquity and numerous transgressions.

The Lord was genuinely aware of the plight of His people. He knew about the distress and shame they felt over the indignities they suffered. God reminded

the exiles that the injustices they endured were the consequence of them having sinned greatly and incurring an enormous amount of guilt. Nonetheless,
the Lord declared that their time of trouble would eventually come to an end.
Those who forced God's people into captivity would experience exile. Likewise,
those who had plundered the Israelites would be pillaged. In contrast, the
Lord pledged to heal the nation's wounds and restore it to health. The people
of Jerusalem would no longer be considered as outcasts whom others glibly
abandoned.

In verse 18, God promised He would completely reverse the circumstance
of the exiles. They would return to Judah and be empowered to rebuild their
"tents" or dwelling places. Even their bygone homes would become the object
of the Lord's "compassion." The latter term renders a Hebrew verb that denotes
the presence of God's tender affection and mercy. Moreover, He would enable
the returnees to "rebuild" Jerusalem and the cities of Judah on their former
"ruins." Similarly, Jerusalem's palace, as well as the nation's fortified enclaves,
would be reestablished where they once stood.

B. Enabling God's People to Flourish: vss. 19-20

*"From them will come songs of thanksgiving and the sound of rejoicing. I will add to their numbers, and
they will not be decreased; I will bring them honor, and they will not be disdained. Their children will be
as in days of old, and their community will be established before me; I will punish all who oppress them.'"*

It's not difficult to imagine the intense joy the former exiles would feel once
they resettled their families in Judah. Whereas before there was grief and
mourning over being in captivity in Babylon, Jeremiah 30:19 anticipated a
future time in which the returnees expressed "thanksgiving" and "rejoicing"
through "songs." Previously, foreign invaders had moved scores of God's people
from the promised land. Yet in a future day of restoration, the Lord would cause
the population of Judah to increase.

In the preceding decades, the enemies of the exiles held them in utter
contempt. But God promised that a time was coming when He would replace
such disdain with "honor" for His people. Then their "children" (vs. 20) would
prosper as in earlier times (for example, when David and Solomon reigned).
Moreover, the Lord would reestablish the former political and religious institu-
tions of the covenant "community." Judah would be so secure that God would
visit with punishment any foe who tried to mistreat His people.

C. Commissioning a New Leader: vs. 21

*"Their leader will be one of their own; their ruler will arise from among them. I will bring him near and
he will come close to me, for who is he who will devote himself to be close to me?' declares the LORD."*

According to Jeremiah 30:21, a "leader" would "arise" from among the returnees to Judah and oversee them. Also, in God's grace, He would grant this "ruler"
permission to approach Him, perhaps on special occasions to pray and obtain

guidance. Ezra 1 reveals that, in 537 B.C., the Lord worked through Cyrus, Persia's king, to authorize a Jewish official named Sheshbazzar to lead a group of exiles from Babylon to Judah. Then, Ezra 3:8 discloses that, in 536 B.C., God raised up another leader named Zerubbabel, along with Jeshua the high priest, to lead the people in their temple rebuilding efforts.

Some scholars have speculated that Zerubbabel and Sheshbazzar were the same person, but this is highly improbable. Zerubbabel was likely born during Judah's exile in Babylon. He was a grandson of Jehoiachin, one of the last Davidic kings, who had died in Babylon (1 Chron. 3:17-19). Jehoiachin had been honored in exile (2 Kings 25:27-30), and it was natural that his descendant would be highly respected in the Jewish community.

Through the Old Testament prophet Haggai, the Lord declared that He was appointing Zerubbabel for a special mission of high honor (Hag. 2:23). While Zerubbabel did have a claim to the throne of Israel, the Persian domination of Judah during that time prevented him from assuming the monarchy. In all likelihood, Haggai was looking forward to the Messiah, who would come through Zerubbabel (Matt. 1:12). Jesus is the "Son of the Most High" (Luke 1:32) who Gabriel revealed to Mary would sit on David's "throne."

This interpretation is further supported by the Lord's designation of Zerubbabel as "my servant" (Hag. 2:23). In Isaiah, the Lord repeatedly referred to the Messiah by that title (Isa. 41:8; 52:13; 53:11). The Lord also said He would make Zerubbabel His "signet ring" (Hag. 2:23). A signet ring contained an official seal that served as a signature carrying the full authority of the owner of the signet ring. For instance, when Pharaoh appointed Joseph the governor of the land, he gave his signet ring to him as a symbol of his new office (Gen. 41:42). The royal signet ring gave the bearer the full authority of the ruler.

This act was symbolic of God's reestablishing the messianic line after the exile in Babylon. In contrast to earthly rulers, the Messiah came for the eternal benefit of the lost. His divinely appointed mission was to serve others and to lay down His life so that the lost could receive His promise of salvation (Matt. 20:28; Mark 10:45). Jesus, the King of kings and Lord of lords (Rev. 17:14; 19:16), humbled Himself by becoming the penalty for our sins so that we might inherit eternal life.

D. Living in a Covenant Relationship with God: vs. 22

"'So you will be my people, and I will be your God.'"

During the Israelites' time of captivity in Babylon, it was understandable that they might have doubted whether God still loved them and considered them His chosen people. Hosea 2:23 declares that the Lord, in faithfulness to His ancient covenant, would have mercy and show compassion on the wayward Israelites. Furthermore, in their day of restoration, they would realize once again that the Lord was their God and they were His people (Jer. 30:22). In short, the Lord promised to abide with, watch over, and provide for the returnees from exile. Their joyous and heartfelt response would be to remain loyal to God and obedient to His will. As Christians, it is also important for us to acknowledge God in all that we do and remain steadfast in our devotion to Him.

Discussion Questions

1. When Jeremiah prophesied, what was the plight being experienced by God's people?
2. How would God bring about the restoration of His people?
3. Why was it important for the former exiles to know that the Lord was their God?
4. How can believers demonstrate that they are totally committed to serving God?
5. In what ways does God bless believers? How might they use His blessings to help others?

Contemporary Application

As fallen human beings, we can sink quite low into sinful behavior. This was true of God's chosen people before they were exiled to Babylon. Perhaps at times we might feel, as did the captives in Babylon, that we are beyond the scope of God's restorative touch. Yet those feelings must be challenged with the truth about who God is and what He is capable of doing.

Any god I use to support my latest cause, or who fits comfortably within my understanding or experience, will be a god no larger than I and thus not able to save me from my sin or inspire my worship or empower my service. Any god who fits the contours of me will never really transcend me, never really be God.

Donald W. McCollough wrote those words in *The Trivialization of God*. The author's remarks emphasize the need for us to remember that God is greater than we can ever conceive Him to be. Thousands of years ago, He promised to restore the exiles in Babylon. Even today, He can enable us to experience spiritual renewal in loving relationship with Him.

In short, a lowercase "god" cannot be the same as our uppercase "God." This truth is important for us to recall, especially when we think about God's ability to pick us up when we have fallen down and to restore our lives when we are overwhelmed in the midst of their ruins. His infinite and incomprehensible grace provides the spiritual building material we need to reclaim our shattered lives. Only He is big enough and powerful enough to do the job.

A Promise of Restoration

Scripture

Background Scripture: *Jeremiah 31*
Scripture Lesson: *Jeremiah 31:31-37*
Key Verse: *"The time is coming," declares the* LORD, *"when I will make a new covenant with the house of Israel and with the house of Judah."* Jeremiah 31:31.
Scripture Lesson for Children: *Jeremiah 31:31-37*
Key Verse for Children: *"They will all know me, from the least of them to the greatest," declares the* LORD. Jeremiah 31:34.

Lesson Aim

To spiritually flourish as a result of knowing God intimately.

Lesson Setting

Time: 587 B.C.
Place: Judah and Jerusalem

Lesson Outline

A Promise of Restoration

   I. God's Promise of a New Covenant: Jeremiah 31:31-34
      A. *The Distinctive New Covenant: vss. 31-32*
      B. *The Blessings of the New Covenant: vss. 33-34*
  II. God's Assurance of Israel's Existence: Jeremiah 31:35-37
      A. *Israel's Permanence as a Nation: vss. 35-36*
      B. *God's Unwavering Commitment to Israel: vs. 37*

Introduction for Adults

Topic: *Hope for Tomorrow*

Life is filled with ups and downs, joys and disappointments. We tend to become weary when there are more losses than gains and more failures than successes. In that situation, we can begin to feel as if life is hopeless.

It's possible that for the upright living during the time of Jeremiah, things looked pretty bleak. Sin was rampant, idolatry seemed in vogue, and the disadvantaged were being exploited. Worst of all, people ignored and disobeyed God.

Jeremiah 31:31 reveals that in the future, the Lord would establish a "new covenant" with His people. Verse 33 pictures God inscribing His moral code on their hearts. The close relationship between God and His people would be undergirded by the people's intimate understanding and application of the law.

Even today, under the new covenant the Son inaugurated, everyone who trusts in Him can know the Father intimately. Indeed, God's pardon creates the possibility of transforming all interpersonal relationships within a congregation with forgiveness, patience, and hope.

Introduction for Youth

Topic: *Begin with a Fresh Start*

Teenagers learning to drive a car achieve the goal of obtaining a driver's license because they have more than one opportunity to pass the driving test. If we flunked everyone who rear-ended another car or ripped off the side molding of the garage door, very few individuals would be licensed drivers.

God made it clear to Jeremiah that, even though His people would be judged for their sins, in the future He would usher in a new society in which people would prosper because they loved and obeyed Him. Since we know that this is God's wise and loving plan, how much better for us if we get in step with it now!

The world might scoff at this idea of a fresh start. Yet believers know from God's Word that it is true. Remember, God's promises are sure to happen. Of this we can be certain!

Concepts for Children

Topic: *An Awesome Promise!*

1. God promised to bring His people back to their homeland.
2. God promised to help rebuild His people's nation.
3. God promised to make a new agreement with His people.
4. God promised that His people would truly know Him, that He would forgive them, and that they would obey Him.
5. God also wants to love and forgive us, and it's possible when we trust in Jesus for salvation.

Lesson Commentary

I. GOD'S PROMISE OF A NEW COVENANT: JEREMIAH 31:31-34

A. The Distinctive New Covenant: vss. 31-32

"The time is coming," declares the LORD, "when I will make a new covenant with the house of Israel and with the house of Judah. It will not be like the covenant I made with their forefathers when I took them by the hand to lead them out of Egypt, because they broke my covenant, though I was a husband to them," declares the LORD.

As we learned in last week's lesson, the collection of oracles recorded in Jeremiah 30–33 has been called the Book of Consolation or Comfort. It contains two sections, the first dealing with the restoration of Israel and Judah (chaps. 30 and 31), and the second with the faith and assurance of God's future blessing of His people (chaps. 32 and 33). Based on 32:1, some date the entire section to 587 B.C. The Babylonians had laid siege to Jerusalem, and they had already conquered other Judean cities. Even the efforts of Egypt to intervene could not prevent the fall of Jerusalem (37:4-5).

It was in the midst of this dismal situation that Jeremiah spoke words of comfort. Chapters 30 and 31 are remarkable for their emphasis on a better future when a reunited Israel would be back in the land and living out a new relationship with the Lord. This relationship would be established by a new covenant. Beginning in 31:23, God declared through Jeremiah that one day He would free His people and lead them back to their hometowns. When God restored His people, the returnees would ask Him to bless Jerusalem and the sacred hill on which His temple stood.

Three key pieces of information are discernable from verse 23. First, the Lord was going to send His people away into captivity. Second, at some point in the future, He promised to end their period of exile and enable them to come back to Judah. Third, the temple and the hill on which it stood would be characterized by righteousness and sacredness. In that day of restoration, city dwellers, farmers, and shepherds would live together in peace and joy (vs. 24). Regardless of their occupation, even those who felt tired and worn out would find renewed energy and strength (vs. 25).

Israel's future depended on God's love. His love made it possible for Israel to again be pure and chaste like a virgin. Like parents gathering their children, the Lord would gather His people. Also, like shepherds watching over their regathered flock, the Lord would watch over His people. Verse 26 suggests that the prophet received his divine revelation in a dream. It was an amazing vision of what God planned for His people in the future. Jeremiah learned that God would greatly increase the number of people, along with livestock, living in the land of promise (vs. 27). In the past, the Lord had uprooted and torn down the nation. In the future, however, God would plant and rebuild it (vs. 28).

There was a popular proverb in use among the exiles. The maxim said that if parents ate sour grapes, this caused the children to grind and wear out their teeth from the bitter taste (vs. 29). The exiles were using the proverb to claim that their generation was being punished with captivity because of the sins previous generations of Judahites had committed. This application of the proverb was based on a misunderstanding of Numbers 14:18. It teaches that the actions of one person could adversely affect several generations of family members.

In the ancient Near East, it was typical for intergenerational families to live within the same household. Tragically, the severe consequences of one person's behavior could adversely impact the lives of other family members up to several generations (Num. 16:31-34). It would be incorrect to conclude, however, that God's judgment was not due to personal sin. The Lord revealed that He would judge each person for his or her own misdeeds, not those of anyone else (Jer. 31:30). Because His treatment of people was objective and fair, they lived or died according to their own deeds. This meant that each person was individually responsible for his or her actions. Thus guilt would not be transferred from one generation to the next.

"Covenant" is a critical term in the Book of Jeremiah. In chapter 11, the term appears five times, where the prophet reminded the people that the coming judgment was simply the consequence (or curse) of breaking their mutual agreement with God. In chapters 31–34, the word "covenant" appears 16 times, contrasting the blessings of the new covenant with the curses of the old. The primary way people in the ancient Near East understood interpersonal relationships was by a legally binding obligation. Although the term "covenant" included both the concept of a modern-day contract or treaty, it was a much broader idea. To people in Bible times, a covenant extended to any relationship that involved responsibility: marriage, parenthood, and even friendship. That is why the entire Mosaic law could be summed up as love—love to God with all one's being, and love for one's neighbor as for oneself (Matt. 22:37-40).

Jeremiah 31:31-34 represents the apex of the prophet's ministry. By declaring, "the time is coming" (vs. 31), Jeremiah indicated that the new (or renewed) covenant would be part of a future age of blessing. More than a century before (722 B.C.), the Assyrians had defeated and removed the residents of Israel (2 Kings 17:5-6). Even though Israel no longer existed as an independent nation, it would be included along with Judah in the new covenant. This indicated that the new covenant would be for all God's people. The problem with the old covenant that God made with Israel at Mount Sinai was that God's chosen people continually broke it. This remained the case, even though the Lord had miraculously delivered them from Egypt and remained faithful to them (Jer. 31:32). The new covenant would have to address the problem inherent in the old one and compensate for the inability of the people to perform up to God's standards.

B. The Blessings of the New Covenant: vss. 33-34

"This is the covenant I will make with the house of Israel after that time," declares the LORD. "I will put my law in their minds and write it on their hearts. I will be their God, and they will be my people. No longer will a man teach his neighbor, or a man his brother, saying, 'Know the LORD,' because they will all know me, from the least of them to the greatest," declares the LORD. "For I will forgive their wickedness and will remember their sins no more."

Whereas before God's people disobeyed Him, under the new covenant they would obey Him. It was as if He were inscribing the moral code on their hearts and minds (Jer. 31:33). The close relationship between God and His people would be undergirded by the people's intimate understanding and application of the Mosaic law to the emotional, intellectual, and ethical aspects of their lives. Jeremiah is the only Old Testament prophet who spoke specifically about the new covenant that Jesus inaugurated (Matt. 26:28).

Perhaps one of the most precious truths contained in the new covenant is the promise that the Lord "will be their God, and they will be [His] people" (Jer. 31:33). This pledge is reiterated in Revelation 21:3-4. In John's vision of the new Jerusalem, he learned that, in the eternal state, God will permanently dwell, or tabernacle, among the redeemed of all ages. The various scourges of human existence will not occur in the eternal state. In fact, all unhappiness must, of necessity, be gone from life when God dwells with His people. The new order of things—which will be undergirded by the new covenant—will permit no sadness. It is no wonder we read in 22:20, "Amen. Come, Lord Jesus."

Some, in their zeal to stress the importance of the new covenant, have tried to disparage the old covenant. Nonetheless, a careful reading of Scripture indicates that there was nothing wrong with the Mosaic covenant that the Lord had graciously given to Israel. It was never God's intent that the law of Moses be used as a means to obtain salvation. Instead, forgiveness of sins has always been the Lord's gracious gift to those who have humbled themselves before Him in faith (Gen. 15:6; Rom. 4:3). The law was God's way of pointing out the moral pathway that believers should walk (Rom. 7:7-8; Gal. 3:19, 24).

Thus, the problem with the covenant ratified at Mount Sinai was not in God's provision, but rather in Israel's response. The people had continually violated their legally binding obligation. Time and again through the priests and prophets, God had called the Israelites to repent, but any change of heart they underwent was soon abandoned (2 Kings 17:7-23). For example, in the days of Jeremiah, King Josiah destroyed the idols that were in the land (23:4-20). But soon after this godly ruler died, the people turned back to worshiping the idols of the neighboring countries (vss. 31-32, 36-37). Tragically, the calloused hearts of the people remained unchanged. Only God Himself could radically transform the hearts and minds of His people.

Consequently, a new covenant was needed. The Lord described the essential difference between the covenants by saying that the new one would be internal, while the old one was external. The new covenant represented a sacred relationship, while the old one was more of a legal document. The old one was written on tablets of stone, while the new one would be written on human hearts (2 Cor. 3:3). Once the law of God could be implanted within the inmost being of people, their relationship with God could be permanent. The Lord showed Jeremiah a time when all His people, regardless of class distinctions, would directly know Him (Jer. 31:34). This verse signifies more than a mere intellectual awareness of theological truths about God. Implicit is the notion of being wholeheartedly committed to the Lord and steadfastly obedient to His will. When that day finally arrived, the role of prophets such as Jeremiah would become obsolete. The people would no longer need someone to exhort them to love and serve the Lord.

A critical aspect of this new relationship between God and His people hinged on the forgiveness of sins. God's law could not be written on hearts stained by iniquity. The people's hearts required cleansing so they could be changed. Once the Lord had forgiven them, He would deliberately forget their sins. Consequently, interpersonal relationships would be transformed by the reality of God's forgiveness. His refusal to recall the sins committed by His people would enable them to relate to one another with forgiveness, patience, and love. Sin remains the insurmountable human problem. No matter how hard people try, they can do nothing to defeat sin. Hope rests entirely on God's love and forgiveness. Thankfully, the Father sent His Son to die for our sins (and rise again) so that we might be forgiven and enjoy the benefits of the new covenant. On the basis of the Son's atoning sacrifice, the Father declares to us, "Your sins are forgiven." That is the wonderful news of the Gospel!

II. GOD'S ASSURANCE OF ISRAEL'S EXISTENCE: JEREMIAH 31:35-37

A. Israel's Permanence as a Nation: vss. 35-36

This is what the LORD says, he who appoints the sun to shine by day, who decrees the moon and stars to shine by night, who stirs up the sea so that its waves roar—the LORD Almighty is his name: "Only if these decrees vanish from my sight," declares the LORD, "will the descendants of Israel ever cease to be a nation before me."

In Jeremiah 31:35, the Lord vowed that Israel would continue to exist as a nation. "LORD Almighty" is more literally rendered "Yahweh of armies" and depicts Him as a divine warrior who maintains absolute control over everything and everyone in the world. As the Creator of the universe, God had the ability to fulfill His promise to His chosen people. For instance, the all-powerful Lord established the sun to light the day and ordained that the moon and stars would brighten the night. He is the same sovereign King who sets the sea in motion so that its waves clap like thunder as they roll across the ocean's billowing surface.

According to 51:15, God used His awesome power to establish the earth. He also utilized His unfathomable wisdom to set the world firmly in its place. Moreover, by means of His infinite understanding, the Lord spread out the heavens. Verse 16 reveals that when God's voice thunders, rains pour down from the sky. He also effortlessly causes the clouds to arise from distant horizons. Furthermore, as it rains, the Lord makes bolts of lightning flash, and He unleashes the wind from His storehouses. This naturally occurring phenomenon signified God's ability to guarantee a future for Israel and Judah as one people ruled by their Creator. Just as God would never undermine the fixed ordering of the cosmos, so too He would never allow Israel to cease to exist as a nation in His sight (31:36).

Clearly, the new covenant promises recorded in chapter 31 were originally addressed to God's Old Testament people. Yet some mistakenly think that because of Israel's unbelief, God has completely pushed the nation aside and transferred to the church all His promises to Israel. Many Christians, however, maintain that what God pledged to Israel would some day be fulfilled. Israel—God's Old Testament people—would yet receive His promised blessings. Also, Christians—God's people through faith in the Messiah—can receive God's spiritual blessings now. Thus, Jeremiah 31 contains truths about the nature and workings of God that believers of any time in history can study to their advantage.

B. God's Unwavering Commitment to Israel: vs. 37

This is what the LORD says: "Only if the heavens above can be measured and the foundations of the earth below be searched out will I reject all the descendants of Israel because of all they have done," declares the LORD.

God used the poetic expressions appearing in Jeremiah 31:37 to stress His strong commitment to His people. Rhetorically speaking, if the infinite could be measured or the unfathomable could be investigated, only then would there be any possibility that God would reject His people. In verse 38, Jeremiah prophesied about the coming kingdom age and the rebuilding of Jerusalem.

The phrase "the days are coming" suggests a rebuilding in the messianic age and not just the rebuilding that came after the exile in Babylon. Jeremiah described the renovation in concrete terms. He named sites along the wall, listing them from the Tower of Hananel near the northeast corner of Jerusalem and proceeding counterclockwise around the city (vss. 38-40). The prophet declared that this rebuilt Jerusalem will "never again be uprooted or destroyed." Since the Romans destroyed Jerusalem in A.D. 70, it is likely that this was Jeremiah's glimpse of the new Jerusalem, God's eternal dwelling with His people.

Discussion Questions

1. Why did God determine it was important to make a new covenant with His chosen people?
2. Why did Israel repeatedly violate the Mosaic covenant?
3. In what ways had Israel sinned against the Lord?
4. How might believers draw comfort from knowing that God is all-powerful?
5. How does the new covenant change the way believers relate to God and to one another?

Contemporary Application

Jeremiah said that a time was coming when there would be profound change. People would know the Lord and His Word. They would also love Him and others unconditionally. This was good news intended to bring comfort and hope to those living in the prophet's day. His oracle still gives hope to us when we sometimes feel weary.

Several years ago I had the opportunity to pick peaches in an orchard. At one point, I came across a limb that had fallen from one of the trees. Although it had peaches on it, the fruit was rotten and shriveled up. Because the limb was no longer attached to the tree, it had lost the ability to produce a good crop of fruit.

The same thing is true of believers. As long as they abide in Jesus and the new life He offers, they will produce spiritual fruit. For example, they will be godly individuals and witnesses for the Lord. Tragedy results, however, when they allow their spiritual communion with the Son to weaken. They are not as fruitful as they ought to be, and their testimony to others is severely damaged.

Some believers are uncomfortable with the idea of abiding in the new life the Father offers through faith in the Son. They are used to doing things on their own and in their own way. This is a disastrous policy to adopt, however, when it comes to the spiritual life. If people rely only on themselves, it is impossible for them to overcome immoral habits and resist the forbidden cravings of their sinful nature. Only by remaining in the Lord Jesus will they have victory over the things of the world.

Abiding in the new life that the Savior offers is a matter of faith. Believers know that it is important to do, and they depend on the Lord for the strength to remain in touch with Him. They should not take this truth lightly. If they allow themselves to drift away from Jesus, they will become spiritually barren. It is only as they draw close to the Father and live in vital union with His Son that they will grow spiritually and flourish.

A Fresh Start

Scripture

Background Scripture: *Jeremiah 32*
Scripture Lesson: *Jeremiah 32:2-9, 14-15*
Key Verse: *"For this is what the LORD Almighty, the God of
Israel, says: Houses, fields and vineyards will again be bought
in this land."* Jeremiah 32:15.
Scripture Lesson for Children: *Jeremiah 32:2-9, 14-15*
Key Verse for Children: *"I will surely gather [the people]
. . . and let them live in safety."* Jeremiah 32:37.

Lesson Aim

To recognize that even when life seems bleak, God
does not give up on us.

Lesson Setting

Time: 587 B.C.
Place: Judah and Jerusalem

Lesson Outline

A Fresh Start

   I. Purchasing of a Field: Jeremiah 32:2-9
      A. *Imprisoned in the Palace Courtyard: vs. 2*
      B. *Dire, Prophetic Warnings: vss. 3-5*
      C. *A Divine Directive to Buy Some Property: vss. 6-9*
  II. Anticipating Future Economic Activity:
      Jeremiah 32:14-15
      A. *Preserving Important Documents: vs. 14*
      B. *Possessing Property Once Again: vs. 15*

Introduction for Adults

Topic: *Property for Sale*

The situation for the people of Jerusalem was bleak as Nebuchadnezzar surrounded the city with his army. Even as Jeremiah was a political prisoner in the palace courtyard, he was willing to sacrifice his personal desires and ambitions for the good of others.

Florence Nightingale (1820–1910) also exemplified this mind-set. At age 17, she felt God calling her to serve Him. She found her place of service in nursing, which in the early 1800s was done mostly by untrained volunteers. During the Crimean War (1853–1856), Nightingale and 38 nurses whom she trained, organized hospitals for 5,000 wounded British soldiers. She established the first real nurses' training, fought for sanitary hospitals in Britain, and helped make nursing the respectable profession it is today.

But Nightingale felt uncomfortable when Queen Victoria and Parliament honored her. She explained that she was doing God's work. "Christ is the author of our profession," Nightingale said about nursing. She later refused a national funeral and burial in Westminster Abbey when it was promised as a reward for her work. She only wanted to be buried with her family in a rural churchyard with a simple service.

Introduction for Youth

Topic: *A Risk for a New Future*

Thousands of years ago, Jeremiah was jailed in the guardhouse that was attached to the king's "royal palace" (Jer. 32:2). What kept the prophet going? It was his faith in God and the prophet's courage to remain devoted to God's people. Jeremiah had no earthly prospects for a brighter future. Yet he refused to quit, for he knew that trusting and obeying the Lord was his highest goal.

Many adolescents experience times of crisis in their lives—losing a loved one, moving to a strange place, struggling to make ends meet, and so on. Saved teens also know that peers who do not share their faith in the Lord Jesus sometimes treat them like outcasts. They should be encouraged to remain loyal to their Christian faith and heritage. They can do so knowing that the Lord will be with them every step of the way.

Concepts for Children

Topic: *Better Times Are Coming*

1. King Zedekiah put Jeremiah in jail for telling the truth.
2. Even though Jeremiah was in jail, he still told the truth.
3. God told Jeremiah that better times were coming for His people.
4. Jeremiah did not let his troubles keep him from obeying God.
5. God is pleased when we choose to obey Him.

Lesson Commentary

I. PURCHASING OF A FIELD: JEREMIAH 32:2-9

A. Imprisoned in the Palace Courtyard: vs. 2

The army of the king of Babylon was then besieging Jerusalem, and Jeremiah the prophet was confined in the courtyard of the guard in the royal palace of Judah.

Jeremiah 32 and 33 were written during the horrible 18-month siege of Jerusalem by Nebuchadnezzar (587–586 B.C.). At this time, Zedekiah was in his tenth year on the throne of Judah (32:1). As the Babylonian army tightened its grip on the city, Zedekiah imprisoned Jeremiah in the "courtyard" (vs. 2) adjacent to the guardhouse that was attached to the king's "royal palace." Evidently, Jeremiah was a political prisoner who was permitted to receive visitors and conduct business. Verses 3-5 explain why Zedekiah confined Jeremiah to the palace compound.

The events that led up to the fall of Jerusalem are detailed in 2 Kings 25 (see also 2 Chron. 36:17-20; Jer. 52:4-27). On January 15, 588 B.C., the Babylonian army laid siege to Jerusalem (2 Kings 25:1). The siege lasted for 18 months, interrupted briefly when Pharaoh Hophra led an Egyptian army north in a futile attempt to relieve Judah (vs. 2; see also Jer. 37:5-8; Ezek. 17:15). On July 18, 586 B.C., when famine conditions in Jerusalem had reached desperate proportions, the northern city wall was breached by the Babylonian army (2 Kings 25:3-4). The army of Judah attempted to escape Jerusalem by night through a gate on the southeast corner of the city. They fled across the Kidron Valley, over the Mount of Olives, and down into the Arabah, the deep valley containing the Jordan River and the Dead Sea. On the plains of Jericho, about 15 miles from Jerusalem, the forces of Babylon overtook and captured the exhausted defenders of Judah's capital (vs. 5).

The troops of Judah were scattered and Zedekiah was captured (vs. 6). Nebuchadnezzar had not been personally at the siege of Jerusalem. He had remained at his base camp at Riblah in northern Syria, probably to deal with the Phoenician cities of Tyre and Sidon. Zedekiah was taken to Nebuchadnezzar at Riblah, where Zedekiah's sons were executed in his presence before he was blinded and taken to Babylon. The Lord had prophesied about Zedekiah through Ezekiel: "I will bring him to Babylonia, the land of the Chaldeans, but he will not see it, and there he will die" (Ezek. 12:13).

On August 14, 586 B.C., roughly a month after Jerusalem fell to the Babylonians, Nebuzaradan, the commander of Nebuchadnezzar's imperial guard, arrived in the captured city with instructions for destroying it. He burned the temple, the royal palace, and every home. When structures made of limestone blocks are burned, the stones become crumbly from the heat and useless for rebuilding. Finally, all of the troops under Nebuzaradan's command set about dismantling the walls of Jerusalem (vss. 8-10). The distribution of workers during Nehemiah's rebuilding efforts in 445 B.C. suggests that the destruction was more thorough on the east and north sides of the city and less along the west and southwest (Neh. 3).

After completing the devastation of Jerusalem, Nebuzaradan took three groups of people into exile to Babylon: the survivors of Jerusalem's residents, the inhabitants of the towns and countryside of Judah, and those who had deserted to the Babylonians during the siege (2 Kings 25:11). Jeremiah reported only 832 exiles at this time (Jer. 52:29). The prophet must have counted some highly specific segment of what the writer of Kings described as a mass deportation. The peasantry of Judah was left to till the land and keep it from reverting to a wilderness (2 Kings 25:12).

In 597 B.C., when Jehoiachin was deported, the Babylonians had taken the gold and silver utensils from the temple. Then, in 586 B.C., under Nebuzaradan, they made the extraordinary effort necessary to cut up and remove from the ruins of Jerusalem the large bronze items of the temple. They confiscated every bronze utensil from the temple, no matter how humble its use. They also found other items of gold and silver, perhaps newly made since the previous raid (vss. 13-15). The two bronze pillars Solomon had cast to grace the entrance to the temple were the most impressive items the Babylonians took away (vs. 16). As when the columns were made (1 Kings 7:47), there was no practical means to weigh the quantity of brass involved when they were broken up.

In the course of his mopping-up activities in Jerusalem, Nebuzaradan arrested Seraiah the chief priest, Zephaniah the next senior priest, the three directors of temple security, the most senior military commander still at large, five surviving members of Zedekiah's government, an official charged with mobilizing the citizenry of Judah, and 60 of his organizers (2 Kings 25:18-19). Nebuzaradan transported this last group of prominent captives to Nebuchadnezzar at Riblah, where they were all executed (vss. 20-21).

B. Dire, Prophetic Warnings: vss. 3-5

Now Zedekiah king of Judah had imprisoned him there, saying, "Why do you prophesy as you do? You say, 'This is what the LORD says: I am about to hand this city over to the king of Babylon, and he will capture it. Zedekiah king of Judah will not escape out of the hands of the Babylonians but will certainly be handed over to the king of Babylon, and will speak with him face to face and see him with his own eyes. He will take Zedekiah to Babylon, where he will remain until I deal with him, declares the LORD. If you fight against the Babylonians, you will not succeed.'"

"Zedekiah" (Jer. 32:3) was 21 years old, just three years older than his deposed nephew, Jehoiachin, when he became king (2 Kings 24:18). He reigned for 11 years, from 597 to 586 B.C. His mother, Hamutal from Libnah, had also been King Jehoahaz's mother (23:31). Like his predecessors, Zedekiah did evil in the eyes of the Lord. The quality of his kingdom only validated God's intention to remove the people of Judah from His presence in the promised land (24:19-20).

Zedekiah figures prominently in the Book of Jeremiah. The monarch consulted with the prophet (21:1-2) and even begged for Jeremiah's help (37:3), but Zedekiah never had the courage to do what he knew was right. While the king seemed to want Jeremiah, the man of God, on his side, Zedekiah had lost his independence and much of his power to aristocrats around him. In fact, these ungodly counselors in the royal court always got their way (38:1-5). One contingent of those advisers convinced Zedekiah that he could rebel against the Babylonians, who had put him in power (2 Kings 24:17).

Zedekiah shuttled ambassadors between Jerusalem and the capitals of Edom, Moab, Ammon, Tyre, and Sidon to discuss allegiance to Babylon (Jer. 27:3). In 595 b.c., Nebuchadnezzar faced a rebellion in Babylon. It may have been at that time that Zedekiah and the other small nations around him decided they could break from Babylonian control. In 589 b.c., Pharaoh Hophra ascended the throne in Egypt and declared his independence from Babylon. The Lachish letters, 21 pottery fragments with military messages on them, reveal that Hophra was in communication with the commander of Zedekiah's forces in southern Judah. Jeremiah consistently bore witness to Zedekiah that the Lord wanted Judah to submit to Babylon (Jer. 27:12-14).

When the Babylonians temporarily lifted the siege of Jerusalem to deal with Pharaoh Hophra's approaching Egyptian army (Jer. 37:5; Ezek. 17:15), Zedekiah asked Jeremiah to pray that the siege would be over for good (Jer. 37:3). Instead, the prophet declared that the Babylonians would soon be back (vss. 6-8). When Jeremiah tried to leave Jerusalem to attend to some property in his hometown of Anathoth (1:1), he was arrested as a deserter to the Babylonians (37:11-13). Next, he was beaten and put in a dungeon, where Zedekiah visited the prophet, hoping to hear a favorable message from the Lord (vss. 14-17). As before, Jeremiah repeated his oracle of judgment and protested the injustice of his imprisonment (vss. 18-20). In response, the king transferred Jeremiah to a better cell in the courtyard of the guardhouse and ordered that he be fed as long as rations held out (vs. 21).

During this period of Jeremiah's confinement, Zedekiah censured his political prisoner for his dire, prophetic warnings (32:3). Yet Jeremiah remained unrelenting in his assertion that the Lord would deliver Jerusalem into the hand of Nebuchadnezzar. Moreover, Jeremiah had the courage to declare that Judah's king would be unsuccessful in his attempt to flee from the Babylonian army. Rather, God would allow Zedekiah to be delivered to Nebuchadnezzar's control. The Hebrew phrase rendered "speak with him face to face" (vs. 4) denotes a scene of harsh interrogation in which Zedekiah would be forced to answer personally to his captor for his insurrection. Jeremiah prophesied that Zedekiah then would be carried off to Babylon (vs. 5; see also 52:11).

At the time of Jeremiah's call in 626 B.C., God challenged Jeremiah to prepare himself for the resistance he would encounter when he began to prophesy a message of judgment. He would have to stand against the tide of public opinion and resist every tendency to be afraid (1:17). The Lord promised to make Jeremiah like an impregnable fortress in the face of attacks by Judah's kings, government leaders, priests, and ordinary people (vs. 18). God promised the prophet that no matter how frequently or viciously his opponents attacked him (for example, Zedekiah), they would not overcome Jeremiah. The Lord would always be with the prophet to deliver him (vs. 19).

When the Lord wanted to proclaim judgment and doom on His people, He took Jeremiah from his mother's womb and shaped him into an instrument He could use (vs. 4). What kind of man was Jeremiah? Was he as tough as nails, impervious to criticism, and eager to blast away at sin? No. He had none of the credentials we might associate with a prophet foretelling imminent destruction. Instead, Jeremiah possessed a sensitive soul. He anguished—just as God did—over the devastation coming to his people. All the same, Jeremiah stood firm—just as the Lord did—for the truth.

C. A Divine Directive to Buy Some Property: vss. 6-9

Jeremiah said, "The word of the LORD came to me: Hanamel son of Shallum your uncle is going to come to you and say, 'Buy my field at Anathoth, because as nearest relative it is your right and duty to buy it.' Then, just as the LORD had said, my cousin Hanamel came to me in the courtyard of the guard and said, 'Buy my field at Anathoth in the territory of Benjamin. Since it is your right to redeem it and possess it, buy it for yourself.' I knew that this was the word of the LORD; so I bought the field at Anathoth from my cousin Hanamel and weighed out for him seventeen shekels of silver."

While Jeremiah remained imprisoned, he received an oracle from the Lord (Jer. 32:6). The prophet had a cousin named Hanamel, who was the son of Shallum, Jeremiah's uncle (vs. 7). Hanamel owned a field in Anathoth, which was located about three miles northeast of Jerusalem. Anathoth was one of the 45 cities previously allotted to the Levites from the territory belonging to the tribe of Benjamin (Josh. 21:18). While the Babylonians laid siege to Jerusalem, Hanamel asked Jeremiah, as Hanamel's "nearest relative" (Jer. 32:7), to exercise his "right" and fulfill his responsibility as a guardian of the family interests (or kinsman-redeemer) to purchase the property.

Leviticus 25:25-55 provides the scriptural backdrop for Hanamel's request (see also Ruth 4:3-4). The Mosaic law stipulated that if the owner of a tract became so destitute that he had to sell his land, the nearest male relative had the "right and duty" (Jer. 32:7) to purchase it. This transaction was intended to keep the property within the possession of the extended family. In the year of Jubilee, the original owner regained control of the land (Lev. 25:13-17). The implication is that Jeremiah would only be obtaining permission to use the property, not permanently own it.

As God had revealed, Hanamel visited Jeremiah while he was imprisoned and asked that he fulfill his obligation as the family guardian. This incident confirmed to the prophet that he truly had received an oracle from the Lord (Jer. 32:8). From a financial standpoint, the transaction seemed absurd. Yet, despite this, the "Sovereign LORD" (vs. 25) directed His spokesperson to purchase the field with "silver" and the acquisition confirmed by witnesses. In obedience to God, Jeremiah paid his cousin 17 "shekels" (or about seven ounces; vs. 9) of "silver" for the property. In the ancient Near East, the shekel was the basic weight used for financial transactions. Nonetheless, archaeological evidence indicates that there was no uniform standard established for the shekel's size, weight, and value.

II. Anticipating Future Economic Activity: Jeremiah 32:14-15

A. Preserving Important Documents: vs. 14

"This is what the LORD Almighty, the God of Israel, says: Take these documents, both the sealed and unsealed copies of the deed of purchase, and put them in a clay jar so they will last a long time.'"

In the presence of witnesses, Jeremiah "signed and sealed the deed" (Jer. 32:10) of purchase. Also, "scales" (that is, a beam balance) were used to weigh out the "silver." Two copies of the "deed of purchase" (vs. 11) were drafted. The first sheet of papyrus was sealed with wax, and the second was left unsealed (to be used for future reference, if required).

On the first copy were recorded the "terms and conditions" of the transaction. Next, Jeremiah gave both copies to his trustworthy friend and personal scribe, "Baruch" (vs. 12), the son of a man named "Neriah" (36:26). Looking on were Hanamel, along with the "witnesses" (32:12) who had put their names on the sealed document and the "Jews" (or Judeans) sitting in the courtyard of the guardhouse. Then, Jeremiah relayed the Lord's "instructions" (vs. 13) to Baruch. Specifically, he was to place both the "sealed and unsealed copies" (vs. 14) of the "deed" in a pottery "jar" so that the documents would be preserved for a "long time" (that is, until the return of the exiles to Judah from captivity in Babylon).

B. Possessing Property Once Again: vs. 15

"For this is what the LORD Almighty, the God of Israel, says: Houses, fields and vineyards will again be bought in this land.'"

The reason for the divine directive is that the sovereign Lord, who declared Himself to be the "God of Israel" (Jer. 32:15), promised to bring about the restoration of His chosen people from captivity. Jeremiah's purchase symbolized the Lord's pledge that in a future day, a righteous remnant would once again buy "houses, fields and vineyards" in their ancestral homeland.

Discussion Questions

1. What kind of king was Zedekiah?
2. Why was the army of Babylon besieging Jerusalem?
3. Why did God direct Jeremiah to purchase property owned by his cousin?
4. In what ways have you seen God use vexing events in your life to shape your character?
5. What negative influences from your past must you resist in order to grow spiritually?

Contemporary Application

Who could imagine that God would direct Jeremiah to buy his cousin's field even as Jerusalem and Judah were being overrun by the Babylonians? Yet this is what the Lord wanted the prophet to do. And he recognized that God would use this symbolic act to signal to His people that even in their bleak circumstance, He would restore them to their homeland.

In the early 1970s, I attended a Christian youth seminar, where I heard the remarkable testimony of a young man. Kurt was a popular senior at his high school because of his good looks and cheerful personality. One early evening, Kurt took his father's car to a friend's house, where he and three of his peers secretly loaded the car with cans of beer. Then, as they drove around town, they got drunk.

Meanwhile, the roads were becoming slippery from the rain that was now falling heavily. Just when the car neared a fast-food restaurant, Kurt lost control and swerved out of his lane. His car smashed into the side of another car that was coming out of the parking lot of the restaurant. Kurt banged his head on the steering wheel and lost consciousness.

Later, in the hospital, Kurt learned that the injuries to him, his friends, and the driver of the other car were minor. Tragically, though, two passengers in the other car had both died. Incredibly, the victims were Kurt's mother and younger sister. Even more incredibly, his father was at his son's side, having already forgiven him.

At first, Kurt insisted that he was not responsible for the incident. He blamed the weather for the accident, his friends for getting him drunk, and God for letting it happen. Thereafter, Kurt's life speedily went downhill. He became a heavy drinker and often took drugs. As soon as he graduated, he left home. He couldn't keep a job for long, and he often got into fights in bars.

Finally, Kurt hit bottom when he was arrested for brawling. That night, he broke down, confessed his sins, and asked God for forgiveness. Kurt's father, who had never given up praying for his son and was always ready to be there for him with his love, picked Kurt up the next morning. Since then, Kurt has been close to both his earthly and heavenly fathers.

An Incredible Pledge

Scripture

Background Scripture: *Jeremiah 33*
Scripture Lesson: *Jeremiah 33:2-11*
Key Verse: *"'I will restore the fortunes of the land as they were before,' says the LORD."* Jeremiah 33:11.
Scripture Lesson for Children: *Jeremiah 33:2-11*
Key Verse for Children: *"'I will restore the fortunes of the land as they were before,' says the LORD."* Jeremiah 33:11.

Lesson Aim

To trust God to make our lives whole, regardless of the challenges we face.

Lesson Setting

Time: 587 B.C.
Place: Judah and Jerusalem

Lesson Outline

An Incredible Pledge
I. Coming to Terms with a Dreary Present: Jeremiah 33:2-5
    A. *God as Creator: vs. 2*
    B. *God as Judge: vss. 3-5*
II. Awaiting a Blessed Future: Jeremiah 33:6-11
    A. *The Promise of the Exiles' Return: vss. 6-7*
    B. *The Promise of the Exiles' Pardon: vs. 8*
    C. *The Promise of Future Renown: vs. 9*
    D. *The Promise of Restored Fortunes: vss. 10-11*

Introduction for Adults

Topic: *Laughter Will Return*

In Jeremiah 33:9, the Lord declared that one day Jerusalem and its inhabitants would bring Him "renown, joy, praise and honor." Then, all the surrounding nations would witness the marvelous things God had done for His people.

During their town's annual autumn parade, two or three churches made magnificent floats—so good that often one of them took home first prize. It was their way of informing the public that the joyful worship of God was still a viable option for many people.

Then, as time went on, the floats these congregations made gradually disappeared. Why? It's because they required too much work to build and there were not enough people who volunteered to make them.

Making floats, of course, is just one way we can share with others the joy we have in the Lord Jesus. Sometimes we can celebrate with music that has a Christian emphasis. On other occasions, we can give praise to the Lord through acts of service. Regardless of what we do, our focus should remain on God and not ourselves.

Introduction for Youth

Topic: *Return to the Original*

"It's too late! I can't make it!" Young people often say such things after they have wasted their academic opportunities. For example, they might wish they had made better grades in high school so they could get into the college of their choice.

When it comes to the things of eternity, it's never too late to start over. Every day is a fresh opportunity to break from our sinful past and renew our commitment to God. He is always willing to extend His love and forgiveness to us.

The second oracle Jeremiah received from God emphasizes this truth. Jeremiah's peers had sinned greatly, but one day God would restore an upright remnant to the promised land. Then God would pardon them and enable them to start over. The Gospel likewise tells us that our Lord is the God of new beginnings. When we turn to Jesus in faith, He opens the door to abundant, satisfying, and eternal life.

Concepts for Children

Topic: *A Gift of Healing and Hope*

1. The people in Jerusalem were under attack.
2. The people in Jerusalem were terrified.
3. God reminded His people that He would be with them.
4. God promised that one day He would bless His people.
5. We can thank God for being with us.

Lesson Commentary

I. COMING TO TERMS WITH A DREARY PRESENT: JEREMIAH 33:2-5

A. God as Creator: vs. 2

"This is what the LORD says, he who made the earth, the LORD who formed it and established it—the LORD is his name."

Last week, we learned that Jeremiah was confined as a political prisoner in the palace courtyard. At this time, the Babylonians had laid siege to Jerusalem (Jer. 32:2). We also found out that while imprisoned, Jeremiah received an oracle from the Lord (vs. 6). According to 33:1, as the prophet remained incarcerated, he received a second oracle from God. Jeremiah introduced this divine message with the statement, "This is what the LORD says" (vs. 2). An examination of how the phrase is used in Scripture indicates that it is the hallmark of a prophet's message from God (for example, see also Isa. 7:7; Jer. 2:5; Ezek. 5:5).

The Hebrew noun rendered "LORD" (Jer. 33:2) is *Yahweh*. It was a deeply personal name that carried implications of the covenant relationship between God and the Israelites. Exodus 3:14 is the only place in the Old Testament where the significance of the name is clarified. The name "I AM" comes from the Hebrew verb *hayah*, which means "to exist" or "to be." In essence, the name *Yahweh* signifies that God is pure being. He is the eternally self-existent one. As was noted in lesson 2, when the noun rendered "Almighty" appears with "LORD" (32:14), the emphasis is on God as an invincible warrior who protects His chosen people. Also, when the noun translated "Sovereign" occurs with "LORD" (for example, see vs. 17), it highlights God's complete control over history and international events. As the sovereign Ruler, He always accomplishes His will.

The Book of Jeremiah gives repeated emphasis to God as the Creator (10:11-13; 51:15-16). He is the Lord who "made the earth" (33:2), as well as shaped the planet and firmly "established" it. These truths are also found throughout the Psalms. For instance, Psalm 104 (along with Job 38 and Psalms 8 and 29) produces a magnificent poetic and musical commentary on the creation. Even the structure of Psalm 104 draws praise in that it is modeled quite closely on the day-by-day creation events recorded in Genesis. Indeed, as the psalmist described in grandiose detail the daily acts of creation, he seemed to preach in glowing terms that what God created on each day is reason enough to praise Him. It is clear that the poet used the various stages of creation as his starting points for praise. But as he developed each creation-day theme, there is a constant anticipation for more, especially for the later days of the creation.

B. God as Judge: vss. 3-5

"'Call to me and I will answer you and tell you great and unsearchable things you do not know.' For this is what the LORD, the God of Israel, says about the houses in this city and the royal palaces of Judah that

have been torn down to be used against the siege ramps and the sword in the fight with the Babylonians: 'They will be filled with the dead bodies of the men I will slay in my anger and wrath. I will hide my face from this city because of all its wickedness.'"

Jeremiah 33:3 directs our attention to the prayers uttered by God's people. When virtuous individuals such as Jeremiah petitioned the Lord for justice and righteousness to prevail, He promised to answer their requests. Elsewhere, the Hebrew participle rendered "great and unsearchable things" is used to refer to a nation's fortified cities and walls (Num. 13:28; Deut. 1:28; 9:1; Josh. 14:12). But in Jeremiah 33:3, the emphasis is metaphorical and denotes the Lord's inscrutable, mysterious ways (see also Isa. 48:6). The latter includes God's revelation to Jeremiah that He was going to allow Jerusalem to be razed (Jer. 33:4-5) and His people later to be restored to the promised land (vss. 6-26). These are breathtaking truths that the Lord first had to disclose to Jeremiah before he could declare them to God's people.

In Romans 11:25, Paul referred to Israel's hardening as a "mystery." Of the 27 times the Greek noun translated "mystery" is used in the New Testament, 21 are from Paul's hand. The word "mystery" in the Bible is used to refer to something that was previously unknown, but had now been revealed. Often, Paul used the word "mystery" as synonymous with the Gospel. In Romans 11:33-36, the apostle closed off this chapter with a glorious doxology. He was in awe because God's plan of salvation for all people—Jew and Gentile—demonstrated His infinite wisdom and knowledge. Just as Jeremiah 33:3 declares, God's judgments are unsearchable and His paths beyond tracing out. Paul quoted from Isaiah 40:13 to show that God was the wise planner who brought all this about. No one counseled Him. God was under no obligation to repay anyone because no one has ever provided Him with anything. He alone is the comprehensive source of all things to whom belonged unending glory.

Previously, late in 609 or early in 608 B.C., the Lord instructed Jeremiah to deliver a warning to the worshipers at the Jerusalem temple. Following God's directions, the prophet positioned himself at the temple gate (perhaps the New Gate; see Jer. 26:10), where he could address the people who came to worship there (7:2). Though they attended temple activities, their religion was nothing but insincere ritual. Jeremiah challenged them to live in ways that were consistent with their apparent worship (vs. 3). The prophet also warned his peers that trusting in the temple would not keep them safe and that those who said it would were false prophets (vs. 4). Simply chanting the phrase "the temple of the LORD" was believed to ward off destruction. The pious were convinced that God would never allow His own temple and city to be destroyed.

Jeremiah 33:4-5 discredits all false hopes of safety. Already, as the siege of Jerusalem dragged on, the desperate inhabitants had dismantled their "houses" (including those built into or right next to the city's walls) and "royal palaces." In turn, they used these building materials to create a thicker, sturdier structure in a final attempt to strengthen Jerusalem's defenses (Isa. 22:10). Ultimately, the frantic efforts made by Jerusalem's defenders would prove futile against a relentless foe. God, in His "anger and wrath" (Jer. 33:5), would use the Babylonians to slaughter Jerusalem's warriors. The Lord would abandon His people because of all the evil deeds they and their predecessors had committed in His sight.

In ancient conflicts, siege warfare played a major role. City walls kept invaders out, but they could also isolate the inhabitants within. By laying siege to a city, an attacking army could cut off the defenders' food, supplies, and—if possible—water. A siege could be a long and tedious means to weaken a city, but certain tactics helped the process along. Iron-tipped battering rams were swung from ropes or rolled forward on wheels to break through the city gates. Soldiers dug trenches beneath city walls to weaken their foundations. When they burned the support beams, the walls would collapse. Fires were also set against the base of the wall to weaken the sandstone or limestone blocks.

A favorite Babylonian tactic was to build up a ramp of soil and debris against the weakest point of a city's wall. It could take months, but eventually the attackers could rush up the ramp and over the city's walls. Meanwhile, they denuded the surrounding countryside of trees to acquire material for building the ramp. Another result was that the process demoralized the defenders. With towers rolled into place, attackers could shoot arrows at defenders from the same height as the top of the wall. While archers cleared defenders away from the wall, soldiers climbed numerous ladders in an attempt to overrun the top.

II. Awaiting a Blessed Future: Jeremiah 33:6-11

A. The Promise of the Exiles' Return: vss. 6-7

"'Nevertheless, I will bring health and healing to it; I will heal my people and will let them enjoy abundant peace and security. I will bring Judah and Israel back from captivity and will rebuild them as they were before.'"

The dreary circumstance detailed in Jeremiah 33:2-5 stands in sharp contrast to the blessed future foretold in verses 6-11. The Hebrew term rendered "nevertheless" (vs. 6) is more literally translated "look" or "behold" to emphasize God's unwavering commitment to one day restore the exiles in Babylon to their homeland. The reference in verse 7 to "Judah and Israel" indicates that the Lord would bring back from "captivity" His previously divided people and enable all of them to "rebuild" their towns (3:18).

This amazing turn of events remained true, even though the Lord permitted Nebuchadnezzar's army to destroy Jerusalem and its temple (30:8, 16; 32:36-37). When the time came for the remnant to return to Judah, God pledged to "bring health" (33:6) to Jerusalem and "healing" to its people. Indeed, their lives would be overflowing with "peace and security." A comparison with 30:17

suggests that the Lord had in view both the spiritual and political well-being of the returnees. This signifies a dramatic reversal of the divine judgment God brought on the promised land (8:21-22).

B. The Promise of the Exiles' Pardon: vs. 8

"'I will cleanse them from all the sin they have committed against me and will forgive all their sins of rebellion against me.'"

God's promises of restoration were not intended to ignore the harsh reality of what brought about the exile of His people to Babylon. Specifically, generations of them were guilty of sinning against the Lord, and He had to spiritually purify them from their iniquity. God also declared His intent to pardon the exiles for all their transgressions against Him (Jer. 33:8). We find a similar emphasis in 1 John 1. Verse 8 discloses that those who declare themselves to be free of "sin" were self-deceived and not abiding in God's "truth." Oppositely, if they acknowledged their sins to God, He remained "faithful and just" (vs. 9) to pardon the guilt of their sin and cleanse them from their "unrighteousness."

C. The Promise of Future Renown: vs. 9

"'Then this city will bring me renown, joy, praise and honor before all nations on earth that hear of all the good things I do for it; and they will be in awe and will tremble at the abundant prosperity and peace I provide for it.'"

God declared that once the exiles in Babylon were restored to Judah, all the surrounding "nations" (Jer. 33:9) would learn about the remarkable outcome. In turn, all the "good" the Lord did for the upright remnant would bring Him fame, glory, and "honor." Moreover, as His "renown" spread to the Gentiles, they would "tremble" with "awe," especially at the sight of the "prosperity and peace" God poured out on the returnees. Hosea 3:5 reveals that they too would begin to earnestly "seek the LORD," submit in reverence to Him, and experience the fullness of His "blessings."

D. The Promise of Restored Fortunes: vss. 10-11

"This is what the LORD says: 'You say about this place, "It is a desolate waste, without men or animals." Yet in the towns of Judah and the streets of Jerusalem that are deserted, inhabited by neither men nor animals, there will be heard once more the sounds of joy and gladness, the voices of bride and bridegroom, and the voices of those who bring thank offerings to the house of the LORD, saying, "Give thanks to the LORD Almighty, for the LORD is good; his love endures forever." For I will restore the fortunes of the land as they were before,' says the LORD."

As the Babylonian siege continued, the holdouts in Jerusalem realized that the enemy would eventually succeed in breaking through the city's defenses. After all, the invaders had laid waste to the "towns of Judah" (Jer. 33:10) so that they lacked any inhabitants, whether people or animals. The desolation of the nation was a harbinger of the destruction Nebuchadnezzar would bring to Jerusalem. That outcome notwithstanding, the Lord revealed that a future day was coming when Judah's cities and Jerusalem's streets would no longer be empty. Instead, they would be filled with people and animals.

Furthermore, the activity of the inhabitants within these population centers would produce an assortment of sounds, including the following: "joy and gladness" (vs. 11), marriage celebrations, and the jubilant songs of worshipers as they brought their "thank offerings" to the rebuilt Jerusalem temple. The latter group would invite all who heard them to express their gratitude to the Lord of heaven's armies. Their motivation for doing so was the goodness of God and His eternal, steadfast "love" (Pss. 106:1; 118:1; 136:1). His unfailing compassion was demonstrated in restoring the prosperity of Judah as it was before the exile of God's people. It would also signify a reversal of His judgment on the promised land and its inhabitants (7:34; 16:9; 25:10).

Ezra 3 records the efforts of the returnees to Jerusalem to rebuild the altar and temple of the city. We learn that they were so eager to worship God that they wanted to begin offering sacrifices right away, even before the temple foundation had been laid. The people were earnest, however, about rebuilding the temple for worship. They hired masons and carpenters and made arrangements to have timber sent from Lebanon. Then, when the temple foundation was laid, the priests and Levites took up their trumpets and cymbals to praise the Lord in the tradition King David had established. As the priests and Levites thanked the Lord for His goodness and unfailing love to His people, there were mixed emotions among the worshipers.

Many attendees shouted with joy for what God had done and for this first step in rebuilding the temple. However, a number of older residents, who could remember the splendor of Solomon's temple, wept when they saw the less spectacular new structure in its beginning stages. At the celebration, the sounds of the shouting and the weeping mixed together. Both Haggai (Hag. 2:3) and Zechariah would find themselves addressing a segment of the population discouraged by "the day of small things" (Zech. 4:10). But in the second month of 536 b.c., the dominant mood among the returned exiles still was great joy (Ezra 3:13). Even people at a considerable distance could hear the resounding noise of a community of people who dared to take the Lord at His word and risk everything they had to go to ruined towns and farms and trust Him to take a remnant, plant them, and grow a nation.

Discussion Questions

1. Why did the Lord stress that He is the creator of the earth?
2. What unfathomable truths was God revealing to Jeremiah?
3. Why would it be necessary for the Lord to spiritually cleanse and forgive His people?

4. When you compare the good times with the difficult times you have experienced, how do you choose to deal with these realities?

5. Why is focusing on the positive aspects disclosed in God's Word so critical to having a perspective that pleases God?

Contemporary Application

The second oracle Jeremiah received from the Lord served as yet another reminder of His commitment to one day restore His people to Judah. God, in His eternal love, would bring this about and nothing would prevent it from happening. What would it be like for the returnees to be restored to their homeland? It was as if an erasure had taken place and a fresh page had been inserted.

Imagine someone giving you a book containing a record of every word you had ever spoken, every deed you had ever done, and every thought you had ever entertained. Now imagine that with the book you were handed an eraser and were told that you could remove any of the book's contents that you wished and that the actuality of the facts themselves would also disappear with the erasing. Of course, we can't erase our past. But we don't need to, for Jesus has done something much more effective. He makes a "book exchange" for us when He extends His grace to us and we receive it.

Jesus' unmerited favor works like this. His life record book has no wrongs in it. When He gave His life on the cross, it was actually an exchange He was providing for us—His book for ours. He took the consequences for our ugly, embarrassing record and credited us with His clean record. That's the beginning of an amazing transformational process in which God makes our lives whole. As a result of His grace, God forgives our past and in doing so brings renown to Himself.

But beyond that, God continues to provide us with "new starts" in our lives when we fall (as in cheating or lying) or when our world falls around us (from something like a death or a divorce). We have the promise that "his compassions never fail. They are new every morning" (Lam. 3:22-23).

Choosing to Rejoice

Scripture

Background Scripture: *Job 1; Psalm 56; Habakkuk 1–3*
Scripture Lesson: *Habakkuk 2:1-5; 3:17-19*
Key Verse: *Yet I will rejoice in the LORD, I will be joyful in
God my Savior.* Habakkuk 3:18.
Scripture Lesson for Children: *Job 1:1, 13-21; Psalm
56:9-11*
Key Verse for Children: *In God I trust; I will not be afraid.*
Psalm 56:11.

Lesson Aim

To stress that God wants us to abandon our sins and
faithfully serve Him.

Lesson Setting

Time: Around 605 B.C.
Place: Judah and Jerusalem

Lesson Outline

Choosing to Rejoice
   I. God's Response to Habakkuk: Habakkuk 2:1-5
       A. *God's Use of the Wicked: vs. 1*
       B. *God's Judgment of Babylon: vss. 2-5*
  II. Habakkuk's Response to God: Habakkuk 3:17-19
       A. *Rejoicing in the Lord: vss. 17-18*
       B. *Finding Strength in the Lord: vs. 19*

Introduction for Adults

Topic: *The Rewards of Patience*

Don and Joyce's teenage son had already been through two surgeries to relieve pressure on his brain caused by a tumor. He faced a third operation. While on a business trip, they met a woman whose brain tumor had disappeared just before she was scheduled for surgery. She told them, "If you and your son had faith, he would be healed too."

Don and Joyce and their son and two daughters struggled to understand God's ways, just like Habakkuk did when God told him that the pagan Babylonians were going to invade and destroy God's people. In Habakkuk's case, God revealed that he would judge the Babylonians and that the prophet should patiently live by faith. Therefore, Habakkuk rejoiced and found strength in the Lord.

But what about Don and Joyce and many other Christians who try to understand why God has brought suffering into their lives? They get no clear words from the Lord. They get a variety of messages from other people.

In the end, such people decide to patiently live by faith. Habakkuk believed the word of God. The prophet's country was not spared, but he found new resources of joy and strength in the Lord. That has been the experience of Christians who work through their difficulties in light of what they know to be true about the Lord.

Introduction for Youth

Topic: *Choice: To Trust or Not to Trust*

How many times do we feel torn and troubled like Habakkuk over the prevalence of evil in the world? When our faith is under fire, we would rather run than stand and fight.

Habakkuk's quarrel with God instructs us to continue believing, even when we feel weak and unqualified for the life of faith. No Christian ever feels up to the task. But that should not deter us in our quest to remain faithful to the Lord.

God does not expect us to get As in all of life's courses. (Jesus, for example, worked with people who stumbled miserably but never quit.) God wants us to be honest with Him about our fears. He can give us the courage to move ahead, despite the obstacles and disappointments we may face along the way.

Concepts for Children

Topic: *Overcoming All Troubles*

1. Satan lied when he said hateful things about Job.
2. Satan did mean things to Job.
3. Job became very sad.
4. Even when we feel sad, God is with us.
5. God is also our source of strength in times of trouble.

Lesson Commentary

I. GOD'S RESPONSE TO HABAKKUK: HABAKKUK 2:1-5

A. God's Use of the Wicked: vs. 1

I will stand at my watch and station myself on the ramparts; I will look to see what he will say to me, and what answer I am to give to this complaint.

Habakkuk and possibly Obadiah ministered in a period that ranged from approximately 663 B.C. until about 586 B.C. The northern kingdom of Israel had already fallen to the Assyrians, who posed a continual threat to Judah until they fell decisively to the ruthless Babylonians in 612 B.C. Habakkuk ministered toward the end of Josiah's reign, before Babylon's rise to power. Economic conditions during this time were excellent as Judah enjoyed its last period of prosperity and promise of spiritual revival. Yet Judah's rapid decline into wickedness after the death of Josiah shows that the renewal did not go far below the surface—something God enabled Habakkuk to see.

A reading of Habakkuk suggests that the writer was both a poet and a prophet, as well as a person of deep emotional strength. For instance, his hatred of sin compelled him to cry out to God for judgment (1:2-4). Habakkuk's sense of justice also led him to challenge God's plan to judge the nation of Judah through the Babylonians (1:12–2:1). The prophet learned that God, in His sovereignty, uses even pagan nations and leaders to accomplish His purposes. Consequently, Habakkuk decided to recall God's faithfulness and rely on His promises, regardless of how desperate the circumstance might appear. The last chapter records a remarkable statement of faith as Habakkuk reaffirmed his confidence in God.

In 1:13, the prophet was especially pointed in voicing his adverse feelings toward God's decision to use the Babylonians to punish the faithful in Judah along with the oppressors. When the Babylonians conquered nations, they swept everyone up "like fish in the sea" (vs. 14). As a result of God's apparent indifference, the people in these lands, including Judah, were as defenseless as cornered fish before an experienced fisherman using every means possible to produce a large catch (vs. 15). By deploying hooks, nets, and dragnets, this laborer brought in many fish and rejoiced at his success. Similarly, the Babylonians' achievements in taking many captive brought great delight to their hearts.

Verse 16 pictures this fisherman worshiping and sacrificing to his nets. Likewise, the Babylonians ascribed divine honor to their weapons and glorified themselves rather than God. Their military conquests had provided food for a luxurious lifestyle that made them feel self-sufficient and above accountability to any higher being. Habakkuk summed up his argument by asking how much longer God would let the Babylonians persist in their evil ways (vs. 17). Though the Lord had shown Habakkuk a powerful army that ruthlessly devoured nations in its path, God had not yet revealed their destiny. After Habakkuk stated his case before the Lord, the prophet stood "watch" (2:1), waiting for an answer to his questions. The image here is one of a guard standing on the walls of Jerusalem, keeping an eye out for a possible military response to a political challenge. The prophet had presented his complaint in faith, not skepticism, and fully expected God to respond.

As hard as it might have been for Habakkuk to accept, sometimes the Lord allowed the innocent to suffer as He punished evildoers for their transgressions. Whether one is considering wicked attitudes, actions, or aims, this evil results from the absence of the moral perfection that God originally intended to exist in the world. Ultimately, only God knows why He has allowed evil to exist in the world. It nevertheless remains true that the Lord might use evil to bring home to us the distressing fact of our mortality, to warn us of greater evils, to bring about a greater good, or to help defeat wickedness. The last two reasons are especially evident in the cross of Christ. Despite the tragedy of the Messiah's suffering on the cross, His atoning sacrifice resulted in a greater good (namely, the salvation of the lost) and the defeat of evil (for instance, sin and death).

B. God's Judgment of Babylon: vss. 2-5

Then the LORD replied: "Write down the revelation and make it plain on tablets so that a herald may run with it. For the revelation awaits an appointed time; it speaks of the end and will not prove false. Though it linger, wait for it; it will certainly come and will not delay. See, he is puffed up; his desires are not upright—but the righteous will live by his faith—indeed, wine betrays him; he is arrogant and never at rest. Because he is as greedy as the grave and like death is never satisfied, he gathers to himself all the nations and takes captive all the peoples."

God not only gave Habakkuk an answer, but also commanded him to engrave the "revelation" (Hab. 2:2) legibly on "tablets" (possibly made of stone, wood, clay, or metal). Doing this would enable heralds to read the oracle of judgment correctly and quickly proclaim it to others. The Lord would punish Babylon for its sins and bring deliverance for His people. Because God's message awaited a future and certain fulfillment (vs. 3), it was especially important that it be transmitted through a permanent record. Though the judgment of Babylon and the deliverance of God's people would not come immediately, the Lord asked the upright remnant to wait for it. God promised that it would assuredly take place. From a human standpoint, it would seem like an unreasonable delay, but from God's perspective the fulfillment would arrive on time. Despite the prolonged wait, the outcome was certain.

Nebuchadnezzar was possibly the most illustrious of ancient Babylon's rulers. The son of Nabopolassar and the king of the Babylonian Empire from 605 to 562 B.C., Nebuchadnezzar was a powerful monarch who would stop at nothing to bring neighboring countries into submission. His forces were known for their military drive and their savage treatment of conquered peoples. From the outset of Nebuchadnezzar's reign, the Lord used the pagan king to discipline

His wayward people. While the arrogant ignored God's message of judgment for the wicked and deliverance for His people, the righteous lived by faith (vs. 4). For a period of time, circumstances would appear contrary to what one would expect from a holy God. But those who waited and remained faithful to the Lord would not be disappointed in the final results. They would eventually see God's promised salvation (Rom. 1:17; Gal. 3:11; Heb. 10:38-39).

God began His sentence of judgment on the Babylonians by saying, "Indeed, wine betrays him" (vs. 5). Ancient writers confirm that the Babylonians were addicted to strong drink. In fact, Babylon was overthrown in the state of drunkenness and bravado described in this passage (Dan. 5). Moreover, God revealed to Habakkuk that the Babylonians were egotistical and restless. Their "greed" (Hab. 2:5) was as large as the grave's appetite for cadavers. Also, just like "death," the aggressors' craving for dead bodies seemed insatiable. It appeared as if no one could determine the number of battlefields filled with the corpses of warriors from surrounding nations whom the Babylonians had slaughtered.

A time was coming when the nations once terrorized and enslaved by the Babylonians would take up a "taunt" (vs. 6) against them. "Ridicule and scorn" refers to riddles of a mocking nature. The idea is that Babylon's former victims would deride it with songs laced with contempt. The Hebrew term rendered "woe" was used in funeral laments and conveyed the notion of impending death. With respect to Babylon, it would be like pointing a finger at the nation and shouting, "You are doomed!" One reason is that the wicked rulers had amassed stolen goods. Understandably, the victims wondered how long such an atrocity would continue, so great was their pain and despair. The phrase "makes himself wealthy by extortion" is more literally rendered "the person who makes himself heavy by debts." It reinforces the previous charge that the Babylonians used blackmail to get rich from others. Goods taken in pledge kept piling ever higher, suggesting there was no limit to the greed of the profiteers.

The Babylonians' debtors—namely, those whom they previously robbed and terrorized—one day would suddenly be the attackers. In a metaphorical sense, the creditors would rise up in anger to bite their tyrants. In this role reversal, the former victims would wake up and cause the Babylonians to tremble, especially as the oppressed pillaged their tormentors (vs. 7). There is a sense of ironic justice at work here. The Babylonians were guilty of plundering many nations (vs. 8). But there were some survivors, and one day this remnant would turn around and rob the former plunderers. The revenge was justified, for Babylon had shed innocent blood. In addition to murder, the wicked used violence to destroy lands, cities, and their inhabitants.

II. HABAKKUK'S RESPONSE TO GOD: HABAKKUK 3:17-19

A. Rejoicing in the Lord: vss. 17-18

Though the fig tree does not bud and there are no grapes on the vines, though the olive crop fails and the fields produce no food, though there are no sheep in the pen and no cattle in the stalls, yet I will rejoice in the Lord, *I will be joyful in God my Savior.*

Even though Habakkuk 3 is called a "prayer" (vs. 1), in its form and language this passage is closely related to the Psalms. For instance, Habakkuk echoes the terminology and imagery of hymns expressing lament, such as Psalms 18 and 77. Even some phrases used from Psalms are used in Habakkuk 3. "On *shigionoth*" (vs. 1) is an obscure literary or musical term about which little is known. Some think it indicates a highly emotional poetic form. The title of Psalm 7 is the only other time the term appears in the Old Testament (in the singular form).

"*Selah*" (Hab. 3:3, 9, 13) is often used in the Psalms. The term possibly indicates the spot for a brief musical interlude or a short liturgical response by the congregation (for example, Ps. 3:2). "For the director of music" (Hab. 3:19) is a liturgical note that appears in the headings of 55 psalms. It might have designated that the piece was to be used in the temple worship or recited by the leader of the choir. "On my stringed instruments" (Hab. 3:19) is a liturgical note appearing in the heading of several psalms (for instance, Pss. 61; 67). The term comes from a Hebrew verb that means "to strike a cord," and might indicate the manner in which a stringed instrument (such as a harp or lyre) was used to perform the musical piece.

Habakkuk 3:2 is the prophet's formal petition. Verses 3-15 recall the Lord's past dealings with His people, and verses 16-19 express trust and confidence in God's preservation of the upright. Habakkuk knew the testimonies of God's mighty acts as celebrated in song, as well as in feasts and festivals of Israel. These displays of divine power included the exodus from Egypt, the miracles of the Red Sea, and the conquest of the promised land. In verse 2, Habakkuk asked the Lord to once again help His people in their time of great need. In the midst of God's punishment of Judah at the hand of the Babylonians, Habakkuk begged the Lord to "remember mercy." Expressed differently, the prophet wanted God to turn from His anger, be gracious to His people, and rescue them from their plight.

As Habakkuk meditated on God's work in human affairs, he was overcome with an awe-inspiring sense of the greatness of the Lord. Accordingly, in verse 3, the prophet used figures from God's past intervention on His people's behalf to paint a picture of their future redemption. Habakkuk took these images from the deliverance of God's people from Egypt and the conquest of Canaan. Habakkuk declared that the Lord was the same holy God who came from Teman and Paran to help His people from slavery in Egypt. Teman was a district in Edom, but the name was sometimes used for the entire country. Paran was in the hill country along the western border of the Gulf of Aqaba. In Judges 5:4, the Lord is said to have marched from Edom to help His people, and in Deuteronomy 33:2, Paran is mentioned in connection with the Lord's appearance at Sinai.

The glory of God, which protected and led Israel from Egypt through the wilderness (Exod. 40:34-38), was another physical display of the divine presence. The prophet declared that the brightness of God's glory covered the heavens and His praises were heard throughout the earth (Hab. 3:3). The prophet noted that the brilliant light of God's glory was more intense than the sun and also that light flashed from His hands and hid His mighty power (vs. 4). We can almost hear the prophet exclaim, "What an awesome God we serve!"

Habakkuk knew that the Lord was going to discipline the people of Judah and that it wasn't going to be a pleasant experience. The prophet also realized that God's discipline and mercy were both part of His divine entourage. Perhaps recalling earlier events in Israel's history—where God frequently used "plague" (vs. 5) and "pestilence" against enemies (Exod. 5:3; 9:15; Deut. 32:24)—Habakkuk noted that dreadful diseases and plagues marched in front of and followed behind the Lord. Indeed, the entire universe responded in fear at the approach of almighty God (Exod. 15:14).

Habakkuk declared that when the Lord stopped His movement, the earth shook, and when He stared, the nations trembled (Hab. 3:6). Only Israel's God—the all-powerful Lord—could shatter "the ancient mountains" and level the "age-old hills." Such phenomena as earthquakes, volcanic eruptions, and landslides served as reminders that the entire planet and its inhabitants were at God's disposal (Isa. 40:12).

Habakkuk 3:17 reveals the desolation the Babylonians would bring on Judah. Fig trees would be so damaged they would not blossom. Likewise, grape plants would fail to produce fruit on their withered vines. Olive groves and grainfields would become barren. Flocks of sheep and herds of cattle would be decimated by the Babylonian onslaught. Despite the hardships that awaited the people of Judah, Habakkuk determined that it was best to trust God's sovereign handling of the circumstances.

The prophet declared he would find his joy in the Lord (vs. 18). This reveals the depth of his faith in God. Habakkuk also asserted he would exult in the God of his salvation. Rather than look to earthly powers and idols for relief from foreign oppression, the prophet would focus his confidence and joy on his Redeemer and Lord. All earthly rulers and governments are subject to failure and defeat. Consequently, if the people of Judah had looked to powerful kings and armies for deliverance, they would have been deeply disappointed. Only God had the ability to rescue them from danger and watch over them in times of trouble. Unlike trusting in earthly powers, God's people would never be disappointed for placing their confidence in Him.

B. Finding Strength in the Lord: vs. 19

The Sovereign Lord is my strength; he makes my feet like the feet of a deer, he enables me to go on the heights. For the director of music. On my stringed instruments.

The prophet announced in Habakkuk 3:19 that the Lord and God of Israel was his source of strength. As long as he depended on the all-powerful Ruler of the universe, God's spokesperson would not stumble, but remain sure-footed as a deer (2 Sam. 22:34; Ps. 18:33). Even if he were to walk on dangerous mountain slopes (metaphorically speaking), God would watch over him.

Discussion Questions

1. What was the nature of the complaint Habakkuk voiced to God?
2. In what ways did the Babylonians demonstrate extreme arrogance?
3. How did Habakkuk describe the harsh judgment awaiting Judah?
4. What does it mean for believers to walk by faith in devastating circumstances?
5. How is it possible to rejoice in the Lord when life is filled with anguish?

Contemporary Application

Economic affluence and spiritual poverty—does that description of life in ancient Babylon sound contemporary to you? In the time of Habakkuk, the Babylonians commanded unparalleled power and prosperity. Equity and piety, however, were absent from their lives. The people tried to fill their inward emptiness with material riches rather than with a vital relationship with God. In addition, they misused power and privilege to oppress the nations around them.

Despite the 2008 global financial crisis, modern Western civilization continues to enjoy remarkable prosperity. Yet, as most people pursue wealth and power, many no longer feel any need for God's direction. Society has become morally bankrupt, turning away from ethical standards that previous generations recognized as valid. Meanwhile, God calls us to examine our own lifestyle and priorities in light of His values. The exhortation to us today is similar to the prophetic summons of ancient times. We are to turn from our sins and live in a godly manner.

In his classic text *Whatever Became of Sin?*, Karl Menninger tells about a stern-faced man who stood on a city street corner and watched pedestrians hurry by. Every few minutes, the man would lift one arm and solemnly point to an individual and exclaim, "Guilty!" An observer said the effect on people was eerie. They would hesitate, glance at the man, and hurry off.

In a sense, we need to be like that stern-faced man. However, instead of pointing at other people, we need to acknowledge the attitudes and priorities in our own lives that conflict with God's values. Along with admitting our guilt, we can ask God to empower us to change our ways. In turn, He enables us to examine ourselves as candidly as the stern-faced man judged some of the people who passed by him. Indeed, with God's help, character transformation is possible.

Awaiting Vindication

DEVOTIONAL READING

1 Chronicles 16:28-34

DAILY BIBLE READINGS

Monday October 6
Job 19:13–21 Forsaken by Family and Friends

Tuesday October 7
Psalm 10:1–11 Why Do You Stand Far Off?

Wednesday October 8
Isaiah 44:1–8 Do Not Fear

Thursday October 9
Psalm 57:1–6 God's Purpose for Me

Friday October 10
Psalm 57:7–11 My Heart Is Steadfast

Saturday October 11
1 Chronicles 16:28–34 Love That Endures Forever

Sunday October 12
Job 19:1–7, 23–29 My Redeemer Lives!

Scripture

Background Scripture: *Job 19; Psalm 57*

Scripture Lesson: *Job 19:1-7, 23-29*

Key Verse: *"I know that my Redeemer lives, and that in the end he will stand upon the earth."* Job 19:25.

Scripture Lesson for Children: *Job 19:1-6, 23-27; Psalm 57:2-3*

Key Verse for Children: *God sends his love and his faithfulness.* Psalm 57:3.

Lesson Aim

To recognize the importance of affirming God in our troubles as well as our blessings.

Lesson Setting

Time: During the second millennium B.C.
Place: The land of Uz

Lesson Outline

Awaiting Vindication

    I. Job's Impatience with His Counselors: Job 19:1-7

        A. *Feeling Afflicted: vss. 1-2*

        B. *Feeling Reproached: vss. 3-4*

        C. *Feeling Vilified: vss. 5-6*

        D. *Feeling Abandoned: vs. 7*

    II. Job's Assurance of Being Vindicated: Job 19:23-29

        A. *Recording Statements for Posterity: vss. 23-24*

        B. *Looking to God for Redemption: vss. 25-27*

        C. *Anticipating Justice from God: vss. 28-29*

Introduction for Adults

Topic: *Confident of Redemption*

Anna was blind from birth. Everything she knew and accomplished in life she owed to her parents' sacrifice and dedication. When her mother fell ill, Anna was distraught. She had never seen her mother. She knew only her voice and touch.

For months Anna sat with her mother in a nursing home, holding her hands and talking to her. But her mother had lost her speech and could not respond. Nevertheless, Anna held on firmly every day, speaking words of comfort and hope.

In times of suffering, we hold on to each other and especially to God. Even when God does not seem to reply to our cries, we follow the example of Job by continuing to trust in our Redeemer. Faith drives us to prayer and worship every day. In the darkness, we keep pursuing the light by faith. We claim our Savior's promise that nothing can separate us from His love (Rom. 8:31-39).

Introduction for Youth

Topic: *Hope Faces Misery*

One of the basic therapies for strengthening hand, wrist, and arm muscles is squeezing a rubber ball tightly several times a day. At first we feel the tension and pain, but gradually our muscles respond, and we are able to function normally. This exercise is prescribed after injuries or surgeries—incidents and events we would prefer to avoid. In cases like these, holding fast to a rubber ball is a discipline that produces results.

God sometimes takes us through tough times to strengthen our spiritual muscles (so to speak). He knows how flabby we get when we neglect our worship and obedience to His good and perfect will. But when He gets our attention, we respond with therapies that give us new love and zeal for Him.

Job's account tells us that it is possible to be faithful to God, even when hard times come. We surmount our difficulties by the Spirit's indwelling power and presence.

Concepts for Children

Topic: *A Special Friend*

1. There are days when life seems horrible to us.
2. This can leave us feeling sad.
3. Even in difficult moments, God is our friend.
4. During sad times, God still loves us.
5. No matter how hard things get, God always cares for us.

Lesson Commentary

I. Job's Impatience with His Counselors: Job 19:1-7

A. Feeling Afflicted: vss. 1-2

Then Job replied: "How long will you torment me and crush me with words?"

After the prologue to Job (chaps. 1—2), chapter 3 records Job's complaints about his anguishing circumstance. This is followed by a series of dialogues he had with his friends, which are recorded in chapters 4 through 27. Job's three counselors were likely princes and sages in each of their own areas.

Eliphaz's name was derived from an Arabic word meaning "God is the victor." He was from Teman, an Edomite city south of Canaan that was known to be a center for philosophical discussions. Teman is the only hometown of the three comforters that can be definitively located today. Bildad's name came from a Hebrew phrase meaning "Baal is Lord." Bildad may have been a descendant of Shuah, Abraham's youngest son by his wife Keturah. His tribe of Shuhites probably made their home somewhere east of Canaan, but the precise location of their settlement is unknown (Gen. 25:2, 6). Zophar is translated as "little bird." His tribe was from Naamah, perhaps a small town in Arabia.

Job 19 features Job's reply to Bildad's second speech (chap. 18) and includes what might be called four stanzas: (1) Verses 1-6: Job showed his impatience with his counselors. (2) Verses 7-12: Job felt abandoned and opposed by God. (3) Verses 13-20: Job blamed God for alienating him from his friends and family. (4) Verses 21-29: Job declared his hope in a Redeemer. The first stanza of this chapter sums up what might be called Job's fifth persecution. His first persecution was the loss of his servants and property; the second, the loss of his children; the third, his physical suffering; the fourth, the foolishness of his wife; and the fifth, the ongoing torment of his advisers. Prior to this point in Job's conversations with his friends, he was able to scoff at or show some indifference toward their admonitions. But after Bildad's cruel speech, Job had apparently reached his limit. In anguish, Job asked how long he had to endure being tortured by Bildad's reproach and pulverized by his condemnation (vs. 2).

B. Feeling Reproached: vss. 3-4

"Ten times now you have reproached me; shamelessly you attack me. If it is true that I have gone astray, my error remains my concern alone."

Job claimed that his counselors had "reproached" (Job 19:3) him "ten times" with no cause. The Hebrew verb translated "reproached" implies that Job felt insulted and humiliated by the shameless verbal attacks he received from his advisers. By saying "ten times," Job probably was not referring to the actual number of incidents in which his friends had rebuked him. More likely, he was indicating his feeling that they had turned against him completely (see also Gen. 31:7, 41; Num. 14:22; 1 Sam. 1:8). While desiring some sort of pity from his peers, Job had received, instead, their unrelenting harassment and condemnation.

What we see portrayed throughout Job is how damaging words can be in a counseling context. This is especially true in regard to people who are suffering. Contrary to Satan when he brought the devastation recorded in chapters 1 and 2, Job's advisers did not lift a finger against him. But their words caused him great pain—perhaps greater mental and emotional anguish than that produced by all else that had happened to Job. All along, he maintained his innocence, despite the fact that his friends alleged he had morally strayed from the path of virtue and integrity (19:4). Even if he had erred in some minor way, Job maintained that the guilt of any unintentional missteps rested with him. In short, he was telling his counselors to mind their own business.

C. Feeling Vilified: vss. 5-6

"If indeed you would exalt yourselves above me and use my humiliation against me, then know that God has wronged me and drawn his net around me."

Job accused his advisers of exalting themselves at his expense. In Job 19:5, the Hebrew verb rendered "exalt" indicates that the three friends clung to an insolent and lofty attitude. Even worse, they seized on the disgrace caused by Job's physical and emotional suffering to insist that he was guilty of blatantly sinning against God. Job countered that God, by allowing Job to be afflicted without a cause, had mistreated him. Job referred to part of a hunter's equipment when he claimed that God had encircled and ensnared Job like an animal in a "net" (vs. 6).

It is worth noting that Job's apparent accusation is premised on the condition of his counselors' being exalted above him. Job knew that if God exalted these men while unfairly punishing him, this would seem unjust and wrong. Evidently, Job was attempting to answer Bildad's earlier rhetorical question, "Does God pervert justice?" (8:3). In effect, Job declared that if it's simply a matter of good being rewarded and sin punished, then God must be unjust, for the three advisers had no reason to be exalted above Job, who maintained his righteousness. Like any of us, Job did not know God's plan. Consequently, Job had only an incomplete picture. We should be able to empathize with Job's anger when we realize the intense anguish he was experiencing. Nevertheless, the text suggests we need to look at Job's statements not as a direct attack on God, but rather as an indictment of the skewed theology of Job's counselors.

D. Feeling Abandoned: vs. 7

"Though I cry, 'I've been wronged!' I get no response; though I call for help, there is no justice."

As Job continued his response to Bildad, Job expressed his feelings in two ways. First, he felt abandoned by God (Job 19:7). Second, Job felt as though God was opposed to him and attacking him with an army (vss. 8-12). The Hebrew noun translated "wronged" (vs. 7) indicates that an extreme violation of justice had occurred. Even though Job might shout for "help," he received no answer from God. Of course, Job's feeling of isolation is understandable. He knew he had lived in a virtuous manner, and yet he had been struck down. Previously, God had been Job's friend and his source of security. But now God seemed to be Job's enemy, for God exposed Job to all sorts of danger. Even though he had boldly cried out for relief from his suffering, God remained silent.

Next, Job dramatized his feeling that God was at war with him. Job did so by describing the events of this conflict in reverse order. So, if verses 8-12 are read from end to beginning, we can follow in sequence a successful military campaign in all its drama and detail. While Job was camped in his tent, God's troops surrounded and laid siege to his dwelling (vs. 12). God's anger built against Job, whom He considered His enemy (vs. 11). The army of the Lord attacked and destroyed Job's once-secure dwelling place (vs. 10). Having captured Job, God's forces humiliated him by stripping him of his crown and honor (vs. 9). Finally, the troops under God's command confined Job's movements, thus making him a prisoner of war (vs. 8).

Many of the details in Job's depiction of battle echo what he had said earlier or what he would say later. For instance, his portrayal of being held captive (vs. 8) is similar to 3:23, which records Job's expression of feeling as though God had hedged him in. Another time Job complained, "You fasten my feet in shackles" (13:27). In 19:9, Job said God in His anger had removed a "crown" from Job's "head." Here, he said he felt like a king who had been conquered by God's forces. In more than one of Job's speeches, he referred to himself as a ruler. For example, Job compared himself to a monarch when he stated, "I chose the way for them and sat as their chief; I dwelt as a king among his troops" (29:25).

Apparently, Job was growing increasingly hopeless in his situation. To him, it was as though God in His wrath had diminished Job's assurance just as swiftly and as powerfully as He could uproot a tree (19:10). To Job, this circumstance felt like a travesty of justice. Another source of severe distress for Job was his sense of alienation from other people. It seemed as though he stood alone in the world. No one was willing to defend his actions before God's apparent judgment, and Job's alienation from others appeared all the more to be a betrayal.

Job was at his lowest point now, feeling as disgraced, rejected, and tired as at any stage in the account of his struggle. From the onset of Job's misery to this place in the narrative, he had been searching for anyone—even one person—to stand up for him. But it seemed as if everyone was gone. To dramatize his alienation further, Job listed the people who had deserted him. These included his brothers and acquaintances (vs. 13), his relatives and friends (vs. 14), his guests and female servants (vs. 15), his personal servant (vs. 16), his wife and brothers (vs. 17), little boys who mocked Job (vs. 18), and his most intimate friends (vs. 19). In effect, Job was completely alone.

Even though Job deserved to be honored as an esteemed leader, his horrible disease brought him scorn and disdain. When Job was denied one of the common courtesies of ancient society—namely, a young person's respect for an elder—Job must have known that he had sunk from a position of utmost respect to that of a pitiful outcast. Those bound to serve him avoided him, and those whom he thought loved him and enjoyed his companionship refused to give him their solace and affection. Job summed up his miserable condition by declaring bitterly that he was all alone with his deteriorated body. No doubt due to his illness, he had lost so much weight that he was down to just "skin and bones" (vs. 20). Evidently, Job had lost his teeth as well, due to the disease, so that all he had left in his mouth were toothless gums.

II. Job's Assurance of Being Vindicated: Job 19:23-29

A. Recording Statements for Posterity: vss. 23-24

"Oh, that my words were recorded, that they were written on a scroll, that they were inscribed with an iron tool on lead, or engraved in rock forever!"

Perhaps in desperation Job pleaded with his counselors to take "pity" (Job 19:21) on him. He hoped that his description of being unjustly persecuted by God would finally soften the calloused hearts of the three advisers. Of course, this was not the first time Job had pleaded for them to be merciful. He had appealed for their devotion in an earlier speech (6:14). What Job wanted was their friendship and compassion. What he was getting instead was their disapproval and condemnation. So Job complained that they were harassing him even as God was (vs. 22). In Job's mind, his counselors were trying to take on the role of God as judge. This can especially be seen in Eliphaz's earlier assumption that he was speaking for the Lord: "Are God's consolations [referring to the words of Job's advisers] not enough for you, words spoken gently to you?" (15:11).

Despite their sincere intentions, the admonishment offered by Job's peers failed miserably. Rather than consoling Job or prompting him to seek God's mercy, their words were annoying and destructive. In a metaphorical sense, the derisive comments voiced by Job's advisers were devouring his soul. So Job asked whether they would ever be satiated with his "flesh" (19:22). He was using a Semitic expression in which consuming someone's flesh referred to slander. With death an apparent certainty, Job cried out for the means to make a permanent record of his claim to be innocent. As he yearned for an enduring way to defend his integrity, Job expressed his desire to write his words on a "scroll" (vs. 23), chisel them in "lead" (vs. 24), or engrave them in "rock." That way, those who came after Job would know and concur with his case, and perhaps he would be vindicated, even if it was long after he was gone.

B. Looking to God for Redemption: vss. 25-27

"I know that my Redeemer lives, and that in the end he will stand upon the earth. And after my skin has been destroyed, yet in my flesh I will see God; I myself will see him with my own eyes—I, and not another. How my heart yearns within me!"

After many sorrowful expressions of despair, Job uttered perhaps the greatest words of hope recorded in his book. In his deepest anguish, when all his loved ones had deserted him, Job expressed faith in one last hope—an even greater one than having his claim of innocence chiseled on a rock. He placed his confident expectation in a "Redeemer" (Job 19:25), in which the underlying Hebrew verb refers to a protector and vindicator. (For background information, see Lev. 25:25-55 and the comments in lesson 3 on the kinsman-redeemer.) Throughout the Hebrew Scriptures, God is often seen as the Defender of the oppressed and the Savior of the exploited (Ps. 103:2-4; Prov. 23:10-11). Job was convinced that even though he faced eventual death, his divine Advocate would take His stand on the earth, like a witness in a courtroom, to acquit Job of guilt, affirm his integrity, and restore his honor.

Moreover, Job asserted that even after his lifeless body had decayed in the grave, he somehow would be raised from the dead and meet God (Job 19:26; see also 14:10-14). Indeed, Job would personally see his Defender with his own "eyes" (19:27). Bible scholars think that the idea of an advocate—namely, someone to champion one's case before God—was prevalent in Job's day. Despite his present anguish, he was overcome with the thought of God vindicating him in the afterlife. Even though Job did not spell out any details of his longed-for resurrection, he clearly believed it would happen because of God's intervention.

At times, the Hebrew verb translated "redeemer" (vs. 25) referred to a "blood avenger," that is, a member of a victim's family who had the responsibility to obtain justice from the person who killed his relative. The objective of the vindicator, as it would have been in Job's case, was to obtain justice, not retribution. Job clearly saw himself as the target of unwarranted accusations. Figuratively speaking, he had been verbally murdered, and he was calling for an advocate to represent him in the court of justice. Later, Job would learn that it was God who was his Redeemer, Friend, and Provider. At this point in Job's life, having God reveal Himself as Job's vindicator was his heart's intense desire.

C. Anticipating Justice from God: vss. 28-29

"If you say, 'How we will hound him, since the root of the trouble lies in him,' you should fear the sword yourselves; for wrath will bring punishment by the sword, and then you will know that there is judgment."

At the end of Job's response to Bildad, Job directed his comments to his advisers. He realized that even after his declaration of eventually being vindicated by a Redeemer, Job's peers were still mired in their erroneous views. So he admonished them not to pursue him in a misguided attempt to convince him of presumed sin. After all, they were mistaken to conclude that his sufferings were due to transgression in his life (Job 19:28). He also warned his three friends that since they had misjudged him, God would punish them more severely for their iniquity (for example, "by the [edge of the] sword"; vs. 29). Here we see Job resolutely maintaining that he was innocent of any wrongdoing. His desire for his counselors to be punished shows that he still had a glimmer of hope that there could be some measure of justice in the world.

Discussion Questions

1. Why did Job feel tormented by his three friends?
2. Why did Job believe he was innocent of any wrongdoing?
3. Why did Job conclude that God had abandoned him?
4. What promises from Scripture reassure you of God's unfailing love for you?
5. How can knowing that God is your Redeemer encourage you in your daily life?

Contemporary Application

Throughout Job's life, he had been faithful to God. In turn, God had consistently blessed Job and been gracious to him. Suddenly, though, Job could not fathom why God would not come to His servant's aid during the darkest days of his life. Job remained loyal to God, but He no longer seemed to care about Job.

Maybe you, too, have been faithful to God for years. Then, all at once, you have been blindsided by some unexpected trial or painful circumstance. Perhaps you're wondering some, or all, of the following questions: *Have I sinned or displeased God? Am I supposed to be learning something from this (because right now, I don't see the point)? When will this end? Why doesn't God do something to help me? Why does it appear as if other people who do not serve God seem to breeze through life without a hitch? What's going on here? Where is God's love and comfort?*

On the one hand, Job felt as if God had shut out His servant from His grace. On the other hand, Job refused to let go of his faith in God. Job was able to remain loyal to God, even in troubled times, by remembering God's character, as Job had known it in better days. Job was willing to receive both the good and the bad in life. He trusted that God was supremely wise and in control. This remained true no matter how topsy-turvy life appeared to Job in his trials.

It's the same for us. This week's lesson encourages us to find a way to focus on who God is. This includes who He says He is in His Word and who He has shown Himself to be to us in the past. As we do so, He gives us the ability to remain loyal to Him, regardless of the troubles we face. And when all is said and done, one day we will arise from our difficulty to find ourselves redeemed by our Creator.

Longing for Justice

Scripture

Background Scripture: *Job 5; 24; Psalm 55:12-23*
Scripture Lesson: *Job 24:1, 9-12, 19-25*
Key Verse: *I call to God, and the LORD saves me.*
Psalm 55:16.
Scripture Lesson for Children: *Job 5:1, 8-16; Psalm 55:16, 18*
Key Verse for Children: *I call to God, and the LORD saves me.* Psalm 55:16.

Lesson Aim

To understand that God allows us to speak freely to Him.

Lesson Setting

Time: During the second millennium B.C.
Place: The land of Uz

Lesson Outline

Longing for Justice

I. The Presence of Injustice: Job 24:1, 9-12
   A. *Delayed Judgment: vs. 1*
   B. *Oppression of the Destitute: vss. 9-12*
II. The Demise of the Wicked: Job 24:19-25
   A. *A Tragic End: vss. 19-20*
   B. *No Assurance of Life: vss. 21-25*

Introduction for Adults

Topic: *Defiant Faithfulness*

An elderly man—not a believer—suffered a heart attack after a personal disaster. His Christian daughter appealed to him to repent. Could he not see God's hand in what had happened? Absolutely not, the man said. It was just bad luck.

Some people reach the point in their lives where God no longer figures in their thinking. How important it is for Christians to show by example that God is the only one who really counts. When we seek Him in times of trial, we set a powerful example for others to follow.

Admittedly, some of us may be hampered by the fear of God becoming angry with us for telling Him about negative emotions or thoughts we harbor. In Job's time of trial, he felt free to tell God what was on his heart (Job 24:1). We can also communicate openly with God in our distress, yet at the same time show respect for Him.

Introduction for Youth

Topic: *Will Justice Reign?*

Community tragedies, especially when they involve children and youth, invariably draw people closer together. Outpourings of love and support for the suffering play a major role in personal and community recovery. Schools and businesses employ grief counselors.

When tragedies happen, we are forced to reflect on our faith, just as Job did (Job 24:1). The big question always seems to be "Why?" We must avoid glib answers and admit limited knowledge. At the same time, we can confess our faith and hope in the Savior. As we live for Him, others might be drawn to us.

Like Job, we must also develop strong disciplines of obedience to God and love for His Word. We can only be an effective witness for Jesus in times of tragedy if we have a treasure of Scripture in our hearts (Ps. 119:11).

Concepts for Children

Topic: *A Brighter Day Is Coming*

1. Job felt as if his life had been turned upside down.
2. Job believed that God would hear his prayers.
3. Job turned to God for help.
4. God gave Job the strength to remain faithful.
5. We can ask God to help us when we face difficult situations.

Lesson Commentary

I. THE PRESENCE OF INJUSTICE: JOB 24:1, 9-12

A. Delayed Judgment: vs. 1

"Why does the Almighty not set times for judgment? Why must those who know him look in vain for such days?"

The question of Job's authorship had been debated for centuries, and no one has come up with evidence for his or her view that satisfies everyone. The main reason for this uncertainty is that the book neglects to identify its author. In fact, the complexity of the language makes it difficult even to determine a specific period of time within which the discourse was written. Bible critics tend to view Job as a work of fiction. Some conjecture an Israelite took a foreign epic and made it stylistically palatable for a Hebrew audience. Others suggest the book was stitched together by a number of people over an extended period of time.

In contrast to such critical theories, one long-held view maintains that Job was indeed a historical person, and that he wrote the book himself sometime after his ordeal. If this is the case, the account of an encounter between God and Satan in the prologue of the book could have come to Job only by divine revelation. Another traditional view holds that, while Job was a historical person, someone else wrote his account. Some think the writer personally knew Job and made keen observations and carefully recorded the poetic speeches. Others suggest the writer lived some years after Job and put his account together in poetic form based on what he knew about the historical person. Whatever view is taken, it is evident that the author was both divinely inspired and possessed literary genius.

Concerning when Job was written, there is no conclusive evidence that has been found. Some have suggested an early date because of the fact that the book makes no mention of the patriarchs, the 12 tribes of Israel, or Moses. This leads some to think that the book originated in the time before Moses (about 1566–1446 B.C.). If so, then Job is the oldest book of the Bible. As such, it offers us insight into people's conceptions of God before they possessed written revelation. Some Bible scholars propose much later dates for the writing of Job. Some say it was penned during the reign of Solomon (970–930 B.C.), while others are far more general, saying it was composed sometime between the lives of Moses and Ezra. Whatever view is taken, the writer was undoubtedly a skillful poet from the covenant community. While the numerous details in Job indicate that the events occurred during the patriarchal era, the literary evidence suggests that the book was produced sometime later during an era when wisdom flourished.

A number of interesting and illuminating facts about Job can be obtained from Scripture. The Bible reveals that he was a spiritually mature person (Job

1:1, 8; 2:3). He was also the father of many children (1:2; 42:13) and the owner of many herds (1:3; 42:12). Scripture portrays Job as a wealthy and influential man (1:3), a priest to his family (1:5), and a loving, wise husband (2:9). He was both a person of prominence in community affairs (29:7-11) and someone known for his benevolence (29:12-17; 31:32). In addition, Job was a wise leader (29:21-24) and a farmer (31:38-40).

As was noted in lesson 6, a series of three speeches are recorded between Job and his three counselors. The first round occurs in chapters 4 through 14; the second round takes place in chapters 15 through 21; and the third round is found in chapters 22 through 27. In the final cycle of speeches, Eliphaz and Bildad spoke, with Job responding to each of them. Zophar did not speak in this last round, and no explanation is given for why he remained silent. By now in the book, Eliphaz seems to have lost his patience with Job, and he blamed Job's woes on his great and endless wickedness (as Eliphaz saw it). Yet Eliphaz also said that all Job had to do to regain peace and prosperity was to submit to God's will (chap. 22).

Job responded by saying he wanted to talk to God directly, even though it seemed to Job that God was nowhere to be found. Job felt both confident and terrified, trusting that he could withstand God's judgment, and yet knowing God could do as He pleased (chap. 23). Next, Job probed more deeply God's providence over earthly matters. The burning issue for Job was God's presumed indifference in the prevalence of misdeeds and injustices in the world. Job openly asked why it appeared as if the "Almighty" (24:1) did not appoint a time of "judgment" for the wicked, and why the godly had to wait "in vain" for a day of reckoning to occur. "Almighty" renders the Hebrew term *Shaddai*, which appears 31 times in the book. While scholars debate the exact origin and precise meaning of the word, its use in Scripture reminds us that God is supremely powerful. His invincibility encourages believers to serve Him faithfully and with integrity (Gen. 17:1).

B. Oppression of the Destitute: vss. 9-12

"The fatherless child is snatched from the breast; the infant of the poor is seized for a debt. Lacking clothes, they go about naked; they carry the sheaves, but still go hungry. They crush olives among the terraces; they tread the winepresses, yet suffer thirst. The groans of the dying rise from the city, and the souls of the wounded cry out for help. But God charges no one with wrongdoing."

Job 24:2-12 records a series of injustices that occurred in Bible times. For instance, verse 2 notes how the evildoers "move boundary stones," which were used to mark the precincts of a landowner's property. God regarded those who illegally changed these long-standing landmarks as thieves who stole acreage and livestock from their neighbors to enlarge their own estate (Deut. 19:14; 27:17; Prov. 22:28; 23:10). Job 24:3 highlights a circumstance in which the wicked ruthlessly exploited "orphans" and "widows" by seizing what little they had (for example, a donkey or an ox) until they paid their debts. In the ancient Near East, orphans and widows were at an extreme disadvantage, for they had no extended family members to care for them. Also, many in society viewed widowhood with reproach.

Tragically, a widow without legal protection was often vulnerable to neglect or exploitation. Moreover, it was far too common for greedy and unscrupulous agents to defraud a destitute widow and her children of whatever property they owned. There were three primary ways a widow could provide for the financial needs of herself and her children. First, she could return to her parents' house; second, she could remarry, especially if she was young or wealthy; and third, she could remain unmarried and obtain some kind of employment. The last prospect was rather bleak, for it was difficult in the patriarchal era for a widow to find suitable work that would meet the economic needs of herself and her family.

Verse 4 reveals that the impoverished were forced to hide themselves to escape further oppression. These displaced groups of people were like "wild donkeys" (vs. 5) who roamed through a barren "wasteland" in search of "food" to feed their starving "children." At times, the vulnerable of society were driven to eke out a living by gleaning through the "fields" (vs. 6) and vineyards of the wicked rich. Because the poor were also homeless, they spent their nights without clothing to provide them with warmth and protection from the "cold" (vs. 7). Violent "mountain rains" (vs. 8) soaked the dispossessed of society, and they huddled in the cracks of rocks as makeshift shelters.

Evildoers brazenly confiscated nursing babies from their penniless mothers. In turn, these infants were sold to liquidate the mothers' debt (vs. 9). The wicked rich coerced society's outcasts to wander "naked" (vs. 10), and wealthy landowners seized the bundles of grain their day laborers harvested, leaving them to starve. Even though the homeless pressed out olive oil among the terraced groves of trees, they did not benefit from their hard labor. Others endured "thirst" (vs. 11) while expending lots of energy to crush out the juice from grapes in wine vats. In the cities, the pleas of the "dying" (vs. 12) and the cries of the "wounded" for "help" could be heard. Yet, despite their affliction, it seemed as if God ignored the petitions of the downtrodden and did not charge anyone with abusing them.

In Ecclesiastes 4:1-3, Solomon provided a somber assessment of the various kinds of oppression that repeatedly occurred on earth. Included were acts of tyranny and injustice committed throughout human history. The victims of such cruelty lamented over their plight, but there seemed to be no one to comfort them. Because their oppressors wielded tremendous power, potential deliverers were unable or unwilling to rescue the victims of maltreatment (vs. 1). It was distressing enough that life could seem vexing. But even more tragic was the circumstance when one group of individuals abused another group.

Solomon considered people who had died long ago, noting that they seemed better off than those who were still alive. In this way of thinking, the deceased escaped the misfortune of being oppressed. To Solomon, it was ironic that the dead experienced a greater degree of happiness than the living (vs. 2). Yet an even greater paradox was the perceived advantage of never having been born (6:3). The reason is that they had not witnessed and experienced the "evil" (4:3) that people committed on earth. "Evil" renders a Hebrew adjective denoting actions that are vicious, injurious, or malignant in character.

II. THE DEMISE OF THE WICKED: JOB 24:19-25

A. A Tragic End: vss. 19-20

"As heat and drought snatch away the melted snow, so the grave snatches away those who have sinned. The womb forgets them, the worm feasts on them; evil men are no longer remembered but are broken like a tree."

Job 24:13-17 provides a more personalized description of the evildoers who preyed on the vulnerable in ancient times. For example, they openly defied the light-filled truth of God's Word. They neither understood its teaching nor followed the direction it instructed the upright to heed (vs. 13). At the crack of dawn, murderers awoke to kill the indigent, and they used the cover of darkness to steal from the impoverished (vs. 14). Similarly, adulterers waited for twilight to arrive to commit sexual sin without being seen (vs. 15). Likewise, thieves avoided the light of day, instead choosing the camouflage of the night to vandalize "houses" (vs. 16). Indeed, they were more at home in the darkness than in the light of day (vs. 17).

Some think that Job could not have spoken what appears in verses 18-24, since the monologue so closely agrees with what his advisers previously declared. Nonetheless, it is legitimate to regard this portion of chapter 24 as part of Job's petition for God to vindicate the righteous and judge the wicked. For instance, Job observed that evildoers were as insignificant as scum carried away by river currents. Their "vineyards" (vs. 18) were under God's curse so that neither they nor others would dare enter their property.

Those who transgressed God and incurred His wrath were as transient as "melted snow" (vs. 19) dissolved by "heat and drought." *Sheol* is the Hebrew noun rendered "grave" and refers to the abode of the dead. In Job's day, it was believed to be a dismal place where the deceased were cut off from God and people alive on earth. Verse 20 declares that the wombs of the mothers who bore the unrighteous abandoned all memory of them. Even worse, maggots devoured their rotting corpses, and their wrongdoing was destroyed like a "tree" overturned by a windstorm.

B. No Assurance of Life: vss. 21-25

"They prey on the barren and childless woman, and to the widow show no kindness. But God drags away

the mighty by his power; though they become established, they have no assurance of life. He may let them rest in a feeling of security, but his eyes are on their ways. For a little while they are exalted, and then they are gone; they are brought low and gathered up like all others; they are cut off like heads of grain. If this is not so, who can prove me false and reduce my words to nothing?"

Job 24:21 provides the justification for the miserable end awaiting the wicked (as poetically described in verses 18-20). These evildoers targeted women who were "barren and childless" (vs. 21) and abused widows. As noted earlier, both groups were among the most defenseless members of society. Verse 22 declares that God would make the wicked pay for their crimes. Like a mighty warrior, He would sweep them away. Even though they might rise up for a season, their days were numbered. Admittedly, God might permit some wealthy criminals to enjoy a false sense of "security" for a while (vs. 23), but He constantly scrutinized whatever they did. Though the unrighteous might prosper, suddenly they would be disgraced. They would waste away like discarded weeds and be cut down like stalks of "grain" (vs. 24). Job ended his monologue by asking his friends whether they could deny the validity of his assertions and demonstrate that what he declared was worthless (vs. 25). The presumption is that he spoke the truth.

Psalm 1 is just as pointed in contrasting the fate of the wicked and the righteous. The psalm opens with a prognosis that "blessed" (vs. 1) are the prospects of those who reject the beliefs, thoughts, and behavior of evildoers. In that God bestows His favor on the virtuous for following His ways, they are promised a deep-seated, lasting joy that is not disrupted by the typical difficulties of living. Even in the worst of situations, their inner happiness remains.

The delight of the upright endures because, from the negative aspect, they reject the ways and advice of the "wicked." The joy experienced by the godly persists because, from the positive aspect, they delight in and meditate on the "law of the LORD" (vs. 2). To those who put their trust in God, His decrees are not a burden. His ordinances guide them, make their lives better, and help them acknowledge their dependence on God. Indeed, the upright flourish like trees "planted by streams of water" (vs. 3), so that whatever they undertake succeeds. This does not mean, of course, that they are promised health and wealth. Rather, it means that they receive and achieve the most worthwhile objectives of life. As a result of putting divine wisdom into practice, they reap the benefits of God's approval.

The psalmist next conveyed how the "wicked" (vs. 4) forfeit these benefits because of their disregard for God. They are described as wind-driven "chaff." In the threshing of grain, the crushed sheaves were tossed into the air, where the wind blew away the lighter, dryer husks, leaving only the grain to fall to the ground. In this way the eternal worthlessness of evildoers is portrayed. Verse 5 reveals their inability to bear up under God's searing "judgment." Their instability comes as a result of their degenerate lifestyle. The first psalm concludes with words of promise for the "righteous" (vs. 6) and words of warning for the "wicked." The promise is that the Lord safeguards the godly in their way. In contrast, He undermines the sinful priorities and behavior of the unrighteous. The promise comforts those who put their faith in the Lord, for they realize that He knows them intimately, that He cares for them actively, and that He provides guidance for their lives. Those who refuse to trust in God are warned about facing one dead end after another.

Discussion Questions

1. Why did Job at first assume that God was indifferent to the crimes of the wicked?
2. Why were the poor without food or clothing?
3. What was the basis for Job's belief that God would one day bring an end to the wicked?
4. How can believers affirm that only God has answers to the complex questions of life?
5. How can believers be certain that they are walking in God's ways?

Contemporary Application

Often a crisis of faith is a God-given opportunity for us to demonstrate what it means to follow the Lord and allow Him to carry our pain and loss. Paul said that one reason he had suffered was so that he might comfort others in their trials (2 Cor. 1:3-7). That is true for all Christians.

When calamity struck Job and his family, he and his three friends wrestled with the question of whether God was fair. His advisers took the view that God was punishing him, that he must have done something wrong to deserve such evil. Job disagreed, not only because he felt certain of his own integrity, but also because the wicked actually seemed to prosper, not suffer (Job 12:6).

Most significantly, Job rejected the conventional view that the world is orderly and that everything is arranged according to just principles. His tragedy was not just, for his upright and virtuous life did not result in good fortune. He was a living testimony to the fact that tragic things can happen to godly people.

This realization, though, only brought Job back to the original question concerning God's fairness (24:1). If the wicked prosper and the righteous suffer, where is justice in the world (vss. 2-17)? Job concluded that the seemingly easy life of the wicked was very temporary and that sooner or later it would all fall apart (vss. 18-24). Job maintained that, in the end, God would humble the proud, enable those with integrity to receive His blessings, and thereby establish justice. Thus, He is indeed fair (vs. 25).

Receiving God's Blessing

Scripture

Background Scripture: *Job 42; Psalm 86*

Scripture Lesson: *Job 42:1-10*

Key Verse: *"I know that you can do all things; no plan of yours can be thwarted."* Job 42:2.

Scripture Lesson for Children: *Job 42:1-6, 10; Psalm 86:1-4*

Key Verse for Children: *"My ears had heard of you but now my eyes have seen you."* Job 42:5.

Lesson Aim

To learn that humility comes from recognizing who God is.

Lesson Setting

Time: During the second millennium B.C.

Place: The land of Uz

Lesson Outline

Receiving God's Blessing

    I. Job's Repentance before God: Job 42:1-6

        A. *An Opportunity to Reply: vs. 1*

        B. *An Admission of Limited Knowledge: vss. 2-3*

        C. *An Acknowledgment of Guilt: vss. 4-6*

   II. God's Restoration of Job: Job 42:7-10

        A. *Censuring Job's Friends: vss. 7-8*

        B. *Blessing Job Abundantly: vss. 9-10*

Introduction for Adults

Topic: *Who's in Control?*

How much time do we spend crying out to God for answers, and how much time do we spend listening to God? Unfortunately, we are much better at demanding than at listening.

The outcome of Job's experience forces us to listen. Under the probing searchlight of God's questions, we must take a fresh look at ourselves and our pride. Too often we listen only when God has laid us aside and caught our attention. How much better it is for us to sharpen our spiritual eyes and ears by faithful prayer, worship, and study of God's Word.

Job repented when he heard from God (Job 42:6). Job's response enables us to see that we need to abandon our pride. Furthermore, we have to learn to repent of wrong attitudes, of exalted views of ourselves, and of trying to bring God down to our level. Job points us in the right direction toward a healthy regard for our awesome God and toward an appropriately humble view of ourselves.

Introduction for Youth

Topic: *Good Results in Due Time*

Youth today grow up in a culture that says we can control our destinies, we can fix anything, and, given time and technology, we can explain everything. Our culture teaches the superiority of human intellect and technical prowess, so the idea of God is irrelevant.

How hard it is then for teenagers to confess, as Job did, that there are some things beyond human understanding, that some things are "too wonderful . . . to know" (Job 42:3). Pride says we comprehend it all and we can do anything. Christian humility says God is greater than we are and we will one day have to answer to Him for our thoughts and deeds.

At the same time, God has given us ample evidence for faith and humility, as opposed to pride and self-sufficiency. We must encourage teens to look for the Lord's good and gracious hand in the created world about them. They must look at the universe through the spiritual eyes of faith. Then focus their attention on the demonstration of the Father's love and power in the death and resurrection of His Son for our sins.

Concepts for Children

Topic: *An Unexpected Gift*

1. God invited Job to talk to Him.
2. Job said that he had a lot to learn about God.
3. God forgave Job for saying incorrect things about Him.
4. God poured out His gift of love on Job.
5. God is pleased to answer our prayers.

Lesson Commentary

I. JOB'S REPENTANCE BEFORE GOD: JOB 42:1-6

A. An Opportunity to Reply: vs. 1

Then Job replied to the LORD.

Throughout Job's long ordeal, it seemed as if God was distant, silent, and uncaring. Finally, as 38:1 states, God came out of a "storm" and responded to Job. Perhaps the phenomenon was a whirlwind not unlike the one that had killed Job's children (1:18-19). No indication is given that Job actually saw the Lord, only that Job heard God's voice. The Lord did not, however, give Job an explanation for his suffering. Nor did God list Job's sins, as his friends possibly would have wanted. Instead, God just exposed Job to the wonders of His power and creation. With great effectiveness, God's words demonstrated how limited is human knowledge, no matter how the counselors went on and on about their own vaunted wisdom. In the end, none of Job's questions were answered specifically. Nonetheless, after hearing the Lord's declarations, Job was drawn back to complete faith in and worship of his Creator and Savior.

The description of creation and the natural world in the Book of Job is harmonious with the opening chapters of Genesis. Both portray God as the Author and Architect of the universe. Out of nothing, He brought into existence the light and darkness, the dry land and the sea, the birds and the animals. Through what God declared in Job 38, He taught His "servant" (1:8; 2:3) to accept the Lord as God. No mere human could understand all the workings of the universe, much less control it. Therefore, God called upon Job to put aside all his idle speculation and to accept God's dominion over all things.

In chapter 39, the Lord offered glimpses of wild animals and birds, and asked Job what control he had over them. Brought to Job's attention were lions, ravens, mountain goats, deer, wild donkeys, wild oxen, ostriches, warhorses, hawks, and eagles. The intent of God's menagerie was to show Job that, regardless of the ferociousness or peculiar nature of the creatures, all are under His supreme control and care. As the Lord pointed out various aspects of the universe, He had pushed Job to consider the outer limits of His creation. We can easily understand how dumbstruck Job must have become at hearing God's words.

B. An Admission of Limited Knowledge: vss. 2-3

"I know that you can do all things; no plan of yours can be thwarted. You asked, 'Who is this that obscures my counsel without knowledge?' Surely I spoke of things I did not understand, things too wonderful for me to know."

In God's first major speech (38:2–39:30), He had exposed Job to His power over the natural universe. In the Lord's second speech (40:7–41:34), He presented to Job His lordship over the moral universe. God's intent was to encourage

Job to rely upon and rest in the Creator's omnipotence. Job's two replies are recorded in 40:3-5 and 42:1-6. He laid aside his rage as well as his stance of stubbornly challenging the Lord. At several points during his suffering, Job had dared to question God's justice by suggesting that the Lord was not running the universe in the way Job thought it should be run. But now, obviously chastened by what God had told Job, he replied humbly and with reverence (40:3).

Job acknowledged that he was insignificant when compared to God's overall scheme of creation (vs. 4). In light of all God had told Job, he felt ashamed that he had ever raised his voice. To register his regret for saying too much, Job went on to promise that he would place his hand over his mouth in order to say no more. Indeed, he had nothing to add to what he had already stated (vs. 5). After hearing the voice of God, Job seems to have lost his desire to vindicate himself. He knew God is all-powerful and that nothing can hinder His plans (42:2). In God's mighty hands, all things—even justice for the suffering—would be worked out eventually.

Job went on to apologize for his earlier attitude and behavior. He referred specifically to statements God had made in His speeches. For instance, Job quoted God's reprimand at the beginning of His first speech. God had asked on what basis Job dared to question the Creator's wisdom, especially knowing how oblivious Job was concerning the vast universe (vs. 3; see also 38:2). Now Job admitted his ignorance. His answer was simple and contrite. He was guilty of prattling on about marvels too mysterious for him to comprehend (42:3). In the end, all Job's understanding, reasoning, and doubting had to give way to faith.

In addition to teaching about God's nature and humanity's suffering, the Book of Job might have had in mind some of the following purposes: to establish that we simply do not know enough about God and His ways to question His wisdom or justice; to expose the theological position that says "people suffer in proportion to their sins" as a shallow and erroneous doctrine; to prove that God—because He is all-powerful and all-knowing—can make use of any means and any situations to bring about His purposes; to demonstrate that God does not abandon those who suffer, but communicates with them as He chooses; to explain that, regardless of circumstances, people must accept God on His own terms; to suggest that believers can remain upright even in the midst of physical agony, emotional confusion, and spiritual testing; and to teach the wisdom of people's complete submission to the will of God.

C. An Acknowledgment of Guilt: vss. 4-6

"You said, 'Listen now, and I will speak; I will question you, and you shall answer me.' My ears had heard of you but now my eyes have seen you. Therefore I despise myself and repent in dust and ashes."

Job still knew nothing about Satan's challenge at the beginning of the drama. Job also had no idea God was allowing him to be tested so as to show Satan that Job was "blameless and upright, a man who fears God and shuns evil" (1:8). Job didn't even know that he had basically passed the test—even though he, like his four friends, had talked too much and had made a fool of himself before God. For the most part, Job was still in the dark—except now he knew unmistakably that the Lord created and sustains the universe, and that He manages the moral order. Furthermore, Job must have now realized that God would keep His servant close to His heart.

In 42:4, Job referred to a statement God had made at the beginning of both major speeches. God had ordered Job to listen because He was going to ask questions (38:3; 40:7). Before God's interrogation of him, Job said, he had only known about God. For example, Job had known the Lord through what His servant had learned from tradition and from what others had told him. Perhaps Job was referring specifically to the words about God he had heard from his counselors. But all such words conveyed only indirect knowledge about the Lord. Through God's interrogation, Job experienced the Lord and His holy nature firsthand. Job learned about God's power and righteousness by being allowed to enter the Lord's sacred presence and listen to His voice. Even though Job didn't actually see God, he felt as though he had met the Lord face-to-face (Job 42:5; see also Job 19:25-27; Pss. 25:14-15; 123:1-2; 141:8).

Most likely, the only reaction Job could have had to this experience was to loathe himself, that is, to see his own knowledge, self-assessment, and arguments for the nonsense they were (Job 42:6). His words "I despise myself" could also be translated, "I reject what I said." In this case, Job might have intended to take back all the spiritually rebellious statements he had made in his speeches to Eliphaz, Bildad, and Zophar. Job also reproached himself "in dust and ashes," which drew attention to his humiliation and insignificance (Gen. 18:27; Job 2:8, 12). But his sorrow should not be taken to be regret for the host of sins his counselors had accused him of committing. Job was correct in his opinion that his miserable condition was not a result of personal transgressions. In addition, he had learned from God that life and suffering are far more complex and mysterious than he or his friends had ever imagined.

Job's repentance, therefore, was for boldly questioning God's wisdom, justice, and ability to manage human affairs (Job 40:2, 8-9). Job wanted the Lord to know that His servant had experienced a dramatic change in his attitude. In this context, the Hebrew verb translated "repent" (42:6) denotes more than confessing one's sins. It also means to "console oneself" or to "be comforted." In essence, Job discarded all his previous, false notions about and bitter accusations against God. Moreover, Job was placing his assurance in the truth that God was not his enemy but his Friend and Redeemer.

II. GOD'S RESTORATION OF JOB: JOB 42:7-10

A. Censuring Job's Friends: vss. 7-8

After the LORD had said these things to Job, he said to Eliphaz the Temanite, "I am angry with you and your two friends, because you have not spoken of me what is right, as my servant Job has. So now take seven bulls and seven rams and go to my servant Job and sacrifice a burnt offering for yourselves. My servant Job will pray for you, and I will accept his prayer and not deal with you according to your folly. You have not spoken of me what is right, as my servant Job has."

The concluding portion of Job (42:7-17) was written in narrative form like the introduction (chaps. 1–2). In the epilogue, God scolded Job's friends and ordered them to make a sufficient and satisfactory offering as a sign of their repentance and to atone for their errant counsel. The conclusion also includes the account of how God restored Job's prosperity—in fact, giving him more than he had previously possessed. Before Job's restoration took place, God voiced His anger with Job's three counselors—Eliphaz, Bildad, and Zophar. Curiously missing from the group is Elihu.

Sometime after the Lord taught Job about His dominion over the universe, God spoke to Eliphaz, who may have been the community leader and eldest among the friends of Job. God not only announced His anger with Job's three friends, but the Lord also stated the cause of His anger. He told Eliphaz that he and his peers had declared falsehoods, not truths, about the Creator (vs. 7). How surprised these three advisers must have been! They likely assumed that they had been speaking on God's behalf. Now they learned that they were facing the brunt of His anger because of their erroneous words.

God told Eliphaz that Job had escaped condemnation because he had spoken what was "right." But how could God say this when He had just accused Job of obscuring His counsel (vs. 3)? After all, Job had ranted and raved, as well as questioned God's justice. In short, Job had spoken in ignorance. The Hebrew verb translated "right" denotes what is firm, fixed, or established. One option is that God commended Job for taking the risk of being honest in voicing his feelings openly to the Lord. A second possibility is that God was praising Job for his sincerity. A third alternative is that God was simply saying Job was correct about his alleged sins not being the cause of his suffering. In retrospect, it seems that both Job and his counselors were partly correct and partly incorrect. Job was right about the fact that he was not suffering as a punishment for his sins, but he was wrong in questioning God's justice. Job's counselors were right about God's control over the universe, but they were wrong to assume Job's suffering was linked to some hidden trespass. Certainly, both Job and his advisers had a limited view of God and His plan for the world.

Eliphaz, Bildad, and Zophar must have been stunned when they learned that it was they, not Job, whom God required to offer a sacrifice as a sign of their repentance. The Lord told them to go to Job, taking with them "seven bulls and seven rams" (vs. 8; in which "seven" denotes a complete number). In Job's presence—so that God's "servant" could look on—the three "friends" (vs. 7) were to sacrifice these animals. This was a large "burnt offering" (vs. 8) to make, perhaps indicating how seriously God took their error. As part of the ceremony, Job would "pray" for them so that God would not deal harshly with them for their "folly." At this point God repeated His judgment that the three counselors had not spoken the truth, in contrast to Job, who had done so.

B. Blessing Job Abundantly: vss. 9-10

So Eliphaz the Temanite, Bildad the Shuhite and Zophar the Naamathite did what the LORD told them; and the LORD accepted Job's prayer. After Job had prayed for his friends, the LORD made him prosperous again and gave him twice as much as he had before.

Job's three discredited friends obeyed what the Lord had commanded them. Job prayed for their forgiveness, and God answered His servant's prayer (Job 42:9). Presumably, it was soon after this ritual was completed that the Hebrew text literally says God "returned the captivity of Job" (vs. 10). This clause means that the Lord restored the prosperity Job previously lost. Indeed, God doubled His servant's former wealth. The Lord did so, not coincidentally, but only after Job prayed for his friends. In his newfound wisdom and humility, Job obeyed his Creator, and He graciously and abundantly bestowed on Job both inner and outer healing.

The final verses of Job show in dramatic fashion just how magnificent was his restoration. Not only was his prosperity doubled, but also his relatives, who had remained distant throughout his ordeal, returned to his side to comfort him. Moreover, as they returned, each bore expensive gifts for Job—"a piece of silver and a gold ring" (vs. 11)—and joined him in a meal of celebration. Verse 12 states that "the LORD blessed the latter part of Job's life more than the first." Some of those blessings are then listed, beginning with Job's flocks. Those flocks included 14,000 sheep, 6,000 camels, 2,000 oxen, and 1,000 donkeys. In all, Job's livestock was replenished so that he owned at least 23,000 animals!

The book closes with a brief summary of the rest of Job's life. The warm and tender relationships that Job certainly missed during his period of suffering apparently were a mainstay for the remainder of his years. Job died at the age of 140, after seeing "his children and their children to the fourth generation" (vs. 16). The phrase telling that Job died "old and full of years" (vs. 17) expresses that he passed away in a dignified and peaceful manner, having come to the end of a fulfilling life.

In retrospect, the message of the book is that God is sovereign, regardless of what happens to the wicked or the righteous. Job had endured his test. He had shown his uprightness and unselfishness. In the end, God chose to bless His servant. He did so not necessarily to teach Job or anyone else a lesson, but simply because it was His pleasure. As far as Satan's original challenge to God is concerned (1:9-11; 2:4-5), Job not only withstood Satan's onslaught, but Job also won the contest the accuser had proposed. Job demonstrated that a person can love the Lord simply because He is God, and not because that person expects a reward for all his or her efforts.

Discussion Questions

1. How did Job come to the realization that God is all-powerful?
2. Why did Job presume to speak about matters that he did not understand?
3. How did Job come to terms with the ignorant assertions he had made?
4. Why is human pride such a hindrance to receiving spiritual insight from God?
5. What is necessary to live a holy life despite not knowing all the answers?

Contemporary Application

Job's account has been analyzed over and over again from both secular and Christian standpoints. In some reviews, God is still blamed for not answering Job's complaint. How hard it is for some people to walk by faith and trust in God!

However, we must be cautious about offering glib answers to hurting people. The silence of God is sometimes deafening to them. Above all, we must not assume that some sin is the cause of their suffering. Usually, it's better to sit quietly with them and to pray with them than it is to try to figure out why they are suffering.

Physical pain and grief are heavy loads to bear. As Christians, we have much to learn about how to comfort one another. Job's account is one piece of biblical evidence that people suffer for unknown reasons. His experience also encourages us to humbly recognize who God truly is and to believe in Him, no matter what.

As Christians, we have a significant advantage that Job did not have. We know Jesus suffered and died for our sins (John 1:29, 36; 1 Pet. 1:18-19). We also realize that nothing can separate believers from the Father's love in His Son (Rom. 8:35-39). Rather than debate the mysteries of God's dealings with Job, we would do well to encourage one another to "grow in the grace and knowledge" (2 Pet. 3:18) of our Savior.

God's Glory Returns

Scripture

Background Scripture: *Ezekiel 40:1–43:12*

Scripture Lesson: *Ezekiel 43:1-12*

Key Verse: *The glory of the Lord entered the temple through the gate facing east. Then the Spirit lifted me up and brought me into the inner court, and the glory of the Lord filled the temple.* Ezekiel 43:4-5.

Scripture Lesson for Children: *Ezekiel 43:1-12*

Key Verse for Children: *The glory of the Lord filled the temple.* Ezekiel 43:5.

Lesson Aim

To discover that God wants us to live in a manner characterized by holiness.

Lesson Setting

Time: 573 B.C.

Place: Babylon

Lesson Outline

God's Glory Returns

I. The Return of the Lord's Glory: Ezekiel 43:1-5
  A. *Arriving at the East Gate: vs. 1*
  B. *Seeing God's Glory Return: vss. 2-3*
  C. *Watching God's Glory Fill the Temple: vss. 4-5*
II. The Purpose of the Vision: Ezekiel 43:6-12
  A. *Abandoning Detestable Practices: vss. 6-9*
  B. *Pointing Out the Temple's Holy Design: vss. 10-12*

Introduction for Adults

Topic: *Seeking a Place of Peace*

Many believers have sung the hymn "Holy, Holy, Holy" at one time or another. That hymn of praise, which is based on Revelation 4:8, rightly portrays God as the only one who is absolutely holy—"only Thou art holy, there is none beside Thee." We are reminded that we will always fall short of God's holy standard, which is "perfect in power, in love and purity."

But the preceding truth doesn't mean we think of holiness as some heavenly concept with no earthly application. On the contrary, Ezekiel 43:1-12 urges God's people to be holy. Admittedly, this emphasis on holiness is not popular, even in the church, but it is necessary. After all, if we don't teach God's standards and exhort that they be followed, the sins of the world might become the sins of the church. Then, instead of being a sanctuary characterized by peace, our congregations will soon become filled with turmoil and dissention.

Introduction for Youth

Topic: *Glorious Light and Clear Sacred Places*

Is it really possible for saved adolescents to live in a way that is characterized by holiness, especially around their unbelieving peers? The following story can give regenerate teens the insight they need to be successful in doing so.

A minister who was visiting a coal mine noticed a pure white flower growing at one of the tunnel entrances. When he asked the miner with him how the flower stayed white, the miner said, "Throw some coal dust on it." When the minister did, the dust slid right off of the flower's smooth surface, so it remained white. That's how the youth in our congregations should be in the world, namely, individuals who remain holy in an unholy place.

Concepts for Children

Topic: *Majesty in the House*

1. God told Ezekiel that His people would one day have a new house of worship.
2. Ezekiel learned that God's people would worship Him in this special place.
3. Ezekiel was to tell God's people to obey Him.
4. Ezekiel let God's people know that He would always be with them.
5. God is also always with us and helps us to live for Him.

Lesson Commentary

I. THE RETURN OF THE LORD'S GLORY: EZEKIEL 43:1-5

A. Arriving at the East Gate: vs. 1

Then the man brought me to the gate facing east.

Ezekiel, whose name means "God strengthens," was the son of Buzi, a priest of the family of Zadok (Ezek. 1:3). What is known about Ezekiel's life comes from the information he gives in his book. Also, his prophecies contain dates more specific than almost any others in the Old Testament. This makes it possible to correlate Ezekiel's declarations with Babylonian records and date many of the prophet's oracles (for example, see 1:1-3; 8:1; 20:1; 24:1; 26:1; 29:1, 17; 30:20; 31:1; 32:1, 17; 33:21; 40:1). In 597 B.C., when Ezekiel was about 25 years old, the Babylonians took him into exile with Jehoiachin and about 10,000 other Jews (2 Kings 24:10-17). When Ezekiel was 30 years old and living in the Jewish colony of Tel Aviv on the Kebar River (near the ancient city of Nippur), he heard God's call to be His prophet (Ezek. 1:2-3; 3:15; about 593 B.C.).

Apparently, Ezekiel was a person of some stature among the leaders of his people, for the prophet's home became a central meeting place (3:24; 8:1; 14:1; 20:1). Ezekiel was married. But 10 years into the exile, his wife died suddenly, perhaps of the plague (24:15-18). The couple was evidently childless. Throughout Ezekiel's ministry, which continued until 571 B.C. (29:17), he tried to help his fellow exiles deal with the fact that they were far from their homeland. He taught them that the Lord was close at hand to sustain them during their time of displacement. Ezekiel's oracles, like those of Jeremiah, fall into three major categories: declarations against Israel, especially before the fall of Jerusalem in 586 B.C. (chaps. 1–24); pronouncements against the nations, such as Egypt and Tyre (chaps. 24–32); and words of consolation for Israel's future, including visions of a restored nation and a new temple (chaps. 33–47).

Throughout the Babylonian captivity, the nation of Israel was as dead as bleached bones strewn about a sun-parched valley floor (37:1-3, 13). It was the consummate picture of destruction so thorough that no rational person could possibly envision this nation ever coming to life again. There was no precedent. No nation in history had ever risen from the ashes after having come to such a devastating end. But other nations worshiped deities made out of wood, stone, and metal. In contrast, Israel served the living Lord of the universe. What great hope Ezekiel's words must have brought to the people of Israel. He had already prophesied about restored land, a reunified nation, and renewed fellowship with the Lord. But there was even more to come. Chapters 33–39 paint a picture of the new life the Israelites could expect when they were returned from exile, restored to their land, and reunited in fellowship with God. Then, chapters 40–48 explain the form this new life would take.

Sometime in 573 B.C., on the twenty-fifth anniversary of his exile to Babylon, Ezekiel was supernaturally transported to Jerusalem (40:1). There the prophet received a remarkable and detailed vision of a future temple to be built in Israel's restored land. The vision has been interpreted in four main ways: (1) This was supposed to be the temple built by Zerubbabel in 520–515 B.C., after the return from the Babylonian exile, but it fell short of Ezekiel's blueprint; (2) The temple is symbolic of the Christian church's earthly glory, blessing, and true worship of God in the present age; (3) The temple is a symbolic description of the final form of God's kingdom when His presence and blessing fill the whole earth; and (4) Ezekiel's temple is a literal, future sanctuary that will be built in Israel during the 1,000-year reign of the Messiah on earth. Chapters 40–42 report that Ezekiel saw the future temple measured with a reed that was ten feet, four inches long. An angel sent by the Lord guided the prophet through the temple. During the tour, Ezekiel was given detailed measurements and descriptions of the entire sanctuary complex, including the temple proper and the chambers in the inner court.

Ezekiel not only described to the exiles the newly constructed temple, but also presented the sanctuary as an important sign that God would indeed dwell among His people once again, just as He promised He would. Ezekiel explained how a newly established service of worship would provide the means of access to God. Finally, the prophet unveiled the grand divisions and blessings of the new land awaiting the people of Israel. About 18 and a half years earlier, Ezekiel had witnessed in a vision the departure of God's glory through the gateway Solomon built into the retaining wall directly east of where his temple stood (also called the "King's Gate" in 1 Chron. 9:18). Then the divine glory continued to move eastward across the Kidron Valley to the Mount of Olives (Ezek. 10:18-19; 11:22-23). Led by the same angelic emissary who had taken him through the temple, the prophet saw the return and reentry of the Lord into the new temple "through the gate facing east" (43:1). What joy Ezekiel must have felt to see God's presence in the midst of His people once again. The prophet surely longed, as most believers do, for the time when the glorified Lord will return to live among His people forever.

B. Seeing God's Glory Return: vss. 2-3

And I saw the glory of the God of Israel coming from the east. His voice was like the roar of rushing waters, and the land was radiant with his glory. The vision I saw was like the vision I had seen when he came to destroy the city and like the visions I had seen by the Kebar River, and I fell facedown.

The Hebrew noun rendered "glory" (Ezek. 43:2), when applied to God in Scripture, refers to the radiant manifestation of His being. Expressed differently, it is the brilliant revelation of Himself to humanity. This description is borne out by the many ways the word "glory" is used in the Bible. For example, brilliant light consistently went with manifestations of God (Matt. 17:2;

1 Tim. 6:16; Rev. 1:16). Moreover, the word "glory" is often linked with verbs of seeing (Exod. 16:7; 33:18; Isa. 40:5) and of appearing (Exod. 16:10; Deut. 5:24), both of which emphasize the visible nature of God's glory.

Jewish rabbis later described the glory of the Lord abiding with Israel as *shekinah*, from the Hebrew word for "dwelling." God's *shekinah* dwelt with the Israelites in the wilderness period, came to Solomon's temple when it was built, and then departed when the temple was destroyed. One tradition of the rabbis says that God's glory returned to heaven, while another says that some of the *shekinah* remains even today in the Western (or Wailing) Wall in Jerusalem, the last remnant of Herod's temple. The Fourth Gospel depicts Jesus as God's *shekinah* returned to earth (John 1:14). In a similar vein, Paul said it was possible to see God's glory in Jesus when He was on earth and that believers have the promise of sharing in that glory (Rom. 5:2). The latter will occur at the resurrection, when the bodies of believers are transformed into the same kind of glorified body that Jesus had after His resurrection (1 Cor. 15:35–57; Phil. 3:20–21).

In Ezekiel's vision, he saw the glory of Israel's God appearing from the east (Ezek. 43:2). Most likely, the gateway located on the eastern side of Solomon's temple was the main entrance to the court of the sanctuary (Exod. 27:13). The sound of the Lord's presence was comparable in intensity to waves crashing against the shore. Moreover, the entire landscape radiated God's "glory" (Ezek. 43:2). This apparently signified His power and majesty. The prophet mentioned that this vision was like others he had seen previously (vs. 3). The vision regarding the destruction of the city is recorded in chapters 8–11, while those by the Kebar River may be found in chapters 1 and 10.

In Ezekiel's first vision, he saw an awesome, ice-blue "expanse" (1:22) that glistened like crystal. The prophet also heard a voice coming from the dome-shaped platform (vs. 25). Above the vault was a blue, sapphire-shaped royal seat (vs. 26; see also 10:1). Furthermore, on this chariot-throne was a figure who resembled a human being (1:26). The torso and head of the figure Ezekiel saw had the appearance of glowing, yellow amber in the middle of a fire. Also, from the waist down, the Lord looked like a burning flame, while all around Him was a "brilliant light" (vs. 27). His dazzling "radiance" (vs. 28) was as bright-hued as a "rainbow" that appears after a storm (Gen. 9:12–16). When the prophet realized he was gazing on the "glory of the LORD" (Ezek. 1:28), he fell face downward on the ground in submission and worship (3:23; 9:8; 11:13; 43:3; 44:4). For the rest of Ezekiel's life, he would carry the memory of his surreal encounter with the Creator-King.

C. Watching God's Glory Fill the Temple: vss. 4-5

The glory of the LORD entered the temple through the gate facing east. Then the Spirit lifted me up and brought me into the inner court, and the glory of the LORD filled the temple.

We can only imagine the wonder and excitement Ezekiel must have felt as he witnessed the glorious presence of the Lord enter through the eastern gateway of the temple (Ezek. 43:4). This episode signified that God's approval and blessing rested on the sanctuary. Next, the prophet felt his body being lifted up by the Spirit and placed within the inside courtyard of the temple. Then, as the prophet looked on, the Lord's glory completely engulfed the sanctuary (vs. 5).

Prior to the Babylonian captivity, the Jerusalem temple was the central religious institution in Israel. For instance, the sanctuary was the locale where the Lord manifested His holy presence in Israel. It was also the place where sacrifices were made in response to God's gracious choice of Israel as His people. In the temple, they could spend time in prayer. Moreover, its design, furniture, and customs were object lessons that prepared them for the Messiah.

Additionally, the sanctuary had important political and economic roles to play in Israelite society. It was the institution that held together the entire covenant community—the past as well as the present and the future. Moreover, the sanctuary gave political identity to the people. Access to its courts identified who was properly a citizen and who was excluded. From an economic perspective, rooms in the temple functioned as a treasury—in effect, the society's bank. Because of the temple's demands for tithes and offerings, a large portion of the nation's economy passed through the sanctuary personnel and storehouses.

II. THE PURPOSE OF THE VISION: EZEKIEL 43:6-12

A. Abandoning Detestable Practices: vss. 6-9

While the man was standing beside me, I heard someone speaking to me from inside the temple. He said: "Son of man, this is the place of my throne and the place for the soles of my feet. This is where I will live among the Israelites forever. The house of Israel will never again defile my holy name—neither they nor their kings—by their prostitution and the lifeless idols of their kings at their high places. When they placed their threshold next to my threshold and their doorposts beside my doorposts, with only a wall between me and them, they defiled my holy name by their detestable practices. So I destroyed them in my anger. Now let them put away from me their prostitution and the lifeless idols of their kings, and I will live among them forever."

As the Lord's glory returned to the rebuilt temple, His emissary stood beside Ezekiel. Next, he heard someone else speak to him from within the sanctuary (most likely God, whose sacred name, out of reverence, is left undisclosed; Ezek. 43:6). The prophet is addressed as "Son of man" (vs. 7) more than 90 times in this book. This title was used quite frequently of Jesus to call attention to His true humanity. In Ezekiel's case, it was a reminder that he was a mere mortal who served the all-powerful Lord of the universe. The prophet learned that God was accepting the new temple as His throne and dwelling place among the Israelites (1 Sam. 4:4; 2 Sam. 6:2; 2 Kings 19:15; 1 Chron. 13:6; Pss. 80:1; 99:1; 132:13-14; Isa. 37:16). Ezekiel also discovered that since the sanctuary was to be God's permanent place of residence among His people (Ezek. 43:7, 9), no defilement of any kind would be allowed there.

Before the Exile, the rulers and people of Israel had desecrated God's "holy name" (vs. 7) by revering pagan deities in the Jerusalem temple (8:1-18). The meaning of the Hebrew noun rendered "their prostitution" (43:7, 9) is unclear. Certain forms of idol worship involved shrine prostitutes. Some have suggested that is the meaning here. Others, however, understand the term in a figurative sense as signifying the "spiritual adultery" of God's people. The nation is often portrayed in Scripture as an unfaithful spouse enticed away from the Lord by pagan deities. The Israelites also profaned the Lord by offering sacrifices at funeral pillars set up to venerate their deceased monarchs. The phrase, "the lifeless idols of their kings" (vss. 7, 9), probably refers to the practice of placing the tombs of Israelite rulers on the same hill as the temple. In earlier times, the monarch's palace and the temple were connected, but separated by a wall (vs. 8). Thus, Ezekiel was told that the shameful tradition of placing the kings' memorial graves (as well as their living quarters) near the sacred precincts, where vile deeds often occurred, would no longer be tolerated.

B. Pointing Out the Temple's Holy Design: vss. 10-12

"Son of man, describe the temple to the people of Israel, that they may be ashamed of their sins. Let them consider the plan, and if they are ashamed of all they have done, make known to them the design of the temple—its arrangement, its exits and entrances—its whole design and all its regulations and laws. Write these down before them so that they may be faithful to its design and follow all its regulations. This is the law of the temple: All the surrounding area on top of the mountain will be most holy. Such is the law of the temple."

God directed Ezekiel to describe to the exiled Israelites the divine design of the reconstructed temple and the nature of the religious observances to be practiced there (Ezek. 43:10-11). The plans upon which Israel's earlier sanctuaries were built also originated with God. By disclosing a clear picture of God's ideal blueprint for the people, Ezekiel would prompt them to recall the glory of Solomon's temple. Also, by writing it all down in their sight, the prophet would remind them of their iniquities, which brought the Lord's judgment upon them. Moreover, the people would be motivated to return to God in obedience with a desire to follow all of the decrees and statutes instituted in the new temple (chaps. 40–42).

Ezekiel described the new temple, God's future dwelling place, in terms and depictions the people could easily understand. God wanted His people to see what was in store for those who lived in faithful obedience to Him. The hard road of sin ultimately leads to judgment, as Israel learned all too well. But the pathway of obedience to the Lord leads to blessing, joy, and a peace that only God can give. God emphasized that maintaining the holiness of the future temple was supremely important. Indeed, the entire region on the mountaintop where the sanctuary was placed would be "most holy" (vs. 12). Holiness was the basic "law" of the Lord's new temple, because He is absolutely holy.

Discussion Questions

1. Why had God's glory previously departed from the Jerusalem temple?
2. In what way was the vision Ezekiel saw like the previous ones he had experienced?
3. Why did God emphasize that His people must never again profane His "holy name" (Ezek. 43:8)?
4. What does it mean to live in a holy manner?
5. How can believers use God's Word to help them live holy lives?

Contemporary Application

Ask three friends what image comes to mind when they hear the word *holy*, and you'll likely get three very different answers. Maybe one will see the face of this century's best-known spiritual leaders—a person known for an outspoken faith and a lifestyle beyond reproach.

Another might imagine monks cloistered in some mountaintop monastery far away from the cares of daily living. These would be people so caught up in visions of heaven that they are removed from the rough-and-tumble struggles "ordinary" folks must face. On the negative side, a third friend might picture individuals whom they describe as being "holier than thou." Put another way, these are people so certain about their own righteousness that no one else can measure up to their standards.

But what would be greater than asking your closest friends, "What comes to mind when you hear the word *holy*?" and listening to them sincerely reply, "You"? True, relatively few Christians will establish worldwide reputations for their faith or devote every moment of their waking lives to prayer and worship. Even in Ezekiel's day, the exiles in Babylon struggled to live in ways that were characterized by holiness.

And yet, God calls all of His spiritual children to be holy. The new temple that Ezekiel described was intended to motivate his peers to remain obedient to the Lord. And now, the Spirit of the Lord abiding in believers encourages them to be unwavering in their commitment to God. As this week's lesson indicates, being holy is not impossible. Also, it is not connected to those with robes and halos. Holiness is a natural characteristic of those who wholeheartedly follow the Creator.

God Accepts His People

Scripture

Background Scripture: *Ezekiel 43:10–46:24*
Scripture Lesson: *Ezekiel 43:13-21*
Key Verse: *"At the end of these days, from the eighth day on,
the priests are to present your burnt offerings and fellowship
offerings on the altar. Then I will accept you, declares the
Sovereign LORD."* Ezekiel 43:27.
Scripture Lesson for Children: *Ezekiel 43:13-21*
Key Verse for Children: *"These are the measurements of the
altar in long cubits."* Ezekiel 43:13.

Lesson Aim

To appreciate the lasting significance of Jesus and His
atoning sacrifice at Calvary.

Lesson Setting

Time: *573 B.C.*
Place: *Babylon*

Lesson Outline

God Accepts His People
  I. The Dimensions of the New Altar:
      Ezekiel 43:13-17
      A. *The Base Section of the New Altar: vs. 13*
      B. *The Next Three Sections of the New Altar: vss. 14-17*
  II. The Regulations for Offering Sacrifices:
      Ezekiel 43:18-21
      A. *The Command to Offer Sacrifices: vs. 18*
      B. *The Specific Sacrifices to Be Offered: vss. 19-21*

Introduction for Adults

Topic: *A Sign of Hope*

Restoration follows cleansing. That principle works when we take a bath, when we confess our sins, and when we forgive each other and give up our grudges. How pleasant it is to put on clean clothes. How much more delightful it is to be restored to God and one another.

Before we apply soap to our bodies, we have to be convinced that we need a shower. The spiritual counterpart of this is that we must admit that we really have offended God and other people by our behaviors. That's the hard part.

Many people are unconvinced that they need to be spiritually renewed. They refuse to admit the consequences of their sins. They fail to see the necessity of the cleansing that Jesus offers them through His atoning sacrifice at Calvary.

Through Ezekiel's prophecy about the new temple, its altar, and the sacrifices to be offered on it, the prophet declared that God provides forgiveness and complete restoration to those who come to Him in humility and faith. Even today, the Lord is our only hope for a future in which we can be pardoned and reconciled to Him.

Introduction for Youth

Topic: *An Opportunity to Meet God*

As the years and decades passed by for the exiles in Babylon, life must have seemed bleak. Then they heard Ezekiel declare to them God's amazing plan for a new temple and altar. Many of the specific instructions the Lord conveyed through Ezekiel were reminders of God's commitment to meet His people's deepest spiritual needs.

For New Testament believers, Jesus is the One who satisfies their longing to be restored to fellowship with God. When they trust in Jesus, they experience new life. Their rebelliousness and unbelief are supplanted by obedience and dependence, and their hatred is exchanged for unconditional love.

The world might scoff at the idea of receiving new life in the Son. However, believers know from God's Word that this is a reality. Remember, lasting inner renewal cannot be purchased with money or earned by doing good deeds. The lost must put their faith in Jesus, who atoned for their sins at Calvary.

Concepts for Children

Topic: *A Place of Hope*

1. God's people were far away from their homeland.
2. At times, God's people felt sad because they lived in a strange place.
3. God let His people know that He still loved them.
4. God also let His people know about the wonderful future He had planned for them.
5. God loves us so much that He has great plans for us too.

Lesson Commentary

I. THE DIMENSIONS OF THE NEW ALTAR: EZEKIEL 43:13-17

A. The Base Section of the New Altar: vs. 13

"These are the measurements of the altar in long cubits, that cubit being a cubit and a handbreadth: Its gutter is a cubit deep and a cubit wide, with a rim of one span around the edge. And this is the height of the altar."

In last week's lesson, we learned that when Ezekiel was 30 years old and living in the Jewish colony of Tel Aviv on the Kebar River (near the ancient city of Nippur), he heard God's call to be His spokesperson (Ezek. 1:2-3; 3:15). Ezekiel's prophecies began with "the fifth year of the exile" (1:2), and concluded with "the twenty-fifth year of our exile" (40:1). Based on these chronological pegs, it is possible to deduce that Ezekiel's ministry started on July 31, 593 B.C., and his ministry ended around March 26, 571 B.C. (29:17). By this reckoning, Ezekiel prophesied for approximately 22 years, from age 30 to 52.

In Ezekiel, at least two major structural features are evident. The first of these is the chronological presentation of significant events, visions, and oracles. This chronological arrangement is paralleled by a presentation of the material based on content. As was noted in lesson 9, the central theme of chapters 1–24 is the judgment of Judah, while that of chapters 33–48 is Judah's future restoration. Between these two major focal points, in chapters 25–32, Ezekiel pronounced God's judgment upon pagan kingdoms. The content of Ezekiel's prophecies was delivered through a variety of literary means. These included symbolic actions, allegories or parables, and most importantly, visions. In broad outline, the first vision focused on the presence of God's glory in Babylon (1–3), the second on the judgment of Jerusalem (8–11), and the third (37) and fourth visions (40–48) on the future restoration of Judah.

Strange visions like spinning wheels and a valley of dry bones that come to life have caused many readers of Ezekiel's prophecy more than a little puzzlement. Also, not surprisingly, these visions have generated wildly different interpretations of many passages. The problem of understanding Ezekiel's prophecies has a long history. At least as early as the late fourth and early fifth centuries, the great Bible scholar Jerome offered numerous apologies in his commentaries for an inability to better explain difficult passages. But for the reader who is willing to dig a little deeper into Ezekiel's prophecies, there is a wealth of spiritual insight into God's patient involvement and dealings with His people during this dark period of Israel's history.

For example, in last week's excursion through 43:1-12, we learned about Ezekiel's vision of a new temple whose design originated with God. This was also the special place where the glory of God returned. He revealed to His spokesperson that because the reconstructed sanctuary would serve as the divine throne and dwelling place, the Lord would not permit any kind of defilement within its precincts. As a result of Ezekiel disclosing this information to the exiles in Babylon, they would be compelled to abandon their sinful ways and return to God in obedience. This included heeding all the "regulations and laws" (vs. 11) pertaining to the new temple.

With the completion of the rebuilt sanctuary and the divine glory filling it, worship services would begin. To set the stage for this, Ezekiel detailed the dimensions of the future altar (vss. 13-17; see also 40:47). Next, he presented the regulations for offering sacrifices on the altar (43:18-27 and the Bible lesson commentary that appears below). The measurements for the altar, like those for the temple itself, were given to Ezekiel in great detail. To avoid any confusion, the prophet was even informed that the dimensions were in "long cubits" (vs. 13).

A "long" or royal "cubit" was approximately 21 inches in length, while a short cubit measured about 18 inches. A "handbreadth" was about three inches long, and a "span" was approximately nine inches in length. The altar, which was probably made of dressed stones, consisted of four stages or platforms, including the "gutter" or base section on the very bottom. This design resembled a Mesopotamian ziggurat, which was a type of symmetrical step-pyramid. The altar's lowest base level was 21 inches high and extended 21 inches out from the next higher platform on all sides. It had a nine-inch rim or molding all around it.

B. The Next Three Sections of the New Altar: vss. 14-17

"From the gutter on the ground up to the lower ledge it is two cubits high and a cubit wide, and from the smaller ledge up to the larger ledge it is four cubits high and a cubit wide. The altar hearth is four cubits high, and four horns project upward from the hearth. The altar hearth is square, twelve cubits long and twelve cubits wide. The upper ledge also is square, fourteen cubits long and fourteen cubits wide, with a rim of half a cubit and a gutter of a cubit all around. The steps of the altar face east."

The next level up from the base of the altar was a stone platform three and a half feet high. It also extended 21 inches out from the next higher platform on all sides. The third level, just beneath the horned altar itself, was seven feet high with a surrounding ledge, in a "gutter" (Ezek. 43:14) design like the base, 21 inches wide. This third level was 24 and a half feet long on each side with a "rim" (vs. 17) or molding 10 and a half inches high.

The topmost level of the altar complex, the "altar hearth" (vs. 15) or altar proper, was also seven feet high like the platform below. But it was distinguished by a 21-inch horn or stone projection at each of its four corners. The top level measured 21 feet on each side (vs. 16). The entire altar complex had "steps" (vs. 17) on the east side that led up to the top of the altar. This was actually forbidden by the Mosaic law (Exod. 20:26). But at a height of 19 feet—nearly two stories—the altar would be impossible to reach without them.

Since the dawn of human history, people offered sacrifices to God. For instance, at the end of the growing season, Cain (the first son of Adam and Eve) brought some of his harvest as an offering to the Lord (Gen. 4:3). Likewise, Abel (Cain's brother) offered to the Lord "fat portions" (v. 4) taken from "some of the firstborn" sheep of his herd. Later, after the great Flood, Noah presented "burnt offerings" (8:20) to God to express his gratitude for the Lord's deliverance of him and his family. Each of the Old Testament patriarchs, Abraham, Isaac, and Jacob, often built altars on which they made offerings to the Lord as a demonstration of their faith in His covenant (12:7–8; 13:18; 22:9; 26:25; 33:20; 35:1, 3, 7).

Be that as it may, it was not until the Israelites had camped in the Sinai desert that the Lord instituted formal sacrifices among His people. Moses instructed the Israelites to make five different types of sacrifices: burnt, grain, fellowship, sin, and guilt offerings (Lev. 1:1–7:21). In the Old Testament, sacrificial animals were laid out on the altar hearth. The blood of the animal was smeared on the altar horns (Exod. 29:12; Lev. 4:7, 18). The horns of the altar were also regarded as places of refuge (1 Kings 1:49-53). If an individual were in mortal danger because of some wrong done to another, grasping the horns of the altar was supposed to prompt mercy from the person seeking revenge. This act was presumably symbolic of God's gracious acceptance of Israelite sacrifices offered in atonement for the people's sins.

II. THE REGULATIONS FOR OFFERING SACRIFICES: EZEKIEL 43:18-21

A. The Command to Offer Sacrifices: vs. 18

Then he said to me, "Son of man, this is what the Sovereign LORD says: These will be the regulations for sacrificing burnt offerings and sprinkling blood upon the altar when it is built."

Ezekiel 43:18 introduces the statutes Israel's all-powerful Lord wanted His people to follow when they offered sacrifices on the altar in the reconstructed temple. These sacrifices included "burnt offerings," as well as splashing "blood" against the altar. In a sense, Ezekiel's vision here was looking backward and forward at the same time. It looked backward to the time of Moses when the imperfect sacrificial system was first instituted. It also looked forward to the Messiah's perfect sacrifice, which fulfilled the potential and promise of the imperfect animal sacrifices. The Israelites could approach God and receive forgiveness for their sins only because of Calvary. Today, it is still the only means by which we can gain acceptance by God and experience complete pardon from sin (Rom. 3:25-26).

B. The Specific Sacrifices to Be Offered: vss. 19-21

"You are to give a young bull as a sin offering to the priests, who are Levites, of the family of Zadok, who come near to minister before me, declares the Sovereign LORD. You are to take some of its blood and put it on the four horns of the altar and on the four corners of the upper ledge and all around the rim, and

so purify the altar and make atonement for it. You are to take the bull for the sin offering and burn it in the designated part of the temple area outside the sanctuary."

In Ezekiel's vision, it was revealed that a seven-day ritual administered by the priests, from the "family of Zadok" (Ezek. 43:19), who were members of the tribe of Levi, would be required to consecrate the altar of the new temple to God (vs. 26). The Zadokite priesthood originated when Solomon set aside the priestly line of Eli by deposing Abiathar and putting Zadok in his place (1 Kings 2:26-27). God had already condemned the priesthood of the house of Eli because of Eli's two worthless sons, Hophni and Phinehas (1 Sam. 2:30-36).

The Lord indicated that the altar would be truly purified after "blood" (Ezek. 43:20) from the sin offering was applied to "the four horns of the altar," the "four corners" of the platform below the altar hearth, and on the "rim" of the base. After the blood of a young, domesticated "bull" (vs. 21) was used for this sacrificial purpose, the carcass of the animal was supposed to be burned in a specific place outside the "sanctuary." Everything in temple worship had a precise purpose, place, and order. God required that it all be done exactly as He instructed.

Many interpreters of Scripture object to the idea of the reinstatement of sacrifices in the new temple and thus view Ezekiel's description of future sacrifices as symbolic rather than literal. They argue that to reinstate animal sacrifices in the last days implies that the Messiah's death was somehow deficient. They point out that according to Scripture, Jesus' atoning sacrifice was the permanent remedy for sin, making all further animal offerings unnecessary (Rom. 6:10; Heb. 9:12; 10:10, 18). Other Bible scholars think the problem is solved when the function of Ezekiel's sacrifices are properly understood. For instance, they explain that animal sacrifices could not take away sin. These interpreters assert that the only way to be saved in any age is by grace through faith in the shed blood of the Son (Heb. 10:1-4, 10).

Proponents of the latter view note that even after the church began at Pentecost, Jewish Christians still offered sacrifices in Herod's temple, perhaps as memorials to the Savior's death (Acts 2:46; 21:26). In the new temple, say these interpreters, animal sacrifices also serve as memorials honoring the ultimate, efficacious sacrifice of the Son. The conclusion of the matter is essentially the same as the controversy surrounding the building of the new temple. Whether understood symbolically or literally, the Israelites no doubt simply took Ezekiel's message at face value. The message was clear. The worship and fellowship with God that His chosen people had lost because of divine judgment for sin would one day be restored.

In the biblical era, there were three orders in the hierarchy of priests: the high priests, priests, and Levites. Whereas the Levites were subordinate sanctuary officials who supervised the minor duties of the temple, the priests were associates of the high priests. Priests were to come from the tribe of Levi and had to be without any physical defect. They were organized into 24 divisions that served the sanctuary in rotation. Each of the divisions ministered for a week, beginning on the Sabbath, except during the annual feasts, at which time all the priests served together.

The ceremony of consecration of the priests was much like that for the high priest, but not as elaborate. The clothing of the priests included a tunic, breeches, and a turban—all of which were made with white linen, as well as a white linen girdle embroidered with blue, purple, and scarlet. The chief duties of the priests were the care of the sanctuary vessels and the sacrifices at the altar. But the priests also taught the Mosaic law, watched over the physical health of the nation, and administered justice.

Under the old covenant, the sacrificial system was God's provision for reconciling sinful people to Himself. Even though God prescribed these sacrifices, they had limitations. They were external rituals and ceremonies, and they were not able to change the hearts of the worshipers. Also, the sacrifices needed to be repeated, because they could not atone for future sins. Only sins already committed were covered. Moreover, repetition was required to atone for any sins committed since the last sacrifice was made.

Another weakness was that from the time the Lord gave the law of Moses until the time of the Messiah's death and resurrection, believers had to go through priests to have access to God. If someone needed atonement for sins, only a priest could offer a sacrifice in that person's behalf. Also, if someone wanted to sacrifice an animal to God, the priest was required to offer it on the altar. Furthermore, only once a year, on the day of Atonement (that is, Yom Kippur), the high priest entered the most holy place, stood before the ark of the covenant, and made atonement for the sins of the people.

The Book of Leviticus reveals the following five basic facts about Old Testament sacrifices: (1) They were made to God alone and thus required the choicest animals and produce; (2) They were God's provision for humankind's approach to Him; (3) Unlike most pagan religions, they were usually performed by the worshiper and the priest together; (4) They were limited in their effectiveness; pardon was effected by God, not the blood of bulls and goats; and (5) They represented a substitution. Often the death of an animal was regarded as taking the place of the one who brought the sacrifice. But Jesus alone, the only perfect sacrifice, was qualified to serve as the substitute for sin that deserved death.

In this regard, "atonement" is one of the most important words in all of Scripture. Ezekiel twice refers to making atonement for the altar (Ezek. 43:20, 26). The root meaning of the Hebrew verb for atonement, *kaphar*, is "to cover over." Throughout Scripture, atonement is closely related to the concept of "reconciliation," that is, bringing together those who were estranged or enemies. In the Old Testament, the blood of rams and goats "covered over" the sins of Israel. But the purpose of blood atonement was not merely to conceal sins from sight. It was meant to pay the ransom price required for canceling out the debt and penalty owed by sin. That said, the blood of rams and goats was only a symbol of Jesus' sacrificial death, the perfect "Lamb of God" (John 1:29, 36). His sacrifice alone was sufficient to stamp out the debt owed by sin (1 Pet. 1:18-19).

Discussion Questions

1. What function would the altar serve in the new temple?
2. What was the theological purpose of the sacrifices offered on the altar?
3. In what sense did Ezekiel's vision of the altar look backward and forward in time?
4. Why are the Old Testament sacrifices no longer necessary?
5. What did Jesus accomplish by His once-for-all-time sacrifice?

Contemporary Application

In Ezekiel's vision of the new temple, he received divine instructions concerning the altar upon which sacrifices were to be offered. As a result of what he recorded, the exiles in Babylon learned that the Lord could not be accessed apart from an offering of atonement. From the New Testament, believers learn that when Jesus allowed Himself to be sacrificed at Calvary, He atoned for the sins of the world (1 John 2:2).

In previous generations, we used to derive much strength and support from family and friends. But for many families today, divorce and frequent relocation have severed the supportive ties upon which former generations relied. There are adults who feel lonelier now than they ever did before. Some are unable to socialize as much as they would like because of their demanding work schedules. Others are unwilling to take the risk of getting to know people because they fear being rejected or misunderstood.

In the midst of these difficulties, it's easy to wonder whether there really is anyone who cares about the struggles, shortcomings, and difficulties we experience. In an increasingly impersonal world, there's also a heightened need for personal contact and emotional support. One of the great needs today is for people to know that God cares about them and will never abandon them.

For the believer, the Lord Jesus meets their deepest spiritual needs. As our perfect atoning sacrifice and faithful High Priest, who ministers before the Father's throne of grace, Jesus is sympathetic to our concerns and burdens. Rather than letting us shrink back from God in times of distress because we think our problems are insignificant or we're unworthy, Scripture encourages us to receive timely help from the Savior (Heb. 4:14-16).

God Revives His People

Scripture

Background Scripture: *Ezekiel 47:1, 3-12*

Scripture Lesson: *Ezekiel 47:1, 3-12*

Key Verse: *"Swarms of living creatures will live wherever the river flows. There will be large numbers of fish, because this water flows there and makes the salt water fresh; so where the river flows everything will live."* Ezekiel 47:9.

Scripture Lesson for Children: *Ezekiel 47:1, 3-12*

Key Verse for Children: *"Where the river flows everything will live."* Ezekiel 47:9.

Lesson Aim

To eagerly wait for the day when we will spend eternity with the Lord.

Lesson Setting

Time: 573 B.C.

Place: Babylon, Jerusalem

Lesson Outline

God Revives His People

  I. The River's Presence: Ezekiel 47:1-5
      A. *The Entrance of the Temple: vs. 1*
      B. *The Depth and Breadth of the River: vss. 3-5*
  II. The River's Power: Ezekiel 47:6-12
      A. *The Presence of Many Trees: vss. 6-7*
      B. *The Presence of Life and Activity: vss. 8-11*
      C. *The Healing Power of the River: vs. 12*

Introduction for Adults

Topic: *Life Needs Water*

The television series *Extreme Makeover* showcases everyday people who undergo a series of cosmetic procedures and supposedly have their lives changed forever. One season included two sisters who struggled with cleft palettes and underwent nearly 40 surgeries; a colorful bull rider who had his teeth knocked out and wanted to be transformed into an urban cowboy; and a female rock musician who spent her days hiding behind her shocking stage appearance. These and other participants recuperated at the "Makeover Mansion," a luxurious residence tucked away in the Hollywood Hills, complete with stunning views, a swimming pool, fully equipped home gym, and plasma televisions.

This prime-time version of a new start on life is a far cry from what we find revealed in Ezekiel 47:1-12. God doesn't promise to remodel our dying physical bodies. And we aren't going to be given a lavish estate that will eventually decay and fall apart. What the Lord has in store for us—spiritual fruitfulness and healing—is far better and will be everlasting.

Introduction for Youth

Topic: *More than Enough*

In 1990, the comedy *Home Alone* appeared in movie theaters. The film is about eight-year-old Kevin McAllister, who is accidentally left behind when his family takes off for a vacation in France over the holiday season. Once he realizes they've left him home by himself, Kevin learns to fend for himself. He eventually has to protect his house against bumbling burglars Harry and Marv, who are planning to rob every house in Kevin's suburban Chicago neighborhood.

In the eternal state, God does not leave the redeemed all alone in their celestial home to fend for themselves. As we learn from Ezekiel 47:1-12 (the focus of this week's lesson), He makes His dwelling place among them and graces them with His overflowing, glorious presence. He removes every trace of vice, permitting only what is virtuous to remain. Best of all, His people reign with Him forever. Now that is Good News worth sharing!

Concepts for Children

Topic: *A Flowing River*

1. Ezekiel saw a vision of a river flowing from God's house.
2. God gives us His message in His Word and His actions.
3. God used water as a symbol of new life.
4. Ezekiel's vision gave the people hope for a wonderful new life.
5. This new life would be healthy and satisfying.

Lesson Commentary

I. THE RIVER'S PRESENCE: EZEKIEL 47:1-5

A. The Entrance of the Temple: vs. 1

The man brought me back to the entrance of the temple, and I saw water coming out from under the threshold of the temple toward the east (for the temple faced east). The water was coming down from under the south side of the temple, south of the altar.

In the previous two lessons, we learned that in 573 B.C., on the twenty-fifth anniversary of Ezekiel's exile to Babylon, he was supernaturally transported to Jerusalem. There the prophet received a vision of a new temple to be built in Israel's restored land (Ezek. 40:1-4). Chapters 40–43 contain a thorough description of the reconstructed sanctuary. The new service of worship in the temple is detailed in chapters 44–46. This is followed in chapters 47–48 by a picture of the new land of Israel, with its life-giving river, its boundaries, and its divisions. Taken all together, the revelation is a dazzling portrait of a bright future ahead for God's people.

In Ezekiel 44, God revealed to His spokesperson the routine operation of the future temple. The Lord's angelic guide discussed the duties of its appointed ministers, the priests and Levites, and the means of their support. Chapter 45 delineates the allotments of the new land reserved for the priests, Levites, the whole house of Israel, and the prince. The identity of the "prince" (vs. 7) is impossible to determine with certainty. Some think He is the Messiah, but this cannot be since this prince needs a sin offering (vs. 22) and he has sons (46:16). Others conjecture the prince is King David, or some other human representative of the Messiah in the government of the kingdom age to come (34:23-24; 37:24).

In any case, chapter 46 gives God's directions to the Israelite princes for proper conduct toward the people of the nation. There are also instructions on the required preparation and procedure for presenting offerings and celebrating holy days. Ezekiel's tour of the future temple ended with the angelic guide bringing the prophet back to the entrance of the sanctuary (47:1). As he stood in the temple's inner courtyard, he saw a life-giving river flowing from it.

In Ezekiel's vision of the future temple, the sacred enclosure "faced east." The prophet noticed that water also flowed east from beneath the threshold, or entrance, of the temple. The stream passed to the right of the altar of sacrifice on its south side, continued east through the courtyard, and then exited from the sanctuary complex. The angelic guide escorted God's spokesperson outside the temple through the north gateway. From there, the two went around the wall of the compound to the gate that faces east. A small stream of water could be seen trickling out from the south side of the gate (vs. 2).

The presence of water flowing from the future temple brings to mind the river that flowed from Eden to water its orchard and suggests that the end-time sanctuary will be the center of God's new creation (Gen. 2:10). The perennial streams of the garden were a source of life-sustaining refreshment. The lushness of this Edenic paradise forms the backdrop of Psalm 46:4. A figurative "river" and its "streams" are depicted as bringing joy to the "city of God." The latter is none other than the special, holy dwelling place of the "Most High."

A corresponding depiction is found in Joel 3:18. The Lord promised the remnant that in the time of restoration, the mountains of Zion would drip with sweet wine, the hills would "flow with milk," and Judah's ravines would "run with water." A spring would flow out from the temple of the Lord and water the parched "valley of acacias" (possibly located in the plains of Moab, northeast of the Dead Sea). The language used here is an embellished way of describing the overflowing blessing that God would shower on His people in the kingdom age.

Accompanying God's abundant provision is forgiveness of sin. In the future, He who is the spring of life-giving water (Jer. 2:13; 17:13) not only declared that bountiful streams would "flow out from Jerusalem" (Zech. 14:8), but also that a fountain would be opened up to "the house of David and the inhabitants of Jerusalem" (13:1) to "cleanse them from sin and impurity." Ultimately, through Jesus and the Holy Spirit, believers find this abundance of pardon (John 7:37-39). The eternal life Jesus offers amply satisfies the spiritual thirst of people forever (10:10). Indeed, God's gift of salvation is comparable to a fountain of water that vigorously wells up in believers in an inner, unending, and overflowing supply (4:14).

B. The Depth and Breadth of the River: vss. 3-5

As the man went eastward with a measuring line in his hand, he measured off a thousand cubits and then led me through water that was ankle-deep. He measured off another thousand cubits and led me through water that was knee-deep. He measured off another thousand and led me through water that was up to the waist. He measured off another thousand, but now it was a river that I could not cross, because the water had risen and was deep enough to swim in—a river that no one could cross.

As the angelic guide led God's spokesperson in an eastward direction, the escort used a "measuring line" (Ezek. 47:3) he held in his hand to mark off a "thousand cubits" (or 1,750 feet) downstream. Then the guide led Ezekiel through the water, which was up to his ankles. Next, the escort measured off another "thousand cubits" (vs. 4) downstream. As the two waded through at this point, the water came up to the prophet's knees. After another thousand cubits, the water came up to his waist. Just one thousand cubits downstream from there, the current had become an impassible river. The water was deep enough to swim in, but too deep to walk through (vs. 5). The series of measurements appearing in these verses contribute to a larger, complex scenario that symbolically depicts God's abundant provision. The latter includes the promise of forgiveness, new life, and fruitful service in His kingdom.

In a corresponding way, Isaiah 55 reassured the captives in Babylon of God's abundant provision. In this case, the Lord called out to the remnant as if He were a street vendor selling food and water. Life for the exiles may not always have been good, but it was at least secure and familiar. A return to Judah would involve unknown hardships and hazards. Thus, God promised spiritual benefits if the exiles would take the risk of returning. God had many blessings to offer His people, including water, wine, and milk. He urged His people to obtain His goods, but to do so without spending any money (vs. 1). The idea is that they were to take freely from Him what they normally would have had to pay for. This is a marvelous picture of God's unmerited favor, which is otherwise known as grace.

The Lord tried to persuade His potential customers to stay away from His competitors. He warned that if the people did not buy what He was selling, they would be spending their money without getting what they needed and would be laboring without satisfaction. Expressed differently, if they stayed in Babylon, their lives would be spiritually unproductive. But if they listened to Him and partook of His spiritual food, their souls would thrive immensely (vs. 2). The Lord urged the exiles to pay attention to what He declared. If they heeded Him, they would enjoy life to the fullest. In fact, by obeying God, the people would receive the benefits of the "everlasting covenant" (vs. 3) He made with David. "Faithful love" spotlights the unconditional nature of the covenantal promises. God's unfailing mercies to David were held out to all his descendants who lived uprightly.

In the doxology appearing in Ephesians 3:20-21, Paul likewise stressed the abundance of God's gifts to believers, the power He makes available to them, and the relationship between Jesus and His church. God's ability to meet the deepest needs of His spiritual children far exceeds any request we can make in prayer or could even imagine. This point is emphasized by the Greek adverb rendered "immeasurably more," which could also be translated "superabundantly." In other words, there is no limit to what the Father can do on behalf of those who trust in His Son. All of this is brought about through divine "power," which is present in the lives of believers (2 Pet. 1:3-4). To such a God, Paul ascribed glory in the church and in His Son, who has made all these blessings possible. The apostle ended his prayer with a mighty crescendo of praise to God. Then, like the whisper of an orchestra's strings dying away, Paul added his "amen" (Eph. 3:21), meaning "so let it be."

The preceding truths are also emphasized in the doxology the apostle recorded in Romans 16:25-27. Paul declared that the all-powerful Lord was sufficiently able to strengthen believers in accordance with the proclamation of the Gospel. The latter was the message the apostle and his colleagues announced about the Lord Jesus. Furthermore, the Good News was in harmony with prophecies about the Messiah recorded in the Old Testament. As the apostles and evangelists heralded the Gospel, the Spirit enabled many to believe and obey the truth. This amazing outcome was due to the incomparable wisdom of God and prompted Paul to offer praise to the Lord.

II. THE RIVER'S POWER: EZEKIEL 47:6-12

A. The Presence of Many Trees: vss. 6-7

He asked me, "Son of man, do you see this?" Then he led me back to the bank of the river. When I arrived there, I saw a great number of trees on each side of the river.

The angelic guide asked whether Ezekiel had been paying attention to the unfolding vision (Ezek. 47:6). The answer is that the prophet had carefully noted everything he saw. When the escort led Ezekiel back to the riverbank, he was surprised by the sight of a "great number of trees" (vs. 7) growing on both sides of the river. Such abundance is reminiscent of the Garden of Eden, where God caused all kinds of beautiful, fruitful trees to grow. In the middle of this pristine orchard stood the tree that gives life (Gen. 2:9). In Ezekiel's vision of the new temple, the river and its orchard indicated the Lord's intent to transform Jerusalem and its environs into a paradise-like garden.

B. The Presence of Life and Activity: vss. 8-11

He said to me, "This water flows toward the eastern region and goes down into the Arabah, where it enters the Sea. When it empties into the Sea, the water there becomes fresh. Swarms of living creatures will live wherever the river flows. There will be large numbers of fish, because this water flows there and makes the salt water fresh; so where the river flows everything will live. Fishermen will stand along the shore; from En Gedi to En Eglaim there will be places for spreading nets. The fish will be of many kinds—like the fish of the Great Sea. But the swamps and marshes will not become fresh; they will be left for salt."

The angelic guide explained to Ezekiel that the water flowed eastward through the desert to the Jordan River valley and emptied into the stagnant, filthy Dead Sea (which is approximately 25 percent saline). In so doing, the salty water became fresh and pure (Ezek. 47:8). The Hebrew text of this verse literally reads "the waters become healed," which is figuratively expressive of the power of God to bring about restoration and renewal. Just as in the original creation the earth teemed with life (Gen. 1:20-25), so too swarms of living creatures would one day flourish wherever the river from the temple flowed.

Unlike today, the Dead Sea would become the habitat for "large numbers of fish" (Ezek. 47:9). Also, as hard as it is to currently imagine, people would fish on the shore of the sea from En Gedi (located about midway along the western shore of the Dead Sea) to En Eglaim (possibly near the northwestern corner of the Dead Sea; vs. 10). Moreover, they would spread out their nets on the coast to dry. Indeed, there would be as many different kinds of fish swarming in the Dead Sea as the aquatic life populating the Mediterranean Sea. The only exception would be the "swamps and marshes" (vs. 11) along the shore. These waters would remain briny, so that people could extract salt from it, perhaps for use in temple sacrifices (43:24).

C. The Healing Power of the River: vs. 12

"Fruit trees of all kinds will grow on both banks of the river. Their leaves will not wither, nor will their fruit fail. Every month they will bear, because the water from the sanctuary flows to them. Their fruit will serve for food and their leaves for healing."

The angelic guide revealed that all kinds of "fruit trees" (Ezek. 47:12) would flourish on both sides of the river's banks. Amazingly, the leaves of these trees would never wither, and they would always bear fresh fruit on their branches. "Every month" a new crop would be ready for God's people to enjoy. This was made possible by the water from the temple, which streamed continuously to the orchard. People would harvest the luscious fruit to eat and use the "leaves for healing." This depiction of agricultural abundance signifies the extent to which God intended to restore His people to their homeland after the exile.

Revelation 22:1-5 draws upon similar imagery to describe the eternal state. John, while exiled on the island of Patmos (1:9), saw a pure "river" (22:1) containing the "water of life." The river was crystal clear, and it flowed from God's throne down the "middle" of the city's main thoroughfare. The river and its water are a symbol of the fullness of eternal life that proceeds from the presence of God. To those living in the hot and dry climate of Palestine, this scene would be a vivid image of God's ability to satisfy their spiritual thirst (John 4:7-14; Rev. 22:17).

John noted that a "tree of life" (Rev. 22:2) grew on "each side of the river." Some think the Greek noun rendered "tree" (vs. 2) should be taken in a collective sense to refer to an orchard lining both sides of the riverbank. In either case, the tree bears 12 different kinds of "fruit," with a new crop appearing each "month" of the year. The fruit gives life, and the "leaves" are used as medicine to heal the "nations." The presence of health-giving leaves does not mean there is illness in heaven. Rather, the leaves symbolize the health and vigor that believers enjoy in eternity.

In the new creation, the Father and the Son are seated on their thrones, and the redeemed worship and serve them continually (vs. 3). God establishes unbroken communion with His people, and He claims them as His own (vs. 4). The end of history is better than the beginning, for a radiant city replaces the Garden of Eden, and the light of God's glory drives out all darkness. There is neither idleness nor boredom in the eternal state, for God gives His people ruling responsibilities (vs. 5). Revelation, as the final book in Scripture, assures us of God's enduring purposes and should also increase our longing for communion with the Lord.

Discussion Questions

1. What did Ezekiel see at the entrance to the temple?
2. Why do you think the angelic guide progressively measured off the riverbank?
3. What was the significance of the orchard growing on both sides of the river?
4. What kind of spiritual life does the Father make available to us through faith in His Son?
5. In what ways is the Lord able to bring about spiritual wellness in our lives?

Contemporary Application

In Ezekiel's vision of the new temple, he learned about a river streaming out from under the sanctuary and flowing east. Yet, this was no ordinary stream. It enabled many trees and creatures to flourish in its life-sustaining waters (47:1-2). The healing power of the river is a reminder of God's unlimited ability to enable us, as Jesus' followers, to thrive spiritually. Indeed, we eagerly wait for the day when we will spend eternity with the Lord.

Unlike other world religions, Christianity is the only one that centers on what the Father has done for us in His Son. Every other religion is based on what people presume to do for themselves and for God. Scripture says it is just the opposite. Regardless of how high and admirable humanly contrived ideals may be, any religion or philosophy that does not follow the one true God can never hope to fulfill its own standards. All it takes is one sin to make us fall short of God's glory (Gal. 3:10; Jas. 2:10-11).

In contrast, the Gospel proclaims the only viable way. God Himself must save us, because we can never save ourselves. The Messiah—God incarnate—did just that. He suffered incredibly and was crushed so that we might be redeemed (Isa. 52:13–53:12). As echoed in this week's Scripture passage from Ezekiel, because of Jesus' redemptive work, we are healed (1 Pet. 2:24).

As John Bunyan portrayed in his famous allegory, *Pilgrim's Progress*, the Messiah is holding the pardon document in His hand. It is already a done deal. All we need to do is take it. And once we are pardoned, we must tell others how to take it, too!

God Transforms His People

Scripture

Background Scripture: *Ezekiel 47:13-23; Acts 2:37-47*
Scripture Lesson: *Ezekiel 47:13-23*
Key Verse: *Peter replied, "Repent and be baptized, every one
of you, in the name of Jesus Christ for the forgiveness of your
sins. And you will receive the gift of the Holy Spirit."*
Acts 2:38.
Scripture Lesson for Children: *Acts 2:37-47*
Key Verse for Children: *All the believers were together and
had everything in common.* Acts 2:44.

Lesson Aim

To share God's gift of a new spiritual beginning with
others.

Lesson Setting

Time: 573 B.C.
Place: Babylon, Jerusalem

Lesson Outline

God Transforms His People
  I. The Boundaries of the Land: Ezekiel 47:13-20
      A. *The Command to Divide the Land: vs. 13*
      B. *The Specific Boundaries on Each Side: vss. 14-20*
  II. The Distribution of the Land: Ezekiel 47:21-23
      A. *Allocating the Land by Tribes: vs. 21*
      B. *Including Foreigners in the Allotment: vss. 22-23*

Introduction for Adults

Topic: *A New Beginning*

What do Andrew Carnegie, Henry Ford, Luther Burbank, and Charlie Chaplin have in common? Each rose from an impoverished background and became a superachiever in his field.

Carnegie came to America as an immigrant and rose to become one of the wealthiest businesspersons in America. Ford's interest in machinery while living on a Michigan farm started a revolution to the motorcar industry.

Burbank's lack of a formal education did not prevent him from becoming a world-class breeder of plants. Last, Chaplin overcame his impoverished childhood to become a famous star of silent movies. All these persons, at one point, felt they had little to contribute to the world.

Ezekiel 47:22-23 reminds us that regardless of our backgrounds, God can work in our lives to do good for His glory. His grace is that inclusive. As we submit to His will, we have an opportunity not only to make a new start, but also to share with others how God can enable them to do so, too.

Introduction for Youth

Topic: *God's Gift of New Starts*

Ezekiel's vision of the new temple also included details about the land where it was located. The Lord disclosed to His spokesperson what the boundaries of that land would be and how it would be distributed. Amazingly, both "native-born Israelites" (Ezek. 47:22) and resident "aliens" would be "allotted an inheritance."

At times, we might think God's gift of a new start applies to others, not us. Our circumstantial limitations can feel disqualifying, and we might conclude that God has disregarded us. Or perhaps a personal failure leads us to believe that God has written us out of His plan and purpose.

This week's lesson is a reminder that God uses His unlimited power in many ways: to create, to disclose the future, to save, to fulfill His Word, and to use whomever He wishes for His purposes. He can even bring about a new beginning in our lives. He also can use us in extraordinary ways to reach others with His message of love and grace. None of our limitations limit God. He delights to demonstrate His power through us.

Concepts for Children

Topic: *A New Start*

1. On the day of Pentecost, Jesus sent the Holy Spirit.
2. The Spirit is a special gift to help Jesus' followers.
3. The coming of the Spirit was powerful.
4. Jesus' followers knew the Spirit had come, for He did special things.
5. The Spirit enables us to share the Good News about Jesus with others.

Lesson Commentary

I. THE BOUNDARIES OF THE LAND: EZEKIEL 47:13-20

A. The Command to Divide the Land: vs. 13

This is what the Sovereign LORD says: "These are the boundaries by which you are to divide the land for an inheritance among the twelve tribes of Israel, with two portions for Joseph."

In last week's lesson, we learned about Ezekiel's vision of a life-giving river that flowed from the new temple (Ezek. 47:1-12). This week we turn our attention to the boundaries of the promised land (vss. 13-20) and its distribution to the 12 tribes of Israel. God's spokesperson discovered that the land would be fully restored to the order and oversight that God decreed. Also, the land would be divided equally among the nation's "tribes" (vs. 13). The tribe of Levi was the one exception, since its members lived on a designated portion of the sacrifices offered in the rebuilt temple (44:28-31; 45:1-8; 48:8-14). So, in order to keep the number of Israelite tribes at 12, Joseph's tribe was divided into two. This meant that one portion of Joseph's allocation would go to Ephraim and the other to Manasseh.

Genesis 48 provides the biblical context for the double portion of land going to Joseph's tribe. The year was 1859 B.C., and the place was Egypt. The patriarch, Jacob, was ill and near death, so he summoned his sons to his bedside (vss. 1-2). Even Joseph came from his palace with his two boys. Jacob knew that his time was short, so he performed the traditional duty of blessing his sons. This meant he divided the inheritance among them and invoked God's favor upon them. Since Jacob's family was in covenant with the Lord, the belief that their descendants would one day possess the promised land lies behind Jacob's words.

The patriarch began his speech by addressing Joseph, telling how almighty God had blessed Jacob long ago at Luz or Bethel (48:3-4; see also 28:10-22). The Lord had promised that Jacob's descendants would become numerous. In light of that blessing, Jacob claimed Manasseh and Ephraim as his own sons. Any other sons Joseph might have would remain Joseph's own. They would not be equal with their uncles, as Manasseh and Ephraim were (vss. 5-6). The Hebrew verb rendered "blessed" (vs. 15) literally means "to kneel." When used of God toward people, the term generally refers to His bestowing a rich and abundant life on someone. Also, when used of people blessing people, the verb usually signifies a desire that God would shine His favor on a particular individual or group. Finally, when the verb describes people blessing God, it is an expression of praise to Him in recognition of His goodness and grace.

In the blessing that Jacob conveyed to Joseph and his two sons, the patriarch made reference to the covenant-keeping God of Abraham and Isaac. Many years earlier, God came to Abraham in a vision and declared that He was the patriarch's shield of protection as well as the One who would reward him in great abundance (15:1). Later, the Lord referred to Himself as almighty God and instructed Abraham to serve Him faithfully and live a blameless life (17:1). The testimony of Jacob's grandfather and father was that both of them lived faithfully in the Lord's presence (15:2; 48:15).

Like other people of faith, the patriarchs believed that God exists and that He rewards those who earnestly seek Him (Heb. 11:6). Their trust in the Lord enabled them to sojourn as foreigners in Canaan and embrace the covenant pledges connected with the promised land. They could live in this way because they looked forward to the heavenly city of the eternal God (vss. 7-16). Indeed, the lives of Abraham, Isaac, Jacob, and Joseph were all characterized by unwavering faith in the Lord (32:17-22). They and others like them died with the assurance that God would bring to pass everything He declared He would do (vss. 39-40).

It is this perspective of faith that lay at the heart of Israel's statements to Joseph and Ezekiel's vision of the fully restored temple and land to Israel. As the end of Jacob's life drew closer, he could genuinely affirm that the Lord had been his shepherd (Gen. 48:15). When Jacob first ventured from Canaan to Paddan Aram, God pledged to watch over him and prosper him (28:10-22). Two decades later, as Jacob prepared to return to Canaan, the Lord promised to be with him (31:3). Before the patriarch's reunion with Esau, Jacob had a life-changing encounter with God's angel (vss. 24-30). Then, as Israel made the journey to Bethel, the Lord appeared to him and spoke reassuringly to him (35:1). Upon Israel's arrival, almighty God again appeared to him and reiterated the covenant promises (vss. 11-13).

Even in the matter involving Joseph, Jacob believed the Lord was sovereignly at work to bring about His will. Indeed, the patriarch was convinced that the angel sent by God had protected and delivered him from all harm. It may be that Jacob thought the divine blessing he was conferring on Joseph's sons would be mediated through this angelic representative. It was Jacob's expressed wish that they would be identified by the names of Abraham, Isaac, and Israel. An additional implication is that as the Lord enabled Joseph's sons to increase greatly on the earth and become a mighty nation, they would also preserve the honor associated with the names of the patriarchs (48:16). Ezekiel 47:13 reveals that Jacob's deathbed aspiration concerning Ephraim and Manasseh would endure into the future.

B. The Specific Boundaries on Each Side: vss. 14-20

"You are to divide it equally among them. Because I swore with uplifted hand to give it to your forefathers, this land will become your inheritance. This is to be the boundary of the land: On the north side it will run from the Great Sea by the Hethlon road past Lebo Hamath to Zedad, Berothah and Sibraim (which lies on the border between Damascus and Hamath), as far as Hazer Hatticon, which is on the

border of Hauran. The boundary will extend from the sea to Hazar Enan, along the northern border of Damascus, with the border of Hamath to the north. This will be the north boundary. On the east side the boundary will run between Hauran and Damascus, along the Jordan between Gilead and the land of Israel, to the eastern sea and as far as Tamar. This will be the east boundary. On the south side it will run from Tamar as far as the waters of Meribah Kadesh, then along the Wadi of Egypt to the Great Sea. This will be the south boundary. On the west side, the Great Sea will be the boundary to a point opposite Lebo Hamath. This will be the west boundary."

The division of the promised land into equal portions among Israel's 12 tribes was in accordance with God's promise to the patriarchs that their descendants would inherit the entire region (Ezek. 47:14). For instance, Genesis 12:7 records God's appearance to Abraham (Abram) when he was 75 and the Lord's pledge to give Canaan to the patriarch's offspring. Ten years later, when he was 85, God again appeared to Abraham. On this occasion, the Lord made a covenant with the patriarch and defined the extent of the land his descendants would receive. The territory lay between the river of Egypt (probably one of the seasonal rivers in the Negev) in the south to the Euphrates River in the north. At that time, this land was occupied by ten people groups (15:18-21).

Thirty-one years after that, when Abraham was 116, God once more reiterated His promise to the patriarch (22:17). The Lord declared that He would give Abraham innumerable descendants, that they would be victorious over their foes, and that through the patriarch's offspring all nations on earth would experience God's blessing. One hundred and twenty one years later, when Jacob was 77 years old, his father, Isaac (the son of Abraham), pronounced a blessing on his son, Jacob. He learned that he would receive the divine blessings originally given to Abraham. This included the promise of many descendants, who would one day occupy Canaan (28:3-4).

Centuries after that, during the reigns of David and Solomon, God brought to pass what He previously pledged to the patriarchs. For instance, at the dedication of the Jerusalem temple Solomon had built, those who attended the ceremony came from "Lebo Hamath to the Wadi of Egypt" (1 Kings 8:65), that is, a domain extending from the Euphrates River to the border of Egypt (Num. 34:1-12; 2 Sam. 8:3; 1 Kings 4:21; 1 Chron. 13:5; 2 Chron. 9:26). These boundaries roughly correspond to the borders recorded in Ezekiel 47:15-20. On the eastern section of the promised land, the boundary started at the source of the Jordan River south of Damascus and extended south to the shore of the Dead Sea. Toward the west, the Mediterranean Sea formed the border. The northern boundary began near Tyre and extended east to a spot north of the Sea of Galilee. In the south, the border proceeded from an area below the Dead Sea to the Wadi of Egypt (that is, the Wadi el-Arish, about 50 miles southwest of Gaza) on the coast of the Mediterranean Sea.

More specifically, while the exact location of the "Hethlon road" (vs. 15) remains undetermined, a locale on the Lebanese coast has been proposed. The precise whereabouts of "Lebo Hamath" has been debated, though it is generally said to refer to Lebweh, which is roughly 45 miles north of "Damascus" (vs. 16). This well-known city is located northeast of Mount Hermon, while "Hamath" is located 120 miles north of Damascus. "Zedad" (vs. 15) is commonly identified with Sadad, which is about 67 miles northeast of Damascus. "Berothah" (vs. 16) is said to refer to Bereitan, which is approximately 30 miles northwest of Damascus.

Some think "Sibraim" is the same as Sepharvaim (2 Kings 17:24; 18:34), though this remains disputed. "Hazer Hatticon" (Ezek. 47:16), which means "the middle court," is considered a variant name for "Hazar Enan" (vs. 17). The latter has been identified with Kuryetein, which is approximately 60 miles northeast of Damascus. "Hauran" (vs. 16) refers to a district east of the Jordan River and the Sea of Galilee and southeast of Mount Hermon. Though there are numerous conjectures for the location of "Tamar" (vs. 18), it is mostly identified with Ain Husb, which is 23 miles southwest of the Dead Sea in the Arabah. Finally, "Meribah Kadesh" (vs. 19) is about 50 miles south of Beersheba and in Numbers 34:4 is identified with Kadesh Barnea.

II. THE DISTRIBUTION OF THE LAND: EZEKIEL 47:21-23

A. Allocating the Land by Tribes: vs. 21

"You are to distribute this land among yourselves according to the tribes of Israel."

In 1406 B.C., the Lord used Joshua to lead the Israelites in the conquest of Canaan. During this extended military operation, which is recorded in Joshua 1–12, God demonstrated to the inhabitants exactly who He was. In particular, His miraculous display of power over nature put to shame the pagan deities of the Canaanites. Next, the division of the promised land is summarized in Joshua 13–21. By enabling His chosen people to settle Canaan, God fulfilled His promise to Abraham. In Ezekiel's vision of the new temple and restored land, the Lord revealed to the remnant that one day they would have the opportunity to divide the territory among Israel's 12 tribes (Ezek. 47:21).

B. Including Foreigners in the Allotment: vss. 22-23

"You are to allot it as an inheritance for yourselves and for the aliens who have settled among you and who have children. You are to consider them as native-born Israelites; along with you they are to be allotted an inheritance among the tribes of Israel. In whatever tribe the alien settles, there you are to give him his inheritance," declares the Sovereign LORD.

In Ezekiel 47:22, the mention of resident "aliens" reveals that, in a future day, the faith community would include both Jews and Gentiles. Furthermore, God disclosed to Ezekiel that the foreigners living among the remnant would be considered as "native-born Israelites" (Lev. 19:34; 24:22; Num. 15:29; Isa. 56:3-8). This amazing display of welcoming outsiders as equals included them receiving an "inheritance" (Ezek. 47:22) allotment along with God's chosen people. Verse 23 states that the foreigners were to be given some land within the "tribe" in which they took up residence. This directive was not optional, either, for it came directly from the "Sovereign Lord."

A foretaste of this inclusiveness occurred in A.D. 30 on the day of Pentecost (Acts 2). The name *Pentecost* comes from a Greek word meaning "fiftieth." The festival fell on the fiftieth day after the Passover Sabbath. Along with the festivals of unleavened bread and tabernacles, Pentecost was one of the three great Jewish religious holy days. The population of Jerusalem swelled during each of these festivals as pilgrims streamed into the city from all over the Roman Empire. The risen Lord had commanded His disciples not to immediately leave Jerusalem but to wait for the arrival of the Spirit (Luke 24:49; Acts 1:4). In obedience to Jesus, His followers were "all together in one place" (Acts 2:1).

Ten days after Jesus ascended into heaven, the Holy Spirit came upon Jesus' disciples as they assembled in one location. Some think His followers were at that moment in one of the courts of the Jerusalem temple (Luke 24:52-53), while others maintain that the disciples were in the upper room of a house (Acts 1:13). Observable evidences of the Spirit's arrival included the sound of wind, the appearance of what looked like tongues of flame resting on each disciple, and supernatural empowerment to speak in tongues. Because the Spirit enabled the disciples to converse in other languages, God's message of salvation reached people from many nations that day. These foreign Jews, along with Gentile converts, were amazed to hear locals fluently speaking in dialects from around the empire.

When the Spirit spoke to the multitude through Peter in a powerful sermon, many people became deeply convicted of their sin and asked the apostle what they should do. He instructed them to turn away from sin, be baptized in Jesus' name, and receive His forgiveness. About 3,000 people accepted the message that day and were baptized. The Father would use them to take the good news of salvation in the Son back with them to their homelands. Even the people who did not respond to Peter's message were filled with wonder at what they heard and saw. Miraculous signs were evidence of God's power and presence with the believers.

Moreover, the believers were devoted to the issues that made them one: hearing the teaching of truth, fellowship and the Lord's Supper, corporate worship in the Jerusalem temple, and prayer. It did not matter whether Jesus' followers were native-born Jews or foreigners. In harmony with the directives recorded in Ezekiel 47:22-23, as the faith community focused on their common devotion to the Savior, they freely shared their material goods with the needy in their midst. Because both love and unity characterized the lives of these believers, each day more and more people put their trust in the Messiah and were saved. The Savior's disciples recognized that one of their responsibilities was to help people in whatever way possible. By doing this, they gave evidence of the Spirit's presence in their lives and showed that He had transformed them from selfish individuals into members of a caring community.

Discussion Questions

1. Why did God stress to Ezekiel that it was the "sovereign LORD" (Ezek. 47:13, 23) who was speaking to the prophet?
2. In specifying the boundaries for the land, how was God being faithful to the promise He made to the patriarchs?
3. Why would God decree that foreigners living among the Israelites were to receive an allotment of the promised land?
4. Why is it important for believers to share what they have with one another?
5. How can believers show that the good news about the Lord is meant for all people to receive by faith?

Contemporary Application

Ezekiel 47:13-23 details the boundaries of the promised land and its distribution among Israel's 12 tribes. But God's blessings would not be restricted to only one group of people. Even foreigners who trusted in and obeyed the Lord would be included in the divine inheritance.

The Spirit's coming on the day of Pentecost provides a foretaste of what is to come. Acts 2 records Peter's declaration that the Father, through His Son, freely offers redemption to the lost. In turn, those who believe in Him experience a new beginning within a faith community where Jesus' followers can gather and support one another.

The preceding description of life for God's spiritual children appears to be so idyllic that we might think it's impossible to reproduce today. Wouldn't it be wonderful, we say, if thousands were saved every day? Wouldn't it be great if we shared our possessions, prayed together, and worshiped and witnessed in unity?

Of course, our immediate response would be *yes*, but then we confess that such things just do not happen that way in our churches. We admit defeat without really considering how God can bring about a fresh start for believers. For instance, the Holy Spirit dwells in God's people and enables them to tell others about Jesus' death and resurrection. The Lord calls believers to unity, generosity, prayer, and worship. When they confess their need for spiritual power, God answers.

Perhaps our problem is that we do not desire these things as much as we say we do. Perhaps we have higher priorities and goals for ourselves and our churches. It is only when we put Jesus and His people first in our lives that we will see the Lord adding to our congregations those who are being saved.

God Frees His People

Scripture

Background Scripture: *Psalm 33; Isaiah 52:1-2, 7-12*

Scripture Lesson: *Isaiah 52:1-2, 7-12*

Key Verse: *How beautiful on the mountains are the feet of those who bring good news, who proclaim peace, who bring good tidings, who proclaim salvation, who say to Zion, "Your God reigns!"* Isaiah 52:7.

Scripture Lesson for Children: *Psalm 33:1-9, 20-22*

Key Verse for Children: *For the word of the LORD is right and true; he is faithful in all he does.* Psalm 33:4.

Lesson Aim

To be encouraged by recalling God's faithfulness and trusting His promises.

Lesson Setting

Time: 740–700 B.C.

Place: Judah

Lesson Outline

God Frees His People

I. Anticipating Freedom from Captivity: Isaiah 52:1-2
  A. *The Command to Wake Up: vs. 1*
  B. *The Command to Be Free: vs. 2*

II. Heralding a Message of Deliverance: Isaiah 52:7-12
  A. *A Proclamation of Peace and Salvation: vss. 7-8*
  B. *A Song of Joy: vss. 9-10*
  C. *An Assurance of Divine Protection: vss. 11-12*

Introduction for Adults

Topic: *Seeking Words of Hope*

One of the unfortunate characteristics of adults is our tendency to forget. We record in our mobile devices phone numbers, bank account information, tasks to do, and birthdays so we won't forget. Some of us are better at remembering than others, but everyone slips now and then.

Another regrettable inclination is that we tend to dwell on the negatives that happen to us or are verbalized to us. If someone tells us we're stupid, that remark sticks much longer than if someone praises us for providing the correct answer. Psychologists suggest that it takes seven positive statements to make up for one negative statement. In light of this ratio, we are certainly in need of hearing and delivering some encouraging statements.

Isaiah 52:1-12 provides us with hope by offering us reminders of God's faithfulness. Here we also encounter words of encouragement that we can share with others. The latter includes the "good news" (vs. 7) of the Father's "peace" and "salvation," which He graciously offers and which can be freely received through faith in the Son.

Introduction for Youth

Topic: *From Hopeless to Hopeful*

What do you do with a broken-down car that needs repairs and paint? You see beyond the wreck and envision a sparkling new paint job and a motor that purrs sweetly down the road. You give that car all the sweat you can muster because you have high hopes for it and yourself.

Perhaps if we were writing Isaiah's sermons today, rather than comparing God to an attentive parent, we would compare Him to a sensitive, careful, hardworking, and loving mechanic. That's because we bestow the same kind of love on our cars that parents do on their children.

The main point is that God can bring about restoration and healing in the lives of youth, especially if they submit to His will. He has wonderful plans for them that they can't even imagine. Metaphorically speaking, God can take their dings and dents, and all the misfirings of their cylinders, and make a beautiful automobile out of their lives. Through faith in His Son they can make a fresh start down the road to hope!

Concepts for Children

Topic: *Trusting and Rejoicing*

1. God wants us to sing to Him.
2. God wants us to be joyful when we sing.
3. We can thank God for loving us.
4. We can praise God for taking care of us.
5. We can invite our friends to also trust and praise God.

Lesson Commentary

I. ANTICIPATING FREEDOM FROM CAPTIVITY: ISAIAH 52:1-2

A. The Command to Wake Up: vs. 1

Awake, awake, O Zion, clothe yourself with strength. Put on your garments of splendor, O Jerusalem, the holy city. The uncircumcised and defiled will not enter you again.

In Isaiah 51:1—52:12, we read how God, through Isaiah, spoke to the Jews in exile long after the prophet's day. The Lord reminded the remnant of His faithfulness by utilizing the metaphor of rocks being drawn from the same quarry. Put another way, God's chosen people were all descended from Abraham through Isaac and Jacob (51:1-2). As God had called Abraham while he was living in Ur, and out of one person had produced many descendants, God would call the exiles out of Babylon and multiply them. Indeed, God's children can always find strength for present circumstances by remembering God's faithfulness in the past.

There was great comfort in the Lord's promise. Even though the Babylonians had left Judah in a desolate state, God would make the promised land as the Garden of Eden, and its inhabitants would be filled with joy and gladness. God's blessings would benefit everyone and would outlast the heavens and earth (vss. 4-6). So even though the exiles in Babylon were subject to the reproach and insults of others, they were not to fear. Their enemies would be destroyed, yet the Lord would never die (vss. 7-8).

Isaiah enthusiastically called upon God to rise to action and demonstrate His power as He had done in the past with Egypt, which was symbolized by the mythological monster Rahab (vs. 9). The prophet reveled in how the Lord had clothed Himself with strength in days gone by, especially during Israel's exodus. To Isaiah it seemed that the return from Babylonian captivity would be the same, with those whom God had rescued returning to Judah and replacing their sadness with joy (vss. 10-11). It is always this way with God's salvation, namely, unparalleled gladness, regardless of the worldly circumstances. Verses 12-16 contain God's response to the remnant. They were not to be afraid of what mere people can do. In fact, the wording of verses 12-13 suggests that to fear worldly concerns ironically represents a type of pride. This being the case, why should the exiled Jews be afraid of people, who die, who wither like the grass and fade away?

In verse 9, the Lord is twice called to "awake" and use His strength on behalf of the remnant. In verse 17, this summons is turned back upon Jerusalem, but this time in anticipation of the royal city's deliverance. Conquered Jerusalem is represented as a drunken woman who is staggering about, unaided by her children. Now, under Babylonian captivity, she had by choice drained the cup of God's wrath and become drunk with His judgment. Certainly, none of

Jerusalem's children could come to her aid (vs. 18), for they too had drunk from the cup of God's wrath and were as immobile (or completely helpless) as an antelope caught in a net (vs. 20).

The exiles could not even help themselves. Indeed, they all had experienced "double calamities" (vs. 19). This means God's judgment on His people had been thoroughly sated. Because Jerusalem had endured "ruin and destruction, famine and sword," the city was consequently inconsolable. God, in response to this pathetic state, offered encouragement and a promise. He had always defended His people (vss. 21-22), and He pledged He would remove the cup of wrath from Jerusalem. The day would come when the exiles would never again drink from God's judgment. In fact, He would pass it to the tormentors, who mocked and mistreated God's people, and make them drink fully of His wrath (vs. 23).

Once more, in 52:1, God's wake-up-call rejoinder is proclaimed to the remnant. "Zion" is exhorted to arise and dress herself in "strength." Likewise, "Jerusalem" is directed to robe herself with beautiful garments, that is, priestly attire characterized by "splendor." Doing so was in keeping with the "holy" status of the city, where the temple was located. The latter truths suggest that when God rescued the exiles from captivity, He would fortify and purify them. The "uncircumcised and defiled" is a reference to the Jews' pagan oppressors. The Lord pledged that a day was coming when tyrants would no longer bother the remnant.

B. The Command to Be Free: vs. 2

Shake off your dust; rise up, sit enthroned, O Jerusalem. Free yourself from the chains on your neck, O captive Daughter of Zion.

Next, Isaiah told the Jewish exiles to throw off the dirt covering them. In the ancient Near East, sitting in "dust" (Isa. 52:2) was a sign of mourning. The prophet's command was that the remnant was to cease their lamenting over their captivity, tragic as it was, for it would end. Isaiah also commanded the exiles to get up, sit upon a throne, and remove the "chains" of their captivity. They could do so, for they knew that God would deliver and honor them. The good news is that the Father's claim upon His spiritual children is the same today. Through our faith in the Son, we too belong to the Father and are guaranteed an eternal inheritance (John 1:12-13; Eph. 1:13-14).

Often our insecurities can be symptomatic of a self-absorption, in which our fear drives us to see ourselves as the center of the universe. But when we consider ourselves realistically within the context of God's design, true humility allows us to appreciate His sovereignty, instead of grasping at the straws of our own need to be in control. Who are we, anyway? We're either the children of the all-powerful Lord or nothing more than pathetic, foolish mortals (1 Cor. 1:23-31). God calls us to humbly trust in Him, the Creator of the universe.

II. HERALDING A MESSAGE OF DELIVERANCE: ISAIAH 52:7-12

A. A Proclamation of Peace and Salvation: vss. 7-8

How beautiful on the mountains are the feet of those who bring good news, who proclaim peace, who bring good tidings, who proclaim salvation, who say to Zion, "Your God reigns!" Listen! Your watchmen lift up their voices; together they shout for joy. When the LORD returns to Zion, they will see it with their own eyes.

In Isaiah 52:3, the Lord declared to the Jewish captives that when He "sold" them into exile, He received no payment. Appropriately, He would redeem the remnant without being compensated. Expressed differently, Babylon offered no "money" for acquiring the chosen people, and they would now be released from Babylon for nothing. Moreover, God would claim the exiles as belonging exclusively to Him. Isaiah illustrated God's meaning by briefly reviewing the history of Israel's past oppressions. The Hebrews had been slaves in Egypt, and more recently the Assyrians had invaded Judah (vs. 4). In both instances, the Lord had gloriously delivered His people. This brief history lesson showed that no oppressor of the Jewish remnant had any legitimate claim on them.

Now the captives were enslaved by the Babylonians, who made a habit of ridiculing and slandering God's name (vs. 5; see also Rom. 2:24). Just as the Lord had delivered His people from the Egyptians and the Assyrians, so now He would rescue the Jews from the Babylonians. When that deliverance came, the chosen people would realize that the Lord had foretold this remarkable event and had accomplished it. In that day, the remnant would "know" (Isa. 52:6) God's name. Put another way, they would recognize the Lord's identity as their Deliverer and Redeemer (49:26). They would also come to see that He alone had brought about their amazing deliverance from captivity in Babylon.

Isaiah 52:7-12 foretells the glorious return of the exiles to their homeland. In Bible times, a messenger would survey the horizon and then rush from the location of a major battle and report the "good news" (vs. 7) of the conflict's aftermath to an anxious ruler and his court officials (2 Sam. 18:26). In Isaiah 52:7, the herald does not announce the outcome of a military clash, but of the release of God's people from captivity in Babylon to return to Jerusalem. Isaiah observed how delightful it was for the messenger's "feet" to travel over the "mountains" in order to declare "peace" and "salvation." With the ending of oppression for the remnant and the commencement of their rescue, they would experience firsthand that God, as a triumphant warrior, had established His sovereign reign over Zion (Ps. 93:1; Isa. 40:9; 41:27; Rev. 19:6).

Nahum 1:15 records a similar declaration of Judah's deliverance from the threat of Assyria. Most scholars believe that Nahum prophesied around 654 B.C., when Nineveh was still at the peak of its power. Some, however, place the time of his ministry closer to the fall of Nineveh around 625 B.C. This would have been about 13 years before the city fell to the Babylonians. In the days of

Nahum, a "command" (vs. 14) constituted a formal pronouncement. Once it had gone out to the people, it could not be taken back or altered. God's oracle sealed the demise of the Assyrians. He would not fail to do what He promised.

The destruction of the leadership in Nineveh was to be accompanied by the elimination of their idolatry. The Assyrian kings ruled by the apparent favor of their idols and credited these pagan deities for their many victories. It was essential that the false gods and temples be demolished along with the monarchs to demonstrate the futility of idolatry. The news of the demise of these rulers brought rejoicing to the people of Judah, who had been oppressed by their reigns of terror. The "good news" (vs. 15) of "peace" meant that Judah could "celebrate" its feasts without fear of interference from Assyria. The kings of Nineveh would never again invade the promised land.

In Romans 10:15, Paul quoted Isaiah 52:7 and Nahum 1:15 to emphasize the importance of proclaiming the Gospel. Some of his Jewish readers might have tried to argue that they and their ancestors never had a fair chance to hear and respond to God's announcement of salvation. To answer such a challenge, Paul asked a series of rhetorical questions that point to the necessary process of hearing the message of the Savior and responding to it in faith (Rom. 10:14-15).

Though the questions are listed in reverse order, Paul's point was that God first sends a preacher. The preacher proclaims the message, the people hear the message, and some believe. Verses 16-21 reveal that God indeed sent His word through His messengers on numerous occasions, but not all the Jews responded favorably. What kinds of messengers were sent? Certainly the Old Testament prophets had been dispatched to communicate God's Word to Israel. The Father sent the Son as Prophet, Priest, and King. The Son commissioned the apostles to herald the Good News, first to the Jews and then to the Gentiles. From this information we see that in verse 15, Paul used the words of Isaiah 52:7 and Nahum 1:15 in reference to those who preached the Gospel. They came with a message of release from the oppressive captivity of sin.

Centuries earlier, the return of God's people from captivity in Babylon to Jerusalem would show that the Lord was in control of the affairs of nations, even powerful ones such as Babylon. In ancient times, just as there were messengers who would run to deliver important news to awaiting rulers, so also there were "watchmen" (Isa. 52:8) stationed on the city walls (Ps. 127:1; Isa. 62:6-7). One of their jobs was to look out for incoming messengers. In our passage, the guards in Jerusalem are pictured awaiting the arrival of messengers. When they reach their destination, the watchmen "shout" (52:8) in joyful unison at the realization that the exiles would return to the city. A little later, the guards see God Himself leading the procession of Jews back to "Zion."

B. A Song of Joy: vss. 9-10

Burst into songs of joy together, you ruins of Jerusalem, for the LORD has comforted his people, he has redeemed Jerusalem. The Lord will lay bare his holy arm in the sight of all the nations, and all the ends of the earth will see the salvation of our God.

Because of the joyous event described in Isaiah 52:7-8, the "ruins of Jerusalem" (vs. 9) were exhorted to shout and rejoice together. There was good reason to sing, for the Lord would deliver, protect, and console His beleaguered people (44:23; 49:13; 55:12). Also, all the surrounding "nations" (52:10) would recognize this amazing redemption as a demonstration of the Lord's royal power. Even the remotest regions of the planet would become aware of God's strong and "holy arm" (Exod. 6:6; Isa. 40:4; 45:22).

C. An Assurance of Divine Protection: vss. 11-12

Depart, depart, go out from there! Touch no unclean thing! Come out from it and be pure, you who carry the vessels of the Lord. But you will not leave in haste or go in flight; for the Lord will go before you, the God of Israel will be your rear guard.

In view of the divine promises of deliverance and restoration, the exiles in Babylon would have a choice to make. Given the freedom to leave, they would have to decide whether they wanted to stay in Babylon or risk taking the long journey back to Judah and participating in the difficult rebuilding period. Life in Babylon had become comfortable for the exiles. But of course their spiritual health depended upon their fleeing from the defiling atmosphere of Babylon and setting themselves toward the blessings promised by God.

One can almost hear Isaiah calling joyously across time to the exiles, exhorting them to "depart" (Isa. 52:11) from the land of their captivity. The "unclean thing" spoken of here probably refers to pagan religious objects in Babylon. Those who carried the "vessels of the Lord" were likely the priests and Levites, who reclaimed the articles of the temple that had formerly been seized by Nebuchadnezzar (Num. 3:6-8; 2 Kings 25:14-15; 2 Chron. 5:4-7; Ezra 1:7-11; 5:14-15). In a way, God also calls believers today to separate themselves from the spiritual impurities of the world (Jam. 4:4-6; 1 John 2:15-17). After all, the Lord desires Jesus' followers to be holy and distinct from the world (1 Pet. 1:13-25). Even in the midst of such a clear victory by God, the reminder to remain pure must be remembered.

For the preceding reasons, Paul quoted Isaiah 52:11 to urge the believers in Corinth to separate themselves from the wickedness around them. In return for the believers' purity, God promised that He would receive them. The Christian life is not a barren list of regulations. Instead, it is a relationship. God calls us away from the evil practices around us so He can enjoy fellowship with us and we can enjoy communion with Him and His people. The Lord is not seeking to diminish our joy. Rather, He wants to make it greater through the blessing of our walk with Him.

Isaiah 52:12 reveals that the remnant leaving Babylon and heading for Judah would not be forced to "leave" quickly or depart in a panic. In contrast to the Israelites' departure from Egypt (Exod. 12:33, 39), the exiles did not have to fear pursuit and recapture, because the Lord would be with them. Indeed, just as God had been their "rear guard" (Isa. 52:12) in the exodus with the pillar of cloud and fire (Exod. 13:21-22; 14:19-20), so too He would protect them as they returned to their homeland (Isa. 42:16; 48:20; 49:10; 58:8).

There are some notable comparisons between our passage and the Exodus account. In both cases, God's people were enslaved by powerful nations (Exod. 3:7-10; Isa. 40–66); God's mighty power was displayed in delivering His people from bondage (Exod. 7:5; Isa. 52:10); the offending nations were judged by the hand of God (Exod. 6:28–7:6; Isa. 51:23); God acted as His people's rear guard in the journey home (Exod. 14:19–20; Isa. 52:12); and there was joyful singing upon deliverance (Exod. 15:1-21; Isa. 52:9).

Discussion Questions

1. Why did God exhort His people to clothe themselves with strength?
2. In what dramatic way would the Lord make His name known to the exiles?
3. Why was the ruined city of Jerusalem urged to burst forth in a joyful shout?
4. What are some ways believers can renew their confidence in the Lord?
5. How do God's words of consolation offer believers hope when they go through hard times?

Contemporary Application

The good news that God had planned a glorious return to Judah for the Babylonian captives was perceived by Isaiah as a reason to "shout for joy" (Isa. 52:8). There was no reason, either, to doubt God's wisdom or His goodness. He had everything under control. Also, in His good time and way, He would rescue and preserve His people (vss. 10-12).

Thousands of years have passed since Isaiah proclaimed this good news to a distressed and troubled nation, but affliction and doubt still weigh down the hearts of those who look around and see gloom instead of looking above in faith to see God. Like Isaiah, we know that God redeems from bondage those who believe in the Redeemer. He sets free the captives who trust in the Lord Jesus. Moreover, He liberates those who accept the Good News, that "if the Son sets you free, you will be free indeed" (John 8:36).

In a spiritual sense, we can be "watchmen" (Isa. 52:8) who issue a wake-up call to our unsaved contemporaries. The Lord can use us to declare the wonderful message that the distress and doubting experienced by the lost can be discarded forever when they embrace the Messiah by faith. The power to offer them this hope is in our hands!

Worship the Messiah

Scripture

Background Scripture: *Hebrews 1:1-9*
Scripture Lesson: *Hebrews 1:1-9*
Key Verse: *The Son is the radiance of God's glory and the
exact representation of his being, sustaining all things by his
powerful word.* Hebrews 1:3.
Scripture Lesson for Children: *Hebrews 1:1-9*
Key Verse for Children: *"Let all God's angels worship
him."* Hebrews 1:6.

Lesson Aim

To sort out the implications of worshiping Jesus as God.

Lesson Setting

Time: Between A.D. 64–68
Place: Possibly Rome

Lesson Outline

Worship the Messiah

   I. Jesus' Superior Work: Hebrews 1:1-3
     A. *The Father's Disclosures through the Prophets: vs. 1*
     B. *The Father's Message through His Son: vs. 2a*
     C. *The Son as Divine Creator: vss. 2b-3a*
     D. *The Son's Redemptive Work: vs. 3b*
  II. Jesus' Superiority over Angels: Hebrews 1:4-9
     A. *The Son's Superior Name: vs. 4*
     B. *The Son's Unique Relationship to the Father: vs. 5*
     C. *The Angels as Worshipers and Servants of the Son:
       vss. 6-7*
     D. *The Son as Divine Ruler: vss. 8-9*

Introduction for Adults

Topic: *Better than Angels*

Until his retirement in 1981, Robert Jastrow was the director of NASA's Goddard Institute for Space Studies. In his book entitled *God and the Astronomers*, Jastrow took note of the "scientist who has lived by his faith in the power of reason," only for "the story" to end "like a bad dream." The scientist has "scaled the mountains of ignorance, he is about to conquer the highest peak; as he pulls himself over the final rock, he is greeted by a band of theologians who have been sitting there for centuries!"

Where do we learn about God, the One who created and sustains all things? The writer of Hebrews does not point us to angels or any other created being. Instead, the author points us to Jesus Christ, who is "the radiance of God's glory and the exact representation of his being" (Heb. 1:3). As your students get to know the Son better, they will come to know the Father too (John 14:9).

Introduction for Youth

Topic: *Who's in Charge?*

"She's the spitting image of her mother!" "He's a virtual clone of his father!" And on it goes, as well-intentioned friends and family members congratulate a couple on the birth of their newborn daughter or son. While such statements might be slight exaggerations, they remind us that we resemble our parents in many ways.

The writer of Hebrews went beyond such sentiments when he talked about the Son. We learn in 1:3 that the Lord Jesus reflects God's glory. Indeed, everything about the Son exactly represents the Father. Moreover, Jesus sustains the entire universe. As the saved adolescents in your class become more and more like Jesus in their thoughts and actions, in turn they will reflect the glory of God in their lives.

Concepts for Children

Topic: *Like Father, Like Son: Honor Him*

1. Long ago, God spoke to His people in many different ways.
2. Now God has spoken to us through Jesus.
3. Jesus shows us exactly what God is like.
4. Jesus can make us clean from our sins.
5. Jesus wants us to worship Him.

Lesson Commentary

I. JESUS' SUPERIOR WORK: HEBREWS 1:1-3

A. The Father's Disclosures through the Prophets: vs. 1

In the past God spoke to our forefathers through the prophets at many times and in various ways.

While it is virtually certain that the Letter to the Hebrews was written to Jewish Christians in the first century A.D., it is impossible to tell with certitude just where those believers lived. Alexandria, Egypt, is one place that some experts have suggested. The identity of the author is also shrouded in mystery. At one time or another, scholars have suggested all the following people as the writer of this letter: Barnabas (by Tertullian), Paul, Luke (by John Calvin), Apollos (by Martin Luther), Priscilla, and Clement of Rome (one of the church's early theologians).

Whoever penned the letter had a keen command of Greek and a razor-sharp intellect. The author of Hebrews set his course in chapter 1 by testifying to Jesus' supremacy over all things. The letter reminds readers of God's ways under the old covenant and affirms the Father's new and better way in the Son. Themes common throughout the letter are incarnation, redemption, perseverance, faith, and mutual love among believers.

Some professing Jewish Christians, who were recipients of this letter, may have been on the brink of relinquishing their commitment to the Lord Jesus. They had begun to consider leaving the church and reintegrating fully into the Jewish synagogue worship of the day. In response to their circumstances, the writer of Hebrews encouraged them to remain firm in their faith in the Messiah.

To portray Jesus' superiority, the author compared the incompleteness of God's revelation through the Old Testament prophets with the completeness of His revelation through His Son. Various prepositional phrases in verse 1 indicate some of the characteristics of God's communication: the timing was long ago; the target was our spiritual ancestors; the medium was through the prophets; and the methods were diverse and varied.

The following lists some of God's creative and varied means of communicating with the people of Old Testament times: through miracles (Exod. 3:2-6); through the Urim and Thummim (28:30); through direct speech (Num. 12:8); through angels (Judg. 6:11-12); through a soft whisper (1 Kings 19:11-13); through dreams (Job 33:14-18); through family circumstances (Isa. 8:1-4); through catastrophes (45:7); through visions and parables (Hos. 12:10); through symbolic actions (Ezek. 4:1-7); and through prophets (Heb. 1:1).

The implication is that God has always been active in history. Regardless of the manner in which the Lord communicated, He conveyed His message to people of faith, and those spokespersons for God passed on His inspired declarations to others. Though acknowledging these ancient revelations for what they taught people about God, the author implied that they were fragmentary and transitional. At most they pointed to a time when the Father would reveal Himself fully and finally in His Son, Jesus of Nazareth (John 1:14, 18; 14:9).

Still, the author of Hebrews did not intend to diminish the value of God's revelation through the Hebrew prophets. The fact that the writer considered them the transmitters of God's revelation is evidence of just how much respect he held for these faithful servants of the Lord. For all that, the same God who had revealed Himself in a limited way during the Old Testament era now had disclosed Himself completely and absolutely in the Messiah.

B. The Father's Message through His Son: vs. 2a

But in these last days he has spoken to us by his Son.

The author said the full and final revelation of God had come in the form of His incarnate Son. The phrase "in these last days" (Heb. 1:2) would carry a special significance for the Hebrew readers, who probably interpreted the phrase as meaning that Jesus, as the Redeemer, had ushered in the messianic age. Jesus is not merely the end of a long line of Old Testament prophets. He is the One for whom the Hebrews had waited for centuries (Mark 15:43; Luke 1:25, 38; 23:50-51). He is the complete and superlative revelation of God's being.

C. The Son as Divine Creator: vss. 2b-3a

Whom he appointed heir of all things, and through whom he made the universe. The Son is the radiance of God's glory and the exact representation of his being, sustaining all things by his powerful word.

Having pointed out Jesus' distinction as the Son of God, the author of Hebrews proceeded to explain ways in which God's revelation through the Messiah is superior to all previous disclosures from the Lord. To show this superiority, the writer made a number of statements describing the Son. First, the Father appointed His Son as "heir of all things" (Heb. 1:2). In Hebrew culture, the firstborn son was the highest ranked of all children. Therefore, he was also the family heir. Jesus is the heir, owner, and Lord of the whole created order.

Second, it is through the Son that the Father "made the universe." The Greek noun rendered "universe" not only refers to the heavens and the earth, but also to the temporal ages (11:3). Before time and matter were created, the Messiah eternally preexisted, and He reigns supreme over all space throughout the eons of history. Third, the Son is the "radiance" (1:3) of the triune God's glory. This does not mean Jesus is merely a reflection of the Lord's majesty. Because the Messiah is God Himself, He is the source of God's glory. In Jesus' incarnation, He unveiled to humankind the splendor of the divine (John 1:14).

Fourth, the Son is the "exact representation" (Heb. 1:3) of the triune God's being. The Greek noun in this verse was used in pagan literature to refer to objects (such as coins or seals) that exactly reproduced the imprint and contours of the die from which they were cast. Regarding Jesus, who He is corresponds exactly to that of the Godhead. Thus He alone is the precise image of God's essence (Phil. 2:6; Col. 1:15; 2:9). While the Son is one with the Father and the Spirit in terms of Their being, there remains a distinction of the divine Persons of the Trinity. Fifth, not only did the Son create the universe, but He also holds it together by His powerful command (Col. 1:17). Through His sustaining royal decree, He enables the cosmos to achieve its God-ordained purpose. Clearly, the Son has a continued interest in the world and loves it. For that reason, He is carrying it toward the fulfillment of His divine plan.

D. The Son's Redemptive Work: vs. 3b

After he had provided purification for sins, he sat down at the right hand of the Majesty in heaven.

At the heart of God's plan was to make redemption freely available to the lost. The Son died on the cross to wash away the stain of our sins from us (Rom. 4:25; 2 Cor. 5:21; 1 Pet. 1:18-19). The Greek noun rendered "purification" (Heb. 1:3) denotes a thorough cleansing that brings about spiritual renewal. The idea is that through Jesus' atoning sacrifice at Calvary, He removed the defiling presence of sin from the very core of our innermost being (9:14; 10:22).

The writer expressed his thoughts in the past tense to emphasize that the Messiah's redemptive work on our behalf has already been accomplished. Because He completed the task for which He was sent (John 3:16; 17:4), He was granted the place of highest honor—at God's "right hand" (Heb. 1:3). Jesus did once and for all what the Hebrew priests were required to do on a regular basis (9:26-28). Now, as our great High Priest, the Son continually applies to us the "purification for sins" (1:3) He obtained at the cross. This enables us to worship in God's presence (4:14-16).

II. JESUS' SUPERIORITY OVER ANGELS: HEBREWS 1:4-9

A. The Son's Superior Name: vs. 4

So he became as much superior to the angels as the name he has inherited is superior to theirs.

Because the Son has come to earth and sacrificed His own life for the sins of the world (1 John 2:2), He is to be considered superior to all things. This includes the angels (Heb. 1:4), who were the object of intense speculation within first-century Judaism. Angels are spirits (vs. 14) who are in heaven (Matt. 22:30) sent to earth as messengers by God. They are mighty (Ps. 103:20) and powerful (2 Thess. 1:7) and possess great wisdom (2 Sam. 14:20). Ordinarily they are invisible to us (2 Kings 6:17), though they have appeared as humans (Luke 24:4).

The duties angels perform are varied. They serve God by serving us (Heb. 1:14). Moreover, angels provide us protection (Dan. 6:22), guard us (Ps. 91:11), guide us (Acts 8:26), and help us (Dan. 10:13). In addition to the elect angels who worship and serve the purposes of God (1 Tim. 5:21; Heb. 1:6), there are also fallen angels who serve the purposes of Satan (Rev. 12:7-9).

The Hebrew people had long held angels in high esteem because these heavenly beings were instrumental in giving the law at Mount Sinai (Heb. 2:2; see also Acts 7:38, 53). The author told the Hebrews that God's Son is absolutely higher in rank than all angels (Heb. 1:4). To emphasize his point, the writer said Jesus' name is superior to that of the angels (Phil. 2:9-11). To Jews, a name summed up all that a person was—his or her character and even profession. For this reason, the author explained that Jesus' essence and work were far superior even to those of the heavenly beings.

B. The Son's Unique Relationship to the Father: vs. 5

For to which of the angels did God ever say, "You are my Son; today I have become your Father"? Or again, "I will be his Father, and he will be my Son"?

Having made numerous statements about the superiority of God's Son, the author of Hebrews then quoted various Old Testament Scripture passages to show how and why Jesus is superior to the angels. The writer apparently intended to imply that Jesus, as the Messiah, is to be seen throughout the Hebrew Scriptures (Luke 24:27, 44). The writer began this series of quotations with a question: "For to which of the angels did God ever say" (Heb. 1:5).

Quoting first a messianic psalm (Ps. 2:7) and then 2 Samuel 7:14, the author indicated that the Father had never singled out an angel and applied to that being the exalted status He had accorded His Son (Heb. 1:5). In the first quotation, the writer made a clear distinction: the angels are created heavenly beings, but Jesus is the only Son of God, the long-awaited Messiah who gives salvation to those who trust in Him. Even though the second quotation originally referred to Solomon, the author of Hebrews applied it to the Messiah. Jesus enjoys a unique, one-of-a-kind relationship with the Father (John 1:14, 18), something the angels cannot claim.

C. The Angels as Worshipers and Servants of the Son: vss. 6-7

And again, when God brings his firstborn into the world, he says, "Let all God's angels worship him." In speaking of the angels he says, "He makes his angels winds, his servants flames of fire."

The writer of Hebrews referred to Jesus as God's "firstborn into the world" (1:6). Here the idea is not of the Messiah being first in order of birth, but highest in rank. The Son's unique relationship as an heir to God the Father is depicted in this verse. As God's firstborn heir, Jesus is the source of both righteousness and eternal life for all those who will come after Him—in essence, for all those who place their faith in His atoning work.

Bible scholars dispute the source of the quotation in verse 6. Some say it was taken from Deuteronomy 32:43 of the Septuagint (a pre-Christian Greek version of the Hebrew Scriptures) and was not included in other ancient texts of the Bible. Others say it was taken from Psalm 97:7, and still others say the author of Hebrews combined the Deuteronomy and Psalm passages. Whatever the case, the writer's purpose in using the quotation was to indicate that the Son is worthy of the angels' worship in the same way that the Father and the Spirit deserve the angels' veneration. The quotation also affirms the Son's essential deity. This worship of the Son was no small matter. Indeed, all of God's angels would participate in venerating Jesus.

While still addressing the Son's superiority to angels, the author then cited a quotation—the Septuagint version of Psalm 104:4—describing the character of the angels (Heb. 1:7). In the original Hebrew version, that psalm's verse appears to describe the wind and lightning of a storm as God's servants. The Septuagint version, however, identifies angels as God's servants, and that's the point the author of Hebrews wanted to make. They are much lower in existence than the royal Son of David, who is enthroned in the heavens as the eternal Creator and King (vss. 10-12).

D. The Son as Divine Ruler: vss. 8-9

But about the Son he says, "Your throne, O God, will last for ever and ever, and righteousness will be the scepter of your kingdom. You have loved righteousness and hated wickedness; therefore God, your God, has set you above your companions by anointing you with the oil of joy."

While the angels are God's servants, Jesus is God's Son and the divine King. This truth is stressed in Hebrews 1:8-9, which contain a quotation from Psalm 45:6-7. Here we find one of the Bible's strongest affirmations of Jesus' deity. In Hebrews 1:8-9, the Son is addressed as God. Also, His royal status is alluded to in the words "throne," "scepter," and "kingdom." As the Father's representative and co-regent, the Son rules over all creation forever. His scepter symbolizes His regal authority, which is characterized by justice and equity. Because these virtues are the basis of His unending rule, He enjoys an infinitely exalted status as the true and everlasting King (Rev. 19:16).

The latter emphasis can be found in the phrase "oil of joy" (Heb. 1:9). The allusion is to an ancient Israelite practice of anointing the head of a king with olive oil at his coronation. The event was a time of great celebration and re-newed hope. The ultimate focus, of course, is Jesus Christ, who reigns as King over the cosmos. Like the Father, the Son loves righteousness and hates wicked-ness. Because of these characteristics, the Father set His Son above all other people and beings and anointed Him to carry out the most sacred function of all time—to bring people to salvation.

Verses 10-12 quote Psalm 102:25-27. The poet declared that at the dawn of time, Yahweh (the covenant-keeping God of Israel) laid the foundations of the earth. Likewise, He made the heavens with His hands. We learn from Hebrews 1:10 that the Messiah acted as God's agent in Creation (John 1:1-3; Col. 1:15-17). One day, the heavens and the earth will perish and disappear. The Son will roll up the Creation like a worn-out robe that is to be discarded and replace this tattered garment with a new heaven and earth (2 Pet. 3:10-13; Rev. 21:1). In contrast, the Son (like the Father and the Spirit) will remain the same through-out all eternity (Heb. 1:11-12).

In verse 13, the writer quoted Psalm 110:1. In ancient Israel, the verse was applied to each successive monarch in the dynasty of David. Various New Testament references understand the Messiah to be the ideal Davidic king to which the verse ultimately points (Matt. 22:43-45; Mark 12:36-37; Luke 20:42-44; Acts 2:34-35). The Lord Jesus is God's vice-regent who sits in the place of honor at His right hand. The Father has pledged to humble the enemies of the Son and force them into subservience, as if they were a footstool under His feet (Heb. 1:13). No angel has such a privilege given to them. In fact, angels have a lesser role as "ministering spirits," serving those who are saved through faith in the Son (vs. 14).

Discussion Questions

1. In what sense is the Son the complete and final revelation of the Father?
2. What did the writer of Hebrews mean when he declared Jesus to be the radiance of God's glory?
3. In what ways is the Son's superior status to angels emphasized?
4. Why does Jesus deserve our unwavering commitment?
5. What are some ways we can worship the Son, both individually and corporately?

Contemporary Application

When we read the opening verses of the Book of Hebrews, we learn that Jesus is supremely great. Our natural response should be to worship the risen Lord. Admittedly, though, there are times when we do not feel inclined to do so. In those instances, our will should direct the actions of our hearts.

One reason we should worship Jesus is that Scripture commands us to do so. At first we might react negatively to this. But we can see the wisdom of the biblical directive when we realize how inclined we are to worship ourselves and others, rather than the Lord (Rom. 1:25).

Another reason for worshiping Jesus is that it remains such an integral part of our relationship with Him. He created and saved us to adore Him. When we give praise to the Messiah, we will come to know and enjoy Him more. Additionally, we should worship Jesus out of love and gratitude. He loved us enough to die on the cross for our sins. We in turn demonstrate our love by adoring Him as our divine Creator and King.

Finally, we should worship the Son in order to be united in love with other believers. Too often we want to base our unity in the faith on how much we like one another, rather than on our common relationship with our Savior. Worship brings us back to the true basis for our unity in the faith.

Shout for Joy

Scripture

Background Scripture: *Psalm 95:1-7a*

Scripture Lesson: *Psalm 95:1-7a*

Key Verse: *Come, let us sing for joy to the* LORD; *let us shout aloud to the Rock of our salvation.* Psalm 95:1.

Scripture Lesson for Children: *Psalm 95:1-7a*

Key Verse for Children: *Let us come before [God] with thanksgiving and extol him with music and song.* Psalm 95:2

Lesson Aim

To praise God for His greatness and goodness.

Lesson Setting

Time: Written sometime before the Exile (586 B.C.*)*

Place: Jerusalem

Lesson Outline

Shout for Joy

   I. A Call to Joyful Praise: Psalm 95:1-5

      A. *The Exhortation to Praise God: vss. 1-2*

      B. *The Reason to Praise God: vss. 3-5*

  II. A Call to Heartfelt Submission: Psalm 95:6-7a

      A. *The Exhortation to Submit to God: vs. 6*

      B. *The Reason to Submit to God: vs. 7a*

Introduction for Adults

Topic: *Sing a Song of Praise*

The men's boardinghouse had a weekly meeting convened by the owner. The residents were expected to attend. More than that, they were invited to tell about something that God had done in their lives.

Of course, a few attendees were not too keen about this idea. But something always happened after those meetings. The stories about fresh encounters with God were like blood transfusions. The accounts injected spiritual vitality into those who were just going through the same old religious routines.

Every gathering of believers can benefit from testimonies of how God has been powerfully at work among His people. That's why Psalm 95 (the focus of this week's lesson)—which is a hymn of worship and praise—is so invigorating and life-changing. We all need to contemplate specific ways we can extol the Lord, for doing so helps to keep our love for Jesus from growing cold.

Introduction for Youth

Topic: *Sing His Praises*

"Declare his glory among the nations" has been the theme of student missionary conventions. Thousands of students have responded to the command. They have given their lives to serve Christ where His name is not known, loved, and obeyed. These dedicated young people have changed countless communities and brought hope to innumerable people.

When we sing a joyful song of praise to God for what He has done for us (Ps. 95:1-2, 7), we should also think about people locally and around the world who have no reason to sing. Some have never heard the Good News of Jesus, while others have rejected it. In either case, we should continue filling our hearts with the truth that Jesus is the "Rock of our salvation" (vs. 1), as well as our "Maker" (vs. 6) and Shepherd (vs. 7). Doing so will keep us from hardening our hearts to the needs of the lost around us.

Concepts for Children

Topic: *Make a Joyful Noise*

1. God wants us to sing songs to Him.
2. God wants us to tell Him we love Him.
3. God wants us to be thankful that He takes care of us.
4. God wants us to let others know that He is our Creator.
5. God wants us to tell others about the wonderful things He has done for us.

Lesson Commentary

I. A CALL TO JOYFUL PRAISE: PSALM 95:1-5

A. The Exhortation to Praise God: vss. 1-2

Come, let us sing for joy to the LORD; let us shout aloud to the Rock of our salvation. Let us come before him with thanksgiving and extol him with music and song.

The Psalms are songs and prayers that give deep expression to Israel's faith. Perhaps more than any other part of Scripture, the Psalms tell us what it feels like to walk in the way of the Lord. The traditional Hebrew title of the Psalms is *Sepher Tehillim,* meaning "Book of Praises." But the title "Psalms" had become attached to the book by the first century A.D. The Greek words translated "Psalm" and "Psalter" once referred to stringed instruments. In time, though, the terms came to mean songs accompanied by those instruments.

The outpourings of many poets, living over a period of hundreds of years, flow together to make up the Psalms. Probably groups of these psalms were collected at different times. By the third century B.C., the book had received its final form, presumably through the efforts of temple musicians. The best-known author of psalms was David. More psalms—nearly half the book—are attributed to him than to any other author. Furthermore, historians recorded that David was "Israel's singer of songs" (2 Sam. 23:1) and that he organized the sanctuary's music program (1 Chron. 15:3-28). In addition to David, several other people are claimed to be authors by the psalm titles. These are Moses, Solomon, Asaph (a Levite choir director), the Sons of Korah (a group of Levite musicians), Heman the Ezrahite (founder of the Sons of Korah), and Ethan the Ezrahite (probably also called Jeduthun). Of the several authors, only David is represented in each of the book's major divisions.

Old Testament scholars have noted the similarity of forms and themes among many of the psalms. In turn, they have tried to classify the poems according to their literary type. For instance, due to the fact that Psalm 95 places specific emphasis on extolling the Lord (vs. 1), some specialists consider it a praise or worship psalm. Yet, because the writer acknowledges God as the supreme King (vs. 3), others categorize the piece as a royal or enthronement psalm. Still others label the composition as a prophetic hymn, since it reiterates themes found in the Old Testament prophets. Moreover, the incidents the psalm revisits from Israel's past (namely, the episode that occurred at Meribah and Massah; vs. 8) lead some to designate the song as a historical psalm.

In all likelihood, the original context for the psalm would have been a gathering of Israelites at the Jerusalem temple. The worship leader would have been a priest or a Levite. He summoned the faith community to revere the Lord (vss. 1-3), to heed His will (vss. 6-7), and to remain unwavering in their commitment to Him (vss. 8-11). Like other Hebrew poems, this one exhibits a distinguishing characteristic called parallelism. This term simply means that two (or some-times three) lines of the poetry are, in one way or another, parallel in meaning.

For instance, verse 1 reflects equivalent parallelism, in which the second line repeats the thought of the first. More specifically, the summons for congregants to sing joyfully to the Lord is synonymous with the call to shout out praises to God. The second stanza refers to the Lord as the "Rock" of Israel's "salvation." The depiction is that of a rocky summit that provides protection. For God's people, He was comparable to a lofty fortress where they could find refuge from temporal threats (Pss. 18:2; 31:2; 62:2, 6; 89:26; 92:15; 94:22). In 95:2, the second stanza not only repeats the thought in the first, but also advances it. The worship leader invites the assembled Israelites to enter God's presence with an attitude of "thanksgiving." Additionally, they are directed to shout out praises to Him with "music and song." The idea is that both gratitude and celebration mark the sacred gathering.

B. The Reason to Praise God: vss. 3-5

For the LORD is the great God, the great King above all gods. In his hand are the depths of the earth, and the mountain peaks belong to him. The sea is his, for he made it, and his hands formed the dry land.

Psalm 95:3-5 explains why the Israelites who had assembled at the Jerusalem temple were to offer praise to the Lord. Verse 3 declares Him to be the "great God" and adds that He is the "great King" who is superior to all the false "gods" venerated by Israel's pagan neighbors (Exod. 15:11; Pss. 5:2; 82:1; 97:9). In 1 Corinthians 8, Paul noted that idols are nothing more than humanly made ob-jects and that they represented no real existence or power (vs. 4). Nonetheless, many people believed that they existed. The apostle stated that people wor-shiped all sorts of "gods" and "lords" (vs. 5), some of which they venerated as objects they could see and some of which they believed to exist in heaven. That said, Paul revealed there is only one God and one Lord (vs. 6; see also Deut. 6:4).

The apostle further described God as the Father, who was the source of all creation, and the Lord as Jesus Christ, through whom all creation came into ex-istence. In addition, the apostle noted that the believer lives for God alone and gets his or her power to serve the Father from the Son. Psalm 95:4-5 declares similar truths. Believers learn that even the "depths of the earth" are under the Creator's authority and control. Likewise, He reigns supreme over every aspect of the "mountains," including their "peaks." Similarly, because Israel's God made the "sea" and the "dry land," all of it belongs to Him (24:1-2; 96:4-5). This biblical view of reality sharply contrasted with the mind-set that prevailed throughout the ancient Near East. Supposedly, a different god or goddess con-trolled a particular region of the heavens or the earth. Even various aspects of life (including a person's birth, death, livelihood, and so on) belonged to a different patron deity.

II. A Call to Heartfelt Submission: Psalm 95:6-7a

A. The Exhortation to Submit to God: vs. 6

Come, let us bow down in worship, let us kneel before the Lord our Maker.

In Psalm 95:1, the worship leader invited the assembled Israelites to express joyful praise to the Lord. Similarly, in verse 6, the congregants were summoned to "bow down in worship," as well as to "kneel" in the presence of their "Maker." The emphasis is on completely submitting to the Lord, who not only created the universe, but also brought Israel into existence. He reigned supreme over the entire cosmos and redeemed His chosen people so that they might humbly submit to His will and worship Him alone.

What is worship? It is ascribing worth, respect, or praise to the Lord. In ancient times, the Israelites worshiped God in a variety of ways. Their expressions of praise were formal and informal, structured and unstructured, solemn and joyous. They would glorify God through song, prayer, and the study of Scripture. There are incidents mentioned in the Old Testament where God was worshiped on an individual basis (Gen. 24:26). However, corporate worship seems to have been more common (Exod. 33:10; 1 Chron. 29:20).

Both instrumental music and singing were integral parts of worship (2 Chron. 5:11-13). The Israelites also praised God through dancing (Exod. 15:20; 2 Sam. 6:14) and the clapping of hands (Ps. 47:1). Such emotions as gladness (Ps. 42:4) and rejoicing (Lev. 23:40; Deut. 16:11) were present when God's people worshiped Him. These expressions of joy were accompanied by an attitude of reverence (Ps. 95:6).

There are a variety of Hebrew terms used in the Old Testament for worship. *Saha* (sha-CHAH; the term rendered "worship" in verse 6) means to prostrate oneself. *Hallel* (ha-LAL) means to acclaim, boast of, or glory in, and is used in passages where homage is given to God for His wonderful acts and qualities. *Yada* (yah-DAH) means to praise or give thanks and is used in passages where God's works or character are being acknowledged. *Zamar* (zah-MARE) means to sing praise or to make music and is used in passages where God is being revered for who He is and what He has done. Finally, *sabah* (shah-BACK) means to praise or commend and is used in passages where God is worshiped for His mighty acts and abundant goodness.

B. The Reason to Submit to God: vs. 7a

For he is our God and we are the people of his pasture, the flock under his care.

In Psalm 95:7, the worship leader declared to the assembled Israelites that the Lord was their God. In a metaphorical sense, He was their Shepherd, and they were the "people of his pasture," as well as the "flock under his care." David stated similar truths in Psalm 23. He was himself a shepherd in Israel, and his familiarity with the shepherd's life permeates this poem. He compared himself to a sheep on the mountains of Israel, tenderly cared for and kept by his Shepherd (vs. 1). In David's opening confession, he acknowledged that the God of the universe can be known in a warm, personal relationship. In ancient times, shepherds were responsible for the total care of their sheep. That theme emerges in this hymn. Because David knew God as his Shepherd, he had everything he needed to be an effective servant for the Lord.

The implications of David's shepherding imagery are profound, for sheep in Bible days typically were at the mercy of the elements and wild beasts. The safety of sheep had to be maintained on a day-by-day and moment-by-moment basis. Like a sheep exposed to the perils of life, David had tasted danger when various enemies threatened his life. Despite these difficult circumstances, David knew that his Shepherd, the King of Israel, would provide everything he needed. David had complete confidence in God's protection, guidance, and provision. While we may not have experienced the same kind of outdoor life that David did, his imagery still moves us to reflect on our own relationship with God. We feel the intensity of David's emotions toward the Lord. David's poem, along with Psalm 95:6, invites believers from all walks of life to examine how they relate to God.

David described with vivid poetic imagery what it was like to be fed and watered by his Shepherd. The Lord allowed David to rest in green, fertile pastures, having grazed to his fill. Israel's God led David to quiet pools of fresh water so that his thirst could be satisfied (23:2). The image is one of total satisfaction, contentment, and peace. When we allow God, our Shepherd, to guide us, we have contentment. This is because He knows the "green pastures" and "quiet waters" that will restore us. We can reach these places only by following Him obediently. Otherwise, if we rebel against the leading of our Shepherd (an issue dealt with in Ps. 95:7-11 and Heb. 3:7–4:13), we will bring frustration, dissatisfaction, and sadness into our lives.

An able shepherd would lead his flock along the paths where they needed to go. David knew firsthand about being restored in his soul and about turning to paths of righteousness (Ps. 23:3). For example, after the prophet Nathan confronted David with his sin of adultery (2 Sam. 12:1-14), David repented and entered on a course of moral restoration. Such restoration brought honor to God. Psalm 23:4 is the thematic center of this song of trust. Here we find David referring to God in a direct, reverent manner and declaring his confidence in the Shepherd-King's abiding presence.

David knew that, while he trusted in the Lord, he was not immune from the trials of life. The psalmist referred to these as "the valley of the shadow of death." This was a vivid way of alluding to a life-threatening situation. David compared his experiences to the sheep's being comforted by the shepherd's rod and staff. A typical Israelite shepherd would carry a "rod," or club, to defend against predators. He would also be equipped with a "staff," or crook, to control the sheep. For these reasons his presence would comfort his sheep, just as God's powerful and disciplining presence comforted David.

The positive biblical pictures of a shepherd focus on those who care for the welfare of their animals. The best shepherds provided veterinary care, drove off wild animals, knew their animals by sight, led their charges to the right kind of grassland, and lived as good stewards of their responsibilities. Perhaps these shepherds are the reason why throughout the ancient world "shepherd" was a recognized image or title for a nation's leader (Jer. 23:1-4; Ezek. 34:11-16). David's faith in the Lord's protection sustained him throughout each harrowing incident he encountered in his life.

There are times when a shepherd in ancient Israel might have to lead the flock through a narrow gorge. Such could be a dangerous place, especially as the evening shadows hid bandits or fierce beasts. David's own experiences matched this imagery, for he often had to flee for his life to the mountains and caves of Judah. Yet even in those dark times, when it seemed as if his life would be snuffed out, God protected David. Because he knew his Shepherd, David did not experience paralyzing fear.

At Psalm 23:5, the figure of the Lord changes from a shepherd with his sheep to a host of a banquet. This host entertained David lavishly. David's head was anointed with perfumed oil in the traditional way of showing honor to a guest. The table was spread with food, and David's cup was kept filled with wine. Meanwhile, David's enemies were present to look with envy upon his happiness, in the way captive enemies would be forced by ancient kings to observe their victory celebrations.

Throughout David's life, he had to endure pain, suffering, and threats to his life. God enabled him to overcome these with strength and courage. Death, however, was a different matter. It could not be overcome by conventional human means. Only the God of life, Israel's Shepherd-King, could enable David to face death with the assurance of eternal comfort in God's presence. David poetically expressed these thoughts when he declared that God's goodness and unfailing love would "follow" (vs. 6; literally "pursue") him throughout his life. David would not have to beg the Lord for evidences of His care. God would be eager to give them. Knowing this enabled David to entrust his eternal future with the Lord.

The feast David described earlier was more than a victory celebration. It was also the seal of his alliance with God. David realized that he had not come to the Lord's house for one meal only. He had come to live "forever." This does not mean that David expected to take up residence in the Jerusalem sanctuary. Rather, it means he looked forward to eternal communion with God. In the final verse of this psalm, we see that believers dwell with God in eternity. Their perfect Shepherd-King promises to guide and protect them throughout their life and to bring them to His heavenly home forever.

God's lavish treatment of David is indicative of the loving care that the Lord provides for His people. Jesus echoed this theme when He urged His followers to live for God and make His kingdom their primary concern, for the Lord would give them all they needed from day to day to serve Him (Matt. 6:33). Paul voiced a similar sentiment in Philippians 4:19, "My God will meet all your needs according to his glorious riches in Christ Jesus."

Discussion Questions

1. What feelings do you experience when you worship the Lord?
2. How can believers cultivate an attitude of thanksgiving as they sing praises to God?
3. Why is it important for Christians to affirm that the Lord reigns supreme over all the so-called "gods" (Ps. 95:3) of the world?
4. In what sense is the Lord our Shepherd, and we are the "flock under his care" (vs. 7)?
5. What obvious ways have you seen God care for you—protect you, provide for you, and so on—in the past?

Contemporary Application

Giving praise to God is not something that happens in isolation, nor is it simply a matter of being caught up in a spirit of contagious enthusiasm. Proper adoration comes in response to the revealed greatness of God's character and works (Ps. 95:3-5). Apart from that, we would not know about God's supremacy or grandeur, and therefore could not rejoice in these truths (vss. 1-2).

The poet described God's character and explained some of His awesome deeds on behalf of His people. This included Him protecting His people (vs. 1) and providing for them (vs. 7). Apart from God's Word, we would not know these marvelous truths.

From Scripture we also learn about God's holiness, love, and mercy. An examination of the world informs us that there is a great and intelligent Designer behind the universe (Rom. 1:19-20). But apart from the Bible we would never know the true purpose for Jesus' death on the cross and could never guess that He promises us eternal life.

In John 4:24, Jesus declared, "God is spirit, and his worshippers must worship in spirit and in truth." As we consider the importance of giving praise to God, we must not forget that rejoicing is based on the revealed truths of His character and works. Indeed, the jubilant praise called for in Psalm 95:1 resulted from a consideration of God's unique authority, glory, and salvation.

Offer God Praise

Scripture

Background Scripture: *Luke 2:1-20*
Scripture Lesson: *Luke 2:8-20*
Key Verse: *The shepherds returned, glorifying and praising
God for all the things they had heard and seen, which were
just as they had been told.* Luke 2:20.
Scripture Lesson for Children: *Luke 2:8-20*
Key Verse for Children: *"I bring you good news of great joy
that will be for all the people. Today in the town of David a
Savior has been born to you; he is Christ the Lord."*
Luke 2:10-11.

Lesson Aim

To stress that the Savior's birth is for all people.

Lesson Setting

Time: Around 6 to 5 B.C.
Place: Nazareth and Bethlehem

Lesson Outline

Offer God Praise
   I. The Announcement of the Angel: Luke 2:8-14
      A. The Shepherds and Their Flocks: vs. 8
      B. The Angel of the Lord: vss. 9-12
      C. The Heavenly Host: vss. 13-14
  II. The Visit of the Shepherds: Luke 2:15-20
      A. To Bethlehem: vss. 15-16
      B. To Spread the Word: vss. 17-18
      C. The Response of Mary: vs. 19
      D. To Praise God: vs. 20

Introduction for Adults

Topic: *Spontaneous Joy!*

Charles Schultz's *Peanuts* characters frequently give insight into human nature. As a bewildered Charlie Brown thinks about Christmas, Lucy comments, "Who else but you, Charlie Brown, could turn a wonderful season like Christmas into a problem?"

For many, Christmas is a problem to be endured rather than a holiday to be celebrated. Exhaustion from too much activity exaggerates family tensions. Parents are tired, and children are anxious. A demoralizing Christmas might also result from feelings of loss or incompleteness. Living with memories of happier holidays past, an elderly person might long for those who have died or are far away. The single person might feel miserably alone at Christmas, when everyone else seems to have someone. Even dreary weather can contribute to the Christmas blues.

Although your students may not put their feelings into words, they will bring some of these thoughts to your class. Use this lesson to focus on the good news of Jesus' wondrous birth as the gift of God's kept promise. Giving Jesus the central focus can turn a gloomy holiday into a joy-filled occasion.

Introduction for Youth

Topic: *Go Tell It on the Mountain!*

In our culture of plenty, we find it hard to find a Christmas gift that an adolescent really needs. But if we plan ahead, we can find something that is surprisingly desirable. When that happens, the giver is as happy as the receiver.

Perhaps that's how the angels felt when they delivered Good News to the shepherds. At least we know the shepherds were surprised. We also know they valued the news because they rushed off to Bethlehem to worship the Christ child.

The Christmas account is, after all, God's monumental surprise. His people had waited centuries for some word from their prophets, but there was none. Then suddenly, seemingly out of nowhere, the Good News of the ultimate Shepherd came not from a prophet but from humble shepherds.

Never count God out of the picture. He will surprise you and do far more than you can ask, think, or even dream about (Eph. 3:20).

Concepts for Children

Topic: *Praise for the Newborn King*

1. Joseph and Mary traveled to Bethlehem to be counted.
2. Mary gave birth to Jesus and placed Him in a manger.
3. During the night, an angel told shepherds about the Christ child.
4. The shepherds went to see baby Jesus and praised God for the gift of His Son.
5. We can also thank God for sending His Son to us..

Lesson Commentary

I. THE ANNOUNCEMENT OF THE ANGEL: LUKE 2:8-14

A. The Shepherds and Their Flocks: vs. 8

And there were shepherds living out in the fields nearby, keeping watch over their flocks at night.

Luke 2:1 introduces Jesus' birth by setting it in its historical context. The author mentioned the emperor of Rome, Caesar Augustus. This refers to Octavian, who had established a reputation for being administratively skillful and adroit. As a result of an imperial edict issued by the Roman Senate, Caesar directed that the inhabitants of the empire be registered for the purpose of collecting taxes. The census was not so much to count people as to determine who owed taxes and who could serve in the Roman army (though Jews were not subject to military conscription).

This was the first registration taken when Quirinius was military governor of the Roman province of Syria (vs. 2). Caesar relied upon high-level administrators such as Quirinius to ensure that inhabitants throughout the empire journeyed to their hometowns to be registered (vs. 3). At Jesus' birth, the eternal God invaded temporal human affairs by using secular rulers and events to accomplish His purposes.

Even such a seemingly unimportant individual as Joseph was affected by the Roman census (vs. 4). At the time, Joseph was living in Nazareth, a town situated in lower Galilee. To comply with the census, Joseph had to travel about 90 miles—at least a three-day journey—from Nazareth to Bethlehem, the town of his ancestors (and possibly those of Mary; vs. 5). Bethlehem was the ancestral home of David, and it was there that Samuel the prophet anointed David as Saul's successor (1 Sam. 16:1, 13; 17:12). Micah 5:2 foretells that Bethlehem would be the birthplace of the Messiah. The verse discloses that the origins of the Savior were in the distant past. This probably means that He would come from the royal lineage of David, who had been dead for more than two centuries in Micah's day. But the prophet's words may also hint at the eternal nature of the Ruler.

At the time Joseph made the journey, he was betrothed to Mary (Luke 2:5). In Jewish culture, betrothal was as legally binding as marriage itself. Evidently, Mary was living with Joseph as his wife, though they had not yet consummated their relationship (Matt. 1:24-25). Because Mary was almost ready to give birth to Jesus, the trip from Nazareth to Bethlehem was not the best time for her. But there was no way Joseph could delay the journey. So, they decided Mary should go with him.

While Joseph and Mary were in Bethlehem, Mary prepared to deliver her child (Luke 2:6). Suitable accommodations were difficult to find because the town was overflowing with travelers who sought to register in the census. The "inn" (vs. 7) could have been a guest room in a private home or a space at a public outdoor shelter, but it was probably not a large building with several individual rooms. Like many peasant children, Mary's son would have been washed in a mixture of water and olive oil, rubbed with salt, and then wrapped in strips of linen. These would be placed around the arms and legs of the infant to keep the limbs protected. Mary then laid her child in a trough used for feeding animals. We discover that the world's Messiah would not mobilize the militant Zealots to throw off the Roman yoke. Instead, the Christ child came to serve (Matt. 20:28; Mark 10:45), as well as to seek and to save the lost (Luke 19:10).

An angel announced the Messiah's birth to ordinary shepherds, not the powerful rulers or religious leaders (Luke 2:8). Since shepherds in Bible times lived out in the open and were unable to maintain strict obedience to the law of Moses, they generally were considered to be ceremonially unclean. As a result, they were despised by religious legalists and were typically excluded from temple worship. Custom didn't even allow shepherds to serve as witnesses in legal cases. Interestingly, these shepherds may have been watching over flocks reserved for temple sacrifices in Jerusalem. Why, then, did God single out these Bethlehem shepherds? Perhaps He wanted to make a theological point. It's not normally the influential or the elite whom God chooses, but those who call for help and place their trust in the Lord.

B. The Angel of the Lord: vss. 9-12

An angel of the Lord appeared to them, and the glory of the Lord shone around them, and they were terrified. But the angel said to them, "Do not be afraid. I bring you good news of great joy that will be for all the people. Today in the town of David a Savior has been born to you; he is Christ the Lord. This will be a sign to you: You will find a baby wrapped in cloths and lying in a manger."

According to Luke 2:9, an angel of the Lord suddenly appeared near or in front of the shepherds, and the radiance of God's glory surrounded them. The sight of the angel terrified the shepherds. But the heavenly emissary reassured them with good news of a joyous event (vs. 10), namely, the birth of Israel's "Savior," "Messiah," and "Lord" (vs. 11). (This combination of terms appears nowhere else in the New Testament.) The one who eternally existed in regal splendor had been born that night in Bethlehem. Indeed, He who is sovereign and all-powerful would make redemption available to humanity, including the weak and oppressed—even society's outcasts. Military and political leaders during those times were frequently called "lord" and "savior." But Jesus was unique, being the Anointed One of God.

The Gospel is always "good news of great joy" (vs. 10) for everyone who receives it by faith. The "good news" is that God loves us despite our sinful thoughts, words, and deeds (John 3:16-21; Eph. 2:1-10; 1 John 4:10). Jesus was born to die on the cross for our sins, but He would not stay dead (1 Cor.

15:3-4). It is His victory over death through His resurrection that gives us life (vss. 56-57). "Great joy" (Luke 2:10) is experienced when we trust in the Son, who reconciled us to the Father (2 Cor. 5:17-21). He bestows on us eternal life (John 3:36), His Spirit (Eph. 1:13-14), unrestricted access to His throne of grace (Heb. 4:14-16), a promise that the Son is always with us (Matt. 28:20), and the assurance that the Father will complete the work He begins within us in union with His Son (Phil. 1:6).

The angel encouraged the shepherds to find the Christ child lying in a manger, wrapped snugly in strips of cloth (Luke 2:12). In fact, this would be a sign from the Father validating the birth of His Son, the Messiah. It's worth mentioning that *Christ* is a word borrowed from Greek. It means "Anointed One," signifying divine commissioning for a specific task. In Old Testament times, kings and priests were anointed with oil as a sign of their divine appointment. The Hebrew word for the Anointed One is translated *Messiah*. It was used of the promised one who would deliver Israel from oppression. Most Jews thought He would be a political leader. They did not consider that His mission might be to free them from sin.

C. The Heavenly Host: vss. 13-14

Suddenly a great company of the heavenly host appeared with the angel, praising God and saying, "Glory to God in the highest, and on earth peace to men on whom his favor rests."

Stories about the shepherds make them out to be profane on the one hand or deeply faithful on the other. Though it's hard to know for sure, we can at least assume they were familiar with God's messianic promises. (The angel's announcement would have otherwise meant nothing to them.) We can also marvel at God's wisdom, love, and grace in choosing these rugged individuals (rather than the religious elite in Jerusalem) as the ones who first heard the good news of Jesus' birth.

We can imagine the shepherds staring in amazement, trembling, and trying to grasp the significance of the angel's announcement. Suddenly the night sky exploded with the sounds of "the heavenly host" (Luke 2:13). This was a large group of angels who offered a hymn of praise to God. And what a joyful carol it has become! We can only imagine the glory and praise that must have filled the nighttime sky. The news was simple. The angels gave glory to God and said His peace remained on those with whom He was pleased.

The idea of verse 14 is not so much a general feeling of goodwill toward all people as it is of God's favor resting on those who experience inner peace through faith in Christ (Rom. 5:1). The reference to God's favor in Luke 2:14 reminds us of His grace made available to all humankind through the Savior (Eph. 2:8-9). To some the idea of being at peace with God seems far-fetched, especially in a world continually plagued by war. But the absence of peace can be traced to humanity's stubborn refusal to accept God's Son as their Savior.

The potential for harmony is there, and God's offer of peace still stands. In fact, His grace extends to all who repent of their sin and trust in the Messiah for salvation.

II. The Visit of the Shepherds: Luke 2:15-20

A. To Bethlehem: vss. 15-16

When the angels had left them and gone into heaven, the shepherds said to one another, "Let's go to Bethlehem and see this thing that has happened, which the Lord has told us about." So they hurried off and found Mary and Joseph, and the baby, who was lying in the manger.

We don't know how long the angels sang and whether any others saw them. Most likely they did not stay very long with the shepherds. Also, the biblical text leaves the impression that the angels did not reveal themselves to anyone else. Thus, God's Good News was committed into the hands of a small number of shepherds, not to those who had the power to command obedience, such as the emperor of Rome.

As was noted earlier, the shepherds' initial response to the unusual sights and sounds was fear. But following the words about the birth of the baby, and after the praise of the angelic host, the shepherds moved from fear to curiosity (Luke 2:15). The angel had told the shepherds the specific location and situation of the holy birth. Now they decided to travel to Bethlehem and see for themselves what the Lord had told them about it. It's not easy to convey in English the urgency of the shepherds' words. We might paraphrase it by saying, "Come on, let's hurry and see Him, before it's too late!"

So, the shepherds hurried off and successfully found Mary and Joseph (vs. 16). The shepherds also saw the baby lying on the bed of hay. These most common of all people had the privilege of being the first on record to see the holy child. We can only guess as to what the shepherds said to Joseph and Mary. Obviously, they told the couple about the angels. Perhaps the excitement of the shepherds filled Joseph and Mary with wonder and prompted them to rehearse the ancient messianic prophecies, especially that the Savior was to be born in Bethlehem (Mic. 5:2).

B. To Spread the Word: vss. 17-18

When they had seen him, they spread the word concerning what had been told them about this child, and all who heard it were amazed at what the shepherds said to them.

Today, as soon as babies are born, their parents get on the phone to call relatives and friends. They might also share the information by using email or text messages. But in ancient Bethlehem, the good news could only be spread by word of mouth. In the case of the shepherds, after they had seen Jesus, they became instant evangelists. Being in His presence must have convinced them that what the angel had said to them was true. Indeed, the shepherds felt compelled to tell every person they met that they had seen the Messiah (Luke 2:17).

We can imagine the shepherds saying, "Angels told us the Messiah has been born in Bethlehem, and we went to see for ourselves. We found Him lying in a bed of hay and wrapped in strips of cloth." Regardless of what they actually said, their key point would have been that they had found the Savior. It's no wonder all who heard them were amazed (vs. 18). The shepherds could have responded differently to the wonderful things they had seen and heard. They could have been so paralyzed by fear that they told no one about the wonders. The shepherds could have remained quiet. Thankfully, they spread the good news about the Messiah's birth.

Those who heard the news were astonished. The Greek verb translated "amazed" (vs. 18) conveys the idea that when the people heard the testimony of the shepherds, chills ran down their spines. As with most listeners, some believed, while others probably dismissed the message as nonsense. The latter may have occurred because the information came from lowly shepherds, not from religious leaders and experts. Perhaps from the day of Jesus' birth, the announcement of His advent was an enigma to many. We can imagine skeptics wondering whether the news sounded too good to be true. For people of faith, the answer is clear. The Father had sent His Son into the world so that the lost might be saved.

C. The Response of Mary: vs. 19

But Mary treasured up all these things and pondered them in her heart.

Not only were the people of Bethlehem left to figure out what had happened, but so also was Mary, Jesus' mother. What was Mary to make of all this? The angel Gabriel had previously spoken to her, and she had willingly submitted to the Lord (Luke 1:26-38). But now that the birth of the Christ child had actually occurred, what was Mary to think? In addition, she had to reflect on the angel's announcement to the shepherds concerning the advent of the Messiah. Luke was very specific in describing how Mary responded. She "treasured up" (2:19) all that had happened and "pondered them in her heart."

Most likely, this was a time of intense contemplation for Mary in which she sought to fathom the significance of the momentous events unfolding before her. This search for understanding remained true even though Mary did not fully comprehend all the ramifications of the events that were happening around her. She probably also spent much time in prayer and in conversation with Joseph. Doing these things would have helped Mary to make sense out of the angel's message, Jesus' birth, and the shepherds' account. Before the birth of Jesus, everything may have seemed theoretical to Mary. But now it was reality. The Christ child had been born!

D. To Praise God: vs. 20

The shepherds returned, glorifying and praising God for all the things they had heard and seen, which were just as they had been told.

The shepherds returned to their fields, but they were changed. How could they help but praise God for what they had seen (Luke 2:20)? Joy in heaven and on earth was the suitable reaction to the birth of the Savior. Today, media outlets seem to highlight accounts of catastrophes, deprivations, and distress. Much "news" is the same old story that has been told by people for centuries. Human sin has made a mess of God's wonderful creation. That's why all of us should reflect on God's gift to humanity—Jesus Christ. He came to earth to offer salvation to all people, regardless of their gender, race, or social status. Jesus is the Lord's gift to all who realize their need for Him to deliver them from their bondage to sin.

Discussion Questions

1. What were the shepherds doing when an angel of the Lord appeared to them?
2. What was the joyous good news the angel announced to the shepherds?
3. What sign did the angel give to the shepherds concerning the Christ child?
4. How should we respond to the account of the shepherds' encounter with the Christ child?
5. Why is it important for us to glorify the Father for the gift of His Son?

Contemporary Application

Popular Christmas cards picture the place where Jesus was born as a clean and quiet spot. This depiction couldn't be further from the truth. The Savior's surroundings most likely were dark, smelly, and dirty. This isn't the atmosphere we would expect for the birthplace of our Savior, the King of heaven. From this we see that we shouldn't limit God by our expectations. Despite the filth of our sin-darkened world, He is still at work.

As we reflect on this week's lesson, we see that God revealed the birth of His Son to seemingly insignificant shepherds in a field. This reminds us that Jesus is the Savior of all people, not just the elite and powerful. He comes to anyone with a heart humble enough to accept Him by faith. Extraordinary qualifications are not necessary, for Jesus welcomes us just as we are.

The first account of Jesus in Luke's Gospel is of a tiny, helpless baby. But this is not how the Messiah remained. He grew to be an adult, lived an amazing life, died for us, and ascended to heaven. One day He will return as King of kings to rule the world, judge the wicked, and reward the upright. Let's make sure we don't continue thinking of Jesus merely as a baby in a manger. Because He is our Lord, He deserves our utmost obedience and highest praise.

Affirm the Savior's Power

DEVOTIONAL READING

Mark 9:15-24

DAILY BIBLE READINGS

Monday December 22
Hebrews 11:1-6 By Faith We Please God

Tuesday December 23
Luke 8:19-25 Where Is Your Faith?

Wednesday December 24
Mark 9:15-24 I Believe; Help My Unbelief

Thursday December 25
John 1:1-9 The Light Overpowers Darkness

Friday December 26
Matthew 17:14-20 A Mustard-Seed-Sized Faith

Saturday December 27
Matthew 15:21-31 Great Is Your Faith

Sunday December 28
Matthew 14:22-36 Oh You of Little Faith

Scripture

Background Scripture: *Matthew 14:22-36*

Scripture Lesson: *Matthew 14:22-36*

Key Verse: *When they climbed into the boat, the wind died down. Then those who were in the boat worshiped him, saying, "Truly you are the Son of God."* Matthew 14:32-33.

Scripture Lesson for Children: *Matthew 14:22-36*

Key Verse for Children: *"Truly you are the Son of God."* Matthew 14:33.

Lesson Aim

To recognize that Jesus has the ability to meet our deepest needs.

Lesson Setting

Time: A.D. *29*

Place: Sea of Galilee and Gennesaret

Lesson Outline

Affirm the Savior's Power

  I. The Setting of the Episode: Matthew 14:22-24
      A. *Dismissing the Crowd: vs. 22*
      B. *Fighting Heavy Waves: vss. 23-24*
  II. The Savior Walking on the Water: Matthew 14:25-36
      A. *A Reassuring Word: vss. 25-27*
      B. *A Moment of Doubt: vss. 28-31*
      C. *An Expression of Worship: vss. 32-33*
      D. *An Opportunity to Minister: vss. 34-36*

Introduction for Adults

Topic: *Believing in the Savior*

Life is filled with hardships, many of which are unexpected and unavoidable. It's in these tough, overwhelming circumstances that Christian faith swings into action. We find that Jesus is loving, wise, powerful, and trustworthy. How exciting it is to discover that, even in life's darkest moments, the Lord is there to watch over and provide for us.

Christians sometimes say, "Oh, that wouldn't matter to Jesus." Or, "It's too trivial to pray about." But we soon learn that nothing is inconsequential to the Lord. He invites us to experience the great privilege of praying to Him about everything, not just major crises. In fact, we grow the most spiritually when we place all of our needs in His hands.

This week's study of Jesus walking on the water and healing scores of people brings us fresh insight concerning the ability He has to meet our needs. We learn that nothing is impossible for Him to do for us (Luke 18:27).

Introduction for Youth

Topic: *Surprised by Power*

The teenager and his father returned to the car after fishing for a couple of hours, only to discover that the car keys were nowhere to be found. They searched everywhere and finally the father said, "Let's pray and ask Jesus to help us find those keys." So the two did just that, and in a matter of minutes the keys turned up.

Was this a minor miracle? Regardless of our response, the lesson is clear. Our faith in Jesus covers all areas of our lives. Faith is not confined to the church building, the Sunday worship services, or the youth meeting. Rather, Jesus wants us to trust Him in every circumstance of life.

Jesus encountered people at the point of their greatest needs. He used incidents such as His walking on the water to teach His disciples to trust Him more (Matt. 14:22-33). There were also opportunities for the crowds to receive His healing touch (vss. 34-36). By studying the way Jesus ministered to others, we are encouraged to depend on Him more in our trying situations.

Concepts for Children

Topic: *What Power!*

1. Jesus told His followers to get into a boat and go across a lake.
2. Jesus' followers were scared when a storm overtook them.
3. Jesus came to His followers and told them not to be afraid.
4. Jesus' followers worshiped Him as God's Son.
5. Jesus wants us to trust Him, no matter what happens to us.

Lesson Commentary

I. THE SETTING OF THE EPISODE: MATTHEW 14:22-24

A. Dismissing the Crowd: vs. 22

Immediately Jesus made the disciples get into the boat and go on ahead of him to the other side, while he dismissed the crowd.

The episode in which Jesus walked on the water is preceded by Him feeding over 5,000 people in a remote area near Bethsaida (Luke 9:10, 12). The latter was a town on the northeast shore of the Sea of Galilee. Both events occurred in the spring of A.D. 29, which was the third year of Jesus' earthly ministry. It was a time in which the civil and religious authorities increasingly opposed Jesus. For instance, Matthew 14:1-12 states that Jesus' forerunner, John the Baptizer, was beheaded by Herod Antipas a few months earlier. Antipas ruled over Galilee and Perea from 4 B.C. to A.D. 39. Based on reports he received about Jesus' preaching and miracles, Antipas incorrectly surmised that Jesus was the Baptizer "risen from the dead" (vs. 2).

The precarious situation prompted Jesus to leave the area by boat (vs. 13). He felt a need to get away and spend some time by Himself in prayer (perhaps to reflect on John's beheading; vs. 23). That said, Jesus was unable to remain alone for long, even in a relatively unpopulated region. Large crowds of people had heard of His whereabouts and followed Him on foot from the nearby towns of Galilee (vs. 13). Indeed, when Jesus arrived at the shore of the lake and began to disembark, He spotted many people already there waiting for Him (vs. 14). This incident indicates that Jesus was tremendously popular among the people and that they looked to Him to fill a spiritual void in their lives.

What Jesus wanted most was to be alone and pray. Yet, when He saw the needy people, He was moved with "compassion" (vs. 14) for them. This means He was filled with pity and concern for the disadvantaged all around Him. So, with heartfelt love, Jesus willingly cured the "sick" of their afflictions. The implication is that He deferred the fulfillment of His own desire for solitude and prayer. As the day wore on, Jesus' disciples recommended that He dismiss the crowds so they could go to nearby towns to purchase food for themselves. His followers noted that the locale was isolated and that it was "already getting late" (vs. 15), perhaps referring to late afternoon. Undoubtedly, the disciples were concerned about the crowd of hungry people, but the Twelve might have also felt irritated and inconvenienced by the lingering presence of so many needy people.

The Savior indicated that it was not necessary for the multitudes to be dismissed. Instead, He told the Twelve to give the people food (vs. 16). This wasn't at all what the disciples expected or wanted to hear from Jesus. Nevertheless, His followers investigated their resources to see whether there was any way they could obey His surprising instructions. In the end, though, they had to report that all the food they had were five small, round loaves of barley bread and two small, dried or pickled fish (vs. 17; see also John 6:9, 13). These were common elements in the diet of the Galilean poor. Jesus used this episode to challenge the disciples' faith in God to provide what was needed (John 6:6). By their focus on entirely natural means to resolve the problem—human resources that were clearly inadequate—the Twelve demonstrated that they were not trusting in the Lord.

What was inconceivable to Jesus' followers was not beyond His ability to do. Accordingly, He told them to bring what little food they had to Him (vs. 18). Jesus then directed the Twelve to have the crowds recline on the grass (vs. 19). As the Savior fixed His gaze heavenward, He took the meager amount of food and blessed it. Perhaps Jesus said something similar to the following refrain, which would have been offered in that day during the celebration of the Passover Seder (ceremonial meal): "Blessed are you, O Lord our God, King of the universe, who brings forth bread from the earth" (see David's prayer of thanksgiving recorded in 1 Chron. 29:10-13). Next, as Jesus broke the loaves of bread, He gave them to His disciples, who in turn distributed the food to the hungry people. Imagine the amazement of the Twelve as Jesus handed them one loaf after another!

Jesus miraculously multiplied the bread and fish to such an extent that the hunger of the large crowd was completely satisfied. In fact, His provision was so abundant that His disciples filled 12 baskets with the leftover pieces of food (Matt. 14:20). That was one basket for each disciple! These were not small wicker baskets, but rather large, heavy ones used for carrying sizeable quantities of food and other supplies. Jesus performed a genuine miracle, for about 5,000 men, not counting all the women and children, were fed (vs. 21). In the culture of Jesus' day, men often ate separately from women and children. Some Bible scholars think that when the women and children are included in the count of people, the number fed that day might have been several times more than 5,000.

As the day drew to a close, Jesus directed the Twelve to get into a boat without Him and cross over to the other side of the Sea of Galilee. This would have been the northwest shore of the lake, near the Plain of Gennesaret. Meanwhile, the Savior dispersed the crowds (vs. 22). The Greek verb rendered "made" means to compel someone to act in a certain manner and hints at the presence of a crisis. We learn from John 6:14 that the miraculous supply of food prompted many to wonder whether Jesus was the prophet that Moses referred to in Deuteronomy 18:15 and 18. In their desperation, the people wanted to force Jesus to be their king (John 6:15). But the kind of ruler they wanted, a brigand who would overthrow Israel's oppressors, was not in God's plan (John 18:36–37; Acts 1:6; Rom. 14:17).

B. Fighting Heavy Waves: vss. 23-24

After he had dismissed them, he went up on a mountainside by himself to pray. When evening came, he was there alone, but the boat was already a considerable distance from land, buffeted by the waves because the wind was against it.

After Jesus sent the crowds away, He ventured up the side of a mountain to spend the night in prayer (Matt. 14:23). As the sun set over the horizon, Jesus was finally alone with the Father. We don't know what Jesus prayed about. Jesus might have talked to the Father about the needs of the people, the direction of the Son's earthly ministry in the face of growing opposition, and His upcoming crucifixion. Certainly, the Savior recognized the importance of spending private time with His Father in prayer.

While Jesus was beginning to pray, His disciples had already gone far out on the lake. As the Twelve made their way, a gale-force wind sent huge waves crashing against the sides of the boat (Matt. 14:24; John 6:18). At times on the Sea of Galilee, the sudden appearance of violent storm episodes occurred. Evidently, the disciples spent most of the night fighting the elements as they tried to cross. Despite their efforts, they only went about three miles, which placed them near the middle of the lake (Mark 6:47; John 6:19).

The Sea of Galilee is not really a sea in the same sense as the Mediterranean Sea and other large bodies of water are called "seas." Instead, the Sea of Galilee is actually a pear-shaped lake lying below sea level, being 6 miles wide, 15 miles long, and approximately 150 feet deep. During the Old Testament era, it was known as the Lake (or Sea) of Kinnereth. Later, it became know as Lake Gennesaret, the Sea of Tiberias, and the Sea of Galilee. In the time of Jesus, the steep hills that surround most of the lake's shoreline were prime locations for villages. Despite its relatively small size and unpredictable, often violent weather, the lake was vital to the economy of the local villages. Even today, fish from the Sea of Galilee are as important to modern Israelis as they were to the people living in the area when Jesus ministered.

II. THE SAVIOR WALKING ON THE WATER: MATTHEW 14:25-36

A. A Reassuring Word: vss. 25-27

During the fourth watch of the night Jesus went out to them, walking on the lake. When the disciples saw him walking on the lake, they were terrified. "It's a ghost," they said, and cried out in fear. But Jesus immediately said to them: "Take courage! It is I. Don't be afraid."

It was the "fourth watch of the night" (Matt. 14:25) when Jesus saw the trouble embroiling His disciples. In ancient times, the night was divided into "watches," that is, time periods used by watchmen to regulate their shifts. The Jews divided the night into three watches: (1) sunset to about 10:00 P.M.; (2) about 10:00 P.M. to about 2:00 A.M.; and (3) about 2:00 A.M. to sunrise (Exod. 14:24; Judg. 7:19; Lam. 2:19). In contrast, the Romans had four watches: (1)

sunset to about 9:00 P.M.; (2) about 9:00 P.M. to about midnight; (3) about midnight to about 3:00 A.M.; and (4) about 3:00 A.M. to sunrise. Our verse reflects the Roman practice.

In the hours preceding dawn, Jesus came to rescue His friends. He didn't take a boat, though, for He didn't need one. He came to the Twelve by walking on the lake (Matt. 14:25; Mark 6:48). Not even the wind, waves, and gravity could stop the One who is the Lord of all creation (Job 38:8-11; Pss. 29:3-4, 10-11; 65:5-7; 77:19; 89:9; 107:23-32; Isa. 43:2, 16). While God used Moses to part the waters of the Red Sea, not even the famed leader, liberator, and lawgiver of Israel could claim authority and control over the elements the way Jesus did.

Jesus' form appeared mysteriously out of the darkness like a ghost, and He seemed as if He intended to pass on ahead of the fishing boat (Mark 6:48). The disciples' minds must have turned to the old Jewish superstition that a spirit seen at night brings disaster. In this case, they mistook Jesus for an apparition (Matt. 14:26; Mark 6:49-50). It seems that whenever the Savior was absent, the Twelve fell into distress through lack of faith. Jesus quickly calmed their fears. Undoubtedly, the familiar sound of His voice identifying Himself reassured His disciples that they would not be harmed (Matt. 14:27; John 6:20). Jesus' declaration, "It is I" (Matt. 14:27), is more literally rendered "I am" (Matt. 14:27). This might be an intentional allusion to Exodus 3:14, where God made Himself known to Moses as "I AM WHO I AM" (Isa. 43:10; 51:12).

B. A Moment of Doubt: vss. 28-31

"Lord, if it's you," Peter replied, "tell me to come to you on the water." "Come," he said. Then Peter got down out of the boat, walked on the water and came toward Jesus. But when he saw the wind, he was afraid and, beginning to sink, cried out, "Lord, save me!" Immediately Jesus reached out his hand and caught him. "You of little faith," he said, "why did you doubt?"

Peter took Jesus at His word by boldly asking the Savior to allow His disciple to venture out on the water toward Him (Matt. 14:28). When Jesus gave Peter permission to do so, he initially exercised great faith by leaving the boat (vs. 29). For a moment, he could actually walk on the water (vs. 29). Perhaps at first Peter felt exhilarated. But when he shifted his attention from Jesus to the tempestuous wind, Peter became terrified, began to sink into the water, and shrieked, "Lord, save me!" (vs. 30).

Despite Peter's alarm, Jesus remained in full control of the situation. He quickly extended His hand and took hold of Peter. The Savior wasted no time in focusing on Peter's real problem. He had allowed doubt to squash his faith (vs. 31). If Peter had remained unwavering in his trust, he would have experienced no difficulties. From this incident, Peter (and the rest of the Twelve) learned that any task done for Jesus must be accompanied by faith in Him from start to finish (John 15:5). The episode also reminds us of our need for faith throughout our spiritual lives. Faith is not only necessary for conversion. Living day by day with Jesus requires us to trust Him to take care of us. Admittedly, this is difficult when we see the risks that are involved. Yet we can persevere if we remain focused on our all-powerful Savior.

C. An Expression of Worship: vss. 32-33

And when they climbed into the boat, the wind died down. Then those who were in the boat worshiped him, saying, "Truly you are the Son of God."

The moment Jesus and Peter returned to the fishing boat, the turbulent wind ceased (Matt. 14:32). The Twelve, now completely dumbfounded over what had taken place (Mark 6:52-53), fell prostrate in worship before the feet of the Messiah. As they did so, they exclaimed, "Truly you are the Son of God" (Matt. 14:33). This messianic title emphasizes the special and intimate relationship between Jesus and the Father (3:17; 16:16; 27:54). The title also spotlights Jesus' unwavering commitment and obedience to the Father's will. As the second Person of the Trinity, Jesus is equal with the Father (and the Spirit), exercises divine prerogatives, and is worthy of our trust, obedience, and adoration.

D. An Opportunity to Minister: vss. 34-36

When they had crossed over, they landed at Gennesaret. And when the men of that place recognized Jesus, they sent word to all the surrounding country. People brought all their sick to him and begged him to let the sick just touch the edge of his cloak, and all who touched him were healed.

After the crisis had passed, the fishing boat landed and moored at Gennesaret (Matt. 14:34). This was a fertile plain located on the northwest bank of the Sea of Galilee. According to local belief, the numerous mineral springs in the area could heal the infirm and crippled who flocked to them. When the people of the region recognized who Jesus was, they told others who lived there that He had come (vs. 35). Consequently, a large crowd hurriedly carried all who were sick to Him to be healed. The crowds were so desperate and needy that they begged to simply touch the edge of Jesus' cloak (or loose outer garment) in the hope that they might be cured (vs. 36). He granted the people's requests and healed all who touched Him.

Jesus performed many miracles during His earthly ministry, some of which are not recorded in the Gospels. His miracles were extraordinary expressions of God's power. When Jesus performed a miracle, God directly altered, superseded, or counteracted some established pattern in the natural order. The miracles of Jesus served several purposes. First, they confirmed His claim to be the Messiah. Second, they validated His assertion that He was sent by God and represented Him. Third, they substantiated the credibility of the truths He declared to the people of Israel. Fourth, they encouraged the doubtful to put their trust in Him. Fifth, they demonstrated that the One who is love was willing to reach out to people with compassion and grace.

Discussion Questions

1. After feeding over 5,000 people, why did Jesus compel His disciples to get into a fishing boat?
2. How important was it for Jesus to spend time in prayer?
3. After Peter left the boat and began walking on the water to Jesus, what prompted Peter to doubt?
4. Why is it important for believers to give Jesus their heartfelt devotion?
5. How can the divine authority of Jesus give us confidence in life's most difficult circumstances?

Contemporary Application

By this time, Jesus' disciples had seen Him heal many people. And yet, when they saw Him walking on the water in their direction, they responded with fear, not faith (Matt. 14:26). Nonetheless, Peter's call to Jesus for help (vs. 30) indicated that Peter and the rest of the Twelve thought Jesus had the ability to rescue them from whatever plight they encountered.

That said, Jesus' followers struggled with doubt (vs. 31). Even when they declared Him to be the "Son of God" (vs. 33), they still did not completely grasp exactly who He was (Mark 6:51-52). Jesus' mastery over the storm should have signaled to His disciples that He is God incarnate. After all, in the Old Testament, God is described as the One who controls the natural world and the seas (Ps. 93:3-4; Isa. 51:10; Hab. 3:8-10).

We have all faced severe storms in our lives. These might involve the loss of a job, the death of a loved one, or the onslaught of a frightening disease. Regardless of the nature of these trials, it is virtually impossible for us to avoid them. And they have a way of pushing us to the limits of our faith.

Whatever our needs, Jesus offers to meet them. The question we face is whether we have the courage to believe that He can help us. In other words, it's not a matter of what Jesus can do but rather of our willingness to trust Him every step of the way.

A Model Prayer

Scripture

Background Scripture: *Luke 11:1-13*
Scripture Lesson: *Luke 11:1-13*
Key Verse: *"When you pray, say: 'Father, hallowed be your name, your kingdom come.'"* Luke 11:2.
Scripture Lesson for Children: *Luke 11:1-13*
Key Verse for Children: *"When you pray, say: 'Father, hallowed be your name, your kingdom come.'"* Luke 11:2.

Lesson Aim

To appreciate the importance of prayer in our lives as believers.

Lesson Setting

Time: A.D. *29*
Place: Judah

Lesson Outline

A Model Prayer

  I. A Model Prayer: Luke 11:1-4
      A. *Asking for Guidance on How to Pray: vs. 1*
      B. *Worshiping the Father: vs. 2*
      C. *Petitioning the Father: vss. 3-4*
  II. An Encouragement to Pray: Luke 11:5-13
      A. *Being Bold in Prayer: vss. 5-8*
      B. *Being Persistent in Prayer: vss. 9-10*
      C. *Being Assured of God's Concern: vss. 11-13*

Introduction for Adults

Topic: *Finding the Right Words*

People learn new skills all the time. For instance, they like to talk about how they learned to use different types of electronic equipment, including laptops, smart phones, and tablet devices. We laugh about the mistakes we made and how we inadvertently wiped out some important information. We keep taking refresher courses to upgrade our computer skills.

Learning to pray is like that, because praying is a new skill. It's not something you fall into. Prayer is a developed discipline that expresses our sincere piety. Prayer takes the same kind of training and discipline. While we pray, we learn more about it and find new pleasure in it, but it requires time and concentration.

Prayer is not like technology, however, because anyone can pray. That's because prayer is having a conversation with the Father (Luke 11:2). But in order for it to be satisfying, we have to think about what we say and how we say it. We have to use our best thoughts and skills, conditioned by a proper attitude (vss. 3-4).

Introduction for Youth

Topic: *Talk to Your Father*

The concept of prayer as conversation with the Father has tremendous appeal (Luke 11:2). We have to take prayer out of the realm of stuffy, pious jargon. We have to show saved teens that prayer is not limited to the people who do the praying in public services. Rather, prayer pleases God because it shows that we love Him and His fellowship.

Many times Christian adolescents pray for the first time on retreats or in small campus and church groups. They touch levels of intimacy in prayer because they are vulnerable to each other, more so than many adults. Therefore, our concern is not with the right words and tone of voice, but in practicing our faith with honesty and integrity. That's what Jesus talked about.

Our goals for youth are to cultivate strong daily prayer habits, as well as quality prayer in fellowship groups. Then as they pray, they can develop the needed spiritual muscles for standing up in spiritual battles (vss. 3-4).

Concepts for Children

Topic: *Here's How We Do It!*

1. God loves to hear His children talk to Him in prayer.
2. God wants us to talk to Him about all of our fears and needs.
3. When we ask God to forgive our sins, we must also forgive those who have wronged or hurt us.
4. It is helpful to pray with our parents and friends.
5. By praying every day, we grow stronger in our faith.

Lesson Commentary

I. A MODEL PRAYER: LUKE 11:1-4

A. Asking for Guidance on How to Pray: vs. 1

One day Jesus was praying in a certain place. When he finished, one of his disciples said to him, "Lord, teach us to pray, just as John taught his disciples."

Numerous scholars have noted that the theme of prayer is strong in the Gospel of Luke, as exemplified by this week's Scripture passage. In 11:1, we learn that one day Jesus was praying in an unnamed spot. According to 10:38, the Savior and His disciples were continuing on their way to Jerusalem, where He would be crucified (9:51; 13:22; 17:11; 18:31; 19:11, 28). They spent a short while in Bethany (10:38), which was about two miles from Jerusalem and was also the hometown of Mary and Martha (John 12:1-3).

Sometime after that, Jesus' disciples were with Him as He spent time in prayer with His heavenly Father. When Jesus finished, one of the Twelve asked Him to teach them how to pray, just as John the Baptizer had done for his followers (Luke 11:1). In that day, Jewish groups would typically express their corporate identity by means of a distinctive prayer. Evidently, the disciples of John the Baptizer had adopted a prayer as their own, and now Jesus' followers requested from Jesus the opportunity to do something similar.

B. Worshiping the Father: vs. 2

He said to them, "When you pray, say: 'Father, hallowed be your name, your kingdom come.'"

In response, Jesus outlined a model prayer (Luke 11:2-4). This is traditionally known as the Lord's Prayer (see also the longer version in Matt. 6:9-13). But it is more accurately understood as the Disciples' Prayer, for it represents how Jesus' followers should approach God. A fuller understanding of what Jesus taught can be obtained by considering both Luke's and Matthew's versions of the Lord's Prayer. We discover that God wants us to address Him in a way that reflects our close, personal relationship with Him (Rom. 8:14-17; Gal. 4:4-7). Like a father, God has authority over us, and yet at the same time He loves us and wants to give us what we need to be effective in our service for Him. Because He lives in heaven, He is transcendent (namely, going beyond our earthly existence) and has the ability to grant our requests.

The Greek phrase rendered "hallowed be your name" (Luke 11:2) emphasizes how important it is for us to honor and revere the Lord, as represented by His holy name. So, the initial focus of prayer is not on our personal needs, but on God's glory. The one who prays also desires that God's rule over His creatures would extend to its fullest bounds and that people on earth would come to obey the Lord as perfectly as do the angels in heaven. Some think that the reference to "kingdom" denotes a time when Jesus will physically rule over the earth. They maintain that the official rejection of Jesus did not negate the promises to Israel regarding the kingdom. Others, however, think that this kingdom refers to Jesus' spiritual rule and that the disciples would someday share close fellowship with Jesus at a future time in this realm.

C. Petitioning the Father: vss. 3-4

"'Give us each day our daily bread. Forgive us our sins, for we also forgive everyone who sins against us. And lead us not into temptation.'"

Luke 11:3-4 indicates that we are to look to God for our needs (not our greeds)—no matter how basic—on a day-to-day basis. Accordingly, while our foremost priority should be giving God the honor that is due Him, there's nothing wrong with asking Him to give us the things we think we need, whether they are material or spiritual in nature. Three personal requests are delineated in the Lord's Prayer.

The first petition is for bread, which was a staple of the Jewish diet in Jesus' day. Bread stands for all the basic needs people have. The second personal request is for forgiveness. The Father is the One who can cancel our spiritual debts because the Son paid them in full on the cross. But as Jesus stated, before we ask God to pardon our sins, we should first forgive the wrongs others have done to us. The third request is for protection from temptation and Satan. This reminds us that we should ask for God's help in preserving our spiritual health.

II. AN ENCOURAGEMENT TO PRAY: LUKE 11:5-13

A. Being Bold in Prayer: vss. 5-8

Then he said to them, "Suppose one of you has a friend, and he goes to him at midnight and says, 'Friend, lend me three loaves of bread, because a friend of mine on a journey has come to me, and I have nothing to set before him.' Then the one inside answers, 'Don't bother me. The door is already locked, and my children are with me in bed. I can't get up and give you anything.' I tell you, though he will not get up and give him the bread because he is his friend, yet because of the man's boldness he will get up and give him as much as he needs."

Perhaps the model prayer Jesus offered prompted some of His disciples to wonder how confident they should be in bringing small, personal matters to God. Also, if it is permissible for God's spiritual children to make specific requests to Him, then why doesn't He appear to answer all their petitions? These are some of the concerns Jesus addressed in His parable on being bold in prayer. From this story, they learned that if they prayed, God would answer.

Jesus' parable recorded in Luke 11:5-8 differs from other stories He told in that He made His point by means of contrasts, rather than similarities. In particular, God is not like the friend or the father in these stories, but rather different from them. The parable about the unexpected guest spotlights a typical, though embarrassing, situation in the time of Jesus.

It's late at night when a hungry traveler arrives at the home of a friend and requests some food to eat. The friend, however, does not have anything to feed his friend. And since showing hospitality was important in that culture, the friend would feel ashamed if he could not satisfy his guest's request for a meal. This prompts the host to go to a neighbor around midnight to pester him for a loan of three loaves of bread (vss. 5-6). In a simple Galilean village such as this, in which women baked bread in common courtyards, all the residents would know who had a fresh supply of bread.

In Jesus' parable, the head of the household told his neighbor not to bother him. The former explained that the wooden door was already bolted shut, and he and his children were in bed. Moreover, the homeowner declared that he was unable to get up and give his neighbor anything to eat (vs. 7). This scene can be better understood with some background information about the typical sleeping arrangements of a home in Jesus' day.

The dwelling was probably a peasant's cottage made up of one large room that served the entire family's needs. The bedding was kept in a recessed part of a wall and taken out at night and spread on reed mats on the floor. The parents would sleep in the center of the room, with the male children positioned on the father's right-hand side and the female children on the mother's left-hand side. Even with a modest-sized family, the father's getting up would have disturbed the whole household, especially any children sleeping closest to him.

As noted earlier, it was a matter of cultural honor for a neighbor to be a good host to visitors. Thus, the host in Jesus' parable continued to nag his friend for food to give to the hungry traveler. The Savior noted that the inconvenienced fellow would not comply with the request out of friendship. Instead, he caved in to the demand because of the neighbor's "boldness" (Luke 11:8). Indeed, the worn-down head of the household gave his neighbor not just three loaves of bread, but whatever he requested.

The Greek noun rendered "boldness" is used only here in the New Testament. It denotes a lack of sensitivity to what others would consider proper. Such ideas as "shamelessness," "impertinence," and "impudence" are wrapped up in the NIV translation. Other possible renderings include "sheer persistence" and "shameless audacity." The idea is that the neighbor gave his friend as much bread as he needed because the man kept harassing him. In addition, the head of the household possibly wanted to avoid the shame that would come from a breach of hospitality (Prov. 3:27-28).

It would be incorrect to infer from Jesus' story that God will eventually answer our prayers if we keep pestering Him. He is not like a sleepy man who does not want to be troubled and has to be shamed into responding. In reality, our heavenly Father is completely opposite the friend in the house. Jesus' point is that if this man was willing to respond to the pleas of his friend, how much more willing is God to give us the things we really need. He is not reluctant to give us what we ask, but instead is eager to do so.

James 4:2-4 adds further insight regarding the issue of prayer. In the last part of verse 2, James explained that his readers did not receive what they desired because they left God out of their pursuits. Perhaps these believers recognized the selfish or immoral nature of what they desired, so they felt that asking God's assistance would be futile. Of course, if this was true, they would have been correct. Some of those who did make their requests known to God were attempting to use prayer as a means of self-gratification. Their motives were impure because they sought pleasure for its own sake—not the pleasure one derives from implementing the will of God (vs. 3).

James' anger over this matter is revealed by his reference to his readers as adulterous or unfaithful people (vs. 4). He used this harsh tone in order to shock his readers into an awareness of what they were really doing. Again, James drove his point home with a question: "Don't you know that friendship with the world is hatred toward God?" To be friends with the world—that is, to court its godless beliefs and value systems—is to make oneself an enemy of God. As we see in John 17:15 (to be studied in next week's lesson), Jesus asked His Father not take believers out of the (physical) world, but to protect them from the evil one who cultivated worldly thinking.

B. Being Persistent in Prayer: vss. 9-10

"So I say to you: Ask and it will be given to you; seek and you will find; knock and the door will be opened to you. For everyone who asks receives; he who seeks finds; and to him who knocks, the door will be opened."

In moments of discouragement or distress, believers can receive consolation and encouragement from their heavenly Father. Although He is the all-powerful and sovereign Lord, they should not be timid or fearful about praying to Him, for Jesus will intercede on their behalf (Heb. 4:14-16; 1 John 2:1). Likewise, believers should not worry about petitioning God in a religiously acceptable manner or framing their words in exactly the proper way, for the Spirit will help them to communicate with the Father (Rom. 8:26-27).

So, it was fitting for Jesus to encourage His followers to pray. He stated that when they asked the Father for something, it would be given to them. This meant He delighted to hear and answer their requests. It also meant the disciples were totally dependent on the Lord. The more they looked to God to meet their needs, the less inclined they would be to covet what others had. Whatever Christians sought from God would be found, and whatever door of ministry opportunity they accessed in His will would be opened to them (Luke 11:9). The idea of knocking suggests that a sense of urgency should accompany the disciples' praying. The Greek verb tenses used in this verse (present imperatives) indicate continuous action—keep on asking, keep on seeking, and keep on knocking.

The Savior explained that His followers need not fear being rejected or ignored, for the Father would answer their petitions (vs. 10). Moreover, Jesus' comments implied that His followers were to persist until the answer came. Perseverance in prayer would produce tangible results, for no prayer went unheard or unanswered by God (18:1). The Lord would neither disregard the petitions of His children nor treat them as insignificant. In fact, their prayers were important and would get His personal attention. It would be mistaken to assume from what the Son said that the Father would fulfill unbiblical requests. In that regard, Luke 11:9-10 (see also Matt. 7:7-8) are not a blank check that God issues to people for them to fill in as they please. Before the Lord answers a believer's request, she or he should be seeking to live and pray in His will (1 John 5:14-15).

C. Being Assured of God's Concern: vss. 11-13

"Which of you fathers, if your son asks for a fish, will give him a snake instead? Or if he asks for an egg, will give him a scorpion? If you then, though you are evil, know how to give good gifts to your children, how much more will your Father in heaven give the Holy Spirit to those who ask him!"

Jesus ultimately intended His comments to encourage, not discourage, His followers to pray. The Savior illustrated His Father's eagerness to fulfill the requests of His children by referring to the sensible practices of all parents. Normally when a child asked for a fish, a reasonable parent would not hand her a water snake, for that would be cruel and insensitive (Luke 11:11). Moreover, if a child asked for an egg, he would not get something as inappropriate and harmful as a scorpion (vs. 12; see also Matt. 7:9-10). Similarly, God is not cruel and insensitive toward His children. Rather, He is kind and reasonable in handling their requests.

Human beings, who are fallen and inclined to do evil, understand how to give beneficial and appropriate things to their children. This being true, believers were to consider how much more their heavenly Father would do for them when they brought their requests to Him. He would always give them what was sensible and appropriate to meet their needs for that moment. This includes virtues such as righteousness, purity, and wisdom (Matt. 7:11; Jas. 1:5). Luke 11:13 specifies that the Holy Spirit is the ultimate good gift we can receive from God. From the Spirit believers receive wisdom and guidance to live in a godly manner in a fallen world (1 Cor. 2:10-16).

Jesus' teaching unveiled the heart of God. The Savior revealed that the Father was not stingy, selfish, or begrudging. Likewise, His children did not have to grovel and beg as they brought Him their requests. They knew He was a compassionate Father, who understood their needs and cared for them deeply. If human parents could be kind to their children, God, the heavenly Father of believers, was infinitely more considerate in hearing their petitions and meeting their needs.

Jesus' teaching serves as a reminder about the true nature of God. He is not a reluctant stranger who has to be coaxed and harassed into bestowing His gifts. Neither is He a malicious tyrant who takes vicious pleasure in playing tricks on others. Nor is God like an indulgent grandparent who provides whatever anyone asks of him. Rather, God is the believer's heavenly Father and the Lord of an eternal kingdom. He is the One who graciously and willingly bestows the good gifts of His kingdom in answer to our prayers (Jas. 1:17).

Discussion Questions

1. What are the key aspects of Jesus' model prayer?
2. In Jesus' parable, what prompted one friend to go to another friend and request some food?
3. In what way is the Father in heaven unlike the reluctant neighbor?
4. What time of the day is best for you to pray?
5. What are some of your recent prayers that God has answered?

Contemporary Application

Praying is talking to God (Luke 11:2). The act of praying does not change what God has purposed to do. Rather, it is the means by which He accomplishes His will. Talking to God is not a method of creating a positive mental attitude in ourselves so that we are able to do what we have asked to be done. Instead, prayer creates within us a right attitude with respect to the will of God. Prayer is not so much getting God to do our will as it is demonstrating that we are as concerned as He is that His will be done (Matt. 6:10).

Perhaps the most unpopular concept regarding the practice of prayer is persistence (Luke 11:9-10). Whatever our misgivings about coming before the all-knowing, all-powerful God with the same specific petitions over and over, persistence is scriptural (vss. 5-8). God does not become more willing to answer because of perseverance. Rather, the petitioner might become more capable of receiving God's answer to his or her request. Also, perseverance can clarify in our minds deep-seated desire from fleeting whim. Additionally, talking to God about the deepest desires of our heart can prepare our soul to more fully appreciate the answer He gives to our request.

Thanksgiving is to be a regular part of our prayer life (1 Thess. 5:18). Expressing gratitude is an aspect of praise in which we convey appreciation to God. It should spring from an appreciative heart, though it is required of all believers, regardless of their initial attitude. We can thank God for His work of salvation and sanctification, for answering our prayers, and for leading us in the path of righteousness (Phil. 1:3-5; Col. 1:3-5). We can also express gratitude to God for His goodness and unending mercy and for leading us to spiritual victory in Christ (Ps. 107:1; 1 Cor. 15:57).

Jesus Prays for Us

Scripture

Background Scripture: *John 17:1-26*

Scripture Lesson: *John 17:6-21*

Key Verse: *"That all of them may be one, Father, just as you are in me and I am in you. May they also be in us so that the world may believe that you have sent me."* John 17:21.

Scripture Lesson for Children: *John 17:6-21*

Key Verse for Children: *"I protected [my followers] and kept them safe by that name you gave me."* John 17:12.

Lesson Aim

To learn that Jesus prayed for His followers to be united.

Lesson Setting

Time: A.D. *30*

Place: Jerusalem

Lesson Outline

Jesus Prays for Us

    I. Jesus' Prayer for His Disciples: John 17:6-19

        A. *Making the Father Known: vs. 6*

        B. *Operating as the Father's Spokesperson: vss. 7-8*

        C. *Safekeeping the Disciples: vss. 9-12*

        D. *Setting Apart the Disciples as Holy: vss. 13-19*

    II. Jesus' Prayer for All Believers: John 17:20-21

        A. *Expressing Concern for Future Believers: vs. 20*

        B. *Seeking a Unified Faith Community: vs. 21*

Introduction for Adults

Topic: *A Friend in High Places*

A certain efficiency expert finally met the woman of his dreams. Because the specialist was a busy person, he decided to use his management and administrative skills to help him in his courtship.

The professional quickly sat down at his computer and prepared a note saying, "I love you." Then he had 365 copies made, each addressed to his newfound love. He then instructed his office staff to send one note each day for the coming year. At the end of the 365 days, he planned to propose to the woman. The notes went out as the expert had instructed. A year later, he called the woman and was surprised to learn that she planned to marry the postman!

Jesus never treats us in an impersonal way. As we discover in John 17 (the focus of this week's lesson), He is always at hand. Jesus has no perfunctory consideration of our needs, but constantly intercedes for us.

Introduction for Youth

Topic: *Together as One*

In the film *Oh God!*, George Burns starred as "God," who supposedly came in human form and appeared to a young man played by John Denver. As the appearances and miracles increased, the man's commitment deepened, causing him to be ostracized by his friends.

"God" finally decreed that He would not put in any more appearances. This decision prompted the young man to lament that he would never be able to talk with "God" anymore. In turn, "God" responded, "You talk, I'll listen."

John 17 records Jesus' farewell prayer. He asked that His all-powerful and glorious Father in heaven would listen to His spiritual children. And unlike the character played by George Burns, God not only listens, but also protects His children. Moreover, He enables them to be united and with one voice bring His message of truth and love to a lost and dying world.

Concepts for Children

Topic: *Pray for Protection*

1. Jesus prayed for all His followers.
2. Jesus prayed that His followers would be safe.
3. Jesus prayed that His followers would be filled with joy.
4. Jesus prayed that His followers would help each other.
5. Jesus prayed that His followers would tell others about Him.

Lesson Commentary

I. JESUS' PRAYER FOR HIS DISCIPLES: JOHN 17:6-19

A. Making the Father Known: vs. 6

"I have revealed you to those whom you gave me out of the world. They were yours; you gave them to me and they have obeyed your word."

John 13 through 17 records Jesus' farewell discourse to His disciples in the upper room, accompanied by a final meal known as the Lord's Supper. At the end of that event, Jesus lifted His eyes toward heaven and prayed aloud to His Father. According to Jewish custom in the first century A.D., this was a common posture for prayer. Jesus used this stance on other occasions (Matt. 14:19; Mark 7:34; John 11:41).

John 17 contains Jesus' longest recorded entreaty. In it He prayed for Himself (17:1-5), the disciples who were with Him (vss. 6-19), and everyone who would later come to believe in Him (vss. 20-26). Indeed, Jesus prayed for all of us as He was about to take our place on the cross. Jesus began the prayer by noting that the divinely appointed "time" (vs. 1) had arrived. Jesus was aware that He was about to die at Calvary, and He knew the cross would be the consummation of His earthly ministry. Ironically, the cross meant something considerably different to Jesus than it did to the people of His day. From their perspective, the cross was a symbol of disgrace, but to Jesus it meant the path to heavenly glory.

The hour was at hand for the Father to "glorify" His Son, especially as Jesus glorified the Father on the cross. Jesus' request denotes a claim to being God, for God never shares His splendor with anyone else (Isa. 42:8; 48:11). The religious leaders in Jerusalem thought they had authority over Jesus. Supposedly, His humiliating death at Calvary would be proof of their supremacy. In truth, however, the Father had given the Son "authority" (vs. 2) over all humanity. His gift of eternal life to the lost exemplified that authority. Though Jesus seemed to hang helplessly on the cross, through His sacrificial death, He was able to grant eternal life to those whom the Father had given to Him.

In Jesus' prayer, He defined "eternal life." It is not mere endless existence, but a personal relationship with the Father based on knowing Him as the one true God (Deut. 6:4; Mark 12:29; 1 Cor. 8:6; 1 Thess. 1:9; 1 Tim. 1:17). The emphasis here goes beyond an intellectual understanding to living in intimate fellowship with the Creator (1 John 1:3-4). Moreover, we can know the Father only through faith in the Son, Jesus the Messiah (John 1:14, 18; 14:9; 20:31), whom the Father sent as His emissary (3:34; 4:34; 13:20). So, eternal life is a growing relationship with God that begins, not just when the believer dies, but at the moment of his or her conversion (1:12-13; 3:3, 5).

Jesus' next statement assumed that He would complete His redemptive work on the cross. His decision to die at Calvary was irrevocable. Though He had the choice not to place His life in the hands of His enemies, Jesus was firm in His resolve to finish the task His Father had assigned Him. Jesus always performed His duties on earth with the intent of glorifying His Father in heaven. Even now, as Jesus prayed, He was confident that the completion of His work on earth would bring honor to His Father (John 17:4). In light of this truth, it is significant that Jesus' last words on the cross were, "It is finished" (19:30).

Jesus asked His Father to "glorify" (17:5) Him. Put differently, Jesus asked for the same splendor He had enjoyed with the Father before the creation of the universe. The Son's glorification would occur in the Father's presence after the Son was raised from the dead and exalted to the Father's right hand in heaven (Rom. 1:4; Phil. 2:9-11; Heb. 1:3). Jesus' entreaty reveals two significant attributes of His deity. First, He is not a created being, but has always existed (John 1:1; 8:58; 16:28). Second, the Son is equal with the Father (and the Spirit) in that they share the same divine majesty. In essence, Jesus was saying what He had publicly acknowledged before: "I and the Father are one" (10:30).

As Jesus' disciples listened to His prayer, He spoke extensively on their behalf. He knew that they were about to face the worst crisis in their lives. His death and their temporary abandonment of Him would rock their fragile faith. So the Son devoted the major portion of His high-priestly prayer to entrust His followers into the hands of His Father. Even before Jesus had "revealed" (vs. 6), or disclosed, the Father's holy character to the disciples, they belonged to God. In fact, God had taken them from the "world" and given them to His Son (6:37, 44-45; 15:16, 27). Jesus commended them for having kept God's Word. Despite their impending but brief lapse in faith (Matt. 26:56; Mark 14:50), they had been and would be obedient to the truth about the Father, which the Son unveiled through His teachings and miracles.

B. Operating as the Father's Spokesperson: vss. 7-8

"Now they know that everything you have given me comes from you. For I gave them the words you gave me and they accepted them. They knew with certainty that I came from you, and they believed that you sent me."

Not only Jesus' disciples, but also everything that belonged to the Son came from the Father (John 17:7). In contrast to the religious elite, the Eleven had finally understood that all they knew about the Son had the Father as its source. The disciples' comprehension was based on their receiving and believing the message that Jesus—the Father's spokesperson—had imparted to them (1:12). Though their understanding was not yet complete, they were convinced that the Son had come from heaven and that the Father had sent Him to earth to proclaim eternal truths. Jesus understood that the Eleven had much more to learn and that their faith needed to be strengthened. Yet, Jesus also knew that He could count on their devotion. After all, His Father had given them to the Son and they truly believed in Him (17:8).

C. Safekeeping the Disciples: vss. 9-12

"I pray for them. I am not praying for the world, but for those you have given me, for they are yours. All I have is yours, and all you have is mine. And glory has come to me through them. I will remain in the world no longer, but they are still in the world, and I am coming to you. Holy Father, protect them by the power of your name—the name you gave me—so that they may be one as we are one. While I was with them, I protected them and kept them safe by that name you gave me. None has been lost except the one doomed to destruction so that Scripture would be fulfilled."

Jesus made it clear that He was praying for the Eleven and not for the rest of the "world" (John 17:9), which was opposed to God. This did not imply a lack of concern for the world or other people. Jesus wanted the Eleven to know His specific concern for them, they who would glorify Him by being the first to take the Gospel to the lost. These disciples belonged to the Father, and He had specifically given them to the Son. As the Father had released them into His Son's care, now He was giving them back into His Father's care.

Jesus stated that the Father owned whatever belonged to the Son. Likewise, the Son owned everything that belonged to the Father. Jesus' statement included the Eleven (John 17:10). A mere mortal could not legitimately make such a claim, so the Son was clearly declaring here His equality with the Father (and the Spirit). Furthermore, the disciples heard Jesus express His confidence in them by stating that "glory" had come to Him as a result of them following Him. Perhaps at times over the past three years they felt doubtful about what they had accomplished for the Savior. They might have even thought that Jesus was annoyed with their inability to grasp His teachings. Now, however, they knew that the Messiah was pleased with them, for they had brought and would bring honor to Him.

Jesus was not going to be with His disciples much longer, but He was returning to His Father in heaven. For a brief period, the Eleven would be left alone in the world. Without the Son they would need protection from people and circumstances that could cause unbelief and disunity among them. They would also need protection from human and supernatural enemies who would oppose their efforts to declare the Good News to the lost. So Jesus petitioned His Father to guard His disciples by the "power of [His] name" (vs. 11).

Jesus' reference to God as the "Holy Father" is striking because a similar statement is not recorded anywhere else in the Gospels (though see 1 Pet. 1:15-16; Rev. 4:8; 6:10). Evidently, Jesus was focused on God's righteousness when He asked His Father to use His supreme power and authority to protect the disciples (John 17:25). Indeed, no form of evil could stand in the presence of God's upright character, as denoted by His sacred name. Jesus, however, was not implying that God's name is a magic formula that people can use to wield supernatural power. Rather, God's name reveals His awesome splendor, which is epitomized by righteousness, truth, and love. The Father shared all these attributes with the Son (as well as the Spirit).

Just as the three Persons of the Trinity were united in thought and purpose, so too Jesus prayed that His disciples would be characterized by such unity (vs. 11). Indeed, the primary purpose of God's protection of Jesus' disciples was the preservation of their unity, which they had as regenerate members of Christ's spiritual body (John 15:4-5; 1 Cor. 12:12-13). While Jesus was with His disciples, He preserved them as a unified group and guarded them from outside threats (John 10:28-29). The supernatural power behind the name the Father had given the Son enabled Him to keep His disciples from denying Him (17:12). Only one of them was lost.

Early in the evening, before much of Jesus' farewell discourse, Judas Iscariot had left the upper room (13:21-30). Now Jesus described Judas as the disciple who had been lost (17:12). Evidently, the remaining eleven could not figure out who was the "one doomed to destruction." Yet Jesus knew that at that very moment Judas was betraying Him for 30 silver coins (Matt. 26:14-16; Mark 14:10-11; Luke 22:3-6). As a consequence of this wicked act, which Scripture had foretold, Judas was headed for eternal ruin. While Jesus did not state the Old Testament passages He had in mind, Psalm 41:9 is a likely candidate (John 13:18). The fulfillment of biblical prophecy does not mean that the Father forced Judas to betray the Son, especially since Judas decided to do this evil deed on his own. That said, God used Judas' treachery to accomplish His greater redemptive plan.

D. Setting Apart the Disciples as Holy: vss. 13-19

"I am coming to you now, but I say these things while I am still in the world, so that they may have the full measure of my joy within them. I have given them your word and the world has hated them, for they are not of the world any more than I am of the world. My prayer is not that you take them out of the world but that you protect them from the evil one. They are not of the world, even as I am not of it. Sanctify them by the truth; your word is truth. As you sent me into the world, I have sent them into the world. For them I sanctify myself, that they too may be truly sanctified."

Jesus continued to pray aloud in the presence of the Eleven so that they might be completely filled with His "joy" (John 17:13). In the brief time left before the Son returned to the Father, He wanted to encourage the Eleven with His final words, which would always be a source of delight for them. It was important for Jesus to give His disciples His joy because they would bear the brunt of the world's displeasure.

Since Jesus had given His followers God's Word—that is, His full revelatory message—the "world" (vs. 14) hated them (15:18-25). Though Jesus' disciples did not belong to the world, the Son did not ask the Father to deliver the Eleven "out of the world" (17:15). They had a mission to fulfill, and they could not accomplish it if they were removed from the earth. Nevertheless, Jesus did pray for the protection of His disciples from the "evil one." Jesus did not pray that the Eleven be freed from hardship and persecution, but that they would not fall under the corrupting influence of Satan's control. Once more, Jesus emphasized in His parting prayer that He and His disciples did not belong to the "world" (vs. 16). While the Eleven listened, they could not miss the implication of Jesus' statement. They had come to learn that unsaved humanity neither owned nor controlled the Savior. Likewise, the pagan world system had no legitimate claim on His followers.

Previously, in verse 11, Jesus referred to God as the "Holy Father." Now in verse 17, the Son asked the Father to "sanctify" the disciples through the "truth," which Jesus equated with divine revelation, including His own teachings. The Greek verb rendered "sanctify" means to "dedicate" or "set apart." In brief, Jesus asked His Father to use the truth of His Word to separate the disciples from evil and consecrate them for a life of service. Just as the Father had appointed the Son to perform His earthly ministry (3:17; 10:36), so too Jesus commissioned His disciples to proclaim His message of redemption throughout the earth. To ensure their success, Jesus consecrated Himself by dying on the cross (17:19; see also 1:29, 36; 10:17-18; 11:49-52; 18:11; 19:30). Jesus did not mean He had to make Himself more pure. Instead, He was affirming His commitment to finish the Father's plan of redemption so that believers could be pardoned, justified, and made holy (Rom. 4:25; 1 Cor. 1:2).

II. JESUS' PRAYER FOR ALL BELIEVERS: JOHN 17:20-21

A. Expressing Concern for Future Believers: vs. 20

"My prayer is not for them alone. I pray also for those who will believe in me through their message."

The scope of Jesus' farewell prayer broadened as He focused on those who would come to faith as a result of the Good News the Eleven proclaimed (John 17:20). Previously, Jesus had spoken about the "message" He had taught His disciples, but now He referred to the truth they would herald to the lost (Matt. 28:18-20; Mark 16:15-16; Luke 24:45-47; Acts 1:8). So, Jesus' petitions in John 17:20-26 were for all future believers, including those who follow Jesus now.

B. Seeking a Unified Faith Community: vs. 21

"That all of them may be one, Father, just as you are in me and I am in you. May they also be in us so that the world may believe that you have sent me."

Jesus' prayer for believers today is that we be unified in our faith. He prayed that our unity be like the oneness that He has with the Father and the Spirit (John 17:21). Jesus was not calling for all believers to be the same in every way, just as the three Persons of the Trinity are not identical. Instead, Jesus was praying that all believers would bond together in mutual love while preserving our distinctiveness. Furthermore, Jesus prayed that as the world sees believers dependent upon God, many would come to believe that the Father did in fact send the Son to earth to die for their sins. They would recognize that God loves them just as much as He loves His Son (3:16).

Jesus also spoke about the "glory" (17:22) He had given His disciples and that the Father had given the Son. Jesus was apparently referring to His earthly mission, which would eventually lead to His death at Calvary. The path of the cross does not end in worldly honor, but in the recognition that only God can give. Jesus mediated this divine glory to His disciples so they would be unified in the same way the Father, the Son, and the Spirit were one. In fact, Jesus' holy presence indwells believers even as the Father indwelled the Son. "Complete unity" (vs. 23) among believers shows the world that the Father actually sent the Son and that the Father loves the lost just as much as He loves the Son.

Discussion Questions

1. In what ways did Jesus make the Father known to the disciples?
2. Why did Jesus pray that the Father would protect the disciples?
3. What role does God's Word have in sanctifying believers?
4. Why is it important to emphasize that God's Word is truth?
5. Why did Jesus stress the importance of believers being unified?

Contemporary Application

In Jesus' prayer toward the end of His farewell meal, He expressed His concern for each of His followers. This included His desire that they all be united. Many surveys have shown that those who are not saved reject Christianity because they see both the global church (as a whole) and local congregations (in particular) as nothing but quarreling, bickering people.

The Christian writer Charles H. Brent once said, "The world is too strong for a divided church." That is one reason why Jesus prayed for all His followers to be united. It is also why Jesus wanted us to know that He prayed for oneness among believers. The Savior knew that we must put aside our petty differences lest the world overwhelm us. Moreover, He wants us to pray and work daily for harmony within His spiritual body.

It would be incorrect to conclude from Jesus' prayer that all Christians should be replicas of one another. Jesus would not have us disregard our distinctive traditions, nor have us all worship and serve Him in exactly the same manner. As long as belief in Jesus as our Lord and Savior defines who we are, we can express our devotion and service to Him according to our uniqueness.

Even though we are individuals, we can still remain spiritually united in the Son. A football team has members with distinctive responsibilities and roles. Unless they exhibit teamwork as they play, their opponents will completely defeat them. Likewise, when Jesus' followers are united in the "fellowship of the Holy Spirit" (2 Cor. 13:14), the Son will lead them to certain victory over the challenges they face daily.

Jesus Intercedes for Us

Scripture

Background Scripture: *Hebrews 4:14–5:10*
Scripture Lesson: *Hebrews 4:14–5:10*
Key Verse: *We do not have a high priest who is unable to
sympathize with our weaknesses, but we have one who has
been tempted in every way, just as we are—yet was without
sin.* Hebrews 4:15.
Scripture Lesson for Children: *Hebrews 4:14–5:10*
Key Verse for Children: *[Jesus] offered up prayers.*
Hebrews 5:7.

Lesson Aim

To find consolation in Jesus as our great High Priest.

Lesson Setting

Time: Before A.D. 70
Place: Possibly Rome

Lesson Outline

Jesus Intercedes for Us
  I. Our Compassionate High Priest: Hebrews 4:14-16
      A. *The Exhortation: vs. 14*
      B. *The Basis for the Exhortation: vss. 15-16*
  II. Specific Qualifications for High Priesthood:
      Hebrews 5:1-4
      A. *Divinely Appointed: vs. 1*
      B. *Empathetic with Others: vss. 2-3*
      C. *Divinely Called: vs. 4*
  III. Jesus' Qualifications for High Priesthood:
      Hebrews 5:5-10
      A. *Divinely Chosen: vss. 5-6*
      B. *Characterized by Reverence and Piety: vs. 7*
      C. *Designated in the Line of Melchizedek: vss. 8-10*

Introduction for Adults

Topic: *Someone's on My Side*

To approach God boldly is not to approach Him flippantly. Some people are so casual with God that they take His name in vain. In contrast, some people are so unfamiliar with God that they find it hard to pray to Him.

Christians enjoy confidence before the Father because they know the Son has opened the door to fellowship with Him (Heb. 4:16). God is holy, yet He gave His Son to save us from judgment and death. The only way we can approach the Father without fear is through His Son. In fact, no one comes to the Father except through His Son (John 14:6).

We can pray and worship with boldness because Jesus sits at the Father's right hand. Jesus intercedes for us as our merciful and faithful High Priest. Because He is our heavenly representative, we are freed to worship God with joy.

Introduction for Youth

Topic: *Jesus Cares about Me*

Brian's case was fairly typical. His parents divorced, and he lived with his father, who had a hard time building a good relationship with him. Brian got into trouble at school. He developed emotional problems and was hospitalized. To put it simply, Brian could not fill the vacuum in his life caused by a broken family.

Many adolescents rightly ask, "Who cares for me?" They lack strong family ties. They don't have any good friends. They wander fruitlessly from one activity to another and often get into deep trouble.

Without sounding sanctimonious, we should try to introduce teens like Brian to Jesus. In order to do so, we must enjoy a vibrant faith ourselves. We must be able to explain how Jesus makes a difference as our "great high priest" (Heb. 4:14), even when no one else seems to care.

Concepts for Children

Topic: *What a Gift!*

1. Like us, Jesus experienced pain and sadness.
2. In times of difficulty, Jesus prayed to God.
3. Jesus obeyed God, even when life seemed hard.
4. Jesus can help us when we feel afraid, weak, or hurt.
5. Jesus can give us the strength we need to obey God.

Lesson Commentary

I. OUR COMPASSIONATE HIGH PRIEST: HEBREWS 4:14-16

A. The Exhortation: vs. 14

Therefore, since we have a great high priest who has gone through the heavens, Jesus the Son of God, let us hold firmly to the faith we profess.

The Letter to the Hebrews is a pep talk to a group of professing Christians who had evidently lost their initial enthusiasm for the Christian faith. The recipients of the letter had apparently failed to progress in spiritual understanding and discernment. They seemed to be growing more discouraged and apathetic. They had even begun to question whether they should remain committed Christians or revert to their old religious ways and traditions. To help his readers make the right choice, the author of Hebrews pointed to Jesus as the perfect revelation of God. In essence, the author encouraged his readers to make the best choice—to abide in the eternal salvation of the Lord Jesus, even if it has trials and tribulations, rather than to renounce what is true.

In 4:12-13, the writer stressed that everything we think, say, and do is completely exposed to God. This sobering truth emphasizes our need for a sympathetic High Priest, one who can meet our deepest needs. As was noted in lesson 10 from the last quarter, from the time the Lord gave the law to Moses until the time of Jesus' death and resurrection, believers had to go through priests to have access to God. If someone needed atonement for sin, only a priest could offer a sacrifice in that person's behalf. If someone wanted to sacrifice an animal to God, the priest had to offer it on the altar. Also, once a year, on the day of Atonement, the high priest entered the most holy place, stood before the ark of the covenant, and expiated the sins of God's people. To say the least, this was a limited and imperfect system.

The need for a priesthood is rooted in people's consciousness of sin. Those whose hearts and lives had been stained by transgression could not enter the presence of a holy God. They needed a mediator, a go-between, a representative—someone who could approach God with sacrifices and prayers on their behalf. The priest was authorized to come before God and intercede on behalf of the people. Prior to Moses' receiving the law at Sinai, the office of priest was filled by the family patriarch or the head of the tribe. For instance, Abraham, Isaac, and Jacob built altars, offered sacrifices, and consecrated themselves and their households.

Once the Israelites had gained independence from Egypt, God gave laws governing every aspect of life. His laws relating to worship defined the place, the forms, and the leaders (priests) of Hebrew worship. The priests were to be from among Aaron's descendants and were to be free of physical defects. Priests were required to dress in designated attire and to live in strict obedience to the law.

Besides upholding the civil and religious codes that applied to all Israelites, they had to execute those laws applying to their vocation as priests.

The high priest was at the top of this religious hierarchy. While in general priests represented the people before God, the high priest was their supreme representative. He was uniquely consecrated to God through the anointing of his head with sacred oil (Lev. 8:12; 21:10; Ps. 133:2). Other priests had oil sprinkled only on their garments, but the high priest became the anointed representative of the people before God.

In the Letter to the Hebrews, Jesus is presented as the believers' great High Priest. Perhaps 4:14 might be regarded as the thesis statement of the entire epistle. Indeed, there is no other strong and straightforward declaration about Jesus' priesthood in the rest of Scripture. The author had touched on Jesus as our High Priest in 2:17 and 3:1, but at this point in the letter, the topic becomes a controlling concept. By calling Jesus a "great high priest" (4:14), the writer implied Jesus' superiority to all the generations of Jewish high priests.

Though the high priests were the only ones permitted to pass beyond the final curtain of the tabernacle or temple into the most holy place, Jesus has passed through the heavenly regions and taken His lawful place at the right hand of the Father. Many think this is a reference to Jesus' ascension into heaven. The Hebrews were beginning to lack spiritual steadfastness. The writer thus urged them to unyieldingly embrace their faith in "the Son of God." As was noted in lesson 4, this significant biblical title for Jesus highlights the special and intimate relationship that exists between the first and second persons of the Trinity (Matt. 16:16; Luke 1:35). "Son of God" indicates that Jesus is to be identified with the Father and considered fully and absolutely equal to Him (and the Spirit; see John 5:18; 10:30, 36).

B. The Basis for the Exhortation: vss. 15-16

For we do not have a high priest who is unable to sympathize with our weaknesses, but we have one who has been tempted in every way, just as we are—yet was without sin. Let us then approach the throne of grace with confidence, so that we may receive mercy and find grace to help us in our time of need.

A key reason we, as believers, can put our trust in Jesus is that He can "sympathize with our weaknesses" (Heb. 4:15). He became one of us and experienced life just as we do. In fact, Jesus faced all the sorts of temptations we do. But unlike us, our High Priest remained "without sin" (John 7:18; 8:46; 1 Pet. 1:19; 2:22; 1 John 3:5). Some might think that because Jesus never sinned, He cannot really empathize with our weaknesses. But only a person who has never sinned has experienced and resisted the full force of temptation. Unlike the rest of sinful humanity, Jesus never yielded to the enticements He experienced.

As one who lived through trials and tribulations on this earth, Jesus is able to understand what believers endure. The innocent one, rather than turning haughtily away from transgressors, invites such people to "approach" His

Father's "throne of grace" (Heb. 4:16). They can do so with confidence, not as a result of what they have achieved, but in what the Lord Jesus has accomplished for them. His ability to understand us, His proximity to the Father, and Jesus' reconciling act on the cross embolden believers to draw near in their time of need to "receive mercy and find grace to help."

The writer's exhortation to persevere in the pilgrimage of faith is grounded in his argument. He maintained that the Old Testament itself testified to the imperfection of the covenant at Sinai and its sacrificial system. This, in turn, pointed ahead to a new High Priest—Jesus Christ. The Messiah is better than the mediators, sanctuary, and sacrifices of the old order. In association with Jesus, there is greater grace and glory. Also, He is the guarantee of this better covenant bond, for He links believers inseparably with the Lord of grace.

II. SPECIFIC QUALIFICATIONS FOR HIGH PRIESTHOOD: HEBREWS 5:1-4

A. Divinely Appointed: vs. 1

Every high priest is selected from among men and is appointed to represent them in matters related to God, to offer gifts and sacrifices for sins.

Having stressed Jesus' ability to serve as our Redeemer and Advocate, the writer of Hebrews next discussed the nature of the high-priestly office in ancient Israel. He noted that the nation's religious leaders chose a high priest from a pool of qualified men (namely, the descendants of Aaron) and appointed him to that office (5:1). This means that no person could lobby to be a priest. The eligibility for priestly service was already settled by God's choosing (vs. 4). The high priest represented his fellow Israelites in matters pertaining to God. Specifically, he offered "gifts" (vs. 1; which were voluntary) and "sacrifices" (which were required) for their sins.

B. Empathetic with Others: vss. 2-3

He is able to deal gently with those who are ignorant and are going astray, since he himself is subject to weakness. This is why he has to offer sacrifices for his own sins, as well as for the sins of the people.

The author of Hebrews noted that the priests had weaknesses of their own. For this reason, they could understand the frailty of the ones they were representing, offer kindly direction to the ignorant, and gently admonish the wayward (5:2). Also, a priest's sinful nature required him to offer sacrifices to atone for his own misdeeds as well as for those of the people he represented (vs. 3).

C. Divinely Called: vs. 4

No one takes this honor upon himself; he must be called by God, just as Aaron was.

Hebrews 5:4 stresses that the high-priestly office was a sacred duty, and it was an honor to serve in this role. Consequently, to seize control of this office would be a sign of disrespect for God, who had graciously instituted it. The Bible records several instances in which disaster occurred when someone tried to perform high-priestly duties without authorization.

The author of Hebrews noted that in addition to being descended from Aaron, the high priests were to be free of physical defects. As we noted earlier, God established the priesthood in Israel as a way of giving His people access to Him. The Lord used the institution of the priesthood to teach His people that they needed a mediator between themselves and Him. This prepared God's people for Jesus, who would reconcile them to the Lord (Rom. 5:10-11; 1 Tim. 2:5).

III. JESUS' QUALIFICATIONS FOR HIGH PRIESTHOOD: HEBREWS 5:5-10

A. Divinely Chosen: vss. 5-6

So Christ also did not take upon himself the glory of becoming a high priest. But God said to him, "You are my Son; today I have become your Father." And he says in another place, "You are a priest forever, in the order of Melchizedek."

The writer of Hebrews explained that Jesus did not take it upon Himself to assume the high priesthood, but rather was called to the office by God (5:5). To illustrate this, the author of the epistle first quoted Psalm 2:7. The idea is that the Father declared Jesus to be His Son when He raised Him from the dead (Acts 13:30; Rom. 1:4). Consequently, only the Son has a right to minister as High Priest in heaven. The writer of Hebrews then quoted from Psalm 110:4 to emphasize that the Father appointed His Son to a unique high-priestly office. Jesus' priesthood was not in the Aaronic line. He is a High Priest forever in "the order of Melchizedek" (Heb. 5:6). Melchizedek foreshadows the Messiah.

Aside from Psalm 110:4, Genesis 14:17–20 is the most extensive passage in the Old Testament concerning Melchizedek. The writer of Hebrews summarized the biblical data by noting that Melchizedek was the monarch who ruled over the city-state of Salem (later Jerusalem). In addition, he ministered as a "priest of God Most High" (Heb. 7:1). The key factor is that Melchizedek was both a king and priest. Here was an individual outside the boundaries of God's revelation to Israel and yet he worshiped the Lord.

The author recounted how Melchizedek met with Abraham (probably before 2000 B.C.) when the patriarch was returning from his victory over the kings of Elam, Goiim, Shinar, and Ellasar. During their meeting, Mechizedek blessed Abraham. The patriarch, from whom God promised to build the nation of Israel, responded by presenting Melchizedek with a tenth of the spoils he had taken in his victory over the four kings (vs. 2). In ancient times, the person who collected the tithe was considered to be greater than the one who presented it. Also, the person who blessed was thought to be greater than the one who received the blessings (vss. 4-7). The implication is that Melchizedek was higher in rank than Abraham, along with all his descendants, including Levi and the priesthood originating from him (vss. 8-10).

The recipient of Abraham's gift was both a "king of righteousness" (vs. 2) and "peace." As it stands, there is no record in Scripture of Melchizedek's parents and ancestors. It is almost as if the life and priesthood of this person had no beginning or ending. In these ways, he prefigured the "Son of God" (vs. 3). Based on the Greek phrase rendered "without father or mother," there is the possibility of incorrectly concluding that Melchizedek was a preincarnate appearance of the Messiah. But this supposition misunderstands the actual intent of the author of Hebrews. He was making a sophisticated, nuanced comparison between Melchizedek and the Lord Jesus. For instance, like Melchizedek, there was no record of the Messiah's priesthood beginning or ending. Yet, unlike Melchizedek, it was because there really is no beginning or ending to Jesus' high-priestly ministry. The implication is that our King-Priest according to the royal "order of Melchizedek" (vs. 17) was superior to all Levitical priests.

B. Characterized by Reverence and Piety: vs. 7

During the days of Jesus' life on earth, he offered up prayers and petitions with loud cries and tears to the one who could save him from death, and he was heard because of his reverent submission.

In Hebrews 5:7, the writer directed his readers' attention to the time in the Garden of Gethesemane when Jesus anguished over the prospect of having to die on the cross (Matt. 26:36-44; Mark 14:32-40; Luke 22:39-44). With loud cries and tears, Jesus appealed to the One who could deliver Him from the clutches of death. Because Jesus honored and obeyed the Lord, God the Father answered the Son's request by raising Him from the dead (Rom. 1:4).

C. Designated in the Line of Melchizedek: vss. 8-10

Although he was a son, he learned obedience from what he suffered and, once made perfect, he became the source of eternal salvation for all who obey him and was designated by God to be high priest in the order of Melchizedek.

The author, in Hebrews 5:8, may have been alluding to Jesus' temptation in the desert as well as to the crucifixion when he wrote about Jesus' afflictions. In the process of His suffering, Jesus "learned obedience." This does not mean Jesus turned from disobedience to obedience. Instead, it means that He obeyed God in a way that He had never done before, that is, as a human being. Verse 9 says that Jesus was "made perfect." This does not mean that Jesus was ever morally imperfect. The writer was stressing that Jesus' human experience entered a new realm of fullness and completion as a result of overcoming temptations and dying on the cross.

Whereas Aaron and his successors offered many sacrifices that could never really atone for sin, Jesus offered one perfect sacrifice—Himself—to expiate transgressions forever. Also, whereas the Aaronic priests served for a limited time, Jesus' priesthood abides forever (7:23-28). Though the Jewish religion with its Aaronic priesthood might have looked appealing to the initial recipients of the author's epistle, the former paled in comparison to Jesus and His eternal, heavenly priesthood. Jesus' life of learned obedience and His victory over sin offset the disobedience of Adam (Rom. 5:19). That is why Jesus could become the source of "eternal salvation" (Heb. 5:9) for all who "obey him." Stated another way, Jesus lives forever to intercede as the believer's "high priest" (vs. 10).

Discussion Questions

1. How does Jesus demonstrate that He is our great High Priest?
2. How is it possible for Jesus to identify with our struggles when He never succumbed to temptation?
3. Why did God establish the priesthood in Israel?
4. How did God's mercy and grace help you in your relationships this past week?
5. What is the best way to respond when you recognize your need for God's mercy and grace?

Contemporary Application

Does Jesus really care? This is a question that frequently crosses our minds when we face tough times. The devil immediately sows seeds of doubt, suggesting that, if Jesus really loved us, we would not be going through a difficult experience. Intellectually, we know Jesus cares, but it is difficult to allow that fact to override our emotional pain, doubts, and fears. That's one reason why the teaching about Jesus as our High Priest is so important and valuable.

When we're down, we can tell Jesus how we feel and that we know He experienced what we are called to endure. Because He suffered as one of us in His humanity, we know we are not alone. He has gone before us, and He wants us to come to His Father's heavenly throne for help. We find great encouragement for ourselves and others when we ask Jesus to show us what it means to obey in the midst of suffering. And we have a significant message of hope to those who have never known Jesus as their High Priest.

Our confidence to approach God's throne is not based on any merit of our own. We have access to the Father because of what the Son, our great High Priest, has already done at Calvary. We can have confidence in our Christian life because we have a Savior who understands us and takes an active interest in our well-being. Most important, He's here for us right now.

Pray for One Another

Scripture

Background Scripture: *James 5*
Scripture Lesson: *James 5:13-20*
Key Verse: *Confess your sins to each other and pray for each
other so that you may be healed. The prayer of a righteous man
is powerful and effective.* James 5:16.
Scripture Lesson for Children: *James 5:13-18*
Key Verse for Children: *Pray for each other.* James 5:16.

Lesson Aim

To affirm the power of prayer.

Lesson Setting

Time: The early 60s of the first century A.D.
Place: Jerusalem

Lesson Outline

Pray for One Another

I. Praying in All of Life's Circumstances:
James 5:13-18
A. *Praying in Times of Joy and Suffering: vs. 13*
B. *Praying in Times of Illness: vss. 14-15*
C. *Praying Earnestly and Effectively: vss. 16-18*

II. Restoring Wandering Believers: James 5:19-20
A. *Wandering from the Faith: vs. 19*
B. *Bringing Back the Wanderer: vs. 20*

Introduction for Adults

Topic: *Powerful and Effective Living*

During Haddon Robinson's tenure as president of Denver Seminary, lawsuits were brought against the school. Because he was named in one of the suits, Robinson had to give a deposition. For two days, prosecutors relentlessly grilled him as they questioned his motives and tried to cast everything he said in a negative light.

Robinson not only faced legal problems, but he also had to deal with attacks against his reputation. For example, a disgruntled former employee of the seminary spread false statements about Robinson throughout the community. Robinson and his wife responded to the devastating emotional pain they experienced by bathing their circumstance in prayer (something enjoined in James 5:13).

Looking back on this trying ordeal, Robinson wrote, "If anything good for me came out of this painful time, it was the overwhelming sense of my need of God. I felt completely vulnerable. Although I was not guilty of any legal negligence or failure, I felt more in need of grace than ever."

Introduction for Youth

Topic: *Help, I'm in Trouble!*

Oswald Chambers (1874–1917) was a Scottish minister whose teachings on the life of faith have endured to this day. He observed that prayer is hard work. "There is nothing thrilling about a laboring man's work but it is the laboring man who makes the conceptions of the genius possible; and it is the laboring saint who makes the conceptions of the Master possible. You labor at prayer and results happen all the time from His standpoint. What an astonishment it will be to find, when the veil is lifted, the souls that have been reaped by you, simply because you had been in the habit of taking your orders from Jesus Christ."

As God did with Chambers, He also upholds us during joyful and sad times in our lives (Jas. 5:13). As we invest energy and effort on our knees in prayer, the Lord gives us the strength to remain faithful to the work He has called us to do (vs. 16).

Concepts for Children

Topic: *Giving and Receiving*

1. We can pray to God when we are sad.
2. We can sing praise to God to express our joy.
3. God wants us to pray for those who are sick.
4. God might heal the sick because we prayed for them.
5. When we have done something wrong to others, we need to ask God to forgive us and ask the person to forgive us too.

Lesson Commentary

I. PRAYING IN ALL OF LIFE'S CIRCUMSTANCES: JAMES 5:13-18

A. Praying in Times of Joy and Suffering: vs. 13

Is any one of you in trouble? He should pray. Is anyone happy? Let him sing songs of praise.

James 5 opens with a volley of accusations aimed at wealthy people who were morally bankrupt. Though successful in their economic pursuits, they were indicted for their disregard for God's righteous principles. In the end, rather than enjoying their riches, the affluent would be condemned by their wealth. In the same way James addressed the boasting merchants in 4:13-16, the author called on the self-indulgent rich to listen attentively (5:1).

While the prosperous were usually envied for their abundant assets, James had only contempt for their status and condemnation for their failure to be good stewards of what God had entrusted to them. "Cry your eyes out," he in effect told them, for the judgment of their ill-gotten gain was going to come down upon them. This is not a call to repentance as we saw in 4:9. Rather, it is an intense emotional reaction to the coming judgment. The author's comments resemble the Old Testament prophets' condemnation of the immorally rich (Isa. 23; Ezek. 27).

Unlike eternal treasures, which can be stored in heaven, earthly wealth is transient (1 Tim. 6:17). For instance, hoarded possessions rot, and fancy clothes make fine meals for moths (Jas. 5:2; see also Matt. 6:19-21). Gold and silver are regarded throughout the world as standards of real, tangible wealth. Technically speaking, these metals cannot rust or even corrode. Perhaps James 5:3 uses the image of corroding gold and silver as a metaphor to emphasize the eternal worthlessness of temporal opulence.

Wealthy figures in the Bible, such as Abraham and Job, show that it is possible to be materially rich and still maintain a sense of dependence upon God. In the Letter of James, the condemnation of the affluent was directed toward the way in which some gained their fortune and then spent it entirely on themselves. The rich whom the author addressed not only exploited the poor, but refused to pay them as well (vs. 4). The prophets were clear on the matter of the timely payment of wages and equitable treatment of the poor (Amos 8:4-7; Mal. 3:5). The cries of these exploited workers had reached the all-powerful Lord of heaven's armies, so retribution was on its way.

In their quest for riches, the wealthy often took the poor to court on trumped-up charges in order to rob them of what little they had (Jas. 2:6). With no influence or connections, the poor were unable to resist. James charged the rich oppressors of the poor with living in ease at the expense of others. By doing this in excess, the wicked were unknowingly preparing themselves like fattened animals for the slaughter (5:5). The author's initial Jewish readers would have known very well the fate of fattened animals—the altar of sacrifice. This was a fitting end for people who brought unjust condemnation and sometimes death on those too powerless to defend themselves (vs. 6).

Having dealt with the wicked rich, the author turned his attention to the persecuted poor. While he chastised the wealthy, he offered impoverished believers words of consolation. "Be patient" (vs. 7), James told them, until the Lord Jesus' return. The poor had suffered all manner of economic and social injustice. When the Savior came back, however, these wrongs would be addressed. The righteous Judge would overturn and reverse all inequitable judgments against His followers. As an illustration of patience, James offered the example of farmers. In order to have a successful harvest, it was essential for them to patiently wait for both the autumn rains at planting time and the spring rains as crops were maturing. They had no control over these rains, but showers would come in God's good time and produce a crop.

In light of the Lord's impending return, James admonished harshly treated believers to wait patiently, strengthen their hearts, and not seek retribution when wronged (vs. 8). While revenge might seem to promise relief from the pain of injustice, it only deepens the sense of emptiness, for it is never satisfying. At the same time, these Christians were also to stop grumbling among themselves or risk facing God's judgment. When dealing with an abusive person who is more powerful than ourselves, it is easy to vent our frustration on people who have done nothing to us. Because the Judge (the Lord Jesus) can return at any moment, we should be especially careful how we speak to one another (vs. 9).

Next, James turned to the Old Testament prophets as an example of patience in times of adversity (vs. 10). As they spoke out on God's behalf, they were often persecuted and insulted. Many lost their lives. James took it for granted that his readers knew that those who persevered in trials would be blessed (vs. 11). As a classic example of perseverance, the author cited Job. This is the only mention of this Old Testament luminary by name in the New Testament (though Paul quotes from the Book of Job in 1 Corinthians 3:19). The point of James using Job's account as an illustration was to remind believers that God has a purpose He wishes to accomplish in every trial and tribulation—even though His people might not understand His purpose.

The author warned his readers not to make frivolous oaths (Jas. 5:12). Not all pledges are necessarily forbidden by this verse. Only vows made lightly or in a blasphemous and profane way are forbidden. Many people invoke flippant oaths in an attempt to increase their credibility. Admittedly, there are examples of the use of oaths in Scripture to validate the truth of one's claim (Exod. 22:11; Matt. 26:63-64; Rom. 1:9). But the point in James 5:12 is that if a person trusts the Lord, there is no need for invoking any type of oath by making reference to heaven (the throne room of God), earth (the footstool of His feet; see Isa. 66:1), or any other aspect of creation. When a person appealed to any of these entities while making an oath, they became as binding as if the individual had invoked the name of the Lord. If a person's word is truthful and honest, then a simple yes or no (which reflects unambiguous language) should be all that is necessary. James reflected the teaching of Jesus in this matter (Matt. 5:33-37). Ignoring this command would result in the condemnation of the flippant oath taker.

James concluded his letter with an emphasis on prayer. Prayer is the most potent action a believer can take in time of trouble. Prayer ought to be a Christian's reflexive response to all of life's problems—accompanied with praise to God for His bountiful gifts. The author employed a series of questions as springboards for conveying some important principles of prayer to his readers. The Greek verb rendered "trouble" (Jas. 5:13) in the first question refers to physical pain, hardship, or distress that comes from any source. The author used the same word in verse 10 when describing the trials of the prophets. The matter of offering songs of praise (a type of prayer) in response to happiness is easy to understand. The difficulty, however, comes in times of sickness.

B. Praying in Times of Illness: vss. 14-15

Is any one of you sick? He should call the elders of the church to pray over him and anoint him with oil in the name of the Lord. And the prayer offered in faith will make the sick person well; the Lord will raise him up. If he has sinned, he will be forgiven.

If a Christian is ill, God should be the first healer to whom he or she turns. It is also a faith action to turn to other members of the church body. The elders should be available for counsel and comfort and be willing to help the afflicted in any way possible (Jas. 5:14). Elders were leaders in the early church. They are first mentioned in Acts 11:30 as the recognized leaders of local congregations (1 Tim. 3:1-7; 5:17; Titus 1:6-9). Once called, the elders were to pray over the sick and anoint them with oil in the Lord's name. The oil symbolized the presence of God (Ps. 23:5). But in Bible times, it was also thought to contain some medicinal properties (Luke 10:34).

Since olive trees, which grew even in rocky places, produced much oil, olive oil came to be regarded as a special gift from God. This oil was also associated with the outpouring of God's Spirit. Anointing with oil customarily accompanied the consecration of individuals to God's service. It was used to dedicate prophets (1 Kings 19:16), priests (Lev. 8:12), and kings (1 Sam. 16:13; 1 Kings 1:34). The use of oil for healing is seen in Jesus' parable of the good Samaritan. As we will learn in lesson 10, the Samaritan first bound the wounds of the man who had been mugged and then poured in oil and wine (Luke 10:34). Apparently, it was for the same purpose that the 12 disciples took oil for healing when Jesus sent them out two by two on a ministry mission (Mark 6:13).

James 5:15 says that if the elders had faith when they prayed for the sick, they would get well. In fact, the Lord would restore the afflicted to health. "Faith" primarily refers to a person's belief or trust in God. The term is also used in the New Testament to refer to the body of truths held by followers of Christ. This second use became increasingly prevalent as church leaders and scholars defended the truths of the faith against the attacks of false teachers. As James made clear in his epistle, genuine faith is evidenced by more than mere words. It leads to a transformed life in which the believer reaches out with the Savior's love to others in need.

Some have understood verse 15 to teach that complete physical health is always assured through prayer. Whenever illness strikes, the Christian should pray in faith as a guarantee for healing. If illness persists (in this view), then the prayer must not have been offered in genuine faith. Others see the verse as teaching cooperation between prayer and medicine (the anointing with oil), between God and a physician. According to this view, just prayer or just medicine alone is less than a full prescription for renewed health. Together they are a powerful remedy for serious illness.

An important question concerns what is meant by the Greek verb rendered "sick." In verse 14, the term denotes a state of incapacity or weakness and is used in the New Testament for physical illness as well as for weakness of faith or conscience (Acts 20:35; Rom. 6:19; 14:1; 1 Cor. 8:9-12). So, James could have meant either sicknesses of the body or the spirit. This reminds us that there are times when physical illness might have a spiritual cause, namely, sin. The remark in James 5:15 about forgiveness of sin might be a reference to an illness brought on by personal sin in the believer's life. In this case, the writer assured the sick that the prayer of faith would result in forgiveness and spiritual restoration. Of course, the use of the word "if" implies that sometimes illness is not the result of personal sin. Irrespective of the details, God is not limited as to the methods He might employ in restoring health to ill believers. Also, with regard to prayer, God answers only according to His will. Sometimes God's will does not include physical healing (2 Cor. 12:7-9).

C. Praying Earnestly and Effectively: vss. 16-18

Therefore confess your sins to each other and pray for each other so that you may be healed. The prayer of a righteous man is powerful and effective. Elijah was a man just like us. He prayed earnestly that it would not rain, and it did not rain on the land for three and a half years. Again he prayed, and the heavens gave rain, and the earth produced its crops.

All of us need some kind of healing, whether physical, spiritual, or emotional, and we should be able to turn to other believers for help. This includes confessing our sins to each other, as well as praying for each other (Jas. 5:16). The acknowledgment of sins among believers helps to promote wellness and wholeness of individuals and relationships. In particular, believers draw their fellow Christians toward a deeper, more mature walk with the Savior. Members of the community of faith also deepen their commitment to one another in the bonds of Christian love. This verse does not signify a call for indiscriminate airing of a believer's every shortcoming. The Holy Spirit should always be given complete charge over the matter of conviction and confession of sin. He will lead the believer in the knowledge of which sins to confess in private prayer and which to confess in the company of other believers.

In any case, whether public or private, one truth is clear, namely, that prayer is a powerful and effective means of accomplishing the will of God. The Lord especially uses the earnest prayer of righteous believers (those who are characterized by virtue and integrity) to produce wonderful results in the lives of believers. As was his practice, James offered an illustration to support his point. This time it was Elijah, an Old Testament prophet with the same human frailties that we have. This person, who was just like us, prayed earnestly that no rain would fall, and none fell for three and a half years (vs. 17; see also Luke 4:25). Then, when he prayed again, rain fell from the skies and made the crops grow (Jas. 5:18; see also 1 Kings 17:1; 18:41-46). Because prayer is our most powerful tool, it should be our first option in responding to a crisis, not a last resort. It only makes sense to rely on God's power, which is infinitely greater than our own.

II. RESTORING WANDERING BELIEVERS: JAMES 5:19-20

A. Wandering from the Faith: vs. 19

My brothers, if one of you should wander from the truth and someone should bring him back.

The author's final appeal to his readers concerned individuals who had wandered from the way of truth. Some think James 5:19 refers to those who claimed to be Christians but whose faith was spurious (Heb. 6:4-6; 2 Pet. 2:20-22). Others think James 5:19 is dealing with genuine believers who have strayed into sinful patterns. In either case, when anyone belonging to a congregation wanders from the path of moral rectitude, it is the duty of God's people to seek out the wayward and bring them back into the fellowship—through prayer, counseling, friendship, or whatever it takes. When sinners are turned back from their error-prone ways, it means they have been rescued from the path of destruction.

B. Bringing Back the Wanderer: vs. 20

Remember this: Whoever turns a sinner from the error of his way will save him from death and cover over a multitude of sins.

For some, the "death" (Jas. 5:20) being averted is interpreted as eternal separation from God (Rev. 21:8). For others, James 5:20 denotes avoiding the experience of premature physical death (1 Cor. 11:29-32; 1 John 5:16). When the wayward are spiritually restored, it signifies the forgiveness of many sins (Jas. 5:20). Often, the process includes godly sorrow that leads to repentance and salvation (2 Cor. 7:10). Most likely, there will also be the confession of sin, which brings about divine pardon and cleansing from all unrighteousness (1 John 1:9). James provided his readers with the valuable instruction necessary for progress on the road to spiritual restoration and growth. Whether the issue was taming the tongue or persevering in persecution, all that a believer needed to grow in holiness was found in the One who answered the prayers of the faithful.

Discussion Questions

1. Why is prayer appropriate in times of trouble?
2. Why are ill believers encouraged to summon the elders of the church?
3. What is the purpose of anointing an ailing believer with oil in the name of the Lord?
4. In what way is Elijah an example of someone who prayed humbly and earnestly?
5. How can concerned believers restore the wayward to the truth?

Contemporary Application

As this week's lesson emphasizes, prayer works. Anyone who prays regularly would agree. It is our strongest communication link with the God who created us. It is a powerful means for giving voice to our faith. Most important of all, God can use our prayers to change the world. Clearly, our petitions matter.

Hands, feet, back, and pocketbook—these are some of the means that come to mind when we think of helping our fellow Christians. They enable us to comfort, carry, accompany, and contribute. They are solid, tangible realities. Beside them, the ethereal act of prayer can seem like little more than nice words spoken more to comfort the person doing the petitioning than to actually accomplish anything real.

Yet James 5:16 points out that a committed believer's prayer can produce powerful results. Powerful is hardly the way to describe nice words whose sole purpose is to offer psychological comfort to those who pray them. No, prayer changes things. Instead of being the last thing we do—when all other avenues are exhausted—it should be the first thing we do in every situation.

Prayer can be effective in more ways than we might realize at first. For instance, while prayer might not change our circumstances, it can alter our response to those circumstances. In contrast, prayer might change our circumstances. As we pray, our lives will reflect our prayerful hearts. We will find ourselves more in tune with the needs of others and better able to meet them because of our deeper walk with God. Our spiritual maturity will enrich our own lives even as it extends to those to whom we minister, bearing fruit in many ways as it touches the lives of others.

Fasting while Serving

Scripture

Background Scripture: *Daniel 1:5, 8-17; Matthew 6:16-18; 9:9-17*

Scripture Lesson: *Daniel 1:5, 8-17; Matthew 6:16-18*

Key Verse: *When you fast, put oil on your head and wash your face, so that it will not be obvious to men that you are fasting, but only to your Father, who is unseen; and your Father, who sees what is done in secret, will reward you."* Matthew 6:17-18.

Scripture Lesson for Children: *Daniel 1:5, 8-17; Matthew 6:16-18*

Key Verse for Children: *"Give us nothing but vegetables to eat and water to drink."* Daniel 1:12.

Lesson Aim

To learn that we can obey God even in complex situations.

Lesson Setting

Time: About 605–602 B.C. (Daniel) and 28 A.D. (Matthew)

Place: Babylon (Daniel) and Galilee (Matthew)

Lesson Outline

Fasting while Serving

I.   Daniel's Integrity: Daniel 1:5, 8-17
  A.   *The Education for Royal Service: vs. 5*
  B.   *The Request Made by Daniel: vs. 8*
  C.   *The Official's Alarm: vss. 9-10*
  D.   *The Suggestion Offered by Daniel: vss. 11-14*
  E.   *The Blessing of God: vss. 15-17*
II. Secret Fasting: Matthew 6:16-18
  A.   *Being Pretentious while Fasting: vs. 16*
  B.   *Being Humble while Fasting: vss. 17-18*

Introduction for Adults

Topic: *The Cuisine of Resistance*

To aid you as you speak this illustration, you could ask an appropriate member of your class to bring in a variety of fishing lures. Holding several where the class can see them, remind the students that most lures don't look at all like food a fish would enjoy. They merely offer shiny or colorful surfaces that catch a fish's attention. Attracted by the novelty, the fish swims over to investigate. The fisherman knows there's nothing for the fish in his lures but danger and potential death. But the fish is not smart enough to figure that out.

Satan's temptations are like fishing lures. They catch our attention. But we end up getting hurt, sometimes seriously. In many situations we face, determining to follow the right course can be difficult, but like Daniel, we must be obedient to God in all things. And we have the assurance of Scripture that He will not allow us to be tempted beyond what we can withstand. In fact, when we are enticed to sin, the Lord will show us a way out so that we can endure (1 Cor. 10:13).

Introduction for Youth

Topic: *Refusing the Royal Treatment*

Every temptation promises saved teens relief from some form of "hunger" inside them. In their weakest moments, what allures them most might involve eating, spending, or lusting (to name a few possibilities).

One way for believing adolescents to get through sinful enticements is this: look steadily at what is being offered and ask whether the activity is really what they want. If they let that question sink in, they can discover, as Daniel did, a deeper need beneath their pressing desire of the moment: their hunger for unconditional love and fulfillment. As Daniel learned while in captivity in Babylon, it's a need only God can meet.

Concepts for Children

Topic: *Less Is Better*

1. Daniel and his friends had to choose whom to obey.
2. Daniel chose to follow God no matter what might happen.
3. God gave Daniel respect from the palace official.
4. People could see that Daniel made the right choice.
5. God blesses those who faithfully obey His Word.

Lesson Commentary

I. DANIEL'S INTEGRITY: DANIEL 1:5, 8-17

A. The Education for Royal Service: vs. 5

The king assigned them a daily amount of food and wine from the king's table. They were to be trained for three years, and after that they were to enter the king's service.

When Judah fell and Josiah was killed in a battle with Egypt in 609 B.C., Josiah's eldest son, Jehoiakim, was made king of Judah by Pharaoh Neco. For four years, Judah was an Egyptian vassal nation until Nebuchadnezzar defeated Egypt at Carchemish in 605 B.C. That same year, the Babylonian king swept into Judah and captured Jerusalem (1:1). He had Jehoiakim, who was in the third year of his reign, carried off to Babylon. Nebuchadnezzar also ordered treasures from the temple in Jerusalem sent back home and placed in the shrine of his pagan deity (vs. 2). The idol referred to was probably the chief Babylonian god, Bel, also called Marduk.

In keeping with a common practice of the time, Nebuchadnezzar had the best educated, most attractive, most capable and talented among Judah's citizens sent back to Babylon. In essence, only the poorer, uneducated people were left behind to populate conquered lands (2 Kings 24:14). Included among those deported from Judah to Babylon were Daniel, Hananiah, Mishael, and Azariah (Dan. 1:3, 6). Most likely, they would have been about 14 or 15 years of age at this time. Nebuchadnezzar commanded Ashpenaz, who was in charge of the king's court officials, to bring in some of the Israelites. The king specifically wanted to see members of Judah's royal family and others who came from the ranks of nobility (vs. 3). Nebuchadnezzar was obviously looking for the captives with the highest aptitudes and abilities. He wanted young men of such physical and mental superiority that they would be qualified for service to him (vs. 4).

Ashpenaz was charged with teaching the young men the Babylonian language (Akkadian) and literature. The latter was written in cuneiform (a complex, syllabic writing system made up of wedge-shaped characters) and mainly engraved on clay tablets. The intent was to assimilate the captives into their new culture. Additionally, they were to undergo an intensive, three-year study program to prepare them for royal service. The course of study most likely included mathematics, history, astronomy, astrology, agriculture, architecture, law, and magic.

During this time, the young men would receive a daily ration of delicacies from the royal kitchen (vs. 5). But because Daniel was certain the monarch's provisions would bring ritual uncleanness, he made up his mind not to partake of them. Daniel's concern undoubtedly centered on the realization that the king's food was not prepared in compliance with the law of Moses. Even the simple fact that it was prepared by Gentiles rendered it unclean. The king's diet included pork and horseflesh, which were forbidden by the Mosaic law (Lev. 11;

Deut. 14). Furthermore, the Gentile monarch's food and wine would have been offered to Babylonian idols before they reached his table. Consuming anything offered to pagan deities was strictly forbidden in Exodus 34:15.

B. The Request Made by Daniel: vs. 8

But Daniel resolved not to defile himself with the royal food and wine, and he asked the chief official for permission not to defile himself this way.

The number of captives enrolled in the king's educational program is not stated. Only the names of the four young men from Judah are given. All four of the names referred to and honored the God of Israel in some way. In Hebrew, the ending "-el" means "God" and "-iah" is an abbreviation for "Yahweh." The God-honoring names of the four men could indicate that they all had God-fearing parents. But since their captors wanted their patron idols to be honored (for instance, Marduk, Nebo, and Ishtar) rather than the God of Israel, the names of the four youths were changed (Dan. 1:6-7).

Daniel, meaning "My judge is God," was changed to Belteshazzar, possibly translated "Bel, protect his life" or "Lady, protect the king." Hananiah, meaning "Yahweh is gracious," became Shadrach, possibly translated "The command of Aku" (the Sumerian moon-god) or "I am very fearful [of God]." Mishael, meaning "Who is what God is?" was changed to Meshach, possibly translated "Who is what Aku is?" or "I am of little account." Azariah, meaning "Yahweh has helped," became Abednego, possibly translated "Servant of Nego" (a corruption of the name of the god Nebo, elsewhere called Nabu, the god of writing and vegetation) or "Servant of the shining one."

If changing the names was a ploy to shift the young men's allegiance from the God of Israel to the gods of Babylon, it failed. For instance, Daniel made up his mind not to defile himself by breaking the Mosaic law. "Resolve" (vs. 8) translates a Hebrew phrase that literally means "placed on his heart" and refers to a determined, committed stand. When Daniel took this position, it was simply the natural result of a lifelong pledge to be obedient to God's will in every situation. With boldness and courage, Daniel asked Ashpenaz for permission not to eat the king's delicacies or drink his wine. Evidently, Daniel's three companions shared his resoluteness and made the same commitment as well.

C. The Official's Alarm: vss. 9-10

Now God had caused the official to show favor and sympathy to Daniel, but the official told Daniel, "I am afraid of my lord the king, who has assigned your food and drink. Why should he see you looking worse than the other young men your age? The king would then have my head because of you."

Both Daniel 1:8 and 9 contain a phrase that can be rendered "the commander of the officials" or "the chief of the eunuchs." The earliest-known eunuchs lived in Mesopotamia, where they worked as servants in the women's quarters of the royal household. They could also serve as palace or government officials, even generals. They were castrated in the belief that this would make them more compliant to their superiors. While the Hebrew term for "eunuch" appears 47 times in the Old Testament, it is used in the technical sense of a castrated man on only 28 of those occasions. The rest of the time it appears to be used more broadly to refer to an official representative of the king. Its use in Daniel is probably meant to emphasize the official capacity of those who cared for Daniel, rather than their physical state.

As was noted earlier, Ashpenaz was in charge of the court officials (vs. 3). According to verse 9, God caused the overseer to be sympathetic to Daniel. Despite the respect, kindness, and compassion of Ashpenaz, he was afraid of violating the edict of his master, the king. We previously learned from verse 5 that Nebuchadnezzar had assigned the trainees a regular amount of "food and wine" that his servants prepared for him. Ashpenaz realized the monarch would hold him responsible if Daniel and his three Israelite peers looked malnourished in comparison to the other young men their age. The chief official also knew he would be decapitated for neglecting his duties (vs. 10).

D. The Suggestion Offered by Daniel: vss. 11-14

Daniel then said to the guard whom the chief official had appointed over Daniel, Hananiah, Mishael and Azariah, "Please test your servants for ten days: Give us nothing but vegetables to eat and water to drink. Then compare our appearance with that of the young men who eat the royal food, and treat your servants in accordance with what you see." So he agreed to this and tested them for ten days.

Since Daniel got nowhere with Ashpenaz, the young Israelite captive turned his attention to the guardian or warden placed over him by the chief official (Dan. 1:11). The petition was for the guardian to put Daniel and his friends on a 10-day trial diet. In the Old Testament, the number 10 was sometimes used as an ideal figure to denote completeness. Daniel proposed that the four be given nothing but vegetables to eat and water to drink (vs. 12). The Hebrew noun for "vegetables" meant "that which grows from sown seed." Thus, grains, bread made from grain, and even fruit would also have been included. Since no plants were designated unclean by the law of Moses, there was no danger of ceremonial defilement with this diet.

At the end of 10 days, the warden could compare the appearance of the test subjects with that of the young men who were eating the royal delicacies. Based on what the guardian saw, he would decide what to do with Daniel and his friends (vs. 13). The warden agreed to Daniel's proposal (vs. 14). Perhaps the guardian was reassured by Daniel's confidence that the Jews would fare better on the vegetarian diet than those who ate the king's food. In any case, the warden probably reasoned that 10 days was not enough time for the health of the four youths to suffer any permanent damage.

E. The Blessing of God: vss. 15-17

At the end of the ten days they looked healthier and better nourished than any of the young men who ate the royal food. So the guard took away their choice food and the wine they were to drink and gave them vegetables instead. To these four young men God gave knowledge and understanding of all kinds of literature and learning. And Daniel could understand visions and dreams of all kinds.

At first, Ashpenaz worried that Daniel and his friends would become pale and thin compared to the other youths their age (Dan. 1:10). But at the end of the 10 days, the four looked healthier in appearance and their bodies looked better nourished than the rest of the young men who had been eating the royal delicacies (vs. 15). So after that, the warden removed the rich foods and wines from their diet and instead gave them only vegetables to eat (vs. 16).

Daniel managed to negotiate his way to an acceptable solution to a difficult problem. He undoubtedly petitioned the Lord for divine guidance in this matter. That he received God's assistance is obvious. Daniel's very life depended on his faith. Since he requested a specific amount of time, a specific method, and a specific result, he knew that only God could bring the necessary results. In one sense, Daniel was pitting God against the Babylonian king himself. Daniel would have seen in the Babylonian literature he was being taught many stories in which the gods and goddesses affirmed the king as a deity. So the Lord was the ultimate reason for the success of Daniel's plan.

This incident illustrates the truth that God blesses those who obey and trust Him. Perhaps the lesson was not lost on the Israelite people as a whole. They had disobeyed God's laws and were severely judged because of it. Their nation was destroyed, and they were now captives. Daniel and his friends, on the other hand, obeyed God by refusing to eat Nebuchadnezzar's food. They did this even though they knew their stand might cost them their lives. But because of their faithfulness and obedience, the four youths experienced God's blessing and continued to thrive even in a hostile, ungodly environment.

While Daniel and his three friends were being groomed for service in the royal court, God was preparing them for service to Him and to His people. The Lord gave the four Israelites "knowledge and understanding" (vs. 17). They had a special ability to reason clearly and logically and to approach any subject with insight and discernment. Under royal tutelage and with divine assistance, the four youths excelled in a wide range of subjects in the arts and sciences. Daniel, however, surpassed all the other students in a special field. God gave him insight into all kinds of dreams and visions.

II. Secret Fasting: Matthew 6:16-18

A. Being Pretentious while Fasting: vs. 16

"When you fast, do not look somber as the hypocrites do, for they disfigure their faces to show men they are fasting. I tell you the truth, they have received their reward in full."

Before delivering the Sermon on the Mount (Matt. 5–7), Jesus traveled throughout Galilee and proclaimed the Good News of the kingdom. He taught in the synagogues and healed large numbers of people. During this time, His popularity grew considerably, with many people following Him from all over Palestine and its surrounding regions (Matt. 4:23-25 and similar observations made in lesson 4). In chapter 6, Jesus targeted a variety of pious acts the religious leaders performed in a hypocritical manner. This included charitable giving (vss. 1-4), praying (vss. 5-15), and fasting (vss. 16-18). Whereas Jerusalem's elite participated in various rituals to gain attention from other people, Jesus emphasized the importance of worshiping God discreetly and serving others without fanfare.

In verse 16, the reference to fasting referred to abstaining from eating for a limited period of time. Throughout the Scripture, we can see that God's people fasted for a variety of reasons: to express grief over the death of a loved one or a leader (1 Sam. 31:13), to petition God for a matter of great urgency (2 Sam. 12:15-23), to humble oneself before God (1 Kings 21:27-29), to seek God's help (2 Chron. 20:1-4), to confess sins (Neh. 9:1-2), and to prepare oneself spiritually (Matt. 4:1-2). Fasting was difficult, requiring self-discipline and sacrifice. It gave God's people the opportunity to devote more time to spiritual pursuits. It said to God, in effect, that the matter they were bringing before Him was more important than anything else, even eating.

The Greek noun rendered "hypocrites" (6:16) originally referred to an actor on a stage. It eventually came to denote individuals who pretended to be something they were not. In the moral realm, they were religious leaders characterized by duplicity and pretense. For instance, whenever the hypocritical religious leaders of Jesus' day fasted, they would look dreary and gloomy. They deliberately disfigured their faces by heaping ashes on their heads and disheveling their hair and beards. The intent was to let everyone know they were doing something pious. Yet any admiration they received would be their only reward.

B. Being Humble while Fasting: vss. 17-18

"But when you fast, put oil on your head and wash your face, so that it will not be obvious to men that you are fasting, but only to your Father, who is unseen; and your Father, who sees what is done in secret, will reward you."

In New Testament times, people would perfume their heads with olive oil and splash their faces with water to help rejuvenate and invigorate them. Jesus instructed His followers to put oil on their heads and wash their faces when they fasted (Matt. 6:17). They were to look refreshed and joyful, not sullen and unkempt, so that others might not realize they were fasting. In other words, they were supposed to hide their fasting. But their unseen heavenly Father would know, and He would reward whatever they did in private (vs. 18). Whatever righteous acts we do, whatever service we render to others in the name of the

Lord, we should do all things out of our love for God and not to receive people's applause. Otherwise, the latter will be all the benefit we get out of our pious deed. So instead we should "play" to an audience of one, namely, God.

Discussion Questions

1. Why did Daniel resolve not to defile himself by eating food and wine provided by Nebuchadnezzar?
2. Why would Daniel take the risk of approaching the guardian with the proposal of a vegetarian diet?
3. What was the basis for the superior intellectual abilities of Daniel and his three friends?
4. What is the connection between being humble and serving others in Jesus' name?
5. Why can we never impress God with our righteous acts, such as fasting?

Contemporary Application

Daniel faced two choices. He could succumb to Nebuchadnezzar's edict and defile himself by eating food forbidden by Mosaic law. Or Daniel could remain obedient to God and risk the displeasure of the Babylonian king.

As Christians, we sometimes find ourselves in situations where being faithful to Jesus' teachings is not easy (for example, those concerning fasting in Matt. 6:16-18). In fact, the pressure from others to disobey God can be so intense and the circumstances so complicated that it can be difficult for us to know the right option to choose in certain situations.

For instance, what if a Christian is attending the funeral of a close relative who belonged to a pagan religion? The family members expect, and a few even insist, that the Christian participate in all the funeral ceremony rituals. The Christian wants to honor the relative's memory, but thinks some of the rituals might conflict with biblical teachings. How would any of us make sure that we remain obedient to God in this complex situation while also demonstrating our Christian compassion?

We might choose one of several options. Some of us might not attend the ceremony at all. Others of us might attend, but not participate in any aspects of the ceremony. Still others might attend but refrain from those rituals we are certain violate the teachings of our faith. Determining the right course can be difficult in many situations we face. Yet like Daniel, we must remain obedient to God under all circumstances.

Serving God and Others

DEVOTIONAL READING

Matthew 22:34-40

DAILY BIBLE READINGS

Monday February 2
*Matthew 19:16-22 If You
Wish to Be Perfect*

Tuesday February 3
*James 2:8-13 Mercy Triumphs
over Judgment*

Wednesday February 4
*Joshua 22:1-6 Keep the
Instruction of Moses*

Thursday February 5
*Philippians 2:1-5 Look to the
Interests of Others*

Friday February 6
*Matthew 22:34-40 The
Foremost Commandment*

Saturday February 7
*Galatians 5:10-17 Live by
the Spirit*

Sunday February 8
*Luke 10:25-34 Who Is My
Neighbor?*

Scripture

Background Scripture: *Luke 10:25-34*
Scripture Lesson: *Luke 10:25-34*
Key Verse: *[Jesus asked,] "Which of these three do you think
was a neighbor to the man who fell into the hands of robbers?"
The expert in the law replied, "The one who had mercy on
him." Jesus told him, "Go and do likewise." Luke 10:36-37.*
Scripture Lesson for Children: *Luke 10:25-34*
Key Verse for Children: *"Love the Lord your God with all
your heart'. . . and, 'Love your neighbor as yourself.'"*
Luke 10:27.

Lesson Aim

To be proactive in showing compassion on the needy.

Lesson Setting

Time: A.D. *29*
Place: Perea, east of the Jordan River

Lesson Outline

Serving God and Others
  I. The Question about Eternal Life: Luke 10:25-28
      A. *The Legal Expert's Question: vs. 25*
      B. *The Answer Found in the Mosaic Law: vss. 26-28*
  II. The Parable of the Good Samaritan:
      Luke 10:29-34
      A. *The Question about Neighborliness: vs. 29*
      B. *The Insensitivity of a Priest and a Levite: vss. 30-32*
      C. *The Compassion of a Samaritan: vss. 33-34*

Introduction for Adults

Topic: *Do We Know Our Neighbor?*

Booker T. Washington, the noted African-American educator, was taking a walk with a Caucasian friend when a pedestrian roughly elbowed Washington into the gutter. His friend was furious and asked him, "How can you tolerate such an insult?" Washington replied, "I defy any man to make me hate him."

This is what true Christian love does—it defies all the bitterness and hatred in the world. It also sweeps aside all the barriers that separate people. Because Jesus makes a difference in our social relationships, Christians can extend the love of God to others.

Jesus' parable of the good Samaritan forces us to look deep inside ourselves. How easy it is for us to say we love God, but then do nothing for our neighbors. Also, how hard it is for us to cast aside our own desires for the sake of helping those in great need.

Introduction for Youth

Topic: *May I Help You?*

The expert in the Mosaic law who questioned Jesus was experienced in creating diversion, and, sadly, many people today follow his tactics. They find it relatively easy to talk about spirituality. But they find it difficult to stick to the main point, namely, their need for Jesus to save them from their hypocrisy and self-righteousness.

It's a huge step for us to confess that we aren't good enough to merit eternal life. Perhaps that's why some people talk about the sins of others without ever facing the reality of their own transgressions. They have no desire to repent of their misdeeds and be saved. And they have no interest in being kindhearted to their enemies.

From the parable of the good Samaritan we learn three principles about loving our neighbor. First, lack of love is often easy to justify, even though it is never right. Second, our neighbor is anyone of any race, creed, or social background who is in need. Third, love means acting to meet the person's need.

Concepts for Children

Topic: *Helping Others*

1. A teacher asked Jesus about getting eternal life.
2. The teacher knew the most important commands in the Bible.
3. The teacher asked Jesus to explain what it meant to be a neighbor.
4. Jesus told a story to show how a neighbor is someone who helps another person.
5. As Jesus' followers, we should help other people.

Lesson Commentary

I. THE QUESTION ABOUT ETERNAL LIFE: LUKE 10:25-28

A. The Legal Expert's Question: vs. 25

On one occasion an expert in the law stood up to test Jesus. "Teacher," he asked, "what must I do to inherit eternal life?"

Luke 10:25 states that one day a Jewish legal expert (that is, a scribe) asked Jesus a question to test Him. In Jesus' day, scribes were members of a learned class who studied the Mosaic law and served as copyists, scholars, and teachers. At first all the priests in Israel were responsible for the study and communication of this legal code. But this function eventually passed to the scribes. Their official interpretation of the meaning of the law gradually became more important than the law itself. Before A.D. 70, large numbers of priests in Jerusalem served as scribes. Because they were not paid for their services, they had to earn a livelihood in another way. Though some of the scribes were Sadducees, the bulk of them came from the ordinary priestly ranks (such as merchants, carpenters, flax combers, and tentmakers).

One striking distinction between Jesus and the scribes of His day was the difference between their tendency to make many laws out of a few and His gift for making few laws out of many. They had identified a law for every Hebrew letter (613 of them) in the Ten Commandments. Generally, they emphasized laws about external behavior, such as maintaining cleanness and keeping the Sabbath. Jesus, by contrast, summarized the entire law very briefly—love God (Matt. 22:37). Jesus knew that the Father did not give the law to burden people with endless rules, but so that they would love Him. Obedience should be an outgrowth of love for God.

The scribe who questioned Jesus asked, "What must I do to inherit eternal life?" (Luke 10:25). According to John 17:3 (which was covered in lesson 6), eternal life is not mere endless existence, but a personal relationship with the Father based on knowing Him as the one true God (Deut. 6:4; Mark 12:29; 1 Cor. 8:6; 1 Thess. 1:9; 1 Tim. 1:17). Furthermore, we can know the Father only through faith in the Son, Jesus the Messiah (John 1:14, 18; 14:9; 20:31), whom the Father sent as His emissary (3:34; 4:34; 13:20). The legal expert's question in Luke 10:25 reflected the popular Jewish approach to finding favor with God. Most Jews thought one had to earn God's favor by doing good works. They couldn't fathom that eternal life is God's free and immediate gift to those who come to Him in repentance and faith (Rom. 6:23; Eph. 2:8-9).

In Romans 9:30-33, Paul contrasted the way in which unsaved Gentiles and Jews responded to the proclamation of the Gospel. By the time the apostle wrote this epistle, he had been on three missionary tours and preached the Gospel to Jews and Gentiles. While many Gentiles trusted in the Messiah and thereby received righteousness through faith, most Jews became increasingly hostile toward the Gospel. The Gentiles, who were not looking for righteousness, nevertheless found righteousness by faith (vs. 30). The Jews pursued righteousness, but one that was based on human merit, not God's grace (vs. 31).

Such an attempt is futile because one must keep the entire Mosaic law perfectly to attain righteousness through observing it (Jas. 2:10). The fact is, not a single human being (outside of the Lord Jesus) has ever perfectly kept the law. Yet, out of pride, many Jews kept trying to earn favor with God. They stubbornly refused to admit their inability to keep the law and turn to God in faith for forgiveness through Jesus the Messiah. Many Jews kept tripping over the "stumbling stone" (Rom. 9:32), which was the Messiah (1 Pet. 2:4-8).

B. The Answer Found in the Mosaic Law: vss. 26-28

"What is written in the Law?" he replied. "How do you read it?" He answered: "'Love the Lord your God with all your heart and with all your soul and with all your strength and with all your mind'; and, 'Love your neighbor as yourself.'" "You have answered correctly," Jesus replied. "Do this and you will live."

No doubt the scribe wanted to discredit Jesus by outwitting Him in public debate. But Jesus reversed the situation for the legalist. Instead of saying something that might sound like a contradiction of the law, Jesus asked the scribe to use the law to answer his own question (Luke 10:26). We can imagine Jesus pointing to the phylactery (a small square leather box or case) on the scribe's forearm or forehead, in which was written the compendium of the law.

In response, the scribe quoted Deuteronomy 6:5, which emphasizes love for God (Luke 10:27). Together "heart," "soul," "strength," and "mind" are a way of saying "entire being." Every part of us should be involved in our devotion to God. The basis for doing so is found in Deuteronomy 6:4. Moses told the Israelites to "hear," or listen carefully to, a divinely revealed insight: "The LORD our God, the LORD is one." As the NIV margin note shows, the Hebrew can be translated in several different ways. Other possibilities include "The LORD our God is one LORD" and "The LORD is our God, the LORD is one."

For centuries in Jewish tradition, Deuteronomy 6:4-9 has been known as the *Shema'.* These verses contain the fundamental truth of Israel's religion and are the creed of Judaism. The name *Shema'* was given to these verses because the word "Hear" at the beginning of the passage is translated from the Hebrew word *shema'.* Pious Jews today recite the *Shema'* several times a day. In fact, early rabbis called for Jews to recite these verses once in the morning and once in the evening. Jesus called the instruction given in the *Shema'* the greatest commandment (Matt. 22:37-38) and the most important (Mark 12:29-30). Deuteronomy 6:4-9 may be the most often quoted verses from the Bible.

The scribe next quoted Leviticus 19:18, which says we are to love our neighbors as ourselves. The idea is that we need to work out our love for God in daily life. A supreme love for God will always find expression in unselfish love for others. The importance of doing the latter is seen in Jesus' statement recorded in Matthew 22:40, namely, that the entire Old Testament depends on loving God and others. Expressed differently, the Mosaic legal code is illumined and deepened by the presence of Christlike love (Matt. 5:17; 7:12; Rom. 8:4; 13:8-10). Furthermore, just as the Savior loved us and gave His life for our eternal benefit, we also should reach out to others in a caring manner (1 John 4:9-12). We must always use the two principles of a supreme love for God and an unselfish love for others to test the priorities by which we order our daily lives. If we fail these tests, then our life, and even our religion, will bring little fulfillment.

Jesus approved of the scribe's response and urged him to put his insight into action (Luke 10:28). Then Jesus said, "Do this and you will live." This is the exhortation of the law (Lev. 18:5). But since no sinner can obey it perfectly (Jas. 2:10), the impossible demands of the law are meant to drive us to seek divine mercy (Gal. 3:23-24). The scribe should have responded with a confession of his own guilt. Instead, he arrogantly tried to vindicate himself. The problem, then, was not with the law's commands. Rather, it was with the scribe's inability to keep them. Similarly, our total failure to heed God's laws makes it impossible for us to merit eternal life. Because of our indwelling sin nature, we are powerless to live in a perfectly virtuous manner. Accepting this fact drives us to Jesus for forgiveness, eternal life, and an upright standing in God's presence. We cannot partake of Jesus' saving grace until we are convinced of our inability to earn eternal life by our own efforts.

II. The Parable of the Good Samaritan: Luke 10:29-34

A. The Question about Neighborliness: vs. 29

But he wanted to justify himself, so he asked Jesus, "And who is my neighbor?"

The scribe felt uncomfortable with his own answer. Perhaps he knew that his behavior didn't measure up to the standard he had quoted. So, he raised a technicality, hoping to account for and vindicate his failure. He would be glad to love his neighbor, he implied, if only Jesus would tell him who his neighbor was (Luke 10:29). In Jesus' day, the widespread opinion among scribes and Pharisees was that one's neighbors only included the upright. Supposedly, the wicked were to be hated because they were enemies of God. The religious leaders defined the wicked as sinners (such as tax collectors and prostitutes), Gentiles, and especially Samaritans. Psalm 139:21-22 was used to legitimatize this view.

It's true that a love for righteousness will lead to a hatred of evil. However, this does not excuse being hostile and malicious toward sinners. The upright should abhor the corrupt lifestyle of the lost, but never harbor a vindictive loathing of them as human beings. Instead, the godly should display a brokenhearted grieving over the sinful condition of the lost. Such is undergirded by a genuine concern for the eternal condition of the unsaved (Matt. 5:44-48; Luke 6:27-36). Tragically, the scribes and Pharisees had made a virtue out of being antagonistic toward the sinful. The result was a renunciation of Leviticus 19:18, the command to love one's neighbor. The parable Jesus told shattered the legalistic notion of hating one's enemies.

B. The Insensitivity of a Priest and a Levite: vss. 30-32

In reply Jesus said: "A man was going down from Jerusalem to Jericho, when he fell into the hands of robbers. They stripped him of his clothes, beat him and went away, leaving him half dead. A priest happened to be going down the same road, and when he saw the man, he passed by on the other side. So too, a Levite, when he came to the place and saw him, passed by on the other side."

Luke 10:30-35 is known as the parable of the good Samaritan. Jesus used parables as a favorite teaching technique. The parables were effective because they appealed to the entire person by touching the emotions, challenging the mind, and igniting the imagination. The Synoptic Gospels record 40 parables told by Jesus. They are short stories and sayings drawn from everyday life. But Jesus used these parables to communicate spiritual truths that may have been unfamiliar to His audience. He would start by commenting on something in the physical world and then compare it to something in the spiritual realm. Jesus' parables usually emphasized one primary concept that could be applied in a variety of ways. In fact, not all the details of a parable necessarily had significance. This observation serves as a caution against reading too much into a parable.

The story Jesus used in response to the scribe concerned a man who traveled from Jerusalem to Jericho. Jesus' listeners would immediately recall that notorious stretch of road. In less than 20 miles it descended nearly 3,600 feet. It had plenty of hazardous twists and turns and steep inclines, with rocks and caves lining the way. The road's conditions gave robbers ample opportunity to prey upon travelers. That's what happened to the traveler in Jesus' story. Some men beat him, robbed him, and left him lying by the side of the road (vs. 30). But the wounded man was not alone for long. Three travelers passed by in turn: a priest, a Levite, and a Samaritan.

Many priests and Levites lived in Jericho. So perhaps we should imagine the priest returning home to Jericho after serving at the temple in Jerusalem. When he came along, he saw the victim, beaten and bloody. Now the priest was faced with a decision: to help or refuse to do so. Sadly, he chose not to help (vs. 31). Whatever reasoning he used in making his decision was inadequate to justify shirking his duty to show mercy to a hurting person (Mic. 6:8). Next, a Levite came along. He was a member of a group that was responsible for maintaining the temple and its furniture and utensils. Like the priest, he too may have been coming from (or going to) the temple on religious business. And he, too, chose not to help the injured traveler (Luke 10:32). Likewise, the Levite was guilty of being unmerciful. The priest and the Levite saw no connection between their temple worship and the needs of the beaten traveler. Though the religious leaders affirmed their love for God, they denied by their actions the importance of loving their fellow human beings. Such hypocrisy was abhorrent to God.

C. The Compassion of a Samaritan: vss. 33-34

"But a Samaritan, as he traveled, came where the man was; and when he saw him, he took pity on him. He went to him and bandaged his wounds, pouring on oil and wine. Then he put the man on his own donkey, took him to an inn and took care of him."

A Samaritan was the third person to come upon the injured man. Samaritans were Jews who had intermarried with people from other nations following the deportation of much of the Israelite population by the Assyrians 750 years before Jesus (2 Kings 17:24-41). Over the following centuries, racial prejudice and a history of animosity fueled an intense rivalry between Jews and Samaritans. The Jews bitterly hated the Samaritans, for the Jews prided themselves on their supposedly "pure" ancestry. Additionally, Jews despised Samaritans for their hybrid religion. Samaritans accepted the Torah (the five books of Moses), but inserted some of their own interpretations. Also, they worshiped on Mount Gerizim rather than on Mount Zion in Jerusalem (John 4:20).

Given this climate of animosity, the Samaritan in Jesus' parable could have rationalized failing to assist the injured man more easily than the priest and Levite did. But the Samaritan did not do that. Instead, feeling deep pity, he decided to help the stranger (Luke 10:33). The Samaritan was thorough in the assistance he gave. He began by administering first aid. He bandaged the man's wounds, pouring on oil (which acted as a salve) and wine (which acted as an antiseptic). Then the Samaritan turned his donkey into a makeshift ambulance. He transported the man to an inn (vs. 34). Finally, the Samaritan arranged to pay the man's expenses. Since one denarius was equal to a laborer's daily pay, the two silver coins (denarii) that the Samaritan paid would probably have lodged the wounded man for several days (vs. 35).

At the end of the parable, Jesus asked the scribe which of the three passersby—the priest, the Levite, or the Samaritan—was a neighbor to the robbed man (vs. 36). The scribe correctly answered, the one who had assisted the man in distress. Jesus told the scribe to act the same way (vs. 37). Society has fragmented as people have held each other at arm's length. Consequently, many people today have retreated behind the security and seclusion of their own doors. They don't want others to intrude, and they don't want to get involved with others. But Jesus called us to be neighbors, to interact with others. We cannot be spiritual hermits and adequately love our neighbors. We have to be involved.

The scribe had asked how far he had to go to love others. But Jesus turned the question around. Instead of "Who is my neighbor?" (vs. 29), the question became, in effect, "How can I be a good neighbor?" (vs. 36). The lesson Jesus taught is that we become good neighbors by showing mercy to everyone we encounter (vs. 37). Though Jesus' parable takes place in a rural setting, it speaks to a number of urban issues: racial and ethnic divisions, violent crime, and even the struggle of small businesses to remain solvent. The Samaritan—the good neighbor—does not eliminate these problems, but he does act as an agent of mercy to overcome them in small but effective ways. The Samaritan's example challenges us to consider how we can be good neighbors to others, regardless of their racial, economic, social, political, or ethnic background. Ultimately, God is interested in mercy, not maintaining prejudice.

Discussion Questions

1. Why do you think the legal expert sought to put Jesus to the test?
2. Why did the scribe try to justify his actions?
3. What did the Samaritan sacrifice to get involved with the wounded traveler?
4. What rationalizations might busy Christians make to avoid assisting others?
5. How do you feel after you've stopped to help someone in need?

Contemporary Application

Like the specialist who confronted Jesus about eternal life (Luke 10:25), there is a lawyer's instinct in all of us that seeks careful definitions of our Christian duties. This suggests we suffer from a cold creedalism that can strangle tangible expressions of love.

However, God's command to love all people transcends legal niceties (1 John 4:21). We cannot separate our duties to others from our duties to God. Saying the right words, praying the right prayers, and singing the right hymns cannot make up for a lack of love (1 Cor. 13:1-3).

We have to confess our coldness and our preoccupation with ourselves. And we have to admit how hard it is to find the time and resources to be good Samaritans to wounded people. Together, we must encourage one another to make our churches places where love springs into action. Otherwise, we may look outwardly holy (like the priest and Levite), but be inwardly full of hypocrisy (like the scribe).

In making the commitment to extend mercy to those who need help, we must realize that we are all at some time one of the people in Jesus' parable—the wounded person, the passerby, or the helper. We are more likely to help others if we remember the last time someone helped us. If we maintain a safe distance from those in need, we can avoid feelings for them, but Jesus tells us we don't have an excuse good enough to stay on the other side of the road (so to speak). We should stop, cross over, and extend mercy to anyone we have the opportunity and resources to help.

Serving the Least

Scripture

Background Scripture: *Matthew 25:31-46*

Scripture Lesson: *Matthew 25:31-46*

Key Verse: *"The King will reply, 'I tell you the truth, whatever you did for one of the least of these brothers of mine, you did for me.'"* Matthew 25:40.

Scripture Lesson for Children: *Matthew 25:31-46*

Key Verse for Children: *"I tell you the truth, whatever did for one of the least of these . . . you did for me."* Matthew 25:40.

Lesson Aim

To treat others as if they were Jesus.

Lesson Setting

Time: A.D. *30*

Place: Mount of Olives outside Jerusalem

Lesson Outline

Serving the Least

   I. The Sheep and the Goats: Matthew 25:31-33

      A. *The Coming Judge: vs. 31*

      B. *The Determination: vss. 32-33*

  II. Those on Jesus' Right: Matthew 25:34-40

      A. *The Promise of the Kingdom: vs. 34*

      B. *The Deeds of the Blessed: vss. 35-36*

      C. *The Questions Asked by the Blessed: vss. 37-39*

      D. *The Response Given by the Lord: vs. 40*

 III. Those on Jesus' Left: Matthew 25:41-46

      A. *The Pronouncement of Judgment: vs. 41*

      B. *The Failures of the Condemned: vss. 42-43*

      C. *The Questions Asked by the Condemned: vs. 44*

      D. *The Response Given by the Lord: vss. 45-46*

Introduction for Adults

Topic: *Meeting Others' Needs*

Several years ago, when King Abdullah succeeded his father, King Hussein, on the throne of Jordan, he decided to discover the needs of his people. The monarch assumed several roles in disguise, such as taxi driver, moneychanger, and so on. The people he worked with had no idea they were serving their king.

We recognize something similar taking place in Jesus' parable of the sheep and the goats. The sheep had no idea they helped Jesus, and the goats had no idea they refused to come to His aid. How many times do we make the same mistake? We simply do not recognize that by helping needy people, we are ministering to our Lord and King.

Introduction for Youth

Topic: *Talking to Strangers*

A group of Christian college students decided to find out what it was like to be homeless. They spent several weekends living among the homeless in Chicago by sleeping outside at night on cardboard pallets and scrounging for their food.

This incident reminds us that young people generally have a keen sense of helping others. They organize food drives and walk, run, and swim for charity. They go overseas to build houses, drill wells, and teach people to read.

In the parable of the sheep and the goats, Jesus said these sorts of activities really count with Him. The idea is that by investing our lives by helping others, we serve Him. Conversely, by refusing to help others in need, we also refuse to minister to our Savior.

Concepts for Children

Topic: *Serving Others*

1. One day Jesus will come back to earth.
2. When Jesus comes again, He will separate believers from unbelievers.
3. Jesus will bless His people with eternal life.
4. In contrast, those who reject Jesus will experience unending sadness.
5. Jesus wants us to help others through deeds of kindness.

Lesson Commentary

I. THE SHEEP AND THE GOATS: MATTHEW 25:31-33

A. The Coming Judge: vs. 31

"When the Son of Man comes in his glory, and all the angels with him, he will sit on his throne in heavenly glory."

Matthew's Gospel includes five major discourses or lengthy sections that end with a specific formula. The first is usually called the Sermon on the Mount (chaps. 5–7; see lesson 5 for more information). The others are chapters 10, 13, 18, 24, and 25. (Matthew 23 is a long speech without the usual ending.) Because Jesus was sitting on the Mount of Olives when He taught the material in chapters 24 and 25 to His disciples, it has been called the Olivet Discourse. It contains some of the most noteworthy prophetic passages in all of Scripture.

Following the parable of the wise and wicked servants (Matt. 24:45-51), Jesus told three more parables related to His return: the parable of the 10 virgins (25:1-13), the parable of the talents (vss. 14-30), and the parable of the sheep and the goats (vss. 31-46). All of these stories have to do with being ready for Jesus' return by remaining faithful to Him. Each of these parables, however, has a slightly different slant. In the parable of the 10 virgins, Jesus called His disciples to exercise foresight and wisdom as they prepared themselves for His return. In the parable of the talents, Jesus stressed that His followers were to be wise stewards of all He had entrusted to their care.

Lastly, in the parable of the sheep and the goats, Jesus revealed that the righteous would be rewarded for their concern and hospitality, while the wicked would be punished for their indifference. In the final parable that Jesus delivered on the Mount of Olives, He provided a few details about what His return would be like. First, Jesus would come in "glory" (vs. 31), or divine splendor, no longer simply appearing as an ordinary human being. Second, He would bring with Him "all the angels," who would no doubt serve as His assistants (2 Thess. 1:7). Third, Jesus would "sit on his throne in heavenly glory" (Matt. 25:31), meaning He would rule in splendor.

The expression "Son of Man" occurs over 80 times in the Gospels and spotlights both Jesus' lowly humanity and heavenly origin (Ps. 8:4; Ezek. 2:1; Dan. 7:13). On the one hand, "Son of Man" is associated with the glory and triumph of the Messiah at His second coming (Matt. 16:27-28; 25:31; Mark 14:62; Luke 22:69; Acts 7:56). On the other hand, the title is connected with the suffering of God's Servant on the cross (Matt. 17:22-23; Mark 8:31; Luke 9:22; John 3:13-15). In a similar vein, Paul referred to Jesus as the "last Adam" (1 Cor. 15:45) and the "second man" (vs. 47) to draw attention to His representative role over the human race as its Lord, Judge, and Savior (Matt. 13:41-42; 19:28; Acts 17:31; Rom. 2:16).

B. The Determination: vss. 32-33

"All the nations will be gathered before him, and he will separate the people one from another as a shepherd separates the sheep from the goats. He will put the sheep on his right and the goats on his left."

Once Jesus was seated on His glorious throne, all the nations would be gathered in His presence. Then He would segregate them into two groups (Matt. 25:32). Expressed differently, the purpose of the judgment would be to set apart the righteous from the wicked. Only God can do that with perfect justice. We know from the parable of the wheat and the tares that during the church age, there would be a commingling of true and false disciples (13:30). Even until the end time of judgment, the good would coexist alongside the bad. Nonetheless, when the Messiah gathered together all humanity, then the separation would come.

Jesus compared the setting apart of humans to the way a shepherd would separate sheep from goats. In ancient Palestine, sheep and goats often grazed together during the day. When night came, however, they were herded into separate folds. That was because the goats, unlike the sheep, could not easily endure the cooler night air and thus had to be grouped to keep warm. The point of the comparison lies in the fact that sheep and goats were separated at the end of the day. As the Shepherd of judgment, Jesus would put the "sheep" on His right and the "goats" on His left (vs. 33).

Some think this separation might refer to a custom practiced by the Sanhedrin or Jewish Supreme Court. Acquitted prisoners were sent to the right of the leader of the court, while those who were convicted were placed on the left. More generally, in ancient times, the right hand was commonly understood as a place of honor or special favor. The left hand, by contrast, was regarded as a place of lesser favor or, in more extreme cases, the absence of any favor whatsoever.

There are two primary ways of understanding Jesus' parable. Some say the "nations" (vs. 32) refer to all peoples, while others claim they refer to Gentiles only. One group thinks the judgment occurs at the conclusion of history. In contrast, the second group says it takes place when Jesus comes to set up a kingdom on earth. For those in the first group, the judgment determines who goes to heaven and who goes to hell. Oppositely, those in the second group say the judgment concerns who enters Jesus' earthly kingdom and who does not.

II. THOSE ON JESUS' RIGHT: MATTHEW 25:34-40

A. The Promise of the Kingdom: vs. 34

"Then the King will say to those on his right, 'Come, you who are blessed by my Father; take your inheritance, the kingdom prepared for you since the creation of the world.'"

The remainder of Jesus' parable describes what He would do with the sheep (or the righteous) and the goats (or the wicked) once He has them separated. First,

He commented on the sheep (Matt. 25:34-40) and then the goats (vss. 41-45). While seated on His throne, Jesus would reign and judge as King. He would address those on His right side as "blessed by my Father" (vs. 34). God would favor them in the blessing they received as an inheritance from Him, namely, the kingdom of heaven. Jesus described this kingdom as having been "prepared for you since the creation of the world." All along it has been a part of God's plan to bless the righteous with His kingdom. Upon Jesus' return, it would be time for the plan's fulfillment.

"Kingdom" in verse 34 translates *basileian* [bah-sih-LAY-ahn], from which we get our English word *basilica*. The term refers to the rule of God over His creation. The Bible describes God's kingdom as being heavenly (2 Tim. 4:18), unshakable (Heb. 12:28), and eternal (2 Pet. 1:11). Scripture describes the richness of God's kingdom in a variety of ways. It is inseparably linked to righteousness, peace, and joy (Rom. 14:17). The kingdom of God is associated with suffering and patient endurance (Rev. 1:9), supernatural power (1 Cor. 4:20), promise (Jas. 2:5), glory (1 Thess. 2:12), and the "renewal of all things" (Matt. 19:28). God's kingdom is not the product of human striving or invention (John 18:36). It is given as a gift (Luke 12:32) and humbly received (Mark 10:15). The Lord brings His people into His kingdom (Col. 1:13), makes them worthy of it (2 Thess. 1:5), and preserves them for it (2 Tim. 4:18).

The divine kingdom embraces all who walk in fellowship with God and do His will. It is governed by God's laws, which are summed up in our duty to love God supremely and love others as ourselves (see last week's lesson for further development of this theme). Also, this kingdom, which the prophets announced and Jesus introduced, would one day displace all the kingdoms of this world, following the return of the Messiah. How can formerly sinful people share in the divine kingdom? It's because they have trusted in God's Son, whom He sent to earth to die for humanity's transgressions (John 3:16). The believers' place in God's kingdom is assured because they are forgiven in union with the Son (Eph. 1:7). And their hope of salvation is sure because it rests on the finished redemptive work of their great High Priest (1 Pet. 1:3-5 and the commentary appearing in lesson 7).

B. The Deeds of the Blessed: vss. 35-36

"For I was hungry and you gave me something to eat, I was thirsty and you gave me something to drink, I was a stranger and you invited me in, I needed clothes and you clothed me, I was sick and you looked after me, I was in prison and you came to visit me.'"

Jesus said the righteous would inherit the kingdom because of how they have treated Him. They would have met His needs for food, drink, shelter, clothing, nursing, and visitation (Matt. 25:35-36). These are emphases that anyone at any time in any society can understand, for they are the common concerns of life everywhere. So, the test of faith that stands up under Jesus' inspection would be how we performed deeds of mercy, love, and kindness. After all, this is what Jesus did for people while He was here on earth. Also, His righteous sheep follow His example. They show that their faith is practical and touches the lives of hurting people. Clearly, then, valid Christian faith is more than saying the right prayers or singing approved hymns. It includes standing alongside people in the harshest circumstances.

C. The Questions Asked by the Blessed: vss. 37-39

"Then the righteous will answer him, 'Lord, when did we see you hungry and feed you, or thirsty and give you something to drink? When did we see you a stranger and invite you in, or needing clothes and clothe you? When did we see you sick or in prison and go to visit you?'"

Jesus called His sheep "the righteous" (Matt. 25:37). They were upright because of their faith in the Messiah, and godly living marked their lives because they cared for people in need. The righteous asked a series of good questions in verses 37-39. In their place, we might also wonder when we ever had an opportunity to do such charitable deeds for Jesus. Here we see that Jesus wants us to show His love to others. Even the simplest act of kindness to the seemingly most insignificant person meets with God's approval and will be eternally rewarded.

D. The Response Given by the Lord: vs. 40

"The King will reply, 'I tell you the truth, whatever you did for one of the least of these brothers of mine, you did for me.'"

Jesus said that the deeds the righteous had done "for one of the least of these brothers of mine" (Matt. 25:40) were performed for Him. Put another way, service carried out for Jesus' needy brothers and sisters is the same as service done for Him. This is an astounding truth, for it radically transforms our motivation for performing deeds of mercy. Because elsewhere Scripture clearly teaches that good works do not earn salvation (Eph. 2:8-10; Titus 3:5), we know that the assessment of lifestyle in Matthew 25:40 refers to the results of salvation, not the cause of it. Once we are saved, we should expect to see the fruit of God's grace at work in our lives (Eph. 3:10; Jas. 2:26).

There has been much discussion about the identity of the "brothers" (Matt. 25:40). Some have said they are the Jews; others say they are all Christians; still others say they are suffering people everywhere. Such a debate is much like the lawyer's earlier question to Jesus, "And who is my neighbor?" (Luke 10:29; also, see the corresponding commentary in lesson 10). The point of Jesus' parable is not the *who*, but rather the *what*; in other words, the importance of serving where ministry is needed. The focus of this story about the sheep and the goats is that we should love every person and reach out to anyone we can. Such compassion and kindness glorifies God by reflecting our love for Him.

III. Those on Jesus' Left: Matthew 25:41-46

A. The Pronouncement of Judgment: vs. 41

"Then he will say to those on his left, 'Depart from me, you who are cursed, into the eternal fire prepared for the devil and his angels.'"

Jesus next focused on the goats. Instead of being invited to come, like the ones on the right, the ones on the left would be told to depart. Also, rather than being blessed by the Father, these people would be cursed. Moreover, instead of inheriting the kingdom prepared for the righteous, these people would be consigned to the eternal fire (Matt. 25:41).

God did not prepare hell for people, but for the devil and his angels. God's plan was to redeem and restore human beings, not condemn and destroy them. This was His reason for the cross. From the foundation of the world, He prepared an inheritance for His people (vs. 34). However, people sentenced to the place prepared for the devil go there because they chose to reject the Father's gracious offer of eternal life through faith in His Son—as evidenced by the lack of compassion in their lives (Rom. 9:22; 1 Pet. 2:7-8).

The point Jesus made in Matthew 25:41 is that He barred hypocrites from entering His kingdom. Expressed differently, He did not want people doing good works for show, just so they could get credit. Nor did Jesus want people doing charitable deeds simply as an escape plan to avoid eternal judgment. He desired people to be motivated by a change from the inside out. Jesus also wanted their good works to be expressions of grace, not superficial acts done to somehow tally up points toward heaven.

B. The Failures of the Condemned: vss. 42-43

"'For I was hungry and you gave me nothing to eat, I was thirsty and you gave me nothing to drink, I was a stranger and you did not invite me in, I needed clothes and you did not clothe me, I was sick and in prison and you did not look after me.'"

Just as the righteous would inherit the kingdom for meeting Jesus' needs, the wicked would be consigned to hell for not meeting His needs. They would have been presented with the same opportunities to give Him food and drink and the rest, but they would have chosen not to do so (Matt. 25:42-43). Notice that even though the goats mingled with the sheep, that alone did not make them sheep. To be a sheep, we must be born a sheep. Spiritually speaking, we need a new birth from above (John 3:3). For those who spurn the Messiah, all that remains is for Him to condemn them. It would be a terrifying scene as He issues a verdict of guilty against the unsaved (John 5:22; 9:39; Acts 10:42).

C. The Questions Asked by the Condemned: vs. 44

"They also will answer, 'Lord, when did we see you hungry or thirsty or a stranger or needing clothes or sick or in prison, and did not help you?'"

199

The wicked would be just as mystified as the righteous about when they had the opportunities that Jesus mentioned. They would ask when they chose not to help the Lord (Matt. 25:44). They failed to realize that the basis for judgment would be whether they showed love to others, whom God has created in His image (Jas. 2:15-16; 1 John 3:14-18).

D. The Response Given by the Lord: vss. 45-46

"He will reply, 'I tell you the truth, whatever you did not do for one of the least of these, you did not do for me.' Then they will go away to eternal punishment, but the righteous to eternal life."

Jesus' solemn reply would be that refusing to help others in need is the same as refusing to help Him (Matt. 25:45). Verse 46 concludes both the story of the sheep and the goats. The wicked and righteous have radically different futures. The first group is eternally condemned, while the second group is eternally blessed. Jesus' judgments would be beyond appeal.

Discussion Questions

1. What would be the first act Jesus performs after sitting on His glorious throne?
2. What would be the destiny of those on Jesus' right? Why would this be so?
3. What would be the destiny of those on Jesus' left? Why would this be so?
4. How does Jesus say we can know that our good works are done for the right reason?
5. Who among our family, friends, and coworkers needs the touch of God's love from us?

Contemporary Application

As Jesus approached His crucifixion, He never wavered from judgment. He told His people to get ready, to keep watching, to keep working, and to take care of one another when they were hungry, sick, imprisoned, and so on. In fact, He pictured a grand finale of judgment when He will separate everyone, some to His kingdom and some to eternal fire.

As was noted in the Lesson Commentary, we should not misinterpret the parable of the sheep and the goats to mean that one's eternal state is based upon good works. The New Testament is clear that faith in Christ (or its absence) determines our eternal destiny. Nevertheless, we can take away from this parable the ideas that Jesus eternally rewards service done to Him, that real faith is expressed in good works, and that He counts ministry accomplished on behalf of His people as the same as service done to Him.

So, what acts of service receive the reward of the kingdom? Included are simple acts any of us can do, such as offering a meal to a hungry person and giving a cup of water to a thirsty person. Let's get busy! And let's get ready for Jesus to come!

Serving in God's Strength

Scripture

Background Scripture: *Ephesians 6:10-20*
Scripture Lesson: *Ephesians 6:10-20*
Key Verse: *Put on the full armor of God so that you can take
your stand against the devil's schemes.* Ephesians 6:11.
Scripture Lesson for Children: *Ephesians 6:10-20*
Key Verse for Children: *Put on the full armor of God.*
Ephesians 6:11.

Lesson Aim

To recognize that God alone can equip us for spiritual
warfare.

Lesson Setting

Time: A.D. *60–62*
Place: Rome

Lesson Outline

Serving in God's Strength

   I. Putting on the Armor: Ephesians 6:10-12
      A. *Donning Our Spiritual Armor: vss. 10-11*
      B. *Recognizing Our True Enemy: vs. 12*
  II. Standing with the Armor: Ephesians 6:13-17
      A. *Victory as Our Goal: vs. 13*
      B. *Our Spiritual Arsenal: vss. 14-17*
      C. *Our Dependence on the Spirit: vss. 18-20*

Introduction for Adults

Topic: *Always Be Prepared*

In the movies, fighting evil is simply a matter of having the right equipment. But in real life, spiritual warfare involves a far more powerful weapon—faith in God. Anything less, and it is like waving a plastic wand over an empty top hat and expecting "magic" to happen. There's no power in the plastic. It's merely a prop. Only the trained illusionist can take that empty hat and fill it with a live rabbit.

When it comes to combating evil and sin in our world, the real source of power is the sovereign Lord of all creation. So, to be victorious, we must put ourselves in God's hands. When we do, He promises to give us the spiritual tools we need to stand our ground when the day of evil comes.

The Book of Acts tells us that's what happened in ancient Ephesus (19:11-20), especially as "the name of the Lord Jesus" (vs. 17) triumphed over evil. We can witness those same results today.

Introduction for Youth

Topic: *Armed for Battle*

In Ephesians 6:13, Paul urged us to put on every piece of God's armor so that in the time of evil we will be able to resist our enemy, the devil. As believers, if we don't keep in mind who the real enemy is, we may sometimes begin to wage war on one another, rather than on the true enemy, as the following story shows.

When World War I broke out, the war ministry in London sent a coded message to one of the British outposts in the inaccessible areas of Africa. The message read: "War declared. Arrest all enemy aliens in your district."

The War Ministry received this prompt reply: "Have arrested ten Germans, six Belgians, four Frenchmen, two Italians, three Austrians, and one American. Please advise immediately with whom we're at war."

Concepts for Children

Topic: *Get Ready to Serve!*

1. God wants us to be strong in His power.
2. God wants to protect us against the forces of evil in the world.
3. God can help us serve others by telling them about Jesus.
4. God wants us to pray to Him, even when we don't feel like doing so.
5. As we obey God, He watches over us.

Lesson Commentary

I. PUTTING ON THE ARMOR: EPHESIANS 6:10-12

A. Donning Our Spiritual Armor: vss. 10-11

Finally, be strong in the Lord and in his mighty power. Put on the full armor of God so that you can take your stand against the devil's schemes.

More information in the New Testament pertains historically to Ephesians than to almost any other community of believers. No less than 20 chapters of the Bible describe God's work and His people at Ephesus. For instance, in Acts 18–20, Luke recounted the founding of the church. Also, Paul wrote Ephesians to the congregation and sent two letters, 1 and 2 Timothy, to this young pastor. Moreover, John, as he repeated a message from the Savior, encouraged and warned the Ephesians in a letter preserved in Revelation 2:1-7.

From this information, which covers a period of more than four decades, it seems the Ephesian church was quite productive. According to Acts 19:10, the Gospel spread far inland from Ephesus until both Jews and Greeks who lived in the province of Asia heard the Good News. Revelation and the letters to Timothy show that the Ephesians started several other churches. Also, some historians think that a fugitive slave named Onesimus, who once belonged to Philemon (who lived in Colossae), might have been the same Bishop Onesimus who served at Ephesus around A.D. 110.

As Paul and others ministered at Ephesus, they encountered the spiritual forces of darkness arrayed against the proclamation of the Gospel. The apostle understood the power of evil as much as anyone. He had often been the object of satanic efforts to hurt him and hinder his work. Also, he knew the Ephesian Christians were on Satan's list of targets too. So, in bringing his letter to a close, the apostle focused on the spiritual struggle that they faced. Some people say that Satan and demons are a myth invented by primitive, ignorant people. In contrast, the Bible indicates that the devil and his fallen angels are real and pose a threat to the Christian way of life. Paul said that to withstand their attacks, believers must depend on God's strength and use every item that He makes available (Eph. 6:10).

In verse 11, the apostle exhorted his readers to "put on the full armor of God" so that they could stand firm against all the strategies and tricks of the devil. In other places besides Ephesians, the Bible describes cosmic forces that are at work against God in the world (Rom. 8:38; 1 Cor. 15:24; Col. 2:15; 1 Pet. 3:22). Moreover, Satan is called the "ruler of the kingdom of the air" (Eph. 2:2), and he has this world in his power (1 John 5:19). Believers fight against evil spiritual beings who are part of a hierarchy of power in heavenly and earthly places. The ultimate goal of these evil forces is to destroy the relationship between God and humanity. But one of the major themes of Ephesians is that Jesus is the supreme

Lord of the universe. Once we believe in Him, we can escape defeat by the ruler of this world (1:21; 2:2).

B. Recognizing Our True Enemy: vs. 12

For our struggle is not against flesh and blood, but against the rulers, against the authorities, against the powers of this dark world and against the spiritual forces of evil in the heavenly realms.

The battle Paul described is not a human one, but rather a supernatural one. It involves a hierarchy of evil rulers and authorities in the unseen world and wicked spirits in the heavenly realms (Eph. 6:12). The Greek nouns translated "rulers" and "authorities" indicate that demons have a certain amount of power and influence at the present stage of history. But of course this power is far less than what belongs to Jesus. The Greek noun rendered "powers" once indicated those who aspire to world control. In pagan religions, it was often used of idols and especially of the sun, which was considered a deity. So, Paul's use of the term in connection with the phrase "dark world" might have been meant to suggest that while the demons masquerade as ambassadors of light (good), they are in fact agents of darkness (evil; see 2 Cor. 11:4).

The phrase translated "the spiritual forces of evil in the heavenly realms" (Eph. 6:12) reflects the language of astrology in Paul's day. Astrologers taught that demons live in the heavenly bodies and from there control the destiny of people. The apostle's use of the phrase in this context indicates that believers need not be dominated by demons, but are able to fight against them. It is important for us to recognize that Satan rules a powerful demonic army whose prime objective is to defeat Jesus' followers. In this battle, the devil and his subordinates use whatever devices they have to turn us away from the Lord and back to sin. Christians today are engaged in a spiritual struggle no less fierce than the one that raged in the early years of the church. In fact, our battles are really the continuation of a war begun long ago.

Satan and his demons have adapted their strategies to current situations, but their goals have not changed. They want to prevent the lost from hearing the Gospel; they want to undermine the faith of believers; and they want to thwart Christians from contributing to God's work in the world. The devil certainly is far stronger than we are, but he is infinitely weaker than God. In fact, Jesus' death and resurrection ensure that eventually we will win (1 Cor. 15:57; Col. 2:15). As John explained, every child of God is able to prevail against this evil world, and the believers' victory is achieved through their trust in the Messiah (1 John 5:4), the Son of God (vs. 5).

II. STANDING WITH THE ARMOR: EPHESIANS 6:13-17

A. Victory as Our Goal: vs. 13

Therefore put on the full armor of God, so that when the day of evil comes, you may be able to stand your ground, and after you have done everything, to stand.

Paul told the Ephesians not to delay preparing for spiritual battle. They should put on the "full armor of God" (Eph. 6:13) right away. Then they would be ready in the time of evil, that is, when Satan launches his attack (which is certain to come). Paul was convinced that with the right preparation (and of course courageous fighting), his readers would still be standing and retain their ground when the battle was over. According to traditional military doctrine, the army in possession of the field after a battle is the victor.

As a prisoner in Rome, Paul was chained to a Roman soldier at all times. So, it was natural for him to see his guard as a model and to think of the spiritual struggle in military terms. Undoubtedly, the Old Testament influenced the apostle too, since the Hebrew Scriptures frequently use military images for spiritual realities (Isa. 11:5 and 59:17). Paul's guards probably did not wear full battle dress. But they could easily bring to Paul's mind the times he had seen Roman soldiers fully armed. As every Roman soldier knew, the occasion to dress himself in his protective covering was not when hostilities erupted. Before the battle, he prepared himself by taking up armor and weapons. In Paul's discussion, we are not told to take the offensive against Satan. But he is attacking us. Therefore, we need to look to our defenses and make sure we do not lose any ground to him. Our spiritual successes have been hard-won, and so we should stand firm and fight to hold onto them.

B. Our Spiritual Arsenal: vss. 14-17

Stand firm then, with the belt of truth buckled around your waist, with the breastplate of righteousness in place, and with your feet fitted with the readiness that comes from the gospel of peace. In addition to all this, take up the shield of faith, with which you can extinguish all the flaming arrows of the evil one. Take the helmet of salvation and the sword of the Spirit, which is the word of God.

Having made his plea for preparedness, Paul began describing the six pieces of equipment that the Christian should take into spiritual battle (Eph. 6:14-17). The apostle listed them in the order in which a soldier getting ready for a battle would put them on. The first piece of equipment is the "belt of truth" (vs. 14). A Roman soldier's belt held in his tunic and breastplate and became a place to hang his sword. For Christians, our belt is "truth." This general term might refer to the truth of the Gospel and to our truthfulness in everyday life. Conversely, Satan is a liar and hates the truth (John 8:44; Rev. 12:9).

The second piece of equipment Paul describes is the "breastplate of righteousness" (Eph. 6:14). Roman soldiers wore over the entire front of their torso a large protective plate made of bronze, or, if they were wealthy, of chain mail. The Christian's breastplate is "righteousness." As we draw on the Savior's righteousness, we are able to live devout and holy lives. Also, an upright life is an effective defense against Satan's attacks. Paul didn't specify what the third piece of equipment is, but he was obviously referring to footgear. Roman soldiers wore strong sandals or boots studded with nails for traction while marching.

Similarly, Christians are to be shod with "the readiness that comes from the gospel of peace" (vs. 15). This phrase was probably meant to suggest that our peace with the Father, won by the Son, gives us sure footing in our spiritual battle with Satan.

The fourth piece of equipment is the "shield of faith" (vs. 16). Roman soldiers carried large shields made of wood covered with hide and bound with iron. These shields provided effective protection from blows and even from the burning darts fired at them by their enemies. "Flaming arrows" were often used in sieges of cities. Bows and arrows would effectively hit targets from long range (300–400 yards). If a soldier became terrified of burning darts stuck in his shield, he might throw down his shield and be more vulnerable to attack. Therefore, shields were sometimes dipped in water to extinguish flaming arrows. Faith is more effective than a Roman shield in defending us against Satan's attack, especially as we steadfastly anchor our trust in the Savior (Heb. 6:19-20).

The fifth piece of equipment is the "helmet of salvation" (Eph. 6:17). Roman soldiers wore helmets of bronze and leather to protect their heads. Also, just as Roman soldiers received their helmets from their armor-bearers to put on, so Christians receive salvation from the Lord to use in their conflict with Satan. We look forward to a time when our salvation is complete and Satan is utterly defeated. The last piece of equipment in the Christian's armory is the "sword of the Spirit." For some reason Paul did not mention the long spear that was the Roman soldier's chief offensive weapon. Instead, the apostle referred to the short two-edged sword Roman legionaries carried. Paul compared this weapon to "the word of God." When Jesus was tempted in the wilderness, He used Scripture as a weapon against Satan. The Spirit can also help us use God's Word against the same foe.

C. Our Dependence on the Spirit: vss. 18-20

And pray in the Spirit on all occasions with all kinds of prayers and requests. With this in mind, be alert and always keep on praying for all the saints. Pray also for me, that whenever I open my mouth, words may be given me so that I will fearlessly make known the mystery of the gospel, for which I am an ambassador in chains. Pray that I may declare it fearlessly, as I should.

Prayer is not a piece of spiritual armor for believers. We are not to use prayer just when under attack, but rather we are always to keep in touch with God through prayer and receive power and strength from Him. Accordingly, Paul urged his readers to pray "in the Spirit" (Eph. 6:18). This probably means either to pray in communion with the Spirit or to pray in the power of the Spirit (or both). Paul described some qualities associated with prayer in the Spirit. First, it is frequent. We are to pray "on all occasions" and "always keep on praying." Second, prayer in the Spirit has room for variety. We are to pray "with all kinds of prayers and requests." Third, prayer in the Spirit is well informed. We are to "be alert," that is, on the lookout for needs. Fourth, prayer in the Spirit is unselfish. We are to pray not only for ourselves, "but for all the saints," meaning for all Christians.

This last point mirrors what Paul said in Philippians 2:4. The apostle did not intend for us to overlook our personal needs, but taught that self-centeredness should be replaced by a mind-set that gives equal weight to the welfare of others. It is another way of expressing Jesus' command to love our neighbors as we love ourselves (see Matt. 19:19, as well as the pertinent information in lesson 10). In the midst of intense spiritual warfare, a cooperative effort among believers was imperative, in which they lovingly and humbly upheld one another in prayer.

As an example of a saint for whom the Ephesians could pray, Paul offered himself (Eph. 6:19-20). He did not ask his readers to pray for his release from prison. Instead, he requested prayer for a courageous spirit in proclaiming the Gospel while imprisoned (vs. 19). When Paul arrived in Rome as an inmate about A.D. 60, he was not kept in one of the civil or military prisons. He was permitted to rent his own home, to receive visitors, and to preach the Gospel (Acts 28:30-31). Soldiers of the Praetorian Guard, the emperor's bodyguard unit, took turns watching the apostle while chained to him. Paul was able to share the Good News about Jesus with these soldiers as well as others associated with the apostle's case (Phil. 1:12-14). The imprisonment lasted about two years. During this period, the apostle wrote Philemon, Colossians, Philippians, and Ephesians.

Ambassadors are usually afforded the privilege of diplomatic immunity from arrest. Even though Paul was "in chains" (Eph. 6:20), he saw himself as an ambassador for the Messiah. There was no doubt in the apostle's mind that his imprisonment was a God-given opportunity. It would enable Paul to convey the Gospel to officials high in the Roman government—people he would not otherwise have had an opportunity to meet. The emperor might even have heard his case personally. Since the government officials had the power of life and death over the apostle, he naturally felt some anxiety. But he didn't want unease to prevent him from preaching the Good News clearly and powerfully. So his primary prayer request was for fearlessness and reliance upon God when it came time for Paul to witness at the risk of his life.

Early traditions suggest that Paul was not martyred at the end of the Roman imprisonment during which he wrote Ephesians. One possible scenario for the last years of the apostle's life, based on historical reports and inferences, goes like this: About A.D. 62, Paul was released from house arrest in Rome, either because he was acquitted or because his case dragged on beyond the allowable limit. Then the apostle achieved his long-held goal of taking the Gospel to Spain, the western limit of the Roman Empire. Next, Paul turned east, revisiting cities in Crete, Asia Minor, and Greece. In one of these places or in Rome, the apostle was arrested again and taken to the Mamertime Prison in Rome. The persecution of Christians under Nero was in full swing, so Paul's second Roman imprisonment was shorter and harsher than his first one. But he managed to get off the letters to Timothy and Titus. Between A.D. 65 and 67, the apostle was executed by beheading, and his body was buried along the Ostian Way outside Rome.

Discussion Questions

1. What should believers do when the devil and his subordinates attack?
2. When is the best time to put on God's spiritual armor?
3. What good is truthfulness when fighting against Satan?
4. Of what value is God's Word in the midst of the battle?
5. When did Paul envision believers praying?

Contemporary Application

The "Got Milk?" advertisement campaign, which has been running since it first aired on October 29, 1993, made a valid point: the necessity of an item is never so apparent as when it's missing. Consider the experiences of these individuals.

Loraine, a Christian, knew she lacked a certain degree that would give her an edge in getting a job she really wanted. On her application, she said she held the degree. However, someone who knew about Loraine's education saw her application. They were ready to hire her, but the company called and asked if she held the degree she indicated. In shame, Loraine had to admit that she didn't. Do you have your *belt of truth?*

Devon was busy with the demands of the holiday season when his landlord came to his door to deliver a Christmas card. Devon hoped his visit would be brief, and it was. The landlord announced he had things to get done. Devon wished him Merry Christmas and got back to his work. But a few minutes after the landlord left, Devon noticed on his table an invitation to his congregation's Christmas candlelight service. In his self-centeredness, he'd forgotten that he had been praying for an opportunity to give his landlord the invitation. Do you have your *boots of readiness?*

Bill had been laid off from his job, and Tina's income was just barely paying the bills. Bill was always one of the final candidates for the jobs, but he was never hired. As difficulties pressed in on this young couple, they began to turn on one another in anger and frustration, straining their relationship. At church, they acted as if everything was all right, but in their hearts, they had begun to wonder if God had abandoned them. Do you have your *shield of faith?* In each of these scenarios, Paul couldn't have stressed more strongly our need to put on spiritual armor.

The Lamb of God

Scripture

Background Scripture: *John 1:29-34*
Scripture Lesson: *John 1:29-34*
Key Verse: "*I have seen and I testify that this is the Son of God."* John 1:34.
Scripture Lesson for Children: *John 1:29-34*
Key Verse for Children: *The next day John saw Jesus coming toward him and said, "Look, the Lamb of God, who takes away the sin of the world!"* John 1:29.

Lesson Aim

To humbly point others to the Lord Jesus.

Lesson Setting

Time: A.D. *27*
Place: Jordan River

Lesson Outline

The Lamb of God
   I. The Identification of Jesus: John 1:29-31
       A. *Spotting Jesus: vs. 29*
       B. *Explaining Who Jesus Is: vss. 30-31*
  II. The Baptism of Jesus: John 1:32-34
       A. *The Testimony of John: vs. 32*
       B. *The Declaration of the Father: vss. 33-34*

Introduction for Adults

Topic: *A Reliable Testimony*

Derrick stood center stage in his royal finery as King Lear and read loudly from his well-thumbed script, "If your diligence be not speedy, I shall be there afore you." Then Jack suddenly stepped in front of Derrick, faced the darkened auditorium, and exclaimed, "I will not sleep, my lord, till I have delivered your letter."

"No, no, no," the director called out from the front row. "Jack, you're playing the Earl of Kent, not King Lear." "So?" asked Jack. "So, don't step in front of the king to deliver your line," responded the director. "Otherwise, you're upstaging the play's central figure."

In theater, it is crucial that minor characters not outshine the more important people on stage. It misleads the audience and can potentially damage the scene. A similar principle applies with believers pointing others to Jesus. Our role is to direct the lost to the Savior and not risk drawing attention to ourselves. As we learn in this week's lesson, John the Baptizer gladly took on that role.

Introduction for Youth

Topic: *Let Me Point the Way*

At a University of Chicago religion class, a student declared, "I want to be like John: a voice in the desert, crying for the outcasts, unmasking the hypocrites, and showing sinners the way to righteousness!" Another student echoed the sentiment: "Please, not Jesus! John is my man!"

These remarks represent a desire for a revolutionary leader. But was the Baptizer really such a revolutionary? Or was John the one who humbly pointed to a far more effective leader: Jesus, who is an avenue beyond mere social change? Scripture reveals that John directed the attention of others away from himself to the "Lamb of God" (John 1:29). The Baptizer also spotlighted Jesus' messiahship.

John submitted to Jesus' lordship and His loving way. Jesus' way is based on love, not rebellion. Here we discover that both John and Jesus were far more than social activists.

Concepts for Children

Topic: *Jesus Is the One!*

1. God gave John a special job.
2. God wanted John to tell others about Jesus.
3. John knew his job was very important.
4. John let others know that Jesus is our Savior.
5. God also wants us to talk about Jesus to others.

Lesson Commentary

I. THE IDENTIFICATION OF JESUS: JOHN 1:29-31

A. Spotting Jesus: vs. 29

The next day John saw Jesus coming toward him and said, "Look, the Lamb of God, who takes away the sin of the world!"

John's Gospel has been described as a drama. In particular, the opening portion is considered the prologue (1:1-18). Subsequently, the apostle's account introduced a series of characters, including John the Baptizer (the subject of this week's lesson), Nicodemus, and the Samaritan woman at the well. John skillfully wove Jesus' encounters with these and other individuals into the narrative of the Fourth Gospel to show Jesus as the pivotal figure of the universe. For instance, we learn in verses 1 and 2 that Jesus eternally existed before the dawn of creation and that He, the Father, and the Spirit were inseparable. The text does not say that Jesus, the "Word," is "a god." Instead, we learn that the Son is in every way equal to the other members of the Godhead.

"Word" is *logos* in the Greek. The Greek philosophers used *logos* in various ways, usually to refer to a prevailing rational principle or force that guided the universe. But to John, the *logos* was not an impersonal rational force that remained detached from humanity. John used *logos* to refer to that supreme being who, although equal to the Father and the Spirit, became human and shared in the struggles and hardships of the human race. The person we know as Jesus of Nazareth is the eternal, living Word who spoke all things into existence (Gen. 1). While John 1:3-4 are clear that we owe our physical existence to the Son, the meaning probably goes beyond that to include spiritual life. Jesus shines as our ultimate hope (vs. 5). He alone can offer eternal life in a world filled with depravity and death.

Verses 6-8 explain that John the Baptizer was the key person who testified concerning the Messiah as the light of the world. In doing so, John prepared the hearts of people to accept Jesus as the unique Son of God. The primary purpose of the Baptizer's ministry was to point the lost to Jesus for salvation. By the time the Fourth Gospel was written (around A.D. 85), some individuals held exaggerated views of Jesus' forerunner. While not directly confronting these people, the apostle made it clear that the Baptizer was simply a witness to the light. As verse 9 declares, Jesus is the genuine light who came to shine God's truth in a world bound in the darkness of sin and superstition.

Even though the Son is equal to the Father and the Spirit, the Son came to earth as a human being. However, earth's inhabitants failed to "recognize" (vs. 10) Him as their Maker and Messiah. Ironically, those who owed their every breath to Jesus refused to give Him the honor due His name. Verse 11 emphasizes the tragedy of the rejection. Jesus not only came into the world He created, but also came to the people He had chosen—that is, the inhabitants of Israel. Yet, instead of welcoming Him with open arms, a majority rejected Him.

Thankfully, the narrative does not end there. Some in fact "received" (vs. 12) Jesus and were given the "right" to join God's family as His spiritual "children." The lost enter God's household by grace through a spiritual rebirth (3:3, 5). No one can earn this privilege or be physically born into it (1:13). To accomplish our salvation, Jesus became human and took up residence among us. The Greek verb rendered "made his dwelling" literally means "to encamp," as though Jesus temporarily pitched His tent in our midst. In the Incarnation, God the Son accepted the limitations and conditions of humanity. Those who were close to Him, such as John, saw Jesus' divine glory, especially in His crucifixion. In turn, the apostle testified that Jesus was indeed the one whom the Father sent to live as a human being (vs. 14).

Because John the Baptizer was slightly older than Jesus and began his ministry earlier, many naturally assumed that John was the greater of the two individuals. People in ancient times gave the older person more respect and honor than the younger one. But the Baptizer reversed that custom by proclaiming that Jesus far "surpassed" (vs. 15) him because, in reality, Jesus existed as God the Son for all eternity before He was ever born. In verse 14, the apostle said that Jesus was "full of grace." Then, in verse 16, the apostle expanded on that theme, describing the Messiah as the source of all eternal blessings. God's grace to His people is never depleted. So, while Moses revealed God's justice through the law, Jesus showed us the "grace and truth" (vs. 17) of God Himself.

The apostle stated that no person has seen God at any time (vs. 18). Yet, in the Old Testament, there seem to have been appearances of God. Nonetheless, while people on previous occasions saw special appearances of God (for example, as Moses did on Mount Sinai; see Exod. 33:18-23), these did not reveal God's essential being. The human eye can neither detect His full revealed essence nor survive the direct sight of all His glory. The Father, in His grace, sent His unique and beloved Son to unveil the sublime nature of the Godhead in a way that we could understand. In a manner of speaking, Jesus was God's living image dwelling on the earth (John 14:9; Col. 1:15; 2:9; Heb. 1:3).

John 1:19-23 indicates that because the Baptizer's preaching attracted so much attention, the Jewish authorities in Jerusalem sent a delegation to Bethany, beyond the Jordan River, where John was baptizing (vs. 28). Their job was to investigate and interrogate this unauthorized and unusual teacher, whom they thought posed a threat to their established traditions. John probably addressed the question of whether he was the Messiah many times without even being asked. Since he clearly and emphatically denied being Israel's Savior, the delegation wondered whether John was Elijah, the renowned Old Testament prophet.

In that day, the Jews believed Elijah would appear in Israel before the coming of the Messiah (Mal. 4:5-6). After all, Elijah had not died, but had been taken up by a chariot into heaven (2 Kings 2:11). The Baptizer's rugged characteristics, ascetic behavior, and fiery temperament probably reminded people of the Elijah they knew from Scripture (2 Kings 1:8; Matt. 3:4; Mark 1:6). Based on Deuteronomy 18:15, the Jews also expected a great prophet to appear in connection with the Messiah. Although the Jews of that time were unclear as to whom this spokesperson might be, from the earliest days of the church, Christian scholars have identified Him as the Messiah.

Next, the delegation asked the Baptizer for an answer concerning his identity so they had something specific to report to the authorities in Jerusalem. In response, John applied the words of Isaiah 40:3 to his ministry. That passage pictures someone preparing a road through open and rugged territory so a monarch could travel on a smooth highway. The Baptizer claimed to be nothing more than a voice preparing people for someone who would be much greater than himself. The Pharisees, who were probably part of the original delegation, were unsatisfied with the progress of the interrogation and probed further into the nature of John's ministry. They questioned his authority to baptize, especially since it did not fit with their understanding of the Mosaic law, and no one else had acted in such a dramatic way (John 1:24-25).

John responded to the Pharisees' challenge in a manner that exalted Jesus and diminished John's own importance as the messenger. The other Gospels record that John mentioned the baptism of the Holy Spirit (Matt. 3:11; Mark 1:8; Luke 3:16), but in John 1:26, the Savior's forerunner moved right into the importance of Jesus after briefly mentioning John's baptism with water. John's words seem to indicate that Jesus was in the crowd that day and listening to all that transpired. While the disciples of a rabbi would perform several menial tasks for their teacher, loosening a sandal was forbidden. The task was reserved for the lowest of slaves, who took off a person's sandals to wash that person's soiled feet (13:5). It is significant that the Baptizer's comment—that he was unworthy to be Jesus' slave—is recorded not only in 1:27, but also in the other three Gospels.

The entire Old Testament sacrificial code looked forward to the day when God would provide a "Lamb" (vs. 29) that would atone for the transgressions committed by people. The day after the Jewish delegation's visit, the Baptizer identified Jesus as that Lamb. Some think this refers to the idea of the Passover sacrifice (Exod. 12:21; 1 Cor. 5:7). Others note that the title also fits the imagery of the suffering Servant described in Isaiah 53, who was to be led like a "lamb" (vs. 7) to the slaughtering block. Jesus, the ultimate suffering Servant, was sacrificed as a lamb at Passover (1 Pet. 1:19). In this way, the Father provided the "once for all" (Heb. 7:27) sacrifice of His Son to expiate the "sins of the whole world" (1 John 2:2).

B. Explaining Who Jesus Is: vss. 30-31

"This is the one I meant when I said, 'A man who comes after me has surpassed me because he was before me.' I myself did not know him, but the reason I came baptizing with water was that he might be revealed to Israel."

The Gospel of John is one of the best-known books in the New Testament. It has also been important to the church's understanding of who Jesus is. John's Gospel differs from the Synoptics—Matthew, Mark, and Luke. Those Gospels trace Jesus' career generally in an orderly sequence. However, the Fourth Gospel is made of carefully selected material so that readers might come to a saving knowledge of the Lord Jesus as the Messiah, God's Son (20:31). Certain scholars might praise the fine literary qualities of John's Gospel, but the apostle simply wanted to promote the good news about Jesus of Nazareth. Moreover, the apostle wrote to convince each reader to trust in the Son for salvation.

For instance, we learn that God had earlier revealed to John that the Lord would identify the Messiah through John's baptizing ministry. Because they were related (and possibly cousins; see Luke 1:36), John was most likely already acquainted with Jesus. But it wasn't until John baptized Jesus that John knew for certain that Jesus was the Messiah. In declaring Jesus to be the "Lamb of God" (John 1:29), John was fulfilling his role as the one who heralded the Redeemer. Because He eternally preexisted before His messenger was ever born, Jesus "surpassed" (vs. 30) John in greatness. The Baptizer recognized the amazing privilege that God had given him to make the Messiah known to the people of Israel (vs. 31). Throughout the opening section of the Fourth Gospel, the Baptizer was presented as a great prophet. Yet as God's spokesperson, John bore witness to the fact that Jesus would usher in the reign of the Lord (Matt. 11:9-10; 14:5; 21:26; Luke 1:76; 7:26).

II. THE BAPTISM OF JESUS: JOHN 1:32-34

A. The Testimony of John: vs. 32

Then John gave this testimony: "I saw the Spirit come down from heaven as a dove and remain on him."

At the Savior's baptism, John saw the Holy Spirit appear in bodily form as a "dove" (John 1:32), descend from the sky, and settle on Jesus (Matt. 3:16; Mark 1:10; Luke 3:22). In that culture, the dove was considered a symbol of reconciliation with God (Gen. 8:8,10). Accordingly, the bird became an emblem of peace. The dove also represented tender affection (Song of Songs 1:15; 2:14).

B. The Declaration of the Father: vss. 33-34

"I would not have known him, except that the one who sent me to baptize with water told me, 'The man on whom you see the Spirit come down and remain is he who will baptize with the Holy Spirit.' I have seen and I testify that this is the Son of God."

Most likely, the Spirit's presence in the form of a dove signaled that Jesus was inaugurating the promised age of renewal for the people of God (John 1:33). This includes the Messiah's baptism of believers with the Holy Spirit (Jer. 31:31-34; Joel 2:28-32; Acts 2:16-21). The New Testament reveals that the permanent, indwelling presence of the Spirit in believers started on the day of Pentecost (see Acts 1:5; 2:1-4; 11:15-16 and the Bible commentary in lesson 13) and is now the common experience of all who have repented of their sins and experienced the new birth (Acts 2:38; 1 Cor. 12:13; Gal. 3:2). The Spirit's presence as a dove and the Father's pronouncement concerning Jesus (Matt. 3:16-17; Mark 1:11; Luke 3:22) confirmed His status as the divine, anointed Son (John 1:34).

Accordingly, the Baptizer testified publicly to the people and privately to his disciples that Jesus was the person whom God had chosen to be the Redeemer (Isa. 42:1). Also, with John's blessing, some of his followers eventually became Jesus' disciples (vss. 35-39). That said, the Baptizer made such a profound impression on his generation that a group of his followers formed a sect or community that continued long after his death (Acts 19:1-4). As noted earlier, John was a prophet in the great tradition of Amos and Isaiah. Indeed, John's message echoed the inspired preaching of the greatest of the Lord's spokespersons in Israel and Judah. Furthermore, as the son of Zechariah and Elizabeth, John's priestly family meant that he was related to the aristocracy of Jerusalem. Most importantly, John shouldered his responsibility as Jesus' forerunner with integrity, earnestness, and humility.

Discussion Questions

1. What did John mean when he called Jesus the "Lamb of God" (John 1:29)?
2. In what sense was Jesus, who was born after John, before him in time (vs. 30)?
3. What was the significance of the Spirit's descent in the form of a dove on Jesus (vs. 32)?
4. Why is the baptism of the Holy Spirit an important truth to emphasize?
5. Why is pointing others to Jesus a privilege rather than an obligation?

Contemporary Application

Imagine Prince Fielder—a star first baseman for the Detroit Tigers—choosing you to be his personal assistant and friend during his major-league baseball career. And imagine him promising to share with you everything of value he acquired during his record-setting years as an athlete (including being a four-time All Star player). Your job would be to do whatever he asked of you (and, of course, being the good guy that he is, he wouldn't ask you to do anything illegal or immoral).

At times, Fielder would have you drop him at the airport in one of his expensive vehicles. And there would be times when he'd want you to wash and wax those expensive vehicles. But what about getting a little dirty once in a while? Even if Fielder received recognition and you got the dirty work, it would be a privilege just to say you personally knew him. You'd be investing time and energy in the career of a sports celebrity, right?

But that's not the whole picture. Fielder would treat you as his personal friend. For example, he would take you out to dinner with his family and introduce you to his buddies. Who could ask for a better job? In reality, Jesus' followers don't have to dream up a job like that, for we already have one. We have the privilege of serving the King of kings. And Jesus has promised to share His entire inheritance with us. He even calls us His friends!

We have been invited to share in all that Jesus has accomplished by His life, death, and resurrection. He's the one who has done all the work that makes the hope of eternal life a reality. That's why we, like the John the Baptizer, point others to the "Lamb of God" (John 1:29) and not to ourselves. Even though we, in ourselves, have nothing to offer, Jesus has everything we need and more.

The Promised Advocate

Scripture

Background Scripture: *John 14:15-26*

Scripture Lesson: *John 14:15-26*

Key Verse: *"The Counselor, the Holy Spirit, whom the Father will send in my name, will teach you all things and will remind you of everything I have said to you."* John 14:26.

Scripture Lesson for Children: *John 14:15-26*

Key Verse for Children: *"The Holy Spirit . . . will teach you all things and will remind you of everything I have said to you."* John 14:26.

Lesson Aim

To find comfort in the Spirit's helping, guiding presence.

Lesson Setting

Time: A.D. *30*

Place: Jerusalem

Lesson Outline

The Promised Advocate

  I. The Spirit's Indwelling: John 14:15-21
    A. *Obedience Enjoined: vs. 15*
    B. *Another Counselor Promised: vss. 16-17*
    C. *Jesus' Postresurrection Appearances: vss. 18-20*
    D. *Love's Reality Confirmed: vs. 21*
  II. The Father's Love: John 14:22-26
    A. *The Request for Clarification: vs. 22*
    B. *The Savior's Explanation: vss. 23-24*
    C. *The Spirit's Teaching: vss. 25-26*

Introduction for Adults

Topic: *A Comforter and Much More*

The *Alliance Magazine* recounts the efforts of a missionary in Africa to translate the local dialect into a written form in order to produce the New Testament in that tribe's language. He was frustrated at times, especially when he couldn't find a tribal word to express the consoling ministry of the Holy Spirit.

One day, after three years of searching for just the right phrase, the missionary heard an elderly chief refer several times to a man as "Nsenga-Mukwashi" during a village proceeding. So, after the court closed, the missionary asked the chieftain what that term meant. The aging leader smiled and explained that "Nsenga-Mukwashi" was the title given to the one whose duty it was to represent all the people of the village and to stand up for them when they were in any trouble.

On that particular day, the "Nsenga-Mukwashi" had eloquently pleaded the cause of an old woman who had been unjustly treated. "My people see him as a comforting advocate," said the chief. Immediately, the missionary recognized that here was the term he could use to describe the Holy Spirit's work in the lives of believers. It beautifully expressed the truth that God's Spirit is both the Advocate and Comforter for Jesus' followers.

Introduction for Youth

Topic: *Help Is on the Way*

Students at a large city high school were upset because the adviser for their student council was always a student teacher who took the job for extra pay. The adolescents argued that there was never any continuity. Each year brought new leadership, which lasted only nine months and then changed. All programs halted. The students wondered why they couldn't have a staff member who would not leave them.

Like these students, many youth want an advocate who will not abandon them in the lurch. Many want someone who will be with them for a long period so that there will not be changes or problems. Jesus promised the Spirit—the "Counselor" (John 14:16)—would always be present with His disciples. Since Pentecost, that promise has been fulfilled!

Concepts for Children

Topic: *Help Is Coming*

1. Jesus wants us to love Him.
2. Jesus wants us to obey Him.
3. Jesus has given us the Holy Spirit.
4. The Spirit helps us to know Jesus better.
5. The Spirit helps us to be more loving to others.

Lesson Commentary

I. THE SPIRIT'S INDWELLING: JOHN 14:15-21

A. Obedience Enjoined: vs. 15

"If you love me, you will obey what I command."

During the Last Supper, Jesus encouraged His followers to calm their troubled hearts. The way to do this was to put their trust in the Father as well as in the Son (John 14:1). It is remarkable that Jesus focused on comforting His followers rather than dealing with His own needs. The treachery of Judas and the fickleness of the rest of the disciples did not prevent the Savior from remaining a calming presence among them. Jesus next spoke about heaven, perhaps to further ease the minds of His followers. He referred to heaven as a large house—belonging to His Father—that has plenty of room. Though Jesus was leaving the disciples, He was going there to prepare a place for them. Jesus told the disciples that if this were not so, He would not have made this promise to them (vs. 2). The pledge, however, was true, and so the disciples could count on Jesus one day returning to bring them back with Him to heaven (vs. 3).

Throughout Jesus' public ministry He had been teaching these men what it meant to be His followers. Now He told them that they should know the way to the place where He was going. As they followed that way, they would end up there with Him (vs. 4). Thomas openly expressed his confusion, and he was probably speaking for the other 10 as well. They did not know where Jesus was going, and they did not know the way (vs. 5). How could they? Had not Jesus already said that where He was going, they could not come (13:33)? They were dumbfounded. Jesus' reply to Thomas is the most profound "I am" declaration in the Fourth Gospel. The Savior not only identified who He was, but also made it clear that He is the only possible path to God (14:6). When Thomas asked Jesus the way, Jesus did not hand him a road map and give him directions. Jesus told all of them that He Himself is the way to God. In a few hours some of His followers would see Jesus hanging on a cross and would wonder how this could be true. After His resurrection, they would understand that as the one who died for their sins, He is the only link between God and repentant sinners.

Previously, Jesus' disciples had not fully known Him. They had seen glimpses of His true identity and had a partial understanding of who He was, but they had not fully experienced Him. If they had, they would have known that they were seeing what God the Father is like by seeing the Son. In the coming days, however, they would know Jesus and likewise they would know God (vs. 7). Philip asked Jesus to show the Father to the group. If Jesus would do that for them, they would be satisfied and it would end any doubts they had (vs. 8). Jesus was disappointed that Philip still did not understand His statement about knowing and seeing God.

The disciples had spent nearly three years with Jesus. There was no need for Philip or any of them to ask Him to show them the Father. If they truly knew the Son, they would have known that to see Him was to see the Father's divine nature (vs. 9). Jesus continued to describe His unity with God the Father by asking His disciples whether they believed He was in the Father and the Father was in Him. Jesus was forcing His disciples to consider what would have been outrageous to the Jewish mind—that a person could be one in essence with the Creator—while expecting them to believe it. In fact, Jesus' words and works were a revelation of the triune Godhead, for the Father gave the Son the words He spoke and performed through Jesus the works He did (vs. 10).

Once more Jesus encouraged His disciples to believe that He is in the Father and the Father is in Him. After living with Jesus and experiencing the life He lived, the Eleven should have taken Him at His word. But even if they could not at this point, they could at least base their belief on the miraculous signs they had witnessed (vs. 11). Jesus was presenting faith based on miracles as second best. The supreme foundation of faith is Jesus' proven character, especially when a wished-for miracle did not appear. Jesus told the disciples that those who believed in Him would do even greater things than what He had been doing (vs. 12). Jesus was not saying that they would possess greater powers than He or that they would perform greater miracles. Evidently Jesus was talking about the mighty work of conversion. Whereas Jesus' ministry was primarily confined to Galilee and Judea, they would take the Gospel to distant lands. Yet they could do none of this unless Jesus first returned to the Father.

According to verse 13, when we make our requests known to God through Jesus' name, the Savior Himself will do it. Of course, Jesus was not providing a magical formula to be used as though one were bidding a genie to grant a wish. Nor did Jesus mean that He would always fulfill the request in the way His followers desired. Moreover, Jesus was referring to requests whose primary purpose is to glorify God, and so are in line with God's will. Jesus' statements do not limit the power of prayer. Instead, they require the petitioner to make his or her request consistent with the character of the Son and in accordance with the will of the Father (vs. 14). Since we pray in Jesus' name, He promised that He will do it. Accordingly, Jesus is the one who is glorifying His heavenly Father. The two not only are one, but they also bring glory to each other. Jesus continually stressed that love was integral to the disciples' relationships with each other, with Him, and with the Father. Furthermore, Jesus said that if His disciples truly loved Him, they would obey His teachings (vs. 15). He did not demand obedience to prove our love for Him. Rather, obedience would be a natural result of loving Him.

B. Another Counselor Promised: vss. 16-17

"And I will ask the Father, and he will give you another Counselor to be with you forever—the Spirit of

truth. The world cannot accept him, because it neither sees him nor knows him. But you know him, for he lives with you and will be in you."

Morality for the ancient Hebrews was not an abstract concept disconnected from the present. Rather, it signified ethical imperatives concerning how people of faith should live. As an encouragement to those who would love and obey Him, the Messiah promised that His disciples would have the indwelling of the Holy Spirit. The third person of the Trinity would come and make His home in believers so that their love could be clearly defined and their obedience could be carefully directed. The Greek noun rendered "Counselor" (vs. 16) literally means "a person summoned to one's aid" and originally referred to a legal advocate. Since Jesus did not want to leave His followers alone in this world, He would ask His Father to give them another Comforter.

The Spirit would serve as the believers' adviser, advocate, mediator, and intercessor. Expressed differently, the Spirit comes to the believers' aid to help them meet every challenge to their faith. As the Spirit of truth, He reveals the truth about God, shows what is true, and leads believers into all truth (vs. 17). In these ways, the Spirit remains ever present to help believers understand, accept, and apply what the Redeemer commanded. Jesus was confident that the Father would grant His request and send the Holy Spirit. Though nonbelievers would reject the Spirit, Jesus' disciples would know the Spirit intimately. At Pentecost, Jesus' prayer request was answered. Today, the Spirit takes up permanent residence in believers, and is always available to instruct, convict, and lead.

C. Jesus' Postresurrection Appearances: vss. 18-20

"I will not leave you as orphans; I will come to you. Before long, the world will not see me anymore, but you will see me. Because I live, you also will live. On that day you will realize that I am in my Father, and you are in me, and I am in you."

Jesus assured His disciples that He would not leave them as "orphans" (John 14:18). In fact, after His death and resurrection, He would appear to them several times before His ascension into heaven. These appearances would be only for believers, in order to strengthen their faith and persuade them that He would never leave them alone in this world (vs. 19). After seeing the resurrected Lord, they would learn that the power that raised Him from the dead would be living in them. Since the ever-living Messiah conquered death, they too would be victorious over death through faith in Him. At that time, they would realize that the Son is indeed in the Father and that there is a mutual indwelling of the Son and believers (vs. 20).

Sixty years after John saw Jesus crucified, buried, and ascended into heaven, the Roman authorities exiled the apostle to the island of Patmos (Rev. 1:9). John suddenly saw the Lord again. This time, however, Jesus did not look the same as He did when John leaned against Him at the Last Supper. Once again, here was his closest friend—but now exalted and honored as the glorified Son of God. The Messiah encouraged John not to be afraid, for He is "the First and the Last" (vs. 17). This is a divine title that appears elsewhere in Scripture in reference to the Lord (Isa. 41:4; 44:6; 48:12). It means essentially the same thing as the title "the Alpha and the Omega" (Rev. 1:8).

At the time John wrote Revelation, the Roman government was pressuring believers to renounce the Savior and declare the emperor to be their lord. Jesus' words to John emphasized why it was wrong to do so. All human authorities were mortal and limited, whereas Jesus is immortal and infinite in power. The gods of Rome were lifeless, whereas Jesus is "the Living One" (vs. 18). This means His essential nature is characterized by life. Not even the grave could hold the Savior. Though He died on the cross and was buried in a tomb, Jesus rose from the dead and now lives forevermore. His victory through the resurrection enabled Him to control the keys of death and Hades (the place of the dead). In ancient times, keys were symbols for authority. Also, death and Hades were considered places where people were bound and held captive. Jesus wanted His followers to know that He alone had the power and the authority to free them from the shackles of death and give them eternal life.

D. Love's Reality Confirmed: vs. 21

"Whoever has my commands and obeys them, he is the one who loves me. He who loves me will be loved by my Father, and I too will love him and show myself to him."

Once again Jesus emphasized that it is not enough for believers simply to have affection for Him in their hearts. True love for Him is demonstrated when they keep His commandments in their daily lives. When believers demonstrate this kind of love for Jesus, they enjoy three specific blessings: the love of the Father, the love of the Son, and a deeper knowledge of Jesus (John 14:21).

II. THE FATHER'S LOVE: JOHN 14:22-26

A. The Request for Clarification: vs. 22

Then Judas (not Judas Iscariot) said, "But, Lord, why do you intend to show yourself to us and not to the world?"

Jesus' statements puzzled one of His disciples. His first name was "Judas" (John 14:22), though he was not "Iscariot"—that, is the disciple who earlier had left to betray the Savior (13:30). The faithful disciple named Judas asked Jesus why He would show Himself to the Eleven but not to everyone (14:22). Judas probably voiced the confusion of all the disciples, who expected Jesus to reveal Himself before the entire world as the messianic King of the Jews. How, then, could Jesus claim such glory by revealing Himself to only a select few?

Very little is known about the other disciple named Judas. The Gospel writers listed him as one of Jesus' 12 apostles. He was probably the one whom Matthew and Mark called "Thaddaeus" (Matt. 10:3; Mark 3:18). Luke twice mentioned him as the "Judas of James" (Luke 6:16; Acts 1:13), which could mean that he was the son of James (as the NIV translates it) or perhaps the brother of James the Less. John is the only Gospel writer who made Judas' presence known through a specific action or dialogue (John 14:22). Early church tradition simply notes that he founded a congregation at Edessa in Syria.

B. The Savior's Explanation: vss. 23-24

Jesus replied, "If anyone loves me, he will obey my teaching. My Father will love him, and we will come to him and make our home with him. He who does not love me will not obey my teaching. These words you hear are not my own; they belong to the Father who sent me."

Jesus did not answer Judas' question directly, for the disciples would learn the ultimate purpose of Jesus' earthly ministry soon enough. He was more concerned about their relationship with Him. For a third time He stated that if they loved Him, they would obey His teachings. And once again the Son said that the Father loves those who truly love Him. In addition, both the Father and the Son would come to believers and make their home with them (John 14:23). In contrast, those who did not obey Jesus' teaching showed that they really did not love Him. The words the Son spoke came directly from the Father. So, to accept the Son is to accept the Father, and to reject the Son is to reject the Father (vs. 24). There is no middle ground.

C. The Spirit's Teaching: vss. 25-26

"All this I have spoken while still with you. But the Counselor, the Holy Spirit, whom the Father will send in my name, will teach you all things and will remind you of everything I have said to you."

Within a few hours Jesus would leave His close friends and begin His agonizing journey to the cross. But first He wanted to encourage the Eleven while He still had time to be alone with them. Much of "all this" (John 14:25) we would not know without John's record. Just as the Father had sent His Son into the world, He would also send the Spirit to this world to dwell within Jesus' followers. This Counselor would instruct believers by helping them recall all that Jesus taught. Having been sent in Jesus' name, the Spirit would officially represent Jesus (vs. 26).

Discussion Questions

1. Why did Jesus connect love for Him with obedience to Him?
2. In what sense is the Spirit the believer's Counselor?
3. How is the Spirit the source of truth?
4. Why is it important for believers to affirm Jesus as the source of their eternal life?
5. What are some ways believers can share Jesus' compassion with the lost?

Contemporary Application

Jesus promised His disciples that after His return to heaven, He would send them the Holy Spirit. They would need the Spirit in order to understand Jesus' teachings more clearly and to be strengthened in their spiritual growth and service for God's kingdom.

As the "Spirit of truth" (John 14:17), the third Person of the Trinity is not merely a supernatural force or an abstract concept of God. Though fully divine, the Spirit is also a person, with a passionate desire for our welfare. He is not like a teddy bear upon which we can pour affection yet which never responds to us. Instead, He is our friend, who cares for us far more than even the best of our human friends can offer.

Moreover, the Spirit is not an evil entity that seeks to hold people captive. We are not puppets to God's Spirit. He desires what is best for us, not mindless bondage to His will. While the Spirit seeks to transform us, He does not rob us of our freedom in Christ. Indeed, the Spirit loves us, and He also esteems our individuality within the body of Christ. That is why the Spirit graces each of us with gifts He wants us to use to glorify the Savior and build up His kingdom.

The Spirit, of course, has the mind and power of the triune Godhead. So, no matter how threatening or painful the circumstance we face, the Spirit can help us and guide us through every situation. Furthermore, we have the same needs as those disciples who were Jesus' companions during His earthly ministry. In many instances, our responsibilities and ordeals might not seem as great as theirs. Nonetheless, we still need the presence and power of the Spirit as we continue our journey of faith.

The Spirit of Truth

Scripture

Background Scripture: *John 16:4-15*

Scripture Lesson: *John 16:4-15*

Key Verse: *"I tell you the truth: It is for your good that I am going away. Unless I go away, the Counselor will not come to you; but if I go, I will send him to you."* John 16:7.

Scripture Lesson for Children: *John 16:4-15*

Key Verse for Children: *"When he, the Spirit of truth, comes, he will guide you into all truth."* John 16:13.

Lesson Aim

To draw strength from the Spirit's teaching ministry in our lives.

Lesson Setting

Time: A.D. *30*

Place: Jerusalem

Lesson Outline

The Spirit of Truth

I. Exposing the World's Sin: John 16:4-11
  A. *The Savior's Warning: vs. 4a*
  B. *The Sending of the Spirit: vss. 4b-7*
  C. *The Spirit's Convicting Ministry: vss. 8-11*
II. Making Jesus' Teaching Known: John 16:12-15
  A. *The Spirit's Guidance of Jesus' Disciples: vss. 12-13*
  B. *The Spirit's Glorification of Jesus: vss. 14-15*

Introduction for Adults

Topic: *Sorrow Turns to Joy*

Jesus' disciples were filled with grief over the news that He was returning to heaven to be with the Father (John 16:5-6). Jesus also explained that after His departure, He would send the Holy Spirit (vs. 7). In turn, Jesus' followers would be filled with joy as the Spirit helped them better understand Jesus' teachings and overcome their selfish impulses.

Every adult knows about pain and joy in their lives. And while some have little hope for the future, apparently many more are optimistic. When polled by TIME/CNN and asked what happens after death, 61 percent of Americans felt that they would go to heaven. Joni Eareckson Tada, a quadriplegic since she was 17, trusts in full-body resurrection and the glorification of the body in heaven.

In Paul's letters, he talked about the indwelling presence of the Spirit. For instance, he taught in Ephesians 1:13-14 that the Spirit is given to every follower of Jesus as a pledge of their future inheritance in God's kingdom. Encourage the class members that with the Spirit in their lives, they have the assurance of salvation and the confident hope of one day being resurrected.

Introduction for Youth

Topic: *Never Alone*

Long before we had mobile devices with applications for updating calendars, organizing tasks, and receiving notifications of pending appointments, my mother had a simple time management system. Because she disliked excess paper, she wasn't one to use notes or wall calendars. Instead, she would tell one of her children about an upcoming event and kindly say, "Please remember that for me."

At one point in my young life, I traveled the most with my mother, and so became her appointment book. Upon request, I regurgitated upcoming schedules with speed and accuracy. But I seldom recalled everything.

Our heavenly Father knows the limitations of our minds and our tendency for distraction. So, He graciously provides the Holy Spirit. Along with teaching us "all things" (John 14:26) connected with our salvation, the Spirit's job is to remind us of "everything" Jesus has taught us. What a relief! With the Spirit in our lives, we can remember what Jesus wants us to know.

Concepts for Children

Topic: *You Have Help*

1. Jesus told His followers that He was going to die on the cross.
2. Jesus' followers became sad when they heard this.
3. Jesus said the Holy Spirit would bring honor to Jesus.
4. Jesus said the Holy Spirit would teach Jesus' followers.
5. Jesus wants us to learn from the Holy Spirit.

Lesson Commentary

I. Exposing the World's Sin: John 16:4-11

A. The Savior's Warning: vs. 4a

"I have told you this, so that when the time comes you will remember that I warned you."

John 15 and 16 record additional farewell statements Jesus made to the Eleven in the upper room (13:2; 14:31). In 15:1-17, we find Jesus' well-known discourse about being the true vine. He stressed the importance of His disciples living in vital union with Him, obeying His commands, bearing abundant spiritual fruit, and loving one another. This kind of love was demonstrated by a willingness to lay down one's life for a friend (vs. 13). Indeed, Jesus did this very thing for humankind when He freely subjected Himself to death on the cross. Jesus knew His disciples needed each other's love because of the intense suffering that lay ahead for them (vs. 17).

There was a striking contrast between the love of believers and the hatred of nonbelievers (vs. 18). The world loved those who either renounced the Messiah or were indifferent to His commands. Resistance to the Son or apathy toward Him was an indication of allegiance to the world. Those who followed the Savior did not belong to the world, for Jesus had chosen them and set them apart from the world. The world hated those whom the Messiah had chosen because the world had lost its power over them and could no longer control them (vs. 19). Jesus told His disciples that allegiance to Him brought persecution and peace—never just one or the other. He further explained that those who identified with Him would suffer because their persecutors did not know God (vs. 21).

If the oppressors had known the Father, they would have recognized the Son, because the Father sent Him. Ignorance, however, was no excuse. The revelation of God was given to them through the appearance and teachings of the Son. Because they rejected that revelation, the guilt of their sins remained (vs. 22). Despite the miracles Jesus had performed before His enemies, they still refused to believe in Him. In fact, they despised Him. By hating the Son, they were expressing a deeply felt hatred for the Father (vss. 23-24). Though Jesus' enemies contended that they were upholding God's law by opposing and persecuting the Son, they were actually breaking the very law that bore witness to the Messiah. Jesus quoted from the Old Testament to expose the hypocrisy and treachery of those religious rulers who were hostile to Him (vs. 25; see also Pss. 35:19; 69:4; 109:3). The words of the psalmist found their ultimate fulfillment in the persecution of the Savior.

The Old Testament was not alone in testifying about the Son. As we learned in last week's lesson, Jesus also promised that He would send the Holy Spirit to bear witness to Him (John 14:16-17, 26). Jesus referred to the Spirit as the "Counselor" (15:26) who came from the Father to impart truth. An essential function of the Spirit was to continue to present Jesus as the Messiah to the world. Along with the Spirit, Jesus' disciples also were to testify about Him. This specific command was intended for those who were with Him at the Last Supper, for they had been with Him from the beginning of His public ministry (vs. 27). The principle behind this command is applicable to all believers. As followers of Jesus, believers ought to cooperate with the Spirit in testifying to the world about the Son of God.

Jesus knew that after His ascension, the Eleven would undergo terrible persecution. He also knew they would be expelled from the synagogues and branded as traitors to the Jewish faith (9:22; 12:42). In fact, some would even die at the hands of those who, in their misguided zeal, thought they were serving God (16:1-2). So that Jesus' disciples would not falter in their commitment to Him, He revealed these truths to them the day before His arrest, trial, and execution. When Jesus spoke about the ignorance of His enemies, He was not referring to intellectual knowledge. His adversaries had seen His miracles and listened to His teachings. Jesus had in mind knowledge that comes from being in an intimate relationship with Him and the Father. This type of knowledge was profoundly absent in the hearts of Jesus' detractors (vs. 3). On the eve of Jesus' crucifixion, He now shared these important truths with the Eleven so that when the events He foretold occurred, they would recall His warning and be prepared to act in a godly manner (vs. 4).

B. The Sending of the Spirit: vss. 4b-7

"I did not tell you this at first because I was with you. Now I am going to him who sent me, yet none of you asks me, 'Where are you going?' Because I have said these things, you are filled with grief. But I tell you the truth: It is for your good that I am going away. Unless I go away, the Counselor will not come to you; but if I go, I will send him to you."

Jesus had not previously shared with His disciples important truths about the world's hatred, since His presence was sufficient to strengthen their faith (John 16:4). While He was with the Eleven, His enemies had primarily attacked Him. However, when Jesus left, the situation would change dramatically. His foes would direct their enmity toward His followers. When that time came, the disciples would be able to recall Jesus' warning and remain unwavering in their devotion to Him.

Jesus had mentioned several times that He was returning to His Father. For instance, earlier during Jesus' farewell discourse, Peter had asked, "Lord, where are you going?" (13:36). Then, not long after, Thomas stated, "Lord, we don't know where you are going" (14:5). Even though the Eleven had been distressed about their Lord's leaving them, on the eve of His crucifixion, they were not really concerned about His destination (16:5). Otherwise, they would have pressed the issue to determine the reasons for His departure, which they did not. Instead, they were worried about what would become of themselves without

Him. Here we see that when Christians become too focused on their own fates, they can lose sight of Jesus' ultimate purpose.

The thought of being separated from their Lord deeply saddened the disciples (vs. 6). Jesus said, however, that His leaving was in their best interest. Unless He returned to the Father, He could not send the "Counselor" (vs. 7) to be with them. As was noted in last week's lesson, the Greek noun rendered "Counselor" literally means "a person summoned to one's aid" and originally referred to a legal advocate. Only the Holy Spirit, through His abiding presence, could transform the disciples into the image of Christ. In addition, the Spirit would provide them with the guidance and power to proclaim the Gospel throughout the world. Even today, it is only by the Spirit that believers can accomplish all the ministry that Jesus has prepared for them to undertake.

C. The Spirit's Convicting Ministry: vss. 8-11

"When he comes, he will convict the world of guilt in regard to sin and righteousness and judgment: in regard to sin, because men do not believe in me; in regard to righteousness, because I am going to the Father, where you can see me no longer; and in regard to judgment, because the prince of this world now stands condemned."

The Holy Spirit does not limit His involvement to believers. According to John 16:8, the Spirit also acts as a prosecutor to bring about the world's conviction. The verb the apostle used to describe the convicting work of the Spirit can be translated "to prove wrong." The Greeks used this term to describe the cross-examination of a person who either acknowledged personal guilt or was convinced of the weakness of his or her defense. Both meanings seem to apply in John's text. The Spirit does not merely accuse the world of transgression, but also presents indisputable proof of the world's sinfulness. He establishes the Father's case against unbelievers by putting forward evidence in three different areas: sin, righteousness, and judgment.

In verse 9, Jesus clarified that the reason the Spirit convicts the world about sin is because humanity refuses to trust in the Son. This implies that the central sin of pagan humanity is unbelief, a truth that is stressed time and again in the Gospels. Furthermore, in verse 10, Jesus explained that the Spirit convicted the world about God's righteousness because the latter was manifested in the Son. His return to the Father vindicated His character and established Him as the standard of all integrity (Rom. 1:4; 1 Tim. 3:16). When the Son returned to the Father, He was no longer physically visible to the disciples and the world. It was now the Spirit's responsibility to prove that the unsaved were wrong about the nature and source of divine righteousness.

In John 16:11, Jesus revealed that the Spirit convicted the world of the coming judgment because God has already condemned Satan, the prince of this world. In fact, Jesus' death on the cross and resurrection from the tomb sealed Satan's defeat. Since unsaved humanity has followed the "prince of this world"

(Luke 10:18; 2 Cor. 4:4; Eph. 2:2), the unsaved stood condemned with him. Jesus revealed in John 12:31 that Satan and his demonic cohorts cannot escape divine judgment. Likewise, Colossians 2:15 discloses that the Father, through the crucifixion of His Son, publicly declared the divine intent of judging sinners and their iniquity. According to 1 Corinthians 15:54-57 and Hebrews 2:14-15, even death itself stands condemned as a result of the atoning sacrifice of the Son at Calvary.

II. MAKING JESUS' TEACHING KNOWN: JOHN 16:12-15

A. The Spirit's Guidance of Jesus' Disciples: vss. 12-13

"I have much more to say to you, more than you can now bear. But when he, the Spirit of truth, comes, he will guide you into all truth. He will not speak on his own; he will speak only what he hears, and he will tell you what is yet to come."

The purpose for the coming of the Holy Spirit was not only to convict the world of its guilt, but also to guide Jesus' disciples into a comprehensive understanding of "all truth" (John 16:13) concerning salvation. Jesus wanted to share these truths with His friends, but He knew that what the Spirit would later convey to them would be too much for them presently to "bear" (vs. 12). Jesus might have meant that this knowledge was too difficult for them to understand, or too difficult to emotionally absorb, or perhaps both. Following Pentecost, the Spirit—who is the source of "truth" (vs. 13) and bears witness to it—would help Jesus' disciples understand the significance of His ministry, death, resurrection, and exaltation (1:14, 18; 14:6). The Spirit never worked independently from the Father and the Son. The Spirit would pass along to Jesus' followers whatever He gave to the Spirit.

B. The Spirit's Glorification of Jesus: vss. 14-15

"He will bring glory to me by taking from what is mine and making it known to you. All that belongs to the Father is mine. That is why I said the Spirit will take from what is mine and make it known to you."

Just as Jesus glorified His heavenly Father during His earthly ministry, the primary function of the Holy Spirit's ministry was to glorify the Son (John 16:14). He did this by taking Jesus' teachings and making them known to His followers. Anything the Son conveyed to the Spirit was given to the Son by His Father (vs. 15). This should not be surprising, for there is unhindered communion, concert, and cooperation among the three Persons of the Godhead. Finally, Jesus told His disciples that soon He would be leaving them, but a little later they would see Him again (vs. 16). Jesus was alluding to His imminent arrest, trial, execution, and burial. During that time of adversity, they would abandon Him and not see Him. Then, after Jesus' resurrection, He would appear to them several times before His ascension into heaven.

Admittedly, some think the phrase "[in] a little while" refers either to the coming of the Spirit following the ascension of the Son or to the Messiah's second advent. But, as 14:19 and 16:22 suggest (see also 7:33; 12:35; 13:33), it is more likely that 16:16 is referring to Jesus' postresurrection appearances to His disciples. Indeed, Scripture reveals that He manifested Himself to them several times before His ascension into heaven (Matt. 28; Mark 16; Luke 24; John 20–21; Acts 1:3-8; 9:1-19; 1 Cor. 9:1; 15:5-7).

Jesus' statement about departing, returning, and going to the Father perplexed His disciples (John 16:17). They especially struggled to make sense of His words recorded in verses 10 and 16, which refer to His ascension and crucifixion, respectively. While Jesus had not connected these two events, His followers nonetheless considered them to be linked. Their desire to understand the Savior prompted them to keep on repeating fragmentary portions of His statements (vss. 17–18). Jesus, of course, was receptive to their desire to grasp the significance of His words.

Jesus could see that His disciples wanted to query Him about His statements. While Jesus had supernatural knowledge of all people (John 1:47-48; 2:24-25; 4:17-18; 6:61, 64), the writer of the Fourth Gospel was not necessarily referring to it in 16:19. Most likely, the open back-and-forth dialogue between Jesus' disciples made it obvious that they wanted Him to clarify what He meant when He declared that they would not see Him for a "little while," but then after an unspecified period of time, they again would see Him.

"I tell you the truth" (vs. 20) is more literally rendered "Truly, truly, I say to you." It's as if Jesus was in a courtroom and bearing solemn witness to the facts. In this case, He acknowledged that His crucifixion and burial would cause His followers to wail and lament over what they presumed was His demise. Meanwhile, unsaved humanity—whom Jesus referred to as the "world"—would celebrate their apparent triumph over the "Lord of glory" (1 Cor. 2:8). Though the disciples would be sad for a while, it would not last forever. Indeed, their grief would be turned into joy over the news of the Savior's resurrection from the dead (John 20:20).

Discussion Questions

1. What was the nature of the warning Jesus gave to the Eleven?
2. What are some ways you have seen the convicting ministry of the Spirit at work in the lives of unbelievers?
3. Why do you think unbelievers refuse to trust in Jesus for salvation?
4. In what ways does the Spirit guide believers into "all truth" (John 16:13) concerning the Son?
5. Why does the Spirit seek to bring glory to the Son?

Contemporary Application

John 16 is one of the Bible's chief passages describing the Holy Spirit and His teaching ministry. We learn three main points about Him in this chapter: first, He convicts the world of sin; second, He is the teacher of all redemptive truth; and third, He glorifies the Son.

It is important for saved adults to consider Jesus' words regarding the Spirit's teaching function within the historical context in which the Savior spoke. At that point, the New Testament had not yet been written. So, the Spirit was going to have a key role in the development of the written Word.

Even Old Testament scrolls were scarce and unavailable to the common person. Accordingly, the internalization of oral material was immensely important for early Christians. They needed the Spirit to help them keep the Word hidden in their hearts, just as we do. As the Spirit preserved and communicated Jesus' teachings, as well as the apostles' words about Him, the Spirit brought honor to the Lord.

Furthermore, the Spirit brought discernment to first-century believers, who were trying to avoid false teachers and determine what was true and what was counterfeit (1 John 2:20-27). That same Spirit can guide us today through the maze of cults and false gospels in our world. For this reason, it is prudent for us to draw strength from the Spirit's teaching ministry in our lives.

The Spirit's Presence

DEVOTIONAL READING

Romans 14:13-19

DAILY BIBLE READINGS

Monday March 16
  Mark 13:5-11 The Holy Spirit Speaks

Tuesday March 17
  Acts 10:39-48 Gentiles Receive the Holy Spirit

Wednesday March 18
  Acts 11:19-26 Full of the Spirit and Faith

Thursday March 19
  Romans 14:13-19 Joy in the Holy Spirit

Friday March 20
  Acts 1:4-8 Power from the Holy Spirit

Saturday March 21
  Ephesians 5:15-21 Be Filled with the Spirit

Sunday March 22
  John 20:19-23 Receive the Holy Spirit

Scripture

Background Scripture: *John 20:19-23; Acts 1:4-8; 2:1-4*
Scripture Lesson: *John 20:19-23*
Key Verse: *And with that [Jesus] breathed on [the disciples] and said, "Receive the Holy Spirit."* John 20:22.
Scripture Lesson for Children: *John 20:19-23*
Key Verse for Children: *[Jesus] breathed on [the disciples] and said, "Receive the Holy Spirit."* John 20:22.

Lesson Aim

To overcome any fears we might have in telling others about the risen Lord.

Lesson Setting

Time: A.D. *30*
Place: Jerusalem

Lesson Outline

The Spirit's Presence

  I. The Risen Lord Appears to His Disciples: John 20:19-20
      A. *The Disciples' Fear: vs. 19a*
      B. *The Savior's Greeting of Peace: vss. 19b-20*
  II. The Risen Lord Commissions His Disciples: John 20:21-23
      A. *Sending the Disciples: vs. 21*
      B. *Promising the Holy Spirit: vs. 22*
      C. *Giving the Disciples Authority: vs. 23*

Introduction for Adults

Topic: *An Opportunity to Serve*

If there was no resurrection, the church would have no mission. The church's world mission explodes from the dramatic news that Jesus lives. The church advances on His resurrection power. Paul began the church's great missionary movement convinced that the risen Lord lived in the apostle and energized him.

That's why it is so important to settle the issue of who Jesus is in the way His closest disciples settled it. Unless a person is really convinced that Jesus has risen from the dead, no congregation can inspire obedience to Jesus' Great Commission.

Every believer, having met the risen Lord through faith, must ask the next question: "What do You want me to do, Jesus?" This is the product of genuine conversion. This week's lesson shows that ultimately we offer Jesus all we have and are, or we give Him nothing.

Introduction for Youth

Topic: *Peace, Power, and Presence*

Growing up is often a time filled with doubt. We doubt our parents' rules and wisdom. We doubt what older people tell us. *What do they know?* We doubt the basic maxims of life—for example, that it's better to tell the truth and work hard.

But then one day we have to make some big decisions for ourselves. Where do we find the rules that guided our parents and our elders? Are we left to shift for ourselves?

Doubts can be beneficial if they lead us to look for the truth. If we do not investigate the claims of Jesus to be God when we are young, probabilities are good that we will never get around to it later. The Fourth Gospel's account of Jesus' friends cowering behind locked doors and being filled with doubt shows us how much the risen Lord cares, wants to answer our questions, and meets our needs.

Concepts for Children

Topic: *The Gift of Power*

1. After Jesus died on the cross, He rose from the dead.
2. On the first Easter Sunday, Jesus met with His followers.
3. Jesus had a big job for His followers to do.
4. Jesus gave His followers the Spirit to help them.
5. The Spirit is with us as we tell others about Jesus.

Lesson Commentary

I. THE RISEN LORD APPEARS TO HIS DISCIPLES: JOHN 20:19-20

A. The Disciples' Fear: vs. 19a

On the evening of that first day of the week, when the disciples were together, with the doors locked for fear of the Jews.

The account of Jesus' appearance to His disciples is preceded by the discovery of the empty tomb and Jesus' appearance to Mary Magdalene. Like the other Gospel writers, John concluded his account of Jesus' life with His resurrection. Yet John's presentation shows us that Jesus' resurrection was not only a decisive affirmation of Him as God and Savior, but it also left an enduring impression on the people who loved Him and put their faith in Him. John began by focusing on one woman, Mary of Magdala, not on the several women who had also visited the empty tomb, as described by the other Gospel writers. John's exclusive focus on Mary was probably because she was the one who had told John about the empty tomb and had the distinction of being the first person to encounter the resurrected Lord.

Once the Sabbath had ended, Mary hurried to Jesus' tomb early Sunday morning apparently to complete the burial anointing of His body (20:1). She—and the other women with her—wondered how they would be able to move the massive stone away from the entrance. Their concern vanished when they discovered that the rock had already been removed. Though it was still early in the morning, they were able to see that Jesus' tomb was empty. Mary dashed to Peter and John, the disciple whom Jesus "loved" (vs. 2). Mary frantically stated that people had transferred Jesus' body to a place Mary and the other women did not know. Mary had not considered the possibility that God had raised Jesus from the dead. Mary assumed that Jesus' enemies had stolen His body.

Being alarmed by Mary's news, Peter and John ran to Jesus' tomb to see for themselves whether the body was missing (vs. 3). John arrived at the tomb first, where he peered in and saw Jesus' burial clothes (vss. 4-5). Though John was hesitant to enter, Peter rushed by him. Once Peter reached the tomb, he stepped right in and saw the strips of linen that had wrapped Jesus' corpse. Peter also noticed that Jesus' head cloth was neatly folded and separate from the linen strips (vss. 6-7). Robbers would neither have removed the burial clothes nor left them in such order. John followed Peter into the tomb, and when he saw the graveclothes, he "believed" (vs. 8), though the exact nature of his faith remains ambiguous. Evidently, at this point, neither Peter nor John had a full understanding of Scripture's teaching about Jesus' resurrection (vs. 9).

Next, Peter and John left the tomb and returned to their lodgings in Jerusalem (vs. 10). Meanwhile, Mary remained near the empty tomb and wept because she assumed that Jesus' enemies had taken His body (vs. 11). At this point,

Mary leaned forward to gaze into the tomb, perhaps to see for herself that the body was missing, or to confirm in her mind what she had seen before. What Mary saw amazed her. Two angels, robed in white, were in the tomb. One was sitting where Jesus' head had been, and the other where His feet had been (vs. 12). The angels asked Mary why she was weeping. In response, Mary said Jesus' enemies had removed His body to an unknown location (vs. 13). The fact that she couldn't attend to Jesus' body and give Him a decent burial added to Mary's distress.

At that moment Mary sensed the presence of another person. She turned and saw someone standing outside the tomb with her, but she did not realize it was Jesus (vs. 14). Either there was something different about the risen Lord that prevented not only Mary but also others of His friends from immediately recognizing Him (Luke 24:13-31; John 21:4), or they were supernaturally prevented from recognizing Him until the time was right. Initially, Mary thought Jesus was the gardener (John 20:15). In turn, Jesus first addressed Mary as "Woman" as the angels had done. Also, like the angels, Jesus asked Mary why she was weeping. Moreover, Jesus inquired as to whom Mary was seeking.

Previously, Mary had thought that Jesus' enemies might have stolen His body, but now she hoped that this person, whom Mary assumed was responsible for the upkeep of the private cemetery, might have moved Jesus' body. Mary did not answer Jesus' questions, but implored Him to reveal the whereabouts of the Savior's body—if the "gardener" had carried it away. Mary promised to return the body to the tomb herself (which would have been required considerable strength). Just then, Mary recognized the Lord when she heard Him say her name (vs. 16). Mary's immediate reaction was to turn toward Jesus again, but this time to exclaim, "Rabboni!" John translated this Aramaic word to mean "Teacher," but it can also carry overtones of "my dear Lord."

According to Matthew 28:9, when Mary Magdalene and another Mary encountered the risen Lord, they fell to the ground, clasped His feet, and worshiped Him. John 20:17 reports Jesus' instruction to Mary not to cling to Him. Jesus told Mary to get up and convey a message to Jesus' friends. Although He had not yet ascended into heaven, He wanted to assure His disciples that shortly He would be returning to His heavenly Father. The Son spoke about His Father and His God as the disciples' Father and God. Now that Jesus' redemptive work was fully accomplished, the reconciliation between God and His spiritual children was complete. Mary obeyed by rushing to the rest of the disciples and telling them that she had seen the risen Lord. Mary also related the message Jesus had entrusted to her (vs. 18).

After Jesus first appeared to Mary of Magdala, other people encountered Jesus (Luke 24:13-49). John, however, skipped these incidents and went to the evening's events of which he was an eyewitness. Many of Jesus' disciples, which included most of the apostles, had secretly convened to discuss the strange yet marvelous reports that their Lord had risen from the dead. Nevertheless, since they still feared the religious leaders, they bolted the doors (John 20:19). In light of how the civil and religious authorities had treated Jesus, the fears of His closest disciples were well founded.

B. The Savior's Greeting of Peace: vss. 19b-20

Jesus came and stood among them and said, "Peace be with you!" After he said this, he showed them his hands and side. The disciples were overjoyed when they saw the Lord.

In addition to fear, Jesus' disciples suffered horrendous grief. After all, when the authorities arrested Jesus in the garden of Gethsemane, all His followers deserted Him and ran away (Mark 14:27, 50). Understandably, on the Sunday following Jesus' crucifixion, His disciples were still in the shock of mourning. Also, the Feast of Unleavened Bread was still going on, so they would not have left Jerusalem for Galilee. Most likely, they were in the upper room where they had previously met with Jesus. As the disciples talked, Jesus suddenly stood among them (John 20:19). The verse does not explain how Jesus could have entered the house when the doors were locked. Clearly, Jesus' resurrected body had extraordinary powers and capabilities. In 1 Corinthians 15:35-44, Paul explained that the resurrection body is heavenly in origin and glorified in nature.

Jesus greeted His friends by exclaiming, "Peace be with you!" (John 20:19). Although this phrase was a common Hebrew salutation, Jesus probably said it to relieve the disciples' fears at His sudden and unexpected appearance. Luke 24:37-38 mentioned that Jesus' appearance had frightened His followers. To demonstrate that His resurrected body had substance, Jesus showed His disciples His nail-pierced hands and His spear-pierced side (John 20:20). Luke 24:39 adds that Jesus told His disciples to touch Him to see that He had flesh and bones and was not a spirit or a ghost.

Perhaps the disciples should have believed the reports about Jesus' resurrection, but because of the depth of their despair and sorrow, they needed to see actual evidence for themselves. Their shock was so great that they also needed strong assurance. They could not deny Jesus' scars when they saw them. Once the disciples were convinced of Jesus' identity and presence, His friends were overcome with joy (John 20:20). Like Mary, they traveled from the depths of despair to the pinnacle of happiness in a matter of seconds. Even today, the presence of the risen Lord can do that in the life of believers.

II. THE RISEN LORD COMMISSIONS HIS DISCIPLES: JOHN 20:21-23

A. Sending the Disciples: vs. 21

Again Jesus said, "Peace be with you! As the Father has sent me, I am sending you."

Once again Jesus greeted His disciples with a greeting of "peace" (John 20:21)— that is, an impartation of calmness, self-composure, and freedom from terror.

This time, however, the Savior wanted to strengthen the resolve of His disciples to obey His commission and proclaim the message of redemption. In the same way the Father had sent the Son to earth to fulfill His redemptive mission, Jesus was sending His disciples into the world to continue His ministry. This commission, and the peace He provided, are also given to us as believers today.

First, let's consider 14:27. We learn that Jesus would not only leave us the Holy Spirit and His teachings (vss. 25-26, which were studied in lesson 2), but also the Savior's peace. His peace is not like the world's artificial sense of well-being. Jesus' peace does not guarantee the absence of war or difficult circumstances. Jesus' peace is the assurance of God's favor regardless of our circumstances. Since Jesus had repeatedly warned His disciples of His impending departure and the peril ahead for them, He knew they'd be upset. So He urged them not to nurture their feelings of distress and fear, but to allow His peace to calm their spirits and be a source of courage (vs. 27).

Second, let's think about Matthew 28:16-20, which is the premier passage in the Gospels concerning the Great Commission. Just as Jesus had commanded in verse 10, His disciples traveled north from Jerusalem to Galilee to meet with Him. The Eleven were originally from Galilee, and Jesus had spent much of His earthly ministry there. So, it was fitting for the risen Lord to meet them in Galilee. When the disciples saw Jesus, their response was mixed. Some "worshiped him" (vs. 17), which means they recognized Him to be the risen Lord and paid Him homage as the Son of God. Others, however, doubted. Either they were uncertain about whether Jesus truly had risen from the dead or whether the person they were meeting was actually Jesus.

At an unnamed mountain, Jesus declared that the Father had given Him "all authority in heaven and on earth" (vs. 18). Having been completely faithful in His mission on earth, Jesus had proved His right to have such authority (John 17:4-5). This authority was the basis for the commission He was about to give. Jesus entrusted to His friends the responsibility to serve Him as His ambassadors, that is, to "go and make disciples of all nations" (vs. 19). His followers must have been surprised at such a commission. Generally, Jews believed that Gentiles were outside the favor of God, or that if Gentiles were to receive God's favor, they first had to become Jews. But here was Jesus telling His friends to disperse and make disciples of people from all over the globe (Acts 1:8). The Father had thrown His arms wide to graciously receive everyone who loves and believes in His Son.

As Jesus outlined it, making disciples had two aspects: baptizing and teaching. In Jesus' time, Jews performed ceremonial washings on Gentile converts to Judaism. John the Baptizer had been an innovator when he had baptized not Gentiles but Jews who wanted to express repentance from their sins (for more information, see the Bible commentary in lesson 1). Now Jesus adopted baptism for His followers, as a means of showing discipleship to Him. He authorized them to baptize people "in the name of the Father and of the Son and of the Holy Spirit" (Matt. 28:19). Being a follower of Jesus means entering into a relationship with all three members of the Trinity, as represented by their names. Moreover, the disciples were to teach believers to obey all the commandments Jesus had given during His years of ministry on earth (vs. 20). Discipleship means more than just claiming to follow Jesus. It also means actually doing what He said to do. Fulfilling the Great Commission would be difficult. At times, the disciples would encounter disappointment and grief. But the risen Lord gave them—and us—encouragement and hope when He declared, "Surely I am with you always."

B. Promising the Holy Spirit: vs. 22

And with that he breathed on them and said, "Receive the Holy Spirit."

Jesus not only charged His disciples with the momentous commission to proclaim the Gospel, but also empowered them with the Holy Spirit to do it. This was necessary, for the disciples could not possibly carry out Jesus' work without the Spirit's wisdom, protection, and power. In short, there could be no evangelistic mission without the Spirit. Accordingly, Jesus told His friends to wait in Jerusalem until the Spirit fell upon them (Acts 1:4-8). The Greek word for "spirit" is *pneuma*, which literally means "breath." So, in anticipation of the day of Pentecost, it was fitting that Jesus breathed on the disciples to give them the Spirit (John 20:22). Apparently, at Jesus' postresurrection appearance, He gave them a foretaste of what was to come on Pentecost (see Acts 2:1-4, to be studied in lesson 13). The Savior's followers had to be prepared for that momentous occasion, which motivated and made them courageous witnesses, instead of fearful cowards.

C. Giving the Disciples Authority: vs. 23

If you forgive anyone his sins, they are forgiven; if you do not forgive them, they are not forgiven."

Jesus' statement in John 20:23 reveals the heart of the evangelistic work He was commissioning His disciples to perform. It had to do with offering people forgiveness of sins. Jesus' mission was not primarily physical release, but spiritual deliverance. After all, He shed His blood for the remission of sins (Matt. 20:28; 26:28). Also, He came to seek and save the lost (Luke 19:10). This was to be the church's pattern from the beginning—bringing spiritual salvation to a lost and dying world.

The disciples properly used their God-given authority when they faithfully declared the Gospel from the day of Pentecost right through the events described in the Book of Acts. Ultimately, of course, God alone forgives and condemns, depending on a person's response to the Good News. But with this remarkable delegation of ministerial authority, Jesus' followers could and did tell people they were forgiven. When people come to faith in the Son, and accept His death and resurrection for their sins, they may rightfully claim God's forgiveness (1 John 1:9). Also, with the authority of God's Word, we can assure new converts of that truth.

Discussion Questions

1. Why were Jesus' disciples hiding behind locked doors?
2. How would you write the script for the disciples' conversation in their hiding place?
3. Why do you think the disciples were unprepared for Jesus' postresurrection appearance to them?
4. Why is being commissioned by Jesus something not just reserved for full-time Christian workers, pastors, and missionaries?
5. What fears do people today have about the future, and how can Christians help them with the good news of the Lord?

Contemporary Application

At first, when Jesus' disciples saw him, they were overcome with fear. One source of dread was the possibility of their being arrested by the authorities. Another reason for the disciples' alarm was the sight of Jesus suddenly appearing in their midst.

Jesus, fully knowing the terror being experienced by His disciples, first spoke peace to them. Then, to address any doubts they had about His presence and identity, He showed them His hands and side. As a result, the disciples were not only convinced, but also filled with joy.

Next, Jesus commissioned His friends to proclaim the good news of salvation far and wide. He even equipped them with a full measure of His peace and the enduring presence of the Holy Spirit. Now they were fully prepared and empowered to share the Gospel with an unbelieving world.

The Lord's spiritual army cannot march on short rations. The day demands that the people of God be fully equipped—intellectually, volitionally, and emotionally. Doubters in the ranks destroy the army's effectiveness. Jesus demands our all, but emotional responses are insufficient. If our minds and wills are not totally His, no amount of enthusiasm will carry the day.

Therefore, the church's task is to help lost people meet the risen Lord face-to-face, as it were. Those who come to believe in Him like the Eleven did will be prepared for Jesus' mission in the world. Without such a life-changing encounter, our involvement in this mission is doomed to futility and frustration.

The Savior's Arrival

Scripture

Background Scripture: *Mark 11:1-11*

Scripture Lesson: *Mark 11:1-11*

Key Verse: *Those who went ahead and those who followed shouted, "Hosanna! Blessed is he who comes in the name of the Lord!"* Mark 11:9.

Scripture Lesson for Children: *Mark 11:1-11*

Key Verse for Children: *Those who went ahead and those who followed shouted, "Hosanna! Blessed is he who comes in the name of the Lord!"* Mark 11:9.

Lesson Aim

To openly praise Jesus for who He is and what He has done.

Lesson Setting

Time: A.D. *30*

Place: Jerusalem

Lesson Outline

The Savior's Arrival

  I. Jesus' Arrival at Jerusalem: Mark 11:1-3
     A. Dispatching Two Disciples: vs. 1
     B. Giving Preliminary Instructions: vss. 2-3

 II. Jesus' Triumphal Entry into Jerusalem: Mark 11:4-11
     A. Finding the Colt: vss. 4-6
     B. Riding on the Colt: vss. 7-8
     C. Offering Praise: vss. 9-10
     D. Entering the Temple Courts: vs. 11

Introduction for Adults

Topic: *Hail to the Chief*

An old saying warns us, "If you find the perfect church, don't join it, because you'll wreck it." Due to our sinful natures, this is always a possibility. Nonetheless, God calls His purified people to worship in a holy way. After all, there's no room for ungodliness in Christ's body.

When Jesus accepted praise from the crowd, He could have felt good about the situation. But then He witnessed the wretched conditions around the temple, and He decided to risk the crowd's fury. Yes, there was a time to challenge worship that had been corrupted by commercialism. Pure worship was a worthwhile goal that required drastic action.

How easy it is to slip over the line and make worship into a business. This danger lurks everywhere. Therefore, we need constant reminders to purify our hearts before we lavish our praise in worship to the Lord.

Introduction for Youth

Topic: *A Star Is Born*

Pageantry excites young people, whether it's a sports event, a political rally, an art or music fair, or even a religious gathering. In Christendom, Christmas, Easter, and Palm Sunday call for pageantry, including processions, music, and colorful banners. For many years, until politics intervened, the Palm Sunday procession leading from the Mount of Olives into Jerusalem was one of the most exciting religious ceremonies anywhere.

Jesus did not avoid a wild public demonstration when the time was right according to His purposes. His triumphal entry in Jerusalem—what we now call Palm Sunday—signified that He threw down the gauntlet to the nation of Israel. Would the people accept His coming as from heaven, from God above, or would they see Jesus simply as another impostor, a false messiah?

This week's lesson prompts your students to examine their motives in coming to Jesus. If they join the crowd in hailing Him, they must accept all He has to offer and the changes He wants to make in their lives.

Concepts for Children

Topic: *The King Is Here!*

1. Jesus sent two of His followers to a village to bring Him a young male donkey.
2. The two followers went away and found the animal.
3. Jesus rode the animal into Jerusalem while many people praised Him.
4. Jesus returned to a nearby town called Bethany.
5. God is pleased when we praise Jesus for saving us.

Lesson Commentary

I. Jesus' Arrival at Jerusalem: Mark 11:1-3

A. Dispatching Two Disciples: vs. 1

As they approached Jerusalem and came to Bethphage and Bethany at the Mount of Olives, Jesus sent two of his disciples.

A popular misconception about the Gospels is that their main purpose is to provide a comprehensive biography of Jesus' life. In contrast, the chief aim of these accounts is to convey the message of salvation that Jesus brought into the world. The Holy Spirit led each Gospel author to communicate the good news about Jesus in different ways, emphasizing unique aspects of His life and ministry. In writing the Gospel of Mark, its author carefully selected and arranged material he had gathered from a variety of sources. It suited his purposes to ignore all the events of Jesus' life prior to His baptism. But the author described at length many of the later words and works of Jesus. Remarkably, the writer devoted nearly the entire second half of his Gospel to Jesus' last days. Apparently, the author believed that Jesus' ministry, especially His death for sinners, was most important for communicating the message of salvation.

In our current lesson, we jump ahead in Mark's Gospel to what has commonly been called Jesus' "Passion Week." This refers to the final days of His earthly life. It began with a joyous event—Jesus' triumphal entry into Jerusalem as King. Set on a hill some 2,500 feet above sea level, Jerusalem is 33 miles east of the Mediterranean Sea and 14 miles west of the Dead Sea. Because access was difficult and the city lacked natural resources, it at one time enjoyed a relatively protected location. But when a major regional trade route developed through the city, Jerusalem became commercially and strategically desirable to every subsequent political force that came to power.

The following are some key facts about the holy city: it appears in the Bible as early as Abraham (Gen. 14:18), though the site had probably been inhabited for centuries before; it was captured by David and made the capital of Israel; Jerusalem was the site of Solomon's temple and, in the first century, Herod's temple; the city's estimated population in Jesus' day was probably 50,000 (though during Passover, it possibly grew to 120,000); Jerusalem was besieged and destroyed by the Romans in A.D. 70; and the city was relatively small geographically, but had a sizable metropolitan area with numerous suburban towns.

Jesus, having ministered in Perea and the Jordan River area, now headed westward with His disciples by the steep road leading uphill to Jerusalem. On Sunday, the first day of the week preceding Passover, they came to the towns of Bethphage and Bethany. Bethphage was near Bethany, which in turn was located on the southeastern slopes of "the Mount of Olives" (Mark 11:1). Bethany was also about two miles east of Jerusalem near the road to Jericho. Because the

Mount of Olives is approximately 2,700 feet in elevation and thus about 200 feet higher than the city of Jerusalem itself, it commanded a superb view of the city and its temple.

With Passover only a few days away, Jerusalem was already filling up with pilgrims from all over. Jesus, too, was expected to be there. On every hand there were high expectations and high tensions. Undoubtedly, some of Jesus' followers were hoping He would use the great national celebration to claim His place as king of the Jews. The religious leaders were hoping to find an opportunity to arrest and execute Him. Knowing the danger, Jesus could have stayed away. Yet He chose otherwise. He decided to enter Jerusalem—but on His own terms.

B. Giving Preliminary Instructions: vss. 2-3

Saying to them, "Go to the village ahead of you, and just as you enter it, you will find a colt tied there, which no one has ever ridden. Untie it and bring it here. If anyone asks you, 'Why are you doing this?' tell him, 'The Lord needs it and will send it back here shortly.'"

Jesus instructed two of His followers to go into Bethphage. As soon as they entered the village, perhaps just inside the gate, they would find a mother donkey and her colt tethered there. The disciples were to untie the animals and bring them to Jesus (Matt. 21:2). The colt had never been ridden (Mark 11:2). Jesus would ride the colt, but the colt's mother could also have been taken along as a steadying influence, leading the way as the colt followed (Matt. 21:7). If the disciples were questioned by anyone (for instance, the animals' owner or onlookers), they were to explain that Jesus needed the donkeys (Mark 11:3).

We learn in Matthew 21:4-5 that Jesus' entry into Jerusalem on the back of a colt would fulfill Zechariah 9:9. Jerusalem, personified as the "Daughter of Zion," was about to see its long-awaited King—the Messiah—humbly ride into the holy city. In Bible times, unused animals were often taken for religious purposes (Num. 19:2; 1 Sam. 6:7-8). Also, while donkeys were commonly used for transportation, they had come to be associated with royalty and with peace (2 Sam. 16:2; 1 Kings 1:33-34). The Son was unmistakably different from human conquerors. His claim to sovereignty did not rest on political and military subjugation, but on the strength of His character and His obedience to His Father's will. Nowhere did the Son's distinctiveness become more apparent than when He rode into Jerusalem with much acclaim.

II. JESUS' TRIUMPHAL ENTRY INTO JERUSALEM: MARK 11:4-11

A. Finding the Colt: vss. 4-6

They went and found a colt outside in the street, tied at a doorway. As they untied it, some people standing there asked, "What are you doing, untying that colt?" They answered as Jesus had told them to, and the people let them go.

The two disciples left and found the animals standing in a street and tied outside a house (Mark 11:4). As Jesus' followers were untying the animals, some bystanders questioned what they were planning to do (vs. 5). When the disciples repeated what Jesus had said, they were permitted to take the animals (vs. 6). It may be that the donkeys' owner was a follower of Jesus and by prearrangement had agreed to provide the animals to the Lord. The donkey on which Jesus rode into Jerusalem was much different from its stubborn European counterpart. The donkeys of Palestine were more tame and peaceful animals. They had an easy gait and were surefooted. Most were North African in origin, and their color was reddish brown.

People used these animals as beasts of burden, and seldom did the donkeys have riders. When they were ridden, heavy saddles were not placed upon them. Instead, a soft woven covering was placed over their backs and attached with a cord. They accepted almost any reasonable burden placed on them. In Old Testament times, while the people of Israel considered donkeys as objects of wealth, they saw owning at least one beast of burden as necessary for basic survival. The number of donkeys a person owned was often a measure of that person's economic worth. Though the Israelites used donkeys for plowing, the Mosaic law forbade them to yoke a donkey to an ox (Deut. 22:10). The law also prohibited them from eating a donkey's flesh.

B. Riding on the Colt: vss. 7-8

When they brought the colt to Jesus and threw their cloaks over it, he sat on it. Many people spread their cloaks on the road, while others spread branches they had cut in the fields.

The two disciples successfully carried out Jesus' instructions by bringing the donkeys to Him (Matt. 21:6). To show Jesus honor and make Him more comfortable, they placed their cloaks on the animals as a makeshift saddle before Jesus took His seat (Mark 11:7). Presumably, while Jesus sat on the colt, the mother donkey walked beside to calm her offspring (Matt. 21:7). Next, the Messiah started the steep descent into the valley, a route that for years was jammed with thousands of pilgrims coming to Jerusalem for the Passover. The climb from the valley into the city was more gradual. Jesus' ride was a living parable that set forth His claim to be the Messiah. His kingdom was at hand, a rule characterized by peace, love, humility, and gentleness. This monarch was gentle and compassionate, even to the extent of doing good to His enemies. For instance, He bore their persecutions with a gentle, forbearing spirit, even on the cross.

As Jesus rode the donkey, a large crowd of people gathered at the Mount of Olives. Apparently, they sensed that something dramatic was about to happen. Admittedly, the throng included critics (Luke 19:39-40). Even so, the majority of the group was full of high hopes, especially as they came from all over Israel and various parts of the Roman Empire to celebrate the Passover. According to a census taken by Emperor Nero, nearly three million Jews came to Jerusalem for the event. A spontaneous outburst of adulation, welcome, and praise filled the air. People removed their cloaks and spread them on the road (Mark 11:8).

In Jesus' day, most people had very few articles of clothing. Often, what people wore was all they owned. However, the one indispensable and most useful piece of clothing was a cloak. For example, the cloak became a kind of knapsack in which loose items could be wrapped and slung over the shoulder for easy transport. As the Israelites left slavery behind in Egypt, they most likely carried their meager belongings in this fashion. Women used their cloaks as infant carriers, while farmers sowed crops with grain carried in a sack made from a cloak and hung around the neck. At night, a cloak served as a pillow or blanket, depending on the time of year. Moreover, when a special guest came to visit, bound by proper etiquette, a good host might cover the dusty ground with a cloak to provide a place to sit.

As the triumphal procession made its way, other people cut branches off the trees and spread them on the road (Matt. 21:8). This action was a demonstration of respect such as might have been shown to royalty. From ancient times, people in the Middle East have valued the palm tree for its usefulness and beauty. Its branches and leaves are used as ornaments, while its sap is made into sugar, wax, oil, tannin, and dye. People in the Middle East eat its fruit and grind its seed for their camels. They use its branches in the production of mats, roofs, baskets, and fences. To desert travelers, the shade of a palm tree is a welcome sight.

Furthermore, in Bible times, the Jews applied religious symbolism to the palm tree. For example, the psalmist described the righteous as flourishing like the palm tree (Ps. 92:12). Also, in accordance with the Mosaic law, they celebrated the Feast of Tabernacles with palm branches (Lev. 23:40). In the time preceding the New Testament era, the Jews used palm branches in their observance of other feasts as symbols of national triumph and victory. Early Christians adopted this appreciation of the palm tree. John himself noted that people in heaven would pay homage to the Messiah with palm branches (Rev. 7:9), which became a symbol of His victory over death. In fact, the emblem of the palm leaf frequently accompanied the monogram of the Savior on Christian tombs.

C. Offering Praise: vss. 9-10

Those who went ahead and those who followed shouted, "Hosanna!" "Blessed is he who comes in the name of the Lord!" "Blessed is the coming kingdom of our father David!" "Hosanna in the highest!"

The people demonstrated their respect for Jesus by word as well as deed. As they accompanied Jesus on His journey, they hailed Him with such acclamations as "Hosanna!" (Mark 11:9) and "Blessed is he who comes in the name of the Lord!" These praises all come from Psalm 118:25-26. (Psalms 113–118 were usually sung at Passover.) Most likely, the crowds were thinking Jesus would liberate them from Rome. The interjection "Hosanna!" (Mark 11:9) literally means "Save now!" or "Save, we pray!" The use of the expression "Son of David" (Matt.

21:9) was a recognition of Jesus' royal lineage. The statement appearing in Mark 11:10 was a recognition that Jesus came with the authority and approval of God. "Hosanna in the highest!" implied that the angels of heaven were to praise Jesus. In short, the crowd's words proclaimed Jesus to be the Messiah. The irony is that within a week nearly all support for Jesus would melt away. These truths mirror what the shepherds heard on the night of the Savior's birth. They were greeted by a chorus of angels who gave glory to God and announced peace for all who received the Lord's favor (Luke 2:14).

Centuries earlier, God had chosen David to be the first of many successive kings (2 Sam. 7:8-16). But the dynastic rule was broken when Jehoiakim died and his son Jehoiachin was carried away in exile to Babylon (2 Kings 24:15; 25:27-29; Jer. 36:30). Later, the prophets said that God would one day restore David's dynasty (Ezek. 37:24-25; Amos 9:11). By the second century B.C., there began to develop among the Jews a growing expectation for a future anointed leader. The Jewish group who wrote what are known as the Dead Sea Scrolls recorded on some of the documents their belief that three prominent figures would come instead of one—the prophet of Deuteronomy 18:15, 18; a priestly figure named the "Messiah of Aaron"; and a kingly, Davidic figure called the "Messiah of Israel."

In the first century B.C., the Jews longed for an anointed, righteous king who would liberate God's people from their unpopular leaders. Some Jewish writings from this period linked this expected heavenly figure with the day of judgment. By the first century A.D., the Jews wanted freedom from Rome. Expectations ran high that God would raise up a warrior-prince who would throw off the yoke of Gentile rule and usher in a Jewish kingdom worldwide (John 6:15; Acts 1:6). This explains why Jesus was careful not to give false impressions about the exact nature of His messiahship (John 18:33-37). He saw His destiny in terms of service to God and sacrificial suffering (Mark 8:31; 9:31; 10:33-34; Luke 24:45-46).

D. Entering the Temple Courts: vs. 11

Jesus entered Jerusalem and went to the temple. He looked around at everything, but since it was already late, he went out to Bethany with the Twelve.

By the time Jesus crossed from the Mount of Olives to Jerusalem, "it was already late" (Mark 11:11). With darkness coming on, most of the people were beginning to leave the temple, the shops, and the gates, and were heading for their homes or inns. So all Jesus did in Jerusalem on this day was to stop briefly in the temple area.

The phrase "He looked around at everything" in the courts of the sacred complex holds more significance than might at first appear. As the Son of God, Jesus was examining His property to see how it was being used. He said nothing, but from the events of the next day we know He had an opinion (vss. 15-17). For the time being, Jesus left Jerusalem and spent the night in Bethany, perhaps at the home of Mary, Martha, and Lazarus (John 12:1-2). This withdrawal from the city might have been for safety's sake, since Jesus knew it was not yet time for Him to fall into His opponents' hands. It might also have been to dramatize His unwillingness to be a part of what was going on in the temple.

Discussion Questions

1. How do you think the disciples felt about Jesus' plan to enter Jerusalem?
2. Why is it sometimes hard to understand and obey the Lord's instructions?
3. Why did Jesus choose this time to enter Jerusalem in a royal way and accept the praises of the crowds?
4. How can believers show their exuberant, uninhibited praise to the Savior?
5. What impresses you most about this occasion?

Contemporary Application

As Jesus made His triumphal entrance into Jerusalem, He was accompanied by shouts of acclamation from crowds of pilgrims. Parades in honor of Jesus are out of place in most locales today, but His followers still face the obligation to cry, "Hosanna!" wherever they can. Sometimes bringing praise to Jesus requires overt public action, even though it might be embarrassing. At such moments we have to recall the admirable courage Jesus established.

Our having a personal relationship with Jesus is a necessary prelude to praising Him, whether in public or in private. Admittedly, we cannot develop a personal relationship with Him without an investment of our time. Frantically busy as many of us are, we often find it difficult to find time to spend with the Lord. Yet intimacy with Jesus demands that we determine to set aside a regular time each day to commune with Him.

While God has determined that developing our intimacy with Jesus is mainly a private and personal enterprise, He desires that our praise of Jesus often be a public matter. Like the cheering crowds who focused the spotlight on Jesus during His entry into Jerusalem, we must do the same by praising Him openly. That's certainly part of what Jesus intended when He ordered the disciples to be His witnesses. At the minimum, His followers are to bring Jesus and His deeds to the public's attention.

Since Jesus has died for our sins and changed our lives, we should say so. If we have found Him to be the one who hears our prayers, let us report it. Let us joyfully recount every good and perfect deed that Jesus has done. To an age that has lost its way, despairs of finding truth, and seeks to find a life worth living, let us praise Jesus for what He has done for us. In addition, we benefit when we praise the Father for His Son. For in doing so, we are reminded of how wonderfully blessed we are to have Jesus' love and friendship.

Affirming Jesus' Resurrection

Scripture

Background Scripture: *1 Corinthians 15:1-22*
Scripture Lesson: *1 Corinthians 15:1-11, 20-22*
Key Verse: *For as in Adam all die, so in Christ all will be
made alive.* 1 Corinthians 15:22.
Scripture Lesson for Children: *1 Corinthians 15:1-11,
20-22*
Key Verse for Children: *Christ has indeed been raised from
the dead.* 1 Corinthians 15:20.

Lesson Aim

To recognize that Jesus conquered death so that
believers can experience new life with Him.

Lesson Setting

Time: A.D. *55*
Place: Ephesus

Lesson Outline

Affirming Jesus' Resurrection
   I. The Reality of Jesus' Resurrection:
      1 Corinthians 15:1-11
      A. *The Centrality of the Gospel: vss. 1-2*
      B. *The Core Message of the Gospel: vss. 3-4*
      C. *The Savior's Appearance to Many Disciples: vss. 5-7*
      D. *The Savior's Appearance to Paul: vss. 8-11*
  II. The Significance of Jesus' Resurrection:
      1 Corinthians 15:20-22
      A. *Jesus as the Firstfruits: vs. 20*
      B. *New Life in the Son: vss. 21-22*

Introduction for Adults

Topic: *Fully Alive*

Every Easter we celebrate the resurrection of our Lord Jesus Christ. His resurrection also guarantees the resurrection of our bodies. The two cannot be separated. Yet many adults are resigned to the mistaken idea that when they die, they will cease to exist.

Even brilliant, well-educated people assume that one day they will "die like a dog" (that is, as miserably and shamefully as a dog). They cannot conceive of life beyond the grave. They assume that we are no different from the animals, and to claim immortality is foolishness. They cannot see beyond the physical realm of existence.

But the Christian hope of the resurrection—of new life in a new body—gives meaning to every aspect of daily existence. Because Jesus lives, we will also live. More than ever, saved adults need to share the certainty of eternal life in Jesus with hopeless people.

Introduction for Youth

Topic: *True Eyewitnesses*

The hope of the resurrection of believers is not wishful thinking. As Paul declared in 1 Corinthians 15, it is the truth we can count on.

Jesus' resurrection was the foundation of early Christian preaching. The Gospel spread and the church was established because Jesus is alive. Of all religions, Christianity alone claims that its founder was raised from the dead. This claim has been disputed, but never successfully refuted.

Here we discover that faith in Christ is not a close-your-eyes-and-take-the-plunge-and-hope-you're-not-wrong kind of thing. We did not see everything happen with our own eyes. But the facts are recorded for us in Scripture to examine and accept. And even though we have not physically seen Jesus as many did, we can still believe in Him and receive eternal life.

Concepts for Children

Topic: *That's Good News!*

1. Jesus died on the cross for our sins.
2. After that, Jesus rose from the dead.
3. Many people saw Jesus after He rose from the dead.
4. Even Paul had an opportunity to see that Jesus is alive.
5. God wants us to have faith in Jesus, who conquered death for us.

Lesson Commentary

I. THE REALITY OF JESUS' RESURRECTION: 1 CORINTHIANS 15:1-11

A. The Centrality of the Gospel: vss. 1-2

Now, brothers, I want to remind you of the gospel I preached to you, which you received and on which you have taken your stand. By this gospel you are saved, if you hold firmly to the word I preached to you. Otherwise, you have believed in vain.

The first-century A.D. church at Corinth struggled with a number of problems that required Paul's attention. Among these were a growing laxity for discipline, a surge of lawsuits being brought before non-Christian judges, and a spreading propensity for sexual immorality. Also, there was probably some opposition to Paul in the church. Perhaps while the apostle was in the process of writing this epistle, the Corinthian believers sent him a letter in which they asked his advice on a variety of moral and social matters (1 Cor. 7:1). This gave rise to Paul's instruction about maintaining stable marriages, about discontinuing less-than-ethical actions, about what to do and what not to do in public worship, and about the reality of Jesus' resurrection. It may have taken the apostle days or weeks to write this letter.

After Paul concluded his lengthy section on spiritual gifts (a topic discussed in lesson 11), he turned a corner and began talking about another major subject: the resurrection. Probably because of their faulty understanding about what it meant to be "spiritual," some of the Corinthians did not believe in the bodily resurrection of the dead. They might have believed that Christians, after death, live on forever in heaven as spirits. But to them the idea of one's soul being rejoined with one's body was distasteful. The apostle determined he had to correct their theological error.

Paul began his argument by establishing common ground with his readers: they all believed that the Lord Jesus had been raised from the dead. When Paul had arrived in Corinth, he had proclaimed the Gospel—the body of teachings about Jesus and salvation that had been handed down from the first Christians. Paul's readers had not only accepted the Gospel, but had also based their faith squarely upon it (15:1). Furthermore, it was by this Gospel that they would reach final salvation (vs. 2). But now some of them had begun to believe that there is no future resurrection of the dead—an idea contradictory to the Gospel. Paul warned his readers that if they held to that idea, then their Christian faith was made pointless. A little later in the chapter (vss. 12-19), the apostle would explain what he meant.

B. The Core Message of the Gospel: vss. 3-4

For what I received I passed on to you as of first importance: that Christ died for our sins according to the Scriptures, that he was buried, that he was raised on the third day according to the Scriptures.

The Greek noun rendered "gospel" (1 Cor. 15:1) translates *euangelion* (you-ahn-GELL-ee-ahn), from which we get such words as *evangelism* and *evangelical*. The noun literally means "good news." In the New Testament, the Gospel is not merely historical facts about someone who lived long ago. Its message focuses on certain saving acts that were believed and proclaimed by the early church. Specifically, the term is used to refer to the message concerning the life, death, and resurrection of the Lord Jesus. It was also used to refer to the kingdom of God and salvation. The truths contained in the Gospel are not optional to the believer's faith. Rather, they are central to it. What the Gospel teaches is absolutely accurate and true, and thus to be readily accepted by all Christians.

In verse 3, Paul repeated a portion of the Gospel he had preached in Corinth—the part that related to Jesus' death and resurrection. Also, this aspect was of foremost importance. Because of the structure, wording, and content of verses 3-5, many New Testament scholars believe that Paul was quoting an early Christian creed. The first statement in the creed is that the Messiah "died for our sins according to the Scriptures" (vs. 3). Jesus' death was not a tragic accident; it had a purpose—namely, to rescue sinners. Passages in the Hebrew Bible, such as Isaiah 52:13–53:12, foretold Jesus' sacrificial death. Second, Jesus "was buried" (1 Cor. 15:4). Burial in a tomb certified the reality of the Messiah's death. Third, He was raised from death on the third day, just as the Scriptures had foretold. After being buried on Friday afternoon, Jesus was resurrected on early Sunday morning. As for the biblical prediction of this amazing event, such passages as Psalm 16:8-11 and Jonah 1:17 might be in view.

To fully appreciate Paul's teaching here on the resurrection, it is necessary to have some knowledge of the Greek view of life and death. Generally speaking, the Greeks believed the soul was immortal, but the body would not be raised from the dead. In Greek thought, the body was the source of all human sin and weakness. So, death brought release of the soul from its fleshly prison. It was inconceivable, therefore, to accept a process by which the soul would be re-imprisoned. The problem in the Corinthian church was that some could accept the teaching that Jesus had been raised from the dead, but they were reluctant to affirm the bodily resurrection of Christians in general. Paul corrected this theological error by first establishing the certainty of the resurrection and by making the connection between the resurrection of Jesus and that of believers (1 Cor. 15:1-34). Next, the apostle explored key issues surrounding the idea of a bodily resurrection and Jesus' return (vss. 35-37). Finally, Paul made an appeal to his readers to stand firm in their labor for the Lord (vs. 58).

C. The Savior's Appearance to Many Disciples: vss. 5-7

And that he appeared to Peter, and then to the Twelve. After that, he appeared to more than five hundred of the brothers at the same time, most of whom are still living, though some have fallen asleep. Then he appeared to James, then to all the apostles.

In the fourth part in the early Christian creed quoted by Paul, we learn that Jesus, after rising from the dead, "appeared to Peter" (1 Cor. 15:5), and after that to the "Twelve." These appearances proved the reality of the Lord's resurrection (Luke 24:34; John 20:19). Paul expanded the creed he had been quoting by citing additional postresurrection appearances that he had learned about. To begin with, the apostle reported that the Lord had appeared to a group of Christians numbering more than 500. (This appearance is mentioned nowhere else in Scripture.) Since many of these people were still living at the time the apostle wrote, the Corinthians could have had plenty of eyewitness testimonies to the resurrection, if they wanted them (1 Cor. 15:6). Jesus also appeared to His half brother James (vs. 7), who by this time was leader of the Jerusalem church. (Here again, we know nothing more about this appearance.) In addition, Jesus appeared to "all the apostles"—perhaps meaning a larger group than just the Twelve. This might refer to the appearance described in Acts 1:6-11.

D. The Savior's Appearance to Paul: vss. 8-11

And last of all he appeared to me also, as to one abnormally born. For I am the least of the apostles and do not even deserve to be called an apostle, because I persecuted the church of God. But by the grace of God I am what I am, and his grace to me was not without effect. No, I worked harder than all of them— yet not I, but the grace of God that was with me. Whether, then, it was I or they, this is what we preach, and this is what you believed.

Finally, the Lord Jesus appeared to Paul (1 Cor. 15:8). Clearly, the apostle was referring to his meeting with the risen Savior on the Damascus road (Acts 9:3-6). To Paul, this was more than just a vision. He had seen the Lord as surely as had all the other disciples. Many people today doubt or deny Jesus' resurrection. Yet while all the eyewitnesses have now died, there is still abundant biblical and circumstantial evidence that Jesus rose from the dead. In short, it is a historical fact.

As Paul described his own sighting of the resurrected Lord, the apostle called himself "one abnormally born" (1 Cor. 15:8). This translates a Greek noun that literally referred to a miscarriage or a stillbirth. The other apostles had all achieved their status through following Jesus in His earthly ministry. But Paul's entrance into apostleship was unusual, as someone who survived a freakish birth. Some in Corinth might have come to undervalue Paul in comparison to other apostles. Paul agreed that he was the "least" (vs. 9) important of all the apostles. Here Paul was probably making a pun on his Roman name, Paulus, which means "the little one." Indeed, Paul said he didn't deserve to be called an apostle. After all, before getting saved, he had acted like a predator who pursued and tyrannized God's "church" (Acts 8:1; 9:1-2; 22:4; 26:9-11; Phil. 3:6; 1 Tim. 1:12-13).

Yet, despite all that, Paul was an apostle solely by God's grace. The Lord could have punished Paul for persecuting Jesus' followers, but instead He forgave the misguided Pharisee and called him to service. In turn, Paul responded by working harder than any other apostle in spreading the Good News. Again, he was quick to add that this, too, was by God's grace (1 Cor. 15:10). Since Paul was an apostle, he was preaching the same Gospel that all the other apostles were proclaiming. Moreover, it was this Good News through which the Corinthians had come to faith (vs. 11; compare vs. 1). Clearly, Paul meant that if the Corinthians were disbelieving a part of the Gospel—the part about the bodily resurrection of the dead—then they were going against not only him, but also all the rest of the apostles.

II. THE SIGNIFICANCE OF JESUS' RESURRECTION: 1 CORINTHIANS 15:20-22

A. Jesus as the Firstfruits: vs. 20

But Christ has indeed been raised from the dead, the firstfruits of those who have fallen asleep.

In 1 Corinthians 15:12-18, Paul told his readers that if Jesus had not been raised from the dead, their faith would be useless. The apostle argued that all the logical conclusions he had drawn from the Corinthians' implicit denial of Jesus' resurrection were meaningless, since He had been resurrected. Paul firmly asserted that Jesus is the "firstfruits" (vs. 20) of those who would be resurrected. By this the apostle meant Jesus' rising from the dead was the down payment or guarantee that believers who die would also be raised from the dead (Rom. 8:23). In a manner of speaking, Jesus' resurrection was the prototype for the future resurrection of believers.

At harvest time, Israelite farmers took the first and finest portions of their crops and offered them to the Lord (Exod. 23:16, 19; Lev. 23:9-14). The whole nation initially celebrated the offering of the "firstfruits" in the late spring, 50 days after Passover, at the beginning of harvest season. At first, this celebration was known as the Festival of Weeks. Later it became known as *Pentecost*, the Greek word meaning "fiftieth." The celebration was repeated throughout summer as other crops were brought in. The whole purpose of the festival was to give thanks to God for His bounty. It was a time of great rejoicing throughout Israel. In the same way, Paul pictured Jesus' resurrection as just the beginning, the "firstfruits" of the resurrection harvest yet to come. Indeed, Jesus was not only the first to rise from the dead, but He also served as a pledge that more resurrections would one day follow. His resurrection guarantees that all the deceased who placed their trust in Him while alive will someday be resurrected (1 Cor. 15:20).

B. New Life in the Son: vss. 21-22

For since death came through a man, the resurrection of the dead comes also through a man. For as in Adam all die, so in Christ all will be made alive.

In 1 Corinthians 15, Paul's theological point is that the resurrection of the dead is one of the things that would inevitably happen because Jesus was raised. His resurrection set in motion an unstoppable chain of events. As an explanation of this inevitability, Paul set up a comparison between Adam and Christ. The apostle reminded his readers that because Adam sinned, death entered the world. And since the human race is related to Adam through natural birth, sin and death spread to all humanity (Rom. 5:12-21). Even though one man's disobedience brought death to all, in the same way, another man's obedience would result in resurrection to eternal life for all who are spiritually related to Him (1 Cor. 15:21-22).

In verses 23-28, Paul outlined things to come. No exact chronology or timetable is given for the events described here, but nearly 2,000 years have already passed. What is certain is that Jesus promised after His resurrection that He would return for those who "belong to Him" (vs. 23) and raise them from the dead. Even though the Father and the Son (along with the Spirit) are equal in every respect, they each have their own special mission and area of sovereign control. Jesus' important task on earth was to defeat and destroy all evil. On the cross, He triumphed over sin and death. And when Jesus returns at the close of the present age, Satan's "dominion, authority and power" (vs. 24) on earth will be defeated. Moreover, along with Satan's destruction, death—the final enemy of humankind—will be destroyed (vs. 26). In verse 27, the apostle quoted Psalm 8:6 to describe Jesus' total victory over His foes. The verse reflects an ancient practice in which a monarch would symbolize his control over a defeated enemy. First, he would have the antagonist bow down, and then the victor would put his foot on the enemy's neck.

Some commentators have looked at 1 Corinthians 15:23-26 and found a definite sequence for what happens at Jesus' return. According to this view, the dead in Christ will rise first at His return (vs. 23), followed by those believers who are alive at the time, an event sometimes called the rapture. "Then" (vs. 24) Jesus will begin His 1,000-year reign on earth, when the saints rule with Him (Rev. 20:4-6), followed by His conquest of the kingdoms of this world (vss. 7-10). The devil and his cohorts will be defeated, and then death itself will be cast into the lake of fire (1 Cor. 15:26; Rev. 20:14). Others understand the "he must reign" of 1 Corinthians 15:25 as what Jesus is doing now in this age. Put another way, His reign is more spiritual in nature, extending over the entire course of human history. So, Jesus' reign during this present age is His moral rule over the lives of the saints. After such a reign, "then the end will come" (vs. 24).

Discussion Questions

1. Why did Paul think it was important to remind his readers about the Gospel?
2. In what way is our salvation tied to the Gospel?
3. Why is it important for us to hold to the historical resurrection of Jesus?

4. How did Paul experience the mercy and grace of God?

5. How can believers use the truths Paul taught about the resurrection to encourage someone with a terminal illness?

Contemporary Application

When I was a hospital chaplain, I conducted many memorial services for deceased patients and staff members, and I attended many others. I came to realize that our grieving takes on two aspects. One is the normal sadness that comes over the family and friends the deceased person has left behind. The other, less mentioned aspect involves the bereaved grieving because the passing away of the deceased has reminded them of their own impending demise. The Good News is that Jesus rose from the dead. And we who are in spiritual union with Him by faith are promised a new life after death with the Lord in heaven.

In *The Last Battle*, C. S. Lewis's final book in his beloved Narnia children's fantasy series, he offers a refreshing picture of eternal life in heaven: "All of the old Narnia that mattered, all the dear creatures, have been drawn into the real Narnia through the Door," Lewis wrote. "And of course it is different; as different as a real thing is from a shadow or as waking life is from a dream. . . . The difference between the old Narnia and the new Narnia was like that. The new one was a deeper country: every rock and flower and blade of grass looked as if it meant more. I can't describe it any better than that: if ever you get there you will know what I mean."

The popular image of heaven—angels with harps and wings, fluffy clouds, holier-than-thou people clothed in white—is as different from the real heaven as a lightning bug is different from a lightning bolt. That popular image of heaven is not an eternity many people would enjoy. It is certainly not an eternity worth dying for. And yet dying for the lost is exactly what Jesus did on the cross. He then rose from the dead so that believers could live with Him in the real heaven, that "deeper country" of which this life is but a shadow. Because of His victory over death, we can experience true life.

Loving One Another

Scripture

Background Scripture: *1 John 3:11-24*
Scripture Lesson: *1 John 3:11-24*
Key Verse: This is the message you heard from the beginning: We should love one another. *1 John 3:11.*
Scripture Lesson for Children: *1 John 3:11-24*
Key Verse for Children: Love one another. *1 John 3:11.*

Lesson Aim

To reflect Jesus' love for us by loving others.

Lesson Setting

Time: Around A.D. 96
Place: Possibly Ephesus

Lesson Outline

Loving One Another
  I. Belief Validated by Love: 1 John 3:11-15
      A. *The Command to Love, not Hate: vss. 11-12*
      B. *The Contrast between Hatred and Love: vss. 13-15*
  II. Love Demonstrated through Obedience:
      1 John 3:16-24
      A. *Reaching Out in Love to People in Need: vss. 16-18*
      B. *Experiencing Confidence in God's Presence:
          vss. 19-22*
      C. *Uniting Belief and Love: vss. 23-24*

Introduction for Adults

Topic: *We Need Love*

In 1 John 3, the apostle used the word "love" multiple times. First, he described Jesus' great love for us. Then, the apostle emphasized that Jesus' followers would act like Him. Finally, John stressed the importance of believers demonstrating the Savior's love toward others, especially fellow believers.

In 1965, Jackie DeShannon performed the top ten single "What the World Needs Now Is Love." The chorus for this popular song stated that love is "the only thing that there's just too little of" and that "sweet love" is "not just for some but for everyone."

Few people would claim that these sentiments don't apply today. In an era in which people tend to live for themselves and take advantage of others to satisfy their own desires, the world needs a special kind of love. It's not the sort, though, that we hoard for ourselves. We need the love of the Savior, a practical love that seeks the benefit of others, a caring love that is active and sincere.

Introduction for Youth

Topic: *Show Me Love*

What is it like to live in the light of Jesus' love, as 1 John 2:10 emphasizes? Have you ever entered a dark room or an abandoned apartment, turned on the light, and watched the cockroaches scurry away? Living in the light means we do not have to run away when Jesus shines the truth of His Word on our lives. It means we welcome His inspections. According to the apostle John, it means letting the Savior's love guide our conduct.

That's a tough assignment and sometimes we fail to make the grade. But Jesus forgives us when we confess our sins. He pardons our transgressions. That's why it's so important to stay close to Him, whatever our circumstances. Jesus not only tells us how to be compassionate, but also helps us to display kindness when we rely on Him.

Concepts for Children

Topic: *Love One Another*

1. John encouraged us to obey Jesus' teachings.
2. Our behavior shows others that we are Christians.
3. As we live for Jesus, we grow stronger in our faith.
4. Jesus' love in us helps others to see that we belong to Jesus.
5. Our love for others pleases the Lord.

Lesson Commentary

I. Belief Validated by Love: 1 John 3:11-15

A. The Command to Love, not Hate: vss. 11-12

This is the message you heard from the beginning: We should love one another. Do not be like Cain, who belonged to the evil one and murdered his brother. And why did he murder him? Because his own actions were evil and his brother's were righteous.

First John was authored primarily to combat the emerging heresy of Gnosticism, which was influencing the churches in the apostle's day. Key Gnostic teachings included these beliefs: (1) virtue is inferior to knowledge; (2) only a few chosen people can understand the true meaning of Scripture; (3) to explain the existence of evil, God must have had a cocreator; (4) the Incarnation must be rejected because a spiritual deity would not unite with a material body; and (5) there can be no bodily resurrection since the body is evil and the spirit is good (see also the comments on Greek thought appearing in last week's lesson).

John's pre-Gnostic opponents might have been led by a man named Cerinthus. They denied that Jesus was the Son of God who had come in the flesh. To an extent, they denied their own sinfulness and that righteous conduct was necessary to remain in good standing within the church. Apparently, the proponents of these views had once been a part of the established church in Asia Minor, but at some time made a distinct break from this fellowship. It seems members of this subversive group were attempting to lure the faithful away from the apostles' authoritative teachings. For this reason, John wanted to make it clear that these people were false teachers. In fact, he considered them Jesus' archenemies.

In 3:11-24, the apostle wrote about the impact of Christian love. He began by stressing that what Christians believed was validated by the presence of compassion and kindness in their lives. John's message to his readers was not something new, but what they had heard from the beginning of their Christian experience, namely, that God's children were to "love one another" (vs. 11). In fact, the practice of love toward fellow believers was profoundly related to the reality of salvation in a person's life.

Before John told his audience exactly what Christlike love was, he revealed what it was not (see also the Bible commentary in lesson 13 dealing with 1 Corinthians 13). The apostle used an illustration from the dawn of human existence. It is the account of the first murder in history (Gen. 4:2-8). The point of the illustration is that Cain's murder of his brother, Abel, is the exact opposite of genuine love and certainly not the kind of behavior to be found among Jesus' followers. John pointed out that by murdering his brother, Cain proved he was a child of Satan, "the evil one" (1 John 3:12). The reason for Cain's homicidal act was his jealousy and resentment toward Abel's virtuous character as compared with Cain's own ungodliness.

259

Numerous conjectures have been recorded as to why Abel's sacrifice was superior to Cain's. Some think God accepted Abel's sacrifice because, as an animal offering, it involved blood, whereas Cain's, as a type of grain offering, did not. However, we don't have clearly recorded specifications for blood sacrifices until the Book of Leviticus. Others note that Abel's sacrifice was living and Cain's was lifeless, or that Abel's grew spontaneously and Cain's grew by human ingenuity. Perhaps the strongest reason Abel's offering was accepted and Cain's was rejected lies in the attitude of both brothers. Abel offered his sacrifice willingly, and so his was a demonstration of faith (Heb. 11:4). Because of the reference to Cain belonging to the "evil one" (1 John 3:12), Cain's name became associated with the devil and wicked deeds in general. At first, the carrying out of such deeds was referred to as "raising the devil." But some, preferring not to mention Satan's name, substituted "raising Cain."

B. The Contrast between Hatred and Love: vss. 13-15

Do not be surprised, my brothers, if the world hates you. We know that we have passed from death to life, because we love our brothers. Anyone who does not love remains in death. Anyone who hates his brother is a murderer, and you know that no murderer has eternal life in him.

Cain was an illustration of the world. This is the realm of evil, which one day will pass away (1 John 2:15-17). Since the unsaved display the heinous qualities Cain possessed and acted upon, Christians should not be astonished if unbelievers hate them (3:13). Believers should expect the wicked to treat Jesus' followers just as Cain treated his brother. Jesus warned His disciples that they should anticipate that the world would hate them because it hated Him first (John 15:18-19, 25). While the world's hatred of believers is commonplace, the hatred of one Christian for another is inexcusable. Indeed, it was out of sync with the eternal life that comes through faith in the Messiah.

In 1 John 3:14, the apostle connected love to life and hatred to death. The test that one had truly experienced new life in Christ was an ever-deepening love for other believers. God's children naturally had a desire to meet together for prayer and fellowship. In contrast, an unbelieving world wanted no part of such activity. So, to harbor hatred for believers suggested a closer intimacy with the world than with the Savior. Verse 15 is even more blunt in equating hatred with murder and declaring that "eternal life" could not flourish in the toxic soil of a homicidal disposition. Likewise, in the Sermon on the Mount, Jesus equated the hatred of one person for another with spiritual or moral murder, just as He equated lust with adultery (Matt. 5:21-22, 28).

II. LOVE DEMONSTRATED THROUGH OBEDIENCE: 1 JOHN 3:16-24

A. Reaching Out in Love to People in Need: vss. 16-18

This is how we know what love is: Jesus Christ laid down his life for us. And we ought to lay down our lives for our brothers. If anyone has material possessions and sees his brother in need but has no pity on him, how can the love of God be in him? Dear children, let us not love with words or tongue but with actions and in truth.

In 1 John 3:16, the apostle pointed his readers to the Lord Jesus as the most sterling example of unconditional love. The Savior gave His life so that believing sinners might have new life in Him. John 3:16 teaches a similar truth. The Father, being motivated by His infinite love for lost humanity, sent His "one and only Son" to die for the sins of the world. God summons all people to put their faith in Messiah—not only assenting to what He said as true, but also entrusting their lives to Him. Those who believe in the Savior do not suffer eternal separation from God, but enjoy a reconciled, deeply satisfying relationship with the Son and His heavenly Father.

The apostle declared that because the Lord Jesus gave His life on the cross to redeem the lost, His disciples should be ready and willing to demonstrate self-sacrificing love for their fellow Christians (1 John 3:16). Admittedly, not many believers will be called to literally sacrifice their lives for another believer. Nonetheless, as verse 17 reveals, Jesus' followers can show their unconditional love by meeting the needs of others. This includes believers giving sacrificially of their material resources. Christlike love should prompt God's children to display empathy and concern for others in need of the basic necessities of life—such as food, clothing, and shelter. God's love demands nothing less. Christians who refuse to be moved by the need of others reveal an absence of divine love in their hearts.

Today it is often said that talk is cheap. Apparently, it was no different in John's time. For that reason, the apostle warned his readers that mere verbal expressions of love with no actions were useless in the face of dire need (vs. 18). Actions indeed speak louder than words. James 2:15-16 makes a similar point about seeing others who are desperate for food and clothing and responding with nothing more than a pious-sounding farewell. If God's children refuse to help the impoverished, especially when believers have the means to do something, what good is their professed faith in God? The desire and practice of actively meeting the physical needs of others is an indication of whether a person's faith is genuine. Believers who put their faith into practice can be assured that they are active participants in divine truth. They can also be confident that they are doing the Father's will and demonstrating the Son's compassion.

B. Experiencing Confidence in God's Presence: vss. 19-22

This then is how we know that we belong to the truth, and how we set our hearts at rest in his presence whenever our hearts condemn us. For God is greater than our hearts, and he knows everything. Dear friends, if our hearts do not condemn us, we have confidence before God and receive from him anything we ask, because we obey his commands and do what pleases him.

A great sense of failure or inadequacy might result when believers compare their faith in action to the high standard set by the Lord Jesus. In this regard, the hearts of His followers might condemn them, even though they have been performing the practical acts of love referred to in 1 John 3:16-18. The apostle reminded his readers that, as practicing Christians, they were not only abiding in the truth of the Gospel, but also dwelling in the comforting presence of God (vs. 19). Even when His children felt a false sense of guilt, they could draw consolation from the truth that their heavenly Father knew everything about them. In fact, His knowledge exceeded that of their troubled hearts (vs. 20). Jesus' followers might have an oversensitive spirit to their own inadequacies, when they should be resting in the sufficiency of God's grace. In this instance, anxious believers ought to find repose in the knowledge that an all-compassionate God is aware of their genuine acts of faith.

John associated the serenity that comes from being in God's loving hands with confidence in prayer. As a result of performing deeds of mercy and kindness, believers could find peace for their troubled consciences and approach God's throne with confidence in prayer (vs. 21). As they did so, they could rest assured that God would hear and respond to their requests (vs. 22). In order for their petitions to be answered, the habitual conduct of their lives had to be characterized by submission and obedience to God. John was by no means suggesting that occasionally keeping God's commands and sporadically doing His will were sufficient grounds upon which to expect answers to prayer. Those who played fast and loose with God's boundaries for living and displayed little regard for His will had no claim upon Him. God was not a genie who existed to grant the selfish desires of humankind. Instead, He was the moral Governor of the universe who deserved unquestioning obedience from those He created.

C. Uniting Belief and Love: vss. 23-24

And this is his command: to believe in the name of his Son, Jesus Christ, and to love one another as he commanded us. Those who obey his commands live in him, and he in them. And this is how we know that he lives in us: We know it by the Spirit he gave us.

In 1 John 3:22, the apostle told his readers that effective prayer was based in large part upon obedience to God's Word. Verse 23 draws attention to the Creator's supreme two-part command. God's children were directed to trust in His Son, the Lord Jesus, for eternal life and be unconditionally loving to one another. This is the first explicit reference to faith in John's epistle. Evidently, the false teachers of John's time insisted that "Jesus" and "the Messiah" were separate individuals. In contrast, the apostle taught that the historic person, Jesus of Nazareth, is identical with the Messiah, God's Son (John 20:31; 1 John 4:15; 5:5). To put one's trust in Jesus' name meant to believe in everything that it represented. This included affirming Jesus as being fully human and fully divine. Faith in the Son's name also involved appropriating His redemptive work on the cross for oneself and depending upon the Spirit to help God's children mature.

The command to show unconditional love was previously mentioned in 1 John 2:7-11. The directive was first truly realized in the Son and then in His followers. John made reference to this truth in terms of the true light of the Messiah already shining brightly. Because the apostle saw the victory of light over darkness as something previously begun, he urged his readers to hold fast to what they had already heard and not be influenced by the teaching of the opponents. The commandment to love others did not belong to the old era that was passing away. It belonged to the new era of righteousness that was introduced by Jesus' incarnation and made possible by His atoning work on the cross. It followed that any professing Christian who claimed to follow Jesus but harbored hatred toward others was still living in the old era of darkness (1 John 2:9).

Believers who demonstrated genuine love for others were living in the light of the new era in the Messiah. And because of this, there was nothing in them that would cause others to stumble (vs. 10). Professing believers, however, who nursed grudges and cultivated bitterness remained spiritually darkened. These people lost their bearings, especially as they stumbled around in the dark (vs. 11). John minced no words about the vileness of abiding in the darkness of sin and the virtue of dwelling in the light of the Savior. Darkness was the haunt of all that was unrighteous and corrupt, while light was the haven of whatever was pure and wholesome.

In 3:23, the apostle brought faith and love together in the same context. Both concepts are commanded, both are elements of God's will for believers, and both are tests of genuine Christian profession. There is a kind of progression in John's development toward the twofold command to believe in Jesus' name and to love other believers. As His disciples performed acts of Christian love and gained confidence in prayer, they were in fact obeying God's commands (2:3; 5:2-3). They were also living a life of faith in Christ, one that demonstrated their active belief in the name of Jesus.

In 3:24, John discussed the concept of mutual abiding—the believer in the Son and He in the believer. This truth is evident in the parable of the vine and branches (John 15:1-17). The apostle revealed that obedience is the basis for living in vital union with the Messiah. Furthermore, in 1 John 3:24, the apostle stated that the claim to abide in the Son was validated by a believer's fidelity to three foundational commands: (1) believing in the Savior; (2) loving one another (vs. 23); and (3) living in a godly manner (vss. 7-10). Abiding in Jesus was not an assertion that could be successfully made without convincing evidence. For instance, such a claim must be accompanied by a confession that Jesus is the Son of God and Savior of the world, as well as by a life characterized by unconditional love for other believers and the practice of personal holiness.

In general, how could believers know that the Savior abided in them? The indwelling Spirit was the source of the believer's assurance. He enabled repentant sinners to believe the truth about the Messiah's person and work (2:20, 27; 4:1-6). The Spirit also empowered believers to fulfill God's will, live righteously, and love their fellow Christians (Gal. 5:16, 22-23). So, the presence and power of the Spirit in the lives of believers was the crucial evidence that Jesus was one with them. Since the Spirit was characterized by faith and love (4:1-16), it made sense that He enabled Christians to fulfill the two-part command given in 3:23.

Discussion Questions

1. Why is it important for believers to love one another?
2. Why does unsaved humanity tend to hate God's children?
3. When believers demonstrate Christlike love to others, how does it impact their witness?
4. How can believers obtain divine consolation when they feel a sense of false guilt?
5. Why did John place a strong emphasis on believing in the name of the Son?

Contemporary Application

John pointed to Jesus' voluntary death on the cross as the supreme example of love (1 John 3:16). Why was Jesus willing to lay down His life for the sins of the world? And why did He offer Himself as the sacrificial lamb? Surely, it wasn't because of the character or conduct of those for whom He died.

Israel's misdirected religious leaders had successfully bargained with the Roman authorities for the Messiah's death. The mob rejected Jesus, calling instead for the release of a notorious criminal. Even one of Jesus' own inner circle of followers betrayed Him for money, while another, when pressed, vehemently denied even having known Him.

Jesus was sworn at, spat upon, and ridiculed. He was so badly beaten before He was finally nailed to the cross that He was almost unrecognizable. Why didn't He just call an army of angels and destroy the mocking crowds? He owed these people nothing. According to this week's Scripture passage, it was love, pure and simple, that prompted Jesus to die on the cross.

Jesus welcomes us as His spiritual children and wants us to reflect His unconditional mercy, forgiveness, and compassion. When we love as He does, we show that we truly belong to Him. And others take notice.

Each day, we have opportunities to demonstrate Jesus' love. And each time an opportunity presents itself, we have a choice to make. The Spirit enables us to focus on the love Jesus has demonstrated to us. As an expression of gratitude for His love, we find the courage and strength, despite our emotions, to act in loving ways toward others.

Recognizing God's Love

Scripture

Background Scripture: *1 John 4–5*
Scripture Lesson: *1 John 4:13–5:5*
Key Verse: *Everyone who believes that Jesus is the Christ is born of God, and everyone who loves the father loves his child as well.* 1 John 5:1.
Scripture Lesson for Children: *1 John 4:7-18*
Key Verse for Children: *Dear friends, since God so loved us, we also ought to love one another.* 1 John 4:11.

Lesson Aim

To appreciate that the Father showed His love for us by sending His Son.

Lesson Setting

Time: Around A.D. 96
Place: Possibly Ephesus

Lesson Outline

Recognizing God's Love

  I. God's Demonstration of His Love: 1 John 4:13-21
      A. *The Father Sending the Son: vss. 13-15*
      B. *The Source of the Believers' Confidence: vss. 16-18*
      C. *The Importance of Showing Love: vss. 19-21*
  II. Love for God and His Children: 1 John 5:1-5
      A. *The Trio of Faith, Love, and Obedience: vss. 1-3*
      B. *The Source of the Believers' Victory: vss. 4-5*

Introduction for Adults

Topic: *Beloved Child*

An older carpenter prepared to retire. He told the contractor for whom he worked about his plans to stop building and to enjoy a more leisurely life with his wife and extended family. He would miss the paycheck, but he needed to retire. They could get by.

The contractor was sorry to see his good worker go and asked whether he would build just one more house as a personal favor. The carpenter agreed, but in time it was easy to see that his heart wasn't in his work. He grew careless and took shortcuts on quality. It was an unfortunate way to end his career. When the carpenter finished the house, the contractor handed him the front-door key. "This is your house," the contractor said. "It's my gift to you in appreciation for all your dedicated work."

If the carpenter had known he was building his own house, he would have done it all so differently! We build our lives every day by the way we express God's love to those around us (1 John 4:20-21). Our love should be like the love of Jesus—only the highest quality—so that our lives will be like His, too.

Introduction for Youth

Topic: *Loving My Brothers and Sisters*

We like to sing, "They'll know we are Christians by our love," which is straight from the teaching of Jesus. But how much harder it is to practice the words. Any group of Christian teens is bound to include some who are not especially lovable. In fact, they may turn us off by their rude behavior.

Yet we cannot dodge the hard commands of Jesus and John. To love is our inescapable imperative and the source of one of God's greatest blessings. Failure to do so negates our Christian profession. Perhaps we need to confess our bad attitudes and listless behavior. Out of our weakness we must ask Jesus to make us more loving toward others, including those who may turn us off.

Concepts for Children

Topic: *Showing God's Love*

1. God is filled with love.
2. Love comes from God.
3. God loved us by sending His Son.
4. God loved us by giving us His Spirit.
5. God wants us to show His love to others.

Lesson Commentary

I. GOD'S DEMONSTRATION OF HIS LOVE: 1 JOHN 4:13-21

A. The Father Sending the Son: vss. 13-15

We know that we live in him and he in us, because he has given us of his Spirit. And we have seen and testify that the Father has sent his Son to be the Savior of the world. If anyone acknowledges that Jesus is the Son of God, God lives in him and he in God.

First John 4:7-12 begins the apostle's third significant discourse on the subject of Christlike love. (The first was given in 2:7-11 and the second in 3:11-18.) This is also the third time in his letter that the apostle employed love as the supreme test of Christian commitment and character. Furthermore, in 4:7-12, John gave three significant statements about the essence and nature of God. The apostle had previously revealed that "God is spirit" (John 4:24) and "God is light" (1 John 1:5). In 4:7-12, he described what is perhaps the supreme quality of the Lord's character, "God is love" (vs. 8). While false teachers believed that God is a spirit being and that He is light, they also taught that God is passionless and thus incapable of love.

John stated that if Christlike love is not present in an individual, then that person cannot possibly have an intimate knowledge of God. Though the phrase "born of God" is not present in verse 8 as it is in its counterpart in verse 7, John was likely talking about someone who has not trusted in the Savior, and is thus incapable of showing divine, unconditional love. Believers should love one another because God is the source of love and because He is in fact the essence of love. In verse 8, John was referring to an aspect of God's character. It would be theologically incorrect, however, to declare "love is God," for love is not the sole quality that absolutely defines the nature of the Lord.

We learn in verse 9 that the Father sent His Son into the world in order to make salvation available to all. "One and only" translates a Greek adjective that means not only "unique," but also "especially treasured." The idea is that the Father demonstrated the reality of His love by sending His cherished Son to die on behalf of sinful humanity. The Father's decision has nothing to do with humanity's love for Him. The initiative was all on God's side. In fact, Jesus' atoning sacrifice for sin is the supreme demonstration of God's love (vs. 10).

One of the most significant of Jewish festivals was the day of Atonement (Yom Kippur). At this annual celebration, the high priest entered the holy of holies to offer sacrifices for the sins of the people. Hebrews 2:17 pictures Jesus' death in terms of this festival. In His crucifixion, He was the real sacrifice, while those offered on the Day of Atonement were only shadows. By offering Himself on the cross, the Son presented Himself before the Father as the final, all-sufficient payment for the sins of the world.

The superlative example of Christian love is the Father's passion displayed in the Son's sacrificial death. Any expression of Christian love is only a response to the love God showed us first. Since God loved us so much, then "we also ought to love one another" (1 John 4:11). Expressed differently, if Jesus loved us sacrificially, then it is our duty to love each other in the same way.

No human being has ever seen God in all of His essential character. However, as Christians express mutual love, the invisible God manifests Himself through their acts of caring and tenderness (vs. 12). This is another reason given by John as to why believers should love one another. God still loves today and that love is revealed in our time when Christians love one another. In sum, God's love originates in Himself, was perfectly demonstrated in His Son, and is now perfected in God's own people when they genuinely love one another.

In verse 13, the apostle continued his discussion of the mutual abiding of a believer and the Lord Jesus. *Meno* (MEE-know) was one of John's favorite Greek words to describe the nature of the believer's relationship with God. Most often translated as "remain," "abide," "live," or "continue," this term occurs 112 times in the New Testament. Of these occurrences, 66 are found in the writings of John (40 in the Gospel of John, 23 in 1 John, and 3 in 2 John). Some scholars have suggested that *meno* actually signifies something beyond simple fellowship with God. The progression is given as (1) knowledge of God, (2) fellowship with God, and finally, (3) abiding in God. Clearly, John desired the deepest possible relationship between God and His children.

For proof that this mutual abiding is in effect, one has to look for the work of the Holy Spirit in that believer's life. Obedience to the two-part command to believe in the Messiah and love one another is a direct result of the Spirit's work within a believer's heart (Rom. 5:5; 1 John 3:24; 4:2). So, a Christian's Spirit-prompted obedience is the real evidence that a believer and the triune God abide in one another. The apostle had just told his readers that if we are characterized by Christlike compassion and kindness, then the invisible God lives in us, and His love for us is brought to full expression in our love for others (1 John 4:12).

The preceding experience validates our testimony that the Father sent His Son to be the Savior of the world (vs. 14). In practical terms, while God is invisible to the eye, He becomes visible in a spiritual sense when His indwelling presence is evident in the mutual love between believers. In light of what the apostle just said, he told his readers that anyone who acknowledged that Jesus is the Son of God was indwelled by God and in turn dwells in God (vs. 15). Here again is a test or evidence of mutual indwelling. Life-changing belief in the deity of the Savior suggests obedience to Him and surrender to His will.

B. The Source of the Believers' Confidence: vss. 16-18

And so we know and rely on the love God has for us. God is love. Whoever lives in love lives in God, and God in him. In this way, love is made complete among us so that we will have confidence on the day of judgment, because in this world we are like him. There is no fear in love. But perfect love drives out fear, because fear has to do with punishment. The one who fears is not made perfect in love.

John rounded out his discussion by declaring that believers know how much God loves them, and they have put their trust in the God of love. As Christians live in a community of mutual love with other believers, it results in an intimate experience of God's love and a renewed faith in that love. As before, John reaffirmed the truth that everyone who abides in love experiences intimate fellowship with the Lord (1 John 4:16).

According to the apostle, abiding in love would also produce boldness on the day of judgment (vs. 17). Paul similarly described a time of evaluation in which the works of all believers would be judged. This is commonly known as the judgment seat or *bema* (bei-MAH). In ancient Greek literature, the judgment seat usually referred to a chair or throne set up in a public place. From this spot, judicial decisions and other official business were conducted.

At the judgment seat of Christ (1 Cor. 3:10-15), those spiritual "buildings" of believers that are constructed with imperishable materials will be left standing and their builders will be given a reward. Those buildings constructed of consumable materials will be reduced to ashes and their owners will suffer loss—while still being saved. Bible scholars differ on the nature of this "loss." Some claim it is regret when they have no works of any quality to present to Christ. Others say this loss will involve diminished responsibility in the kingdom of God and withholding of reward that might have been theirs if they had acted more faithfully.

Paul said the fires of God's omniscience and justice would test the believer's works. The apostle used the metaphor of an ongoing construction project to illustrate the "materials" with which Christians could build their lives. The indisputable foundation was faith in the Lord Jesus. Those who demonstrated a life of obedience were like contractors who selected the best stones available to construct their building. Those who compromised the commandments of God and wavered in their commitment were like laborers who used easily consumed materials such as wood, hay, and straw to shore up their structures.

As we live in God, our love for one another grows more perfect and is made complete among us (1 John 4:17). This unselfish kindness is the same compassion that God, who is love, reproduces in His children by placing His Spirit in them. If this love is perfected in the believer's life on earth, it will produce a confidence to approach the judgment seat of Christ without shame or regret. The basis for this confidence is the believer's present likeness to the Son, and in this particular case, a likeness to His love.

As was John's habit, he followed the positive aspect of the preceding spiritual truth with its negative counterpart. The apostle noted that fear is the opposite of confidence before the Savior at His coming (vs. 18). If a believer anticipates the judgment seat of Christ with fear of some impending punishment, love has not been made complete in that believer's heart. The full flowering of God's love is incompatible with fear. Perfected love expels anxiety from the heart.

C. The Importance of Showing Love: vss. 19-21

We love because he first loved us. If anyone says, "I love God," yet hates his brother, he is a liar. For anyone who does not love his brother, whom he has seen, cannot love God, whom he has not seen. And he has given us this command: Whoever loves God must also love his brother.

The catalyst for loving other believers (and likewise for having confidence at Christ's return) is the love God first showed for us (1 John 4:19). Christians who love other believers also love God. The real proof that a Christian loves God, in John's estimation, is the love he or she demonstrates to fellow believers (vs. 20). A Christian's love for other believers (who are visible) proves his or her love for God (who is invisible).

While it is easy to proclaim, "I love God," John pointed out that genuine piety is demonstrated by Christian love. The one who claims to love God while hating other believers, said John (in his typical bluntness), is a liar. These people are also commandment breakers, because God had established that we must love not only Him, but also our Christian brothers and sisters (vs. 21). Here the two objects of Christian love are joined together. Love for God cannot be separated from love for our fellow believers in Christ.

II. LOVE FOR GOD AND HIS CHILDREN: 1 JOHN 5:1-5

A. The Trio of Faith, Love, and Obedience: vss. 1-3

Everyone who believes that Jesus is the Christ is born of God, and everyone who loves the father loves his child as well. This is how we know that we love the children of God: by loving God and carrying out his commands. This is love for God: to obey his commands. And his commands are not burdensome.

Throughout his first letter, John offered his readers three tests designed to gauge their relationship with their heavenly Father. These were (1) belief; (2) love for God and fellow believers; and (3) obedience to God's commands. The apostle's three tests are vitally connected. The genuine Christian believes in God's Son, loves God and His children, and obeys God's commands. All three, according to John, are hallmarks of the new birth. Of course, the basis of our fellowship with the Father and other believers is belief in Son (1 John 5:1). This common belief in the Messiah unites God's children to Him and to each other in love.

John told his readers that the new birth brings us into a parent-child relationship with God. This naturally involves love for Him who reached out to us and saved us, even though we were undeserving. Next, the apostle went on to suggest that what is true in a human family is also true in the spiritual family. Love for the Father naturally leads to love for the Father's children. Like the people in our biological families, we love other Christians just because they are "family." From John's perspective, it is as impossible to love the children of God without loving Him as it is to love God without loving His children (vs. 2).

Besides love for fellow believers, John identified one other inescapable result of loving God: obedience to His commands (vs. 3). As the Bible commentary in lesson 13 explains, love for God has less to do with emotions than with an unconditional obedience to His will. Just as love for fellow Christians is expressed not "with words or tongue but with actions and in truth" (3:18), so real love for God is actively demonstrated by keeping His commands.

James, in his letter, wrestled with spurious claims to faith. For instance, 2:18 anticipates an imaginary objector declaring, "You have faith; I have deeds." The idea is that there are two equally valid types of faith—one that simply believes and another that acts on that belief. James challenged the idea that genuine, saving faith has no effect on the way a person acts. In short, trusting in the Messiah is authenticated by doing kind deeds to others. Just as James taught, John insisted that genuine faith and good works go hand in hand. Moreover, God's commandments do not weigh down believers because the Spirit gives them the ability to obey the Lord (1 John 5:3).

B. The Source of the Believers' Victory: vss. 4-5

For everyone born of God overcomes the world. This is the victory that has overcome the world, even our faith. Who is it that overcomes the world? Only he who believes that Jesus is the Son of God.

Unsaved humanity views God's commandments as an unbearable drag. In contrast, those experiencing the new birth triumph over the world (1 John 5:4). This includes overcoming the false beliefs and practices of those opposed to the Gospel. Indeed, this conquest has already been accomplished through the faith Christians have in Jesus as the "Son of God" (vs. 5). Put another way, faith in the full divinity and humanity of the Savior is Christians' best defense against a dark world system controlled by Satan. Indeed, this truth is their greatest weapon and strongest shield (Eph. 6:16).

Discussion Questions

1. What role does the Spirit play in our lives as Christians?
2. How much do you depend on the Spirit to show God's love to others?
3. Why is it important for us to rely on God's love as we live for Him?
4. Why is it impossible for love and hatred to coexist in our lives as God's children?
5. What is the connection between faith in the Lord Jesus and overcoming the world?

Contemporary Application

In 1 John 4, "love" is defined in terms of the Father sending His Son to die on our behalf. This love neither wavers over time nor is it a whimsical feeling.

Instead, God's love is an intelligent display of compassion that acts with purpose. With repsect to loving sinful humankind, God's mercy and kindness are self-sacrificial and willingly seek the eternal good of the lost at great personal cost.

There has never been, and never can be, a greater gift-giving than the Father sending His Son into the world. Our experience of God's love begins through faith in the Messiah. It is at that moment that the Lord forgives our sins and restores our relationship to Him. We also inherit the privilege and responsibility of loving others with that same kind of love. In his first letter, John explained that key principle.

As we examine the Father's love for us, we find three characteristics we should also have. First, His love is not based on our being lovable or worthy of love. Second, the Father held nothing back in giving what was precious to Him—namely, His Son as our atoning sacrifice. Third, God's love is not a onetime expression, but an ongoing commitment. God's unending love for us equips us to live in love. Moreover, our compassion for other people allows them to discover the depth of God's love and sets them free to love in return.

Remaining Vigilant

Scripture

Background Scripture: *1 John 5:6-12, 18-20; 2 John*
Scripture Lesson: *2 John*
Key Verse: *Watch out that you do not lose what you have
worked for, but that you may be rewarded fully.* 2 John 8.
Scripture Lesson for Children: *1 John 5:6-12, 18-20*
Key Verse for Children: *[Whoever] has the Son has life.*
1 John 5:12

Lesson Aim

To remain committed to the truth Jesus taught about
Himself.

Lesson Setting

Time: Around A.D. 96
Place: Possibly Ephesus

Lesson Outline

Remaining Vigilant
  I. Recognizing the Truth: 2 John 1-6
      A. *Living in the Truth: vss. 1-3*
      B. *Walking in the Truth: vss. 4-6*
  II. Remaining Committed to the Truth: 2 John 7-13
      A. *The Presence of Charlatans: vs. 7*
      B. *The Importance of Apostolic Teaching: vss. 8-11*
      C. *The Desire for a Future Visit: vss. 12-13*

Introduction for Adults

Topic: *Fraud Alert*

The young professional made fun of the owl in the taxidermist's window. "Oh, even I could stuff one better than that," he bragged to his buddies. "That bird hardly looks real at all!" Then the live bird turned to him—and blinked.

Sometimes things are not as they appear. Would you be able to tell a decorative bird from the real one? How about a false teacher from a true one? As 2 John emphasizes, believers have to keep on the lookout for spiritual impostors. One way to recognize them is their denial of the truth Jesus taught about Himself.

From the apostle's letter we discover that even the early church faced the threat of religious frauds. They claimed to speak for the Savior but denied He had come in the flesh (vs. 7). It's no wonder John warned his readers not to share in the evil work of these heretics (vs. 11).

Introduction for Youth

Topic: *Beware of Deceivers*

When Mason graduated from college, one of his professors expressed disappointment that he had not been able to shake what he called Mason's "Sunday school" faith. The academic had assumed that when Mason got a college education, he would outgrow his childhood beliefs.

Mason, however, learned how to grow in and defend his faith, because in college he joined a Christian group and studied the Bible, prayed, and told other students about the truth Jesus taught concerning Himself. When Mason's faith was attacked in class, he consulted the library shelf where Christians had placed a number of scholarly books that held the Bible to be true and trustworthy.

Keeping the faith required commitment, perseverance, knowledge, and Christian fellowship. Mason knew he could not go through college in neutral as far as his faith was concerned. If he did not spiritually grow, he would coast into indifference and unbelief. So, he shifted into first gear by "walking in the truth" (2 John 4) and finished the race.

Concepts for Children

Topic: *The Gift of Life*

1. Jesus came to earth as a real person.
2. The Father wants us to put our trust in Jesus.
3. We have eternal life by believing in Jesus.
4. Jesus helps us not to sin.
5. No matter where we are, Jesus watches over us.

Lesson Commentary

I. RECOGNIZING THE TRUTH: 2 JOHN 1-6

A. Living in the Truth: vss. 1-3

The elder, to the chosen lady and her children, whom I love in the truth—and not I only, but also all who know the truth—because of the truth, which lives in us and will be with us forever: Grace, mercy and peace from God the Father and from Jesus Christ, the Father's Son, will be with us in truth and love.

In his second letter, John continued to teach on the importance of love and the destructiveness of false teaching. This time, however, he seems to have written to a specific congregation, whereas 1 John was intended for a more general audience. While the writer of 2 John has traditionally been identified as the apostle John, the author of the letter referred to himself simply as "the elder" (vs. 1). Given the authoritative tone of the epistle, it is unlikely that the reference is to the pastor of some unidentified local church. Also, since this letter is believed to have been written around A.D. 96, during the twilight of John's life, the title "elder" might well have been an affectionate name for the only surviving member of the apostolic band of 12. The intended audience obviously knew this person.

The letters of 1 John and 2 John are similar in style and content. This also suggests that the same person wrote the two letters. Furthermore, no compelling reason has ever been given for rejecting the tradition of the early church that the writer of this letter was John the apostle. The identity of the intended readers of the Second Letter of John has posed more difficulty for interpreters of Scripture than the identity of the author. Who were the "chosen lady and her children" (vs. 1)? No personal names are given in the correspondence. In contrast, three specific individuals are named in 3 John (to be studied in next week's lesson).

There are two possibilities worth considering. Either the designation "chosen lady and her children" (2 John 1) was a literal reference to specific individuals known by the apostle, or else it was a figurative representation of a church in Asia Minor. If the terms are taken literally, the interpretation is clear. The chosen lady was an unidentified individual Christian woman. The children were her natural offspring and the chosen sister mentioned in verse 13 was her natural sibling. If the expression is understood figuratively, then the "chosen lady" was a particular church. In the latter case, the "chosen sister" of verse 13 was a different body of believers, perhaps John's church at Ephesus. Also, in a figurative understanding of the verse, the chosen lady's children would represent the members of the congregation.

The letter's contents are more appropriate for a church (or churches) than for an individual Christian. Also, female personification is a common practice in Scripture. The church, for example, is frequently referred to as "the bride of Christ" (2 Cor. 11:2; Eph. 5:22-33; Rev. 19:7). Also, the people of Israel are called the "Daughter of Zion" (John 12:15). Consequently, it is best to understand the letter as addressed to a body of believers, even though the possibility that it was addressed to a particular Christian woman within that body cannot be completely ruled out.

So, if John's intended audience was indeed a church, then the members of that congregation faced the same sorts of problems as the Christians to whom 1 John was addressed. In 2 John, the apostle again sounded warnings about the charlatans who denied the Messiah (compare 2 John 7 with 1 John 2:18, 22–23; 4:1-3). Once more, the apostle admonished his readers to obey God's commands, particularly the command to show unconditional love to one another (compare 2 John 5-6 with 1 John 2:3-9; 3:14-18, 23).

The elder began his second letter with an affirmation of his love for the church and its members. This compassion was shared by "all who know the truth" (2 John 1). This seems to imply that this particular congregation was well known to other churches. The truth about the Savior compelled John and others to love this body of believers (vs. 2). Furthermore, the truth, as revealed in the Son, is the basis of all Christian love. For John, truth is more than objective facts (or "secret knowledge" as taught by the religious frauds). Truth indwells believers and enables them to show kindness to others in an unconditional, unselfish manner.

Jesus commanded His followers to love their neighbors and even their enemies (Matt. 5:43-48). But as John taught in his first letter, Christians are also united by a special bond of love. The spiritual glue that cements that mutual love is the truth of God. For this reason, God's truth must never be compromised. Believers do not necessarily love each other because they have compatible personalities or share the same interests. Instead, their mutual affection is due to them clinging to the same essential truths about the Messiah. The importance of this observation is made evident by the apostle's use of the Greek noun rendered "truth" four times in the first three verses of 2 John.

The apostle, in wishing his readers "grace, mercy and peace" (vs. 3), used a greeting common in the New Testament (see, for example, 1 Tim. 1:2; 2 Tim. 1:2). "Grace" speaks of God's unmerited favor toward sinners and the bestowing of blessings we do not deserve. "Mercy" has to do with divine compassion and the withholding of judgment that we do deserve. "Peace" speaks of the inner serenity that comes from being in a reconciled and growing relationship with God. What is interesting in the apostle's greeting is his declaration that grace, mercy, and peace "will be with us in truth and love" (2 John 3). As before, the apostle emphasized the spiritual qualities he desired for his readers. If they experienced the heavenly virtues of truth and love, they could anticipate the grace, mercy, and peace that come from knowing the Father through faith in the Son.

B. Walking in the Truth: vss. 4-6

It has given me great joy to find some of your children walking in the truth, just as the Father com-
manded us. And now, dear lady, I am not writing you a new command but one we have had from the
beginning. I ask that we love one another. And this is love: that we walk in obedience to his commands.
As you have heard from the beginning, his command is that you walk in love.

John wasted no time getting to the two concerns that prompted him to write
this second letter. His first concern was for the inner spiritual life of this church,
specifically that they continue to walk in obedience to God (2 John 4-6). The
apostle's second concern had to do with the external doctrinal danger posed by
false teachers and that John's readers staunchly resist their heresies (vss. 7-11).
His two concerns were closely intertwined. A vibrant, inner spiritual life is always
the best defense against doctrinal error. A believer who is not walking closely
with the Lord is vulnerable not only to temptation, but also to wandering from
the path of divine truth.

John began the main body of his letter by stating that he was overjoyed to
know that some of the members of this church were "walking in the truth"
(vs. 4). This, plus the apostle's expression of love for the congregation (vs. 1),
suggests that John had either interacted personally with these Christians on
another occasion or that he had received some detailed report about their
spiritual progress. Like Paul, who began many of his letters with expressions of
thanksgiving and joy, John launched the heart of his epistle on a positive note
of affirmation.

This expression of joy was qualified. Only some of the believers to whom
he wrote were living according to God's truth. Perhaps some of the people in
this congregation had already been swayed by the spiritual charlatans and had
left the fellowship—or worse, had remained and were influencing others. The
expression "walking in the truth" includes believing all that God has revealed
in His Word, especially in regard to the Incarnation. In a practical sense, living according to the truth involves conforming one's life to apostolic teaching.
Walking in the truth is an act of obedience, because God commands it.

John continued with the subject of God's precepts by using the word "command" three more times in verses 5 and 6. First, the apostle pointed out that
what he wrote to this church was not some new expectation of believers, but
one that was known to his readers from the earliest days of their Christian
experience (compare 1 John 2:7–8; 3:11). In fact, this message was as old as
the Gospel itself. In this regard, John encouraged his readers to follow Jesus'
teaching as first delivered by the apostles, and reject the newly arrived heresies
of the false teachers. Here again John addressed the question about the nature
of Christian love. The apostle's definition of love is once more stated in terms of
obedience to God (2 John 6). Believers who sincerely desire God's best for their
fellow Christians must act in accordance with God's revealed will. At its heart,

Christlike love is not just a matter of feeling, but also of doing. It is not a result of warm sentiment, but of unselfish service. This is what it means to fulfill God's command to "walk in love."

II. REMAINING COMMITTED TO THE TRUTH: 2 JOHN 7-13

A. The Presence of Charlatans: vs. 7

Many deceivers, who do not acknowledge Jesus Christ as coming in the flesh, have gone out into the world. Any such person is the deceiver and the antichrist.

John had just admonished his readers to walk in truth and love. He next addressed one of the key reasons why this was so important. Many false teachers, who denied the incarnation of the Son, were living among the people. These "deceivers" (2 John 7; which could also be translated "ones who lead astray") were a danger to the apostle's readers. The charlatans were numerous and their doctrine was deadly. The false teachers' rejection of the Messiah's coming in the flesh and taking on a human nature was tantamount to driving a stake into the heart of God's plan of salvation. After all, if Jesus were not truly human, then there could be no sacrificial death and no atonement for sin.

Anyone who denied the doctrine of the Incarnation was "the deceiver and the antichrist." The prefix "anti" means "opposed to." The antichrists opposed the Messiah and His teaching. The false teachers present in John's day were an indicator that human history had passed into "the last hour" (1 John 2:18). The phrases "last hour" or "last days" in the New Testament usually refer to the historical time period following Jesus' earthly ministry. The coming of many religious frauds heralded the final stage of humanity's experience on earth. The charlatans John referred to in his letters were a group of individuals who had sold out to the ungodly world system (4:5). While the apostle's original readers were aware of prophecies concerning the Antichrist, who would appear at the end of time (1 John 2:18; Rev. 13:1-10), they needed to be aware that before then many others would come who shared that evil one's enmity for the Savior.

B. The Importance of Apostolic Teaching: vss. 8-11

Watch out that you do not lose what you have worked for, but that you may be rewarded fully. Anyone who runs ahead and does not continue in the teaching of Christ does not have God; whoever continues in the teaching has both the Father and the Son. If anyone comes to you and does not bring this teaching, do not take him into your house or welcome him. Anyone who welcomes him shares in his wicked work.

The apostle warned his readers to be on the lookout for spiritual frauds and to be aware of the danger of their teaching (2 John 8). The consequence of compromise with their malignant doctrine was the potential loss of eternal reward. The apostle also warned about those who turned aside from the truth and failed to remain in agreement with what the Messiah taught about Himself.

In rejecting the Son, they also spurned the Father (vs. 9). Perhaps there was an imminent danger of defection among the congregation's members.

John contrasted those who depart from the truth with those who continue in it. The faithful have "both the Father and the Son." God remains in close fellowship with those who remain faithful to the truth about Jesus' incarnation. In John's view, the believer who "continues in the teaching" is linked in vibrant fellowship with the Father and the Son. Clinging to God's truth is an essential ingredient for the maintenance of one's spiritual life and for progress in growth and maturity.

John insisted that it was necessary for believers to have nothing to do with spiritual charlatans (vs. 10). Traveling preachers, teachers, and philosophers were common in New Testament times. In the Christian community, itinerant believers routinely sought and usually found hospitality in the homes of fellow Christians (3 John 5-8). It was regarded as an important Christian duty to take them in when they came to town. For instance, Paul found accommodation with Aquila and Priscilla while he performed missionary service at Corinth (Acts 18:1-3). Both pastors and laypersons alike were expected to show hospitality (Rom. 12:13; 1 Tim. 3:2). Peter admonished believers to "offer hospitality to one another without grumbling" (1 Pet. 4:9).

Showing hospitality was not a call for Christians to entertain their believing friends, but to take in itinerant missionaries in need of food and shelter. This practice not only strengthened fellowship among Christians, but also fostered the spread of the Gospel. For all that, this kind of hospitality was not to be shown to false teachers, for to do so would enable them to expand their destructive efforts. The section on hospitality in a late first- or early second-century A.D. document called *The Didache* (or *The Teaching of the Twelve Apostles*) gave instructions on how to discern between true and false teachers.

John warned his readers about people who came to them for hospitality but did not bring God's truth with them. The Greek verb rendered "bring" (2 John 10) can also be translated "carry." The picture is of someone who shows up at the door seeking hospitality, but whose luggage does not include God's truth. These religious frauds hauled around lies wherever they traveled. Christians, who were faithful to God's truth, were forbidden to show hospitality to anyone who denied what Jesus taught about Himself. The apostle told his readers not only to refuse hospitality to false teachers, but also to refuse to even wish them well. The verb translated "welcome" is akin to wishing one "Godspeed." To do so was to have a part in the charlatans' "wicked work" (vs. 11).

C. The Desire for a Future Visit: vss. 12-13

I have much to write to you, but I do not want to use paper and ink. Instead, I hope to visit you and talk with you face to face, so that our joy may be complete. The children of your chosen sister send their greetings.

The apostle closed his letter by telling his readers that while there was much he could write to them, he preferred a face-to-face meeting over paper and ink correspondence (2 John 12). The apostle's paper was probably made from the papyrus reed. The pith was cut into strips and laid at right angles. Next, it was pressed and pasted together to make sheets of writing material. The Greek adjective translated "ink" literally means "black." The apostle's "ink" was a compound made of charcoal, gum, and water. John was confident that by personally meeting with his fellow believers, their mutual joy would be made "complete" or fulfilled. The apostle signed off with greetings from members of a "sister" (vs. 13) church who, like the members of the congregation to whom he was writing, were chosen by God's sovereign grace.

Discussion Questions

1. What is God's truth, and why is it so important to uphold?
2. How have you recently lived out the truth that abides within you?
3. What is the link between believing the truth and being compassionate to others?
4. What was the nature of the false teaching being promoted by religious frauds?
5. What can believers do to remain anchored to the truth Jesus taught about Himself?

Contemporary Application

Second John reveals that faith in the Son includes an understanding of who He is as the incarnate Messiah. It also involves a complete reliance upon Him for salvation and an overcoming lifestyle. If we allow the erroneous teaching of religious frauds to confuse us, we will experience spiritual defeat. Only Jesus has triumphed over sin and offers us the power we need to escape the threat of charlatans and their ungodly influences.

Heresy manifested itself in many forms in the early history of the church. And it was one of Satan's most effective tools to mislead people. Many were lured out of fellowship with the body of Christ by the attractive lies of those who subtly subverted the truth. Little has changed today. Members of cults still deny divinely revealed truth about the Savior. Also, many people continue to be led astray by the heresy of modern-day deceivers.

The best defense against such false teaching is for Christians to remain under the umbrella of sound Bible doctrine. The way to accomplish that is to pay careful attention to apostolic teaching. Walking in obedience to God's commands and staying on the path of divine truth has never been more important.

Promoting the Truth

Scripture

Background Scripture: *3 John*
Scripture Lesson: *3 John*
Key Verse: *We ought therefore to show hospitality to such men
so that we may work together for the truth.* 3 John 8
Scripture Lesson for Children: *3 John*
Key Verse for Children: *You are faithful in what you are
doing for the brothers.* 3 John 5

Lesson Aim

To work together to advance God's truth.

Lesson Setting

Time: Around A.D. *96*
Place: Possibly Ephesus

Lesson Outline

Promoting the Truth

  I. Attending to the Needs of Others: 3 John 1-8
     A. *Remaining Faithful to the Truth: vss. 1-4*
     B. *Caring for Itinerant Ministers: vss. 5-8*
  II. Contrasting Two Approaches to Ministry:
     3 John 9-14
     A. *Censuring Diotrephes: vss. 9-10*
     B. *Commending Demetrius: vss. 11-12*
     C. *Desiring a Future Visit: vss. 13-14*

Introduction for Adults

Topic: *Let's Work Together*

Some of history's great battles were lost because troops deserted, in some cases to the enemy. For instance, the first American president, General George Washington, was plagued by deserters. Some of his soldiers got tired of the bitter struggle, left camp, and went home. The fight for independence evidently wasn't worth it to them.

Churches have also suffered losses from deserters and deceivers. These are individuals who abandoned their commitment to God's truth and mistreated believers. In John's day, this was a life and death issue. The tiny congregations had no resources other than the faithfulness of their members. Many wavered and reverted to paganism.

Perhaps today it's too easy to drop out. We think we won't be missed. We think there are others to take our place and do our work. But when that attitude takes over, our churches suffer, and the individuals who leave often weaken spiritually or turn away. We must remain loyal because we need each other.

Introduction for Youth

Topic: *Live According to the Truth*

Third John reveals that the Christian life (or walk) can be reduced to simple principles—obedience and love. As we grow in our intellectual understanding of our faith, we also grow in how to live our faith.

Sometimes, though, the situation works the other way around. When we dare to live our faith in front of others, we find that our understanding grows as well. It turns out that we believe what we do, as well as do what we believe.

A young man entered a university terrified that he would lose his faith. He was determined to follow Jesus. After his first year, he told his Christian friend, "You know what? They threw me to the lions, and I survived. Now I'm really convinced that my Christian faith is true!"

Concepts for Children

Topic: *Sharing the Truth with Others*

1. John wrote a letter to his friend Gaius.
2. John was happy that Gaius showed love to some Christians.
3. John asked Gaius to help other Christians who visited him.
4. John warned Gaius about a mean person named Diotrephes.
5. John said that all believers should help each other learn the truth about God.

Lesson Commentary

I. ATTENDING TO THE NEEDS OF OTHERS: 3 JOHN 1-8

A. Remaining Faithful to the Truth: vss. 1-4

The elder, To my dear friend Gaius, whom I love in the truth. Dear friend, I pray that you may enjoy good health and that all may go well with you, even as your soul is getting along well. It gave me great joy to have some brothers come and tell about your faithfulness to the truth and how you continue to walk in the truth. I have no greater joy than to hear that my children are walking in the truth.

John's third letter paints a picture of what church life was like in the first century A.D. We read about three individuals—Gaius, Diotrephes, and Demetrius—who collectively exhibit strong spiritual qualities and serious character defects. In many respects, it is a portrait of the church today. Contrary to what many believe, life in the decades after Jesus' resurrection was not some kind of spiritual ideal, free from posturing and strife. Rather, the church was like a growing adolescent who has to deal with the trials and challenges that maturity inevitably brings.

This epistle, like the apostle's second one, is brief and deals with the issue of itinerant ministers and how they should be received. The key concepts of Christian truth and love as they relate to hospitality are also addressed in both letters. There are, however, significant differences between 2 John and 3 John. While 3 John opens with the writer's self-description as "the elder" (vs. 1; compare 2 John 1), the recipient in this case was not a church personified as a woman and her children, but a specific individual named Gaius. Furthermore, the messages of the two letters present opposite sides of the same subject—Christian hospitality. In John's second letter (which was studied in lesson 9), the apostle instructed the church to refuse hospitality to false teachers who denied Jesus' incarnation. But in the apostle's third epistle, he commended Gaius for showing hospitality to teachers of God's truth. Together, the two letters present a balanced view of Christian hospitality.

Third John opens in a distinctive way. Absent is the customary wish for grace and peace found in other New Testament correspondence. Even so, at the conclusion of the epistle, the apostle did wish "peace" (vs. 14) to Gaius. All that is known for sure about Gaius is his name. But it is probable that he was a leader in the church to which he belonged, since John candidly discussed the matter of Diotrephes with Gaius (vss. 9-10). It is clear that the aged apostle felt genuine affection for Gaius. This is revealed by the apostle's reference to "my dear (or beloved) friend" (vs. 1). John was especially pleased with the unwavering commitment Gaius demonstrated to the truth Jesus taught about Himself. John's inclusion of Gaius among the apostle's spiritual "children" (vs. 4) could mean that Gaius was one of the apostle's converts.

In any case, John was pleased with the spiritual health he found in Gaius, as seen in his devotion to theological orthodoxy (vs. 2). John also cared about the state of physical health Gaius experienced. The Greek verb rendered "good health" is translated in the Gospel of Luke (which was written by a physician) as "healthy," "well," and "safe and sound" (Luke 5:31; 7:10; 15:27). In 3 John, we learn that the apostle not only cared about the spiritual well-being of his fellow Christians, but also about their physical condition. In this way, he was imitating the Lord Jesus, who throughout His public ministry showed concern for the physical problems of people He encountered. In 3 John 2, there is clear biblical precedent for believers praying about the physical needs of their spiritual brothers and sisters.

From traveling missionaries (vs. 3), whom John had sent (vs. 5), he learned about the fidelity Gaius maintained for God's truth. This delegation of itinerant ministers (perhaps led by Demetrius; see vs. 12) had visited Gaius and had witnessed the depth of his spiritual character. Perhaps Gaius provided lodging for them in his home. If so, this gave the evangelists an even more personal look at his godly demeanor and lifestyle. His character included two notable traits as reported by the missionaries. First, Gaius had been faithfully living according to God's truth (vs. 3). Put another way, his doctrine was sound, and he had not been swayed by the false teachers in his region.

Second, Gaius was well known for his practice of Christian love (vs. 6). Expressed differently, Gaius lived out what he believed. No one disputed his theological orthodoxy and heartfelt compassion for others. Indeed, his piety and integrity were so obvious that even strangers quickly recognized these virtues (vs. 5). The apostle was overjoyed to learn how his child in the faith was grounded in God's truth. John's parental affection and concern for the spiritual development of his children extended to all of his readers (vs. 4). As a pastoral leader in the early church, nothing brought the apostle greater joy than to know that his children were adhering to the truth first delivered by the Lord Jesus.

B. Caring for Itinerant Ministers: vss. 5-8

Dear friend, you are faithful in what you are doing for the brothers, even though they are strangers to you. They have told the church about your love. You will do well to send them on their way in a manner worthy of God. It was for the sake of the Name that they went out, receiving no help from the pagans. We ought therefore to show hospitality to such men so that we may work together for the truth.

The apostle again addressed Gaius as his beloved "friend" (3 John 5). Also, the apostle once more commended Gaius for his cordial reception of itinerant ministers who came to his faith community. In this way, Gaius was obedient to a command given to all Christians (Rom. 12:13; Heb. 13:2; 1 Pet. 4:9). The Greek verb translated "hospitality" (3 John 8) means "to support" or "to receive warmly." This is precisely what Gaius had done. He had welcomed into his home fellow Christians, whom he did not know, and provided for their physical needs at his own expense. Verse 6 indicates that this display of hospitality was not a onetime occurrence. It was something Gaius did faithfully as a regular ministry. His generosity to traveling missionaries showed his devotion to God's truth.

The itinerant ministers returning to John reported to his community of believers in Ephesus about the hospitality Gaius had shown. Possibly during one or more church services, the traveling missionaries spoke openly about both the faithfulness of Gaius to God's truth and the generous way in which Gaius had welcomed the evangelists (vs. 3). The apostle encouraged his child in the faith to continue providing for these believers in a way that honored and pleased God. This included supplying the missionaries with adequate provisions for their journey ahead. John explained that this should be done because the ministers had traveled on behalf of the "Name" (vs. 7). The latter was a reference to the Lord Jesus (John 1:12; 3:18; Rom. 1:5; 1 John 2:12). His name represented the Son of God and His work of salvation. Moreover, those who serve the Savior in ministry represent Him and are worthy of the support of other Christians (1 Cor. 9:1-18; Gal. 6:6; 1 Tim. 5:17-18).

It would have been inappropriate for these itinerant ministers, as Jesus' representatives, to seek the support of unbelievers, those who held no regard for the "Name" (3 John 7). So, as a matter of policy and practice, the evangelists neither sought nor received help from "pagans." Even in our day, it seems ethically wrong for missionaries to solicit financial aid from non-Christians, especially those to whom the Gospel is freely offered. Since traveling teachers did not seek support from unbelievers, it was all the more necessary for Christians to provide these ministers with assistance (vs. 8).

John presented Gaius with three reasons to cordially receive Jesus' ambassadors. First, they were fellow members of the Father's spiritual family and faithful workers who ministered in the name of the Son. For this reason alone, the evangelists deserved due honor and the support of the Savior's disciples. Second, the missionaries' only means of obtaining financial assistance was from the hospitality of believers. After all, if the evangelists received no help from unbelievers, who was left to aid Jesus' ministers? Third, by supporting the itinerant ministers, their fellow believers became coworkers with them in spreading God's truth. Unlike the religious frauds described in 2 John, these missionaries proclaimed the Gospel wherever they went. Put another way, when believers helped meet the needs of Christian missionaries, Jesus' disciples in fact became their partners in the evangelistic enterprise.

II. CONTRASTING TWO APPROACHES TO MINISTRY: 3 JOHN 9-14

A. Censuring Diotrephes: vss. 9-10

I wrote to the church, but Diotrephes, who loves to be first, will have nothing to do with us. So if I come, I will call attention to what he is doing, gossiping maliciously about us. Not satisfied with that, he refuses to welcome the brothers. He also stops those who want to do so and puts them out of the church.

In 3 John 9-10, the apostle commented on the thorny problems caused by Diotrephes. Here was a leader whose character was the exact opposite of Gaius. John's beloved child in the faith lived according to God's truth, loved his fellow Christians, and was hospitable even toward strangers. In contrast, Diotrephes was arrogant, verbally attacked others with evil accusations, spurned itinerant ministers, and punished those in his church who tried to be hospitable to Jesus' ambassadors.

The apostle stated that he had written to the congregation in which Diotrephes was a leader. But because the upstart insisted on being preeminent in his faith community, he rejected John's pastoral authority and refused to pay attention to the apostle (vs. 9). The problem was not unique to this first-century church. Many congregations since then have suffered disunity and fracture at the hands of church leaders who abused the authority of their pastoral position.

Apparently, even though John's letter had been addressed to the entire congregation, Diotrephes kept it from being read during any corporate gatherings. This inference is supported by the fact that John had to inform Gaius that the apostle had written the letter. Perhaps Diotrephes simply read the letter and then destroyed it without letting anyone else know about it. "Will have nothing to do with us" can also be rendered "does not welcome us as guests." This suggests that John's representatives (the persons mentioned in vs. 5) delivered the letter in question but were denied hospitality by Diotrephes. A rejection of these Christians would have amounted to a repudiation of the apostle and the truth about Jesus he taught.

John knew that in light of Diotrephes' blatant disregard for the apostle's authority, he should probably deal with this matter in person. John's statement in verse 10 that he intended to report some of the abuses committed by Diotrephes suggests a public rather than private rebuke of his practices. John might have confronted Diotrephes privately in a previous letter. If so, it was a reproof Diotrephes had spurned. For this reason, the apostle intended to subject Diotrephes to disciplinary action.

The Greek phrase rendered "gossiping maliciously about us" is more literally translated "disparaging us with evil words." It conveys the idea of making unjust accusations by using vindictive statements. Diotrephes' slanderous allegations were not only wicked, but they were also contradicted by an objective analysis of the facts. It seems that Diotrephes hoped to elevate his own authority in the church by defaming John's integrity. Furthermore, Diotrephes brazenly rejected the apostle's instruction to welcome visiting missionaries, probably because those in question were the apostle's representatives. Diotrephes' abuse of power contrasted sharply with the humble and generous actions of Gaius. Diotrephes went even further in his defiance of John's apostolic authority by penalizing believers who dared to show hospitality to traveling evangelists. The renegade leader did this by casting them out of the church. The power Diotrephes held was such that he could get away with excommunicating Christians who went against his will.

It is unclear what relationship Gaius had with this faith community. One possibility is that he belonged to another local congregation several miles away from Diotrephes' church. It's also possible Gaius was a member of the same faith community Diotrephes tried to control. If so, it is difficult to know whether or how Gaius might have dealt with Diotrephes' abuse of power. Gaius appears to have held a position of rank in his church. Also, the fact that he could afford to routinely entertain visiting Christians suggests he possessed some wealth. Whatever the situation, Gaius was in a position to stand up to Diotrephes. So, John wrote to Gaius to explain what was occurring and how he should deal with the problem.

B. Commending Demetrius: vss. 11-12

Dear friend, do not imitate what is evil but what is good. Anyone who does what is good is from God. Anyone who does what is evil has not seen God. Demetrius is well spoken of by everyone—and even by the truth itself. We also speak well of him, and you know that our testimony is true.

The apostle exhorted Gaius not to copy the "evil" (3 John 11) deeds of individuals such as Diotrephes. Instead, Gaius was to follow the example of those who did what was "good." The theological implication is that the way in which people behaved indicated how they were related to God, the source of good actions (James 1:17). For instance, those whose lives were characterized by kindness and compassion lived in fellowship with the Lord. Oppositely, those wallowing in evil deeds were in spiritual darkness and not abiding in the light of God and His truth (1 John 1:6).

While the apostle censured Diotrephes for his abuse of power, John commended Demetrius for adhering to God's truth. Most of what we know about this believer is found in 3 John 12. According to later church tradition, John appointed Demetrius as a pastor of the Philadelphian church in Asia Minor. In keeping with the Old Testament directive about witnesses (Deut. 19:15), John offered a threefold testimonial to the high character of Demetrius. The first witness consisted of all who personally knew Demetrius. They uniformly spoke well of him (3 John 12). The second witness was the truth of the Gospel. So conformed was Demetrius' life to what Jesus taught that in a personified way it testified in support of Demetrius' godly demeanor. The third witness was that John himself could vouch for the integrity of Demetrius. With this threefold commendation, Gaius was encouraged to receive Demetrius (perhaps the bearer of 3 John) without reservation.

C. Desiring a Future Visit: vss. 13-14

I have much to write you, but I do not want to do so with pen and ink. I hope to see you soon, and we will talk face to face. Peace to you. The friends here send their greetings. Greet the friends there by name.

With much still on John's mind to share with Gaius, the apostle declined further written correspondence in favor of a "face to face" (3 John 13) meeting in the near future (compare 2 John 12). The apostle wished Gaius "peace" (3 John 14) and passed on greetings from friends in the Ephesian congregation. In turn, the apostle asked Gaius to "greet the friends there by name." Here we discover that a shared faith within the worldwide network of believers creates a bond of friendship that accompanies Christians wherever they go.

Discussion Questions

1. Why did John regard Gaius as a dear friend?
2. How do believers demonstrate they are living according to the truth of God's Word?
3. Why is it important for believers to partner with missionaries in the spread of the Gospel?
4. What are some ways Christian leaders can avoid abusing their pastoral authority?
5. Why is it important for believers to be characterized by integrity?

Contemporary Application

One point of application found in 3 John is the importance of showing hospitality to our fellow Christians. The example of Gaius reminds us that a home can be a place of ministry to others who serve the Lord (vss. 5-8). With the modern proliferation of motels and restaurants, the need for hospitality in the home may have diminished. Still, sometimes we should open our doors to strangers and friends in Jesus' name.

The second applicational strand concerns the biblical model of leadership. The dictatorial style practiced by Diotrephes (vs. 9) reflects the mind-set of the world. It defines leadership as the ability to direct the thoughts and actions of others. People are supposedly good leaders if they can command the obedience, confidence, respect, and loyal cooperation of their subordinates. The emphasis is on the followers doing exactly what the leader demands (Mark 10:42; Luke 22:25).

The biblical model for leadership shown by Demetrius is quite different (3 John 12). If people want to be great leaders in the eyes of God, they must unsparingly serve others (Matt. 23:11; Mark 10:43-45; Luke 22:26). They must humbly set aside their desires and minister to the needs of others (John 13:12-15). Their goal is to shepherd the flock of God willingly, not because they are forced to do so (1 Pet. 5:2).

Devout Christian leaders make the Bible their guidebook and the holiness of God their life aim (1 Thess. 4:3; 2 Tim. 4:1-2). They strive to be an example to those whom they are spiritually leading and feeding (1 Pet. 5:3). Their ultimate goal is to please the "Chief Shepherd" (vs. 4), not themselves.

The Gifts of the Spirit

Scripture

Background Scripture: *1 Corinthians 12:1-11*
Scripture Lesson: *1 Corinthians 12:1-11*
Key Verse: *Now to each one the manifestation of the Spirit is given for the common good.* 1 Corinthians 12:7
Scripture Lesson for Children: *1 Corinthians 12:1-11*
Key Verse for Children: *There are different kinds of gifts, ... but the same God works all of them in [everyone].* 1 Corinthians 12:4, 6.

Lesson Aim

To learn that God works through each believer's spiritual gifts.

Lesson Setting

Time: A.D. *55*
Place: Ephesus

Lesson Outline

The Gifts of the Spirit
I. The Source of Spiritual Gifts: 1 Corinthians 12:1-6
  A. *The Question about Spiritual Gifts: vs. 1*
  B. *The Testimony of the Spirit: vss. 2-3*
  C. *The Sovereignty of God: vss. 4-6*
II. The Variety of Gifts: 1 Corinthians 12:7-11
  A. *Spiritual Gifts for the Common Good: vs. 7*
  B. *Diversity of Spiritual Gifts: vss. 8-10*
  C. *Gifts and the Spirit's Control: vs. 11*

Introduction for Adults

Topic: *Unity in Diversity*

How you would feel if you discovered that the gift you gave someone you love had never been unwrapped and opened? The hurt and anger that you would feel might be similar to how God feels when we fail to unwrap the spiritual gifts He has given to each of us.

Regrettably, some adult believers have not unwrapped their spiritual gifts. They don't know what the Spirit has given them, much less have they used these special abilities. They need to understand that God will not shrug off the fact that they have disregarded the spiritual gifts with which He has blessed them.

This week's lesson encourages your students to discover and use their various God-given abilities to minister to others around them. Each spiritual gift brings unique care to meet the needs of other Christians. And each of your class members has one or more of these spiritual gifts.

Introduction for Youth

Topic: *What's My Spiritual Gift?*

In *The Secret Place*, Charlotte Burkholder tells us that fingers in a mitten are in contact with one another, and that each contributes body heat. Therefore, these fingers keep warmer than those in a glove where each finger is wrapped separately.

The preceding observations are a reminder that believers must remain together spiritually and allow each other to contribute to the common good of the church. This is done when every believer uses their God-given spiritual gifts without hesitation (1 Cor. 12:1-11). In short, we are most useful to the Lord and to one another in the body of Christ when we are practicing a "mitten" faith together instead of "glove" living.

Concepts for Children

Topic: *I Am Gifted!*

1. God wants us to trust Him.
2. God wants us to reject sin.
3. God wants us to love Him and other people.
4. God wants us to help others.
5. God's Spirit gives us the strength to do what is right.

Lesson Commentary

I. The Source of Spiritual Gifts: 1 Corinthians 12:1-6

A. The Question about Spiritual Gifts: vs. 1

Now about spiritual gifts, brothers, I do not want you to be ignorant.

As noted in lesson 6, the first-century A.D. church at Corinth was still young when problems like divisions, immorality, immaturity, and instability began to crop up. To address these issues, Paul, who had founded the church about five years earlier while on his second missionary journey, wrote a letter to believers instructing them to live godly lives. Because Paul dealt with a number of practical matters facing the church, this letter is highly relevant to Christians today. In fact, as we study the principles taught by Paul, we might find more than a few similarities between the church at Corinth and the church of the early twenty-first century. We are also likely to discover a number of resemblances between the society of first-century A.D. Corinth and our society today.

Corinth may have been the wealthiest and most important city in Greece when Paul wrote to the Christians living there. Its location near two seaports—the Gulf of Corinth was a mile and a half to the west and the Saronic Gulf was six miles to the east—caused the city to become a busy commercial center. As a mercantile city with a constant influx of visitors from nations around the known world, Corinth also became known as a center for immorality. Greek philosophy was discussed and wisdom was emphasized, but such considerations in no way bridled the debauchery practiced in the city.

In some respects, Corinth's religious makeup helped create this atmosphere of depravity. Though the Jews had established a synagogue near the city's forum, at least 12 temples to various pagan deities existed in Corinth and overshadowed the city's Jewish influence. One of the most famous of these shrines was the temple of Aphrodite (the goddess of love), where at one time more than a thousand priestess-prostitutes served the shrine's patrons. It was into this setting that Paul brought the Gospel while on his second missionary journey. Before leaving the city to continue his trip, Paul established a church made up of a growing number of Christian converts, including both Jews and Gentiles, higher and lower classes, free persons and slaves.

Upon the apostle's departure, the philosophical, sexual, and religious temptations of Corinth took their toll on many of the new Christians, and after a while, began to break down the unity of the church. When Paul got word of the divisiveness and immoral practices arising among the believers, he penned a letter to them in the hope of correcting the problems they were experiencing. He recognized that the Corinthian Christians lived in a city well known for its wickedness and vice, and it was difficult for them not to behave in the same manner as their peers. Faced with such a challenge, the young church was beginning to experience a variety of dangerous problems. To address these issues, Christian conduct became the central theme of Paul's First Letter to the Corinthians.

Paul was at Ephesus when he received the news about what was happening in Corinth. According to 1 Corinthians 5:9, the apostle had sent a previous letter to the congregation, a letter that apparently was not preserved by the early church. Sometime after sending this epistle, Paul received either a personal or a written report from members of Chloe's household about several problems that were threatening the church and its ministry. That's when Paul began composing this letter that would be a vital resource for sustaining the ongoing work of the Corinthian church. A key purpose of the apostle was to explain that Jesus Christ crucified—who embodies the Gospel—creates the church's unity, service, and hope.

Part of that unity is maintained through the presence of "spiritual gifts" (12:1) in the body of Christ. The Greek text is more literally rendered "spiritual things" and can either refer to persons filled with the Holy Spirit or the special abilities He bestows on them to serve others. In verses 8-10, Paul supplied a representative list of spiritual gifts. In this letter, the Greek noun rendered "gifts" is *charismata* (car-ISS-mah-tah). The singular form of this word is *charisma*. Both terms relate to the word *charis* (CAR-iss), which means "favor" or "grace." While *charisma* denotes a personal endowment of grace, *charismata* refers to a concrete expression of grace. The main idea is that the Spirit bestows His gifts of grace on Christians to accomplish God's will (vss. 4-6 and the lesson commentary to follow).

Previously, in 1:5-7, Paul mentioned the spiritual gifts that the Corinthian Christians were diligently exercising. Later in the epistle, the apostle admonished them for misusing their gifts, which was due in part to their being theologically uninformed (12:1). In 1:5-7, Paul expressed gratitude for the spiritual enrichment his readers enjoyed in union with the Savior. The apostle said that in every way they had been blessed with a multitude of gifts. For example, God had given the Corinthians the ability to speak in tongues, to prophesy, to interpret tongues, and to discern spirits. No spiritual gift was lacking in the congregation.

What Paul and his coworkers had declared about the Messiah had been confirmed in the lives of the believers at Corinth. Their behavior was transformed in measurable ways and their service for the Lord was dynamic and effective as they waited for the Second Coming. Yet, from what is said in chapter 14 (see also the Bible commentary in lesson 13), it seems the Corinthian Christians were emphasizing the gift of speaking in tongues almost to the exclusion of all other gifts. Probably, they thought this gift confirmed their mistaken view about their "spiritual" nature. The apostle, hearing about the overemphasis on tongues, taught that a variety of gifts were needed in the church.

B. The Testimony of the Spirit: vss. 2-3

You know that when you were pagans, somehow or other you were influenced and led astray to mute idols. Therefore I tell you that no one who is speaking by the Spirit of God says, "Jesus be cursed," and no one can say, "Jesus is Lord," except by the Holy Spirit.

As previously noted, the believers of Corinth did not have a proper understanding of spiritual gifts (1 Cor. 12:1). So Paul reminded them of how they had once lived as "pagans" (vs. 2). The apostle literally called them "Gentiles" (or non-Jews) to refer to the fact that they were previously unbelievers. He noted that they had by some means been drawn into idol worship, which was prevalent in their city, even though none of the idols could speak a word. Scripture reveals that idols are powerless, lifeless objects (Ps. 115:4-8; Hab. 2:18-19).

In contrast to the idols, the Spirit of God was not mute and was the only true source of divinely-inspired speech. He spoke through Jesus' followers, never directing them to curse the Savior but rather prompting them to confess Jesus as Lord (1 Cor. 12:3). Put another way, the speech empowered by the Spirit was always edifying, never blasphemous. Admittedly, anyone could say either "Jesus be cursed" or "Jesus is Lord." Be that as it may, no one who slandered the Lord was ever enabled by the Spirit to do so. Oppositely, no one who ever affirmed Jesus' divine lordship—and genuinely meant it—did so apart from the Spirit of God (John 20:28; Rom. 10:9; Rev. 19:16). Paul's point seemed to be that having an inspired utterance was, in itself, not most important. Instead, the content of that utterance was what mattered most.

C. The Sovereignty of God: vss. 4-6

There are different kinds of gifts, but the same Spirit. There are different kinds of service, but the same Lord. There are different kinds of working, but the same God works all of them in all men.

In 1 Corinthians 12:4-6, Paul focused on the sovereignty of the triune God in the distribution and exercise of spiritual gifts among believers. For instance, while there are varieties of "gifts," they have their source in the "same Spirit." Also, there are varieties of ministries, yet believers serve the "same Lord." Moreover, even though there are varieties of activities, it is the "same God" who produces all of them in everyone. In these verses, Paul linked each of three synonyms for spiritual gifts and ministries—"gifts," "service," and "working"—with different names for God—"Spirit," "Lord," and "God." In this way, the apostle showed that the variety of spiritual gifts within the unity of the church mirrors the diversity of the Persons within the one divine Trinity.

II. THE VARIETY OF GIFTS: 1 CORINTHIANS 12:7-11

A. Spiritual Gifts for the Common Good: vs. 7

Now to each one the manifestation of the Spirit is given for the common good.

Paul stated that to each believer was given a "manifestation of the Spirit" (1 Cor. 12:7) for use in serving the whole congregation of believers. Peter likewise taught that the Lord had given believers spiritual gifts (such as teaching and preaching) and that they were to use these to serve others (1 Pet. 4:10-11). As previously noted, the Holy Spirit bestows on Christians special abilities to accomplish the will of God. They do not own the gifts. Instead, they are stewards of what God has graciously provided for them. These gifts of grace take various forms, and they are to be faithfully used wherever and whenever possible.

B. Diversity of Spiritual Gifts: vss. 8-10

To one there is given through the Spirit the message of wisdom, to another the message of knowledge by means of the same Spirit, to another faith by the same Spirit, to another gifts of healing by that one Spirit, to another miraculous powers, to another prophecy, to another distinguishing between spirits, to another speaking in different kinds of tongues, and to still another the interpretation of tongues.

In 1 Corinthians 12:8-10, Paul listed nine special abilities, which represent only a few of the many gifts the Spirit has entrusted to Jesus' followers. "Message of wisdom" denotes the ability to deliver profound truths consistent with biblical teaching. Some think "message of knowledge" refers to information received through supernatural means. Others believe it points to the effective application of Bible teaching to people's lives. While all Christians have saving "faith," the reference here is to the display of amazing trust in God regardless of circumstances.

"Gifts of healing" denotes a believer's ability to restore someone else to health through supernatural means. "Miraculous powers" spotlights the ability to perform supernatural acts, that is, signs and wonders. "Prophecy" refers to the proclamation of revelations from God, including predictions of future events. "Distinguishing between spirits" highlights the ability to discern which messages and acts come from the Spirit of God and which come from evil spirits. "Speaking in different kinds of tongues" could be human languages or dialects unknown to the person speaking them (Acts 2:1-12). Others think they are heavenly languages (1 Cor 13:1). Either way, it seems these languages are unintelligible to both the speaker and the hearers (unless they had the gift of interpretation), and are directed to God as prayer or praise (14:2, 14-16). Finally, "interpretation of tongues" (12:10) refers to the ability to translate what was being spoken and clearly explain what it meant to listeners.

In Romans 12:6-8, Paul put forward another, shorter, representative list of seven spiritual gifts. In line with what was said earlier, those with the gift of "prophesying" are to communicate God's revealed truth to believers for their edification. Also, this and the other special abilities mentioned by Paul are to be exercised in accordance with the measure of faith the Lord provides. "Serving" denotes meeting the needs of others in unique ways. "Teaching" points to the communication of biblical truth in a clear and relevant manner. "Encouraging" spotlights the provision of reassurance or admonition as needed. "Contributing" has in mind believers whom the Spirit enables to give significantly to those in need, and they do so generously. "Leadership" refers to a special ability to shepherd and govern the body of Christ, and it is to be done with devotion and enthusiasm. Lastly, "showing mercy" points to the exceptional aptitude some believers have to be warmhearted and considerate, especially as they show the kindness of the Spirit to the disheartened.

Believers often disagree about which gifts are still given by God's Spirit to Christians today. Some argue that all of the gifts described in Scripture are still given to the church because its needs are still the same and because there is evidence of these gifts operating in Christians today. Others maintain that one or more of the gifts ended with the early church, while most of the gifts still exist. For example, some hold that the gift of apostleship died out with the original apostles, but the other gifts are still in operation. Still others think that all of the so-called spectacular gifts—such as miracles, speaking in tongues, and healings—were only given to the early church and not to the church today.

Regardless of which of these views is favored, 1 Peter 4:11 reminds us that as believers diligently help one another and rely on the Father for enabling, they bring Him honor through His Son, the Lord Jesus. For instance, others will see believers ministering in the name of the Son and praise the Father for it. Indeed, the thought of God being honored moved Peter to write a doxology of praise at the end of the verse. Glory and power belonged to the Lord for ever and ever. Peter then affirmed this truth with an "Amen," which might be paraphrased, "So be it!"

C. Gifts and the Spirit's Control: vs. 11

All these are the work of one and the same Spirit, and he gives them to each one, just as he determines.

Paul reminded his readers that they had done nothing to receive the gifts of the Spirit, for He gives them openly and unsparingly according to His sovereign will (1 Cor. 12:11). This meant believers were not to become conceited or divisive because of their gifts. Rather, they were to use their special endowments to help others become better Christians.

Discussion Questions

1. What incentive do believers have to learn more about spiritual gifts?
2. How does coming to faith in Christ free us from idolatry?
3. What are some ways the variety of spiritual gifts in your church have been used for the "common good" (1 Cor. 12:7)?
4. Why is it important to affirm the sovereignty of God in the distribution of spiritual gifts?
5. What are some creative ways you could use your spiritual gifts to minister to others?

Contemporary Application

This week's lesson reminds us that every believer has at least one spiritual gift. Moreover, we discover that God expects us to use these special endowments to serve others, regardless of whether they are believers or unbelievers. In short, the students in your class are called to be faithful stewards of the Spirit's gracious abilities as they minister to others around them.

Many people yearn for the kind of human companionship, support, and fellowship offered in Jesus' spiritual body, the church. Sadly, many times they don't find it because the church seems to be marked by disunity, cliques, and self-centeredness. That's why many of these folks look elsewhere to get their legitimate needs met. They might join service organizations, community groups, and athletic clubs, or spend a lot of time pursuing frivolous entertainment activities.

When congregations do not offer the kind of hospitality people are looking for, they do not seek the Messiah who is supposed to be at the heart of His church. His spiritual body is supposed to be the one social group that transcends all our differences. It's supposed to bear witness to the lost that Jesus can meet their deepest needs. Our witness is only as valid and strong as our visible unity. Our message is heard when we sublimate our differences and cooperatively use our spiritual gifts in a peaceful manner to show Jesus' love to the lost.

The Unity of the Body

Scripture

Background Scripture: *1 Corinthians 12:12-31*

Scripture Lesson: *1 Corinthians 12:14-31*

Key Verse: *For we were all baptized by one Spirit into one body—whether Jews or Greeks, slave or free—and we were all given the one Spirit to drink.* 1 Corinthians 12:13.

Scripture Lesson for Children: *1 Corinthians 12:14-31*

Key Verse for Children: *You are the body of Christ, and each one of you is a part of it.* 1 Corinthians 12:27.

Lesson Aim

To recognize how important every believer is to the life of the church.

Lesson Setting

Time: A.D. *55*

Place: Ephesus

Lesson Outline

The Unity of the Body

    I. The Unity and Diversity within Christ's Body:
      1 Corinthians 12:14-26

      A. One Body with Many Parts: vs. 14

      B. All the Members United Together: vss. 15-20

      C. Every Part Essential to the Body: vss. 21-26

    II. The Importance of Every Believer:
      1 Corinthians 12:27-31

      A. Different Members of Christ's Body: vss. 27-28

      B. Every Gift Essential to the Body: vss. 29-31

Introduction for Adults

Topic: *The Sum Is Greater Than Its Parts*

In the 1938 movie *The Citadel*, Robert Donat plays a talented, idealistic young Scottish physician named Andrew Manson. He is committed to providing medical care to Welsh miners who have tuberculosis. Yet, by the film's conclusion, he is on trial for assisting an unlicensed medical practitioner during an operation.

Manson's accusers claim that the physician forsook his oath in order to help a "quack." They don't seem to care that the operation was a success or that the so-called quack clearly had a gift for medicine. For the critics, medical talents must fit their specific image to be valid. Otherwise, they are disregarded.

Thankfully, God does not operate that way. As Paul stated in 1 Corinthians 12:18, God has placed together all the members of Christ's body in a way that He decided is best. God accepts and works through every believer's unique and valued spiritual gifts.

Introduction for Youth

Topic: *Many Members Equal One Body*

In this week's lesson, we examine the source and purpose of spiritual gifts. We also learn how God grants special endowments to believers so that they can serve the church and glorify the Lord.

As a young woman, Senia Taipale knew that God had given her a gift for comforting others. She felt called to ministry, but she did not believe that God wanted her to be a minister. Others questioned whether she understood God's calling at all. But, in time, God made clear His plans for her gifts.

From 1992 to 2010, Senia oversaw the chaplaincy program at a large Midwestern hospital. She saw it as a perfect fit. "When people are in the hospital, they're worried, stressed," Senia points out. "Patients don't usually have folks who can take the time to come in and just listen to them. A hospital chaplain's job is to get to the patients and listen to their stories. I try simply to be a listener and a companion on the patient's spiritual journey." For that, Senia was uniquely gifted.

Concepts for Children

Topic: *Many Members in One Body*

1. God has made each of us part of the church.
2. Each of us is a special part of the church.
3. Each of us has a job to do in the church.
4. Each of our jobs is very important.
5. God can use us to be loving and kind to others.

Lesson Commentary

I. THE UNITY AND DIVERSITY WITHIN CHRIST'S BODY: 1 CORINTHIANS 12:14-26

A. One Body with Many Parts: vs. 14

Now the body is not made up of one part but of many.

To a church that was emphasizing the gift of speaking in tongues almost to the exclusion of all other spiritual gifts, Paul began a new section of his letter. As we learned in lesson 11, dealing with 1 Corinthians 12:1-11, the apostle reminded his readers that they possessed a diversity of special endowments given to them by the Holy Spirit. Paul not only listed some of these gifts, but also told his readers that the Spirit granted them unique abilities according to His will and for the benefit of everyone. Next, in verses 12-20, the apostle compared the church to the human body to stress that there is unity and diversity within the faith community. While Christ's body has numerous members, it remains spiritually one (vs. 14; see also Rom. 12:4-8).

Paul's list of spiritual gifts was representative, not exhaustive, in nature. His intent was to stress that each special endowment is important to the church. To further emphasize this truth, the apostle drew an analogy between the faith community and a human body. In particular, a human body has many different parts, and yet it is a single entity. Expressed differently, it is a unity made up of diversity. Paul declared that the same situation holds true for the body of Christ (vs. 12). In 1 Peter 2:4-5, the writer used another analogy to convey a similar truth. Individual believers are like "living stones" that are being used to build a single "spiritual house." In turn, the Lord Jesus is the living cornerstone of God's sacred temple.

In 1 Corinthians 12:13, Paul explained that what unites diverse believers in the faith community is their common experience of being indwelt by the Holy Spirit. The apostle described this experience as everyone being "baptized" into a single "body" by "one Spirit." Some think this verse refers to water baptism. However, that would seem to teach that this religious ritual is necessary for salvation—something that is not taught in other passages of Scripture (Acts 10:44-48; 16:29-33). Salvation hinges solely on believing in the Savior (Rom. 9:30; Eph. 2:8-9). Water baptism dramatizes the work of salvation in a person's heart. For this reason, others maintain that Spirit baptism is in view in 1 Corinthians 12:13. In accomplishing this work of grace, God's Spirit places believers into the body of Christ and unites them with the Savior (Rom. 6:3-5).

In the Roman world (as often in ours) ethnic, religious, and cultural distinctions were clearly drawn, thus setting up barriers between people. Paul took note of this situation by mentioning "Jews" (1 Cor. 12:13) and "Gentiles," as well as "slave" and "free." Regardless of one's social status in life, all Christians were part of the same spiritual body. In Galatians 3:26-29, Paul taught a similar set of truths (see also Rom. 10:12; Col. 3:11). We learn that through faith in the Son, all believers become children of God (John 1:12-13). They are spiritually united to the Lord Jesus, and in a metaphorical sense, they have clothed themselves with Him. In this regard, ethnic, religious, and cultural distinctions have no bearing on who becomes a follower of the Messiah. Faith in Him is what makes someone a true child of Abraham and of God. So, those who belong to the Son are also Abraham's spiritual descendants. Believers receive all of God's blessings because of the promise that He made to the patriarch. Included would be forgiveness of sins, a right relationship with God, and eternal life.

B. All the Members United Together: vss. 15-20

If the foot should say, "Because I am not a hand, I do not belong to the body," it would not for that reason cease to be part of the body. And if the ear should say, "Because I am not an eye, I do not belong to the body," it would not for that reason cease to be part of the body. If the whole body were an eye, where would the sense of hearing be? If the whole body were an ear, where would the sense of smell be? But in fact God has arranged the parts in the body, every one of them, just as he wanted them to be. If they were all one part, where would the body be? As it is, there are many parts, but one body.

In 1 Corinthians 12:15-16, Paul described two hypothetical situations in which a part of the human body declared itself independent from the other members on the grounds that it was not like any of them. For example, the foot might say that it did not belong to the body because it was not a hand. In the same way, the ear might declare that it was not connected to the body because it was not an eye. Even if body parts could make such assertions, they would be incorrect. Just putting forward a statement would not automatically make it true.

Of course, Paul wasn't really talking about human body parts. The apostle had in mind believers and their spiritual gifts. He was afraid that someone might think, for example, *I have only the gift of distinguishing between spirits, not the gift of speaking in tongues. So, I must not really be a significant part of the faith community.* Paul taught that even if some Christians reasoned in this way, they would still be a part of the church. Having one spiritual gift rather than another did not disqualify anyone from usefulness in the body of Christ.

The situation Paul was concerned about could happen today. Let's say a believer named Abigail looks around her church at people who are preaching, teaching, and singing (abilities she does not have), and she concludes that she has nothing to offer. Yet she's forgetting her gift of showing hospitality to others in her home. Abigail needs to realize that her special endowment is as valid as any other, and she can provide a service distinct from others whom the Spirit has gifted differently. Every ability bestowed by the Spirit is needed, especially if the faith community is to operate effectively. Likewise, each part of the human body is needed if it is to function appropriately.

A body that is nothing but an eye might see fine, but it is deaf. Similarly, a body that is limited to an ear can certainly hear, but it is incapable of smelling. We might paraphrase Paul's questions in verse 17 according to the subject he had in mind: If everyone in a congregation has the gift of speaking in tongues, how will the members of the church be taught? How will believers receive prophecies from the Lord? How will they even interpret what's spoken in tongues? While the Corinthians might have been emphasizing just one spiritual gift, God was not so foolish as to give them only one. It is similar to the way in which He arranged the human body.

Far from being made up of just an eye or just an ear, the body has every part it needs. That's the judicious way God designed it (vs. 18). With this truth in mind, Paul repeated what he had said before when he explained that the human body has many parts and yet is a unit (vss. 19-20). The Spirit has prudently distributed special endowments among Christians so that the faith community can have a complete and well-rounded ministry. He has given to every believer specific gifts, and they can be certain that He has a good reason for doing so. Somewhere in the overall activity of the church, there's a place where each of our God-given abilities—whether it's administration, mercy, or whatever else—fits perfectly into the Lord's will.

C. Every Part Essential to the Body: vss. 21-26

The eye cannot say to the hand, "I don't need you!" And the head cannot say to the feet, "I don't need you!" On the contrary, those parts of the body that seem to be weaker are indispensable, and the parts that we think are less honorable we treat with special honor. And the parts that are unpresentable are treated with special modesty, while our presentable parts need no special treatment. But God has combined the members of the body and has given greater honor to the parts that lacked it, so that there should be no division in the body, but that its parts should have equal concern for each other. If one part suffers, every part suffers with it; if one part is honored, every part rejoices with it.

In 1 Corinthians 12:21-26, Paul used the body-church analogy in a slightly different way. It appears that here the issue is not the relationship between different spiritual gifts in the body of Christ, but the relationship between different people in the faith community. The apostle started off by saying that one member of the human body cannot declare that it alone is sufficient apart from another member. Verse 21 personifies the eye asserting this to the hand, and the head to the feet. Of course, what Paul meant was that one member of Christ's body could not say he or she did not need another member.

Evidently, the apostle was thinking about the division between rich and poor, which had caused enormous problems at the Lord's Supper in the church at Corinth (11:17-34). The "haves" in the congregation possibly thought they could get along fine without the "have-nots." In no uncertain terms, Paul told the believers who considered themselves to be self-sufficient that they were wrong. By way of analogy, the apostle explained that those members of the human body that appear to be the weakest are essential (12:22). Here he was probably referring to the internal organs. These seem to be weak, since they are protected inside the body. Yet without them and the crucial tasks they performed, the body would die.

Furthermore, a notable effort is made to clothe with great care those parts of the body that are considered "less honorable" (vs. 23). Likewise, those members that should not be seen are afforded more decorum. In contrast, the more "presentable" (vs. 24) members do not require this level of dignity. Here Paul meant that the sexual organs are treated with greater propriety by being clothed. More presentable parts of the body, such as the face, are not covered with garments. Regardless of which portion of the body is considered, Paul was really referring to believers in the faith community. Members who were too little appreciated by others were as important, if not more so, than the others. Perhaps the apostle believed that God is especially gracious to the have-nots of this world.

In keeping with what Paul stated in verse 18, he noted in verse 24 that God arranged the human body in just the right way. For instance, He gave more abundant "honor" to the members that lacked it. God also made the body in such a way that it harmoniously worked together and each part mattered equally to every other part (vs. 25). To draw further attention to this mutual "concern," the apostle noted that when one member of the body is hurting, all the other members suffer along with it. Likewise, if one member flourishes, the rest of the members are filled with joy (vs. 26). That's because the human body is a unit.

From Paul's analogy his readers could recognize that God wanted His children to be characterized by harmony and compassion, not division and indifference. The entire congregation was to do what it could to help its despondent members through tough times. Similarly, Jesus' disciples were to rejoice in the acclaim that an individual believer might receive. Even today, God does not want us to live in isolation from each other. He wants us to take an active interest in one another. The apostle's words are a valuable corrective to our prideful tendencies. As we look about us at those in our church, we might be tempted to discount the value of some believers. But they're a part of us, and none of us can do as well without other Christians as we can with them.

II. THE IMPORTANCE OF EVERY BELIEVER: 1 CORINTHIANS 12:27-31

A. Different Members of Christ's Body: vss. 27-28

Now you are the body of Christ, and each one of you is a part of it. And in the church God has appointed first of all apostles, second prophets, third teachers, then workers of miracles, also those having gifts of healing, those able to help others, those with gifts of administration, and those speaking in different kinds of tongues.

In 1 Corinthians 12:27, Paul reminded his readers that he was really talking about each and every one of them as a member of the "body of Christ." Then, in verse 28, the apostle provided a list of eight items (compare vss. 8-10 and the comments appearing in last week's lesson). The first three items on the list are believers who had certain spiritual gifts, while the last five are special endowments that believers had. Since Paul used the words translated "first of all . . . second . . . third" (vs. 28), some see in this list a ranking of gifts from most important to least important. But the apostle did not carry the numbering pattern through to the end. Also, miracles and healings are mentioned in the reverse of their previous order (compare vss. 9-10). Perhaps, then, it is better to see the list as being random, not ranked, or possibly Paul meant to rank just the first three items.

"Apostles" (vs. 28) is the category to which Paul himself primarily belonged. Apostles were people who helped lay the foundation for Christian churches. "Prophets" refers to those who proclaimed divine revelations, including (though not limited to) predictions about the future. "Teachers" were believers who, with their learning and maturity, instructed others in biblical truth. "Workers of miracles" refers to those who performed signs and wonders. This spiritual gift is followed by believers who healed (or supernaturally restored others to health), Christians who ministered to the spiritual and physical needs of others ("able to help"), believers who were gifted with the ability to lead and guide the church ("administration"), and Christians endowed with the ability to communicate in various "kinds of tongues." Some think Paul placed this gift last because he considered it the least important. Others, however, maintain the apostle placed it last because it was the gift over which he and his readers were having a disagreement.

B. Every Gift Essential to the Body: vss. 29-31

Are all apostles? Are all prophets? Are all teachers? Do all work miracles? Do all have gifts of healing? Do all speak in tongues? Do all interpret? But eagerly desire the greater gifts. And now I will show you the most excellent way.

In 1 Corinthians 12:29-30, Paul asked some rhetorical questions. In doing so, he highlighted several of the items he had just mentioned and expanded on the meaning and significance of spiritual gifts. Repeatedly, he asked whether all Christians had the same special endowment, and each time the appropriate answer was *no*. By emphasizing speaking in tongues, the Corinthians forgot about the diversity of gifts. Each believer had his or her own God-given abilities—all of which were important, for that's how the Spirit wanted it.

Paul concluded this part of his argument with a brief statement in verse 31 that has led to some disagreement among interpreters. Here are three of the most common interpretations. (1) Paul exhorted his readers to earnestly strive for the "greater gifts" appearing at the beginning of his list in verse 28, rather than the lesser ones at the end. (2) Verse 31 should be translated, "but you are eager for the greater gifts" (in which the apostle was making a simple statement of fact, rather than issuing a command). (3) Paul was introducing the teachings he would convey in 14:1-25, after the digression of chapter 13 about the "most excellent way" (12:31) of Christlike love.

Discussion Questions

1. How does the human body represent the diversity and unity within the church?
2. Why would it be wrong for a believer to think he or she is the most important part of Christ's body?
3. Why is it important for all believers to have an opportunity to grow, develop, and use their gifts?
4. What are some ways believers can carry out the ministries of mutual support and caring?
5. How can Christians better accept, love, and learn from other members of Christ's body?

Contemporary Application

The church at Corinth was experiencing several problems in its worship practices. Among them was a lack of understanding about spiritual gifts and their proper usage. Individual self-interest had taken control of their exercise of special endowments from the Spirit. The result was division and disorder within the church (1 Cor. 12:25; 14:33, 40).

Paul addressed the problem in two ways. First, he discussed the origin and variety of the spiritual gifts (12:4-11). Second, the apostle explained their proper function (vss. 12-31). Central to his teaching is the principle that every believer is important to the life of the church. Later, Paul explained that this unity of purpose and ministry can only be maintained through the agency of Christlike love (see chap. 13).

Out of all the diversity we see in the body of Christ, there is spiritual unity that joins all Jesus' followers to Him. Different churches and various denominations are not disparate bodies of Christ. Of course, the church has been organized according to doctrinal, historical, and national differences. But Christ's body transcends all of these human distinctions. What holds the body together is a mutual commitment to Jesus as Lord and Savior.

The Gift of Languages

Scripture

Background Scripture: *Acts 2:1-21; 1 Corinthians 14:1-25*
Scripture Lesson: *Acts 2:1-7, 12; 1 Corinthians 14:13-19*
Key Verse: *What shall I do? I will pray with my spirit, but I
will also pray with my mind; I will sing with my spirit, but I
will also sing with my mind.* 1 Corinthians 14:15.
Scripture Lesson for Children: *Acts 2:1-7, 12;
1 Corinthians 14:13-19*
Key Verse for Children: *All [Jesus' followers] were filled
with the Holy Spirit and began to speak in other tongues as
the Spirit enabled them.* Acts 2:4.

Lesson Aim

To identify ways to create a group worship experience
that is edifying.

Lesson Setting

Time: A.D. *30 (Acts) and 55 (1 Corinthians)*
Place: Jerusalem (Acts) and Ephesus (1 Corinthians)

Lesson Outline

The Gift of Languages
   I. The Spirit's Arrival: Acts 2:1-7, 12
      A. *The Meeting of Jesus' Followers: vs. 1*
      B. *The Appearance of the Tongues of Fire: vss. 2-4*
      C. *The Presence of Devout Jews: vs. 5*
      D. *The Crowd's Confusion: vss. 6-7*
      E. *The Crowd's Mixed Reaction: vs. 12*
   II. The Spirit's Manifestation: 1 Corinthians 14:13-19
      A. *Endeavoring to Interpret: vs. 13*
      B. *Seeking to Understand: vss. 14-15*
      C. *Striving to Edify: vss. 16-17*
      D. *Emphasizing Intelligibility: vss. 18-19*

Introduction for Adults

Topic: *Seeking to Be Understood*

People are usually skeptical if they cannot see evidence of a claim. The nickname of the state of Missouri (the "Show Me State") reflects the attitude of many adults. If we claim that God's Spirit is dwelling in us, then we need to give evidence of His presence. One way to show we have had a genuine and lasting encounter with the Spirit is by the powerful changes in behavior He has made in us (for example, by our trusting in the Savior, shunning sin, and remaining united in love with our fellow believers).

This was the central thrust of Peter's message on the day of Pentecost. Adults need to know that Peter's promise of forgiveness and the indwelling Holy Spirit extended beyond his current audience to future generations and to those living in other lands. Although Peter may not have realized it at the time, his words included the Gentiles as well.

Introduction for Youth

Topic: *Communicating in a Different Language*

Some of the most interesting conversion stories I have heard involve people studying to be ministers. The standard assumption is that these people are already saved. Occasionally, this isn't the case.

There are many reasons why individuals want to train for church leadership. Even teens are known to wrestle with this issue. Sometimes, though, the desire—whether it is to help others, exercise abilities in teaching and counseling, enjoy a position of respect and influence, and so on—is void of God's presence and power.

As we learn in this week's lesson, an individual claiming to be a Christian, regardless of his or her age, is spiritually powerless when not connected with the Savior and operating in the Spirit. What a dynamic change occurs when a young person stops trying to live for God in his or her own strength and starts faithfully serving Him with the limitless resources the Spirit made available on the day of Pentecost.

Concepts for Children

Topic: *Talk, Talk, Talk!*

1. The believers were together when God's Spirit came to them.
2. People from many nations heard the Gospel in their own languages.
3. The Spirit helps us worship God through praise and prayer.
4. God is pleased when our worship of Him is orderly.
5. We can thank God for the different ways we like to worship Him.

Lesson Commentary

I. THE SPIRIT'S ARRIVAL: ACTS 2:1-7, 12

A. The Meeting of Jesus' Followers: vs. 1

When the day of Pentecost came, they were all together in one place.

Luke began his historical account with a description of Jesus' ascension to heaven. Christ's last words to His disciples were His promise to send them the Holy Spirit, who would fill them with power to be Jesus' witnesses in Jerusalem, in Judea, and throughout the globe (Acts 1:1-11). The disciples were obedient to the Lord's command. They returned to Jerusalem to wait until the Spirit came as promised. About 120 followers of the Savior spent 10 days together, praying and encouraging each other. During this time, Matthias was selected to replace Judas Iscariot, who had committed suicide after betraying Jesus (vss. 12-26).

Acts 2:1 reveals that the Spirit came upon Jesus' disciples while they were assembled in one place. In addition to the fact that they gathered together in a single location, this verse implies that the disciples were in agreement in their thinking and purpose on Pentecost. As was noted in lesson 6, the name of this Jewish festival means "fiftieth" and was the second of three main yearly feasts. Passover and Tabernacles were the other two annual festivals requiring the presence of all Jewish males. Pentecost was also known as the Feast of Weeks, the Day of First Fruits, and the Feast of Harvest. The festival was always on a Sabbath day. The feast was celebrated 50 (*pente* in Greek) days after the Passover (Lev. 23:15-16). Some have seen a connection between Pentecost and the giving of the law on Mount Sinai, which may have occurred on the fiftieth day after the Exodus.

Pentecost was a celebration of the grain harvest, a period that lasted about seven weeks. Barley and wheat were the primary harvest foods. The poor and strangers were especially welcome during this festival. During Pentecost, the people would bring their offerings of first fruits to the Lord. A special sacrifice was presented in the temple during this time. A wave offering of new bread made from the recently harvested wheat was presented before the Lord, along with sin and peace offerings. No celebrating was to occur until after this ceremony. Every male Israelite was to appear in the sanctuary. Jews from all over the known world would come to Jerusalem to celebrate this feast of thanksgiving.

B. The Appearance of the Tongues of Fire: vss. 2-4

Suddenly a sound like the blowing of a violent wind came from heaven and filled the whole house where they were sitting. They saw what seemed to be tongues of fire that separated and came to rest on each of them. All of them were filled with the Holy Spirit and began to speak in other tongues as the Spirit enabled them.

All at once and unexpectedly, the disciples heard a sound from heaven that was similar to that of a turbulent "wind" (Acts 2:2). The noise filled the entire house where they were meeting. In the context of this incident, the wind was a physical indication of the presence of the Spirit. In Scripture, wind and breath are common symbols of God's Spirit (Ezek. 37:9, 14; John 3:8). The sight of "tongues of fire" (Acts 2:3) was even more unusual than the sound of the wind, perhaps being reminiscent of the thunder and lighting that accompanied God's giving of the law to Moses on Mount Sinai (Exod. 19:16-19).

The tongue-shaped flames appeared to stand over each disciple's head (Acts 2:3). This incident indicated that God's presence was among Jesus' followers in a more powerful and personal way than they had ever experienced before. The disciples could sense the Spirit's coming audibly (through wind) and visibly (through fire). Moreover, they were filled with the Spirit (vs. 4). As evidence of His presence, the Spirit enabled them to speak in other tongues. Apparently these were actual languages or dialects being voiced by the disciples to the visitors from many countries in Jerusalem. The Spirit had come to empower Jesus' followers to reach out to the lost with the saving message of the Gospel.

Some think Jesus' followers were at that moment in one of the courts of the Jerusalem temple (Luke 24:52-53). In a few instances, Luke uses the Greek word for "house" in Acts to refer to the temple, and Luke's Gospel closes with the statement that the disciples "stayed continually at the temple, praising God" (24:53). Those who hold this view also suggest that the disciples had a better chance of attracting a large crowd in the temple precincts than in the upper room. Others who think the Spirit came upon the disciples in the upper room of a house argue that "one place" (Acts 2:1) more naturally refers back to the space mentioned in 1:13. They also point out that Luke more often uses the common Greek word for temple rather than the word for house. With the entire city of Jerusalem filled with pilgrims, the disciples could have attracted a large crowd by coming down to the street after the Holy Spirit had come upon them.

C. The Presence of Devout Jews: vs. 5

Now there were staying in Jerusalem God-fearing Jews from every nation under heaven.

Jesus' disciples, being enthusiastic in their baptism of power, spilled out into the streets of Jerusalem. As was noted earlier, the population of Jerusalem swelled with pilgrims attending the festival of Pentecost (Acts 2:5). This event proved to be a strategic time for the Father and Son to send the Spirit. Visitors who miraculously heard God being praised in their own languages—and were perhaps among that day's 3,000 converts (vs. 41)—could take the good news of salvation in the Messiah back with them to their homelands.

D. The Crowd's Confusion: vss. 6-7

When they heard this sound, a crowd came together in bewilderment, because each one heard them speaking in his own language. Utterly amazed, they asked: "Are not all these men who are speaking Galileans?"

While the Spirit operates quietly, God sometimes sends visible and audible signs of His work. The wind, fire, and inspired speech all have their roots in Jewish tradition as signs of God's presence. This did not escape the notice of the foreign Jews who heard the sound of tongues-speaking. They were amazed that locals could fluently speak languages from around the Roman Empire (Acts 2:6). With their curiosity aroused, crowds of people quickly gathered together to discuss what could be behind all the commotion. They could tell by the distinctive accent of Jesus' followers that they were mainly from Galilee (vs. 7). In general, the Jews living in Jerusalem looked down upon those from Galilee because it was so far away from the religious center of the nation (John 7:52).

Evidently, the throng operated under the assumption that the disciples spoke only one or two languages. Consequently, they were perplexed that these seemingly uneducated Galileans could speak fluently in so many different native dialects, which in turn could be understood by the diverse group of pilgrims (Acts 2:8). In this amazing turn of events, the Lord began to reverse the confusion that occurred at the tower of Babel thousands of years earlier (Gen. 11:1-9). Whereas then God scattered the human race over all the earth, on the day of Pentecost He brought all sorts of different people back together to hear the message of salvation.

E. The Crowd's Mixed Reaction: vs. 12

Amazed and perplexed, they asked one another, "What does this mean?"

Both ethnic Jews and converts to Judaism heard Jesus' disciples using the crowds' own languages to declare to them the wonderful things God had done. These visitors came from all across the Roman Empire (Acts 2:9-11). At the time when the New Testament was written, the entire civilized world (with the exception of the little-known kingdoms of the Far East) was under the domination of Rome. From the Atlantic Ocean on the west to the Euphrates River and the Red Sea on the east, from the Rhone, the Danube, the Black Sea, and the Caucus Mountains on the north, and to the Sahara on the south, stretched one vast empire under the headship and virtual dictatorship of the emperor.

The pilgrims were excited but confused by the tongues-speaking episode unfolding before them. The crowds kept asking one another what its significance might be (vs. 12). Regrettably, some in the throng took a less charitable view. They crassly joked that Jesus' disciples were drunk from having ingested too much wine (vs. 13). The Savior would use the bewilderment of the pilgrims as an opportunity to shine the light of the Gospel into their sin-filled lives. Moreover, the Spirit empowered Peter to stand before the crowd to explain what they were seeing. He was "with the Eleven" (vs. 14), suggesting that while Peter was the primary speaker, the others all affirmed what he said (vss. 15-36).

Jesus' resurrection was the central message of Peter's sermon. His listeners were so moved that 3,000 converts were added to the church (vss. 37-41).

II. THE SPIRIT'S MANIFESTATION: *1 CORINTHIANS 14:13-19*

A. Endeavoring to Interpret: vs. 13

For this reason anyone who speaks in a tongue should pray that he may interpret what he says.

In 1 Corinthians 14:1-12, Paul taught that one of the main purposes of spiritual gifts—including the speaking in tongues that occurred at Pentecost—was to build up the body of Christ. With that truth in mind, the apostle said the gift of tongues occurring during a worship service, if uninterpreted, did nothing to edify the attendees. This is due to the fact that no one in the congregation could understand what was being said. For this reason, Paul said it was better for believers to proclaim God's truth in a language everyone could understand. Accordingly, the apostle directed tongues-speakers to pray that the Spirit would give them the ability to explain the meaning of what they said (vs. 13). The ability to interpret tongues was, in itself, a spiritual gift (12:10). So, if believers had both gifts, they could speak in tongues and then interpret what had been said for the edification of others.

B. Seeking to Understand: vss. 14-15

For if I pray in a tongue, my spirit prays, but my mind is unfruitful. So what shall I do? I will pray with my spirit, but I will also pray with my mind; I will sing with my spirit, but I will also sing with my mind.

Paul explained that when people spoke in tongues, they prayed with their spirit but not with their mind (1 Cor. 14:14). While the tongues-speaking was no doubt a spiritually uplifting experience, it did not directly involve the intellect. More specifically, it did not contribute to the tongues-speakers' knowledge of the things of God. Given that situation, what was Paul's advice? It was not to neglect either one's mind or one's spirit (vs. 15). Through their tongues gift, the believers in Corinth could pray and sing. (Evidently, some worshipers would offer spontaneous hymns of praise to God, with lyrics in an unknown language.) They could do the same apart from that gift. Undoubtedly, Paul was thinking that the praying and singing in the Spirit were to be done in private. During church worship services, these activities were to be done only in limited amounts and when accompanied by interpretation.

C. Striving to Edify: vss. 16-17

If you are praising God with your spirit, how can one who finds himself among those who do not understand say "Amen" to your thanksgiving, since he does not know what you are saying? You may be giving thanks well enough, but the other man is not edified.

Paul proposed a situation in which a believer in a worship service praised God with his or her spirit through speaking in tongues. The Greek noun rendered "who do not understand" (1 Cor. 14:16) refers to inquirers who were uninitiated in the Christian faith (vss. 23-24). In the absence of interpretation, these outsiders would not know what was being said and so would not know when to affirm the praise with an "Amen" (vs. 16). That would show that others were not being edified, even though the tongues-speaker was praising God (vs. 17).

"Amen" (vs. 16) comes from a Hebrew adverb that means "that which is sure and valid." In Jewish worship during the Old Testament era, participants would say "amen" as a way to affirm or agree with a speaker (Deut. 27:14-26; 1 Chron. 16:36; Neh. 5:13; 8:6; 2 Cor. 1:20; Eph. 3:21; Rev. 5:14). This practice was still common in synagogue worship during the first century A.D., and from there it passed into the worship of the early Christians. One of Paul's arguments against the use of uninterpreted speaking in tongues during worship, was that listeners would not know when to say "amen."

D. Emphasizing Intelligibility: vss. 18-19

I thank God that I speak in tongues more than all of you. But in the church I would rather speak five intelligible words to instruct others than ten thousand words in a tongue.

It would be incorrect to conclude from Paul's previous statements that the tongues gift was unimportant. In fact, the apostle was grateful to God for being personally blessed with this gift. Those in Corinth who were overemphasizing tongues-speaking could not truthfully claim to have experienced it more than Paul himself had (1 Cor. 14:18). However, when it came to a corporate worship service, the apostle would have preferred to speak a brief message that could be understood by others than prattle on for hours making utterances in a tongue that made no sense to his listeners (vs. 19). In church, intelligibility is essential because edification is the goal.

The believers in Corinth had misunderstood the place and purpose of speaking in tongues. So, Paul told them to no longer be like children in their thinking (vs. 20). They needed a more mature understanding of spiritual gifts in general and tongues in particular. Childlike ignorance was desirable when it came to the ways of evil, but not when it came to spiritual gifts. It was time the apostle's readers started thinking like adults on this subject. In verse 21, Paul cited a shortened version of Isaiah 28:11-12 to help the Corinthians grasp the true intent of tongues (see also Deut. 28:49). Isaiah had prophesied that God would use foreigners—the Assyrians—to try to teach the wayward Israelites a lesson. Based on what Paul said next, his point seems to be this: just as the Assyrians' foreign speech failed to turn the Israelites to the Lord, so speaking in tongues would fail to help convert unbelievers.

Paul stated that tongues-speaking was a miraculous "sign" (1 Cor. 14:22) that God used to authenticate His spokespersons to the unsaved. In contrast, the Lord primarily intended prophesying for the benefit of Jesus' followers. The apostle described a situation in which unbelievers and the uninformed visited a Christian worship service. If all the participants were speaking in tongues, the visitors would understand nothing and would think they were witnessing madness, like the mania that was a part of some pagan religious rituals commonplace in that day (vs. 23). In this case, speaking in tongues would be a sign in a negative sense. It would confirm the inquirers' spiritual lostness by repelling them from the Christian fellowship.

Discussion Questions

1. Why were the disciples gathered together on the day of Pentecost?
2. What did Jesus' followers do when they became filled with the Holy Spirit?
3. What are some ways that tongues-speaking can be used to edify believers?
4. What is the God-given purpose of prophesying?
5. If you were an unbeliever, would you find your church attractive and welcoming? Explain.

Contemporary Application

In 1 Corinthians 14, Paul taught that tongues-speaking during a worship service, if uninterpreted, does nothing to build up the church. The reason is that no one in the congregation can understand what is being said. Therefore, the apostle revealed that it was better to proclaim God's truth in a language that everyone can understand.

Paul's objective was to encourage believers to identify ways to create a group worship experience that is edifying. Yet, in order for this to happen, we must be willing to put the concerns and interests of others first. Sadly, though, many professing Christians unconsciously center their lives on themselves. They judge things as good or bad depending on how these things affect only them. Their own needs and desires often come first to them.

Such people attend church for what they can get out of it. They give money and time either out of obligation or for self-glorification rather than the desire to build up others spiritually. Their prayers alternate between complaints over their difficult circumstances and petitions that they might have the gratification of their wants.

Self-centeredness and spirituality, however, are incompatible. Before we can hope to live for the Savior and edify others, we have to put self in proper perspective. That will occur only when we surrender to the lordship of the Son, as about 3,000 converts did on the day of Pentecost (Acts 2:41). When Jesus is the focus of our worship and fellowship, His body will be healthy, we will be fruitful as God's representatives in this world, and we will be one in His Spirit.

The Great Gift of Love

Scripture

Background Scripture: *1 Corinthians 13*

Scripture Lesson: *1 Corinthians 13*

Key Verse: *Now these three remain: faith, hope and love. But the greatest of these is love.* 1 Corinthians 13:13.

Scripture Lesson for Children: *1 Corinthians 13*

Key Verse for Children: *Love never fails.* 1 Corinthians 13:8.

Lesson Aim

To consider ways to show Christlike compassion and kindness to others.

Lesson Setting

Time: A.D. *55*

Place: Ephesus

Lesson Outline

The Great Gift of Love

  I. The Necessity of Love: 1 Corinthians 13:1-3
    A. *Amazing Abilities without Love: vss. 1-2*
    B. *Pious Acts without Love: vs. 3*
  II. The Way of Love: 1 Corinthians 13:4-13
    A. *Love's True Nature: vss. 4-7*
    B. *Love's Permanence: vss. 8-13*

Introduction for Adults

Topic: *Love Never Ends*

In the mid-1980s, I bought my first computer, monitor, and printer. Though certain minor problems arose with the equipment, they were repairable. And I chose to ignore such inconveniences as an aging ribbon.

But a few years later when the computer broke down again, the technician said that he could not repair the equipment, for it had become obsolete. In fact, I learned that it was cheaper simply to scrap the computer and buy a new one than to continue having the old one repaired.

Unlike aging electronic equipment, Christlike love never grows obsolete. While even the most spectacular spiritual gifts will outlive their usefulness, this will never be true of love.

Introduction for Youth

Topic: *Love Is Forever*

Nobel Peace Prize winner Mother Teresa died in the fall of 1997, but her example, words, and works continue to have a lasting influence. The woman who headed a religious community that cared for the victims of disease and starvation and demonstrated unconditional and enduring love for all, declared that the greatest illness in the world was not cancer or leprosy, but a lack of love. She further said that the greatest evil was indifference and intolerance.

Paul declared that the love of Christ is the greatest gift that a believer can pass on to others. In light of Mother Teresa's words and Paul's teaching, how are you going to act?

Concepts for Children

Topic: *The Gift of Love*

1. God loves us very much.
2. God wants us to show love to others.
3. God helps us to be kind to people who are mean to us.
4. God helps us to forgive people who are not nice to us.
5. Love is the greatest gift we can give to others.

Lesson Commentary

I. The Necessity of Love: 1 Corinthians 13:1-3

A. Amazing Abilities without Love: vss. 1-2

If I speak in the tongues of men and of angels, but have not love, I am only a resounding gong or a clanging cymbal. If I have the gift of prophecy and can fathom all mysteries and all knowledge, and if I have a faith that can move mountains, but have not love, I am nothing.

In lessons 12 and 13, we studied Paul's teaching to the Corinthians on the purpose and use of spiritual gifts. In this week's lesson, we look at a digression in the apostle's argument. He stepped aside from the subject of spiritual gifts to discuss Christlike love. As 12:31 reveals, love is not a spiritual gift. Instead, it is the way in which all spiritual gifts should be used. Paul's purpose in chapter 13 was to set the issue of spiritual gifts within an ethical framework. Evidently, he thought the Corinthians were too fascinated with the spiritual gifts (particularly speaking in tongues) and had lost sight of a more basic concern, namely, demonstrating Christlike love.

First Corinthians 13 has been called a hymn of love. It is renowned for being sublime in tone and powerful in content. Because the chapter stands well on its own, some New Testament scholars suggest that Paul composed it separately and later inserted it in this letter. Those who make this suggestion say the apostle used transitional clauses in 12:31 and 14:1 to help chapter 13 better fit into its present context. However, other scholars think Paul composed this chapter at the same time he wrote 1 Corinthians. These specialists argue that the composition fits too closely with what appears before and after to be a work created at an earlier time.

With respect to the Greek language spoken by Paul and his contemporaries, there were three terms used to refer to love. In verse 3, the noun rendered "love" translates *agape* (ah-GAH-pay). The apostle used this term to indicate unselfish compassion and unconditional kindness. Such love is prompted as much by will as by emotion. Also, it seeks to reach out to others in need, even if the object seems unworthy of being loved. *Philia* (fih-LEE-ah) is a second Greek term for love that is used in the New Testament. It primarily indicates the fondness, affection, or affinity that exists between family members or close friends. *Eros* (ERR-os) is a third Greek term for love that was frequently used in secular literature but does not appear in the New Testament. This word indicates passionate love of a sensual nature.

In verse 1, Paul named certain representative gifts and actions and then indicated how they are worthless unless done in love. The first item was the special endowment of tongues-speaking (vs. 1), which his readers most highly prized. There is disagreement among interpreters concerning the meaning of the reference to "tongues of men and of angels." One possibility is that these were actual languages or dialects being spoken by people and angels. A second option is that the tongues were unintelligible words of ecstasy uttered by the person or angel in praise to God. A third alternative is that Paul was speaking in exaggerated terms to include every conceivable form of speech. Regardless of which view is preferred, the ability would have been impressive to the Corinthians. Yet, as Paul noted, if he did not have Christlike love, then his speech would have been useless noise, like that produced in a pagan ritual from a deafening gong or a rattling cymbal.

Paul next referred to three other spiritual gifts: "prophecy" (vs. 2), "knowledge," and "faith." For instance, the apostle might be able to deliver spectacular messages from God. Also, Paul might have insight into all sorts of divine secrets and enigmatic truths. Furthermore, he might have such strong belief that he could dislodge mountains from their foundations. Admittedly, from a human standpoint, these gifts would be impressive. Yet, the apostle argued that in the absence of Christlike love, he was "nothing." In a manner of speaking, Paul would be an absolute zero from the standpoint of God. If no compassion and kindness were present, there would be no redeeming value to the gifted one's actions.

B. Pious Acts without Love: vs. 3

If I give all I possess to the poor and surrender my body to the flames, but have not love, I gain nothing.

In 1 Corinthians 13:3, Paul referred to two pious actions he might perform. The first of these would be parceling out all his possessions to the poor. Throughout the Bible, we see the importance of helping those who lack what they need materially. Unfortunately, we can't be sure about the second action Paul listed, since the manuscript evidence is divided. Some early texts read, "If I . . . surrender my body to the flames." This presumably refers to martyrdom by burning. The problem with the latter reading is that when Paul wrote 1 Corinthians, this form of execution was hardly known for either Jews or Christians. So some have questioned whether this is the original biblical text and meaning.

Other early manuscripts read, "If I . . . surrender my body that I may boast." If this is the original reading, then Paul's meaning is less obvious. One option is that he was referring to delivering up his body to slavery or death and boasting in the Lord for doing so. A second option is that he was talking about serving others without regard for his own welfare and receiving acclaim for such an altruistic deed. In either case, the apostle's point remains the same. He taught that regardless of the nature of the pious acts, if he did not have Christlike love, he would be spiritually bankrupt. Expressed differently, he would not gain anything through what he had given up, no matter how laudable it was. The absence of compassion and kindness would rob Christian service of its eternal value.

II. THE WAY OF LOVE: 1 CORINTHIANS 13:4-13

A. Love's True Nature: vss. 4-7

Love is patient, love is kind. It does not envy, it does not boast, it is not proud. It is not rude, it is not self-seeking, it is not easily angered, it keeps no record of wrongs. Love does not delight in evil but rejoices with the truth. It always protects, always trusts, always hopes, always perseveres.

Paul had previously spoken about himself, but now he personified Christlike "love" (1 Cor. 13:4) for the Corinthians. The apostle did so by using both positive and negative terms to describe godly compassion. Most likely, Paul chose his words carefully to implicitly condemn errors committed by his readers. For instance, the Greek verb rendered "patient" denotes a forbearing spirit, whereas the verb translated "kind" points to acts of benevolence. As Christians, we are to have a long fuse to our temper. We must not retaliate when wronged. Instead, we are to remain steadfast in spirit, consistently responding to others in a gracious and considerate manner.

After describing Christlike love using two positive terms, Paul next used a series of expressions to indicate what love is not and does not do. For example, the Greek verb rendered "envy" signifies the presence of intense jealousy. We are not to resent what others are or have, nor wish to take those things for ourselves. The verb translated "boast" refers to those who brag about themselves, especially by using flashy rhetorical skills. We should never gloat over our own achievements. The verb rendered "proud" literally means "to puff up." We should not be inflated with arrogance.

The Greek verb translated "rude" (vs. 5) means to act in an indecent or shameful way. We should not behave in a disgraceful or dishonorable manner. The reference to "self-seeking" points to an egotistical mind-set that borders on narcissism. We are not to be primarily concerned with getting our own way or seeking what's best for us. The verb rendered "not easily angered" denotes an irritable disposition that becomes annoyed at the slightest inconvenience. We should not let ourselves be provoked to rage by what others do. The verb translated "keeps no record of wrongs" brings to mind individuals who maintain an inventory of how others allegedly have shortchanged them. We should not brood over offenses or keep a scorecard of how many times we have been hurt.

"Delight in evil" (vs. 6) could also be rendered "be glad about injustice" or "rejoice at unrighteousness." We should never encourage wrongdoing by obtaining pleasure in misdeeds. Instead, Christlike love takes delight in God's "truth," especially as it is revealed in the Gospel. Christians should be overjoyed when others promote what's right in God's eyes. Some people seem to take a perverse joy in evil. They like it when someone gets away with lying, cheating, or stealing. But that is not to be our way. We are neither to promote sin nor encourage its practitioners. We are to cheer on goodness and truth.

In verse 7, Paul closed this paragraph with four examples of what Christlike love always does. Together, these illustrations show us that, through godly kindness and compassion, believers have the inner strength to face whatever trials come their way. Love "always protects" means Christians should strive to keep others from evil. Or, if the original phrase is translated, "[love] bears all things," then it refers to believers enduring troubles or persecution. Love "always trusts" could also be rendered "believes all things." The idea is that Jesus' followers should have such faith that they search for what is finest in people and commend what is best about them.

Love "always hopes" indicates there should be no limit to the believers' confidence in the promises of God or in His ability to fulfill them. "Always perseveres" could also be translated "endures all things." The idea is that when tragedy strikes, Christlike love refuses to collapse or quit. Instead, it has the God-given fortitude to persist through whatever hardships it encounters in life. Put differently, the Spirit enables believers to remain strong to the end of the ordeal.

B. Love's Permanence: vss. 8-13

Love never fails. But where there are prophecies, they will cease; where there are tongues, they will be stilled; where there is knowledge, it will pass away. For we know in part and we prophesy in part, but when perfection comes, the imperfect disappears. When I was a child, I talked like a child, I thought like a child, I reasoned like a child. When I became a man, I put childish ways behind me. Now we see but a poor reflection as in a mirror; then we shall see face to face. Now I know in part; then I shall know fully, even as I am fully known. And now these three remain: faith, hope and love. But the greatest of these is love.

Paul revealed that unlike spiritual gifts, Christlike "love" (1 Cor. 13:8) endures forever. While one day even the most spectacular abilities would no longer be needed, this would never be true of love. Expressed differently, even though special endowments would pass from the scene, love would never become invalid or obsolete. For example, "prophecies" would be discontinued. Similarly, "tongues" would come to an end. Moreover, "knowledge" would be set aside.

Paul was contrasting two periods—an earlier one in which the spiritual gifts were needed and a later one when the need for them would expire. That said, interpreters differ over the time scheme the apostle had in mind. One view is that the first period extended between Pentecost and the completion of the New Testament (or the close of the apostolic age), with the second period coming after. Another view is that the first period is the time between Jesus' first and second comings (or the interval between when individual believers live and die), with the second period following that.

Paul explained that the difference between the first and second periods is like the distinction between the partial and the complete, or between the imperfect and the perfect (vss. 9-10). For instance, the spiritual gifts of knowledge and prophecy put believers in touch with God only in a partial way. But in the later period, Christians would be in full and perfect fellowship with Him. Next,

Paul illustrated his meaning by drawing an analogy involving childhood and adulthood (vs. 11). He said that when he was a child, he talked, thought, and reasoned as a child. But now that the apostle had become an adult, he had put those "childish ways" behind him. Childhood is like the first period, and childish ways are comparable to spiritual gifts. Just as childish ways are appropriate for a child, so spiritual gifts are appropriate for believers in the first period. But then (to follow the analogy further), adulthood is like the second period. At that time, Jesus' followers would set aside their spiritual gifts, for these would no longer be appropriate.

In verse 12, Paul used an analogy involving a "mirror." In his day, this would have been a flat piece of highly-polished silver or bronze attached to a handle. The image this metal disc reflected would be quite inferior to the mirrors in use today. In a spiritual sense, the glimpse of God that we get in the first period, as He is made known through our spiritual gifts, is like the imprecise and obscure image produced by a mirror. However, in the second period, our vision of God would not be mediated by our spiritual gifts, for our encounter with Him would be "face to face." This means it would be direct and personal in nature.

Interpreters disagree over Paul's exact meaning here. Was he saying that the vision obtained using a mirror is either blurry or reflected? In other words, do our spiritual gifts give us a flawed sense of who God is, or do they give us an indirect sense? Either way, the contrast between our vision of God (involving our spiritual gifts) in the first period and our vision of Him (apart from our spiritual gifts) in the later period still stands.

Next, Paul switched from the language of sight to that of knowledge. He explained that he (like all believers in the first period) knew God only partially. Even so, the apostle looked forward to a time when he would know God fully. Of course, Paul was not suggesting that human beings would ever have knowledge equaling that of God. The Lord is not limited, as believers are, by conditions of the first period. God already knew Paul (and all other believers) fully.

In verse 13, Paul revealed that the trio of "faith, hope and love" abide for the benefit of God's children. Indeed, these three virtues sum up the Christian life. "Faith" denotes trust in the Savior and commitment to His teachings. "Hope" signifies an unshakable confidence that the Son would ultimately fulfill the Father's promises. And thanks to Paul's explanation, we have a full description of what "love" means.

Some think that faith and hope, like love, are eternal, for they are manifestations of love. Others maintain that Paul included faith and hope in this verse to remind his readers that Christlike love is for now, just as faith and hope are. Yet, when the apostle went on to say that the "greatest of these is love," he signaled that the latter is superior to faith and hope because love lasts forever. In contrast, faith and hope (like the spiritual gifts) are for this age only. According to this view, faith is superfluous in eternity because then believers will be in God's presence. Likewise, hope is unnecessary in the age to come, for then the divine promises will be fulfilled.

Discussion Questions

1. Why are the gifts of prophecy, knowledge, and faith pointless in the absence of love?
2. How is it possible for Christians to be patient and kind when others are rude to them?
3. What enables a believer characterized by love to bear, believe, hope, and endure all things?
4. What was Paul's main purpose in stressing that spiritual gifts are temporary but love is permanent?
5. In what sense will love last forever?

Contemporary Application

To love the way God does involves making a conscious decision. The Lord Himself is the best example of this. As Romans 5:8-10 teaches, God chose to reach out to us in love even when we were His enemies. Despite our sin, God decided to bring peace and wholeness to our relationship with Him.

There will be times when we do not feel like loving other people. It is in those moments that we need to look to God for supernatural help. He is ready and willing to give us the strength to love in a Christlike fashion. But first we must submit ourselves to God's will.

In addition, when God enables us to love despite our desire not to, nonbelievers will see the power of Jesus' love working through and in us. In a morally corrupt society in which people yearn for a power greater than what they have, so as to give them meaning and value, the love of Christ in us will draw them to Him. Here, then, is another reason to choose to love—to surrender our agendas to Jesus' will and shine the light of the Gospel to others.

If we are to be more loving, we must also examine our attitudes and actions. We need to consider how we love others in our ministries and relationships. Furthermore, we should look for ways in which we can be more loving.

Pronouncing God's Judgment

Scripture

Background Scripture: *Amos 2:4-16*
Scripture Lesson: *Amos 2:4-16*
Key Verse: *This is what the LORD says: "For three sins of Judah [and Israel], even for four, I will not turn back my wrath. Amos 2:4.*
Scripture Lesson for Children: *Amos 2:4-8*
Key Verse for Children: *They have rejected the law of the LORD. Amos 2:4.*

Lesson Aim

To remain ethical in all our dealings with others.

Lesson Setting

Time: 760–750 B.C.
Place: Judah and Samaria

Lesson Outline

Pronouncing God's Judgment

I. Judah's Transgressions: Amos 2:4-5
   A. *Rejecting God's Laws: vs. 4*
   B. *Foretelling Destruction: vs. 5*
II. Israel's Transgressions: Amos 2:6-16
   A. *Committing Immorality and Injustice: vss. 6-8*
   B. *Disdaining God's Representatives: vss. 9-12*
   C. *Declaring Disaster: vss. 13-16*

Introduction for Adults

Topic: *Injustice Is Intolerable!*

Sometimes we are prone to jump to indefensible conclusions. For instance, we see others overcome by difficulties and we incorrectly assume that God is judging them for their sins. It's important to remember that God alone knows the reasons why people suffer. We, however, rarely know all the facts.

This doesn't mean, though, that God has left us in the dark about the importance of righteousness and justice. Consequently, we have no excuse for tolerating the kinds of sins against which Amos preached. We know that such vices as idolatry, sexual immorality, bribery, and exploiting the poor (to name a few iniquities) are always wrong.

We also know that a holy God judges sin, and that we suffer personally and our society suffers as a whole when we flout God's teachings in Scripture. That's why we need the sermons that Amos preached to remind us of the kind of behavior God expects from us as His children. We also need these ancient messages because we are prone to stray from God like lost sheep.

Introduction for Youth

Topic: *Are We Responsible?*

A young, successful businesswoman stated, "Most of my friends aren't at all religious, and if they are, they fall into a feel-good spirituality." Her colleague nodded in agreement and then added, "People we work and party with frankly don't feel it's anybody's business how we live or what we do. The main thing is to be happy."

With slight variations, these words express the outlook and values not only of young adults (commonly referred to as Generation Z or the iGeneration), but also of most Americans today. Likewise, these words sum up the attitude of Amos' hearers in Israel in the eighth century B.C. This outspoken prophet's stern warnings were not well received then, and may not be welcomed today. But God's message must be heard!

Concepts for Children

Topic: *Caught in the Act*

1. Amos spoke God's Word.
2. Amos told God's people they had broken His laws.
3. Amos told God's people they were unkind to each other.
4. Amos told God's people that God was unhappy with them.
5. God wants us to treat others with love and respect.

Lesson Commentary

I. JUDAH'S TRANSGRESSIONS: AMOS 2:4-5

A. Rejecting God's Laws: vs. 4

This is what the LORD says: "For three sins of Judah, even for four, I will not turn back my wrath. Because they have rejected the law of the LORD and have not kept his decrees, because they have been led astray by false gods, the gods their ancestors followed."

Amos was a Hebrew prophet from the southern kingdom of Judah whose ministry was directed mainly toward the northern kingdom of Israel (Amos 1:1). The prophecies of Amos were most likely delivered between 760 and 750 B.C. Israel and Judah were politically at the height of their power and enjoying a prosperous economy. Sadly, however, both nations were corrupt. For instance, idols were worshiped throughout the land and especially at Bethel, which was supposed to be a national religious center.

During this time of relative peace and prosperity, some of God's people had accumulated wealth and had begun to exploit the poor. Appropriate forms of worship had become mixed with pagan religious practices borrowed from the surrounding nations. Even when God's people worshiped in the proper way, many went through rituals without any genuine faith in their hearts. They also treated others badly. God used Amos to preach against such vices. God called Amos to warn His people of coming judgment for their sins, which included social injustice, religious hypocrisy, and idolatry. (The truth of Amos' warning was borne out a generation later, when Assyria overran Israel.)

Amos was a shepherd and fig grower, not a prophet by vocation (1:1; 7:14). Even though he may not have had the formal religious training of his professional counterparts, he nevertheless was inspired by the Lord. God called Amos while he was still living in Tekoa, his hometown. This village was located in the rugged sheep country of Judah about 10 miles south of Jerusalem. Undoubtedly, while there, he meditated on God's Word, formed clear judgments, and learned how to be God's spokesperson to His people in the northern kingdom.

The sermons Amos proclaimed reflected his life in the country. Most likely, Amos made several trips to Jerusalem to sell wool and produce. Also, beyond question, that's one place where he observed conditions of wickedness. While his home was farther south, he seemed well-informed about the evils plaguing Israel to the north. For instance, at Bethel, where King Jeroboam had set up an altar and an idolatrous golden calf (1 Kings 12:26-30), Amos announced judgment on nations surrounding Israel, including Judah (Amos 1:3–2:5).

God's spokesperson began each oracle with a stock phrase: "For three sins . . . even for four" (2:4). This refrain didn't mean these nations were guilty of only four crimes. It was simply an expression that indicated a large number.

The offenses Amos mentioned were specific—but not all-inclusive—examples of unethical behavior. "Damascus" (1:3) refers to the capital of Aram or Syria, which was northeast of Israel. "Gaza" (vs. 6) was the southernmost of the five major cities in southwest Canaan belonging to the Philistines. "Tyre" (vs. 9) was a prominent seaport in Phoenicia north of Israel. "Ammon" (vs. 13) was a nation located east of Israel in the Transjordan. "Moab" (2:1) was another Transjordan state situated east of the Dead Sea.

"Judah" (vs. 4) was the last of Israel's neighbors to receive a pronouncement of judgment. The two nations' inhabitants had once been joined. The Israelites and Judahites shared the same ethnic origin, history, and religion. This included the special revelation the Lord gave to His chosen people through Moses at Mount Sinai (Exod. 19–20; Deut. 5; Rom. 3:1-2; 9:4-5). So perhaps a few (though undoubtedly not all) of Amos' Israelite listeners might have become uncomfortable to learn that God refused to rescind His decree of judgment against Judah.

The nation's people had treated the teachings of the Mosaic law with contempt and flouted His ordinances. They were guilty of turning their backs on God and acting in sinful, destructive ways. "False gods" (Amos 2:4) renders a Hebrew noun that literally means "lies." The term could denote the deceptions spread by counterfeit prophets, especially those promoting idol worship. For centuries, idolatry plagued God's chosen people. Even in Amos' day, the inhabitants of Judah (along with Israel) venerated and served pagan deities.

B. Foretelling Destruction: vs. 5

"I will send fire upon Judah that will consume the fortresses of Jerusalem."

Judah was guilty of violating the Mosaic covenant. Not surprisingly, God's oracle of judgment delivered through Amos was conveyed in language reminiscent of Leviticus 26:14-15; Deuteronomy 5:1, 28:15; and 2 Kings 17:15. The Mosaic covenant was the foundation of God's relationship with Israel. The Lord set His affection on this nation in a unique way by choosing its people for Himself and declaring that He would be their God (Lev. 26:12). In the covenant He established, the Lord pledged to guide and protect them. In turn, they were to observe His commands and accept His sovereign rule (Deut. 10:12-22). Israel was to trust that God would give her whatever she needed, especially if she continued to live according to the Mosaic covenant.

Under this binding agreement, the Israelites would prosper if they obeyed the law and they would experience calamity if they disobeyed (Deut. 28:1-68). The law became the precise expression of God's pure and perfect moral standard. It was the measuring stick by which all Israel's actions were evaluated. From these observations it is clear that the Mosaic covenant occupies a central role in understanding the message and theology of the Old Testament. The book of Amos, for example, reveals that the Creator and moral Judge of the universe would not back down from His promises. He would remain loyal either to bless or to punish His chosen people.

Judah's sins were worse than those of other nations because Judah should have known better. After all, others did not know God as the people of Judah did. He manifested His presence among them in the temple at Jerusalem. Since they possessed God's law and had enjoyed His material and spiritual blessings, He held them more responsible for their actions. A "fire upon Judah" (Amos 2:5) is a reference to the terrible devastation and destruction that the nation, like its pagan neighbors, would eventually experience.

The prophecy of Amos was fulfilled when the Babylonians overran Jerusalem, tore down the city's walls, leveled the temple, and took the people into captivity in 586 B.C. (2 Kings 25:1-26). The Judahites should have understood from the sobering declarations of Amos that God takes obedience to His ethical standards seriously. They also should have realized that God would not overlook transgressions committed by His own people, any more than He would overlook the misdeeds of other peoples. One day He would punish all who rebelled against Him.

II. ISRAEL'S TRANSGRESSIONS: AMOS 2:6-16

A. Committing Immorality and Injustice: vss. 6-8

This is what the LORD says: "For three sins of Israel, even for four, I will not turn back my wrath. They sell the righteous for silver, and the needy for a pair of sandals. They trample on the heads of the poor as upon the dust of the ground and deny justice to the oppressed. Father and son use the same girl and so profane my holy name. They lie down beside every altar on garments taken in pledge. In the house of their god they drink wine taken as fines."

Many in the northern kingdom undoubtedly would have been glad to hear about the troubles in store for their enemies, and perhaps even their longtime rivals, the people of Judah. The Israelites may have thought that such judgment would mean things would go better for them. But Amos also had a sobering message for the proud Israelites. Judgment would visit them as surely as it would other nations.

After years of financial setbacks and foreign intrusions, the Israelites finally were experiencing an economic rebound. Unstable international conditions enabled the nation to recover lands lost earlier and to gain control of some major trade routes. Consequently, many people became prosperous and enjoyed lives of luxury. Even though the Israelites thrived outwardly, inwardly their souls had become impoverished. Sin, corruption, and idolatry entangled their lives. The wealthy had gained their riches at the expense of the poor, leaving them even more destitute. The rich mistakenly thought their prosperity was a sign of God's favor.

Despite the schemes of the wealthy Israelites to defraud and take advantage of the weak, they tended to be religious. For instance, the rich celebrated sacred feasts and visited numerous shrines and altars in an attempt to please all the gods and goddesses, not just the Lord of Israel. What they didn't take into account—and what Amos had come to warn them about—was that religious ritual, in itself, did not please God and that idolatry was something He abhorred.

Moreover, the wealthy had not used their material resources to honor God by showing compassion to the poor. For example, the rich had sold the innocent into slavery, including those who couldn't afford to pay their negligible debts— even for an amount worth no more than a "pair of sandals" (Amos 2:6). The wealthy craved what little the innocent had and treated them shamefully to get it. This included stepping on the dirt-covered "heads of the poor" (vs. 7). The next phrase is literally rendered "they turn aside the way of the impoverished." Most likely, this refers to the wicked rich shoving the rights of the afflicted out of the way so that the oppressors could gain some sadistic pleasure from seeing the defenseless suffer.

Amos denounced the sexual sin of a father and son both having intimate relations with a young woman. It remains unclear, though, what the prophet meant in his reference to the "same girl." One strong possibility is that both the father and son went to the same woman at a pagan shrine and had ritual sex with her. In this case, the idolatry practiced by the father not only was being passed down to his son, but was also being perpetuated through the generations. Another possibility is that both the father and son were having intimate relations with the same household servant (likely a poor person) and exploiting her like a prostitute. Obviously, the father was not demonstrating marital purity and was then passing his corrupt morals on to his son.

In either case, such iniquities defamed God's sacred name (that is, His essential character or reputation; see Lev. 18:21; 20:3; 21:6; Jer. 34:16; Ezek. 20:9). Moreover, Amos was correct to censure these immoral practices. After all, the Mosaic law required a man to marry a girl with whom he had sexual relations (Exod. 22:16; Deut. 22:28-29). Likewise, no father and son were to be physically intimate with the same woman (Lev. 18:7-8, 15; 20:11-12). It is worth noting that the worship of Canaanite gods and goddesses often included ritual prostitution as a fertility cult. The pagans thought it helped to increase crop yield and the productivity of livestock.

Amos declared that at religious festivals, wealthy Israelites reclined at pagan altars while wearing the attire they seized as collateral from those unable to pay their paltry debts (Amos 2:8). The Hebrew noun rendered "garments" literally means a "covering" and refers to large, square cloaks. During the day, these items were worn as clothing, and during the night, they functioned as blankets to keep their owners warm. The greed displayed by the wicked rich dishonored the name of God and violated His law. The latter said no one was permitted to keep a person's cloak overnight as a pledge for a debt (Exod. 22:26-27; Deut. 24:12-13).

Amos 2:8 makes reference to righteous people who were being punished by fines. If the sanction could not be paid, the wine of the indigent was taken and consumed by the greedy extortionists in the shrine of their pagan deity. In their greed, these Israelites ignored the law and took even the basic staples of life—food and clothing—from those in desperate straits. The poor and oppressed no doubt would have welcomed the message proclaimed by Amos. They would see that they had not done anything to warrant the abuse they received from their oppressors. The destitute would also have been encouraged to know that the Lord had forgotten neither them nor their terrible plight.

B. Disdaining God's Representatives: vss. 9-12

"I destroyed the Amorite before them, though he was tall as the cedars and strong as the oaks. I destroyed his fruit above and his roots below. I brought you up out of Egypt, and I led you forty years in the desert to give you the land of the Amorites. I also raised up prophets from among your sons and Nazirites from among your young men. Is this not true, people of Israel?" declares the LORD. "But you made the Nazirites drink wine and commanded the prophets not to prophesy."

After describing the moral and religious corruption prevalent in Israel, Amos gave the people a history lesson. First, he reminded them of what God had done to the Amorites (or Canaanites; see Gen. 15:19-21; Josh. 24:11, 15). Their inhabitants once seemed to be as lofty as massive "cedars" (Amos 2:9) and powerful as huge "oaks." In fact, they had occupied Canaan before the arrival of the Israelites. Even though the Amorites appeared to be invincible giants (Num. 13:26-33; Deut. 1:26-28), God had totally wiped out the "fruit" (Amos 2:9) of their branches and completely uprooted their trunk from the ground (Job 18:16; Ezek. 17:9; Hos. 9:16).

Amos next reminded the Israelites of God's past mercies in bringing them out of slavery in "Egypt" (Amos 2:10), leading them for 40 years through the wilderness, and giving them the territory inhabited by the "Amorites" (Exod. 12:17; Num. 21:25; Deut. 8:2). Amos used this information to show how far God's people had fallen from His mercy. Even though the Israelites had sinned, God's grace had opened the way for them to conquer and occupy Canaan. The Lord had given them a verdant land in which to develop a new society based on His laws.

Deliverance from Egypt was for the sake of God's name and so that the Israelites could be His holy people. Yet the Israelites repaid God's goodness by committing further sins, such as coercing the Nazirites to break their vow not to drink wine and gagging the prophets when they tried to declare God's truth (Amos 2:11-12; see also Num. 6:3; Judg. 13:7; Isa. 30:10). The judgments Amos announced were intensified by his referring to God in the first person: "*I* destroyed the Amorite" (Amos 2:9); "*I* brought [Israel] up out of Egypt" (vs. 10); "*I* also raised up prophets" (vs. 11); and "*I* will crush you" (vs. 13).

C. Declaring Disaster: vss. 13-16

"Now then, I will crush you as a cart crushes when loaded with grain. The swift will not escape, the strong will not muster their strength, and the warrior will not save his life. The archer will not stand his ground, the fleet-footed soldier will not get away, and the horseman will not save his life. Even the bravest warriors will flee naked on that day," declares the LORD.

Just as a utility "cart" (Amos 2:13) groaned when bogged down with heavy, mature sheaves of "grain," so too the Lord would press down on the Israelites by allowing them to be thoroughly defeated in battle. No footsoldier, archer, or cavalrymen (including chariot riders) in Israel—not even the fastest, strongest, and bravest among their heroes—would be able to escape or withstand that punishment (vss. 14-16). If the nation's mightiest warriors could not deliver themselves from the impending calamity, what fate awaited the rest of the people? The oracle Amos foretold was the solemn declaration of the Lord.

Discussion Questions

1. Why did God want the people of Judah to obey the teachings of the Mosaic law?
2. In what ways did powerful Israelites deny justice to the destitute?
3. How had the Lord been gracious in the past to His chosen people?
4. Why does God want us to be loving and kind to others in need?
5. What benefits do you see in being ethical with others?

Contemporary Application

God's Word, its truth unchanged through the centuries, still confronts human nature, which also has not changed. While we may not have to confront Canaanite fertility cults in our day, there remain many parallels between our modern culture and ancient Israel. For example, the people of that day despised the law of the Lord. Similarly, many people today scoff at God's Word. The people of ancient Israel embraced the pagan customs of their neighbors rather than the Mosaic law. Likewise, there are many today who have adopted the value system of the world, rather than the ethical standards of God's Word.

Like the people of Amos' time, many today find it difficult to heed the Bible. They resist the idea that Scripture is the ultimate authority on how we should treat others. Some have called the Bible a narrow-minded, unsophisticated book filled with outdated rules and primitive regulations. They say it has no relevance for today, and they do not need God's Word to tell them what to do.

What these people of today do not realize, and what many people of Judah and Israel did not take seriously, is that God offered His Word for our own good in our relationships with others. The Bible provides us with clear principles to follow. Indeed, being faithful to biblical ethics will not only strengthen our faithfulness to God, but will also enrich our relationships with others.

Doing What Is Right

Scripture

Background Scripture: *Amos 5*

Scripture Lesson: *Amos 5:14-15, 18-27*

Key Verse: *"Let justice roll on like a river, righteousness like a never-failing stream!"* Amos 5:24.

Scripture Lesson for Children: *Amos 5:14-15, 18-24*

Key Verse for Children: *Hate evil, love good.* Amos 5:15.

Lesson Aim

To recognize that empty worship does not please God.

Lesson Setting

Time: 760–750 B.C.

Place: Judah and Samaria

Lesson Outline

Doing What Is Right

I. An Exhortation to Repent: Amos 5:14-15
   A. *Seeking What Is Good: vs. 14*
   B. *Promoting What Is Right: vs. 15*

II. A Pronouncement of Divine Judgment: Amos 5:18-27
   A. *A Time of Darkness: vss. 18-20*
   B. *A Rejection of Israel's Religious Festivals: vss. 21-24*
   C. *A Condemnation of Israel's Idolatry: vss. 25-27*

Introduction for Adults

Topic: *Justice Is Not "Just Us"*

A wealthy church member offered his congregation a quarter of a million dollars to build a huge steeple. His offer was declined because such a steeple did not fit the message his church was trying to convey to unbelievers. His was an empty gesture because he had missed the point of his congregation's ministry—that doing what is right for the good of the people comes before building imposing structures.

Amos preached that the spiritual condition of our hearts is more important than how much we put in the offering plate (Amos 5:24). Similarly, Paul taught that even if we give away everything to the poor, but lack love, our offering is meaningless (1 Cor. 13:3).

This is a hard concept to accept, because religious duty is so deeply ingrained in us. That's why Amos is good medicine for our souls. We need to understand what God looks for and what's most important to Him. He wants our love, trust, and obedience, not just our offering of money. The foremost command is to love Him with the totality of our being (Deut. 6:5; Matt. 22:37). When we make that our aim, we will be doing what is right in His eyes.

Introduction for Youth

Topic: *Words Are Cheap*

In Amos' day, it was relatively easy for the Israelites to play the religious game. What they said sounded good, but the way they lived was characterized by evil.

It's also easy for us to pretend we're Christians when we really haven't trusted in Jesus. We want to please our parents, our friends, and our church leaders, so we go along with the game. Perhaps this is one reason why Christian apologist Josh McDowell has asked, *If we were put on trial as a follower of Jesus, would there be enough evidence to convict us?*

At some point, our facade crashes. Sometimes we can put the pieces together. But on other occasions that's not possible. It's better to confess our lack of genuine faith now than to keep pretending otherwise. Besides, God knows us as we truly are, and we cannot fool Him.

Concepts for Children

Topic: *Do What's Right!*

1. Amos took care of sheep.
2. God wanted Amos to tell God's message to the people of Israel.
3. Amos told the people that God wanted them to do what is right.
4. Amos told the people that God wanted them to tell the truth.
5. God is pleased when we obey what the Bible teaches.

Lesson Commentary

I. AN EXHORTATION TO REPENT: *AMOS 5:14-15*

A. Seeking What Is Good: vs. 14

Seek good, not evil, that you may live. Then the LORD God Almighty will be with you, just as you say he is.

In Amos 4, the Lord declared that He would overthrow the Israelites because they persisted in sinning and refused to take advantage of opportunities to repent. God offered a lament for Israel (5:1-3) and called on the nation's inhabitants to change their ways (vss. 4-9). If the people refused to do so, there was coming a time of sadness in the northern kingdom (vss. 16-17). The Lord's judgment of His people was warranted. Consider the fact that injustice prevailed in Israel's court system. When Amos lived, town elders would meet in the city gate (a large passage with adjacent rooms) to resolve legal disputes. God noted that His people hated those who arbitrated in law courts. The Israelites even despised those who spoke truthfully in such settings (vs. 10). In this case, both honest judges and witnesses were detested.

Other examples of the northern kingdom's unjust ways existed. One was the government's insistence on trampling the poor by levying an excessive agricultural tax on their scant crops (vs. 11). Amos is not the only prophet who condemned such injustices. In fact, the exploitation of the poor and needy—a clear violation of the law of Moses (Exod. 23:6-8)—is condemned in several prophetic books (Isa. 1:17; 32:7; Jer. 5:26-29; Mic. 7:3). Meanwhile, the wicked rich built mansions for themselves out of chiseled stone. These expensive structures contrasted with the mud-brick houses of the common people. The wealthy also planted lush vineyards in the countryside (Amos 5:11). Yet the Lord would prevent them from enjoying these symbols of affluence.

Israel's leaders were self-deceived if they thought the Lord was unaware of their rebellious acts. No transgression was too slight and no sin was too minimal. Whether it was tormenting the innocent, taking bribes, or denying the poor of justice in the city gates, God knew everything that occurred, and He refused to look in the other direction (vs. 12). One way of understanding verse 13 is that, because the time was characterized by evil leaders and oppressive practices, the wise kept silent. Such seemed to be the only sensible course of action. Another possibility is that the verse is referring to those who used shrewd tactics to achieve success. In turn, they would lament under the weight of the Lord's judgment. For them, such a time to come would be filled with disaster, not prosperity.

Regardless of how verse 13 is understood, the thrust of verse 14 remains clear. God wanted to avert bringing judgment on His chosen people. And this was possible if they despised evil (including pagan religious practices) and longed for what is right. Promoting justice and shunning lawlessness would lead to life, both temporal and eternal. Undoubtedly, the Israelites wanted the Lord, the Commander of heaven's vast armies, to be with them. Yet this would only be true if they radically amended their ways.

B. Promoting What Is Right: vs. 15

Hate evil, love good; maintain justice in the courts. Perhaps the LORD God Almighty will have mercy on the remnant of Joseph.

Amos 5:15 builds on the emphasis found in verse 14 of seeking what is good by stressing the importance of promoting what is right. For instance, God's spokesperson emphasized the necessity of hating what is vile and loving what is virtuous. The Hebrew verb rendered "hate" denotes a strong abhorrence, in this case for what is morally reprehensible. In contrast, "love" refers to an intense affection, especially for what is upright in character. The point is that "justice," not injustice, was to prevail. This would occur when impartial verdicts in legal disputes were rendered in the city gates. Only then would the all-powerful Creator of heaven and earth be gracious to the upright remnant of Joseph (Isa. 1:9; Joel 2:12-14). Here we see that Joseph, as the most prominent of the 10 northern tribes, represented the entire northern kingdom of Israel.

II. A PRONOUNCEMENT OF DIVINE JUDGMENT: AMOS 5:18-27

A. A Time of Darkness: vss. 18-20

Woe to you who long for the day of the LORD! Why do you long for the day of the LORD? That day will be darkness, not light. It will be as though a man fled from a lion only to meet a bear, as though he entered his house and rested his hand on the wall only to have a snake bite him. Will not the day of the LORD be darkness, not light—pitch-dark, without a ray of brightness?

Because the Israelites had turned away from God, within a generation He would take their nation away from them and scatter the survivors into foreign exile. Amos 5:16 depicts this episode in Israel's history as a time of "wailing" in every street and "cries of anguish" in the open plazas for all the people who perished. Field workers would be exhorted to "weep" and professional "mourners" would be urged to "wail." Verse 17 foretells that even in the "vineyards" there would be lamenting, for the sovereign Lord would pass through and destroy these agricultural estates (the exact opposite experience of the Passover narrative recorded in Exod. 12:12, 23).

Against the backdrop of the preceding declarations, God's spokesperson challenged the Israelites' glibness and smugness about the "day of the LORD" (Amos 5:18). The latter concept runs throughout the prophetic writings. For instance, in the Book of Joel, the day of the Lord is the time of Israel's final redemption, when God would "pour out [His] Spirit on all people" (2:28) and "restore the fortunes of Judah and Jerusalem" (3:1). Here we see that the Israelites saw this time as something like the Exodus, when God destroyed His enemies and brought His people to safety.

Evidently, then, the people expected that God would punish other nations but deliver Israel on the day of the Lord. So, the Israelites were looking forward to that time. But Amos explained that what they longed for would not be a bright episode of deliverance for them. Instead, it would be an ominous occasion of judgment for them. As Christians, we should remember that the New Testament "day of the Lord"—which refers to the second coming of the Savior—will also bring judgment and destruction upon the earth, as well as the glory of Jesus' eternal kingdom.

God's spokesperson used two vivid metaphors to illustrate the intensity of the day of the Lord. First, that time of judgment would be comparable to people running away in terror from a "lion" (Amos 5:19), but encountering a "bear." Falling prey to either animal would be equally life threatening. Second, the period of distress was like individuals escaping to their home. But just when they thought they could safely rest one of their hands on a "wall," a "snake" would unexpectedly appear from a crevice and bite them. In short, the episode would be characterized by gloomy "darkness" (vs. 20), not a bright "ray" of light.

On one level, Amos' concern involved the coming destruction of Israel by the Assyrians, which occurred about 723 B.C. Yet, on another level, the prophet's words might refer to what would happen to the wicked Israelites of his generation (along with all other reprehensible people) in the end times, such as when they are resurrected for final judgment (John 5:28-29; Rev. 20:12). At any rate, Amos implied that if the Israelites did not dispense with their incorrect theology about the day of the Lord, they were in for an unpleasant shock.

B. A Rejection of Israel's Religious Festivals: vss. 21-24

"I hate, I despise your religious feasts; I cannot stand your assemblies. Even though you bring me burnt offerings and grain offerings, I will not accept them. Though you bring choice fellowship offerings, I will have no regard for them. Away with the noise of your songs! I will not listen to the music of your harps. But let justice roll on like a river, righteousness like a never-failing stream!"

Beginning in Amos 5:21, we read the Lord's own declaration that He loathed the Israelites' religious practices. The Hebrew verb rendered "hate" is the same one used in verse 15. Added to this is the verb translated "despise" (vs. 21), which can also be rendered "spurn" or "abhor." Together, these terms indicate that God absolutely rejected His people's idolatrous festivals (Isa. 1:11-14). Even their religious "assemblies" (Amos 5:21) brought Him no pleasure, being more like a putrid stench than a sweet-smelling aroma. So, whether it was informal times of celebration or formal gatherings for corporate worship, the Lord equally detested the way in which the Israelites observed them (Jer. 6:20).

Amos 5:22 singles out three of the five major kinds of offerings prescribed in the Mosaic law. The "burnt" offering could be a bull, ram, or bird that was

wholly consumed by the fire. It was used to show worship, to atone for unintentional sins, and to express commitment to God (Lev. 1; 6:8-13). The "grain"
(Amos 5:22) offering consisted of cereal grasses, flour, oil, incense, bread, and
salt. It was offered to show worship, to recognize God's goodness, and to express
commitment to God (Lev. 2; 6:14-23). The "fellowship" (Amos 5:22; or peace)
offering could be bread or an animal. It was given to show worship, express
thanks, and promote mutual well-being (Lev. 3; 7:11-34).

Israel also had several festivals to commemorate different events in their history. For instance, the Sabbath was celebrated once a week as a time for rest and
worship. Many restrictions on activity were placed upon people for the Sabbath
day. The New Moon festival was observed monthly and was marked by burnt
offerings and the loud blasts of trumpets. The purpose of this holy day was to
celebrate Israel's unity.

The Passover was an annual festival that commemorated Israel's deliverance
from Egyptian bondage. Passover came to be called the Feast of Unleavened
Bread (though the two were originally distinct), since only bread without yeast
was eaten during the first seven days after the Passover. The Feast of Weeks was
another annual festival. Alternate names for this feast include Pentecost and
the Day of Firstfruits. It celebrated the harvest at the completion of seven weeks,
or 50 days (hence the name Pentecost; see Acts 2:1).

The day of Atonement was an additional annual festival. This event focused
on Israel's sinfulness and the people's need to be reconciled with Yahweh (the
covenant name of Israel's God). Today the feast is known as Yom Kippur. The
Feast of Tabernacles was the last of Israel's annual ceremonies. During the seven
days of this festival, people lived in small booths, or tabernacles, to commemorate God's protection and provision. The Feast of Trumpets, or Rosh Hashanah,
celebrated the coming of the new year.

The Lord declared that when the corrupt and hypocritical Israelites brought
to Him various kinds of sacrificial offerings, He would neither accept nor look
upon them with favor (Amos 5:22). Even the performance of sacred music had
become odious to God. Whether songs delivered by a choir or music played on
stringed instruments (such as viols, lyres, or lutes), He refused to listen (vs. 23).
Of course, God had ordained the rituals of worship. Nonetheless, they were
supposed to support personal righteousness, not replace it. The people were
acting as though they worshiped the Lord, but in fact their human relationships
indicated otherwise. For this reason, their external signs of worship, far from
pleasing God, infuriated Him.

The Lord desired real signs of faith and obedience. Also, that is why He
wanted "justice" (vs. 24) to flow like a "river" and upright acts like a "stream"
that never ran dry. The arid Middle East has many riverbeds called wadis,
where water flows only after a rain. Unlike these wadis, Israelite society was to
flow continually with equity for people and rectitude toward God. In the Bible,

the concept of "righteousness" is essentially the same as holiness. Central to the meaning of both words is the idea of acting in harmony with God's character. When this is done by faith, one enjoys a right relationship both with God and with other believers. Accordingly, if "justice" and "righteousness" did not prevail in the religious life of Israel (Matt. 25:31-46; James 1:27; 1 John 3:17-18), not even the remnant could hope to survive the coming time of divine judgment.

Fundamentally, the outworking of righteousness in Scripture is presented in the language of the law court. In the Old Testament period, God sat as Judge while Israel stood before Him as the accused. The laws the Israelites were indicted for breaking were the terms of the covenant agreement the Lord had graciously made with His people (Ps. 9:4; Isa. 33:15; Jer. 11:20; 1 Pet. 2:23). Our religious practices are different from those of the Israelites, and yet we share a common problem with them. We must be careful that we do not come to rely only on external religious acts. God looks beneath the surface of our lives and wants to see that we love His Son and have an enduring commitment to justice.

C. A Condemnation of Israel's Idolatry: vss. 25-27

"Did you bring me sacrifices and offerings forty years in the desert, O house of Israel? You have lifted up the shrine of your king, the pedestal of your idols, the star of your god—which you made for yourselves. Therefore I will send you into exile beyond Damascus," says the LORD, whose name is God Almighty.

Amos 5:25-27 records God's condemnation of Israel's idolatry. Admittedly, some of the details in these verses are debatable, but the basic sense is discernable. The Israelites did not truly worship the Lord. So, He was going to send them into exile far from their homeland. The Hebrew construction of verse 25 indicates that the question God posed demanded a negative response. Specifically, the Israelites of the wilderness generation (more than 600 years before Amos) did not offer sacrifices to the Lord.

Yet Scripture indicates that sacrifices were actually offered on at least two occasions during the wilderness wandering (Exod. 24:4-5; Num. 7). Bible scholars resolve this apparent discrepancy by suggesting that sacrifices were not offered on a regular basis until the nation settled in Canaan. More than one explanation has been given for the reason God posed this question. According to one view, the point is that Israelite disobedience toward God began as early as the wilderness generation. According to another view, the point is that the wilderness generation demonstrated that a relationship between the people and their God was not dependent on the sacrificial system.

Amos 5:26 confirms other Old Testament passages showing that Israelites were involved with false worship. However, it's debated whether the false worship condemned in this verse occurred in the wilderness or in Israel during Amos' time. Some scholars suggest that the Hebrew noun translated "shrine" refers to Sakkuth, the Assyrian god of war who brought either defeat or victory in battle. Others think the noun rendered "pedestal" is associated with Kaiwan, the Mesopotamian deity for the planet Saturn. In any case, the text indicates that the Israelites performed pagan religious ceremonies, probably parading detestable images fixed to the tops of poles (Jer. 8:2; Acts 7:43).

Amos 5:26 also implies that it was foolish of the Israelites to worship idols they had made with their own hands. After all, these objects were powerless and lifeless. Moreover, Israel's idols could not rescue them from God's judgment. For the people's sins, the Commander in Chief of the heavenly host would exile the Israelites "beyond Damascus" (vs. 27). This refers to their deportation to Assyria. From the northern kingdom's perspective, Assyria was located east of Damascus (Syria's capital) on the trade routes of the Fertile Crescent.

Discussion Questions

1. How could the Israelites foster the practice of fairness within their society?
2. Why should believers detest what is evil?
3. Why would God bring anguish on the inhabitants of Israel?
4. Why did God despise Israel's religious festivals?
5. How can believers ensure that their times of worship are pleasing to the Lord?

Contemporary Application

Reading Amos is like reading the newspaper. Corruption, bribery, immorality, and false religion make the headlines every day. We have come to expect such things in the world at large. But there's a big difference between reading the prophecies of Amos and reading the newspaper. Amos revealed not just the sins of the ungodly nations, but also the sins of God's people.

Regardless of whether we are thinking about ancient Israel or contemporary society, sin still separates people from God. The Lord offers His Word, the Bible, to us so that we can live in the way He originally intended. When we follow the ethical precepts of Scripture, our relationship with God is strengthened, not weakened.

The task of being ethical and encouraging others to do the same can sometimes feel overwhelming to us. Remember that just as God used a simple shepherd like Amos to make a significant difference in his generation, so too He can use us to make an impact on our society. Also, just as God gave Amos the strength to obey His ethical standards, so too He enables us to be upright in all our dealings with others.

Ending Complacency

Scripture

Background Scripture: *Amos 6*
Scripture Lesson: *Amos 6:4-8, 11-14*
Key Verse: *You have turned justice into poison and the fruit of righteousness into bitterness.* Amos 6:12.
Scripture Lesson for Children: *Amos 6:4-8, 11-14*
Key Verse for Children: *You have turned justice into poison.* Amos 6:12.

Lesson Aim

To note that smugness and greed have no place in the lives of believers.

Lesson Setting

Time: 760–750 B.C.
Place: Judah and Samaria

Lesson Outline

Ending Complacency

   I. An End to Complacency: Amos 6:4-7
      A. *Acting Smugly: vss. 4-6*
      B. *Facing Exile: vs. 7*
  II. Israel's Impending Defeat: Amos 6:8, 11-14
      A. *The Lord's Abhorrence of Israel's Pride: vs. 8*
      B. *The Overthrow of Israel: vss. 11-14*

Introduction for Adults

Topic: *A Deadly Trio: Selfishness, Greed, and Pride*

Amos 6 reveals that human relationships change when hoarding wealth becomes more important than anything else in life. For instance, friends are looked upon as business contacts. A spouse is regarded as an additional source of income to maintain an elevated standard of living.

Even children are affected by a greed culture, and look upon parents as sources for handouts. Instead of young children learning to help spontaneously or to show kindness without being rewarded, they are often programmed to expect or demand payment for any good deed they might perform. Ultimately, their behavior becomes based on the money that's given to them.

The greed and money lust in our society affects other relationships besides in those families. A preoccupation with amassing possessions makes us prone to bargaining rather than sharing. We learn to calculate what we will do in terms of what it will cost us and what the payoff will be. As we discover from this week's lesson, the best way to break this insidious cycle is to put the Lord first in our lives.

Introduction for Youth

Topic: *Greed Won't Win*

In Amos' day, Israel was divided into two classes: the haves and the have-nots. Those in the first group thought only about themselves and were indifferent to the struggles faced by the second group. God used Amos to censure the ruling elite in Samaria for their smug, indulgent ways.

In his book *Come Before Winter*, Charles R. Swindoll writes, "I don't have many temptations to worship evil things. It's the good things that plague me. It isn't as difficult for me to reject something that is innately bad or wrong as it is to keep those good and wholesome things off the throne."

Although many teens try to meet the demands of living, they seem to pile up like unfolded laundry. Since each day has only 24 hours, Christian young people need to be selective. Meanwhile, their use of the time and energy that God gives them indicates where their priorities lie. This week's Scripture lesson will help young people to understand how they can spend their time and energy in ways that have eternal value.

Concepts for Children

Topic: *Let's Not Be Selfish*

1. The people of Israel were being selfish.
2. We act selfishly when we only care about ourselves.
3. God warned His people about thinking they were better than others.
4. God wanted His people to care about others around them.
5. God is pleased when we share what we have with others.

Lesson Commentary

I. An End to Complacency: *Amos 6:4-7*

A. Acting Smugly: vss. 4-6

You lie on beds inlaid with ivory and lounge on your couches. You dine on choice lambs and fattened calves. You strum away on your harps like David and improvise on musical instruments. You drink wine by the bowlful and use the finest lotions, but you do not grieve over the ruin of Joseph.

Amos 5:18–6:14 presents a litany of somber oracles preceded by the interjection "Woe" (5:18; 6:1). The term means "to cry out against someone or something" and was often used when expressing intense sorrow for the dead (1 Kings 13:30; Jer. 22:18; 34:5; Amos 5:16). As we learned last week, Amos summoned the inhabitants of Israel to mourn over the impending doom they would experience. God was about to judge them for their blatant and unrelenting violations of the Mosaic law. The Lord especially loathed their detestable religious practices. He also took no delight in the offerings they made at their pagan shrines.

Amos 6:1 draws attention to "Zion" and "Mount Samaria" (Mic. 1:5-9). Zion was another name for the temple mount in Jerusalem, the capital of Judah. Zion is first mentioned in 2 Samuel 5:7 as a Jebusite fortress on a hill. After being captured by David, this fortress was called the City of David. Here, Israel's monarch brought the ark of the covenant, thereby making the hill a sacred site (6:10-12). Later, in Israelite theology, Zion became a symbol of the place where the ever-present Creator defended the righteous by vanquishing their foes. Even though Amos' prophetic ministry was primarily directed to Israel, what he condemned also applied to Judah (see Amos 2:4-5 and the Bible lesson commentary appearing in lesson 1).

The mountains of Samaria (3:9; 4:1) refer to the geographic region surrounding the capital of Israel, which was located in the central highlands of the northern kingdom and the locale for pagan shrines (1 Kings 16:24; Isa. 10:11; Mic. 1:6-7). The city of Samaria was about 40 miles north of Jerusalem and 25 miles east of the Mediterranean Sea. On the upside, the capital was over 400 feet above sea level and strategically positioned along the Via Maris, a major trade route connecting Syria with Egypt. On the downside, Samaria lacked an adequate source of fresh drinking water. In fact, the inhabitants had to rely upon a cistern to bring water from a spring about a mile away.

The first half of Amos 6:1 censured those in Judah who felt at ease and rebuked Israel for their false sense of security. Then, in the second half of the verse, the focus shifts entirely to the northern kingdom. The Hebrew verb translated "notable" refers to Israel's overly confident leaders, who thought of themselves as an elite group of princes to whom the nation's inhabitants turned for insight and guidance. Such an arrogant view is reinforced by the reference to Israel as the "foremost nation" among its peers. The ruling class in Samaria refused to consider that other stronger, nearby nations would fall to the onslaught of the Assyrian juggernaut.

Verse 2 draws attention to several "kingdoms" north and south of Israel. Calneh was in south-central Mesopotamia, Hamath was located in northern Syria, and Gath was one of the five cities belonging to Philistines near the coast of southern Canaan. The territory belonging to these cities was not larger than that of Samaria. Likewise, Israel and Judah were no better off than their neighbors. All of them would be subject to the conquest of foreign invaders (for example, Assyria and Babylon). Despite this harsh reality, the leaders of the northern and southern kingdoms deluded themselves into thinking the prophesied time of calamity either would not occur or would happen in the far distant future (Ezek. 12:27).

This false hope bolstered Israel to establish a "reign of terror" (Amos 6:3), which included abuse of the poor. The Lord, through His spokesperson, condemned Samaria's haughty and wicked rulers. While many in the northern kingdom were destitute and suffered mistreatment, their leaders indulged themselves with wealth they had stolen from the poor. According to 3:15, the wicked rich owned summer and winter homes filled with panels and furniture "adorned" with expensive "ivory." Even the "beds" (6:4) on which they reclined were decorated with "ivory." Moreover, they pampered themselves by loafing on "couches." Even worse, they satiated their cravings by feasting on tender "lambs" from the flock and the finest "calves" from the middle of the stall.

The individuals of privilege and rank in Israel congratulated themselves for being as musically gifted as King David (1 Sam. 16:15-23; 2 Sam. 23:1). For instance, Samaria's leaders chanted frivolous songs as they played music on their lyres and lutes. They even thought of themselves as artistic geniuses who created original tunes and strummed them on "musical instruments" they allegedly invented. All the while, they ingested "wine" (vs. 6) from large, costly, sacrificial basins and anointed their bodies with the "finest" scented, perfumed ointments. Tragically, these same decadent princes neither were saddened by the moral decay of their nation nor lamented the impending judgment that was about to fall on the northern kingdom. "Joseph" refers to two of the tribes of Israel, Manasseh and Ephraim (5:6). They were descended from Jacob's son Joseph.

B. Facing Exile: vs. 7

Therefore you will be among the first to go into exile; your feasting and lounging will end.

As noted in the previous two lessons, when Amos lived, Assyria and other potential enemies of the Hebrew people were in a relatively weak condition. This state of affairs allowed Judah and Israel to enjoy a period of economic prosperity and political expansion. From Amos' words it seems that leaders in the two capitals, instead of humbly thanking and obeying God because of their good fortune, prided themselves on their accomplishments and became egotistical.

Moreover, the Israelites whom Amos addressed were living on a material level far above that of the common people. At night, the poor slept on floor mats, while the rich lay about much of the time on fine couches and beds. The poor might go months without being able to afford meat, but the rich regularly ate the best kinds of meat. The poor worked all day just to scrape by, while the rich could spend their time idly dabbling in music. The poor would drink a cup of wine occasionally, but the rich were in the habit of drinking wine by the bowlful. The poor occasionally poured a little oil on their heads to kill the lice, while the rich used the finest lotions when they wanted an anointing. We should note that the practices Amos decried might not have been wrong in themselves. Yet they became vile when they were taken to an extreme and were done at the expense of the impoverished.

The first part of Amos 6:7 is literally translated, "They will go into exile at the head of the exiles." Put differently, among a large number of peoples whom the Assyrians conquered and uprooted from their homelands, the invaders would first lead away the inhabitants of the northern kingdom as their captives. Indeed, the wicked rich in Samaria would be at the front of the long caravans of shackled refugees whom the Assyrians deported. This gloomy outcome would abruptly end the Israelite nobles' pagan religious banquets. Ironically, the upper class—who prided themselves on being first among the nations—would soon be banned from their estates. Also, existence as the slaves of the brutal Assyrians would not be nearly as pleasant as the life the princes of Samaria had taken for granted.

II. ISRAEL'S IMPENDING DEFEAT: AMOS 6:8, 11-14

A. The Lord's Abhorrence of Israel's Pride: vs. 8

The Sovereign LORD has sworn by himself—the LORD God Almighty declares: "I abhor the pride of Jacob and detest his fortresses; I will deliver up the city and everything in it."

In Amos 6:8, the Hebrew phrases rendered the "Sovereign Lord" and the "Lord God Almighty" depicted the Creator as the invincible, divine Warrior and un-contested moral Governor of the universe. Through His spokesperson, God let the Israelites know more about the destruction He would soon be sending their way. It would be a complete defeat for the inhabitants of Samaria. They thought they were safe. Yet, before long, the Assyrians would be beating down Samaria's gates.

To strengthen the credibility and finality of what the Lord had to say, Amos explained that God had sworn an oath on His own authority. First, He announced that He loathed Jacob's arrogance, as seen in the complacency of the northern kingdom's leaders. Second, God declared that He despised the nobility's fortress-like citadels, which they trusted for safety. So, on the one hand, the Israelites were confident their military readiness would be enough to protect them. On the other hand, God would allow foreigners to thoroughly destroy "the city" (probably the capital, Samaria). This meant that all of Israel would be vulnerable to the invaders.

In the ancient world, people took an oath to back up a statement's truthfulness. Oaths were used as a guarantee that a promise would be kept. Sometimes they were even used as evidence in court. Oath takers often called for some punishment to be inflicted upon them if they broke the oath. Israelites would swear by someone greater than themselves, usually their monarch or the Lord. God adapted Himself to a human custom by sometimes making an oath as a guarantee of performance (Heb. 6:17). When His oath was accompanied by a promise of blessing, it was given for assurance. With a promise of judgment, the divine oath amounted to a curse. Since there was no one greater, the Lord swore by Himself (Amos 4:2; 6:8; 8:7).

B. The Overthrow of Israel: vss. 11-14

For the LORD has given the command, and he will smash the great house into pieces and the small house into bits. Do horses run on the rocky crags? Does one plow there with oxen? But you have turned justice into poison and the fruit of righteousness into bitterness—you who rejoice in the conquest of Lo Debar and say, "Did we not take Karnaim by our own strength?" For the LORD God Almighty declares, "I will stir up a nation against you, O house of Israel, that will oppress you all the way from Lebo Hamath to the valley of the Arabah."

After the lines of poetry in Amos 6:8 comes their prose amplification in verses 9 and 10. In a general sense, this passage describes a hypothetical situation in which at first only a small number of people evaded an onslaught, but afterward the enemy killed the rest of the survivors. In a specific sense, verse 9 is understood in at least three different ways: (1) only ten persons remained in a large, wealthy home; (2) only ten members of a household were left alive; or (3) only ten soldiers of an army unit found refuge in a solitary house not destroyed by the invaders.

The exact meaning of verse 10 is also debated. The first part is literally rendered "a man's kinsmen and his burner." Most likely, the same person is being referred to, namely, a relative who is responsible for removing the corpses of the deceased from the house. In turn, this individual would either cremate the dead or burn a memorial fire to honor them before burying the bodies (Jer. 34:5). The second part of Amos 6:10 pictures a lone survivor who is trembling in fear within an inner room of a house and being asked whether there are any other persons alive with him. At first, he answers "no." But then, he urges those who are outside to remain quiet and not call upon the "name of the Lord" (either to ask for a divine blessing on the dead or to request additional help from God). Evidently, the situation would be so traumatic that it would feel too risky to invoke God's name and bring down further judgment on the group (Isa. 48:1).

In Amos 6:11, the poetry resumes with a vivid statement that the sovereign Commander of heaven's armies had issued the decree for the adversary to invade and destroy Samaria. In turn, the Assyrians would pulverize the "great" houses of the rich (undoubtedly financed with stolen wealth) and the "small" homes of the poor. Put differently, the destruction would be so thorough that no household in the northern kingdom would be spared by God's hand of judgment rendered through His instrument, the Assyrians.

The next stanza begins with two ludicrous questions, both of which demanded a negative answer. First, it was preposterous for "horses" (vs. 12) to gallop over jagged, vertical rocks, for the animals would either be severely injured or killed. Also, it was absurd for a farmer to use "oxen" to cultivate boulders. After all, doing so would maim the animals. Despite that, Israel's leaders were guilty of perverting the moral order the Creator intended for the world. For instance, by denying "justice" to the innocent, the wicked rich subverted the restorative potential of the law courts and made it into a poisonous plant. Also, the corrupt rulers so misused the judicial system that what should have been the sweet "fruit" of upright actions literally turned out to be "wormwood," that is, a bitter herb (5:7).

At Mount Sinai, God had made a covenant with the Israelites. Also, He had given them the Mosaic law so that they would know what He expected from them. Moreover, He had shown them mercy after mercy. Yet, despite all this, the upper class of Israel was leading the way in unrighteous behavior. Mixed up with the Israelites' injustice was their pride. Verse 13 describes them as rejoicing in their overthrow of "Lo Debar" and "Karnaim." The first town was located in Gilead near where the Yarmuk River joined the Jordan River, while the second town was situated about 23 miles east of the Sea of Galilee. Evidently, both of these cities were captured or recaptured from the Syrians by the Israelite king, Jeroboam II, during his campaigns of expansion (2 Kings 14:25-28).

Most likely, Amos 6:13 mentions the two preceding towns because of the meanings of their names. The prophet deliberately misspelled the name of "Lo Debar," or Debir, so that it literally meant "no word," that is, "not a thing." The implication is that the Lord regarded as nothing the minor victory over which Israel rejoiced. Also, the name translated "Karnaim" comes from a Hebrew noun meaning "horns." Since horns were a symbol of strength in the ancient Near East (1 Kings 22:11), "Karnaim" (Amos 6:13) probably appears in this verse because the Israelites assumed their victories were achieved by their own military might. Pride in accomplishments becomes sin when it is divorced from recognizing one's dependence upon God. The Israelites were not wrong to celebrate their successes. Their failure lay in taking credit for achievements that God had accomplished through them.

Before long, the Israelites' pride in their conquests would be obliterated. This is due to the fact that the all-powerful Commander of the heavenly host would bring an adversary, the Assyrian Empire, against the entire northern kingdom. The invaders would completely defeat the "house of Israel" (vs. 14) from one end of its border to the next. In particular, the advancing armies would over-run the Israelites from the northernmost extent of their control, represented by "Lebo Hamath" (on the Orontes River in the valley between the Lebanon and Anti-Lebanon mountains), to the southernmost extent of their control, represented by the "valley of the Arabah" (in the far south between the Dead Sea and the Gulf of Aqabah).

Discussion Questions

1. In what ways were the upper class of Israel acting self-indulgently?
2. Why did the Lord detest Israel's fortified citadels?
3. Why would God allow all the homes of the rich and poor in Israel to be destroyed?
4. How are Christian standards of success different from those of the world?
5. How might believers use their wealth or influence responsibly?

Contemporary Application

Amos 6 reveals the futility of striving for things. We learn from the judgment oracles of Amos that the Lord does not accept our divided affection. This is especially so when it comes to deciding who or what is the ruler of our lives. We must choose either our Creator or our possessions. We cannot live for both.

"We seldom think of what we have, but always of what we lack," wrote the 19th-century German philosopher Arthur Schopenhauer. He was probably de-scribing the mind-set of most people. Sadly, at times even Christians succumb to this skewed way of thinking.

Our society constantly bombards us with commercials and advertisements that try to entice us into believing there's something else we need to possess in order to be truly happy. Yet, despite the benefits of having a credit card, lots of people are inundated with debt. It's too easy for them to charge something else they wanted but couldn't afford on one of their half-dozen credit cards.

To counteract an addiction to affluence and the smugness it produces, believ-ers should regularly stop and ask themselves, "Am I living for things or for the Savior? Am I placing too much confidence in things and not enough in the Creator, who sustains me?" A failure on our part to wrestle with these sorts of questions inevitably will undermine our precious communion with the Lord. As Jesus warned, the value of a person's life is not calculated by adding up his or her possessions (Luke 12:15).

Answering to God

Scripture

Background Scripture: *Amos 8*

Scripture Lesson: *Amos 8:1-6, 9-10*

Key Verse: *"What do you see, Amos?" [God] asked. "A basket of ripe fruit," I answered. Then the Lord said to me, "The time is ripe for my people Israel; I will spare them no longer."* Amos 8:2.

Scripture Lesson for Children: *Amos 8:1-6, 9-10*

Key Verse for Children: *[God said,] "I will never forget anything [Israel has] done."* Amos 8:7.

Lesson Aim

To have the courage to speak out against sinful behavior.

Lesson Setting

Time: 760–750 B.C.

Place: Judah and Samaria

Lesson Outline

Answering to God

  I. The Reason for Israel's Judgment: Amos 8:1-6
      A. *A Vision of Ripe Fruit: vss. 1-2*
      B. *A Time of Wailing: vs. 3*
      C. *Acts of Injustice: vss. 4-6*
  II. The Reversal of Israel's Fortunes: Amos 8:9-10
      A. *Darkness over the Land: vs. 9*
      B. *A Time of Intense Mourning: vs. 10*

Introduction for Adults

Topic: *Sin Has Its Consequences*

The people of Amos' day faced a real dilemma. On the one hand, a small group within society enjoyed considerable wealth and privilege. On the other hand, a much larger group struggled to survive the daily grind of impoverishment. Amos called on the ruling class to abandon their worldly ways, beginning with their neglect and abuse of the poor.

Evidently, an intense fear of giving up power and influence prevented the elitists from doing what was right. We sometimes hear the expression "scared stiff." This is an insight about the nature of fear. It wants to paralyze us and take all the action right out of us. If we allow it, it will keep us from taking any risks at all. This especially includes setting aside our wealth and influence for the betterment of the disadvantaged living around us.

Paralyzing fear, worry, and any other self-imposed limitations must be faced for what they are—the opposite of virtuous faith. John knew what it was like for believers to see only their limitations. That is why the apostle encouraged us by saying that "everyone born of God overcomes the world. This is the victory that has overcome the world, even our faith" (1 John 5:4).

Introduction for Youth

Topic: *God's Unchanging Standard*

For many years, running the four-minute mile was held as the ultimate in human athletic performance. Then, on May 6, 1954, Roger Bannister, a 25-year-old British medical student, made history.

While Bannister was running at Iffley Road near Oxford, he broke the standard. As about 3,000 enthusiastic spectators watched, he set a record with 3 minutes 59.4 seconds. The fans went wild when his time was announced. However, the new standard didn't last long. Only 46 days later, an Australian named John Landy knocked 1.5 seconds off the time and established a new world record.

Human standards rapidly change (especially in the arena of sports). Amos reminded his readers that only one standard was permanent—God's. All of us must look to His standard and, with His help, seek to live by it every day.

Concepts for Children

Topic: *God Warns His People*

1. God's people in Israel did many bad things.
2. God often reminded the people to be nice to each other.
3. God was sad because the people chose to be mean.
4. God said that He was going to punish the people.
5. God is pleased when we choose to do what is good.

Lesson Commentary

I. THE REASON FOR ISRAEL'S JUDGMENT: AMOS 8:1-6

A. A Vision of Ripe Fruit: vss. 1-2

This is what the Sovereign LORD showed me: a basket of ripe fruit. "What do you see, Amos?" he asked. "A basket of ripe fruit," I answered. Then the LORD said to me, "The time is ripe for my people Israel; I will spare them no longer."

Amos continued to warn the Israelites about the judgment God would soon be sending their way. Specifically, the prophet related to them four visions. The first two visions—locusts (7:1-3) and fire (vss. 4-6)—both present judgments God agreed to withhold. The third and fourth visions—a plumb line (vss. 7-9) and ripe fruit (8:1-3)—both present judgments God would send.

The plague of locusts is similar to the infestation Joel 1 described. The short-horned grasshoppers were probably migratory or desert locusts. Amos realized that God would dispatch a vast swarm of locusts to attack the northern kingdom. This occurred after the king had received his portion of the grain but before the rest of the crops had been harvested (Amos 7:1). Indeed, the locusts consumed the second crop before the people could do so (vs. 2). Evidently, in Amos' day, Jeroboam II of Israel required that the first harvest of grain (usually done in April, after the rains) be given to him to support his large royal, military, and governmental establishment. This was a kind of tax. A little later in the season, the farmers harvested for themselves what grew up after the first harvest.

Sometimes large numbers of locusts would hatch in the springtime. Then they gathered in swarms and attacked cultivated areas. If the locusts devastated the fields before the Israelites could get the second crop harvested, the people would not have enough grain to feed their cattle through the coming winter months. Amos fully understood what human suffering would be caused by the loss of the second crop, so he interceded on behalf of the Israelites. He cried out to the Lord to forgive the people of the northern kingdom. Amos pointed out that the nation of Israel (referred to as "Jacob") could not survive God's wrath, since it was small in comparison to Him. God responded to His spokesperson's prayer by deciding not to send a locust plague to wipe out Israel's second crop.

Amos' second vision consisted of destruction produced by fire. Amos learned that the judgment God was preparing would consume the depths of the ocean (possibly the Mediterranean Sea), as well as the farm land of Israel (vs. 4). As with the vision of locusts, Amos responded to the second vision by interceding with God on behalf of the Israelites (vs. 5). This time, however, the prophet simply asked God to put a stop to the judgment. Amos once more pointed out that Israel could not survive such a decree, for the nation was frail. The Lord again responded to Amos' prayer by deciding not use fire to incinerate Israel (vs. 6).

Amos' third vision was of a plumb line, which was a builder's tool made of a cord with a stone or metal weight (called a plumb or plumb bob) at the end. When suspended next to a wall, a plumb line could be used to check how close the pitch of a wall was to true vertical. Amos saw the Lord positioned right next to the wall to determine whether it was still straight (vs. 7). The meaning of this sight is made clear by the conversation recorded in verse 8. The plumb line represented God's holy standard of morality contained in the Mosaic law and revealed how out of alignment Israel was in her priorities and actions.

The Lord got Amos to state what was in His hand: a plumb line. Then the Lord said, "Look, I am setting a plumb line among my people Israel" (vs. 8). This meant, symbolically, that God would check the Israelites to see how faithful they were to Him. In short, the northern kingdom would fail the test, for it was out of plumb spiritually due to the unfaithfulness of its rulers and inhabitants to the divine covenant. So, God was now determined to judge the nation. After the earlier visions, Amos had successfully pleaded for mercy on behalf of the Israelites. But now there was no point in him doing so. God refused to overlook His people's transgressions, and He would not step back from His decision.

Verse 9 details that God would destroy the "high places of Isaac," the "sanctuaries of Israel," and the "house of Jeroboam." The nation's religious establishment was corrupted by faithlessness and idolatry, while the governmental establishment was characterized by disobedience to God. Accordingly, now God would ruin both. Probably fewer than 40 years passed before this vision's prediction of devastation was fulfilled. When the Assyrians came against Israel about 723 B.C., they destroyed the places where the Israelites venerated their pagan deities. It did not even take that long before the royal line (or dynasty) to which Jeroboam belonged was cut off. Jeroboam himself seems to have died of natural causes around 753 B.C. (2 Kings 14:29), but his son and successor, Zechariah, reigned only half a year before being assassinated (15:10).

Since Amos' four visions (locusts, fire, plumb line, and ripe fruit) are closely related, one might expect them to follow one right after another. But that's not the case. Instead, between the third and fourth visions comes a historical passage (Amos 7:10-17). God's spokesperson had been delivering most, if not all, his prophecies in Bethel, one of Israel's two main religious centers. (The other one was Dan.) At that time, the head of Bethel's priestly establishment was Amaziah. Not surprisingly, he did not like what the foreigner from the south was declaring. Perhaps Amaziah was most upset at the statements about Bethel that Amos had communicated for God (3:14; 4:4; 5:4-6).

When Amaziah heard Amos' vision of the plumb line, he thought he had a way to dislodge the prophet from Bethel. Amaziah wrote to King Jeroboam II, accusing Amos of plotting against the monarch at the religious epicenter of the northern kingdom (7:10). The provocative wording of the charge was intended to grab the attention of the king. If he was like most rulers, he was constantly on the alert to learn about attempts at rebellion. In his communication to

Jeroboam, Amaziah quoted Amos as predicting the monarch's death and the Israelites' exile (vs. 11). For the first part, Amos had declared that God would raise a sword against Jeroboam's house (vs. 9), whereas Amaziah quoted Amos as saying Jeroboam himself would die by the sword (vs. 11). For the second part, Amaziah accurately communicated the prophet's warning of exile for the nation (5:5, 27).

We don't know what reply, if any, the priest received from Jeroboam. Probably if the king was convinced that Amos posed a threat to his reign, Jeroboam would have ordered the prophet killed. Yet we have no historical evidence that Amos was murdered. On his own initiative, Amaziah derogatorily referred to Amos as a "seer" (7:12) or "visionary" and ordered him to leave Bethel. The priest also ordered Amos to go back home to Judah and earn his living there as a prophet. Evidently, Amaziah suspected that Amos came to Bethel to make money. In that day, prophets sometimes received support by donations from those who heard their pronouncements. Amaziah asserted that one of Israel's major shrines, along with the king's palace, were in Bethel (vs. 13). While true, this description contained a veiled threat that royal power might be used to cleanse the city of the offending prophet.

Amos responded by defending his own prophetic ministry (vss. 14-15) and then prophesying against Amaziah (vss. 16-17). First, Amos stated that he was a layperson, not a professional prophet. He had a thriving agricultural business (namely, herding flocks and tending sycamore fig trees) when God had called him to prophesy to Israel. So Amos did not need money from that activity. Also, since God had appointed Amos as His spokesperson, Amos would not dodge his responsibility. Moreover, even though Amaziah tried to silence Amos, the prophet would not be deterred from his God-given task.

Amos not only had a prophecy for Israel, but also for Amaziah. (Evidently, this oracle was fulfilled at the time of the Assyrian invasion.) Amaziah would be captured and taken away to spend the remainder of his days in "a pagan country" (vs. 17). Since the Hebrew adjective rendered "pagan" literally means "impure," this was a particularly humiliating prospect for a priest who had devoted his life to remain ceremonially clean. Amaziah's wife would not go with him into exile, but would instead stay behind and be forced into prostitution, as often happened after an invasion. The priest's children would be put to death, and his property would be confiscated and split up among others. All this added up to a dismal future. Yet, Amaziah would not be alone in his misery, for the Assyrians would also exile many of his fellow citizens.

With the historical interlude completed, the fourth vision of divine judgment is presented. In some respects it is similar to the third. The fourth vision concerned a "basket" (Amos 8:1) of "ripe" summer "fruit." The basket probably looked like an ordinary harvesting container made out of woven wicker. The produce in the basket may have been any kind of fruit—such as grapes, olives, pomegranates, and figs—that ripened in August and September and was harvested in the autumn. When the Lord asked Amos what he saw, Amos stated that he saw a container filled with fresh, "ripe fruit" (vs. 2).

The prophet's answer opened the way for God to make the play on words that is the point of this vision. Specifically, the Hebrew noun translated "ripe fruit" (*kayitz*; literally "end-of-the-year fruit") sounds like the noun that is translated "ripe" (*ketz*; literally "the end"). God used this coincidence to make His oracle memorable. Just as the summer fruit was ready to be harvested at the end of the summer growing season, so too the national existence of Israel had come to an end. The all-powerful Lord declared that He would "no longer" overlook their transgressions. Moreover, this prophecy, like the vision of a plumb line, shows that there was no stopping the divine judgment. The Israelites' wickedness had gotten to a point where God had to punish it.

B. A Time of Wailing: vs. 3

"In that day," declares the Sovereign LORD, "the songs in the temple will turn to wailing. Many, many bodies—flung everywhere! Silence!"

As with the oracle about a plumb line, the vision of the ripe summer fruit contains a description of what would happen when the prophecy was fulfilled (Amos 7:9; 8:3). Whereas the Israelites had been singing joyful religious songs (even though hypocritically) in their pagan shrine at Bethel, they would one day wail in sorrow over the horrible circumstance that was about to overtake their nation. A large number of Israelite corpses would be scattered all about by the violence of their attackers. (The prediction came to pass at the time of the Assyrian invasion in 723 B.C.) Due to the dreadfulness of this scene, the all-powerful Lord commanded there be a moment of respectful "silence" (8:3) among those who heard Amos' prophecy.

C. Acts of Injustice: vss. 4-6

Hear this, you who trample the needy and do away with the poor of the land, saying, "When will the New Moon be over that we may sell grain, and the Sabbath be ended that we may market wheat?"—skimping the measure, boosting the price and cheating with dishonest scales, buying the poor with silver and the needy for a pair of sandals, selling even the sweepings with the wheat.

In Amos 8:4-6, several acts of injustice are detailed, especially against the destitute. For instance, the wicked rich were guilty of treating the indigent with contempt and seeking to eliminate from the northern kingdom those who were impoverished (2:7; 5:11). The godless even disdained such religious festivals as the "New Moon" (8:5; observed at the beginning of every month with various offerings) and the "Sabbath" (observed at the end of every week). These were to be sacred occasions when any form of work was discontinued. Yet Israel's greedy merchants were eager for these holy days to pass by so that they could reopen their bins and resume selling their "grain" (including barley and "wheat").

The last part of verse 5 is literally rendered "to make small the ephah and to make great the shekel." The ephah was a unit of dry measure used to determine the volume of grain, flour, or meal being sold and bartered. The shekel of silver was the standard unit used to measure weight in the ancient Semitic cultures. Merchants could increase their profits by using an undersized ephah (that is, selling less) and a heavier shekel (that is, to obtain a higher price). Also, by utilizing out-of-balance "scales," corrupt vendors could swindle even more money from their customers (Lev. 19:35-36; Deut. 25:14; Prov. 11:1; Hos. 12:7).

As noted in lesson 1 concerning Amos 2:6, the wealthy misused their material resources by exploiting the poor. The wicked rich also dishonored God by enslaving the innocent. This included trading the poverty-stricken for "silver" (8:6) and the penniless for a "pair of sandals." The dishonest merchants even mixed worthless chaff and other refuse they swept from the ground with "wheat" so they could get more money when they sold the grain to unsuspecting customers.

II. THE REVERSAL OF ISRAEL'S FORTUNES: AMOS 8:9-10

A. Darkness over the Land: vs. 9

"In that day," declares the Sovereign LORD, "I will make the sun go down at noon and darken the earth in broad daylight."

Previously, in Amos 6:8, the Lord declared how much He loathed Jacob's arrogance, as evidenced by the complacency of the northern kingdom's leaders (see the Bible commentary appearing in lesson 3). Now, in 8:7, God used sarcasm to confirm His oath by the "Pride of Jacob" that He would always remember the wicked deeds the rich and powerful in Israel were guilty of committing. Verse 8 draws attention to the inevitability of the coming flood of judgment, in which God would bring upheaval on the nation and its inhabitants.

The convulsions to be felt throughout the land (perhaps produced by an earthquake; see 1:1) were as certain to occur as the yearly flooding (in September) and receding (in October) of the Nile River in Egypt (9:5). As Israel was tossed about and sank after each jarring episode (especially at the hands of the Assyrians; see Isa. 8:6-8), the northern kingdom would "tremble" (Amos 8:8) and its residents would "mourn." In that time of reckoning, the supreme Creator would upturn the natural order by causing the "sun" (vs. 9; which some of the Israelites venerated) to set at midday and the land to "darken" when it should have been bright (perhaps produced by either a solar or lunar eclipse; see also the Bible commentary in lesson 2 on 5:18-20).

B. A Time of Intense Mourning: vs. 10

"I will turn your religious feasts into mourning and all your singing into weeping. I will make all of you wear sackcloth and shave your heads. I will make that time like mourning for an only son and the end of it like a bitter day."

In Amos 8:10, God declared that "mourning" would soon replace Israel's festivals and dirges would supplant their "singing." Moreover, the carnival atmosphere would give way to the wearing of "sackcloth" and the shaving of "heads." Sackcloth was a rough fabric woven from the long, dark hair of camels and goats. The color and coarseness of the material made it appropriate for wearing during times of national calamity. On such occasions, it was also customary for people to demonstrate grief and signal humiliation by shaving their heads. One day, everyone in Israel would be overcome by the bitterness of their misfortune (Jer. 6:26; Zech. 12:10).

Discussion Questions

1. Why had the time of judgment come for Israel?
2. Why would God allow death and destruction to fall on Israel?
3. Why did God refuse to overlook the exploitation of the needy by Israel's ruling class?
4. In confronting society's problems, what approaches might be most effective?
5. What are some of the consequences (whether positive or negative) of confronting sinful behavior?

Contemporary Application

Amos demonstrated courage in confronting the sinful behaviors of Israel. In turn, the prophet's example can be a valuable lesson for us. For instance, Amos did not confront the people of his day out of self-righteous anger or out of a desire for personal fortune and fame. Instead, the prophet confronted others out of obedience to God and a genuine concern for their welfare.

God calls us, as Christians, to confront harmful and sinful behaviors in others, like Amos did (Eph. 5:11). Sometimes, reprehensible actions occur in our society. In those instances, we might feel called to confront by means such as voting, sharing our beliefs with others, or financially supporting just causes.

Personal confrontation can be much more difficult. Since most of us want to be liked, confrontation can threaten that desire. For that reason, we might be tempted to behave the opposite of Amos. We might pretend that everything is all right. Then, we might resent the other person and rob her or him of an opportunity to grow by acknowledging the behavior and changing.

It's also important to consider how to confront others. Is it better to confront a person alone or with a partner (Matt. 18:15-17)? Also, what should be the setting? Since personalities and situations differ, instead of making a hard-and-fast rule, it is wise for us to ask God for guidance in these choices. No matter what the setting or persons involved, a desire to help and an attitude of humility are two important virtues to include in the confrontation.

Censuring False Prophets

Scripture

Background Scripture: *Micah 2*
Scripture Lesson: *Micah 2:4-11*
Key Verse: *Should it be said, O house of Jacob: "Is the Spirit
of the LORD angry? Does he do such things?" "Do not my
words do good to him whose ways are upright?"* Micah 2:7.
Scripture Lesson for Children: *Micah 2:1-4, 12-13*
Key Verse for Children: *Woe to those who plan iniquity, to
those who plot evil on their beds!* Micah 2:1.

Lesson Aim

To avoid a self-focused life and instead show concern
for the needs of others.

Lesson Setting

Time: About 730 B.C.
Place: Judah

Lesson Outline

Censuring False Prophets

   I. Disaster Foretold for Evildoers: Micah 2:4-5
      A. A Lament Song: vs. 4
      B. A Grim Future for the Greedy: vs. 5
  II. An Oracle against Judah's False Prophets:
      Micah 2:6-11
      A. Indicting the False Prophets: vss. 6-7
      B. Censuring Predatory Behavior: vss. 8-9
      C. Announcing God's Judgment on the Wicked:
         vss. 10-11

Introduction for Adults

Topic: *Justice, not Injustice*

Justice is much more than meting out punishment to criminals. In God's view of things, justice requires that we use what we have to help meet the needs of others. Justice also demands that we do not exploit other people to get what we want. Moreover, justice demands that we set aside our materialistic ambitions so that we can address suffering and hardships.

Injustice, then, is more than the absence of justice. It is also the failure to do the right things when we can. In Micah's day, the rich landowners in Judah were guilty of this. They could have helped the impoverished, but the tyrants refused to do so. Instead, they chose to gratify their own selfish desires. Micah's pronouncement of judgment against them shouts to us a powerful message about how easy it is not only to fail the Lord, but also to ignore His warnings.

Introduction for Youth

Topic: *Serving Self or Others?*

Retailers face huge obstacles trying to keep up with the fast-changing tastes of teenagers. One year's fashions are next year's disappointments. The teen market in the West is driven by the impulse to have everything new right away. How hard it is for adolescents to resist this consuming urge. If they are aware of what is happening, they struggle not to be swept along with the idea that we obtain happiness with a brilliant array of designer clothes, fast muscle cars, and high-tech gadgetry.

The greedy land barons in Judah tried to obtain security and happiness by exploiting others, but they utterly failed in their attempt. We cannot afford to follow the foolish example of the wicked rich who were contemporaries of Micah, the prophet. If we put our trust in the Lord Jesus, we are guaranteed eternal joy and peace with Him in heaven. What more could we possibly want?

Concepts for Children

Topic: *Evildoers Will Pay*

1. Micah was a person who told others about God.
2. Micah was sad that some people were unkind to others.
3. Micah said that it was wrong to hurt others.
4. Micah said that God wanted His people to care for each other.
5. We can show love to others because God loves us.

Lesson Commentary

I. DISASTER FORETOLD FOR EVILDOERS: MICAH 2:4-5

A. A Lament Song: vs. 4

"In that day men will ridicule you; they will taunt you with this mournful song: 'We are utterly ruined; my people's possession is divided up. He takes it from me! He assigns our fields to traitors.'"

We know little about Micah, the prophet, apart from his hometown and his time period (Mic. 1:1; compare Jer. 26:18). Micah hailed from Moresheth Gath, a frontier outpost that lay about 25 miles southwest of Jerusalem (Josh. 15:44; 2 Chron. 11:8; 14:9-10; 20:37). Some scholars, however, theorize that Micah spent much of his adult life in the capital. He prophesied during the reigns of three kings of Judah: Jotham (about 750–732 B.C.), Ahaz (about 735–715 B.C.), and Hezekiah (about 715–686 B.C.). This means Micah's career lasted from about 750 B.C. at the earliest to about 686 B.C. at the latest. So, Micah was a contemporary of Isaiah (Isa. 1:1) and Hosea (Hos. 1:1).

After the opening title (Mic. 1:1), the book's content can be divided into three major sections: the Lord's judgment of Israel and Judah (chaps. 1–3); the vision of future restoration (chaps. 4–5); and the promise of kingdom blessings (chaps. 6–7). Micah condemned such sins as idolatry, false prophecy, and oppression of the poor. He also predicted judgment from God, including the downfall of Samaria and Jerusalem (Mic. 1:1, 5-7, 9-16; 3:12). Even though the Creator would punish the northern and southern kingdoms for violating the Mosaic law, He would preserve a remnant of His chosen people and one day restore them to Judah, with Jerusalem as their capital. Micah even foretold the birth of the Messiah (see 6:8, which is covered in lesson 7).

Micah 1:2 constitutes an introduction to the prophecy that follows. God called the peoples of the world to pay attention to the way He would judge His own people—the Israelites and Judahites—because of their disobedience. In turn, Earth's inhabitants would recognize the way God would treat them unless they also turned to Him. Verses 3 and 4 draw attention to a visitation of the Lord in which He descends from heaven and uses the high places as His stepping-stones. Under His feet the mountains melt and the valleys split apart. All this is symbolism for the way God would send judgment on His rebellious people. The leaders and inhabitants of Israel ("Jacob"; vs. 5) and Judah had violated God's covenant by worshiping pagan deities. The mention of the two capitals may mean either (1) that false worship was going on in both cities or (2) that the political leadership of both nations was involved in the sin of idolatry. Perhaps both were true.

For Israel's transgression, God would utterly destroy Samaria, the city's idols, and all that went along with the veneration of false gods and goddesses (vss. 6-7). Evidently, God was foretelling what would happen when the Assyrians captured Samaria. However, at that time the city was not seriously damaged. (It was destroyed 600 years later, then rebuilt.) The second half of verse 7 is not entirely clear. It may mean that Samaria's conquerors would destroy Israel's idols, which had been paid for by pagan religious prostitution, and then the conquerors would reuse the precious metal for their own idols. Or perhaps the verse means that the metal from idols was used by the Assyrian invaders as payment for prostitutes.

Micah would have felt uneasy about foretelling the destruction of Samaria. The thought of it affected him so deeply that he vowed to display signs of mourning publicly (vs. 8). Yet Micah grieved even more because of what Samaria's demise meant for the inhabitants of Judah. The downfall of Samaria showed that God was willing to turn His wrath upon His covenant people when they persisted in sinning against Him. So God's judgment ("wound," vs. 9) upon Samaria threatened Jerusalem, too. As a matter of fact, in 701 B.C., the Assyrians all but overtook Jerusalem the way they conquered Samaria about 22 years earlier.

While Micah predicted that Jerusalem would be threatened with judgment, he also foretold that other cities of Judah would actually be judged. This accurately describes what happened in 701 B.C. The Bible and ancient Near Eastern historical records both agree that the Assyrian emperor, Sennacherib, captured dozens of cities in Judah but failed to capture Jerusalem. Most of the cities in verses 10 through 15 (all except the first) were sites in Judah and targets of the Assyrian invasion. Micah chose to mention most of these cities (all except the last) because of what their names mean or sound like. Put differently, these verses contain a series of puns in which a city's name is linked with the rest of the prophecy related to it. In short, verses 10 through 16 constitute a lament (or mourning song) over the coming destruction in Judah. Also, verse 16 forms a conclusion to the lament, in which Jerusalem is directed to shave her head in mourning for her children. Here is a look ahead to the time when the people of Judah would leave the land for exile—an event that was not caused by the Assyrians in 701 B.C., but by the Babylonians in 586 B.C.

Micah next turned his attention to rich landowners in Judah. God had an appropriate punishment in mind for these sinners. When a prophet pronounced woe upon somebody, it was a warning about impending destruction and death against them. Micah declared that sorrow awaited those who fabricated wicked schemes. They lay awake at night, hatched "evil" (2:1) plans, and then arose at the first light of dawn to enact their offenses. Evidently, no one could stop the scoundrels, since they controlled the levers of power in society. Specifically, Micah had in mind influential leaders in Israel who committed the crime of land grabbing (vs. 2). The Hebrew verb rendered "covet" is the same term used in the Ten Commandments (Exod. 20:17; Deut. 5:21) and indicates that the greed of unscrupulous individuals trampled on the essence of God's covenant with His people. The criminals used fraud (perhaps by manipulating the court system) to seize real estate (including "fields," "houses," and inherited assets) belonging to others.

God was aware of the unlawful acts occurring in Judah. The Hebrew verb translated "plan" in Micah 2:1 is the same term rendered "planning" in verse 3. Because the wicked were guilty of devising corrupt schemes, the Lord would bring adversity upon them. Also note that the same Hebrew adjective is translated "evil" (vs. 1), "disaster" (vs. 3), and "calamity." Previously, the wicked rich got away with abusing others. Yet a time of captivity was coming when the reprobates literally would not be able to "remove [their] necks." They would be like an animal shackled to a yoke that others forcibly placed on its shoulders (Isa. 9:4; 10:27; 47:6; Jer. 27:8; 28:14; Ezek. 34:27). In days gone by, the villains were arrogant and overbearing in depriving people of their property (which God regarded as a permanent, sacred trust; see Lev. 25:10, 13). But in the future day of reckoning, God would see to it that the lawbreakers could "no longer walk proudly" (Mich. 2:3). That outcome was just and suitable, for the divine punishment fit the nature of the human crime.

The Hebrew noun translated "ridicule" (vs. 4) denotes a brief, memorable saying that was filled with disdain and intended as an object lesson for all who heard the maxim. In this case, Micah foretold a time when bystanders would scorn Judah's greedy elite. Also, spectators literally would "wail a bitter wailing," which refers to mocking the land barons with a chant filled with despair. The lament song would proclaim that the oppressors were completely destroyed, for they were guilty of confiscating what belonged to others (vs. 1). In turn, God would use invaders to seize the evildoers' property (including their orchards, vineyards, and grain fields) and allow the conquerors to divide the spoil among themselves (vs. 4). Micah referred to the victors as "traitors" or "apostates" (namely, those who did not worship the Lord), due to the fact that they would act in a defiant and treacherous manner against the people of Judah. This suggests that Micah was looking ahead to the time of the Babylonian captivity.

B. A Grim Future for the Greedy: vs. 5

Therefore you will have no one in the assembly of the LORD to divide the land by lot.

Micah's prophecy not only anticipated the Babylonian captivity, but also the restoration of God's people from exile to their homeland in Judah. It would be a time of rejoicing in which tribal allotments within the promised land would be redistributed to the returnees. There was one group, however, who would not participate in that joyous occasion—the former land barons who treated the innocent unfairly. That said, scholars are divided over what the prediction in Micah 2:5 denotes. Some say it means that the villains would have no descendants among those who would later return from exile and occupy land in Judah. Other specialists think this verse means the reprobates would have no descendants among those who received allotments of God's benefits in the end times.

II. AN ORACLE AGAINST JUDAH'S FALSE PROPHETS: MICAH 2:6-11

A. Indicting the False Prophets: vss. 6-7

"Do not prophesy," their prophets say. "Do not prophesy about these things; disgrace will not overtake us." Should it be said, O house of Jacob: "Is the Spirit of the LORD angry? Does he do such things?" "Do not my words do good to him whose ways are upright?"

Micah was not the only spokesperson in Judah. Some of his peers, such as Isaiah and Hosea, were true prophets, while others were false ones. The frauds spurned Micah's message, because it contradicted their own. For this reason, they tried to shut him up. The last part of Micah 2:6 can be rendered "humiliation will not befall us." In this case, the false prophets meant that the disgrace Micah had foretold for Judah would not occur. The phrase can also be translated, "humiliation will not be turned back." The latter rendering indicates that the false prophets felt personally reproached as long as Micah predicted judgment.

In verse 7, Micah's opponents accused him of being too negative in his theology. They felt that the kind of wrath Micah predicted was inconsistent with God's benevolent nature. Allegedly, the Lord was too patient and loving ever to judge His covenant people (Gen. 19:16; Exod. 34:6; Num. 14:18; Pss. 78:38; 86:15; 108:4; 115:1; 138:2; Lam. 3:22–23; Rom. 2:4). The second half of Micah 2:7 can be interpreted in two different ways, depending on whether one takes it as being spoken by the false prophets or by God. If the self-serving charlatans made this assertion, they were claiming to be virtuous people, whom God would bless, not judge. In contrast, if God made the statement, He was correcting the religious frauds' one-sided view by declaring that He does good only for the upright, not the wicked.

B. Censuring Predatory Behavior: vss. 8-9

"Lately my people have risen up like an enemy. You strip off the rich robe from those who pass by without a care, like men returning from battle. You drive the women of my people from their pleasant homes. You take away my blessing from their children forever."

Micah 2:8 and 9 describe predatory acts the upper class committed against the impoverished people of Judah. Micah charged the rich and powerful of behaving like a foreign adversary toward the poor and powerless of their nation. One minute a group of the destitute would be feeling as safe as soldiers who returned home from war. Then, the next minute, the ruling elite would assault the unwary travelers and steal the cloaks (or outer garments) off their backs, leaving them with only their tunics. One minute a defenseless widow and her fatherless, young children would be enjoying their comfortable home. Then, the next minute, land barons would be ejecting the family from their dwelling and onto the street and keeping the seized property for themselves. "Blessing" renders a Hebrew noun that literally means "glory," "splendor," or "honor" and refers to the highly prized inheritance children were to receive, by law, from their parents. The denial of this right produced untold hardship and anguish for the innocent.

C. Announcing God's Judgment on the Wicked: vss. 10-11

"Get up, go away! For this is not your resting place, because it is defiled, it is ruined, beyond all remedy. If a liar and deceiver comes and says, 'I will prophesy for you plenty of wine and beer,' he would be just the prophet for this people!"

Once again, God promised to punish Judah's tyrants. Those who had stolen homes would be cast out from their homeland (referred to as their "resting place"; Mic. 2:10) and permanently banned from the covenantal community (Deut. 12:10; Ps. 95:11). This is another prediction of captivity. The sins of the despots had "defiled" (Mic. 2:10) the land. Their transgressions had made Judah so unclean that it was as if the land could never be purified. For this reason, God considered Judah to be uninhabitable. Likewise, He would not permit His chosen people to have contact with the land, like any unclean thing. The threats in this verse remind us that the nature of our behavior often determines the consequences of that behavior (Gal. 6:8).

Micah 2:11 contains the prophet's sarcastic description of the kind of seer or visionary the people of Judah really wanted. Those who foretold only times of increased prosperity and affluence (represented by "plenty of wine and beer") were just the type of spokespersons the inhabitants craved. They did not want to hear the stark truths that a prophet like Micah declared. This goes to show that our evaluation of those who preach God's Word should not be based on whether we like their message. Our assessment must be determined by the message's accuracy with Scripture.

After predicting exile for the leaders, inhabitants, and nation of Judah, Micah offered some words of hope. It is the first positive oracle in the book and contrasts sharply with the platitudes voiced by the rival prophets. God's chosen people (collectively referred to as "Jacob" and "Israel" in verse 12) would be gathered together and then led out. The message of hope was for a "remnant." In the Bible, a remnant is usually a group who survives divine judgment because of their faithfulness and therefore inherits the promises and blessings of the Lord. The remnant Micah spoke about would be gathered like sheep in a pen or like a flock in a pasture. The words translated "throng with people" carry the idea of a large crowd's murmuring. Suddenly, there would appear among the throng one who would break through the enclosure and lead the others out (vs. 13). The person is the "king" and apparently is either the same as the "Lord" or associated with the "Lord."

Verses 12 and 13, which seem so straightforward in their meaning, have been read in a number of different ways. Here are four possible interpretations of the passage: (1) The bringing together is the gathering of Judahites in Jerusalem before or during Sennacherib's siege. The breaking through is the miraculous ending of this Assyrian siege. The king is God. (2) The bringing together is the gathering of Judahites in Babylon during captivity there. The breaking through is the Jews' return from captivity. The king is God or perhaps Sheshbazzar. (3) The bringing together is the gathering of Christians in the church. The breaking through is the removal of obstacles to divine blessing for Christians. The king is Jesus. (4) The bringing together is the gathering of Jews to the Jewish homeland in the end times. The breaking through is the removal of obstacles to divine blessing for those Jews. The king is the Messiah.

Discussion Questions

1. What crimes were the land barons in Judah guilty of committing?
2. Why would God allow calamity to overtake Judah and its people?
3. Why did Micah, despite peer pressure, refuse to stop speaking for the Lord?
4. How should believers respond to the presence of injustice in society?
5. How can Christians encourage the unrighteous to trust in the Savior?

Contemporary Application

According to Micah, greatness isn't defined by how much people own or whom they control. In the prophet's day, the fields, houses, and other assets from the underclass seized by Judah's land barons was an outrage in God's eyes. Here we see that having a gigantic home, a spacious corner office, and stockpiles of money to buy whatever we want are not God's goal for us. Instead, it's to be humane and equitable in all our dealings.

Yet selfishness seems to dominate the human heart. For instance, we might spend a lot of time trying to get a "good deal," even though it means not paying folks what their work is worth. We might argue for tax breaks that favor our own income group, with no regard to how they affect others in lower income groups. Or we might simply not pay much attention to our neighbors' needs. We might be oblivious to the hurts and pains of the people who live next door to us or the other people we see every day.

The needs are great, both where we live and around the world. For example, according to UNICEF, nearly 10 million children under the age of five die every year in developing countries from diseases that are largely preventable. With the basics of clean water, clean power, and vaccinations, this number would shrink considerably. What would it mean to be kind, fair, and compassionate in a needy world such as ours?

The bottom line is that each of our actions needs to be regarded with the following question in mind: *Is this the kind, helpful approach Micah would favor or the greedy, self-focused behavior the land barons of Judah would display?* Our world will be better, and our own lives will be improved, the more we take care of others as much as ourselves.

Rebuking Corrupt Leaders

Scripture

Background Scripture: *Micah 3*

Scripture Lesson: *Micah 3:5-12*

Key Verse: *As for me, I am filled with power, with the Spirit of the LORD, and with justice and might, to declare to Jacob his transgression, to Israel his sin.* Micah 3:8.

Scripture Lesson for Children: *Micah 3:5-12*

Key Verse for Children: *"Listen, you leaders of Jacob, you rulers of the house of Israel. Should you not know justice?"* Micah 3:1.

Lesson Aim

To understand that religious activity apart from just behavior is condemned by God.

Lesson Setting

Time: About 730 B.C.

Place: Judah

Lesson Outline

Rebuking Corrupt Leaders

  I. Rebuking Judah's Prophets: Micah 3:5-8
    A. *A False Message of Peace: vs. 5*
    B. *A Coming Time of Despair: vss. 6-8*
  II. Censuring Judah's Leaders: Micah 3:9-12
    A. *A Perversion of Justice: vss. 9-11*
    B. *A Prediction of Disaster: vs. 12*

Introduction for Adults

Topic: *Public Trust Betrayed*

According to statistics issued by the U.S. Department of Transportation's Inspector General, on average about 500 people each year are killed at railroad crossings. Some communities require people to pay steep fines for crossing the tracks when the gates are down. But in many rural areas the only warnings are old, battered "Stop, Look, and Listen" signs.

When Micah began ministering in Judah and Israel, he resembled those warning signs. God had sent him to preach against the transgressions the leaders committed in the southern and northern kingdoms. After hearing him, the civil and religious authorities of both nations had to make a choice.

We can imagine Micah saying that judgment and disaster would come like a roaring freight train. In a sense, he urged God's people not to "cross the tracks." Micah also exhorted them to turn back to the Lord. That same message of repentance and faith runs throughout the Bible and is worthy of our consideration.

Introduction for Youth

Topic: *Crime and Punishment*

The tired mother asked her pastor for advice concerning her son, who repeatedly got into trouble. Time after time the son came to his mother for help, telling her that he loved her. And repeatedly she went to his aid by bailing him out of trouble.

In this case, the young man had lost his car and had no way to get to work. What should his mother do? The pastor thought it was time for the young man to face the consequences of his misbehaviors. If his mother kept "rescuing" him from taking responsibility, most likely he would not change his ways. How hard this truth was for his mother to accept!

This scenario illustrates the way it is for many of us. Perhaps we like to drift through life, thinking we can do what we want and get away with it. However, a prophet named Micah would remind us that God cares about how we live. In His love for us, He will not allow us to continue down a sinful path. He makes us face the consequences of our actions.

Concepts for Children

Topic: *Leaders Who Do Wrong*

1. God put leaders in charge of Judah and Israel.
2. God wanted the leaders to treat everyone nicely.
3. God was displeased that the leaders were nasty to others.
4. God said He would punish the leaders for doing what was wrong.
5. God wants us to be kind to others.

Lesson Commentary

I. REBUKING JUDAH'S PROPHETS: MICAH 3:5-8

A. A False Message of Peace: vs. 5

This is what the LORD says: "As for the prophets who lead my people astray, if one feeds them, they proclaim 'peace'; if he does not, they prepare to wage war against him."

As we learned in last week's lesson, Micah was a prophet from the rural town of Moresheth Gath, which was located in the Shephelah (or fertile lowlands) of Judah about 25 miles southwest of Jerusalem. Micah has the unique distinction of being the only spokesperson whom God sent to both the northern and southern kingdoms. He was also the last prophet whom God dispatched to warn the errant north. Prior to Micah's ministry, the Assyrian empire was in decline. However, as he began to minister, Assyria experienced a resurgence of power. In fact, during Micah's ministry, the 10 northern tribes were carried into captivity (722 B.C.) and Judah became a vassal state to Assyria.

The third chapter of Micah contains three judgment oracles that share several common literary features. For instance, these prophecies concern the same group of individuals who controlled the southern and northern kingdoms. Verse 1 refers to them as the "leaders of Judah" and the "rulers" over the "house of Israel." Each oracle is four verses in length, and each contains the same elements: an opening address (vss. 1, 5, 9); an indictment preceded by the term "who" (vss. 2, 5, 9); and a verdict introduced by the word "then" (vs. 4) or "therefore" (vss. 6, 12).

Moreover, the three judgment oracles emphasize the travesty of justice occurring in Israel and Judah at the hands of its dishonest and inept leaders. In the first oracle (vss. 1-4), God accused the political and judicial authorities of the southern and northern kingdoms of exploiting and abusing the people. God vowed not to hear the prayers of those wicked tyrants. In the second oracle (vss. 5-8), God accused the false prophets of leading the people astray and of modifying their messages, depending on their fee. In the third oracle (vss. 9-12), God again accused all the rulers, priests, and prophets of injustice and cruelty. So, God declared that Jerusalem would be destroyed at the hands of merciless invaders.

In verse 1, Micah rhetorically asked whether it was the responsibility of the ruling elite of the entire to nation to "know justice." "Know" renders a Hebrew verb that denotes the ability to recognize, understand, and teach. "Justice" translates a noun that refers to civil and religious decisions made by magistrates in courts of law. God expected the leaders of the southern and northern kingdoms to comprehend His statutes and discern how to administrate His ordinances equitably. The latter activity included the officials rendering objective, impartial verdicts when they decided cases. The intended outcome would be to punish evildoers and vindicate the oppressed.

Verses 2-4 indicate that the situation in Judah and Israel deviated greatly from God's holy moral standard, as revealed in the Mosaic law. Instead of dealing with the poor, the widowed, and the orphaned in a humane and just manner, the despots of the southern and northern kingdoms maltreated the lower classes. Specifically, the upper echelons of society perverted the legal system by continuously despising what God considered to be "good" (vs. 2) and savoring what He regarded to be "evil." Indeed, the lives of the oppressed were so imperiled that Micah portrayed the magistrates as cannibals who butchered, cooked, and devoured their victims (Pss. 14:4; 27:2; Prov. 30:14; Isa. 9:19-21).

It was as if the wicked skinned alive God's chosen people and ripped their "flesh" (Mic. 3:2) off their bodies. The tyrants were so bloodthirsty that they devoured the innocent. The grisly imagery included the oppressors flaying the "skin" from the defenseless and crushing their "bones" (vs. 3). Even more ghastly is the idea of the tormentors hacking off portions of the cadavers like meat to be "tossed" into a kettle to make cannibal stew. One can only imagine how calloused the magistrates became as they committed their atrocities against vulnerable groups of people. For this reason, when the reprobates cried out to God for help in the day of their calamity, He would refuse to pay attention to their pleas. In a metaphorical sense, the Lord would not even look at them, so appalling were the crimes they committed (vs. 4; see also Deut. 31:17; Isa. 1:15).

The civil rulers were not the only group in Judah and Israel guilty of violating the Mosaic law. Similarly, there were also false "prophets" (Mic. 3:5) who misled the Lord's chosen people. The image here is that of sheep who follow their shepherd. The seers not only claimed to receive messages from God, but also enjoyed the support of the wicked rulers in Judah and Israel. While Micah and his peers (such as Isaiah and Hosea) announced that captivity awaited evildoers, the spiritual imposters assured their benefactors that they were safe. Also, as long as the clients fed and clothed the religious mercenaries, they were eager to preach a message of "peace," health, and prosperity (Jer. 6:13-14; 8:10-11; Ezek. 13:10). Oppositely, the profit-seeking hucksters launched a crusade against those who refused to pay a cent for the pabulum being offered.

Deuteronomy 18:15-22 reveals that God's true spokespersons received His message directly from Him and proclaimed it to the covenant community in accordance with His commands. Unlike rulers and priests, the Lord commissioned His prophets and empowered them to serve as His ambassadors. On some occasions, God chose spokespersons to deliver one or two messages. On other occasions, He selected prophets to minister for a long period of time. Often, God directed His representatives to herald oracles of doom to wayward listeners.

Centuries later, Paul noted that the impostors' master, Satan, often disguises himself as an "angel of light" (2 Cor. 11:14) to coax people away from the truths of God's Word. The apostle was acutely aware of the spiritual warfare that raged around him, especially as he sought to bring God's message of salvation to the lost. Paul realized that Satan did not always appear as a sinister force. Sometimes he posed as a messenger of light in order to make people think that he was promoting the well-being of his victims. Likewise, the devil's surrogates resorted to false teaching, which contained just enough truth to draw in the unsuspecting.

In every era of Christian history, false teachers have arisen, trying to divert people from the truths of Scripture. Their crafty methods have caused many to go astray and have resulted in the destruction of countless lives. Certainly many spiritual imposters have arisen in our own era. Their presence is one reason why it is critical that we study, learn, and apply the teachings of God's Word.

B. A Coming Time of Despair: vss. 6-8

"Therefore night will come over you, without visions, and darkness, without divination. The sun will set for the prophets, and the day will go dark for them. The seers will be ashamed and the diviners disgraced. They will all cover their faces because there is no answer from God." But as for me, I am filled with power, with the Spirit of the LORD, and with justice and might, to declare to Jacob his transgression, to Israel his sin.

As noted in lesson 1 of the December quarter, God used creative and varied means to communicate through His prophets with the people of Old Testament times (Heb. 1:1). This included God interacting with His ambassadors through direct revelation, dreams, visions, and even their personal experiences. Admittedly, there were occasions when God's spokespersons did not grasp certain aspects of the truth they were directed to proclaim (1 Pet. 1:10-12). In those instances, the Holy Spirit worked through subsequent believers to carefully examine and accurately interpret the theological meaning and significance of earlier prophecies (2 Pet. 1:20-21).

The Lord announced through Micah that unlike God's true prophets, the religious imposters would not experience the Spirit's illuminating presence. For example, instead of revelatory "visions" (Mic. 3:6), night would close in on the frauds. Likewise, "darkness" would put an end to their attempts to make predictions by reading various omens (involving astrology, arrows, sticks, the livers of animals, and so on). Evidently, the soothsayers forgot that sorcery and divination were strictly forbidden in Israel (Deut. 18:14). The blackout of God's favor was comparable to the "sun" (Mic. 3:6) going down on the hucksters and the daytime of their spurious activities ending. Those who falsely claimed to be "seers" (vs. 7) would be humiliated. Similarly, others who alleged to be "diviners" would feel reproach. All of them would cover their lips because God refused to give them a favorable reply.

Unlike the profit-seekers, who spouted religious platitudes, Micah declared that he was "filled with power" (Mic. 3:8). He clarified that the divine Spirit was the source of a genuine prophet's strength, especially in vigorously promoting the cause of "justice" in Judah and Israel. The Spirit enabled Micah to boldly announce to the southern and northern kingdoms their "transgression" (or rebellious acts) and "sin" (or offensive crimes). Zechariah 4:6 contains a helpful reminder that whatever God calls His servants to perform are not accomplished by brute force. Instead, it can only take place through the Holy Spirit. With His abiding presence and help, even obstacles that seemed like insurmountable mountains would be plains to God's true spokespersons.

II. CENSURING JUDAH'S LEADERS: MICAH 3:9-12

A. A Perversion of Justice: vss. 9-11

Hear this, you leaders of the house of Jacob, you rulers of the house of Israel, who despise justice and distort all that is right; who build Zion with bloodshed, and Jerusalem with wickedness. Her leaders judge for a bribe, her priests teach for a price, and her prophets tell fortunes for money. Yet they lean upon the LORD and say, "Is not the LORD among us? No disaster will come upon us."

The oracle in Micah 3:9-12 reiterates the indictment God brought against the feckless leaders of Judah and Israel. The magistrates in the southern and northern kingdoms were guilty of abhorring "justice" and perverting what should have been morally upright. Archaeological evidence indicates that a considerable amount of building took place in Micah's day. The Lord declared through His spokesperson that innocent blood was shed in the process and violent acts of injustice were committed against the defenseless.

In particular, Judah and Israel's magistrates issued wrongful verdicts in exchange for bribes. Also, the priests offered religious instruction only when paid handsomely to do so. Even the covenant community's visionaries read omens as a result of being given silver (the standard of currency for economic activity in the ancient Near East). Amid all this fraudulent activity, the wicked had the audacity to claim that they were trusting in God. For instance, they asserted that the Lord manifested His presence in their shrines. So they assumed that no calamity (such as invasions and exile) would overtake them.

These corrupt leaders were counting on Judah's and Israel's historic relationship with the Lord to protect them. They thought to themselves, *How can we be conquered if God is in our midst?* This is an Old Testament example of grace turned into a license to sin. The false messages of these princes and seers created a sense of optimism among the people that was unfounded. Fittingly, since Jerusalem was established and prospered through violence, the city would also be demolished by violence.

During the waning years of the kingdom of Judah, Jeremiah was a voice for the Lord. God warned the leaders and inhabitants of the nation that their spiritual rebellion would ultimately lead to their destruction—that is, unless they turned back to Him and lived righteously, as their ancestors had lived. The true condition of the people is evident in Jeremiah's declaration recorded in 5:31: "The prophets prophesy lies, the priests rule by their own authority, and my people love it this way."

In light of the preceding terrible indictment, God handed down His sentence: Jerusalem would be destroyed (6:1-8). After all, priests and prophets alike said, "'Peace, peace,' . . . when there is no peace" (vs. 14). They had no shame; in fact, "they do not even know how to blush" (vs. 15). God's people were at a spiritual crossroads. The Lord, through His spokespersons, urged His people to follow the path their ancestors took (vs. 16). This route, which was characterized by justice, fairness, and the true worship of God, led to peace. Tragically, the people refused such an option, choosing instead to travel down a rocky slope that led to destruction.

B. A Prediction of Disaster: vs. 12

Therefore because of you, Zion will be plowed like a field, Jerusalem will become a heap of rubble, the temple hill a mound overgrown with thickets.

Because of the transgressions of the corrupt magistrates, greedy priests, and mercenary prophets, the same disaster that loomed on the horizon for Samaria (Mic. 1:6) also awaited Jerusalem (3:12). Foreign invaders would overrun the city, raze its buildings, and demolish its wall. Consequently, Judah's capital would become a rubble pile and its environs would be cleared like an open field.

Moreover, before judgment struck, God's glory would abandon the mount where the temple sat (Ezek. 10), leaving it to be covered with thick brush (in turn, providing habitat for wild animals). When Micah's prophecy reached King Hezekiah's ear, the monarch initiated reforms. As a result, Judah procured a temporary reprieve from God's judgment (2 Kings 18:1-6; 2 Chron. 29–32; Jer. 26:17-19). But Hezekiah's moral reformation only forestalled certain military defeat and captivity. Micah's oracle of judgment was fulfilled in 586 B.C. at the hands of the Babylonians (2 Kings 25:1-21; 2 Chron. 36:17-20; Jer. 39:1-10; 52:4-27).

About a century after Micah first gave his prophecy of Zion's destruction, Jeremiah 26:18 quoted Micah 3:12. This is the only biblical incident in which one Old Testament prophet quoted another prophet and cited the source of the quote. When Jeremiah first predicted that Jerusalem would be demolished, he was imprisoned. Some even sought his execution. Calmer heads pointed out that Micah had made similar predictions without King Hezekiah ordering his death. Tragically, another prophet named Uriah was martyred for preaching the same message (vss. 19-23).

As Jeremiah's prophetic ministry progressed, he lived an increasingly lonely life. He consistently proclaimed an oracle of judgment that would come at the hands of Babylon. Jeremiah advocated submission to Babylon, for he knew that Jehoiakim and Zedekiah were pursuing a pro-Egyptian policy. The prophet was branded as a traitor and accused of treason. He was imprisoned for a time, first in a dungeon cell and then in a muddy cistern (Jer. 37–38). After that, he remained a prisoner in the courtyard of the guard until Babylon captured Jerusalem (38:28). After the destruction of the city, Jeremiah was forced to go to Egypt with a group of survivors who had rebelled against Babylon (43:4-7). Through it all, the prophet remained true to the Lord and the message of judgment He wanted him to deliver.

Discussion Questions

1. Why were the false prophets so eager to proclaim a message of peace?
2. In what way did Micah promote justice among God's people?
3. How had the magistrates over God's people built Jerusalem through bloody crimes?
4. Why is it important for civil and religious leaders to dispense justice?
5. What are some of the characteristics of truly godly leaders?

Contemporary Application

God spoke through His servant, Micah, to His people in Judah and Israel. The Lord warned that their spiritual rebellion would ultimately lead to their destruction—that is, unless they turned back to Him and lived in a humane and just manner.

Rebellion and judgment imply that there is an ethical standard to follow and someone to decide whether we meet it. Such concepts are foreign to many people. In fact, they ridicule the idea that God has revealed certain unchangeable moral laws. They also poke fun at the idea that He judges people according to His standards.

Admittedly, it's hard for God's spiritual children to make any headway in the light of such prevailing opinions. In some cases, it's even hard for Christians to be consistent in the application of God's truths to their lives. For instance, parents struggle to teach their children what is right and wrong.

Imagine that God is the inspector of our conduct. We make decisions every day that have moral and spiritual ramifications. Our choices reflect how we view God's standards. In a figurative sense, He tests the "metal" of our lives. What are we made of? Are we willing to have God evaluate our behavior by the standard of His Word? Do we come forth shining as pure gold? May the Lord give us the grace to stand up under His scrutiny and shine brightly for His glory.

Fostering Godly Virtues

Scripture

Background Scripture: *Micah 6*
Scripture Lesson: *Micah 6:3-8*
Key Verse: *[God] has showed you, O man, what is good.
And what does the LORD require of you? To act justly and to
love mercy and to walk humbly with your God.* Micah 6:8.
Scripture Lesson for Children: *Micah 6:1-3, 6-8*
KEY VERSE for Children: *What does the LORD require of you?
To act justly and to love mercy and to walk humbly with your
God.* Micah 6:8.

Lesson Aim

To learn that God expects a life of justice, mercy, and
humility from His spiritual children.

Lesson Setting

Time: About 730 B.C.
Place: Judah

Lesson Outline

Fostering Godly Virtues

   I. A Dispute with Israel: Micah 6:3-5
      A. *The Divine Question: vs. 3*
      B. *The Divine Perspective: vss. 4-5*
  II. A Threefold Requirement: Micah 6:6-8
      A. *What God Rejects: vss. 6-7*
      B. *What God Requires: vs. 8*

Introduction for Adults

Topic: *Knowing How to Please God*

A father regularly taught his son to do what is right. One day, while they worked together with some other men, the language became increasingly profane. When the youngster joined in the talk, his father reminded him that such language was inappropriate.

Through His spokesperson Micah, God revealed that He expected Israel and Judah to live up to His high moral standards. Instead, people throughout society wallowed in the ways of their corrupt neighbors, allowed immorality and injustice to prevail, and worshiped the Lord hypocritically.

It's perilously easy for those who have been Christians for a long time to go through the motions of worship, prayer, and other religious activities. We forget that God wants us to grow in our love for Him, to mature in our spiritual wisdom and understanding, and to become more like Jesus in our thoughts and actions. This week's Scripture passage helps us to see how dangerous it is to pretend we're walking with God when we're not.

Introduction for Youth

Topic: *Doing What Is Right*

High school students who know early on that they are headed for college get a clear picture of what the universities expect of all applicants. They take various tests to be sure they can compete. They work hard and it pays off, often with valuable scholarships.

The main reason Christians highly recommend studying the Bible is not to pass an exam, but to learn what kind of behavior God desires of them. Unless we saturate ourselves in Scripture, we will fall prey to various popular ideas that are contrary to God's Word and will. Everything we do must be evaluated by what God has revealed in the Bible.

Micah preached against phony religion as well as against other kinds of sins. The prophet declared that God's basic command was to love Him. Micah also noted that God has revealed righteous principles of conduct for our good. When we love God, we can trust Him to take care of us and lead us in the best way, regardless if the ways of the ungodly sound better.

Concepts for Children

Topic: *We Can Be Good*

1. Micah did a great job of telling others about God.
2. Micah said it was important for people to worship God.
3. Micah reminded people to serve the Lord.
4. Micah taught that people should be good to each other.
5. God is more interested in how we treat others than in how much money we give to the church.

Lesson Commentary

I. A DISPUTE WITH ISRAEL: MICAH 6:3-5

A. The Divine Question: vs. 3

"My people, what have I done to you? How have I burdened you? Answer me."

As we learned in the last two lessons, the politics of Micah's day shaped his prophetic message. Both the southern kingdom of Judah and the northern kingdom of Israel had been enjoying a time of peace and prosperity. Yet rather than growing closer to God out of gratitude for this wealth, Judah and Israel had slipped into moral bankruptcy. Those who became prosperous during this time ruthlessly exploited the poor. Consequently, Micah foretold the fall of both Samaria and Jerusalem.

Of all people, the civil and religious leaders of Judah and Israel should have understood how important justice was to the social fabric of their respective nations. The magistrates often heard and settled disputes among the people, and the decisions made by the leaders were final. The people living in Judah and Israel looked to these rulers for justice. Regrettably, though, the princes of the southern and northern kingdoms perverted the administration of the Mosaic law for their personal gain.

The Hebrew verb rendered "listen" (Mic. 6:1) marks off the three major divisions of the book (1:2; 3:1) and signals that it records the Lord's judgment oracle, as delivered by His spokesperson Micah. The verb rendered "plead your case" (6:1) can also be translated "defend yourself." It indicates that what follows in this chapter is a lawsuit speech in which the Lord presents the evidence and renders the verdict against His chosen people for violating the Mosaic covenant. The literary form mirrors that found in international treaties used throughout the ancient Near East. In this imaginary courtroom scene, God is depicted as the plaintiff and prosecuting attorney, Micah is His emissary, the mountains are the jury, and the covenant community is the accused.

In verse 2, the same Hebrew noun is rendered "accusation" and "case" and has a similar range of meanings to the verb translated "plead your case" in verse 1. The noun signifies a controversy or complaint between two parties. In this instance, the Lord was bringing His indictment against His chosen people. This emphasis is reinforced by the verb rendered "lodging a charge," which can also mean "to dispute" or "to contend" (Isa. 2:4; Mic. 4:3). The idea is that God was establishing a legal proceeding against the covenant community based on irrefutable evidence. It might seem odd to us that the Creator would call upon the "mountains" (vs. 1) and the "hills" to testify on His behalf in a cosmic court of law. A clue to the meaning of this poetic passage might lie in the phrase "everlasting foundations of the earth" (vs. 2). The mountains were very old. They had been around throughout the history of Judah and Israel and were silent observers of what God's people had done. Therefore, these inanimate objects were personified as legal witnesses who could agree with the Lord that His people had broken the covenant (Deut. 4:26; 30:19; 31:28; 32:1).

Micah 6:1-2 reflects an ancient Hebrew conception of the universe in which God's people divided the world into heaven, earth, sea, and the underworld (Ps. 82:5; Prov. 8:29; Isa. 24:18). More specifically, they visualized the earth as being a flat, disk-shaped landmass that was completely surrounded by water. Pillars supported the ground, while mountains located on the distant horizon upheld the sky. The sky itself was thought to be a solid dome or tent-like structure on which the celestial bodies (namely, the sun, moon, and stars) were engraved and moved in tracks. In this ancient three-tiered view of the cosmos, rain, hail, and snow (from an immense body of water located above the overarching sky) fell to earth through openings. God's temple was situated in the upper heavens, which in turn rested atop the sky (or lower heavens). The Jerusalem temple was the earthbound counterpart to the divine abode. The realm of the dead was considered a grimy and watery region located beneath the earth and called the underworld (or Sheol).

The reference in Micah 6:3 to "My people" served as a reminder of the covenant relationship between the Lord and the inhabitants of Judah and Israel. The two questions that follow suggest the southern and northern kingdoms believed God had neglected and abused them. This mistaken notion is especially evident in the Hebrew verb rendered "burdened." The idea is that the Lord had wearied and exhausted His people with His unreasonable demands. Understandably, God did not want to leave room for either nation to claim that He—rather than they—were at fault. Judah and Israel could not legitimately argue that the Creator had been unfaithful to the promises of the Mosaic covenant. Neither could the southern and northern kingdoms rightfully claim that the stipulations of the law were either excessive or perverse. So, with the statement "Answer me," God directed His people to confirm their grievances against Him (that is, if they really could; see Jer. 2:5).

B. The Divine Perspective: vss. 4-5

"I brought you up out of Egypt and redeemed you from the land of slavery. I sent Moses to lead you, also Aaron and Miriam. My people, remember what Balak king of Moab counseled and what Balaam son of Beor answered. Remember your journey from Shittim to Gilgal, that you may know the righteous acts of the LORD."

In Micah 6:3, the Lord gave His chosen people an opportunity to substantiate how He had wronged them. The truth is that God had never been unreasonable or burdensome to Judah and Israel. In fact, He had lavished His love on both the southern and northern kingdoms. To prove this, God recounted four areas of His mercy toward the Twelve tribes in their infancy (vss. 4-5). First, God mentioned how He had rescued His people from slavery in Egypt. Between the time of Joseph and Moses, the Israelites spent 430 years in Egypt. The Hebrew verb translated "redeemed" can also mean "to ransom" and calls attention to all that God did on behalf of the Israelites to deliver them from servitude in Egypt. The Egyptians had forced the Israelites to do construction projects, but God used miracles to convince Pharaoh to let the Israelites go (Exod. 1:1–15:21).

Second, God mentioned the leaders He had given the nation. These individuals included Moses, the deliverer (Exod. 3:10), lawgiver (Deut. 4:45), and prophet (18:15); Moses' brother, Aaron, the high priest (Lev. 8); and Miriam, their sister, a prophetess (Exod. 15:20). With such noteworthy servants of the Lord, the Israelites had exceptional guidance.

Third, God recalled the incident in which He preserved the early Israelites from a threat presented by the Moabites. Balak, the king of Moab, had wanted the soothsayer Balaam to curse Israel, but instead God caused Balaam to bless the Israelites (Num. 22–24).

Fourth, God cited the young nation's final journey into the promised land, from Shittim (a plain in Moab on the east side of the Jordan River) to Gilgal (on the west side). During that journey, God parted the Jordan River just as earlier He had parted the Red Sea (Josh. 3–4). By rehearsing these historic episodes, the Lord wanted His people to be certain of His upright acts, including how He had always treated them faithfully and fairly.

II. A THREEFOLD REQUIREMENT: MICAH 6:6-8

A. What God Rejects: vss. 6-7

With what shall I come before the Lord and bow down before the exalted God? Shall I come before him with burnt offerings, with calves a year old? Will the Lord be pleased with thousands of rams, with ten thousand rivers of oil? Shall I offer my firstborn for my transgression, the fruit of my body for the sin of my soul?

Previously, the Lord asked His people what fault they found in Him (Mic. 6:3). Now, a new voice speaks in 6:6 and 7. God's envoy poses as an inquiring worshiper (possibly a priest or other religious official) at the entrance to the Jerusalem temple (Pss. 15:1; 24:3; Isa. 33:14). As a representative of the entire covenant community, he responded to God's accusation in a way that reflected the pathetic spiritual state of His chosen people. The speaker wanted to know what sacrifices the transcendent Lord required to appease His anger for Judah's rebellious acts and Israel's offenses. The petitioner's suggestions begin with the typical and quickly go to the extreme. Did almighty God want His people to bow before Him with offerings and yearling calves? Or should they offer Him thousands of rams and tens of thousands of rivers of olive oil? Or should they sacrifice their firstborn children to pay for the trespasses they had committed?

The last item warrants further comment. Child sacrifice, while probably never common, was known in both Judah and Israel. The pagan inhabitants of the surrounding nations carried out child sacrifices (2 Kings 3:26-27) and this practice crept into the southern and northern kingdoms with the veneration of foreign gods and goddesses. For instance, the pagan deity Molech was especially associated with child sacrifice. Idolaters built a sanctuary to Molech called Topheth (which means "burning place") south of Jerusalem, and there sometimes burnt children (23:10). Undoubtedly, it was to Molech that the Judahite kings Ahaz and Manasseh sacrificed their sons (16:3; 21:6).

Micah 6:6-7 indicate that God's people were quite mistaken in thinking that He would take delight in their innumerable and extreme sacrifices (1 Sam. 15:22; Ps. 51:17; Isa. 1:11-15). Admittedly, the Lord had ordained the sacrificial system for the Israelite people (even though He never approved of child sacrifice). But in this case, the people were clearly using the system to try to buy His favor. They were willing to carry out rituals, but were not truly obedient when it came to dealing with others.

B. What God Requires: vs. 8

He has showed you, O man, what is good. And what does the LORD require of you? To act justly and to love mercy and to walk humbly with your God.

What can mere mortals do to please their Creator? That is the burning question in the heart of every person who approaches the Lord in heartfelt worship. The responses recorded in Micah 6:6-7 were theologically way off the mark, even though they reflected the thinking of unsaved humanity. Against the backdrop of God's redemptive acts, He clarified what He really wanted (vs. 8; see also Pss. 15:2-5; 24:4-5; Isa. 33:15-16). The eternal Creator did not desire to receive meaningless religious acts from His chosen people. Instead, He wanted their thoughts, words, and actions to be characterized by equity and compassion.

God decreed that His people make the following three principles a priority in their lives: (1) to promote justice (that is, honesty and fairness); (2) to let persistent acts of kindness undergird their dealings with one another; and (3) to ensure that reverence, prudence, and obedience were the foundation of their relationship with the Lord (Isa. 29:19; Jer. 22:16; Hos. 6:6; Amos 5:24; Jas. 1:27). These requirements progress from what is external to what is internal and from one's relationship to other people to one's relationship with God. Specifically, in order to be just toward other people, one must display loyal love. Also, such compassion demands a circumspect walk before the Lord. These virtues are ones that believers today ought to strive to fulfill. God still expects His people to treat others with Christlike love and to live in devotion to Him.

The continuing importance of the preceding three characteristics is seen in Jesus' repeating their essence to the hypocritical religious leaders of His day (Matt. 23:23). So, acting in a just manner means we are determined to do God's will—that is, to love Him with all our heart, soul, mind, and strength, and to love our neighbors as ourselves. Also, our resolving with God's help to carry out justice includes revering Him, honoring our commitments to Him and others, and defending the rights of the innocent. To prize mercy involves more than treating others fairly. It signifies unfailing compassion, which is a key attribute of God Himself, who abounds in love (Exod. 34:6; Neh. 9:17; Ps. 103:8). Moreover, God's type of mercy shows empathy to the undeserving, offers spiritual resources to those who are less fortunate, donates to charitable causes, and actively shares with others in need. To relate to God in a humble manner means understanding that we have sinned and are saved by His grace. Furthermore, submission to the Creator involves fellowship, namely, spending time with Him and devoting our motives, goals, and integrity to Him.

Micah 6:9-16 comprises another prophecy in which God listed some crimes committed by His chosen people. These verses also describe the ways in which the Lord would punish them. The oracle begins with Micah's call for his peers to listen to the Lord's words. The "city" in verse 9 is Jerusalem, which represents the covenant community as a whole. The "rod" Jerusalem was to heed was the punishment God would send. The people of Judah (as well as Israel) were far from walking in justice, kindness, and humility before God. Verses 10 through 12 contain a collection of social sins which they were guilty of committing. Verses 10 and 11 indicate that some in Judah had gotten wealthy through dishonest means. They had "ill-gotten treasures." They used "the short ephah." As noted in lesson 4, since an ephah was a measure equal to about three-fifths of a bushel, this means sellers were cheating buyers by measuring out less than the full amount. They also cheated by weighing goods falsely on a scale balance.

In the ancient Near East, merchants used scales to measure goods and even money, since there was no standardized coinage. Scales consisted of two pans suspended from a crossbar. Vendors would put precisely weighted stones in one pan and place the item(s) for weighing in the other. Even though the law of Moses forbade the falsification of weights and measures (Lev. 19:35–36; Deut. 25:13-16), this dishonest practice sometimes occurred. One way to obtain an inaccurate measurement was to shorten the length of one of the arms of the crossbar. Another way was to use falsely marked stones. Some merchants even used two sets of weights in their transactions, one for buying and one for selling.

Micah 6:12 reveals that the wicked rich were violent, and the people lied. These charges perhaps indicate that the elite in society were using force to steal property and that individuals were committing perjury in court to support dishonest business practices. Similarly, people in the contemporary marketplace use all sorts of excuses to justify their cheating. Consider the following three overused slogans: "business is business"; "it's a dog-eat-dog world"; and "you've got to get them before they get you." In contrast, God calls His people to a far higher standard of business integrity.

Verse 13 introduces a description of the ways in which God would punish His chosen people for their crimes. These consequences included hunger, loss, and futility. For instance, the people who tried to get wealthy by dishonest means would have to do without material goods. The sins of the people were not all social; some were religious (vs. 16). Specifically, the Lord condemned the covenant community for following the traditions of Omri and Ahab, who were kings of Israel more than a century earlier. This wicked father and son engaged in and promoted idolatrous religion (1 Kings 16:25-26, 30-33). In Micah's lifetime, the people of Judah were worshiping in the same ways as their counterparts in Israel. Because of this, God was going to give both the southern and northern kingdoms over to ruin.

Discussion Questions

1. In what ways did the people of Judah and Israel believe God had neglected and abused them?
2. What was the nature of the case God brought against His chosen people?
3. Why did God refuse to delight in countless and extreme sacrifices?
4. What does it mean to be fair, merciful, and humble to others?
5. When do you most remember seeing justice, kindness, and modesty being shown by other Christians?

Contemporary Application

When we first become Christians, our relationship with God feels strong. We are eager to do whatever He asks, and we desire to conform our lives to His will. Over time, however, our devotion may wane. We start worrying about our problems and become distracted by the pressures of life. Before long we realize that we are not as close to the Lord as we want to be.

This common situation emphasizes the importance of renewing our relationship with God. As Micah 6 makes clear, the Lord urges us to do this very thing. Because of all the Father has done for us in the Son, we are to give ourselves fully to Him in service for His glory. Also, as we renew our relationship with God, we will be pure and pleasing sacrifices to Him (Rom. 12:1). In turn, when this becomes a reality, our lives will increasingly become characterized by justice, mercy, and humility (Mic. 6:8).

If our relationship with God has weakened to a certain extent, it will take some time for us to renew it. As part of the renewal process, the Lord will bring to mind areas of our lives He wants to change. It might be the way we think, the words we use, or the goals we adopt. Regardless of how God brings about change in our lives, His ultimate aim will be to draw us closer to Him.

At first, the task might seem daunting. But rather than give up altogether, we should take gradual and realistic steps in cultivating the three elements of upright living—justice, mercy, and humility. At times the process will be difficult and costly in terms of what God leads us to do or stop doing. Regardless of the steps that are taken, we can rest assured that it will be well worth our time, effort, and sacrifice.

Experiencing God's Pardon

Scripture

Background Scripture: *Micah 7:11-20*
Scripture Lesson: *Micah 7:14-20*
Key Verse: *Who is a God like you, who pardons sin and forgives the transgression of the remnant of his inheritance? You do not stay angry forever but delight to show mercy. Micah 7:18.*
Scripture Lesson for Children: *Micah 7:14-20*
Key Verse for Children: *[God will] hurl all our iniquities into the depths of the sea. Micah. 7:19.*

Lesson Aim

To accept the promise of God's unfailing love and forgiveness.

Lesson Setting

Time: About 730 B.C.
Place: Judah

Lesson Outline

Experiencing God's Pardon

I. The Promise of Restoration: Micah 7:14-15
   A. *God's Provision: vs. 14*
   B. *God's Power: vs. 15*

II. The Promise of Blessings: Micah 7:16-20
   A. *God's Subjugation of the Nations: vss. 16-17*
   B. *God's Forgiveness and Compassion: vss. 18-20*

Introduction for Adults

Topic: *God Freely Pardons Us*

What are some lessons we have learned the hard way? What stories could we tell about how we suffered because we thought we knew better? It is humbling to admit that we failed because we were too proud and stubborn to listen to someone's advice or to the wisdom of God's Word.

Nevertheless, how thankful we are that God often delivers us from our follies. Also, how marvelous it is to tell others about His grace. We should mention not just our mistakes, but also God's mercy and goodness.

Imagine the prophet Micah assembling the people in Jerusalem so that they could acknowledge their wrongdoing to the Lord. In turn, consider the joy they would feel when God freely forgave them. This is exactly what the Father has done for us in His Son. When we accept the pardon God freely makes available in Jesus, we have the assurance that our misdeeds will not be held against us.

Introduction for Youth

Topic: *God Is Merciful to Us*

Early in 1993, British police accused two ten-year-old boys of the brutal murder of two-year-old James Bulger. The two boys initially claimed they were innocent. Nevertheless, the young defendants responded to police questioning with noticeable inconsistency.

The climax came when the parents of one of the boys assured him that they would always love him. As a result of being confronted with irrefutable evidence linking him with the crime and the assurance of his parents' love, the boy confessed in a soft voice, "I killed James."

Through Micah the prophet, God declared that He knew the sins His people had committed. The Lord also knows about our misdeeds. Yet He still loves us. The presence of His unfailing compassion encourages us, as it did the people of Micah's day, to confess our sins and experience the Lord's abundant forgiveness.

Concepts for Children

Topic: *Forgiveness for All*

1. God's people did what was wrong in His sight.
2. Micah told God's people that He loved them.
3. Micah said that God wanted to forgive His people's sin.
4. God wants us to turn away from our sin.
5. God forgives us when we are sorry for our sin.

Lesson Commentary

I. THE PROMISE OF RESTORATION: MICAH 7:14-15

A. God's Provision: vs. 14

Shepherd your people with your staff, the flock of your inheritance, which lives by itself in a forest, in fertile pasturelands. Let them feed in Bashan and Gilead as in days long ago.

In lesson 5, we noted that Micah 6 and 7 form a literary unit that focuses on the Lord's indictment and restoration of His chosen people. We also learned in lesson 7 that the charges against the covenant community are detailed in 6:1-8, while the guilt and punishment the people received for their transgressions are described in verses 9-16. The first seven verses of chapter 7 are presented as an agonizing lament that details the crimes Judah and Israel committed and how that decadence lead to the disintegration of society. Micah, as the speaker, voiced his thoughts as though he were the only righteous person left within the covenant community. Of course, he was exaggerating. Nonetheless, verses 1-7 indicate that wickedness had become widespread.

Micah began his dirge by comparing himself to someone who was hungry for some fruit to eat (including clusters of grapes and ripe figs). But he arrived at the vineyard and orchard too late, for all the fruit had been harvested (vs. 1). In plainer language, when the prophet looked for faithful rulers, none were to be found either in Judah or Israel. Moreover, it seemed as if all the leaders characterized by moral rectitude had vanished (vs. 2; see also Isa. 5:1-7). The prophet explained that the magistrates from both the southern and northern kingdoms were adept at preying on the innocent like ruthless hunters. Both princes and judges demanded bribes and collaborated to weave together the fabric of their evil plans (Mic. 7:3). Even the most religious among the ruling class were as menacing as a thicket of thorn bushes. For this reason, the time had come for the Lord to visit His people in judgment. When lookouts (such as God's prophets) sounded the warning of approaching danger (that is, divine judgment), panic and "confusion" (vs. 4) would ensue (Jer. 6:17; Ezek. 3:19; Hos. 9:8).

Micah went on to describe the terrible moral state of his society. He noted that no one could be trusted, no matter how close the relationship, regardless of whether it was between neighbors, friends, or spouses (Mic. 7:5). For instance, within Israelite families, long-standing spheres of authority between the generations collapsed. Sons treated their fathers with contempt, while daughters challenged their mothers. Even daughters-in-law opposed their mothers-in-law. At the same time, the "members" (vs. 6) of the same "household" were adversarial toward one another (Matt. 10:21, 34-36; Luke 12:53). In short, rampant godlessness had poisoned the most intimate relationships. Micah 7:7 records the prophet's own testimony of faith in God. Whereas the sentries of verse 4 watched for the approach of calamity, Micah would look to the Creator and wait expectantly for Him to deliver the faithful. Micah was confident that God would respond to His spokesperson's lament (Ps. 55:16-17).

Micah 7:8-20 contains a liturgical hymn of praise for God's deliverance of His chosen people from the oppression of their enemies. In verses 8-10, the prophet spoke on behalf of Lady Jerusalem, in which the holy city (personified as an individual) confessed her faith in the Lord. Next, verses 11-13 present a divine pledge of blessing on the upright remnant. Most likely, the plight experienced by Zion was due either to the Assyrian siege of 701 B.C. or to the Babylonian victory in 586 B.C. The promises applied in part to the rebuilding of Jerusalem after the Babylonian Captivity, but also apply in part to the messianic age.

Verse 8 issues a warning to Lady Zion's adversary—whether a nation or nations that threatened the city—not to be gleeful over her misfortune. Even though Jerusalem experienced the "darkness" of God's judgment, He would become the "light" of her deliverance. For this reason, Zion's foes were foolish to exult over her downfall, especially since Jerusalem would eventually bounce back from her hardship. The city acknowledged that she deserved to endure God's indignation, for she had violated His covenant. Yet the Lord, like a defense attorney, would advocate for Zion and achieve justice on her behalf. So, in the dispute between Jerusalem and her enemies, the Creator would vindicate the city. His blessing included leading her into the "light" (vs. 9) of His deliverance.

Zion's adversary would witness God's goodness to her and be mortified by it. After all, the foe had taunted Jerusalem with the claim that her Lord was either weak or indifferent. But in the day of reckoning, the "enemy" (vs. 10) would be disgraced as God rescued His chosen people. Also, a time of reversal was coming in which, despite Zion's being downtrodden, her tormentors would be in that position. The Creator would see to it that they were crushed underfoot like refuse in the gutter. In Bible times, it was common for city dwellers to dump refuse (including animal and human excrement) in the dirt streets, which functioned as public sewers.

Micah assured Jerusalem that God would allow her to rebuild her "walls" (vs. 11) and expand her territory far beyond the city's surrounding environs. This prophecy seems to look forward, at least in part, to the period after the exile. Furthermore, Micah promised Zion that people would stream to her from distant places, including Assyria, Egypt, the seacoasts, and even the mountains of the earth (vs. 12). This seems to look forward to the messianic era. While God's chosen people would prosper, the pagan nations would experience desolation. Disaster would come to them because of their ungodly behavior. The Bible often associates the Hebrew term translated "desolate" (vs. 13) with divine judgment upon sinners.

The final section of Micah contains several different literary elements. First, God's spokesperson prayed on behalf of the chosen people (vs. 14). Next, the

Lord responded with an assurance (vs. 15). Then, Micah stated confidently that the nations would submit to God (vss. 16-17) and that He would show mercy to His people (vss.18-20). In the opening prayer (vs. 14), Micah depicted the Lord as a "Shepherd" and the faithful remnant as His prized "flock" (Gen. 48:15; Pss. 23:1; 28:9; John 10:11).

The King made it possible for His "inheritance" (Mic. 7:14) to dwell safely in the woodland far from any predators (Ps. 94:14). The Hebrew text of Micah 7:14 more literally says that the covenant community was living "in the middle of Carmel." Carmel is a mountain range famous for its garden-like forests covered with vegetation. Micah also asked for God to let His people feed in Bashan and Gilead. These were lush grasslands on the eastern side of the Jordan River. In certain periods, Israel possessed those territories, but it probably did not control them at the time Micah wrote. So, this request might be a petition for the Lord to one day return those areas to the covenant community.

B. God's Power: vs. 15

"As in the days when you came out of Egypt, I will show them my wonders."

Micah 7:15 appears to be God's response to the prayer recorded in verse 14. The Shepherd-King promised to perform miraculous deeds as in the time of the Exodus. The "wonders" during that earlier time included the ten successive plagues on Egypt, the parting of the Red Sea, the provision of manna and water in the wilderness, and the appearance of God on Mount Sinai. Concerning the ten plagues, these were blood (Exod. 7:17-24), frogs (7:25–8:15), gnats (8:16-19), flies (vss. 20-32), livestock disease (9:1-7), boils (vss. 8-12), hail (vss. 13-35), locusts (10:3-20), darkness (vss. 21-23), and the death of the firstborn (11:1-8; 12:21-30).

Some Bible scholars think the first nine plagues were natural phenomena in Egypt that were miraculous in their intensity and the time of their occurrence. In this case, God used natural means to achieve divine objectives. In contrast, others see these calamities as being more directly supernatural (for example, blood being taken literally). The final plague—the death of the firstborn in Egypt—was unquestionably different. It was clearly outside the realm of the natural and normal experience of the Egyptians. Yet, like the other plagues, it fell upon prince and peasant alike. This most devastating of the afflictions reached even the family of Pharaoh himself.

After the tenth plague occurred, Egypt's ruler, under cover of darkness, called Moses and Aaron and virtually ordered them to take the Hebrews and their animals and go out to the desert to worship God. The once-arrogant pharaoh was even reduced to asking Moses and Aaron to "bless" (12:32) him. In effect, the Egyptian monarch was requesting prayer for himself and his devastated nation. After nine burdensome plagues, capped by a horrific tenth, Pharaoh no doubt had a much-changed opinion of the God he had earlier defied.

Amazingly, after the Hebrews left, Pharaoh's heart was hardened again. So his army headed across the desert in pursuit of the former slaves. But God delivered the Hebrews once more from their oppressors as the Egyptian army followed them into the Red Sea. The antagonists eventually drowned when the waters closed in behind the Hebrews (14:26-31). After witnessing the Lord's awesome power, His chosen people sang a song of adoration (15:1). They extolled the great strength and majestic power of the Creator that resulted in the destruction of the horses and riders of the Egyptian army. God alone was given credit for the deliverance of the Hebrews. Also, for this He was extremely worthy of their praise and exaltation (vss. 2-16).

II. THE PROMISE OF BLESSINGS: MICAH 7:16-20

A. God's Subjugation of the Nations: vss. 16-17

Nations will see and be ashamed, deprived of all their power. They will lay their hands on their mouths and their ears will become deaf. They will lick dust like a snake, like creatures that crawl on the ground. They will come trembling out of their dens; they will turn in fear to the LORD our God and will be afraid of you.

While God's people could expect to benefit from His power, other peoples would not fare so well. The divine Warrior would judge the pagan "nations" (Mic. 7:16) for their iniquities. These transgressions included taunting and tormenting the upright remnant. Appropriately, God would humiliate the tyrants. Specifically, the might of their armies would be ineffective in resisting the Lord of heaven's vast legions. Indeed, His awesome might so astounded them that they would lose all ability to speak or hear.

Genesis 3 reveals that at the dawn of humanity, a serpent tricked the first woman and man to disobey their Creator and eat of the forbidden fruit (1 Tim. 2:13-14). Part of God's curse on the tempter included experiencing the humiliation of slithering on the ground and being forced to ingest dirt as it moved along (Gen. 3:14). In a future day, when the Lord rescued His chosen people from their foes, He would shame the oppressors by consigning them to "lick dust like a snake" (Mich. 7:17). The Hebrew phrase translated "lick dust" might reflect the ancient practice in which defeated kings were made to kiss the feet of their victorious enemies as a sign of subjugation. Micah foretold that in abject disgrace, the vanquished tormentors would "crawl" out of their fortresses like reptiles and approach the sovereign Ruler of the universe with "fear" and "trembling."

The prophet's declaration parallels the truths recorded in Philippians 2:9-11. Paul, after discussing the Son's sacrificial death on the cross (vss. 6-8), shifted the focus to His exaltation. The place of honor that Jesus willingly forsook was given back to Him with the added glory of His triumph over sin and death. In response to the Son's humility and obedience, the Father supremely exalted Jesus to a place where His triumph will eventually be recognized by all living creatures (vs. 9). The apostle emphatically tells us that every person who has ever lived will someday recognize the Son for who He is, namely, the supreme Lord revealed in the Old Testament as Yahweh (Acts 2:33-36).

The "name of Jesus" (Phil. 2:10) signifies the majestic office or position the Father bestowed on the Son, not His proper name. By bowing their knees, every human being and angel will acknowledge Jesus' deity and sovereignty. Also, everyone will confess that Jesus is Lord—some with joyful faith, others with hopeless regret and anguish (vs. 11). Centuries earlier, Isaiah the prophet had announced the words of the Messiah: "Before me every knee will bow; by me every tongue will swear" (Isa. 45:23; see also Rom. 14:11; Rev. 5:13). Philippians 2:6-11 affirms that this universal acknowledgment of Jesus' lordship will ultimately come to pass.

B. God's Forgiveness and Compassion: vss. 18-20

Who is a God like you, who pardons sin and forgives the transgression of the remnant of his inheritance? You do not stay angry forever but delight to show mercy. You will again have compassion on us; you will tread our sins underfoot and hurl all our iniquities into the depths of the sea. You will be true to Jacob, and show mercy to Abraham, as you pledged on oath to our fathers in days long ago.

Micah closed his book with an expression of wonder at God's mercy and confidence in His faithfulness. The prophet's name means "Who is like Yahweh?" and in Micah 7:18 he apparently wove this name into the fabric of his praise to the Lord. This verse and the next one convey the idea that God is gracious toward His chosen people. For instance, He lifts away the guilt and punishment of their iniquity (Exod. 34:6-7; Ps. 30:5). He also passes over the rebellious acts committed by the upright "remnant" (Mic. 7:18), who are His heritage (Pss. 28:9; 33:12; Isa. 19:25; Joel 2:17). Unlike petulant human rulers, the Creator does not hold onto His anger indefinitely. Rather, He is pleased to lavish His "inheritance" (Mic. 7:18) with His steadfast love.

Micah was confident that even though the Lord brought a season of affliction on His people for their violations of the Mosaic covenant, He would once more shower them with His unfailing kindness. Micah revealed that due to God's clemency, He would subdue their misdeeds like a warrior tramples his defeated foes. The prophet also declared that the Shepherd-King would toss their trespasses into the "depths of the sea" (vs. 19). In ancient Near Eastern literature, the sea was a symbol of chaos. The idea is that the Creator would trounce such a despot. In doing so, God would fulfill the pledge He made centuries earlier to the patriarchs—Abraham, Isaac, and Jacob—to bless their descendants with complete and unconditional forgiveness (Gen. 12:2-3; 13:15-16; 15:5, 18-21; 17:4-8; 21:12; 22:17; 28:13-15; 35:10-12).

New Testament believers have also experienced the kind of pardoning love Micah described (Rom. 4:17; Gal. 3:6-29; Heb. 11:12). They know God's faithfulness in both discipline and forgiveness. The main message of the Bible is that we cannot help ourselves—not one bit. Much as we would like to have the key to our own salvation, so we could effect our own rescue, we need to admit to ourselves that we have lost the key and cannot be our own deliverers. But the closing chapter of Micah's prophecy reminds us of some good news. The Creator has the ability to deliver us and become our salvation.

Discussion Questions

1. In what sense was the faithful remnant of Micah's day the flock of God's inheritance?
2. What miracles did the Lord perform to free the Hebrews from Egypt?
3. How will the pagan nations respond to God's vindication of His chosen people?
4. What is the basis for the Lord pardoning our transgressions?
5. What in your life has God completely and unconditionally forgiven?

Contemporary Application

Micah 7:18-19 reminds us that God freely forgives our sin and guilt. It's as if He hurled our transgressions into the depths of the sea, never to remember them again. The good news of God's grace should prompt us to abandon sin in our lives and wholeheartedly seek the Lord. But what does it mean to do so?

Some people believe all one has to do is recite a pious-sounding prayer and that is the end of it. More accurately, seeking the Lord is a process in which God's people individually and collectively turn their hearts to Him in unwavering devotion. It means they go out into the world and make the wonderful news of His pardon and compassion known through their words and deeds. Seeking the Lord means believers dedicate every aspect of their lives to His service.

When we seek the Lord fully, we figuratively hand Him a blank sheet to fill in, with our name signed at the bottom. We orient our minds and hearts to His will. We effectively say no to our sinful ways and yes to His holy desires. At times, we might not feel inclined to seek the Lord as much as we ought. It is in those moments that we should pray to God for a willing mind and heart.

We should not think that seeking the Lord is an entirely personal matter. God wants us to encourage one another to remain spiritually in tune to Him. For instance, when we see our fellow Christians struggling spiritually, we can stand by their side and offer consolation and support. We can also remember to pray for one another and ask that God would enable us to remain loyal to Him and His people.

The Redeemer's Presence

Scripture

Background Scripture: *Isaiah 59; Psalm 89:11-18*

Scripture Lesson: *Isaiah 59:15-21*

Key Verse: *"The Redeemer will come to Zion, to those in Jacob who repent of their sins,"* declares the LORD. Isaiah 59:20.

Scripture Lesson for Children: *Isaiah 59:15-21*

Key Verse for Children: *"The Redeemer will come to Zion, to those in Jacob who repent of their sins,"* declares the LORD. Isaiah 59:20.

Lesson Aim

To experience the redemption the Father offers in His Son, the Messiah.

Lesson Setting

Time: 740–700 B.C.

Place: Judah

Lesson Outline

The Redeemer's Presence

    I. The Recognition of Sin: Isaiah 59:15-16

        A. *The Prevalence of Iniquity: vs. 15*

        B. *The Need to Intervene: vs. 16*

    II. The Redemption from Sin: Isaiah 59:17-21

        A. *The Divine Initiative: vs. 17*

        B. *The Divine Recompense: vs. 18*

        C. *The Lord's Saving Work: vss. 19-20*

        D. *The Everlasting Covenant: vs. 21*

Introduction for Adults

Topic: *The Rescuer Comes!*

It appalled the Lord that all traces of justice and truth had vanished from Judah (Isa. 59:14-15). That is why God would intervene on behalf of the innocent (vs. 16). Indeed, He would do so through His Suffering Servant (53:12).

We cannot read Isaiah's description of the Suffering Servant without sensing that a great miscarriage of justice occurred. We know from the Gospels that the compelling reasons for Jesus' affliction were entrenched religious hatred and the ruling elite's fear of losing their power. They condemned Jesus to die for having exposed their heartless, rigid hypocrisy.

Adults need to know that Jesus allowed Himself to be sentenced to death at the hands of hypocritical authorities so that His saving grace might be made known through the proclamation of the Gospel (Rom. 1:16). Adults also need to understand that it's only through faith in the crucified, risen Savior that they can be forgiven and receive eternal life (Acts 4:12).

Introduction for Youth

Topic: *Our Redeemer Cares!*

God was astonished that there seemed to be no one in Judah either willing or able to rescue the oppressed from their terrible situation. So, the all-powerful God decided He would bring about their deliverance (Isa. 59:16). He would use His faithful Servant to vindicate the cause of the defenseless (53:5, 11).

Jesus' willingness to suffer in order to make salvation available to the lost shows young people that obedience to God is costly. This should come as no surprise, for Jesus said that no one can follow Him without taking the path of self-denial (Luke 9:23). Whenever Christian youth think they can't endure a severe test of their faith, they should recall how Jesus suffered for them (Heb. 12:2-3).

Jesus was far more than a martyr. He was God's sacrificial Lamb (1 Pet. 1:18-19). The one who atoned for our sins was genuinely humble and gracious, even to His enemies (2:23). No one else can enable young people to go through trials with a peace that "transcends all understanding" (Phil. 4:7). And He alone can keep them from spiritually stumbling (Jude 24).

Concepts for Children

Topic: *Be Redeemed!*

1. Isaiah was a person who spoke for God.
2. Isaiah told God's people that He knew they were suffering.
3. Isaiah said that God would save His people.
4. Isaiah let God's people know that He would punish their enemies.
5. We feel joy when we tell others what God has done for them.

Lesson Commentary

I. THE RECOGNITION OF SIN: ISAIAH 59:15-16

A. The Prevalence of Iniquity: vs. 15

Truth is nowhere to be found, and whoever shuns evil becomes a prey. The LORD looked and was displeased that there was no justice.

In Isaiah 58:1-7, God addressed Himself to people who were fasting and showing signs of humility, and yet were also committing sins. This message seems to have been directed primarily to Jews who would be reading it during the postexilic period. After returning to Judah, the people were fasting improperly and breaking the Sabbath law. The Lord told them that the "fasting" He desires includes helping the needy. Next, in verses 8-14, God assured the people that if they were truly repentant, quit harming others, and honored the Sabbath, He would bless them. The blessings would include control of the promised land and success in rebuilding Jerusalem. Otherwise, the Lord would withhold blessings from His people during the period after the exile because they did not offer Him proper obedience.

The people, however, apparently explained God's failure to deliver them from their troubles by declaring He was unable to act. In clear terms, Isaiah stated that this explanation was incorrect and that the people's problems could be traced directly to their own sins (59:1-2). Then the prophet described those misdeeds (vss. 3-8). Isaiah affirmed that God had the ability to rescue His people. But the Lord chose to withhold His help from them because of their sin. Isaiah sought the restoration of his wayward people to God by identifying with them and offering a detailed confession of their transgressions (vss. 9-15).

In verses 9 and 10, we find the tragic characterization of a privileged community that claimed to be God's children. Despite their assertions, they were both spiritually blind and dead. So, what they needed was nothing less than the light and life of God's salvation. Isaiah's response in verses 11-15 is the only viable one to the Lord's just indictment. The prophet confessed that the people had sinned against God and reaped the consequences of a society void of justice, righteousness, truth, and honesty. These principles were especially intended to govern the administration of the nation's decrees and ordinances within its courts of law. Isaiah personified the absence of these building blocks of the nation as people who were being hindered or were struggling in some way.

Previously, in 51:4-6, the Lord's justice and righteousness symbolized the salvation He graciously provided. If His people waited expectantly for the promised deliverance, it would come. Yet, their lack of faith in God prevented the people from experiencing the full extent of the blessing He pledged to give them. In particular, "justice" (59:14) was beaten back and "righteousness" (or "godliness") was nowhere to be found. Similarly, "truth" staggered in the city squares and "honesty" (that is, integrity and rectitude) was shoved aside. Moreover, "truth" (vs. 15) had vanished from the courts, being replaced by lies. Also, the wicked rich plundered those who renounced "evil." Not surprisingly, the all-knowing God was fully aware of the corruption and cruelty taking place among His people, and He found the circumstance to be abhorrent.

B. The Need to Intervene: vs. 16

He saw that there was no one, he was appalled that there was no one to intervene; so his own arm worked salvation for him, and his own righteousness sustained him.

As the Lord looked upon Judah, He not only witnessed the rampant injustice going on, but also noticed that there was no one to intercede on behalf of the innocent in the courts of law. Similarly, God was disgusted to learn that the defenseless were without an advocate to assist them (Isa. 59:16). A parallel thought is recorded in 63:5. In both passages, we discover that the covenant-keeping God of Israel would come to the aid of the oppressed and rectify the injustices they experienced. The Lord would do so by drawing on His all-sufficient resources. With His own powerful "arm" (59:16) He would win "salvation" for His people, and His commitment to promote justice upheld Him in His righteous cause.

In 53:12, we learn that God would use His Servant to intercede on behalf of the "transgressors." He is none other than the Messiah, the One who would bring true deliverance, not from national slavery, but from humanity's more horrible and eternal slavery to sin (42:1, 7). The typical first-century expectations of the Messiah included political agendas, military campaigns, and great fanfare (John 6:14-15). Matthew 12:18-21 quotes Isaiah 42:1-4 to stress that the Messiah was not this type of king. Instead, He would be a quiet, gentle ruler who would bring justice to the nations. Also, as God's chosen Servant, the Messiah would be noted for His encouragement and truth, not violence and trickery (John 18:33-37). As God's Servant, the Lord Jesus brought justice by dying on the cross for sinners. Without His sacrifice, no one could be saved since justice demands that all sinners be punished. When the Messiah returned, He would also bring justice by rewarding good and defeating evil.

In Isaiah 53:5, we discover that God's Servant was wounded because of our "transgressions." The latter renders a Hebrew noun that can also be translated "rebellious deeds" or "acts of insurrection." Moreover, the Servant was "crushed" because of our "iniquities." The reference here includes the guilt and punishment connected with our trespasses. In short, the holy one of God allowed Himself to be profaned and brutalized to bring us "peace" with God. The noun rendered "peace" comes from a term that means health, wholeness, and well-being in every area of life, including people's relationship with God. Moreover, the "wounds" inflicted on the Servant from being beaten would bring spiritual healing to people's sin-sick souls (Ps. 22:16; Zech. 12:10; John 19:34).

First Peter 2:24 refers to Isaiah 53:5 to affirm that believers are healed by the wounds others inflicted on the Messiah. The Greek noun translated "wounds" (1 Pet. 2:24) refers to bruises and welts caused by being whipped or beaten. Based on this verse, some think that physical healing is included in Jesus' atonement. Probably the majority believe that Peter was referring to spiritual healing. The apostle stressed that those who trust in the Son are delivered from their spiritual sickness. In conjunction with Isaiah 53:6, Peter declared that his readers had once been like straying sheep (1 Pet. 2:25). Furthermore, the apostle explained that though the recipients of his letter had once wandered far from the Son, they had returned to Him when they got saved. Indeed, He was their Good Shepherd, the One who laid down His life for them (John 10:11, 14; Heb. 13:20; 1 Pet. 5:4; Rev. 7:17). Jesus is also their Overseer. This means He looks out for their temporal and eternal welfare.

II. THE REDEMPTION FROM SIN: ISAIAH 59:17-21

A. The Divine Initiative: vs. 17

He put on righteousness as his breastplate, and the helmet of salvation on his head; he put on the garments of vengeance and wrapped himself in zeal as in a cloak.

In Isaiah 59:17-19, God is portrayed as an ancient warrior who gets ready to enter battle on behalf of his nation and people. The Lord wears His commitment to justice as a coat of chainmail (a type of armor comprised of small metal rings linked together to create a mesh). Likewise, the "helmet" on God's "head" is His intent to deliver the faithful remnant. This includes vindicating their cause and punishing their oppressors. For this reason, the Commander of heaven's armies clothes Himself with an overcoat of "vengeance" (or retribution) and clads Himself with a mantle of "zeal" for upholding His people's cause. In short, the divine Warrior trounces His enemies and restores the covenant community to its rightful place of honor (Exod. 15:3; Isa. 42:13; 49:25; 52:10). In Ephesians 6:13-17, Paul used the imagery of God's armor to describe the nature of the spiritual battle Jesus' followers wage against the forces of darkness. (See the exposition of this passage in lesson 12 of the December quarter.)

B. The Divine Recompense: vs. 18

According to what they have done, so will he repay wrath to his enemies and retribution to his foes; he will repay the islands their due.

Not everyone would experience God's blessing. In the coming day of judgment, the Lord would punish ungodly Israelites and wicked nations (Isa. 65:6-7; 66:6; Jer. 25:29). As Isaiah 59:18 reveals, God would deal with His foes in an objective and equitable manner. Based on the way in which His "enemies" abused His people, the divine Warrior would dispense His fury. He would even pay back His adversaries to the coastlands, regardless of whether they were near or far away.

In Romans 2:16, Paul declared that the Lord Jesus will be the agent of God's judgment and that His evaluation would focus on secrets of people's hearts. Sometimes people do good things that are actually rooted in selfish intentions. Other times people may appear guilty of a wrongdoing when there was no bad intention. Sometimes people internalize blame for the sins of others. On the great day, all that was hidden will be revealed. Indeed, there will be no second-guessing when it comes to motives. God's judgment will be impartial, perfect, and absolutely just.

John 5:24-27 also teaches that the Father has granted to the Son the authority to judge all humanity. Jesus stated that because believers put their faith in the Father and the Son—both of whom existed in relational unity—they would not be eternally condemned for their sins. Believers could rest assured that they would not come into judgment, for they had already passed from eternal death to life. Jesus also revealed that a time of reckoning was coming. Indeed, from the vantage point of the Lord, it was already at hand. In that day of judgment, the Son of God would summon the righteous to live eternally with Him in heaven. Moreover, Jesus explained that just as the Father had life in Himself, so too He had granted the Son to have life in Himself. In fact, the Father had given the Lord Jesus authority to execute judgment over all humanity due to His status as the Son of man. Only someone who is God and had communed with the other members of the Godhead could make such claims.

C. The Lord's Saving Work: vss. 19-20

From the west, men will fear the name of the LORD, and from the rising of the sun, they will revere his glory. For he will come like a pent-up flood that the breath of the LORD drives along. "The Redeemer will come to Zion, to those in Jacob who repent of their sins," declares the LORD.

Isaiah 59:19 states that people all over the world—from west to east—would see God's saving work on behalf of His faithful remnant. Also, these witnesses to the Lord's redemptive acts would "fear" His "name" and "revere" His "glory." God's name signifies His holy and righteous reputation. Also, His glory denotes His majesty and splendor. Nations from all over the globe would honor and praise the Creator because of His awesome power. The coming of the Lord in judgment would seem like a rushing stream or torrent, and God's "breath" would move it forward like a violent windstorm. Some think that while the initial fulfillment of this prophecy occurred when the Babylonians were destroyed, the ultimate fulfillment awaits the end times.

God would come to the members of the covenant community, not as their Judge, but as their "Redeemer" (vs. 20). These are individuals who had turned away from their transgressions. This verse probably refers initially to God's protection of the returned exiles from Babylon, but ultimately it refers to the Messiah. As was noted in lesson 6 of the September quarter, the underlying Hebrew verb translated "Redeemer" refers to a protector and vindicator. This term is always used for a next of kin who endeavors to safeguard the family interests. For example, if a man was sold into slavery, it was the duty of a blood relative to act as that man's family guardian and buy him out of slavery (Lev. 25:47-49). Jesus is the Kinsman-Redeemer for sin-enslaved humanity. In order for Jesus to become our Savior, He had to become related to the human race by blood. This theological truth indicates the necessity of the Incarnation. Put differently, Jesus became human in order to redeem us (Heb. 2:14-15).

D. The Everlasting Covenant: vs. 21

"As for me, this is my covenant with them," says the LORD. "My Spirit, who is on you, and my words that I have put in your mouth will not depart from your mouth, or from the mouths of your children, or from the mouths of their descendants from this time on and forever," says the LORD.

Isaiah 59:21 might be considered a brief appendix to the preceding verses. God promised to establish an everlasting "covenant" with those whom He redeemed. His "Spirit" and His "words" would remain with them and their "descendants" from that moment onward. This promise seems to refer to the new covenant Jesus established through His atoning sacrifice at Calvary (Jer. 31:31-34; Luke 22:20; and see the Bible exposition appearing in lesson 2 of the September quarter).

In Romans 11:25-26, Paul identified the Redeemer with the Lord Jesus. The apostle revealed that Israel's spiritual stumbling was a "mystery." In Scripture, a mystery is not an enigmatic saying that is difficult to comprehend, but rather is a truth that was previously unknown but had now been revealed and publicly proclaimed. Paul wanted the mystery of Israel's spiritual darkness to be clearly understood by his Gentile readers. By comprehending God's sovereign dealings with Israel, the Gentiles could avoid arrogance over their inclusion in the people of God. In the Lord's sovereign plan, He desired for people of all nations to become a part of His eternal family. In achieving this goal, Israel was set aside for a time and experienced a hardening of the heart until the "full number of the Gentiles" came in. God has a certain complement of Gentiles and Jews among the redeemed.

It is important to understand two facts about Israel's "hardening." First, it is only partial. This means there has always been a remnant of Jews whose hearts have not become hard. Second, this callousness is temporary. It will end when God's sovereignly chosen number of Gentiles have been saved and brought into God's family. Following this time, Paul said, "All Israel will be saved" (vs. 26). What did Paul mean by "all Israel"? Scholars have suggested three possible views: (1) It could be referring to the majority of Jews living in the final generation. (2) "All Israel" could be referring to the total number of God's elect Jews from every generation. (3) It could be referring to the total number of God's elect—both Jew and Gentile—from all generations. (Regardless of which view is correct, "all Israel" would be saved by personal faith in Christ.) To confirm his assertion, Paul blended passages from Isaiah (under the inspiration of the Holy Spirit) to state that Israel would return to God after the Messiah appeared (Isa. 59:20-21; 27:9).

Discussion Questions

1. Why was truth so difficult to find in Judah's law courts?
2. Why did the Lord decide to intervene on behalf of the innocent in Judah?
3. In the coming day of judgment, how would God deal with His foes?
4. What does it mean for believers to "fear the name of the LORD" (Isa. 59:19)?
5. Why is it important for God's spiritual children to "repent of their sin" (vs. 20)?

Contemporary Application

The indictments against God's people in Isaiah 59 are all too familiar. Rather than love the Lord and those He created, we busy ourselves in a flurry of religious activities. The solution is exactly as Isaiah concluded: God's salvation and participating in His new covenant. As verse 21 so aptly sums up, only God's Spirit and His Word in our lives can bring about righteousness. Also, only our Kinsman-Redeemer, Jesus Christ, could fulfill justice and bring us salvation.

The preceding truth, alone, is how we can be righteous and practice righteousness. Anything else amounts to hypocrisy, as illustrated by the pathetic examples of worship that Isaiah saw happening around him. God doesn't want our symbolic sacrifices. Instead, He wants our lives to be given to Him in living worship. Also, He must dwell within us in order for that to happen.

Certainly, those of us who have been saved and have God dwelling within us know that there are times when we still live in less-than-worshipful ways. Even so, God assures His people in Isaiah's age and in ours today that confession and repentance before Him is all that it takes to return to relationship with Him. We are declared righteous through faith in the Son (Rom. 4:23-25). So, we must live as the transformed, upright creatures that we are in union with the Redeemer.

Best of all, we who have God's Spirit are guaranteed that the Lord's righteousness will never depart from us (Isa. 59:21). The Father will use His wonderful riches in His Son to supply us with everything we need in order to be upright (Phil. 4:19)—such as ministering to those in need and promoting the just treatment of others.

A Call to Reform

Scripture

Background Scripture: *Ezra 7:1, 6, 21-28; Jeremiah 7:1-15*
Scripture Lesson: *Jeremiah 7:1-15*
Key Verse: *"This is what the LORD Almighty, the God of Israel, says: Reform your ways and your actions, and I will let you live in this place."* Jeremiah 7:3.
Scripture Lesson for Children: *Ezra 7:6, 21-28*
Key Verse for Children: *Because the hand of the LORD my God was on me, I took courage.* Ezra 7:28.

Lesson Aim

To place our confidence exclusively in God.

Lesson Setting

Time: 609–608 B.C.
Place: Jerusalem

Lesson Outline

A Call to Reform

   I.   False Securities: Jeremiah 7:1-11
      A. *A Summons to Reform: vss. 1-3*
      B. *An Exhortation to Promote Justice: vss. 4-8*
      C. *The Misuse of the Temple: vss. 9-11*
  II. Judgment Pronounced: Jeremiah 7:12-15
      A. *The Example of Shiloh: vs. 12*
      B. *The Nation's Refusal to Repent: vs. 13*
      C. *The Certainty of Exile in Babylon: vss. 14-15*

Introduction for Adults

Topic: *Doing Justice*

The kicking in of their gate awakened an elderly Jewish couple living in Cottbus, Germany. Neo-Nazis shouted, "Come out! We'll beat you all to death!" After the thugs moved on, the emotional fright lingered. What if they returned?

German police offered the couple *Schutzhaft* (a word meaning "protective custody"). In another culture, the couple might have welcomed the offer. But the term *Schutzhaft* is an affront to German Jews. In Hitler's era, the Gestapo used it to round up and jail Jews. "Imagine what memories this triggered for me," the elderly man said. "I couldn't believe my ears."

As Jeremiah 7:1-15 reveals, spiritual blindness can grip individuals, groups, and even nations, especially as they forget God's ways. Today, Christians must be on guard to identify injustice, appreciate its gravity, and root it out. If not, spiritual blindness will inevitably result.

Introduction for Youth

Topic: *Hope or Doom*

The people in Jeremiah's day incorrectly believed the Jerusalem temple would keep them safe from all harm. The Lord's spokesperson declared that this sanctuary would not shield the nation's inhabitants from God's judgment on their sins.

In the days of the pioneers, prairie fires posed a life-threatening problem. Even horses could not outrun the spread of wildfire in open land. So what did the pioneers do when they saw that a prairie fire was on its way? They took a match and burned the grass in a designated area around them. Then they took their stand in the burned area. As the roar of the flames approached, they didn't need to be afraid. Even as the ocean of fire surged around them, they had no fear because fire had already passed over the place where they stood.

When the judgment of God comes to sweep people into hell for eternity, there is one spot that is safe. Two thousand years ago the wrath of God was poured out on Calvary. There the Son of God took the wrath that should have fallen on us. Now, if we take our stand by the cross, we are safe for time and eternity. We do not need to fear, because hell's fires can no longer reach us.

Concepts for Children

Topic: *Be Fair!*

1. Ezra knew the Bible well.
2. Ezra learned from the Bible that God wants us to be fair.
3. Ezra discovered that God wants us to love Him more than anyone or anything else.
4. Ezra taught other people how to be fair.
5. Leaders in our church can teach us from the Bible how to be fair.

Lesson Commentary

I. FALSE SECURITIES: JEREMIAH 7:1-11

A. A Summons to Reform: vss. 1-3

This is the word that came to Jeremiah from the LORD: "Stand at the gate of the LORD's house and there proclaim this message: 'Hear the word of the LORD, all you people of Judah who come through these gates to worship the LORD. This is what the LORD Almighty, the God of Israel, says: Reform your ways and your actions, and I will let you live in this place.'"

Jeremiah chapters 7 through 10 contain a series of oracles from the Lord to Jeremiah that focus on the Jerusalem temple (7:1). As noted in lesson 4 of the September quarter, the people of Judah incorrectly assumed that because of the presence of this sanctuary, God would always lavish His approval on the nation. They also mistakenly concluded that the Babylonians would fail in their attempts to overrun Jerusalem. The Lord used Jeremiah to challenge and discredit the Judahites' false confidence in the temple of God. Scholars have noted the strong overlap in content appearing in chapters 7 and 26. Based on this observation, they conclude that the oracle recorded in chapter 7 might have been delivered during Jehoiakim's reign (609–598 B.C.; see 1:3; 26:1).

Regrettably, King Josiah's extensive reforms died when he did, and the idolatry of the Canaanites rapidly reemerged in Judah during the early reign of Josiah's son, Jehoiakim. So, late in 609 or early in 608 B.C., the Lord instructed Jeremiah to deliver a warning to the worshipers at the temple. Following God's directions, Jeremiah positioned himself by the gate of the sanctuary—namely, the entrance located in the wall that separated the inner and outer courts (perhaps the New Gate; see 26:10). From there, he could address all those who entered the temple complex to venerate God and acknowledge His lordship (7:2).

Even though the Judahites attended temple activities, their religion was nothing but insincere ritual. The Lord of heaven's armies was not fooled by such disingenuous behavior. As the sovereign King of the universe (2:19; 5:14; 6:6, 9), God not only charged His people with hypocrisy, but also threatened to judge them for violating the stipulations of the Mosaic covenant. In 7:3, the Lord exhorted His people to "reform" their lives. The entire pattern of their attitude and conduct needed to be consistent with their apparent worship. If the Judahites changed how they behaved, especially in doing what was right, God said He would allow them to continue to live in the promised land. Otherwise, He would expel them from it (Lev. 26; Deut. 28).

B. An Exhortation to Promote Justice: vss. 4-8

Do not trust in deceptive words and say, "This is the temple of the LORD, the temple of the LORD, the temple of the LORD!" If you really change your ways and your actions and deal with each other justly, if you do not oppress the alien, the fatherless or the widow and do not shed innocent blood in this place, and if you do not follow other gods to your own harm, then I will let you live in this place, in the land I gave your forefathers for ever and ever. But look, you are trusting in deceptive words that are worthless.

In defiance of God's judgment oracle delivered through Jeremiah, the false prophets repeated the slogan, "This is the temple of the Lord" (Jer. 7:4). They deluded themselves and their patrons into thinking that endlessly chanting this incantation would ward off any disastrous outcome. Surely God would not allow His own home to be destroyed—or so they believed. But the Lord's true spokesperson warned the leaders and people of Judah that trusting in the Jerusalem temple would not keep their city and nation safe from destruction. Furthermore, the would-be seers who declared otherwise had uttered fraudulent, useless statements and were not to be trusted.

A century earlier (701 B.C.), the Lord had delivered Jerusalem from the invading armies of Assyria commanded by Sennacherib (Isa. 37:36-37). Later, King Josiah refurbished the run-down temple as a major part of his reform (2 Chron. 34:8-13). In Jeremiah's time, the "temple theology" of the false prophets concluded that none of Judah's enemies could touch the sanctuary—or, for that matter, the people who worshiped there. In contrast, the Lord revealed that the temple was not some sort of magical charm that would turn away evil. The only thing that would protect Jerusalem was the people's obedience to their covenant with God.

Accordingly, the Lord exhorted His people to honor Him with correct beliefs and righteous actions. For instance, they were to deal fairly and humanely with the most vulnerable groups in society (Jer. 7:5). This included ending all forms of exploitation of foreigners, orphans, and widows. God's decree also involved eliminating all aspects of bloodshed, idolatry, and oppression of the powerless (vs. 6). When the leaders and people of Judah honored God by their actions, they would enjoy the only security they needed to continue living in the promised land (vs. 7). But if the rich and powerful tyrannized the defenseless, murdered the innocent, and venerated pagan deities, God would judge them for their crimes. Moreover, no amount of confidence in the erroneous beliefs uttered by religious charlatans would deliver the nation from ruin (vs. 8).

C. The Misuse of the Temple: vss. 9-11

Will you steal and murder, commit adultery and perjury, burn incense to Baal and follow other gods you have not known, and then come and stand before me in this house, which bears my Name, and say, "We are safe"—safe to do all these detestable things? Has this house, which bears my Name, become a den of robbers to you? But I have been watching! declares the LORD.

There are several reasons why the Jerusalem temple was so important to the people living in Judah. The ornate sanctuary was a symbol of God's holiness, His covenant with Israel, and His willingness to forgive their sins. The Lord used the temple to centralize worship at Jerusalem. In the sanctuary, God's people could spend time in prayer. Finally, its design, furniture, and customs were object lessons that prepared the people for the advent of the Messiah. The goodness and grace of God, as represented by the Jerusalem temple, should have prompted the leaders and inhabitants of Judah to revere the Lord exclusively and treat the defenseless in a compassionate and caring manner. Instead, the nation brazenly violated at least five of the Ten Commandments (Exod. 20:1-17; Deut. 5:6-21). Specifically, they were guilty of theft, murder, adultery, lying, and idolatry (Jer. 7:9; see also Hos. 4:2).

"Baal" (Jer. 7:9) was the name of the principal deity of Canaan. Its devotees regarded Baal to be the supreme, cosmic god who controlled the amount of fertility that people, animals, and the land experienced. Israel's pagan neighbors also venerated "other gods." The foremost idols of Aram (or Syria) included Hadad (a storm god), Mot (the god of death), Anath (a fierce goddess of war and love), and Rimmon (a god of thunder). Eshmun (a fertility god) was the chief deity of Sidon. Chemosh (a savage war god) was the principal idol of Moab. Molech (or Milcom, an astral deity) was the chief god of the Ammonites. Dagon (a grain deity) and Baal-Zebub (a god of health and divination) were the foremost idols of the Philistines.

After wantonly disregarding the Mosaic covenant, the people of Judah had the audacity to trot off to the Jerusalem temple to offer sacrifices. The fact that the sanctuary bore the Lord's holy "Name" (vs. 10) meant He had claimed it as His own and exercised complete authority over it (1 Kings 8:41-43; 2 Chron. 6:33). Yet, the nation's leaders and inhabitants desecrated the temple by using it as a pretext for iniquity. Supposedly, the people could breath a sigh of relief as they said, "We are safe" (Jer. 7:10). In response, the Lord asked incredulously, "Safe for what?" Allegedly, it was for them to persist in committing one abhorrent crime after another without experiencing the Creator's wrath.

God declared that He would not overlook the crimes the people of Judah committed. The seriousness of their iniquities is emphasized in the Hebrew text by the placement of the phrase rendered "den of robbers" at the very beginning of verse 11. In short, the Lord announced His house of worship had been defiled by it being turned into a hideout for thieves. This was not an unfounded charge. It was backed by God's personal knowledge of the situation. Later, Jesus quoted part of this verse (along with Isa. 56:7; see Matt. 21:13; Mark 11:17; Luke 19:46). In Jesus' day, money-hungry vendors and bankers had made the Jerusalem temple a haven for their wicked practices. In a display of righteous indignation, He emptied the sanctuary of these despicable people (Luke 19:45).

II. JUDGMENT PRONOUNCED: JEREMIAH 7:12-15

A. The Example of Shiloh: vs. 12

"'Go now to the place in Shiloh where I first made a dwelling for my Name, and see what I did to it because of the wickedness of my people Israel.'"

Babylon's deportation of Judah from the land was the catastrophe looming on the horizon. As Jeremiah 7:7 revealed, if God's people abandoned their evil ways and lived uprightly, He would allow them to remain in Judah. This was the land of promise He had given to their ancestors as a perpetual inheritance. To impress upon the Judahites the certainty of the judgment that awaited them, God noted what had happened to Shiloh many years earlier (vs. 12). This town was located in the hill country of Ephraim, about 20 miles north of Jerusalem. Shiloh was once the center of worship for the 12 tribes of Israel, from the time of Joshua until the end of the period of the judges (Josh. 18:1; Judg. 18:31; 1 Sam. 1:3; 4:3-4). Because the people living there were wicked, God allowed the city to be overthrown.

After David captured Jerusalem and made it the capital of his kingdom, he eventually moved the ark from Shiloh to the holy city. Thereafter, Shiloh lost its importance and the nation abandoned it as the center of worship. However, Psalm 78:56-61 gives the ultimate reason for Shiloh's decline. Asaph stated that because of the Israelites' idolatry and rebellion, God abandoned the tabernacle there. Scripture does not give a specific account of Shiloh's fall. Nevertheless, it is clear that after the Philistines captured the ark of the covenant during Samuel's judgeship of Israel (1 Sam. 4:1–7:1), the enemy destroyed Shiloh around 1050 B.C. The fact that the nation's priests were operating out of Nob during the reign of Saul (22:11) confirms that the Philistines had destroyed Shiloh. The essence of Jeremiah's warning to the people of Judah is clear. The prophet declared that what God had done to Shiloh, He would certainly do to Jerusalem.

B. The Nation's Refusal to Repent: vs. 13

"While you were doing all these things, declares the LORD, I spoke to you again and again, but you did not listen; I called you, but you did not answer."

For generations, the people of Judah had forsaken the Lord and followed after false gods (Jer. 5:7). They had also committed adultery and frequented the houses of prostitutes. Finally, they allowed lust and fornication, rather than the righteous law of God, to rule their lives (vs. 8). Jeremiah was not the only true prophet of God to warn His people of the coming judgment. Others included Zephaniah, who served early during Josiah's reign, and Habakkuk, who served about the time of the events recorded in Jeremiah 26 (early in the reign of King Jehoiakim, when Jeremiah was threatened with death; see also the Bible commentary in lesson 6). The people ignored many of God's spokespersons during this time.

The Hebrew text of 7:13 literally says that God's spokespersons were "rising up early [in the morning] and speaking." The idea behind this idiom is that the prophets whom the Lord sent had called on His people over and over again to repent. But the inhabitants of Judah had refused to listen to God's messengers, and the people continued to offend Him with their idolatry. They seemed to have heard the message so often that they just tuned it out. The people of Judah had not entirely stopped worshiping God. In fact, archaeological evidence dating to this time period from the area of Judah confirms that the inhabitants still venerated the Lord, but often as just another god alongside the old Canaanite and foreign deities.

The preceding practice is called *syncretism.* Pottery inscriptions have been found addressed "To Yahweh and his Asherah," showing that people believed the Lord had a female consort, just like the other pagan gods. Carved goddess figurines also have been unearthed, many from the area of Jerusalem near the site of the temple. Interestingly, almost no figurines have been found dating to the period after the Babylonian exile. Captivity seems to have burned out the corruption from God's people.

C. The Certainty of Exile in Babylon: vss. 14-15

"'Therefore, what I did to Shiloh I will now do to the house that bears my Name, the temple you trust in, the place I gave to you and your fathers. I will thrust you from my presence, just as I did all your brothers, the people of Ephraim.'"

In Romans 3:2, Paul noted the spiritual privilege God's chosen people enjoyed. Specifically, the Jews had been entrusted with the Word of God. Yet with this privilege came a tremendous responsibility. Sadly, many of the Jews in the apostle's day were unfaithful in their responsibility. Indeed, they failed to live up to God's holy standards. The Israelites were also the recipients of God's law on Mount Sinai (Exod. 19–20). The Jews who lived during Paul's day looked upon the law as their most prized possession (Rom. 2:17).

Furthermore, the Jews engaged in temple worship. This was a great privilege in view of the fact that God Himself had "dwelled" in the sanctuary (Ezek. 43:4). In addition, the Jews were recipients of God's promises—especially those He made to Abraham, the father of the Jews (Gen. 12:7). Israel's intimate connection with the patriarchs—Abraham, Isaac, and Jacob—is also mentioned. This is important because it was through the patriarchs that God gave many of His promises regarding the nation of Israel. Most importantly, from the Jews "is traced the human ancestry of the Messiah," whom Paul described as "God over all" (Rom. 9:5).

In Jeremiah's day, despite the importance of the Jerusalem temple, it would not shield God's people from His hand of discipline. The Lord knew the crimes the inhabitants of Judah had committed, and He would deal firmly with them for their wicked ways. The Lord declared that He would allow the promised land and the sanctuary in the holy city to be devastated, just as He permitted Shiloh to be destroyed (Jer. 7:14). The residents of Judah knew that God had allowed the 10 northern tribes—their relatives, the descendants of Ephraim—to be conquered by the Assyrians and deported from their land (2 Kings 17:6, 20).

The Lord promised that He would also thrust the people of Judah from His presence (Jer. 7:15; see also Deut. 28:64-68; 29:28).

Discussion Questions

1. Why did the Lord direct Jeremiah to position himself at the gate of the temple?
2. In what ways had the people of Judah acted unjustly?
3. What precondition did God make for His people remaining in Judah?
4. Why is it pernicious when Christians trust in anyone or anything other than the Lord?
5. Why can't the rituals of worship compensate for the lack of a growing relationship with God?

Contemporary Application

The people in Judah had accepted the erroneous idea that God would not allow disaster to come to the Jerusalem temple or to those who lived near it. The Lord sent Jeremiah to a prominent gate of the sanctuary to declare His message to the inhabitants of Jerusalem (Jer. 7:1-2).

God announced that He would allow His people to stay in Judah only if they abandoned their evil ways. However, if they remained entrenched in wickedness, not even the temple could protect them from His judgment. The Lord would be merciful only if His people treated others fairly, stopped exploiting the disadvantaged, and discontinued their worship of idols (vss. 3-7).

We may not be guilty of these sins, but there are subtle ways we can treat others unjustly. For example, Christian parents can be unfair to one of their children by paying less attention to that child because he or she is not as gifted as the others. Also, believers might act unjustly when they plan church functions and don't invite people who are different from them in some way.

The people of Judah had deluded themselves into thinking they could get away with stealing, murder, adultery, and worshiping Baal (the main fertility god of the Canaanites) because they had the temple in Jerusalem. The Lord said His house of worship had become a hideout for thieves (vss. 8-11; see also Matt. 21:13). This was not a baseless charge. It was backed by God's personal knowledge of the situation.

There is nothing wrong with doing such things as worshiping in church on Sunday, gathering together on Wednesday for prayer and Bible study, and going witnessing in our neighborhoods several times a month. These activities, however, are no substitute for a vital relationship with God. And these activities can never excuse our wrongful treatment of others.

A Call to Obey

Scripture

Background Scripture: *Ezekiel 18; Proverbs 21:2-15*
Scripture Lesson: *Ezekiel 18:1-13, 31-32*
Key Verse: *"Rid yourselves of all the offenses you have committed, and get a new heart and a new spirit. Why will you die, O house of Israel?"* Ezekiel 18:31.
Scripture Lesson for Children: *Proverbs 21:2-8, 10-15*
Key Verse for Children: *To do what is right and just is more acceptable to the Lord than sacrifice.* Proverbs 21:3.

Lesson Aim

To accept that God holds each of us accountable for our behavior.

Lesson Setting

Time: Sometime before 571 B.C.
Place: Babylon

Lesson Outline

A Call to Obey

I. Being Held Accountable for Sin: Ezekiel 18:1-13
   A. *The False Parable Stated: vss. 1-2*
   B. *The False Parable Refuted: vss. 3-4*
   C. *The Example of a Virtuous Person: vss. 5-9*
   D. *The Example of a Violent Person: vss. 10-13*

II. Forsaking Rebellious Ways: Ezekiel 18:31-32
   A. *The Exhortation to Abandon Iniquity: vs. 31*
   B. *The Exhortation to Repent: vs. 32*

Introduction for Adults

Topic: *The Error of Our Ways*

Ezekiel 18 reminds us that the effects of sin can be cumulative and impart moral and spiritual decay from one generation to the next. Yet, we also learn that each person in each generation will answer to God for his or her own moral choices.

In one of my favorite anecdotes from Clarence Day's *Life with Father*, his father tries to sew on a button, stabs himself with a needle, and then blames his wife for his bloody finger and shirt. After all, she was talking to him and spoiled his concentration!

We can all tell similar stories, but it's hard to admit how easily we slip into the blaming mode. That's why it is refreshing to hear someone say, "I'm sorry. It was my fault." We have to learn to say this to others and to God. When we acknowledge our wrongdoing, it brings healing and joy to our lives.

Introduction for Youth

Topic: *A New Heart Builds a Just Community*

How and why adolescents change is the subject of much social research, both by producers of consumer goods and political leaders. The upshot is that it's very hard to change our ingrained ways and habits. Ezekiel found this was true among the Jewish exiles in Babylon. They resented their troubles and complained that God was being unfair to them.

Even saved teens find it hard to accept God's ways as loving, true, wise, and just. When we rebel, we need to confess our sin and ask God to renew us spiritually. He promises to cleanse us of our sin and bring about the transformation needed for us to live uprightly.

As long as we hide behind our excuses and shift blame for our sinful behavior, we'll never be free from its consequences. We'll always be angrily pointing our fingers, hiding, and hurting. Ezekiel 18 reveals that God wants something better for us. He wants to bring us peace and freedom. Yet we can only receive it when we humble ourselves and come clean in His presence.

Concepts for Children

Topic: *Do Right!*

1. The Bible teaches that God wants us to be good people.
2. In the Bible, we learn what God wants us to do.
3. In the Bible, we discover the sins God wants us to stop doing.
4. God will not punish us for the sins of other people.
5. God will bless us when we choose to obey Him.

Lesson Commentary

I. Being Held Accountable for Sin: Ezekiel 18:1-13

A. The False Parable Stated: vss. 1-2

The word of the Lord came to me: "What do you people mean by quoting this proverb about the land of Israel: 'The fathers eat sour grapes, and the children's teeth are set on edge'?"

From 593 to 586 B.C., Ezekiel warned the exiles that Jerusalem would be destroyed and that there was no hope of an immediate return. The news of Jerusalem's fall in 586 B.C. dashed the false hopes of an immediate deliverance for the exiles. From this point on, Ezekiel's prophecies related to Israel's future restoration to its homeland and the final blessings of the divine kingdom. God used Ezekiel to urge the exiles to heed the stipulations of the Mosaic covenant. Through the prophet's teaching, he stressed the holiness and transcendence of God, His grace and mercy toward the righteous remnant, His sovereignty, and individual responsibility for sins committed. Ezekiel revealed that God pledged to preserve a remnant of His people through whom He would fulfill His promises.

In Ezekiel 18:1-2, we learn about a popular proverb that was circulating among the Jews in Jerusalem and Babylon (see also the commentary in lesson 2 of the September quarter). The Hebrew noun rendered "proverb" signified a comparison of some sort, but it came to mean any wise or moralistic saying. Proverbs are usually thought of as short, pithy sayings, while parables are extended stories. But the distinction is not hard and fast among biblical writers. In this case, when the parents ate "sour grapes," allegedly the mouths of their children became numb from the bitter taste of the unripe fruit (Jer. 31:29). Behind this adage was the recognition that normally one person's unpleasant experience could not be transferred to someone else.

Granted, the moral and spiritual decay of one generation might have profound, long-lasting effects upon those who follow (Matt. 23:35-36). But Ezekiel's peers quoted the popular maxim so they could excuse themselves of responsibility. The proverb, which seems to be based on a misunderstanding of Exodus 20:5 and Numbers 14:18, meant that because of the sins of previous generations, the present one was suffering. According to this logic, one generation could blame their troubles on the misdeeds of previous generations. Even more distressing was the fact that the adage, as it was improperly applied by the exiles, asserted that God was punishing their generation for the transgressions their ancestors had committed.

B. The False Parable Refuted: vss. 3-4

"As surely as I live, declares the Sovereign Lord, you will no longer quote this proverb in Israel. For every living soul belongs to me, the father as well as the son—both alike belong to me. The soul who sins is the one who will die."

The phrase "as surely as I live" (Ezek. 18:3) indicates that the Lord was making a solemn oath (5:11; 14:16; 20:3). As noted in lesson 3, since there was no one greater than He, God swore by His own life when He revealed His will. It was His desire that the Jews no longer use the proverb about intergenerational responsibility, for it represented a warped view of how He executed justice. Since God does not punish the innocent for the sins of the guilty, He rejected outright the Israelites' attempt to avoid guilt for their own idolatry and disobedience.

Furthermore, God was offended by His peoples' audacity in hiding behind this patently untrue notion. So the supreme Lord declared that this widespread adage of the exiles would be repeated in Israel no more. In verse 4, God announced that every living entity belonged to Him, including the parent and the child. As the Creator of life, He had the right to execute judgment as He desired. It was His unchanging will that guilt would not be transferred from one generation to the next. Only the person who sinned would die for his or her sins (see also the similar point made in Jer. 31:30).

C. The Example of a Virtuous Person: vss. 5-9

"Suppose there is a righteous man who does what is just and right. He does not eat at the mountain shrines or look to the idols of the house of Israel. He does not defile his neighbor's wife or lie with a woman during her period. He does not oppress anyone, but returns what he took in pledge for a loan. He does not commit robbery but gives his food to the hungry and provides clothing for the naked. He does not lend at usury or take excessive interest. He withholds his hand from doing wrong and judges fairly between man and man. He follows my decrees and faithfully keeps my laws. That man is righteous; he will surely live, declares the Sovereign LORD."

The overriding truth in Ezekiel 18 is that people are held responsible for their own sin, and that guilt is not transferred across generations. To illustrate this fact, God presented three hypothetical situations. He talked about a man (vss. 5-9), his son (vss. 10-13), and his grandson (vss. 14-18). The first example concerned a person of integrity who lived justly and righteously and was fully obedient to God's law (vs. 5). The individual of moral rectitude did not practice idolatry or pagan practices of any kind. Furthermore, he was faithful to laws governing relationships with other Israelites (vs. 6). For example, he maintained sexual purity. This is probably a reference to the Mosaic law's prohibition against adultery, and having intercourse with a woman during her period of menstruation (Exod. 20:14; Lev. 18:19).

Ezekiel described the righteous man as a person who refused to oppress anyone. For instance, he would not keep as collateral for a loan any item the borrower might require, such as a cloak needed for warmth at night (Exod. 22:26). He would never steal from anyone (Exod. 20:15). On the contrary, he gave food and clothing to the needy. This Israelite of exemplary character cared more about giving to others than receiving anything for himself (Ezek. 18:7). In financial matters, if the upright person made a loan to anyone, his dealings were fair (vs. 8). To "lend at usury" meant to charge an exorbitant amount of interest. The phrase "take excessive interest" refers to exploiting the destitute to amass a fortune.

The Mosaic law allowed interest on loans to Gentiles, but not on those made to fellow Israelites (Deut. 23:19-20). Whether the hypothetical loan here was to a Gentile or an Israelite, in either case, the virtuous person's conduct was praiseworthy. It was divine law that guided him in all his financial dealings, not the profit motive. The devout Israelite tried to do what was right and fair in every situation by carefully observing God's statutes and regulations (Ezek. 18:9). This person's outward actions revealed an inner moral character that was firmly based on obedience to the covenant. In keeping with a life based on God's grace, the upright would not suffer judgment for the misdeeds committed by others. We learn from the New Testament that righteousness is not simply a matter of adhering to a checklist of rules. Instead, the believer's life of virtue results from his or her restored relationship with the Father through faith in His Son (Rom. 3:21-31; Eph. 3:8-10; Titus 2:11-14).

D. The Example of a Violent Person: vss. 10-13

"Suppose he has a violent son, who sheds blood or does any of these other things (though the father has done none of them): He eats at the mountain shrines. He defiles his neighbor's wife. He oppresses the poor and needy. He commits robbery. He does not return what he took in pledge. He looks to the idols. He does detestable things. He lends at usury and takes excessive interest. Will such a man live? He will not! Because he has done all these detestable things, he will surely be put to death and his blood will be on his own head."

After Ezekiel discussed the case of the righteous person, he set forth two more hypothetical cases to confirm the principle of individual responsibility. The second illustration supposes that the virtuous father had a cutthroat son (Ezek. 18:10). Unlike his father, the son ate pagan sacrifices on the hilltops and was physically intimate with someone else's wife (vs. 11). The abhorrent crimes this reprobate committed also included murdering the innocent, cheating the impoverished, extorting the defenseless, and venerating idols (vs. 12). God's judgment upon the wicked son was clear and decisive. He would surely be punished for his atrocious behavior. Indeed, death would be the penalty this tyrant experienced for the guilt of his iniquities (vs. 13; see also Lev. 20:9, 11-12, 16, 27). Moreover, the son would derive no benefit from his father's upright character and conduct.

The final hypothetical case presented by Ezekiel involved a third generation. The righteous father's wicked son now had a son of his own. This individual witnessed all the iniquities his father had committed (Ezek. 18:14). But instead of following in his father's evil footsteps, the son followed the example of his upright grandfather (compare vss. 15-17 with vss. 6-9 and 11-13). The conclusion, based on God's principle of individual responsibility, is inescapable. The last son would not die because of his father's wrongdoing. Instead, the virtuous son would live due to his own integrity, not that of his grandfather. Also, the father would receive the just consequences of his evil deeds (vs. 18).

II. FORSAKING REBELLIOUS WAYS: EZEKIEL 18:31-32

A. The Exhortation to Abandon Iniquity: vs. 31

"Rid yourselves of all the offenses you have committed, and get a new heart and a new spirit. Why will you die, O house of Israel?"

Ezekiel 18:19-30 reveals that God judged the Israelites for their own transgressions, not the abominations committed by previous generations. Also, only the Israelites who were obedient to God could expect to escape the judgment of the dark days ahead. Ezekiel explained that through repentance it was possible to escape the coming Babylonian destruction. In God's infinite love and boundless grace toward all humankind, He desired that everyone would turn from their evil deeds to a life of righteous obedience to His commands. So, if the wicked forsook their disobedience and sin and pursued a life of rectitude, they would be delivered from God's judgment upon Israel. But if the upright abandoned their virtuous life for evil, they would die. Also, their past godly deeds would not be remembered. In fact, previous good deeds could not be used like money to buy the Lord's favor.

Regrettably, the Israelite response to God's judgment was to childishly accuse Him of being unfair and unjust. God declared that, on the contrary, it was Israel's ways that were unjust, not His (vss. 25, 29). Through Ezekiel, the Lord repeated the principle that His judgment upon His chosen people would be based on the sin of each individual. The current generation of idolatrous, disobedient Israelites would be responsible for the fall of the nation—not generations past. So the only hope of avoiding calamity was for the people to repent of their sin (vs. 30). By casting away all of their past transgressions, they would not be dragged down and ruined by their iniquity. The Lord questioned whether His people really wanted to be put to death for their sins. Accordingly, He urged them to allow the Holy Spirit to bring spiritual revival among them. Indeed, only He could give each of them a "new heart and a new spirit" (vs. 31; see also 11:19; 36:26, as well as the commentary in lesson 2 of the September quarter on Jeremiah 31:33).

Together, the Greek and Hebrew words for "heart" are used over 900 times in Scripture. In all these references, few are referring to the heart as a literal, physical organ. A rare example of the literal use is found in Exodus 28:29-30, where Aaron was instructed to wear the breastpiece of decision over his heart whenever he entered the Lord's presence in the Holy Place. Almost always, the heart is presented in the Bible as the figurative seat of human intellect, emotions, or will. For example, the intellectual concept is in view in Genesis 6:5, where it is recorded that God "saw how great man's wickedness on the earth had become, and that every inclination of the thoughts of his heart was only evil all the time." This verse is immediately followed by one in which the heart is seen as the center of emotion, for humankind's wickedness so grieved the Lord that "his heart was filled with pain" (vs. 6). The psalmist described the heart as the wellspring of the will when he declared, "Blessed are they who keep his statutes and seek him with all their heart" (Ps. 119:2).

B. The Exhortation to Repent: vs. 32

"For I take no pleasure in the death of anyone, declares the Sovereign LORD. Repent and live!"

Abandoning their sinful ways and embracing the will of the Lord would enable the exiles of Ezekiel's day to think pure thoughts and remain faithful to God. It would also prevent the all-powerful Creator from putting people to death because of their sins. After all, He did not delight in condemning a person. He wanted all people to turn away from the precipice of destruction and live by trusting in and obeying Him (Ezek. 18:23, 32). God longed to give His people a new heart and spirit that would result in renewed hope, purpose, and power in Israel. Only this would bring pleasure to the Lord. But God's offer of grace was refused. So, from the rulers of Israel to the beggar on the street, God's people were destined to feel His wrath.

In verses 23 and 32, Ezekiel dealt with the temporal issue of life and death at the hands of the Babylonian army. But his words reflect the teaching of Scripture elsewhere concerning the weightier matter of eternal life and death. Peter said of the Lord, "He is patient with you, not wanting anyone to perish, but everyone to come to repentance" (2 Pet. 3:9). Even today, God calls us to live according to His values. We need to place our lifestyles and priorities under the focus of His Word and see what is reflected before Him and the world. If we are true to His teachings, then we will please our Lord and draw others to Him. If we are not true, then we need to change our lifestyles, or like the people of Ezekiel's day, we will incur His displeasure. The options could not be clearer.

From our study we see that God does not allow people to blame others for their behavior. No matter how hard we try to shift the fault to others, we cannot escape the fact that one day we will have to answer to the Lord for all we have done. This is a strong incentive for us to freely admit when we have done something wrong. Also, by accepting responsibility, we bring honor to Jesus and His followers. The world respects the rare individual who is not afraid to admit making a mistake. The unsaved will see that not everyone is self-centered and dishonest. God can use our positive testimony to bring those outside the household of faith into His family. Moreover, by accepting responsibility, we leave a godly example for other Christians to emulate. When our fellow believers see us acknowledging our failures, it encourages them also to be honest about their shortcomings. As more and more Christians freely admit their sins, the faith community is spiritually strengthened and matured. The potential for hurt feelings, misunderstandings, and relational divisions is also reduced.

Discussion Questions

1. What was it about the false proverb that disturbed God?
2. How did God pledge to deal with righteous and wicked people?
3. Why were God's people wrong to accuse Him of unfairness?
4. Why does God want us to shun the wicked ways of the world?
5. How are others negatively affected when we refuse to accept personal responsibility for our misdeeds?

Contemporary Application

The "sour grapes" proverb that God's people were circulating among themselves was actually a complaint and an accusation against God. They blamed Him for punishing the second generation of exiled people for the prior generation's sins. God made it clear through Ezekiel that His approach to dealing with sin was on an individual basis. Each person died by his or her own sin or lived by his or her own righteous choices. God did not hold children accountable for sins of parents nor vice versa.

Consider any walk of life, and we will discover how common it is for people to hold others responsible for their bad behavior. Politicians frequently try to shift the blame for their failed policies onto their colleagues. One spouse will attempt to blame the other for all the problems in their marriage. Students might declare that their teachers are responsible for their poor performance in school. Siblings are prone to point the finger of guilt at each other rather than admit when they did something wrong.

Jesus is unlike any person who ever lived. He did not try to hold others accountable for His behavior. Rather, He took full responsibility for His actions. He went even further by willingly accepting the punishment for the sins of humanity. While the rest of the world was busy blaming others for their misdeeds, the Messiah paid the price necessary to save them.

The noble example of our Lord should encourage us to stop blaming others for the things we have done wrong. If we have been unfair or unkind to someone, we should freely admit it. If we have broken a promise we made, we should acknowledge our failure. Regardless of the situation, we should make every effort not to blame others for our misdeeds.

Administer True Justice

Scripture

Background Scripture: *Zechariah 7:8-14; Isaiah 30:18-26*
Scripture Lesson: *Zechariah 7:8-14*
Key Verse: "Do not oppress the widow or the fatherless, the alien or the poor. In your hearts do not think evil of each other." *Zechariah 7:10.*
Scripture Lesson for Children: *Isaiah 30:18-26*
Key Verse for Children: How gracious [God] will be when you cry for help! As soon as he hears, he will answer you. *Isaiah 30:19.*

Lesson Aim

To alter any aspects of our lives that are compromising to God's will.

Lesson Setting

Time: 518 B.C.
Place: Jerusalem

Lesson Outline

Administer True Justice

  I.   The Humane Treatment of Others:
       Zechariah 7:8-10
       A. *Being Fair and Kind: vss. 8-9*
       B. *Eliminating Oppression: vs. 10*
  II. The Reality of Judgment: Zechariah 7:11-14
       A. *The Lord's Anger with His People: vss. 11-12*
       B. *The Lord's Judgment of His People: vss. 13-14*

Introduction for Adults

Topic: *Making a Difference*

Several years ago, a broadcasting company in Finland conducted a contest to find out how many synonyms people could call to mind. First place went to a contestant who came up with 747 synonyms for drunkenness. Someone in prison was awarded second place for sending in 678 words for the same thing. The inmate also won a prize for thinking of 170 synonyms for stealing. Another person knew 203 words for lying. It certainly was an interesting contest!

Now there is nothing wrong with using synonyms. Writers have books of synonyms and refer to them all the time. But we run into a problem when we begin to call sin by other, more polite words. Believers sometimes do that by labeling it as a mistake, a blunder, a weakness, the result of conditioning or environment, or even a disease. However, transgressing God's holy Word is sin—no matter what we call it—and sin can destroy our walk with God.

This week's lesson from Zechariah 7 shows the consequences of compromising with what is contrary to God's will. As you study the Scripture passage with your class, it should renew their willingness to change those things in their lives that might be displeasing to God.

Introduction for Youth

Topic: *Becoming Responsible Persons*

We had lots of rules in college, but I didn't mind. The rules had drawn me to this small Christian school in the first place. I appreciated knowing that a stereo wouldn't be blasting next door while I was writing a term paper or trying to sleep.

A few students, however, had little respect for the restrictions. They stayed out well past curfew, neglected to clean their room before the weekly inspection, and routinely skipped chapel services. In time they became frustrated with the school and their classmates, and resented any school authorities.

The acerbic attitude of those students mirrors the rebellious spirit of the people of Judah living during the time of Zechariah. God had given them rules to live by, but they rejected them. Instead, they wallowed in sin and scorned His attempts to get them to repent. In this week's lesson, we learn about the personal anguish and loss they would experience for their disobedience.

Concepts for Children

Topic: *Be Obedient!*

1. Isaiah told others about God.
2. Isaiah said that God cares about everyone.
3. Isaiah reminded people about God's promises to them in the Bible.
4. Isaiah encouraged others to believe in God and obey Him.
5. God can use us to tell others about His love for them.

Lesson Commentary

I. THE HUMANE TREATMENT OF OTHERS: ZECHARIAH 7:8-10

A. Being Fair and Kind: vss. 8-9

And the word of the LORD came again to Zechariah: "This is what the LORD Almighty says: 'Administer true justice; show mercy and compassion to one another.'"

In 538 B.C., when the exiles returned to Jerusalem under Zerubbabel, they eagerly began work on rebuilding the temple (Ezra 3:7-13). However, after the foundation was finished, the joy turned to discouragement as the enemies of Judah succeeded in stopping the construction (chap. 4). After almost 18 years of inactivity, God called Haggai and Zechariah to encourage the people to finish the temple. Both prophets began their ministry during the second year of King Darius—that is, in 520 B.C. Haggai completed his work that same year with messages that outlined the consequences of disobedience as well the results of obedience. Specifically, obedience brought blessing, while disobedience resulted in discipline.

Like Jeremiah and Ezekiel, Zechariah was both a priest and a prophet. He was born in Babylon and returned to Jerusalem under the leadership of Zerubbabel and Joshua. Nehemiah 12:16 records that Zechariah succeeded his grandfather, Iddo, as head of that priestly family. Apparently, Zechariah's father died early or for some reason was not able to carry on the leadership of the family. Like Haggai, Zechariah encouraged the people to finish building the temple. Even though Zechariah and Haggai were contemporaries, Zechariah's ministry continued on long after that of his counterpart. For instance, in 519 B.C., he experienced a series of eight visions in one night, which are recorded in 1:7–6:8. Then, in 518 B.C., he urged his fellow Jews to repent (chap. 7) and experience the blessings God promised (chap. 8).

Zechariah's message emphasized the spiritual renewal of the returnees. He prophesied in response to a question posed by representatives from Bethel (7:1-2). Former residents of the town were among the first captives to return from Babylon (Ezra 2:28). As noted in lessons 1 and 2, Bethel (which was 12 miles to the north of Jerusalem) previously served as a center of worship for the northern kingdom (1 Kings 12:28-30). Evidently, this remnant quickly rebuilt Bethel and were eager to obey God. The persons named in Zechariah 7:2 came to inquire of the Lord regarding the fasts that had begun during the captivity in Babylon (vs. 3).

While in exile, the Jews instituted days of fasting and mourning to beseech God concerning their condition. According to Jewish tradition, the fasts of each month were matched with events in the following ways (8:19): (1) the fast of the fourth month fell on the ninth of Tammuz, the day when the city walls were toppled (2 Kings 25:3-4; Jer. 39:2); (2) the fast of the fifth month was on the seventh of Ab, when the house of God was burned to the ground (2 Kings 25:8-10); (3) the fast of the seventh month was on the third of Tishri, the anniversary of Gedaliah's assassination (2 Kings 25:25; Jer. 41:1-2); and (4) the fast of the tenth month fell on the tenth of Tebeth, which was the day when Nebuchadnezzar laid siege to Jerusalem (2 Kings 25:1; Ezek. 24:1-2).

Fasting refers to abstaining from eating for a limited period of time. Throughout the Scripture, we can see that God's people fasted for a variety of reasons: to express grief over the death of a loved one or a leader (1 Sam. 31:13); to petition God for a matter of great urgency (2 Sam. 12:15-23); to humble oneself before God (1 Kings 21:27-29); to seek God's help (2 Chron. 20:1-4); to confess sins (Neh. 9:1-2); and to spiritually prepare oneself (Matt. 4:1-2). Fasting was difficult, requiring self-discipline and sacrifice. It gave God's people the opportunity to devote more time to spiritual pursuits. In effect, it said to God that the matter they were bringing before Him was more important than anything else, even eating.

On December 7, 518 B.C. (Zech. 7:1), the delegation from Bethel (vs. 2) went to the prophets (including Zechariah) and priests serving at the Jerusalem temple (vs. 3). The inquirers asked whether their faith community should continue to weep and fast during the "fifth month" (namely, about mid-July to mid-August on the Jewish calendar) on the anniversary of the temple's destruction. They maintained these practices throughout the duration of the captivity. Yet, now that the temple was being rebuilt and Jerusalem was once again inhabited, the delegation wanted to know whether it was necessary to continue these rituals of humiliation and repentance. Even though Scripture did not prescribe these solemn actions, their observance had become sacred to the Jews, and they did not want to discontinue them without the Lord's approval.

The all-powerful Lord, through Zechariah, responded to the delegation's inquiry with a series of rhetorical questions meant for all the returnees, including their civil leaders and priests (vss. 4-5). Evidently, the issue raised by the small group from Bethel was on the minds of all the people living in Jerusalem and Judah. However, the tone of God's rebuke was not what they expected. Behind the Lord's first objection was the purpose of the fasting. The Creator asked whether His people's ritual mourning was truly done for Him (Isa. 1:11; Amos 5:21). It seems that while in Babylon, the exiles had turned the fasting into a time of self-pity. So, instead of feeling sorrow for their sins, they had lamented for themselves and their deplorable circumstances. In short, they had focused solely on their problems, rather than on God and His righteousness.

The Lord's second question brought out the underlying self-interest of the ceremonies observed by the returnees. Specifically, during their holy festivals, their joyful celebrations were motivated by a desire to satiate their bodily appetites (Zech. 7:6). Put differently, their commemorative observances signified legalistic posturing, not heartfelt repentance to God. Just as they feasted for their own enjoyment, they used fasting to indulge their desire for sympathy and comfort. The denial of food had become times of mourning for themselves, not of remorse for how they had sinned against the Lord. Also, when the remnant in Jerusalem and Judah ate and drank, they gave little or no thought to their Creator, who had showered them with material and spiritual abundance.

The problem of meaningless religious exercise was not unique to the returnees of Zechariah's generation. The third question, recorded in verse 7, indicates that the former prophets—such as Isaiah, Jeremiah, and Ezekiel—proclaimed the same sort of message that Zechariah delivered (2 Chron. 36:15-16; Isa. 45:22; Jer. 18:11; Ezek. 33:11). Before the fall of the southern kingdom in 586 B.C., Jerusalem was peacefully inhabited. Also, the nearby cities, along with the Negev (the desert area along the southern boundary of Judah) and the Shephelah (the lowlands in southwest Judah between the central plateau and the seacoast) were populated and flourishing. If the people living during the time of those earlier spokespersons had heeded God's oracles, the captivity and subsequent need for fasting could have been avoided. Furthermore, if such disastrous consequences could come upon a previous generation for their disobedience, then it could certainly occur again to the current inhabitants of the promised land, who were experiencing far less favorable circumstances.

In contrast to the shallowness of attitude shown in the returnees' fasting, Zechariah proclaimed the essence of God's former message to His chosen people. What follows are four commands, two of which are positive and two of which are negative. With these declarations, the Lord's spokesperson summed up the teaching of the earlier prophets (Zech. 7:8). The supreme Commander of heaven's armies directed the residents of Jerusalem and Judah to dispense equitable decisions in their courts of law. This included delivering the oppressed from their tormentors, along with showing steadfast love and kindness to one another (vs. 9). Here we see that "true justice" included more than maintaining a minimal level of fairness in society. It also meant protecting all individuals from inequity and partiality. That is why Zechariah told the returnees to show tender love and loyalty in their relationships with each other.

B. Eliminating Oppression: vs. 10

"Do not oppress the widow or the fatherless, the alien or the poor. In your hearts do not think evil of each other."

As previous lessons this quarter have emphasized, the Lord's prophets denounced oppression (Isa. 1:17; Jer. 5:28; 7:6; Ezek. 22:7; Amos 4:1). The Hebrew verb rendered "oppress" (Zech. 7:10) denotes abuses of power and authority resulting in the maltreatment of the defenseless. Zechariah selected some of the common victims of persecution to illustrate his point: widows, orphans, foreigners, and the destitute. All of them could easily be exploited and abused by the wicked rich. However, God made it clear that any infringement upon the rights of the socially marginalized would bring His wrath.

Not only did God's spokespersons prohibit the returnees from tyrannizing each other, but also the prophets warned against even contemplating the idea of harming someone else. True fasting could not take place if the inhabitants of Jerusalem and Judah were treating the innocent unjustly. This included failing to show love to each other, taking advantage of the weak, or even considering an action that would hurt someone else. The message of showing our faith through how we treat others did not change in the New Testament. For instance, Matthew 5:21-22 reveals that the mistreatment of others begins with a disregard for God and a disdain for people whom He has created in His image.

II. THE REALITY OF JUDGMENT: ZECHARIAH 7:11-14

A. The Lord's Anger with His People: vss. 11-12

"But they refused to pay attention; stubbornly they turned their backs and stopped up their ears. They made their hearts as hard as flint and would not listen to the law or to the words that the LORD Almighty had sent by his Spirit through the earlier prophets. So the LORD Almighty was very angry."

Even though God repeatedly commanded through His prophets the importance of showing justice, mercy, and compassion, the preexilic Israelites spurned the divine oracles. Rather than take God seriously, the people obstinately turned away (Zech. 7:11; see also Deut. 9:6, 13, 27). It's as if they placed their fingers in their ears to prevent themsleves from hearing what the divine spokespersons preached (Ps. 58:4; Isa. 6:10; 33:15). Zechariah's message to the people of his generation was clear. They were not to imitate the behavior of their headstrong and disobedient ancestors, or the returnees might suffer a similar fate.

In keeping with what was said in lesson 11, the Hebrew term rendered "hearts" (Zech. 7:12) denotes the inner desires, attitudes, thoughts, and endeavors of people. Zechariah accused the former generations of making the center of their spiritual life as hard as diamonds. It seems as if nothing could penetrate their souls. Likewise, the preexilic Israelites grew so calloused that they refused to heed the teaching and directives found in the Mosaic law. They also became increasingly desensitized to the oracles the all-powerful Creator heralded by the Spirit through the former prophets. Understandably, this breach of the covenant infuriated the Lord and resulted in Him judging His people.

B. The Lord's Judgment of His People: vss. 13-14

"'When I called, they did not listen; so when they called, I would not listen,' says the LORD Almighty. 'I scattered them with a whirlwind among all the nations, where they were strangers. The land was left so desolate behind them that no one could come or go. This is how they made the pleasant land desolate.'"

In the past, the people of Jerusalem and Judah had refused to pay attention to the Lord's summons to repentance. In turn, God refused to be attentive to them when they cried for help in the midst of their distress (Zech. 7:13). His anger was like a typhoon that swept away the inhabitants of Judah. In turn, they were hurled to faraway locales, where they lived as "strangers" (vs. 14). Because of their transgressions, their once fruitful and populated land became barren. Invaders ravaged the land so extensively that virtually no one traveled through it (Jer. 7:34; Ezek. 12:19).

The preceding dire outcome was one of the curses for breaking the Lord's covenant. For instance, Moses declared in Deuteronomy 28:64-68 that the exiled people would be forced to venerate pagan deities made out of wood and stone. The deportees would also long to return their homeland, but would have no way to do so. They would struggle with anxious hearts and be overwhelmed by the constant fear of death. Each day would feel so horrible that the refugees would wish it were night. But then, nighttime would seem so terrible that they would yearn for it to be day. Even when, out of desperation, they tried to sell themselves as male and female slaves, no would be interested in their offer.

Jeremiah 11:11-14 records a similar warning of the dreadful consequence that awaited God's people for their violation of the Mosaic covenant (vs. 10). Once disaster struck Judah, it would be too late for the people to cry out to the Lord for help. He would not save those who had ignored Him for so long. Of course, they could cry out to their idols, but that would be futile. Though there were as many pagan deities as there were towns in Judah, their sheer numbers could not offset their impotence. False gods and goddesses could not save the inhabitants, and the true God would not deliver them.

Jeremiah's words of prophecy in chapter 11 probably came to him when he had been preaching only about five years. God instructed him to support King Josiah—who was only 26 years old himself—in his efforts to reform the spiritual life of the nation. The monarch had just heard the law of Moses for the first time, following its discovery during temple renovations (2 Chron. 34:14). After repenting of his own neglect of the law, the king attempted to reinstate the covenant that had once existed between the people and the Lord. The king summoned the population of Judah and Benjamin to the temple and read the law to them. He renewed the covenant and "had everyone in Jerusalem and Benjamin pledge themselves to it" (v. 32).

Even though they made a verbal commitment to do what Josiah had commanded, most of the common people had little interest in his reform movement. That is why God prompted Jeremiah to support the covenant renewal movement and tell about the curse that awaited those who broke the covenant. There is no honor in idolatry—whatever its form—only shame. Also, even though the world might esteem such things as greed, immorality, and self-centeredness, God despises them. Accordingly, God pronounced disaster on His people for their repeated and flagrant violations of their covenant with Him (vs. 17).

The lesson for the returnees from exile was that if they continued to disobey the Lord's decrees, as recorded in the Mosaic law, they ran the risk of experiencing God's judgment instead of His blessing. Scripture also teaches that we have the opportunity to choose between right and wrong. Although God has set moral boundaries, He has not confined us within walls to ensure our obedience. We have no physical limitations keeping us from doing things that displease the Lord. Our sole limits are the commands of God's Word. It is only when we acknowledge sin for exactly what it is—disobedience—that we can avail ourselves of God's provision of forgiveness. Knowing and understanding these truths can help to strengthen our commitment to obey the Lord in whatever we do.

Discussion Questions

1. Why was it important for God's people to administer true justice?
2. In what ways had the socially marginalized in Judah been oppressed?
3. Why is it foolish for us to refuse to heed the admonitions recorded in Scripture?
4. Why did God refuse to listen to an earlier generation of His people?
5. Why did God allow the promised land to become desolate for an extended period of time?

Contemporary Application

The Lord gave an important message to Zechariah, which he was to declare to the people of Judah and Jerusalem. God wanted them to remember the terms of the covenant He had made with their ancestors centuries earlier at Mount Sinai.

Over time, it's easy for us to drift away from the will of the Lord in certain areas of our lives. In light of this, it's good to occasionally review the commands of Scripture so that we can remind ourselves how God wants us to be thinking and acting as His spiritual children.

The Lord declared to the Judahites that His commands hadn't changed over the centuries. He had promised that if the Israelites obeyed His commands, He would protect them and bless them with the good things to be found in Palestine. The Lord also declared that if they rebelled against Him, He would bring calamity into their lives.

Likewise, God admonished His people through Zechariah to pay attention to the commands in His covenant. Ever since the Israelites' departure from Egypt, the Lord had been telling His people to obey Him. Yet generation after generation refused to listen, doing instead what their sinful hearts desired. So, God brought on them the calamities described in the covenant.

Despite the passage of time, the importance of obeying God has not changed. When we heed His Word, He is pleased. However, when we transgress the teachings of Scripture, God is displeased and disciplines us because we are His children (Heb. 12:5-11).

Fidelity to the Lord

Scripture

Background Scripture: *Malachi 3:1-12; Matthew 7:12*
Scripture Lesson: *Malachi 3:1-10*
Key Verse: *In everything, do to others what you would have them do to you, for this sums up the Law and the Prophets.* Matthew 7:12.
Scripture Lesson for Children: *Malachi 3:5-12; Matthew 7:12*
Key Verse for Children: *In everything, do to others what you would have them do to you, for this sums up the Law and the Prophets.* Matthew 7:12.

Lesson Aim

To contrast the lifestyles of unbelievers and believers.

Lesson Setting

Time: Around 430 B.C.
Place: Jerusalem

Lesson Outline

Fidelity to the Lord

   I. The Certainty of God's Justice: Malachi 3:1-5
      A. *The Announcement of the Messenger: vs. 1*
      B. *The Messenger's Work of Judgment: vss. 2-5*
  II. The Offer of God's Blessing: Malachi 3:6-10
      A. *The Lord's Summons to His People: vss. 6-7*
      B. *The Lord's Challenge to His People: vss. 8-10*

Introduction for Adults

Topic: *The Change Agent*

Along with Malachi 3:5, the rest of the Bible calls on us to fear God and love Him. Israel feared what they saw and heard at Mount Sinai. And they asked Moses to be their mediator. He agreed, but told them not to cringe in terror. God had come to test them so that their fear of Him would keep them from sin (Exod. 20:18-20). They were to have confidence in God's goodness ("Do not be afraid") and to recognize His awesome holiness so they would not consider sin a minor matter.

So, in the Old Testament, to fear God could refer to having a right relationship with Him, one that seeks to honor and obey Him. This was the sort of relationship that led to wisdom (Ps. 111:10). Malachi's hearers who feared the Lord trusted in His character and made decisions in their lives on the basis of His revealed will. Even today, when we seek to revere and honor God in our thoughts, feelings, and actions, He spiritually blesses us in ways we cannot even begin to imagine.

Introduction for Youth

Topic: *Justice Is Coming*

Malachi reminded the people of Judah that no one was exempt from God's objective evaluation. Those who rejected His Word and lived for themselves faced a bleak eternal future. In contrast, those who trusted in Him, obeyed His Word, and treated others humanely would experience God's abundant favor.

The story is told of a person who died and went to heaven. There Peter showed this individual the mansions of believers. Then the two came to a small shack that Peter said belonged to this person. The shocked individual asked why his reward was so small. In turn, Peter replied, "We did the best we could with what you sent us."

From the preceding observations, we learn that the decisions we make now have eternal consequences. For instance, even after we choose to trust in Jesus for our salvation, we continue to make decisions that either help or hinder our spiritual growth. And more than that, we make choices—such as whether we invite our non-Christian classmate to church with us next week—that can have unending ramifications for others.

Concepts for Children

Topic: *Do Good!*

1. There are people who are unkind to others.
2. God promises to punish evildoers.
3. God gives us the strength to love and obey Him.
4. God helps us to be kind to others.
5. When we do what God wants, our lives are filled with joy.

Lesson Commentary

I. THE CERTAINTY OF GOD'S JUSTICE: MALACHI 3:1-5

A. The Announcement of the Messenger: vs. 1

"See, I will send my messenger, who will prepare the way before me. Then suddenly the Lord you are seeking will come to his temple; the messenger of the covenant, whom you desire, will come," says the LORD Almighty.

Malachi (whose name means "my messenger") arranged his book to reflect arguments between God and His people. Much of it has to do with temple personnel, priests, and Levites. Malachi's message was directed toward the second generation of those who returned from captivity. The Hebrew noun rendered "oracle" (1:1) is a technical term introducing a message from the Lord. The term is derived from a verb that means "to carry." So, the noun originally denoted a burdensome message—namely, one with ominous content. Alternate renderings of the term include "burden," "prophecy," and "divine revelation."

As our studies in the September quarter from the Book of Job indicate, the issue of why the wicked prosper was taken on by a number of Old Testament writers (Job 21:7-26; 24:1-17; Ps. 73:1-14; Eccl. 8:14; Jer. 12:1-2; Hab. 1). While none of the writers offered a comprehensive solution to the problem, they all affirmed that in the end God would indeed punish the wicked and reward the righteous (Job 24:22-24; 27:13-23; Ps. 73:16-20; Eccl. 8:12-13; Jer. 12:7-17; Hab. 2:3; 3:2-19). This was also Malachi's conclusion (Mal. 3:18). While it is often difficult to know why a righteous person is suffering, the problem with the people in Malachi's day was no mystery. The hypocritical questioners were guilty of deliberate sin and therefore were deserving of God's judgment.

In response to the questioning of God's justice, He promised to send His "messenger" (3:1), who would prepare the way before Him. In Hebrew, the phrase rendered "my messenger" is *mal'aki*, which is the same form as the prophet's name. However, in this verse, the herald is an end-time figure who is about to come. According to 4:5, "the prophet Elijah" is the messenger. The New Testament identified this person as John the Baptizer (Matt. 11:10; Mark 1:2), for he came in the power and authority of Elijah (Matt. 11:14; 17:11-12; Luke 1:17). So, John could be a separate personality from Elijah and yet fulfill the Old Testament promise. John's work is described as clearing the way before the Lord (Mal. 3:1). In ancient times, Eastern kings sent emissaries before them in their travels to remove barriers from their path. John's purpose was to remove opposition to the Lord by proclaiming a message of repentance to sinners (see also the Bible commentary in lesson 1 of the March quarter).

A second view states that John did not completely fulfill the prophecy. For instance, when a delegation of priests and Levites from Jerusalem questioned the Baptizer, he denied that he was Elijah (John 1:19-21). The mention of the day of the Lord in connection with Elijah in Malachi 4:5 also shows that an aspect of this prophecy remains to be fulfilled in the future since that day has not yet come. Accordingly, some have identified the two witnesses in Revelation 11:1-14 as Moses and Elijah.

A third view equates the "messenger of the covenant" (Mal. 3:1) with the Lord Himself. Along with the other cases, the heavenly agent enforces God's covenant with His people, who were guilty of violating that solemn agreement. Concerning the Messiah, He came to the Jerusalem temple as a baby and then most notably during the week before His crucifixion. Even in their sin, the people of the postexilic community desired deliverance through the Messiah. Yet, as Malachi proceeded to point out, the people were not ready for the Redeemer's coming.

B. The Messenger's Work of Judgment: vss. 2-5

But who can endure the day of his coming? Who can stand when he appears? For he will be like a refiner's fire or a launderer's soap. He will sit as a refiner and purifier of silver; he will purify the Levites and refine them like gold and silver. Then the LORD will have men who will bring offerings in righteousness, and the offerings of Judah and Jerusalem will be acceptable to the LORD, as in days gone by, as in former years. "So I will come near to you for judgment. I will be quick to testify against sorcerers, adulterers and perjurers, against those who defraud laborers of their wages, who oppress the widows and the fatherless, and deprive aliens of justice, but do not fear me," says the LORD Almighty.

Along with vindication for the righteous, the coming of the Lord ultimately meant judgment for the wicked. The covenant-breaking Judahites, as well as the wicked of all other nations, would find the day of the Lord to be a terrible time of punishment. Although the people of the postexilic community expressed a desire for it, none of them would be able to endure it in their present moral state.

The Lord's judgment at His coming is compared with two purifying agents: fire for metals and soap for clothing (Mal. 3:2). With respect to the "refiner's fire," people in ancient times used intense heat to melt metal. This allowed the dross, which floated to the top, to be scooped off. Concerning the strong "soap," a launderer would rub cloth with lye and trample the material to remove the loosened dirt. Both metaphors indicated that God's intention was not to destroy the nation, but to purify it spiritually. His purpose was to purge out the wickedness in Judah.

In verse 3, the Lord is represented as a smelter who watches both the intensity of the fire and the metal being purified of its dross. The Messiah would cleanse the entire nation, beginning with the Levites, due to their violation of God's covenant (2:7-9). Above all else, the Lord was concerned about the holiness of His people. Once the refining process was complete, God would have an acceptable priesthood to carry out the sacred temple ministry. Because the offerings and gifts would be given from hearts right in the sight of God, they would be acceptable before Him. As in the past (probably the days of Moses and Phinehas), the sacrificial worship of the priests would be pleasing to the Lord (3:4). For us, Jesus' future return will also result in purification and a time of examination before Him (1 John 3:3).

Besides purifying the Levites, God would judge sinful people when He came (Mal. 3:5). Sorcerers—namely, those practicing divination and witchcraft—are the first addressed in the list of wicked behavior. Magical arts prevailed in Judah in postcaptivity days, perhaps due to the influence of the foreign wives. Adulterers included those who divorced their Jewish wives so they could marry idolatrous women. Those who swore falsely were perjurers. For instance, while under oath in a court of law, they gave fraudulent testimony. They also broke promises they had vowed to keep. Malachi's concern for social justice comes out clearly in the last half of his list. Those who treated their servants unfairly in regard to wages are included along with the adulterers, those who oppressed the weak in society (such as widows and orphans), and those who deprived immigrants and resident foreigners of justice. All these examples of evil behavior are traced to one source: a lack of reverence and respect for the Lord.

II. THE OFFER OF GOD'S BLESSING: MALACHI 3:6-10

A. The Lord's Summons to His People: vss. 6-7

"I the LORD do not change. So you, O descendants of Jacob, are not destroyed. Ever since the time of your forefathers you have turned away from my decrees and have not kept them. Return to me, and I will return to you," says the LORD Almighty. "But you ask, 'How are we to return?'"

Scripture reveals that the Creator is absolutely holy (Exod. 15:11; Isa. 5:16; 6:3; Hos. 11:9; Hab. 3:3). On the one hand, God transcends the entire cosmos. Yet, on the other hand, He is near and involved in the lives of His people, along with the rest of the world's inhabitants. In His mercy, the holy one of Israel chose His people and set them apart for Himself. Because of the Lord's moral purity and separation from evil, He abhors all forms of sin. He not only judges the wicked, but also vindicates the upright and cleanses His people of spiritual impurity.

Even though God must judge sinners, His unchanging nature kept the nation of Judah from perishing (Num. 23:19; Deut. 4:31; Ps. 102:27; Jas. 1:17). Put differently, despite the Judahites' violation of the Mosaic covenant, the Lord remained faithful to it, including His preservation of His people. Malachi 3:6 specifically focuses on God's unfailing commitment to the "descendants of Jacob." The name Jacob was understood to mean "he takes by the heel," "he supplants," or "he deceives" (Gen. 27:35-36). In a play on words, Malachi 3:6 indicates that the Judahites were even more deceitful and unfaithful than their ancestor Jacob had been in his youth. Yet, because God would keep the promises He made to His chosen people, the passing away of the current evil generation would not preclude another generation from fearing God and inheriting what He pledged to do long ago. In short, the refining fires would not completely consume the nation (Exod. 34:6-7; Jer. 30:11).

Regrettably, the heirs of the covenant had been unrelenting in their disobedient ways. For a long time, they had ignored and gone astray from the Creator's statutes (Mal. 3:7). Yet, despite their past history of unfaithfulness, if the people repented, God would graciously receive them and return His favor on them. However, instead of abandoning their vices, the people asked why it was necessary for them to return to God. Behind their rhetorical question was the incorrect assumption that they had never really strayed from keeping His ordinances. Expressed differently, in their self-righteousness, the inhabitants of Jerusalem and Judah did not see a need to repent. Though Malachi did not answer the people's question directly, the entire book was about how the covenant community could get right with the Lord.

B. The Lord's Challenge to His People: vss. 8-10

"Will a man rob God? Yet you rob me. But you ask, 'How do we rob you?' In tithes and offerings. You are under a curse—the whole nation of you—because you are robbing me. Bring the whole tithe into the storehouse, that there may be food in my house. Test me in this," says the LORD Almighty, "and see if I will not throw open the floodgates of heaven and pour out so much blessing that you will not have room enough for it."

The Creator called His chosen people to return to Him. One way to do so was in the area of giving, which was an indicator of the covenant community's spiritual condition. Indeed, this issue required immediate attention, for the Judahites were guilty of robbing God (Mal. 3:8). According to the Mosaic law, the people were required to give a tenth of their accumulated wealth to the Lord (the word "tithe" means "tenth"; see Num. 18:21, 24). Without these tithes and additional offerings, the priests and Levites would have been required to turn to secular work to support themselves. The failure of the Judahites to give God what was His due amounted to defrauding Him. Otherwise stated, He equated the faulty stewardship of His people with theft.

The giving of a set portion to the Lord from one's herds, flocks, fruit, and grain was an ancient biblical custom. For instance, Abraham offered a tenth of the spoils to Melchizedek (Gen. 14:20), and at Bethel, Jacob promised God a tenth (Gen. 28:22). Moreover, the Old Testament describes several different tithes God required His people to give. One tithe went to the Levites for their inheritance (Lev. 27:30-33; Deut. 14:22-27). From this tithe, the Levites gave a tenth (that is, a tithe of a tithe) to the priests for their livelihood (Num. 18:21-32). A third special tithe was given every third year to destitute widows, orphans, and foreigners (Deut. 14:28-29).

Nehemiah 13:10 confirms that the tithes were not properly given during the time in which Malachi ministered. It is possible that adverse economic conditions caused the Judahites to decrease their giving. But if that was the case, they only ended up hurting themselves, for their lack of giving led to widespread crop failures and famine. Because of their carelessness in giving, the Lord declared that the entire covenant community was literally translated "cursed with a curse" (Mal. 3:9). The combination of a verb and a noun in the Hebrew text intensified God's censure that the nation in its entirety was guilty of wrongdoing. Furthermore, they were enduring God's displeasure, as evidenced by their inability to flourish and experience wellness in their daily activities.

The solution to the preceding problem was for all the inhabitants of Judah and Jerusalem once again to give the "whole tithe" (vs. 10). The reference to the "storehouse" was a treasury room in the temple that served as a depository for the produce brought by the people. The priests and Levites lived all year from the offerings and tithes that the covenant community brought to the sanctuary. The mention of the "whole tithe" suggests that the people made a pretense of giving a tenth, but were actually giving far less than the minimum amount required of them.

The Lord gave His chosen people a challenge. He invited them to "test" (vs. 10) His faithfulness, which means He wanted them to prove what He pledged to do. If they began faithfully tithing again, He would open wide His heavenly storehouse of "blessing" (vs. 10). The wording of this verse brings to mind the description of the cataclysmic flood that occurred in the days of Noah (Gen. 7:11; 8:2). The all-powerful Creator declared that as a result of the covenant community's action, they would run out of room to stockpile the overflow of His provision. God's amazing proposal ensured a positive outcome to the people's giving. The implication was that their situation was far from hopeless, assuming they accepted the Lord's offer. In turn, His blessing would enable them to continue being generous.

Next, God specified how He would bless His people in return for their renewed obedience in tithing. He would eliminate the insects and pestilence that had been ruining their crops (vs. 11). Evidently, the Judahites had been experiencing agricultural losses due to locust plagues and drought. The restoration of offerings and tithes required a step of faith. The Lord asked that the covenant community begin giving on a poor harvest so that He would bless the next one. Besides resulting in a greater comfort for themselves, the people's renewed acts of giving would also cause God's name to be revered in the surrounding nations (vs. 12). Others would see the change in the Judahites' situation and recognize how the all-powerful Creator had lavished His favor on them. Since He was ultimately the source of their renewed prosperity, He would be glorified in the process.

Some would argue that the church is not under obligation to tithe. Even if this is the case, sacrificial giving remains an important barometer of faithfulness for New Testament believers. For instance, in 2 Corinthians 9:6-8, Paul encouraged his readers to give purposefully and generously. Can Jesus' followers be any less unstinting than their Old Testament counterparts? As in Malachi's day, the Lord's ministry is dependent upon the cheerful and sacrificial giving of His people. Those who are faithful in this regard find that God still blesses the givers. Of course, our purpose in giving is not for God to satiate our greed, but to be empowered by the Savior to give even more to those in need.

Discussion Questions

1. Why were God's people so eager for the "messenger of the covenant" (Mal. 3:1) to come?
2. What would happen to those who persisted in wickedness?
3. In what way is God merciful to us, even when we sin against Him?
4. How had the Judahites robbed God?
5. What are some ways God has recently proved His faithfulness to you?

Contemporary Application

Malachi taught the people of Judah that God's judgment would come. Believers would be spiritually cleansed, while unbelievers would be eternally condemned. After the Lord had done His purifying work, His devoted followers would bring acceptable offerings to Him.

"A thousand years from now who will know—or care?" This saying implies that whatever we decide, it won't make any difference in the long run. Admittedly, for some decisions this is true. Yet other decisions have important, long-term consequences. For instance, what color shirt or blouse a person wears today is not an earth-shaking decision. But what kind of a person someone is, inside that shirt or blouse, is important and might have eternal ramifications, both for them and for others.

God has given us the ability to decide some things for ourselves. Because we live in, with, and among other people, we have to take them into consideration. Also, we obey society's laws. Of course, we must also make personal choices. On what basis do we make those decisions—what to do, how to spend our time, and how to relate to others?

Malachi 3 sets out God's expectations for our living and thinking. God says that He spiritually blesses us for obeying Him. This includes revering Him through our thoughts, feelings, and actions. Likewise, we honor the Lord by reaching out to the lost with the truth of Scripture, treating others with kindness, and doing what we can to help those in need. Ultimately, God is glorified by our decision to live in such a Christlike way.